DICKSON COUNTY HANDBOOK

BY

JILL KNIGHT GARRETT

A Handbook for research in Dickson County, Tennessee

Containing:

Marriages
Wills
Estate settlements
Deeds
Military Records
Vital Statistics
Gazetteer
Chronolgy
Genealogical Miscellany
A Stroll Through History
And other research aids

Copyright 1984
By: Southern Historical Press, Inc.

All rights reserved. No part of this publication may be reproduced, stored in a retrieval system, transmitted in any form, posted on to the web in any form or by any means without the prior written permission of the publisher.

Please direct all correspondence and orders to:

www.southernhistoricalpress.com
or
**SOUTHERN HISTORICAL PRESS, Inc.
PO BOX 1267
375 West Broad Street
Greenville, SC   29601
southernhistoricalpress@gmail.com**

ISBN #0-89308-304-6

Printed in the United States of America

CONTENTS

	Foreword	
	Introduction to Dickson County	1
I	Dickson County Marriages 1805-1836	5
II	Dickson County Marriages 1838-1849	24
III	Dickson County Wills 1804-1856	51
IV	Estate Settlements, 1823-1841	75
V	Dickson County Vital Statistics	99
VI	Deed Records, 1804-1816	114
VII	Military Records	185
VIII	Circuit Court Miscellany	236
IX	Dickson County Gazetteer	241
X	Dickson County Chronology	301
XI	A Stroll Through History	346

FOREWORD

This handbook for historical and genealogical study of Dickson County, Tennessee, is affectionately dedicated to:

                    Iris Hopkins McClain

                            and

                    Lula Belle Hopkins

The first is my mother and the second my aunt. Through the years they have saved clippings, scrapbooks, and all kinds of memorabilia for me and they have answered hundreds of questions. Without their material this book could not have been compiled.

Some sections of this book are manuscripts for proposed works on various phases of Dickson County history. These projects have since been abandoned but it was thought best to include these, incomplete as they might be, in this book.

The selection of people, events, and other facts has been my own and no one else's. The wealth of material available in some cases, other than the vital statistics, marriages, wills, and court records, was more than can be put in this book--particularly in the chronology section. Maybe next time?

The spelling as found in various sources has been retained--this will account for the name being Donegan sometimes, Dunnegan another, or even Dunegon. In the old records names are often hard to decipher and if you question our interpretation, please try to check the original. Many times we felt "that cannot be right", but copied the information as it appeared to us.

                                            JILL GARRETT

Summer 1982
Columbia, Tennessee

INTRODUCTION TO DICKSON COUNTY

In the years before air conditioning, a funeral home in Dickson County furnished cardboard fans to the churches throughout the county during the summer months. A whole generation of youngsters in the 1930s grew up knowing only a nutshell history printed on the back of this fan.

One of these fans has been kept by my family and the brief history might serve well as an introduction to this handbook on Dickson County. The author is not known, but apparently some of the information came from Goodspeed's history of the county written in 1886.

THIS FAN IS THE PROPERTY OF THE CHURCH. PLEASE DO NOT REMOVE. We hope you will find interesting the sketch below of the early history of Dickson and Dickson County, which we have prepared for your information.

The first land entries bear evidence of white men in Dickson County as early as 1786, and between the years 1800 and 1810 many settlers came to the county. Two block houses or forts were built for protection.

In 1800 there were no roads through Dickson County. About 1810 and 1812, a road was established to Nashville. The first man licensed by the County Court to keep a store was John Holland in 1806. The first corn mills were built about 1800.

There were no offices in Dickson County until 1806, when probably the first postmaster was Richard Waugh.

In May 1830 Dickson County was visited by a destructive hurricane. The Court House and Jail at Charlotte were demolished. Charlotte was damaged to the extent of about $30,000.00.

In 1884 the county had a population of about 14,000 people, 2,700 of whom were qualified voters. In 1855 the population was 8,404, 6,286 being white, and 2,118 were slaves.

The county was named in honor of William Dickson, of North Carolina, a United States Surveyor. The county was created out of the counties of Montgomery and Robertson, Oct. 25, 1803. Charlotte, the county seat, was laid off and platted in 1804.

Nothing comparatively can be learned of the religious conditions and happenings in Dickson County prior to the year 1800. At that time the Methodists, Baptists and Presbyterians had organizations in the county. Probably the first church erected in the county was a log building which stood about one-half mile west of where Charlotte now stands, and built in 1804 by the Palm Singers, who, some time before, led by the Rev. Sam Brown, had seceded from the Presbyterian Church.

The Palm Singers were few in number, and as an organization did not live long in this country, and a graveyard marks where the church once stood.

The Cumberland Presbyterian Church had its origin in this county, in a log house, the home of Rev. Samuel McAdoo. This house stood about 6 miles from Charlotte, an old-fashioned double log house, a story and a half high, covered with clapboards, and the clapboards were supported by light poles.

Probably the first Methodist Church was Smyrna Church erected some time in 1810 on Sulphur Fork of Jones Creek.

Among the early schools was one at the forks of the Piney River, with an average attendance of about 25 pupils. The first schools of any importance were located at Charlotte.

Dickson is by far the largest town in the county. It lies 8 miles south of the county seat. The town was laid off and platted by C. Berringer of Alleghany City, Pa, the owner of the land in 1868.

The first building in Dickson was erected during the war by W. H. Crutcher. It was a log house, and stood on the north side of the railroad crossing, later Main Street. Mr. Crutcher also erected another log house, which stood where the home of J. R. Bryan was erected. But before completion both buildings were destroyed by Federal forces then encamped at Cox's Springs, and the material taken to that camp and used in construction for headquarters for troops.

The first merchant in Dickson was Mr. Crutcher, who built a small log store, 16x16, during the latter part of 1865.

Other log houses were erected during the years 1866-1867, one of which was used as a tavern, corner of Main and Murrell streets, opposite the "Press" office, and was conducted by J. C. Martin.

The Dickson Academy was opened in 1885. The only newspaper in Dickson county during these times was published at Dickson, being established in 1881 by Messrs. Conant and Freeman, and had the appropriate name of "The Press."

Previous to "The Press" the "Dickson County Independent" was conducted by Mr. N. B. Morton, being established in 1878, and continued its publication for three years.

Dickson was incorporated in 1870, but was abandoned in 1883, and the records having been misplaced, an account of the proceedings of the town charter cannot be given.

The town was originally called Sneedsville, in honor of a civil engineer who located the first side track at the place, but subsequently changed to Dickson.

The Methodist Episcopal Church, North, was organized in 1867; Methodist Episcopal Church, South, in 1872; United Presbyterian organized in 1871; Old School Presbyterian organized in 1869; Lutheran organized in 1874. Later the Church of Christ was organized and is now one of the largest church organizations of the city; also the First Baptist and the Primitive Baptist have good memberships and modern meeting houses.

The A. F. & A. M. Lodge was removed to Dickson from Beech Grove in 1873; the K. of H. was organized in 1880; the K. & L. H. organized in 1883; the G. T. was organized in 1886; C. O.F. was organized in 1881.

These early high-lights of the town of Dickson make a very interesting background compared with the progress and growth of the city as it is today. The present population of Dickson is about 4,000. (This fan in 1982 is owned by my aunt Lula Belle Hopkins of Dickson, Tennessee.)

It was many years before many people realized that the so-called Palm Singers of this brief history were really Psalm Singers.

Research in Dickson County records will show some errors in the foregoing sketch, but at least the sketch served to spur interest in the historic county by many.

As early as 1784 Russell Gower, Anderson Lucas, and James Russell hunted and camped on Yellow Creek. Dickson County deeds refer to the spot on the creek as "where they hunted". (Dickson County Deed Book A, pages 310, 311, 312.)

As one of the older counties of Middle Tennessee, the county's records have long been important to researchers of early settlers. Unhappily there are some gaps, particularly in the early marriages. The storm of 1830 damaged and destroyed some records. The following account of the tornado is of some interest:

Nashville Banner, 1 June 1830:

> About 10:30 last night the village of Charlotte was visited by a tornado, the violent and destructive effects of which no pen can describe nor can they be adequately conceived except by those who were witnesses to the awful and terrific scene. Our little town is now a heap of ruins. Many, who yesterday had a comfortable home, are now without a place even to shelter, while their clothing and provisions have been swept away in the general wreck.
>
> The wind approached the village from the southwest and, although the appearance of the sky was frightful and one constant glare of lightning inspired awe and alarm, yet no one anticipated, none could anticipate, and even now it is difficult to realize what the ravages of five minutes have produced.
>
> But yesterday we were at ease and comfortably situated; today many are wandering about the streets, not knowing where to go or how to procure the means of supplying their necessities. Many who but yesterday were blessed with health and the full enjoyment of the comforts of life, are now languishing on their beds with broken limbs or mangled bodies, and some with scarce hope of recovery. But 'midst all these calamities, the hand of a Protecting Providence has been displayed in the almost miraculous preservation of our little village.
>
> Dr. Napier's brick corner, occupied by B. A. Collier as a store and by Mr. Glasgow as a tailor shop; a long log building occupied by Voorhies & Smith as a store and Mrs. Clinton as a dwelling house; Judge Humphrey's house, occupied by Dr. B. M. Carter, Thomas Palmer's house, two stories high, including a saddler's shop, etc., dwelling occupied as a grocery by Mr. Massey, and the Post Office; a dwelling occupied by Mr. Betts--these with all the outbuildings and improvements are entirely destroyed. The opposite corner formerly occupied as a shop by Dr. Carter, and the next building occupied by Mr. Smith as a grocery, are likewise gone, with their outbuildings, two stables and three kitchens; James Nesbitt's cotton gin, with a dwelling house and stables on the same lot, are totally demolished.
>
> Robert Livingston's hatter's shop was destroyed, together with other buildings on his premises, except the dwelling house, the chimney of which was blown down. The dwelling of Jacob Voorhies was taken off to a second story, his chimney blown down and all his outbuildings destroyed.
>
> Field Farrar's stable was badly damaged, James Gould had a part of the roof of his dwelling blown off, his kitchen and smokehouse unroofed and chimneys thrown down; Samuel Bowker's house and smokehouse were unroofed; the corn crib attached to the tavern of Thomas Jarratt, occupied by B. C. Robinson, was blown down and one of the buildings unroofed.

The only house in town that entirely escaped injury is that occupied as a store by James Steele & Company, and with all the buildings destroyed, nearly all their contents were swept away and lost.

The Courthouse, a substantial brick building, is a heap of ruins and Mr. William Collier, who was buried beneath the rubbish, was severely injured but yet survives. The jail is nearly level with the ground; Mrs. Eubank is not expected to recover; Mrs. Coffee is badly mangled and unable to move herself; Mr. Glasgow was badly injured, though recovering, and many other persons have received smaller wounds.

According to local tradition Mrs. Coffee was blown into a tree on Petersburg Hill and remained in the tree two or three days until discovered by a passing citizen. She lingered a few days and died of her wounds.

Another recalled that the 1830 tornado blew books and papers from the courthouse and these were scattered in every direction for miles, many being entirely destroyed. Several large books were carried by force of the wind into Cheatham County and afterwards recovered.

The 1886 history of Dickson County notes that during the Civil War some circuit court records were damaged and destroyed "to a considerable extent" and for the first three years of circuit court there are no minute or docket books.

Although licenses and bonds were issued for marriages from the start, it was not until 1815 that the General Assembly passed a law requiring the clerk to preserve marriages. The fact some of the pre-1815 marriages survived in some counties is "probably because the clerk did not get around to throwing them out", says one researcher.

Prior to 1838 all marriage licenses and bonds were kept, but usually in boxes. In January 1838 the General Assembly passed a law requiring the clerk to "keep a well bound book in which they shall register the names of parties, dates of issuances," and record the return. This explains why there are few, or none at all, bound volumes of marriages in the state prior to 1838. Some clerks later recorded the earlier marriages in books, however. (I am grateful to the writings of Jonathan K. T. Smith of Memphis for this information on the early records of Tennessee.)

In recent years the Tennessee State Library and Archives has had a microfilm program to record all the early records in the Tennessee courthouses. To learn what is available in each county, the researcher is urged to check the TSL&A inventories of county records. Much of the material in this book was copied and abstracted from the microfilm of these Dickson County records.

In using this book, the researcher should be aware that the names found in old records are often hard to decipher and that the interpretations are usually my own. The one exception will be the marriage records copied by Mildred Sullivan Gambill, but here we made an effort to compare these with other listings.

I should like to thank my mother, Iris Hopkins McClain, and her sister, Lula Belle Hopkins, for the scrapbooks, records, notes, and other material they let me use--and also for their fine memories of some of the older people living during their childhood or their knowledge of the children of people mentioned in the records of Dickson County.

JILL GARRETT

I

DICKSON COUNTY MARRIAGES

1805 - 1836

The marriages listed in this section were from loose marriage bonds and licenses in the Dickson County Courthouse at Charlotte. These were microfilmed by the Tennessee State Library and Archives.

However, many additions from other sources have been added to the list and the source of documentation will be given at the end of any marriage record not found in the official Dickson County records. These additional marriages (with sources) have been included in this listing in an attempt to fill in some of the gaps in the early marriage records.

1805

John Deason married Elizabeth_____December 1805 in Dickson County. (The date of this marriage is established in a chancery court lawsuit labeled Deason vs Deason 1816 in a box labeled Equity Causes 1818 in the Maury County Courthouse, Columbia, Tennessee. This was a suit for divorce and the bride's maiden name was not given.)

Joshua Weakley married 27 April 1805 to Mary Morrison, daughter of William and Rachel Morrison. (This date comes from the Morrison family Bible included in the pension application of Rachel Morrison, W-1455, widow of William Morrison, soldier of the American Revolution. The original pension application is in the National Archives but a copy was furnished the compiler by Mrs. Geneva Swain, Dearborn, Michigan, through the courtesy of Mrs. Jack Hudson, Dyersburg, Tennessee. All other marriages from the Morrison Bible will be labeled simply the "Morrison Bible".)

1807

Mr. Molton Dickson of Charlotte married to Miss Martha Strong of Dickson County on Tuesday the 3rd inst. (Impartial Review and Cumberland Repository, 14 Feb. 1807. Newspaper.)

1808

Fountain Lester of Logan County, KY, married Miss Sally Fox Napier on the 3rd instant in Dickson County. (Impartial Review and Cumberland Repository, 10 March 1808. Newspaper.)

David Dickson, Esquire, of Dickson County married Miss Eliza McNairy of Dickson County on Thursday the 16th. (Impartial Review and Cumberland Repository, 30 June 1808. Newspaper.)

1809

Jesse Russell married 28 Feb. 1809 to Mary F. Hudson in Dickson County; marriage performed by Rev. Thomas Murrill. (This marriage may be documented by the War of 1812 Pension application W09441 in National Archives; contributed by Mrs. Roberta Russell Graham, Houston, Texas.)

John H. Stone married 30 July 1809 to Sarah Walker. (This marriage appears in the Alsobrooks Bible, once owned by Mrs. Dolly Steele Petty of Hickman County. A copy was given to the compiler by Mrs. Jane Fullerton, Nashville, Tennessee.)

1811

Elisha Turner married ___Sept. 1811 to Susan May in Dickson County. (This date comes from the Turner family Bible recorded in Johnson County Arkansas, in connection with a War of 1812 petition of Susan May Turner. Date of registration was 12 March 1852. This marriage record was contributed by Mrs. Irma Lee Wharton, Clarksville, Arkansas.)

1813

Robert Patterson married Rachel Morrison, daughter of William and Rachel Morrison on 6 Jan. 1813. (Morrison Bible in pension application, see page 5.)

1815

James Camp, merchant of Nashville, married Miss Sally Pearsall, daughter of J. Pearsall, Esquire on June 27. (Nashville Whig, 4 July 1815. Newspaper.)

1817

Edward Pearsall married Perthenia Sherrin on 7 January 1817; solemnized by T. Brown. (License)

1819

"Married in the town of Charlotte on Monday the 11th by Sterling Brewer, Esquire, Mr. Isaac H. Lanier to Miss Betsy Vanleer, daughter of B. W. Vanleer!!" (Town Gazette and Farmers Register, 18 Oct. 1819. Newspaper published in Clarksville, TN.)

Mr. P. Harrison married in Charlotte on Wednesday last to Miss Eliza B. Pannell. (Town Gazette and Farmers Register, 21 Nov. 1819. Newspaper published in Clarksville, TN.)

Robert Nolin married Charity Morrison, 18 November 1819. (Morrison Bible in pension application, see page 5.)

1820

William Lomax married Elizabeth Arrington 1 March 1820 in Dickson County. (Lomax Family History, published 1894, in Tennessee State Library and Archives; it is believed this was being quoted from a Bible.)

1821

Moses Gammill marriage bond to Nancy Adams, dated 12 March 1821. (Bond)

1822

William Grymes married January 1822 in Dickson County to Missoniah ____. (This marriage may be established by a divorce petition found in Dickson County Circuit Court Minute Book A, pages 51, 52. The bride's maiden name was not given in the entry.)

1823

Robert Dickson married Peggy Morrison on 9 November 1823. (Morrison Bible in pension application, see page 5 of this book.)

William Morrison, Jr., married Naomy Knight 11 Sept. 1823. (Morrison Bible in pension application, see page 5 of this book.)

1825

Lemuel Russell married Nancy Myatt 20 August 1825 in Dickson County; marriage solemnized by Hudson Dudley, J. P. (This marriage is documented in the War of 1812 pension application of Lemuel Russell, BLWT 40495 found in National Archives and contributed by Mrs. Roberta Russell Graham.)

1826

Jacob Voorhies to Margaret Farrar, marriage license, solemnized 21 Nov. 1826 by Molton Dickson, J. P.

William S. Murrell to Mary A. M. _____. (This marriage may be documented by her divorce petition filed Sept. 1826 in Dickson County. No date of marriage was given nor was the bride's maiden name given. The divorce was granted in March 1827. This divorce action will be found in Dickson Circuit Court Book A, no page number in the book at this point; researchers should search date of entry instead.)

1826

John Montague to Nancy Elliott 16 November 1826, Dickson County. (This marriage was quoted in the book "Grimes, Cook, and Related Families of Wayne County, Tennessee, 1800-1960", by Jay Cook Grimes, page 104. It is believed this marriage was being quoted from a family Bible.)

Dr. Drew A. Outlaw of Stewart County married in Dickson County to Miss Mary Ann Eliza West. (National Banner, 3 June 1826. Newspaper.)

1827

Philip W. Austin married Polly Dudley 20 September 1827. (This marriage was recorded in the Austin Ciphering Book, owned by Mr. and Mrs. C. W. Austin, Mayfield, Kentucky, and contributed to compiler's collection by Mrs. Austin.)

John Mays to _____, marriage bond dated 2 January 1827. (Note: The bride's name was left blank on the bond.)

Hosey M. B. Ragan, marriage bond dated 22 Sept. 1827 to Elmena Vanhook.

Jacob H. Purkins to Maria Ferrell, marriage license dated 22 May 1827.

Nehemiah Scott to Sally Williams, license issued 26 Sept. 1827.

George W. Shearon to Elizabeth Brewer, marriage license issued 12 Dec. 1827.

Henry S. Palmer of Dickson County married in Louisville, Kentucky, to Mrs. Eliza Sale of Louisville. (National Banner and Nashville Whig, 8 March 1828. Newspaper.)

1828

James R. Allen, marriage bond dated 18 Nov. 1828, to Polly W. Patterson.

Williber Etheaidge, marriage bond dated 24 July 1828, to Lockie Smith. (Note: His name was spelled this way. An entry in Circuit Court records for 3 July 1820 shows his name to be Willoughby Etheridge.)

Theophilas Horn to Patsy Wall, marriage executed 28 Nov. 1828 by William McMurry, J. P.

Thomas Piner to Elizabeth Turner, marriage bond dated 9 Feb. 1828.

John Story to Polly Burgess, bond dated 23 Sept. 1828.

Littleton Story to Polly Baker, marriage solemnized 11 Sept. 1828 by Howard W. Turner, J. P.

Lewis Harmon married August 1828 to Gilly_____. (Petition for divorce filed 1833 in Dickson County. The original petition is in the legislative petitions in the Tennessee State Library and Archives.)

1829

Anderson Gentry married Mary Murrell 5 Feb. 1829, executed by D. Gray.

Alfred Hooker to Martha Clark, marriage executed 26 Dec. 1829 by William McMurry, J. P.

Martin Hunter to Nancy Duke, executed 23 Aug. 1829 by H. Morris. The license was issued 22 Aug. 1829.

Joseph Nall to Nancy Underhill, marriage bond dated 24 Sept. 1829.

Benjamin Meeker to _____, marriage bond dated 27 Sept. 1829. William McCreeney, bondsman. (Note: Bride's name not given on bond.)

Burwell Myatt to Dolly Dudley, marriage executed 1 March 1829 by Hudson Dudley, J. P.

John McCaslin to Elizabeth Davidson, solemnized 30 July 1829 by Hudson Dudley, J. P., issued 29 July 1829.

Absasder Kyle to Margaret V. Hamilton, bond dated 14 Jan. 1829. (Note: His first name could be Alexander; this name hard to decipher.)

Green Jackson to Cathrine Grymes, solemnized 18 March 1829 by George Hightower; license issued 16 March 1829.

James Redden to Sinthey Petty, issued 3 Feb. 1829, solemnized by K. Myatt, J. P.

Charles A. Baker to Nancy Bullion, bond dated 12 August 1829.

John Brock to Nancy Austin, license issued 6 July 1829, solemnized 7 July 1829 by H. Dudley, J. P.

Charles Robertson to Jane Davidson, marriage bond dated 28 Oct. 1829.

James Robertson to Ann M. Ragan, marriage bond 27 August 1829.

Abel Roy to Sally Myers, marriage solemnized 1 Sept. 1829.

William Sellers to Nancy Sanderson, license issued and marriage solemnized 22 August 1829, by D. Gray.

J. W. Shackelford to Mary Clark, marriage solemnized 5 May 1829 by Molton Dickson, J. P.

F. A. Slayden to Susannah W. Adams, marriage bond dated 20 Aug. 1829.

John S. Spencer to Elinor Parrish, marriage bond dated 24 Jan. 1829.

Daniel Taylor to Mary Ann Gentry, marriage executed 3 August 1829 by D. Gray.

Malichi Tidwell to Peggy Meek, marriage solemnized 21 July 1829 by Hudson Dudley, J. P.

David Wade to Martha Record, 23 July 1829, executed by Hudson Dudley, J. P. James R. Napier was bondsman.

Simon Williams to Martha Green, license issued 24 Nov. 1829, executed by S. Turner, J. P., on ___ Nove. 1829. (Note: Date of solemnization not given.)

James Bullock to Elizabeth Donegan, license issued 17 Jan. 1829. Executed by H. Myatt, J. P.

James Carothers to Elizabeth Shaddock, issued 22 July 1829. Executed by William McMurry, J. P.

David Crawford married on the 21st ult. at Laurel Furnace, Dickson County, to Miss Elizabeth D. Fulcher. (National Banner, 18 July 1829. Newspaper.)

1830

Tristam Rye to Margaret G. Drummond, issued 24 Dec. 1830, solemnized 30 Dec. 1830 by M. Dickson, J. P.

Peter Self to Nancy H. Reynolds, issued 8 Dec. 1829, solemnized 10 Nov. 1830 by S. Turner, J. P. (Note: Please note these dates.)

1831

John S. Williams to Sousannah Adams, marriage bond dated 4 Jan. 1831.

Thomas Welch to Eliza Thomas, license issued 19 March 1831; solemnized 24 March 1831 by Molton Dickson, J. P. Hardeman Stone, bondsman.

Benjamin Walker to Patsy Perry, license issued 18 April 1831, executed 21 April 1831.

George Tidwell to Matilda Tidwell, license issued and executed 10 June 1831 by J. Pendergrass, J. P.

Benjamin Murrell to Zaphina Tedford, marriage bond dated 24 March 1831; George W. Tatom, bondsman.

Benajah Gentry to Eliza Murrell, license issued 2 August 1831, executed by David Gray, J. P.

Charles H. Burton to Lucinda Cooksey, marriage bond dated 28 Feb. 1831.

1832

David Crenshaw to Caroline Wilson; license issued 13 Dec. 1832; solemnized 13 Dec. 1832 by J. Voorhies, J. P.

Burket Murrell to Nancy Dotson; marriage bond issued 25 June 1832 with Richard Murrell, bondsman; performed 28 June 1832 by Molton Dickson.

Jos. A. Dickson to Nancy Bell, marriage bond dated 5 April 1832 with C. S. Bowen, bondsman.

Ruben Dickson to Happy Selfe, marriage bond dated 26 April 1832 with Wilkerson Robertson as bondsman.

Elijah Dotson to Patsy Burgess, marriage bond dated 14 Feb. 1832 with Samuel Brown as bondsman.

James J. Dotson to Elizabeth Patterson, marriage license dated 3 Aug. 1832; executed 9 Aug. 1832; Samuel Brown bondsman.

Stephen P. Forsee to Gincy Taylor, marriage license issued 3 Dec. 1832, executed 31 Dec. 1832 by E. A. Misen. Levi McCollum appears as the bondsman on the marriage bond.

Martin Garton to Elizabeth White, marriage bond issued ___Nov. 1832; Alexander White, bondsman.

Reuben Goodwin to Jane Laughlin, marriage bond issued 3 Dec. 1832, with David Aglermore, bondsman. Executed 3 Dec. 1832 by William White, J. P.

James Graves to Eliza Wilson, marriage bond issued 12 August 1832 with Willis Collier as bondsman. W. B. Dotson, J. P., solemnized marriage on 16 August 1832.

Clement Grogan to Elizabeth Wright, marriage bond dated 29 Oct. 1832 with V. S. Allen, bondsman; executed 30 Oct. 1832 by John Grymes, J. P.

Richard B. Hayden to Elizabeth Porter, marriage bond dated 25 May 1832 with Samuel Golladay as bondsman.

Nicholas Haywood to Mary Cunningham, marriage bond dated ___1832 with James Cummings, bondsman.

James G. Hinson to Martha Goodrich, marriage bond dated 1 Nov. 1832 with Thomas H. Hinson, bondsman. Executed 1 Nov. 1832 by H. Parrish, J. P.

Ezekiel Hickerson to Lucinda W. Garrett, marriage bond dated 3 July 1832 with Richard Waugh, bondsman. Executed ___July 1832 by J. W. Napier.

Allen Hunter to Peggy Brinn, marriage bond issued 30 Jan. 1832 with Albert Speight as bondsman; executed 30 Jan. 1832 by Reuben Chaudoin, D. D.

Miles Hutcheson to Malinda Jarrett, marriage bond issued 3 Jan. 1832 with John W. Hutcheson as bondsman; executed 5 Jan. 1832 by J. Pendirgrass, J. P.

Rheuben Jones to Margaret Burgess, marriage bond dated 27 March 1832 with Isham P. Holt, bondsman.

William Lyle to Gracy Spicer, issued 25 May 1832. Bondsman, Jacob _____.

John Medlock to Seletia Hickerson, marriage bond dated 3 July 1832 with Ezekiel Hickerson as bondsman.

Caleb Morgan to Susannah Bledsoe, marriage gond issued 10 March 1832 with John White as bondsman; executed 15 March 1832 by H. W. Turner, J. P.

Burket Murrell to Nancy Dodson, marriage bond issued June 1832 with Richard Murrell as bondsman; executed 28 June 1832 by Molton Dickson, J. P.

William Nalls to Isabell Laughlin, marriage bond dated 8 Feb. 1832 with Lyndon Laughlin as bondsman; executed 9 Feb. 1832 by J. Pendergrass.

William Pinegar to Sally George, license issued 10 Jan. 1832, executed 1832 by K. Myatt, J. P.

Gabriel Petty to Sally Edwards, marriage bond dated 25 Feb. 1832 with George C. Edwards as bondsman.

John A. Petty to Nancy Edwards, marriage bond dated 25 Feb. 1832 with George C. as bondsman. (Note: Bondsman name in question.)

John Potengale to Polly Shelton, marriage bond issued 30 Jan. 1832 with James Atwood as bondsman.

Joseph W. Ragan to Rachel T. Turner, bond issued 29 Aug. 1832 with James Atwood as bondsman.

Mark Robertson to Elizabeth Harris, marriage bond issued 26 Nov. 1832 with Dury Hunter as bondsman.

William E. Renslow to Racheal M. Warters, marriage bond issued 18 March 1832 with John D. Edwards as bondsman; executed by Reuben Chaudoin, 5 April 1832. (Note: Bride's name is given as Phebe M. Warters on the returned marriage license.)

James M. Self to Francis Weaver, marriage bond dated ___July 1832 with Samuel Self as bondsman; executed 23 July 1832 by S. Turner, J. P.

Abner B. Shelton to Susan S. Vick, marriage bond issued ___May 1832 with William B. Bartee as bondsman. Executed by J. W. Napier, no date.

Samuel Spencer to _____(left blank), marriage bond dated ____1832 with Hiram Parker as bondsman.

William Step to Permelia Chadock, marriage bond dated 11 April 1832 with Thomas Matthews as bondsman; executed 19 April 1832 by John Grymes, J. P.

Abraham Stewart to Elizabeth Evins, marriage bond dated 27 Oct. 1832 with William F._____as bondsman; executed by E. A. Medins, no date.

John Stokey (Stokes?) to Permelia Annis Stafford, marriage bond dated 15 Dec. 1832 with Field Farrar as bondsman. Executed 20 Dec. 1832 by J. Voorhies.

Hardaman Stone to Margaret Kennedy, marriage bond issued 12 June 1832 with J. Voorhies, bondsman; executed 14 June 1832 by J. Voorhies, J. P.

Nicholas Taylor, marriage bond to Matilda Farrar, dated 9 Oct. 1832. John Stone, bondsman.

Thomas S. Taylor to Rebecca C. Powers, marriage bond dated 12 March 1832. Nelson McClelland, bondsman.

James M. Tucker to Susan Laughlin, marriage bond dated 18 Feb. 1832. Lyndon Laughlin, bondsman. Marriage executed 22 Feb. 1832 by J. Pendergrass.

Thomas Wadkins to Margaret Bugg, marriage bond dated 9 Jan. 1832 with William Lamaster, bondsman. Executed 9 Jan. 1832 by W. B. Dotson, J. P.

Berryman Walker to Elizabeth Hinson, marriage bond dated 6 Feb. 1832. Henry Gravet, bondsman.

Joel Wall to Lydia Council, marriage bond dated 23 Jan. 1832. License was executed, no date, by William McMurry, J. P.

James West to Sarah J. Sutton, marriage bond dated 1 Oct. 1832 with T. L. Collier as bondsman. Executed 1 Oct. 1832 by John Grymes, J. P.

John M. Wilson to Selina Grover (or Graves), marriage bond dated 6 Dec. 1832 with Joseph C. Dodson, bondsman.

1833

Edward H. Adcock to Elizabeth Petty, marriage bond dated 11 May 1833 with Phillip W. Austin, bondsman.

Henderson Adcock to Dolly Myett, marriage bond dated 13 Feb. 1833 with William H. Johnson, bondsman. Marriage executed 28 Feb. 1833 by Th. Myatt, J. P.

Abraham Adkins to Mary Whitehead, marriage bond dated 6 Feb. 1833 with David Winstead, bondsman. Executed 5 Jan. 1833 by Hewel Parrish, J. P.

William Adkins to Letsey C. Slayden, marriage bond dated 24 March 1833 with Travis E. Slayden, bondsman.

Thomas Bell to Mary Bowen, marriage bond dated 18 June 1833 with George F. Raworth, bondsman.

Thomas Blackburn to Sally Angling, marriage bond dated 28 Dec. 1833, no bondsman given. Executed by Th. Myatt, J. P., no date. (There is a second bond with the same information only on this bond Milton Loftis appeared as bondsman.)

John W. Brown to Polly Myatt, marriage bond dated 8 October 1833 with Benjamin B. Hall, bondsman. Executed 10 Oct. 1833 by L. Russell, J. P.

William Clark to Eve Ann Hull, marriage bond dated 27 April 1833 with John Jones as bondsman.

James Cunningham to Sarah McMurry, marriage bond dated 30 July 1833 with Thomas Cunningham as bondsman. Executed 1 Aug. 1833 by Reuben Chaudoin.

Willie Daniel to Rebecca Bledsoe, marriage bond dated 24 Sept. 1833 with William Young as bondsman.

James Epperson to Delinda Bugg, marriage bond dated 31 Jan. 1833 with Robert Moore as bondsman. Executed 31 Jan. 1833 by E. A. McAdoo.

Joseph F. Griffith to Elizabeth H. Oliver, marriage bond dated 16 May 1833 with James P. Collins and James Oliver, bondsman. Executed 20 May 1833 by Molton Dickson, J. P.

Zachariah Garton to Nancy Carter, marriage bond dated 30 Oct. 1833 by Martin Garton. Executed 31 Oct. 1833 by A. Pullen.

Ethelbert T. Gray to Abetha P. Carter, marriage bond dated 15 Jan. 1833 with N. B. Pullen as bondsman. Executed 16 Jan. 1833 by A. Pullen.

John Harris to Sally Caruth, marriage bond dated 27 July 1833 with James Carruthe, bondsman. Executed 17 July 1833 by John Grymes, J. P.

Americus V. Hicks to Elizabeth Morris, marriage bond dated 24 Jan. 1833 with Thomas J. Miller, bondsman. Executed by L. Russell, J. P.

William Howard to Jane Hadden, marriage bond dated 9 May 1833 with Allen Nesbitt, bondsman. Executed 9 May 1833 by J. W. Napier, J. P.

Joseph Hudgins to Mary Richardson, marriage bond dated 1 Oct. 1833 with Stephen D. Richardson, bondsman.

Thomas Hudgins to Adeline Nesbitt, marriage gond dated 25 March 1833 with Richard Waugh, bondsman.

Jacob Hufft to Mary Ann Bailey, marriage bond dated 8 July 1833 with William Bailey bondsman; executed 8 July 1833 by Whiliam White, J. P. (Dickson County Circuit Court Minute Book A, p. 11 and p. 12 has a petition for divorce for Mary Ann Haft versus Jacob Haft, who were married in Dickson County in 1833.)

George Noland to Nancy Forsey, marriage bond dated 16 Feb. 1833 with Stephen Forsey, bondsman. Executed 21 Feb. 1833 by E. A. McAdoo.

Daniel B. Norris to Mary Balthorp, marriage bond dated 9 Sept. 1833 with Jesse Turner, bondsman.

Parsons Jackson to Margaret Brown, marriage bond dated 5 Sept. 1833 with John Grymes, Jr., bondsman.

Thomas J. Jones to Minerva Underhill, marriage bond dated 22 July 1833 with William Underhill, bondsman. Executed 24 July 1833 by J. Pendergrass.

James P. King to Rebecca _____ (no last name given), marriage bond dated 30 Oct. 1833 with Alfred M. Strayhorn, bondsman.

James Loggins to Nancy Grymes, marriage bond dated 4 April 1833 with William Hightower, bondsman. Executed 5 May 1833 by J. W. Napier.

William J. Mathis to Louise Roberts, marriage executed 12 Dec. 1833 by J. Voorhies.

Charles Mixon to Sarah Bagget, marriage bond dated 2 Oct. 1833 with Isaac Bone, bondsman.

William J. Parker to Minerva Tidwell, marriage bond dated 3 April 1833 with John Parker, bondsman. Executed 3 April 1833 by J. Pendergrass, J. P.

Abner Pinegar to Sally Terry, marriage bond dated 6 Feb. 1833 with Nathaniel Kimbro as bondsman. Executed 6 Feb. 1833 by L. Russell, J. P.

Thomas J. Ragan to Nancy Toller, marriage bond dated 22 Jan. 1833 with William W. Toler, bondsman.

Solomon J. Reynolds to Jane_____, marriage bond dated 15 Jan. 1833; bondsman, James Gosster (?). (Note: The bride's name had been marked out and could not be read.)

Alexander Rascoe to Elizabeth Davis, marriage bond dated 1 June 1833 with William Yeates as bondsman. Executed 2 June 1833 by Molton Dickson, J. P.

George F. Raworth to Elizabeth Jane Dickson, marriage bond dated 27 Nov. 1833 with T. L. Collier and S. Bell, Jr., bondsmen. Executed ___Nov. 1833 by J. W. Napier.

Meredith Roy to Susan Gentry, marriage bond dated 9 Jan. 1833 with James Cocke, bondsman.

David Rushing, Jr., to Jane Turner, marriage bond dated 2 Sept. 1833 with M. T. Ellis, bondsman, and John Norsworthy, bondsman. Executed 25 Sept. 1833 by W. B. Young, J. P.

John R. Simpson to Elizabeth Whistenhunt, marriage bond dated 11 June 1833 with Joseph Dozier, bondsman. Executed 14 June 1833 by Reuben Chaudoin.

John Southerland to Mary Ann Williams, marriage bond dated 9 Apr. 1833 with Henry Southerland, bondsman. Executed 9 April 1833.

John T. Spats to Lenny Harris, marriage bond dated 2 August 1833. (See also the entry following.)

John T. Speight to Lenny Harris, marriage bond dated 2 August 1833 with Washington Hunter, bondsman.

Isaac L. Shelby to Polly Simpson, marriage bond dated 22 March 1833 with William King bondsman.

Solomon H. Shaw to Angeline S. Russ, marriage bond dated 18 Dec. 1833 with Isaiah Perry, bondsman. Executed 18 Aug. by S. H. Peake, M. G.

David Settle to Nancy Nisbett, marriage bond dated 15 July 1833 with B. Gray, bondsman.

John Step to Prudy Shaderick, marriage bond dated ___Jan. 1833 with Thomas Cunningham, bondsman. Executed 20 Jan. 1833 by Jno. Grymes, J.P.

Edmond Terry to Mary Pinigar, marriage bond dated 12 Oct. 1833 with Daniel Z. Pinegar, bondsman. Executed 13 Oct. 1833 by L. Russell.

Jesse Turner to Barsheba Jane Hill, marriage bond dated 6 July 1833 with William W. Norris, bondsman.

Harrison Watson to Polly Tatom, marriage bond dated 11 Nov. 1833 with David Watson, bondsman.

Jefferson S. Watson to Sarah R. Bacon, marriage bond dated 23 Sept. 1833 with James A. Craft and V. S. Allen, bondsmen. Executed 24 Sept. 1833 by Barton Bacon.

David Weakley to Isabella T. Gleaves, marriage bond dated 11 Dec. 1833 with James H. Fuqua, bondsman. Executed 19 Dec. 1833 by Wa. Hunter, J. P.

William Welker to Louisa Anna Bartee, marriage bond dated 9 Jan. 1833 with George T. Cooksey, bondsman; executed 9 Jan. 1833 by J. W. Napier.

1834

George W. Adcock to Kisiah Petty, marriage bond dated 21 Dec. 1834, bondsman, George C. Petty. Solemnized 22 Dec. 1834 by L. Reynolds, J. P. (The official's name is in question.)

Philip W. Austin married 18 March 1834 to Sally Gilbert. (Note: This marriage is in the Austin Ciphering Book owned by Mr. and Mrs. C. W. Austin, Mayfield, Kentucky.)

Charles A. Baker to Julia Dukes, issued 26 Aug. 1834; solemnized 29 Aug. 1834 by Reuben Chaudoin.

Hosey Bennett to Susan Brown, bond dated 1 Sept. 1834 with James West, bondsman; solemnized 17 Sept. 1834 by H. W. Turner J. P.

Wright Blakely to Mary Ann Sharp, marriage bond dated 29 Aug. 1834 with William Redden, bondsman.

Robert Bonds to Eliza Dickson, license issued 17 March 1834; solemnized. (The date of solemnization could not be deciphered.)

John Brock to Francis Tucker, issued 9 July 1834; solemnized 10 July 1834 by J. W. Napier, J. P.

William P. (or T.) Brown to Elizabeth Hunter, marriage bond dated 30 Jan. 1834 with John W. Nite (or Hite) as bondsman; solemnized 13 Feb. 1834 by Reuben Chaudoin.

Benjamin W. Burford to Joyce P. Hardwick, marriage bond dated 12 July 1834 with Elias Moore, bondsman; solemnized 14 July 1834.

Thomas G. Balthrop to Mariah Hinson, marriage bond dated 15 Dec. 1834 with Erasmus J. Ellis as bondsman; solemnized 17 Dec. 1834 by H. Parrish J. P.

James Choate, marriage bond, 1834. (Note: This was all the information on the bond.)

Robert Caldwell to Martha Brigham, marriage bond, dated 25 June 1834 with B. A. Collier, bondsman. Solemnized 26 June 1834 by J. P. Bellamy, J. P.

Ro_____ C_____, marriage bond dated 21 Oct. 1834. (Note: This bride's name could be Elizabeth Crumpler or Crutcher. This bond was terribly waterstained and faded.)

Nathan Collier to Mary Mar____, 28 Feb. (?) 1834. (Note: This was quite faded and stained and this was all that could be deciphered.)

William H. Coltharp to Mary Hogues, marriage bond dated 12 Dec. 1834; Willis Tatom, bondsman. Solemnized 14 Dec. 1834 by W. Hogins, J. P.

Matthew J. Crumpler to Adelade Seals, marriage bond dated 13 Nov. 1834 with Robert H. Brown, bondsman.

Thomas Cunningham to Sally Daniel, marriage bond dated 25 March 1834 with Nathaniel Cunningham, bondsman. Solemnized 9 April 1834 by Rheuben Chaudoin.

George Davidson to Margaret P. McCall, marriage bond dated 12 March 1834 with F. Farrar, bondsman.

Benjamin Darrow, Jr., to Sally Michel, marriage bond dated 18 Sept. 1834 with Thomas J. Kelly bondsman; solemnized 31 Sept. 1834 by H. W. Turner, J. P.

John Eubank to Eliza Crumpler, marriage bond dated 27 Dec. 1834 with W. L. Adamson, bondsman.

Francis E. Fowler to Martha Robertson, license issued 23 April 1834; solemnized 23 April 1834. (Note: The minister or justice of the peace name could not be deciphered.)

James M. Galloway to Louisa Andrews, ____Oct. 1834; Terrell Andrews, bondsman. (This entry very faded and the bride's name is in question.)

Richard Garton to Keziah Parker, marriage bond dated 15 March 1834 with Martin Garton, bondsman; executed 16 March 1834 by Wm. White, J. P.

James Givins (?) to Elizabeth Oliver, marriage bond dated 2 Jan. 1834 with Reuben Givens (Grimes?) as bondsman.

Jeremiah Gray to Rebecca Powers, marriage bond dated 6 June 1834 with Nathaniel Gray, bondsman.

Jeremiah Gray to Rebecca Black, marriage bond dated 6 Sept. 1834 with William G. Gray, bondsman.

George Grove to Delila Goss, marriage license dated 5 Dec. 1834; executed on 7 Dec. 1834. (The minister's name or the name of the justice of the peace was illegible.)

Jefferson Gunn to Malinda Gunn, marriage bond dated 10 Oct. 1834 with Nelson Dunnagan, bondsman; solemnized 10 Oct. 1834 by L. Russell, J. P.

Allen Halliburton to Susan Ray, issued 21 Nov. 1834; solemnized 22 Nov. 1834 by R. P. Halliburton.

Benjamin B. Hall to Mary J. Reader, marriage bond dated 23 March 1834 with R. H. Brown, bondsman.

Joseph Hall to Phebe Holland, marriage bond dated 17 July 1834 with James Watkins, bondsman. (Note: Refer to the Joseph Walker entry also.)

James F. Hardeman to Polly B. Kelly, solemnized 12 Nov. 1834 by J. Voorhies, J. P. (Note: This one was quite faded and hard to read.)

Burgess Harris to Sarah G. White, marriage bond dated 15 Nov. 1834 with Plummer W. Harris, bondsman.

William Hudgins to Polly Brown, marriage bond dated 15 Feb. 1834 with Miles Long, bondsman.

Christopher Hudson to Edny Hogwood, marriage bond dated 24 Sept. 1834 with J. H. Cotham, bondsman.

Doct. Hudson to Araminta Napier, marriage bond 6 Dec. 1834, S. Bell, Jr. bondsman.

William J. Hudson to Miley Yates, marriage bond dated 29 Nov. 1834 with Fanning Yates bondsman; executed by D. Gray, M. G.

Elijah Humphreys to Elizabeth Morris, marriage bond dated 8 March 1834 with Jonathan Fuller, bondsman. Executed by A. Pullen on 8 March 1834.

Burrell Hunter to Hicksey R. Sims, marriage bond dated 14 May 1834 with Isaac Hunter, bondsman. Executed 16 May 1834 by Reuben Chaudoin.

William Irby to Nancy Hasley, license issued 4 August 1834, solemnized 5 August 1834 by H. Parrish, J. P.

William Johnson to Jane Holland, marriage bond dated 20 Dec. 1834, with John Johnson, bondsman. Executed 25 Dec. 1834 by R. Batson, J.P.

Anderson King to Fanny King, marriage bond dated 11 Oct. 1834 with A. J. Myatt, bondsman. Solemnized 11 Oct. 1834 by L. Russell, J. P. (Note: At one point the groom's name appears to be Henry King.)

Samuel Lankerson to Susannah Walker, bond dated 13 Sept. 1834 with William Turner, bondsman. Executed by W. Pendor (?), J. P.

John M. Leggett, 1834. (Note: This was a marriage bond and so faded that this was the only information that could be deciphered.)

James Lewis to Edney Toler, marriage bond dated 13 May 1834 with Archibald Martin, bondsman. Executed 14 May 1834 by H. Parrish, J. P.

Jacob Luther to Elizabeth Anderson, marriage bond dated 31 Dec. 1834 with William Lofton, bondsman.

Adam W. McCallester to Elizabeth Bartee, bond dated ____ with Thomas J. Kelly, bondsman. Executed 8 Aug. 1834 by J. W. Napier. (Note: There was a date on bond, but could not be deciphered.)

Robert W. McClure to Louisa B. West, bond dated 5 Nov. 1834 with Thomas H. Barnes and J. P. Hardwick as bondsmen.

George McCollum to Ann Pearson, solemnized 3 Aug. 1834 by J. W. Napier, J. P.

Ephraim A. Madden to Minerva Drummonds, marriage bond dated 18 Aug. 1834. (Note: This one was water damaged and faded and not all of it could be deciphered. However, in Feb. 1839 Minerva Madden and Ephraim Madden were parties in a suit for divorce. The bill of complaint stated they were married 11 Dec. 1834! Those interested should refer to Dickson County Circuit Court Minute Book A, no page number on this entry was given, so refer to date of entry, Feb. 1839.)

John Meek to Mahala Tidwell, marriage bond dated 24 Jan. 1834 with Benjamin Tidwell, bondsman. Executed 30 Jan. 1834 by L. Russell, J. P.

John Mixon to Peggy Jones, bond dated 24 July 1834. Bondsman's name was illegible.

James Pullen to Elizabeth S. Barnard, bond date illegible; William Thedford bondsman. Executed 20 Feb. 1834 by D. Gray, M. G.

John Parker married Martha ____ 1 Jan. 1835. (Note: This marriage is documented by a petition for divorce in Dickson County Circuit Court Minute Book A, pages 50, 51.)

Bartholomew Richardson to Susan ____, with Jackson Smith, bondsman. Executed 14 July 1834. (Note: The bride's surname was illegible on the microfilm.)

____ R____. (Note: This bond was faded and could not be read.)

David Rutledge to Ann Harris, marriage bond dated 18 Sept. 1834 with William Speight as bondsman; executed 18 Sept. 1834 by William Hunter, J. P.

G. W. Smith to Elizabeth Farrar, bond dated 20 Feb. 1834 with J. Bev Hughes, bondsman.

John N. Scott to Parthenia Norsworthy, marriage bond dated 1 April 1834 with Henry A. B. Williams, bondsman. Solemnized 13 April 1834 by W. B. Dotson, J. P.

John T. Speight to Sinna Harris, marriage bond dated 8 March 1834 with Peterson Andrews, bondsman. Executed 12 March 1834 by William Hunter, J. P.

James Sweany to Caroline Jones, marriage bond dated 10 Feb. 1834, with Benja. Law, bondsman; executed 12 Feb. 1834 by Reubin Chaudoin.

Samuel Sowell to Nancy Adkins, marriage bond dated 1 May 1834 with Abner Adkins, bondsman. Executed 1 May 1834 by H. Parrish, J. P.

James Watkins to Mary Gunn, marriage bond dated 15 May 1834 with William M. Gunn, bondsman.

Joseph Walker, marriage license. (Note: On the inside the name is given as Joseph Hall to Phebe Holland, executed 20 July 1834 by E. A. Headlee.)

Allen Wiley to Elizabeth Johnson, marriage bond dated 27 Oct. 1834 with Lev Wiley as bondsman. Executed by D. Gray, M. G.

1835

M. Clarence Allman of Dickson County married to Miss Elizabeth Allen of Dickson County on the 30th. (National Review, 19 Jan. 1836. Newspaper)

Q. C. Atkinson to Arabella C. West, marriage bond dated 15 Dec. 1835 with B. A. Collier, bondsman.

Mr. Quintus C. Atkinson of Dover, Tennessee, married on the 17th instant by Rev. Mr. Parrish to Miss Arabella C. West, daughter of Colonel Robert C. West of Dickson County. (National Banner and Nashville Whig, 23 Dec. 1835. Newspaper.)

Elias Baggett to Elly Morriset, marriage bond dated 23 July 1835 with Willis Rainwater as bondsman. Solemnized by Benjamin Darrow, Sen., "A Baptist preacher".

Abraham Baughman to Amand Hamilton, marriage bond dated 28 Jan. 1835 with Newt. Crumpler as bondsman.

Gustavus Blockley to Lucresa Choate, marriage bond dated 30 July 1835 with David E. Slayden as bondsman. Solemnized 30 July 1835 by Benjamin Darrow, Sen., Baptist preacher. (Note: The bondsman name could be Daniel E. Slayden instead of David E. Slayden. Daniel and David are alsmot impossible to tell apart in old handwriting.)

William Balthrop, Jr., to Mary Ann Davis, marriage solemnized 30 April 1835 by J. Voorhies, J. P.

Joshua Brown to Mary Hall, marriage bond dated 10 Oct. 1835 with Moses Tidwell as bondsman.

Spartan Bruce to Sally Bartee, marriage bond dated 18 July 1835 with Andrew Nichol as bondsman.

Leuallen Chaudoin to Eliza Jones, marriage license issued 2 Dec. 1835; solemnized 3 Dec. 1835 by W. A. Hunter, J. P. (Note: The groom's name is spelled Shadowen on inside of license. Shadowen is the spelling found today on tombstones in Dickson County although Chaudoin apparently was the original spelling of the name.)

Peter Choate to Elizabeth Choate, marriage bond dated 10 Oct. 1835 by S. J. Choate, bondsman.

Hiram Cornet to Nancy Ashworth, marriage bond dated 13 Aug. 1835 with Arrington Hutchins as bondsman. Solemnized by J. W. Napier, J. P. (Note: Date of solemnization was illegible.)

James Dunigan to Casader Baker, marriage bond dated 27 July 1835 with Lewis Evins as bondsman. Executed 28 July 1835 by L. Russell, J. P.

George Dunnevant to Nancy Gibson, marriage bond dated 15 Dec. 1835.

Joseph Eatherage to Nancy Smith, marriage bond dated 13 Aug. 1835 with Willie Eatherage as bondsman. Solemnized 13 Aug. 1835. (Note: The name of the officiant could not be read. The surname is believed to be correctly Etheridge.)

Felix Fawcett to Jane Bledsoe, marriage bond dated 8 April 1835 with Caleb Morgan as bondsman. Solemnized 21 April 1835 by H. Parrish, J.P.

Francis E. Fowler to Martha Robertson, marriage bond dated 1835 with Charles Robertson as bondsman. (Note: This bond had not been filled in with complete dates. The bride's name is in question also.)

Henry Garton to Monncy Tidwell, marriage bond dated 25 Dec. 1835 with Moses Tidwell as bondsman. Executed 29 Dec. 1835 by _____, J. P. (Note: The officiant's name was illegible.)

R. J. Halliburton to Polly Turner, marriage bond dated 8 Oct. 1835; executed 8 Oct. 1835 by Benjamin Darrow, M. G. (Refer to following entry also.)

R. H. Burton married Miss Mary Turner 9 Oct. 1835, both of Dickson County. (National Review 18 Jan. 1836. Newspaper. For some unknown reason the name Halliburton is found many times as Burton in old records, with a middle initial of H. used.)

Simon Halliburton to Eliza Council, marriage bond dated 22 Oct. 1835. (Note: See following entry also.)

S. H. Burton married to Miss Eliza Council, both of Dickson County on October 26. (National Review, 19 Jan. 1836. Newspaper.)

Jerry Hambrick to Azelia Brown, marriage bond dated 25 Dec. 1835.

William Hand to Rachel Forsythe, marriage bond dated 30 July 1835 with James Carruthers as bondsman. Solemnized 10 March 1835 by Jno. Grymes.

John Hogwood to Teresa Holland, marriage bond dated 25 Sept. 1835 with James Holland as bondsman.

George W. Humphries to Laura Sutton, marriage bond dated 20 Oct. 1835 with Field Farrar, bondsman. Marriage solemnized 29 Oct. 1835 by H. Parrish, J. P. (See following entry also.)

G. W. Humphreys married 29 Oct. to Miss Laurel Sutton, both of Dickson County. (National Review, 19 Jan. 1836. Newspaper.)

John James to Delila Lewis, marriage license issued 14 Jan. 1835; executed 15 Jan. 1835 by H. W. Turner, J. P.

W. C. Jernigan to Nancy G. Holly, marriage bond dated 28 Dec. 1835.

Drury Jones to Minerva Wadkins, marriage bond dated 21 Nov. 1835 with Henry Jones as bondsman. Executed 29 Nov. 1835 by Reuben Chaudoin, who signed certificate 8 Dec. 1835.

George W. Larkins to Elizabeth Martin, license issued ___Oct. 1835.

James Larkins to Nyomy Bowen, marriage bond dated 14 March 1835.

William P. Lewis to Abegal Smitto, marriage bond dated 7 May 1835 with Tho. W. Collier, bondsman. Executed by H. W. Turner, J. P.

Jacob Lincoln to Jerusha Riley, marriage bond ____1835, with Jonathan Fuller as bondsman.

John McWilliams to Elizabeth Tatom, marriage bond issued 10 Sept. 1835 with John Simpson as bondsman.

William Marsh to Sally Spicer, marriage bond 24 July 1835; George W. Tatom, bondsman.

William Matlock to Maria Acuff, marriage bond dated 6 August 1835 with Richard Waugh, bondsman.

Jackson Malone to Nancy Ann Wilson, marriage bond dated 24 Sept. 1835 with James Arrington as bondsman. Executed 24 Sept. 1835 by W. B. Dotson, J. P. (Note: Groom's surname could be Melone.)

Philemon Moorehouse to Eliza Thomason, marriage bond dated 4 July 1835, with John Johnson as bondsman. Executed 6 July 1835 by M. Dickson J. P.

John Murrell to Sarah Harris, marriage bond dated 17 Dec. 1835.

John Murrell to Lucretia Choate, marriage bond dated 13 May 1835 with Jacob Carnes as bondsman. (Note: Groom's name abbreviated Jno. on the bond.)

William H. Morrow to Elizabeth Hill, marriage bond dated 9 Feb. 1835 with Overton L. Parrish as bondsman.

James C. Myatt to Elizabeth Ann Brown, marriage bond dated 9 Oct. 1835 with Andrew J. Myatt as bondsman.

John Norsworthy to Nancy R. Adams, marriage bond dated 26 Nov. 1835 with Willis Norsworthy as bondsman. (See entry below also.)

John Norsworthy of Dickson County married Miss Nancy B. Adams on the 30th. (National Review, 19 Jan. 1836. Newspaper.)

John C. Parker to Patsy Hand, marriage bond dated 31 Dec. 1835. (Note: Refer to page 16 the marriage of John Parker to Martha ___ as established in petition for divorce.)

Joshua Perkins to Susannah Nolen, marriage bond dated 12 Feb. 1835 with Edgy Hooper as bondsman. Executed 12 Feb. 1835 by R. Batson, J.P.

William Phillips to Susan Bartee, marriage license issued 29 Jan. 1835.

William Piner to Elizabeth Shropshire, marriage solemnized 12 March 1835 by J. D. Steele.

William Porter to Matilda Gafford, marriage bond dated 8 April 1835 with Jonathan Fuller as bondsman. Solemnized 8 April 1835 by J. Pendergrass, J. P.

William Pullen to Nancy Ann Hall, marriage bond dated 29 Dec. 1835.

Isaac Ramey to Martha Council, marriage bond dated 6 April 1835 with Mabel Gilbert as bondsman. Executed 7 April 1835 by Jno. Grymes, J.P.

Standford D. Rhea to Harriet Myatt, license issued 14 Jan. 1835; executed by David Gray, M. G., no date of execution.

Sandy D. Richardson to Elizabeth M. Nolin, marriage bond dated 18 Nov. 1835 with Hutson Richardson as bondsman. Executed, but no date can be deciphered. (Morrison Bible has Sandy D. Richardson married 18 Nov. 1835 to Elizabeth M. Nolin. See the following entry also.)

John Ritcherson married 19 Nov. 1835 to Miss Malinda Nolen of Dickson County. (National Review, 9 Jan. 1836. Newspaper.)

Henry R. Rogers to Crissie Burton, marriage bond dated 13 Nov. 1835 with Erasmus J. Ellis as bondsman. (See following entry also.)*

---

*Henry Rogers was one of three brothers who married Halliburtons. His brother Callum Rogers married Nancy Ann Halliburton (but no date for this marriage is known) and Edward Moore Rogers married Lucy Lee Halliburton 11 Jan. 1840, and their marriage is in this book.

Miss Crissy H. Burton married on the 20th to Mr. Henry B. Rogers, both of Dickson County. (National Review, 19 Jan. 1836. Newspaper. Refer also to the entry immediately before this one. Family records show Chrisstie Halliburton, daughter of Martin Halliburton, was born 1812, died 1884, and is buried in Sango Cemetery in Montgomery County, Tenn. She and her husband Henry Rogers once lived in vicinity of Danielsville on Yellow Creek in Dickson County.)

William Sewell to Ann Baker, marriage bond dated 10 Oct. 1835 with William M. Patterson, bondsman. (See following entry.)

Miss Ann Baker of Dickson County married to Mr. William Sewell on the 8th of Oct., both of Dickson County. (National Review, 19 Jan. 1836. Newspaper. See entry above also.)

Edward M. Simpson to Lucinda Johnson, marriage bond dated 5 Jan. 1835 with S. T. King as bondsman.

John Smith to Lydia H. B. Hardwick, marriage bond dated 22 Dec. 1835. Solemnized 22 Dec. 1835 by J. Voorhies, J. P.

William Smith to Elizabeth Sanders, marriage bond dated 11 Feb. 1835 with Francis Larkins as bondsman.

Joseph Spicer to Ann_____, marriage bond dated 8 Jan. 1835 with Samuel Tate as bondsman. (Note: Bride's last name had never been written in but a line had been drawn where surname should have been.)

Travis E. Slayden to Lovy Council, marriage bond dated 20 Nov. 1835. (Note: The marriage was solemnized but the date was illegible. See also following entry.)

Miss Lovy Council of Dickson County married Travice Staden of Dickson County on the 27th. (National Review, 19 Jan. 1836. See entry above.)

Sampson Stewart to Beede Prater, marriage bond dated 11 Feb. 1835 with Francis Lankford as bondsman. (Note: Bride's name given as Beedy Prater on inside of bond.)

John Sullivant to Ara Stroud, marriage bond dated 22 Dec. 1835; executed 24 Dec. 1835 by William White, J. P.

Samuel Tate to Mary Hedge, marriage bond dated 18 April 1835 with Sharp Dunnegan as bondsman. Executed 21 April 1835 by W. B. Dotson, J. P.

Jonathan Thomason to Nancy Smith, marriage bond dated 16 May 1835 with William M. Patterson, bondsman.

Amos Thompson to _____, marriage bond dated 11 May 1835 with John Norsworthy as bondsman. Executed 14 May 1835 by W. B. Young, J. P.

Gladden Tidwell to Sarah Lankford, marriage bond dated 9 Dec. 1835 with Michael Tidwell as bondsman. Executed 9 Dec. 1835 by A. Pullen, J. P.

Elijah Walker to Polly McMillan, marriage bond dated 30 March 1835 with George Brazeal as bondsman.

George Washington Williams to Charlotte Johnson, marriage bond dated 31 March 1835 with James Yeates as bondsman. Solemnized 2 April 1835 by R. Batson, J. P.

Daniel M. Young to Martha A. Baxter, marriage bond dated 3 May 1835 with Jerome B. Hinson as bondsman. Executed 7 May 1835 by H. Parrish, J. P.

1836

Gabriel Andrews to Adalina Mitchell, marriage bond dated 25 Aug. 1836 with W. B. Joslin, bondsman. Solemnized 2 Aug. 1836.

James Armstrong to Mahaley Turner, marriage bond dated 1 Oct. 1836 with John Eubank as bondsman.

Martin Arnold to Jane Burgie, marriage bond dated 29 March 1836 with John Story as bondsman. Solemnized by _____. (Note: Date and J. P. were illegible.)

William Baker to Mary C. Hasley, marriage bond dated 28 April 1836 with William Richardson as bondsman. Solemnized 2 May 1836 by James Daniel, J. P.

Michael Berry to Mary Ann Walker, marriage bond dated 7 March 1836 with John Norsworthy as bondsman. Executed 13 March 1836 by Richard Kindle. (Note: Bride's name is given as Nancy Ann Walker on the license.)

T. C. Binkley to Indiana A. Massee, license issued 25 Oct. 1837. Executed 26 Oct. 1837 by John Eubanks, J. P. (Note: This 1837 license was in with these 1836 marriages.)

Robert H. Brown to Martha Hogan, marriage bond dated 23 Nov. 1836; Tho. J. Kelly as bondsman. Date of execution was illegible. (Note: Bride's surname given as Hogins on license.)

Solomon Carr to Lucinda Bledsoe, marriage bond dated 27 Oct. 1836 with William Lamaster as bondsman.

Howell H. Davidson to Sarah Davidson, marriage bond dated 14 March 1838 with Daniel M. Shearman as bondsman. Executed 15 March 1838 by L. Russell, J. P. (Note: The execution date appeared to be 1838 without question but was with the 1836 records.)

Samuel A. Dains, merchant at Maysville, married on the 18th instant by Howard W. Turner to Miss Sarah Garrett of Dickson County. (National Register, 30 May 1837. Newspaper. This 1837 marriage included here even though it is for another year.)

Nelson Dunnigan to Martha Russell, marriage bond dated 14 Jan. 1836 with Harmon Joiner as bondsman. Executed, no date, by K. Myatt, J. P. (Note: The first name of the bondsman could also be Harris or Harms.)

Field Farrar to Martha W. Wills, marriage license dated 1 July 1836.

Alfred Fughn to Eliza Tinsley, marriage bond dated 29 Nov. 1836 with John Cooper as bondsman. Executed 13 Dec. 1836 by Reuben Chaudoin.

Hesekiah Gray to Sarah Kimbrough, marriage bond dated 12 Oct. 1836 with George W. Gray as bondsman.

Mr. Dillard Hardwick of Charlotte, Tenn., married on July 21 in Choctaw County, Mississippi, to Miss Mary C. Boykin of Mississippi. (National Register, 15 Aug. 1837. Note: Although this marriage took place elsewhere it is included here as it was for a resident of Dickson County.)

Joseph Harris to Sarah Brown, marriage bond dated 1 Dec. 1836 with Willie Jones as bondsman. Executed 8 Dec. 1836 by J. H. Christian, J. P.

Abraham Hasley to Letty Parrott, marriage bond dated 29 Feb. 1836. (Note: Bondsman's name was given but could not be deciphered. Refer also to page 112, 1880 mortalities in this book.)

James W. Hays to Mary Bartee, marriage bond dated 22 Sept. 1836 with J. Eubanks as bondsman.

Charles Houston to Mary G. Roche, bond dated 24 Feb. 1836 with James M. Ross as bondsman. Executed 25 Feb. 1836 by Reuben Chaudoin.

John Humble to Rebecca Hogins, marriage bond dated 14 Sept. 1836 with James K. Clifton as bondsman.

Benjamin Jones to Mary Williamston, solemnized 11 Nov. 1836 by J. Pendergrass, J. P.

Alfred King to Lucy Murrell, marriage bond dated 24 April 1836 with Andrew C. Gunn, bondsman. Executed ___May 1836.

James Landerson to Emaline Landerson, marriage bond dated 28 Feb. 1836. Solemnized 29 Feb. 1836 by M. Carr, J. P. (Note: This bond was very dim on the film.)

Aron Laws to Elizabeth M. Johnson, marriage license dated ___July 1836. Executed by H. B. Moore. (Note: No date of execution given.)

Finis W. Leech to Mary C. Collier, bond dated 15 July 1836 with Robert McNeely as bondsman.

George W. Leigh to Margarett Billups, marriage bond dated 19 Oct. 1836 with Daniel D. Billups as bondsman. Executed. (Note: The execution date was given but too dim to read.)

John Linsey to Susan Duke, marriage license dated ___Sept. 1836. Executed 16 Sept. 1836 by Reuben Chaudoin.

George Lewis to Rachel Christman, marriage bond dated 26 Jan. 1836 with T. J. Collier as bondsman. Executed 26 Jan. 1836 by Jno. Grymes, J. P. (Note: The surname is in question.)

William Long to Nancy Brown, marriage bond dated 1 Oct. 1836 with James Matlock as bondsman. Executed 4 Oct. 1836 by John Colson, J. P.

Thomas McNeiley to Mary Rye, marriage bond dated 29 Dec. 1836 with James McNeilley as bondsman. Executed 29 Dec. 1836 by John Edwards.

William McNeiley to Sophiah B. Bowers, license dated 12 June 1836. Executed 15 June 1836 by Jesse ____. (Note: Surname of officiant was illegible.)

William Miller to Tabbetha Haguewood, license issued 2 July 1836. Executed 5 July 1836. (Note: Name of officiant was illegible.)

C_____Minor to Mary West, marriage bond issued 22 June 1836 with J. P. Hardwick as bondsman.

Robert B. Mitchell to Nancy Payne, marriage license issued 18 Dec. 1836 and executed 22 Dec. 1836 by Jesse Edwards.

James M. Morgan to Martha A. Rhinehart, marriage bond issued 24 May 1836 with A. H. Morgan as bondsman.

Guilford Morris to Araminty Gleaves, marriage bond dated 8 Dec. 1836 with G. W. Duke as bondsman. Executed 13 Dec. 1836 by Reuben Chaudoin.

Thomas Overton to Elizabeth Christian, marriage license issued 2 Sept. 1836.

William M. Paterson to Elizabeth Richardson, bond dated 24 Dec. 1836 with Robert Paterson as bondsman. Executed 27 Dec. 1836 by Thomas Jernigan, J. P.

William K. Petty to Emelina George, marriage bond dated 8 Feb. 1836 with James D. Petty as bondsman. Executed by David Gray, M. G., no date. (Note: Groom's middle initial also appeared to be "R" or "G".)

John S. Reynolds to Lydia Lewis, marriage bond dated 21 Jan. 1836 with William Jarnagin as bondsman. Executed _____. (Note: date of the solemnization was dim and hard to read.)

Charles Robertson to Dolly Crews, marriage bond dated 11 June 1836 with Albert Hunter as bondsman. Solemnized 15 June 1836 by J. W. Christian, J. P.

Daniel Robertson to Nancy Jones, marriage bond dated 28 March 1836.

Archibald Sensing to Rebach Fourd, marriage bond dated 3 Sept. 1836 with Mekindra G. Sensing as bondsman.

Wm. Sensing to Elizabeth Moore, marriage bond dated 24 June 1836 with Thomas McNieley as bondsman. Executed 24 July 1836 by Richard Randle. (Note: Note difference in month here.)

John Stanfield to Nancy Hall, marriage bond dated 1 Nov. 1836 with Isaac Hill as bondsman.

Knot W. Tidwell to Clara Hammond, marriage bond dated 8 April 1836 with Samuel Skipper as bondsman. Executed 10 April 1836 by William White, J. P.

Daniel Thorn to Sarah Green, marriage bond dated 17 Aug. 1836 with Patrick H. Madden as bondsman. (Note: This marriage was solemnized but the date was faded. The groom's name appeared to be Thom in one place.)

David D. Weakley to Cynthia C. Fausser, marriage bond dated 12 July 1836 with John Forsythe as bondsman. (Note: The bride's surname is in question; it was hard to decipher.)

Reubin White to Mary B. Mitchell, marriage bond dated 31 Oct. 1836 with John M. Bibb as bondsman.

MISCELLANEOUS MARRIAGE NOTES

- CASE. In the Tennessee State Library and Archives, Nashville, Tennessee, there is a legislative petition from Dickson County entitled a petition for divorce, Sarah Case from Francis Case, 1820. This might be for a marriage performed in Dickson County but was not checked for this study.

- CLARK. Benjamin Clark married 14 Feb. 1805 to Sarah Larkin. This marriage was quoted in an article in the Dickson Free Press, dated 26 May 1976. The Bible at that time was owned by Mrs. Mary Ann Caldwell of White Bluff. Benjamin Clark was the son of George Clark, who served 1804 on the committee to select the site for the courthouse in Dickson County.

- SULLIVAN. John L. Sullivan was married 1827 in Dickson County to Arrena Thompson. This information was sent to me by the late Mildred Sullivan Gambill of Waverly--she never could find an official record for this marriage but cited the Sullivan biography in Goodspeed's History of Humphreys County as well as the couple being found on 1850 census of Humphreys County. Arrena Thompson Sullivan is buried beside her husband in the Sullivan Cemetery on Big Richland Creek in Humphreys County.

II

DICKSON COUNTY MARRIAGES
1838 - 1849

These marriages were copied from a bound volume of marriages. Some of the entries were difficult to read. Please check all possible variations in spelling.*

1838

Henry Southerland to Elizabeth McCollom, license issued 9 Jan. 1838.

Benjamin Bowen to Wineford Walker, license issued 11 Jan. 1838. Executed by David Gray, M. G.

James Ross to Edy Myatt, license issued 20 Jan. 1838. Executed by L. Russell.

Thomas M. Caldwell to Elizabeth W. Bell, license issued 23 Jan. 1838. Executed 25 Jan. 1838 by Jesse Edwards, M. G.

Aaron J. Parrish to Rebecca C. Dickson, license issued 27 Jan. 1838. Executed 1 Feb. 1838.

John H. Wright to Mary Martin, license issued 29 Jan. 1838. Executed by L. Russell, J. P., 3 Feb. 1838.

Simon McClendon to Carolina Reynolds, license issued 30 Jan. 1838. Executed 30 Jan. 1838 by Thomas Jarnigan, J. P.

William R. Raney to Susanna C. Jarnagin. Executed by James Daniel, J. P., 1 Feb. 1838.

Richard Murphy to Mary E. Lewis, license issued 9 Feb. 1838. Executed 11 Feb. 1838 by James Daniel, J. P. (Note: an earlier copyist of these marriages read the date of issue as 5 Feb. 1838.)

A. D. Cochran to Nancy Bowen, license issued 12 Feb. 1838. Executed 17 Feb. 1838 by L. Russell, J. P. (Note: The bride's name could also be Nancy Brown.)

William E. Ellis to Mary Ann Ellis, license issued 12 Feb. 1838. Executed 5 Feb.1838 by Thomas Jarnigan.

John R. Jones to Rebecca Russell, license issued 19 Feb. 1838. Executed 22 Feb. 1838 by K. Myatt, J. P.

Ervin Swift to Matilda Welker, license issued 24 Feb. 1838. Executed 12 March 1838 by M. W. Gray, M. G. (Note: An earlier copyist read his name as Erin T. Swift.)

M. Dunn to Margaret Foster, license issued 5 March 1838.

A. J. Myatt to Emaline Oakley, license issued 8 March 1838. Executed by L. Russell, J. P., 8 March 1838. (Note: Some copyists often given the name Oakley as O'Kelly in their copies.)

John W. Ragan to Letticia Tycer, license issued 10 March 1838. Executed by John Eubanks, J. P.

James Lee to Serlane Christer, license issued 13 March 1838. Executed 15 March 1838 by L. Russell, J. P.

---

*We checked our listing with two other listings. Differences will be noted. The most reliable former listing of Dickson marriages may be found in "35,000 Tennessee Marriage Records and Bonds".

Howell A. Davidson to Sarah Davidson, license issued 14 March 1838. Executed 15 March 1838 by L. Russell, J. P.

Jeremiah Gray to Polly Ragan, license issued 29 March 1838. Executed 1 April 1838 by K. Myatt, J. P.

Mark Harris to Martha Gentry, license issued 14 April 1838. Executed 19 April 1838 by M. B. Stuart, J. P.

Daniel M. Jones to Mary Dunnegan, license issued 28 April 1838. Executed by Henry Goodrich, Esquire.

John Turner to Sarah C. Parrish, license issued 2 June 1838. Executed 14 June 1838 by H. W. Turner, J. P.

Judge Jackson to Mary E. Rooker, license issued 4 June 1838. Executed 5 June 1838 by M. W. Gray, M. G.

Samuel Bugg to Lucy Sweaney, license issued 7 June 1838. Executed 8 June 1838 by H. W. Turner, J. P.

Pryor H. Smith to Paralee D. Christian, license issued 16 June 1838. Executed 17 June 1838 by H. W. Turner, J. P.

William Creach to Sarah White, license issued 20 June 1838. Executed ___ June 1838 by John Eubank, J. P.

John Austin to Penelope Creach, license issued 25 June 1838. Executed 27 June 1838 by M. B. Stuart, J. P.

William A. Steele to Susannah Stone, license issued 26 June 1838. Executed 28 June 1838 by Willie Miller, J. P.

Richmond Brazzell to Any Evans, license issued 27 June 1838. Executed 28 June 1838 by Henry Goodrich, Esquire.

William C. Glenn to Elizabeth Walker, license issued 3 July 1838. Marriage executed.

William Russell to Tabitha Gunn, license issued 17 June 1838. Executed 18 July 1838 by Henry Goodrich, Esquire.

Jesse Eastes to Margaret Marsh, license issued 19 July 1838. Executed 19 July 1838 by Henry Goodrich, Esquire.

Joseph Chrisman to Margaret Northern, issued 19 July 1838. Executed 19 July 1838 by James Daniel, J. P.

Bennett C. Duke to Martha Jones, license issued 24 July 1838. Executed 25 July 1838 by D. S. Ford, J. P.

Stanford Dunnegan to Alcy Dunnegan, license issued 30 August 1838. Executed 30 August 1838 by L. Russell, J. P.

Benjamin Sims to Kizziah C. Hunter, license issued 10 Sept. 1838. Executed 16 Sept. 1838 by W. Hand, J. P.

Elijah F. Pendergrass to Hannah Sears, license issued 14 Sept. 1838. Executed 16 Sept. 1838 by William White, J. P.

J. M. Miller to Catherine Douglas, license issued 18 Sept. 1838.

Solomon George to Ferebe Holland, license issued 18 Sept. 1838. Executed by D. Gray, M. G., 20 Sept. 1838.

James Hunter to Sarah Jones, license issued 18 Sept. 1838. Executed by Henry J. Binkley, J. P.

William M. Gunn to Mary Ann Puckett, license issued 2 October 1838; executed 8 October 1838 by Henry Goodrich, J. P.

Thomas J. Kelly to Eliza J. Hardwicke license issued 9 October 1838; executed 9 October 1838 by the Reverend James Marshall.

Clayton T. Hall to Martha S. White, license issued 9 October 1838.

Thomas M. Reynolds to Durina Slayden, license issued 10 October 1838; executed 16 October 1838 by H. W. Turner, J. P.

John M. Bibb to Caroline Johnson, license issued 12 October 1838; executed 11 October 1838 by Empson Bishop. (Note dates of execution and issuing.)

Joshua Clarkston to Delila Hand, license issued 15 October 1838; executed 16 October 1838 by D. S. Ford.

Daniel Cathey to Mary Goodwin, license issued 18 October 1838; executed 18 October 1838 by Henry Goodrich, J. P.

Francis E. Fowler to Jane Robinson, license issued 18 October 1838.

Joseph Nesbitt to Caroline Jane Burns, license issued 20 October 1838; executed _____ by M. Berry, M. G.

William J. Spradlin to Lucretia Blockley, license issued 1 Nov. 1838.

William King to Rebecca Tatom, license issued 3 November 1838; executed 4 November 1838 by D. Womack, J. P.

William D. Reynolds to Elizabeth Jane Walker, license issued 8 Nov. 1838.

Hiram Morgan to Sally Stuart, license issued 19 November 1838; executed 20 November 1838 by Henry J. Binkly, J. P.

Jesse Wall to Mary J. Hightower, license issued 21 November 1838; executed 20 November 1838 by Henry J. Binkly, J. P.

A. C. Gunn to Louisa C. Tucker, license issued 23 November 1838; executed 25 November 1838 by John Larkins, J. P.

Albert N. Joslin to Martha A. _____, license issued 25 November 1838.

Thomas Petty to Rebecca Ann Adcock, license issued 24 December 1838; executed by David Gray, M. G.

John W. Hudson to Mary Tilly, license issued 1 December 1838.

Jesse Coleman to Priscilla L. Terry (Perry?), license issued 24 Dec. 1838; executed 24 December 1838 by L. Russell, J. P.

William Fleet to Sally Edwards, license issued 28 Dec. 1838; executed 28 December 1838 by James Daniel, J. P.

Washington Irby to Margaret Smith, license issued 28 Dec. 1838; executed by M. Berry, M. G.

1839

Benjamin McCaslin to Levena Tidwell, license issued 2 January 1839; executed by William White, J. P., 3 January 1839.
(Note: Another person once copied his name as Benjamin F. McCaslin. We found no "F" in our original copy of these marriages.)

Lewis Evans to Rachel Brazzell, license issued 4 January 1839.

Thomas H. Hinson to Catherine Ellis, license issued 8 January 1839.

Washington Winns to Matilda Vineyard, license issued 31 January 1839. (Note: Everyone who has ever copied the Dickson County marriages has come up with a different version of the surname--some using Weems, some Weins. We do not know if the name is Wynn or Winns as it seems to appear. However, the 1850 census of Dickson County shows W. T. Wyms with wife Matilda in the county that year.)

William Adkinson to Mary Ann Jane Mills, license issued 2 Feb. 1839.

Jacob Petty to Nancy Bibb, license issued 11 February 1839.

David Record to Elizabeth Sanderson, license issued 16 Feb. 1839; executed 21 February 1839 by M. B. Stuart, J. P.

Gilbert Marsh to Dolly Cathey, license issued 23 February 1839.

Joseph S. Slayden to Julia Ann Shelton, license issued 8 March 1839; executed 11 April 1839 by William McMurry.

John Holland to Mary Myatt, license issued 12 March 1839; executed 14 March 1839 by K. Myatt, J. P.

Roberts S. Nesbitt to Martha E. Ragan, license issued 16 March 1839; executed by M. Berry, M. G.

Lorenzo Burpo to Arena Lewis, license issued 19 March 1839; executed by H. W. Turner, J. P.

Benjamin R. Craig to Mary G. Lewis, license issued 20 March 1839; executed by H. W. Turner, J. P.

Madison Dunnegan to Manervia Dodson, license issued 30 March 1839; executed 30 March 1839 by L. Russell, J. P.

James McDurmitt to Olif Harris, license issued 2 May 1839; executed 2 May 1839 by D. S. Ford, J. P.

Edward McCormack to Mariah Link, license issued 23 May 1839; executed 23 May 1839 by John Eubank, J. P.

John Welch to Elizabeth Luther, license issued 8 June 1839; executed 9 June 1839 by John McCaslin, J. P.

William Johnson to Susan Richardson, license issued 21 June 1839; executed 23 June 1839 by the Reverend James T. Morris.

Henry White to Martha Parker license issued 5 July 1839; executed 11 July 1839 by D. S. Ford, J. P.

Lewis D. Collins to Sally Ann Hickerson, license issued 10 July 1839; executed 14 July 1839 by John Eubank, J. P.

Jackson Brazzell to Sarah Tatom, license issued 17 June 1839.

Fanning Yates to Elizabeth Murrell, license issued 17 July 1839; executed 25 July 1839 by K. Myatt.

Job P. Doty to Sarah R. Ford, license issued 31 July 1839; executed 4 August 1839 by William Hand, J. P.

John H. Jones to Finetta B. James, license issued 9 August 1839; executed 22 August 1839 by I. C. Blankenship.

Feliso Robertson to Sarah Hunter, license issued 15 August 1839; executed 16 August 1839 by H. J. Binkly, J. P.

Frank Mulhemis to Susan Oliver, license issued 18 Aug. 1839. (Note: This man's name is possibly incorrect. We could not read it and are using an interpretation made by an earlier copyist.)

John C. West to Lueslia Blockly, license issued 19 August 1839. (Note: These names are in question.)

G. G. Paschall to Mary Ann Toler, license issued 21 August 1839; executed 25 August 1839 by John Eubank, J. P.

Absalom Massie to Milberry Matlock, license issued 24 August 1839.

William Lee to Syntha Jordan, license issued 27 August 1839; executed by H. W. Turner, J. P.

Joseph Price to Elizabeth Rose, license issued 10 Sept. 1839; executed by John McCaslin, J. P., 12 September 1839.

Miles Long to Sophia Heard, license issued 19 September 1839.

Moses Tidwell to Nancy McCaslin, license issued 28 September 1839; executed by D. Gray.

B. F. Larkins to Emily I. Bowen, license issued 28 Sept. 1839.

John G. Hill to Caroline Scott, license issued 28 September 1839; executed 3 October 1839 by James Daniel, J. P.

James M. Albright to Margaret S. Halliburton, license issued 29 September 1839; executed 29 September 1839 by Thomas Jarnigan, J. P.

George L. Smith to Mary Larkins, license issued 1 October 1839.

George Russell to Lucinda Mathews, license issued 4 October 1839.

James Gould to Martha W. Farrar, license issued 5 October 1839; executed 6 October 1839 by H. J. Binkly, J. P. (Note: These people are buried in the old City Cemetery in Nashville, Tennessee.)

Willie I. Gunter to Martha Jones, license issued 11 October 1839; executed 11 October 1839 by Cornelius Grimes, J. P.

James Baggett to Nancy Davis, license issued 19 October 1839; executed 21 October 1839 by Benjamin Darrow. (Note: Our original notes show the marriage was not solemnized until 1840, but we now believe this was an error on our part.)

George Russell to Lucinda Matthews, license issued 21 October 1839; executed 21 October 1839 by Cornelius Grimes, J. P.

Henry Hall to Sarah Ferrell, license issued 23 October 1839; executed 23 October 1839 by H. W. Joslin, M. G. (Note: Some copyists have never included the minister's name. Our notes show this name.)

Burgess Wall to Nancy Harvey, license issued 9 November 1839; executed __May 1840 by Jordan Moore, M. G.

John L. Martin to Minerva J. Hobbs, license issued 14 November 1839.

Drury Seals to Susan Oliver, license issued 21 November 1839; executed 21 November 1839 by John Larkins, J. P. (Note: Susan Oliver appears as the bride on a questionable marriage listed on page 27 of this book.)

John Corlew to Susan Leech, license issued 5 December 1839.

James Brown to Ruth Sellars, license issued 5 December 1839; executed 5 December 1839 by William White, J. P.

Isaac Hunter to Nancy Dave, license issued 7 December 1839; executed 10 December 1839 by Joseph Morris, J. P. (Note: An earlier copyist read the bride's name as Nancy Dane.)

James C. Balthrope to Mary Russell, issued 9 December 1839; executed

17 December 1839 by James Daniel, J. P.

Joseph Larkins to Emily Martin, license issued 24 December 1839.

John Burgess to Phebee Watkins, license issued 28 December 1839; executed 29 December 1839 by W. B. Dotson, J. P.

1840

Thomas Gilbert to Elizabeth D. Collier, license issued 2 January 1840.

James M. Baker to Caroline Goodrich, license issued 11 Jan. 1840; executed 14 Feb. 1840 by Thomas Jarnigan, J. P.

William Phillips to Elender Hogins, license issued 11 January 1840; executed by D. Gray.

Edward M. Rogers to Lucy L. Halliburton, license issued 11 January 1840; executed by H. W. Turner, J. P.

Kinderick Myatt to Sinthy Loftis, license issued 14 January 1840.

Robert Leftwich to Emeline Arnold, license issued 15 January 1840.

Thomas Karns to Martha Hall, license issued 20 January 1840.

William M. Mitchell to Surrena Speight, license issued 24 January 1840.

James H. Oakley to Louisa Myatt, license issued 29 January 1840; executed 30 January 1840 by L. Russell, J. P.

George Parnell to Harriet Price, license issued 7 February 1840; executed 7 Feb. 1840 by John McCaslin, J. P.

John W. Green to Nancy Rye, license issued 8 Feb. 1840; executed 16 Feb. 1840 by Thomas Jarnigan, J. P.

Wesley Jackson to Parthenia Cook, license issued 25 Feb. 1840; executed by John Eubank.

George Dunnevin to Anna Waldin, license issued 2 March 1840; executed 3 March 1840.

John M. Biter to Jennette March, license issued 16 March 1840; executed by John Eubank, J. P.

John A. Weakley to Anna Wall, license issued 16 March 1840; executed 19 March 1840 by William Hand, J. P.

James A. Nesbitt to Nancy Long, license issued 19 March 1840; executed by John Eubank.

John E. Ellis to Harriet Henson, license issued 26 March 1840; executed 31 March 1840 by Willie Miller, J. P.

James D. Hudson to Winnefred M. Lane, license issued 4 April 1840; executed by M. Berry, M. G.

Judge W. Crockett to Polly Wall, license issued 31 March 1840; executed 2 April 1840 by W. Hand, J. P.

Thomas Murphy to Sarah Barter, license issued 2 April 1840; executed 3 April 1840 by John Eubank.

John Rye to Mary Jane Davidson, license issued 18 April 1840; executed by Reuben Chaudoin on 20 April 1840.

Henry M. Hutton to Anna Drummonds, license issued 20 April 1840.

Joseph Dave to Caroline E. F. Fowler, license issued 20 April 1840. (Note: Three different copyists have read this name differently; some read it as Joseph Dane; some as Joseph Done; some as Joseph Dave.)

Hamilton Parks to Rebecca Etherley, license issued 25 April 1840.

John G. Crumpler to Elizabeth Caldwell, license issued 21 May 1840.

Cullin Price to Permelia Ann Recce, license issued 21 May 1840; executed 21 May 1840 by John McCaslin, J. P.

Martin H. Cobbler to Mary Ann Smith, license issued 27 May 1840; executed 28 May 1840 by Jesse Edwards, M. G.

Willis Jackson to Mary Hightower, license issued 20 June 1840; executed by John Eubank.

Benjamin Hay to Huldy Tidwell, license issued 22 June 1840; executed 24 June 1840 by E. Bishop.

Minor Bibb to Lydia Pryor, license issued 24 June 1840, executed by M. B. Stuart, J. P., 25 June 1840.

Andrew Price to Dorothy Fletcher, license issued 4 July 1840; executed 5 July 1841 by John McCaslin, J. P. (Note: Three different copyists have read the solemnization date as 5 July 1841.)

Benajah Gentry to Jane Gentry, license issued 15 July 1840; executed 19 July 1840 by M. B. Stuart, J. P.

James C. Hambrick to Mary Fussell, license issued 23 July 1840.

James Tatom to Anne Tatom, license issued 27 July 1840; executed 30 July 1840 by James C. Pullen, J. P. (Note: One person read the justice's name as Peebles.)

Vernon Bibb to Elizabeth Bibb, license issued 30 July 1840; executed 30 July 1840 by Empson Bishop.

Drury Chappell to Rachel Henry, license issued 5 August 1840; executed 5 August 1840 by William White, J. P.

William Bell to Elizabeth Grimes, license issued 5 August 1840; executed 6 August 1840 by R. Chaudoin.

Robert S. B. Gunn to Dolly Dunn, license issued 5 August 1840; executed 11 August 1840 by James C. Pullen, J. P.

William Cane to Mary James, license issued 5 August 1840; executed 6 August 1840 by W. Hand, J. P.

Wesley Williams to Nancy Dickson, license issued 31 August 1840; executed 1 September 1840 by Rev. Benjamin Rawls.

Walter C. Gentry to Nancy Gentry, license issued 3 September 1840; executed 3 September 1840 by Marcus B. Stuart, J. P.

Jesse Walton to Elizabeth Hagwood, license issued 17 September 1840; executed 8 Sept. 1840 by William Hand, J. P.

John H. Shelton to Sophia Patterson, license issued 28 September 1840.

James W. Hunter to Elizabeth Anne Rooker, license issued 6 October 1840.

Jarrett N. Langford to Lyda Sanders, license issued 18 October 1840; executed 18 October 1840. (Note: His surname could be Lankford; her name has been copied by others as Lytha, Sytha.)

Joseph Fuller to Amanda Durin, license issued 14 Oct. 1840. (Note: Some have read his surname as Fulfer.)

Henderson Procktor to Charlotte Spicer, license issued 20 October 1840; executed 21 October 1840 by C. Grymes, J. P.

George B. Lewis to Sarah M. Fly, license issued 20 October 1840; executed 29 October 1840 by James Daniel, J. P.

Benjamin Rye to Mary Anne Valentine, license issued 29 October 1840; executed 29 October 1840 by James Daniel, J. P.

Elijah Davidson to Mary Hudson, license issued 31 October 1840; executed 31 October 1840 by K. Myatt, J. P.

Epps Jackson to Sarah M. Eleazer, license issued 7 November 1840; executed 8 November 1840 by David Gray, M. G.

Robert L. Dunaway to Eveline Allen, license issued 17 Nov. 1840.

Allen Halliburton to Susan Rainey, license issued 21 November 1840.

Manoah Parrott to Cassander Nichols, license issued 5 December 1840; executed 10 December 1840 by James Daniel, J. P.

Joseph F. White to Jane Nalls, license issued 14 December 1840; executed 15 December 1840 by Parion Bishop.

John James to Phoebe Price, license issued 21 December 1840; executed 22 December 1840 by H. J. Binkley, J. P.

Mark Garton to Jensey Tidwell, license issued 21 December 1840; executed 22 December 1840 by M. B. Stuart, J. P.

Martin Cathey to Louisa Creech, license issued 22 December 1840; executed by L. Russell, J. P.

Napoleon F. Wilkins to Mary Anne Steele, license issued 24 Dec. 1840; executed by John Eubanks, J. P.

1841

William Luke to Emeline Hickerson, license issued 1 January 1841; executed by John Eubank, J. P.

William M. England to Luvica Higgenbotham, license issued 9 January 1841; executed by John Eubank, J. P.

James Daughtery to Luvina White, license issued 10 January 1841.

Albert Hunter to Sarah Crews, license issued 11 January 1841; executed 14 January 1841 by William Hand, J. P.

Owen Monroe to Caroline Sweeny, license issued 19 Jan. 1841; executed 20 January 1841 by H. J. Binkly, J. P.

William Spears to Minerva Hudson, license issued 30 January 1841; executed 31 January 1841 by K. Myatt, J. P.

Thomas Wiseman to Stacy Bishop, license issued 2 February 1841; executed 4 February 1841 by James Daniel, J. P.

David W. Adcock to Martha Anne Crow, license issued 2 February 1841; executed 3 February 1841 by J. Pendergrass, J. P.

Robert Layne to Sarah Paschall, license issued 4 February 1841.

Elisha L. Lloyd to Angeline Bowen, license issued 9 February 1841; executed 14 February 1841.

William B. Ross to Mary T. Raworth, license issued 11 February 1841. (Note: One copyist read his surname as Rawls.)

George W. Bruce to Lydia Dunnegan, license issued 15 Feb. 1841; executed 16 February 1841.

James M. Davidson to Sarah Jane Luther, license issued 17 February 1841; executed 28 February 1841 by K. Myatt, J. P.

Albert G. Sweeny to Kisiah Murrell, license issued 18 February 1841; executed 19 February 1841 by G. W. Tatom, J. P.

Thomas Steele to Mary Stone, license issued 1 March 1841.

Blount Dunnegan to Parthena Dunnegan, license issued 11 March 1841; executed 11 March 1841 by L. Russell, J. P.

Anthony G. Lewis to Nancy Hawkins, license issued 16 March 1841; executed 18 March 1841 by W. R. Hicks, J. P.

William Hand to Nancy Hunter, license issued 17 March 1841; executed 18 March 1841 by William Garrett, J. P.

Thomas Smith to Malinda Matlock, license issued 20 March 1841; executed by John Eubank, J. P.

James McEnnerie to Dicy Crumpler, license issued 22 March 1841; executed 23 March 1841 by George Raworth, J. P.

James Jones to Elizabeth Brown, license issued 26 March 1841.

James N. Hunter to Elizabeth Rooker, license issued 26 March 1841; executed 4 April 1841 by George F. Raworth, J. P.

Moses Sears to Lucretia Pendergrass, license issued 1 April 1841; executed 3 April 1841 by J. Pendergrass, J. P.

Jeremiah Bateman to Nancy Morris, license issued 13 April 1841; executed 13 April 1841 by J. Hill, J. P.

Edward S. Young to Sarah A. Irby, license issued 14 April 1841; executed by John Eubank, J. P.

David Wisenhunt (Whisenhunt) to Elizabeth Brown, license issued 16 April 1841; executed ___April 1841 by George F. Raworth., J. P.

Henry Cole to Frances Johnson, license issued 21 April 1841.

Andrew Monk to Cynthia Haley, license issued 29 April 1841; executed 29 April 1841 by L. Russell, J. P.

Henry Whizenhunt to Elizabeth Barnett, license issued 4 May 1841; executed 16 May 1841 by George F. Raworth, J. P.

John Anderson to Polly Hagewood, license issued 18 May 1841; executed 18 May 1841 by William Garrett, J. P.

Memory England to Malinda Hedge, license issued 5 June 1841; executed 6 June 1841 by Joel Erranton, J. P.

William McCoin to Anna Jones, license issued 13 June 1841; executed 14 June 1841 by James Daniel, J. P.

Elida Burns to Lucy Cugh, license issued 16 June 1841; executed 17 June 1841 by Benjamin Darrow, M. G.

Joshua Y. Knight to Elizabeth Anne Parish, license issued 27 July 1841; executed 29 July 1841 by W. R. Hicks, J. P.

George Scott to Elizabeth Jane Richardson, license issued 27 July 1841; executed 28 July 1841 by H. J. Binkly, J. P.

Thomas M. Wheeler to Louisa Tycer, license issued 3 August 1841.

John C. Ashworth to Nancy Cornell, license issued 17 August 1841; executed 17 August 1841 by John Eubank, J. P.

Washington G. L. Buttrey to Mary Lampley, license issued 23 August 1841; executed 26 August 1841 by J. Hill, J. P.

Alexander Southerland to Julia Anne Wilkins, license issued 24 August 1841; executed 24 August 1841 by John Eubank, J. P.

Thomas Jones to Amanda M. Carter, license issued 30 August 1841; executed 9 September 1841 by Marcus B. Stuart, J. P.

Eli Ashworth to Cyrena Hickerson, license issued 31 August 1841; executed 31 August 1841 by John Eubank, J. P.

Ramsey Linsey to Elizabeth Gafford, license issued 9 Sept. 1841; executed 12 Sept. 1841 by William Garrett, J. P.

John D. Halliburton to Julia Anne Parrott, license issued 2 Oct. 1841; executed 3 Oct. 1841 by James Daniel, J. P.

John White to Eliza R. Jackson, license issued 4 October 1841; executed 5 October 1841 by George F. Raworth, J. P.

Oliver McMenn to Elizabeth Redden, license issued 11 October 1841. (Note: This license was returned by Oliver McMenn, stating that the license was never executed as "the girl back out of the engagement 22 June 1842." Another copyist put it "The engagement was broken.")

James Davidson to Kiziah Davis, license issued 15 Oct. 1841; executed 21 Oct. 1841 by M. B. Stuart, J. P.

James Hudgins to Jane Nesbitt, license issued 21 Oct. 1841; executed 21 Oct. 1841 by William Garrett, J. P.

Henry B. H. Williams to Jane E. Coleman, licensed issued 25 Oct. 1841; executed by M. Berry, M. G.

John Marsh to Lucy Goodwin, license issued 28 Oct. 1841; executed 28 Oct. 1841 by G. W. Tatom, J. P.

Alford Dillihay to Mary Newman, license issued 30 Oct. 1841; executed by James Daniel, J. P., 5 Nov. 1841.

James W. Richardson to Nancy Powers, license issued 3 Nov. 1841; executed 4 Nov. 1841 by G. W. Tatom, J. P.

Neil W. Byrne to Martha Anne Norman, license issued 6 Nov. 1841; executed 7 Nov. 1841 by James Daniel, J. P.

Tolbert Slayden to Louisa Shelton, license issued 24 Nov. 1841.

Harvey Nesbitt to Mary V. Hall, license issued 24 Nov. 1841.

William Goodwin to Arena Puckett, license issued 2 Dec. 1841; executed 2 Dec. 1841 by G. W. Tatom, J. P.

Calvin S. Batson to Eveline Ellis, license issued 4 Dec. 1841; executed 9 Dec. 1841 by Rev. William Gutherie.

Ebenezar Larkins to Elizabeth A. Dickson, license issued 15 Dec. 1841; executed 16 Dec. 1841 by W. R. Hicks, J. P.

James R. Kenable to Rebecca C. Tidwell, license issued 15 Dec. 1841; executed 16 Dec. 1841 by K. Myatt, J. P. (Note: Another copyist read his surname as Kemble.)

Robert H. Weakley to Elizabeth Weakley, license issued 15 Dec. 1841. (Note: Refer to March 1842 entries.)

J. W. Green to Mary E. Ragan, license issued 16 Dec. 1841; executed 24 December 1841 by W. R. Hicks, J. P.

1842

James McNeely to Cassander Rye, license issued 12 Jan. 1842.

Simpson A. Norman to Elizabeth Vanhook, license issued 15 January 1841; executed 20 January 1842 by James Daniel, J. P.

Andrew J. Griffin to Anna Welker, license issued 22 Jan. 1841; executed 23 Jan. 1842 by Jordan Moore. (Note: There were both Welkers and Walkers in early Dickson County and they lived in the same area of the county. Sometimes it is impossible to tell the two surname apart in the old records.)

N. M. Hall to Martha J. Cunningham, license issued 27 Jan. 1842; executed 27 Jan. 1842 by M. B. Stuart, J. P.

Joseph Brown to Nancy Southerland, license issued 1 Feb. 1842; executed 1 Feb. 1842 by W. Hand, J. P.

Richard Fowler to Victoria Vanhook, license issued 4 Feb. 1842; executed 7 Feb. 1842 by James Daniel, J. P.

Allen Brazzell to Nancy Baker, license issued 11 Feb. 1842; executed 13 Feb. 1842 by James W. Lloyd, J. P.

Thomas Shelton to Eliza T. Bumpass, license issued 17 Feb. 1842; executed 17 Feb. 1842 by G. W. Tatom, J. P.

John A. Baker to Eliza Walker, license issued 17 Feb. 1842; executed __Feb. 1842 by John Eubank, J. P.

Robert T. Williams to Martha T. Kephart, license issued 18 Feb. 1842; executed 24 Feb. 1842 by Caleb Rooker, L. D.

Warren Hale to Rhoda Hickerson, license issued 18 Feb. 1842; executed by George W. Tatom, J. P.

John Forsythe to Eliza Fane, license issued 21 Feb. 1842; executed 25 Feb. 1842 by W. Hand, J. P.

William Simpson to Emeline Speight, license issued 26 Feb. 1842.

Sharp Dunnegan to Jane Dunnegan, license issued 23 Feb. 1842, executed 23 Feb. 1842 by G. W. Tatom, J. P.

Robert H. Weakley to Elizabeth Weakley, license issued 26 March 1842; executed 6 April 1842 by W. Hand, J. P. (Note: Refer to a license issued also in 1841.)

Joab Hardin to Manerva J. Leech, license issued 27 March 1842; executed 1 April 1842 by John Eubank. (Note: One person who copied these marriages put the execution as "executed last or March or first of April".)

William M. Ellis to Georgia Anne West, license issued 11 April 1842; executed 12 April 1842 by Jesse Edwards, M. G.

A. A. C. Rogers to Eliza Anne Brown, license issued 22 April 1842; executed 1 May 1842 by John McNobs, M. G. (Note: One copyist gave the minister's name as McNabs. A. A. C. Rogers will be found settling an estate in Stewart County during this time period which is another documentation for having three initials.)

James T. White to Nancy F. Richardson, license issued 7 May 1842; executed 8 May 1842 by H. J. Binkly, J. P.

Mathew T. Gentry to Eliza Gentry, license issued 21 May 1842.

Dureon L. Matlock to M. Phillips, license issued 4 June 1842.

Daniel S. Mosley to Frances Holland, license issued 10 June 1842; executed 12 June 1842 by John A. Petty, J. P.

James Johnston to Sarah Carr, license issued 21 July 1842; executed 21 July 1842 by John Brown, J. P.

William Anglin to Susannah Hay, license issued 6 August 1842.

John Ethridge to Margaret McLain, license issued 24 August 1842.

David Waynick to Malinda Dickson, license issued 14 Sept. 1842, executed 14 Sept. 1842 by James G. Hinson, J. P.

John W. Coleman to Elizabeth Gray, license issued 23 Sept. 1842, executed 23 Sept. 1842 by J. C. Pullen, J. P.

Henry A. Bibb to Milberry Massey, license issued 29 Sept. 1842, executed 29 Sept. 1842 by John Eubank, J. P.

James M. Swift to Rebecca McMurry, license issued 12 Oct. 1842, executed 13 Oct. 1842 by J. Moore.

John Miller to Sarah Jones, license issued 13 Oct. 1842, executed 13 Oct. 1842 by John Brown, J. P.

William B. Simmons to Rebecca McClelland, license issued 19 Oct. 1842; executed, no date, no officiant.

Benjamin Link to Martha Caroline Gafford, license issed 26 Oct. 1842, executed 27 Oct. 1842 by William Garrett, J. P.

Elisha Bell to Sarah E. Collier, license issued 27 Oct. 1842, executed 27 Oct. 1842 by Rev. Uriah Smith.

Andrew Jackson Brin to Mary Jane Boyd, license issued 17 Nov. 1842, executed 22 Nov. 1842 by James G. Hinson, J. P. (Note: One copyist read the groom's surname as Brim.)

William H. Thompson to Mary Anne Oliver, license issued 17 Nov. 1842. Executed.

John Crow to Mary Tidwell, license issued 22 Nov. 1842, executed 22 Nov. 1842 by John Brown, J. P.

John M. Boyd to Nancy Anne Clay, license issued 27 Nov. 1842, executed 29 Nov. 1842 by John McCaslin, J. P.

William M. Larkins to Elizabeth Sanders, license issued 10 Dec. 1842, executed 11 Dec. 1842 by Allen Nesbitt, J. P.

Hudson J. Richardson to Rena Hicks, license issued 15 Dec. 1842, executed 15 Dec. 1842 by John Eubank, J. P.

William D. Bateman to Parthenia H. Blunt, license issued 15 Dec. 1842; executed 15 Dec. 1842 by James Daniel, J. P.

John M. Shelton to Martha Lewis, license issued 22 Dec. 1842; executed 20 Dec. 1842 by Ruben Shadowen. (Note: This seems to be first time Chaudoin is spelled as Shadowen, which seems to be the present day spelling of this name.)

Henry D. Jones to Sarah M. Paschall, license issued 23 Dec. 1842, executed 25 Dec. 1842 by William Garrett, J. P.

Albert G. Shelton to Rachel Lewis, license issued 26 Dec. 1842; executed 3 Jan. 1843.

George Coon to Nancy Wallace, license issued 24 Dec. 1842, executed 25 Dec. 1842.

George W. Oakley to Artimeca (Artimissa?) Dicks, license issued 29 Dec. 1842, executed 29 Dec. 1842 by John Eubank, J. P.

William Good to Edney Durard, license issued 29 Dec. 1842.

William Oakley to Elizabeth Pinegar, license issued 31 Dec. 1842; executed 1 Jan. 1843 by James Lloyd, J. P. (Note: Some copyists in the past have read the groom's name as William O'Kelly. We believe Oakley is correct.)

1843

Jesse Newman to Ellinor Bishop, license issued 4 Jan. 1843, executed 7 Jan. 1843 by James G. Hudson, J. P.

Robert Halliburton to Lucretia Tilly, license issued 5 Jan. 1843, executed 5 Jan. 1843.

Randell Mills to Louisa Moore, license issued 5 Jan. 1843, executed 10 June 1843 by W. H. Johnson. (Note: Our date of solemnization agrees with other copies of this marriage record made in the past.)

Ellington Carroll to Sarah E. Daniel, license issued 17 Jan. 1843, executed 28 Jan. 1843 by W. Hand, J. P.

Crafford Lovell to Elizabeth Petty, license issued 30 Jan. 1843, executed 6 Feb. 1843 by John A. Petty, J. P.

Martin Pinegar to Eliza Lee, license issued 3 Feb. 1843, executed 5 Feb. 1843 by John A. Petty, J. P.

Richard Murphy to Araminta Burgess, license issued 4 Feb. 1843, executed 7 Feb. 1843 by James Daniel, J. P.

Benjamin Stone to Mary Jane Napier, license issued 8 Feb. 1843.

Robert Dillihay to Sarah Anne Self, license issued 15 Feb. 1843, executed 16 Feb. 1843 by James Daniel, J. P.

Richard Hartzog to Susannah C. Vanlandingham, license issued 18 Feb. 1843, executed 19 Feb. 1843 by J. Porter, J. P.

Stanford Dunnegan to Caroline Lloyd, license issued 3 March 1843, executed 5 March 1843 by L. Russell, J. P.

J. D. Woodward to Mary Anne Kephart, license issued 4 March 1843, executed 5 March 1843 by Caleb Rooker, L. D.

John Mickel to Sarah C. Smith, license issued 12 March 1843, executed 12 March 1843 by John Eubank, J. P.

Mathew Morgan to Eliza Anne Harris, license issued 13 March 1843, executed 15 March 1843 by William Hand, J. P.

John Matlock to Mary A. Mallory, license issued 14 March 1843, executed 14 March 1843 by John Eubnak, J. P. (Note: One past copyist read her name as Mary Ann Mallory.)

Albert G. Wilson to Sarah S. Hogan, license issued 14 March 1843, executed 16 March 1843 by L. Russell, J. P.

Britton Harris to Mary Mitchell, license issued 18 March 1843, executed 27 March 1843 by H. J. Binkly, J. P.

James Blackwell to Lucy Wallace, marriage executed 28 March 1843 by William Adkins.

Hugh McClerkin to Isabella McMahan, marriage license issued 18 April 1843, executed 18 April 1843 by James Daniel, J. P.

Joseph Shelton to Susan Rice, license issued 20 April 1843, executed 20 April 1843 by R. P. Halliburton, J. P.

James E. England to Nancy Willy, license issued 22 April 1843, executed 23 April 1843 by Allen Nesbitt, J. P.

John Castleman to Lurena (or Lurana) Lankford, license issued 28 April 1843, executed 30 April 1843 by J. Porter, J. P.

Hugh Depriest to Mary Amanda Vanlandingham, license issued 5 June 1843, executed 8 June 1843 by J. Porter, J. P.

Zen Lewis to Didamy Watson, license issued 7 June 1843, executed 7 June 1843 by James Daniel, J. P. (Note: One copyist of the Dickson County marriages read his name as Yen Lewis. This couple will be found on the 1850 census of Stewart County and here one person read his name as Yen Lewis with wife Didamy; another interpreted the name as Zen Lewis with wife Dilday.)

William Watson to Elizabeth Gorin, license issued 10 June 1843.

Augustine Reeves to Aurena Spicer, license issued 15 June 1843; executed 15 June 1843 by Samuel Tate, J. P. (Note: In 1850 this couple will be found listed as Austin and Reena Reeves in Dickson County.)

Andrew J. Waynick to Mary Hill, license issued 4 August 1843, executed 23 August 1843 by R. P. Halliburton, J. P.

Samuel Heath to Julia Anne McCormack, license issued 24 August 1843, executed 24 August 1843 by Allen Nesbitt, J. P.

Samuel Whitsitt to Henrietta E. Trotter. Executed. (Note: No dates, but found in the book between the 24 August 1843 entry and above and the next entry.)

Samuel Boughter to Sarah M. West. Marriage executed by Jesse Edwards, minister. (Note: This marriage is in question on our original copy. The words had been written beside it "Stewart County".)

Moses A. Sutton to Emeline M. Hall, executed 5 Sept. 1843 by John Eubank, J. P.

Samuel Hedge to Sarah Gunn, marriage executed 5 Sept. 1843 by Samuel Tate, J. P.

John T. Lampley to Harriett Lankford, executed ___ Sept. 1843 by J. Porter, J. P.

Marvell M. Petty to Nancy Castleman, license issued 20 Sept. 1843, executed 21 Sept. 1843 by John Brown, J. P.

Thomas N. Williams to Mary A. Norman, license issued 21 Sept. 1843, executed 21 Sept. 1843 by Barham A. Price.

Wilie B. Joslin to Martha Mitchell, license issued **19 Oct.** 1843, executed 19 Oct. 1843 by H. Parks.

Franklin Robertson to Frances M. Dalton, license issued 28 October 1843.

W. R. Taylor to Charlotty Flannery, license issued 8 Nov. 1843, executed 9 Nov. 1843 by J. W. Hedge, J. P. (Note: The minister's name could be I. W. Hedge.)

Edward Smith to Anne Miscon, license issued 15 Nov. 1843, executed 19 Nov. 1843 by James Daniel, J. P. (Note: The bride's name could be Anne Mixon; there were Mixons in the county, but as far as can be determined the surname Miscon is not in the county.)

John McDole to Mary Anne Williams, license issued 15 Nov. 1843, executed 16 Nov. 1843 by B. Darrow, M. G.

Richard A. Estes to Caroline Tatom, license issued 18 Nov. 1843, executed 19 Nov. 1843 by James W. Lloyd, J. P.

William Caldwell to Martha Joslin, license issued 2 Dec. 1843.

Isaac Griffin to Mary I. Hambrick, license issued 5 Dec. 1843, executed 7 Dec. 1843 by Allen Nesbitt, J. P. (Note: The groom's name could be Isaac Giffin as well. Both Giffin and Griffin appear in early Dickson County records.)

George Turner to Edna Lewis, license issued 17 Dec. 1843, executed 17 Dec. 1843 by James G. Hinson, J. P.

Alfred Elliott to Tennessee Smith, license issued 19 Dec. 1843, executed 19 Dec. 1843 by Allen Nesbitt, J. P.

Felix Badger to Amanda Eleazer, license issued 20 Dec. 1843, executed ___Dec. 1843 by E. Hanks, M. G.

Henry Coleman to Frances Burns, license issued 25 Dec. 1843, executed 26 Dec. 1843 by M. Berry, M. G.

Robert T. Clay to Sarah Edwards, license issued 26 Dec. 1843.

John Hayes to Susan McCaslin, license issued 30 Dec. 1843, executed 31 Dec. 1843 by John Brown, J. P.

1844

Thomas Patterson to Delila Holly, license issued 4 Jan. 1844, executed 4 Jan. 1844 by James G. Hinson, J. P.

William H. Hendricks to Lucinda Tilly, license issued 5 Jan. 1844, executed 5 Jan. 1844 by Thomas Palmer, J. P.

John B. Evans to Letticia B. Christian, license issued 6 Jan. 1844; executed 6 Jan. 1844 by Thomas Palmer, J. P.

Mansel Tidwell to Nancy White, license issued 16 Jan. 1844; executed 17 Jan. 1844 by John Brown, J. P.

Benjamin Darrow to Mary Murphy, license issued 18 Jan. 1844, executed 21 Jan. 1844 by William Adkins, J. P.

Waid Hampton to Lucinda Baily, license issued 19 Jan. 1844; executed 21 Jan. 1844 by William Hand, J. P.

Aaron Pinson to Elizabeth Mitchell, license issued 25 Jan. 1844.

Ezekiel N. Parrish to Elizabeth Self, license issued 17 Feb. 1844, executed 18 Feb. 1844 by James G. Hinson, J. P.

John S. Whitsitt to Rizbah Waynick, license issued 22 Feb. 1844, executed 23 Feb. 1844 by R. P. Halliburton, J. P.

Bartlet A. Oakley to Eliza W. Willy, license issued 22 Feb. 1844, executed 12 Feb. 1844, by L. Russell, J. P. (Note: Surname could be O'Kelly.)

F. F. V. Schmittou to Lavina C. Crews, license issued 29 Feb. 1844; executed 29 Feb. 1844 by William Adkins, J. P. (Note: Lavinia Schmittou filed for divorce Feb. 1849, stating she had married Francis F. V. Schimttou in 1844 in Dickson County and that he abandoned her in 3½ months. See Dickson County Circuit Court Minute Book A, p. 268.)

Isaac Hill to Susan Newman, license issued 12 March 1844.

Thomas Hammonds to Lavena Anderson, license issued 14 March 1844; executed 15 March 1844 by John Brown, J. P.

Mathew L. Gentry to Nancy J. Richardson, license issued 16 March 1844. (Note: At least two other copyists have read her name as Nancy I. Richardson.)

Silas Thompson to Anne Gentry, license issued 19 March 1844, executed by John Brown, J. P., 20 March 1844.

Henry Newman to Eliza Parrish, license issued 24 March 1844, executed 24 March 1844 by James Daniel, J. P.

R. N. Q. Hunt to Mary Jane Jackson, license issued 2 April 1844, executed by John Eubank, J. P.

W. H. Horner to Susan Tatom, license issued 6 April 1844; executed 7 April 1844 by James Thedford, J. P.

Benjamin N. Tatom to Sarah Dotson, license issued 27 April 1844, executed 28 April 1844 by Cyrus Murry, J. P. (Note: Some read his middle initial as M.)

Thomas M. Richardson to Mary H. Williams, license issued 30 April 1844.

Elijah Marsh to Polly Harris, license issued 18 April 1844; executed 18 April 1844 by J. C. Anglin, J. P.

Solomon Ridings to Sarah Horner, license issued 18 June 1844, executed 20 June 1844 by L. Russell, J. P.

James Reynolds to Lucy R. Hayes, license issued 25 June 1844, executed 25 June 1844 by Thomas Palmer, J. P.

Paul Duvaugh to Martha Duran, license issued 26 June 1844, executed 27 June 1844 by Allen Nesbitt, J. P. (Note: The two surnames in this entry have been read differently by almost everyone who has ever worked in these marriages. Sometimes his name is read as Duvaul, and hers as Durard, or Durrard.)

Robert Dolton to Mary A. Cook, license issued 29 June 1844.

Portan Pruit to Martha Mosley, license issued 1 July 1844, executed 3 August 1844 by J. C. Anglin, J. P.

Monroe G. Dotson to Sarah E. Brewer, license issued 4 July 1844, executed 4 July 1844 by A. Nesbitt, J. P.

Jesse H. Bryan to Sarah Myatt, license issued 13 July 1844, executed 17 July 1844 by David Gray, M. G.

George W. Scott to Elizabeth Speight, license issued 16 July 1844 executed 17 July by H. J. Binkly, J. P.

Joseph H. Chester to Mary White, license issued 18 July 1844, executed 19 July 1844 by John Xrown, J. P.

James W. Cook to Cynthia A. Walker, license issued 23 July 1844; executed by J. Eubank, J. P.

A. B. J. Turner to Nancy M. Shelton, license issued 30 July 1844.

Samuel Cathey to Lucinda Edwards, license issued 16 August 1844.

Henry Bullion to Sarah Hambrick, license issued 21 August 1844, executed 22 August 1844 by Samuel Tate, J. P.

Thomas Stark to Rebecca Grymes, license issued 29 August 1844, executed 29 August 1844 by William Garrett, J. P.

Jesse G. Holland to Frances C. Hudson, license issued 3 Sept. 1844, executed 8 Sept. 1844 by David Gray, M. G.

Wiley Davis to Nancy Crow, license issued 8 Sept. 1844, executed 9 Sept. 1844 by Empson Bishop, M. G.

James Blackwell to Cintha Bleadsoe, license issued 12 Sept. 1844, executed 12 Sept. 1844 by Banjamin Darrow, M. G.

Ceborn Puckett to Nancy Goodwin, license issued 7 Oct. 1844; executed 7 October 1844 by Samuel Tate. (Note: One copyist noted that the bride gave her name as Nancy Robbs once and Nancy Goodwin once on the returned license. One copyist in the past read the groom's surname as Parker.)

Moses H. Jones to Sarah E. Jones, license issued 21 Oct. 1844, executed 21 Oct. 1844 by Thomas Payne, J. P.

William C. Lampley to Elizabeth White, license issued 4 Nov. 1844, executed 7 Nov. 1844 by J. Porter, J. P.

William H. Wells to Avery Haley, license issued 7 November 1844, executed ___Nov. 1844 by David Gray, M. G.

Hugh McClerkin to Susan Self, license issued 14 Nove. 1844, executed by James Daniel, J. P. (Note: Refer also to a marriage of Hugh McClerkin on page 37 of this book.)

William Carroll to Catherine Williams, license issued 18 Nov. 1844, executed 19 Nov. 1844 by C. Rooker, L. E. M. E. Church.

Jesse Adcock to Polly M. Adcock, license issued 18 Nov. 1844, executed by David Gray, M. G.

Edward T. Southerland to Helena Anne Paschal, license issued 19 Nov. 1844, executed 19 Nov. 1844 by William Garrett, J. P.

James G. Jackson to Susan Eleazer, license issued 21 Nov. 1844, executed 21 Nov. 1844 by J. C. Pullen, J. P.

James B. Stokes to Elizabeth J. Evans, license issued 26 Nov. 1844, executed 28 Nov. 1844 by H. W. Turner, M. G.

A. F. Nesbitt to Nancy Anne Dillehay, license issued 27 Nov. 1844, executed 28 Nov. 1844 by James Daniel, J. P.

John M. Wiley to Marthena Frasher, license issued 3 Dec. 1844, executed 5 Dec. 1844 by David Gray, M. G.

David G. Dotson to Elizabeth Hudson, license issued 14 Dec. 1844, executed 18 Dec. 1844 by Cyrus Murry, J. P.

William Marsh to Nancy Sullivan, license issued 17 Dec. 1844.

Thomas Brown to Jane Gentry, license issued 17 Dec. 1844, executed 19 Dec. 1844 by J. Porter, J. P.

1845

William Bell to Sarah E. Bell, license issued 5 Jan. 1845, executed 5 Jan. 1845 by Jesse Edwards, M. G. (Note: One copyist read her name as Sarah B. Bell.)

William Adcock to Sarah Thedford, license issued 8 Jan. 1845, executed 8 Jan. 1845 by Samuel Tate, J. P.

Thomas L. Holt to Flora A. Kyle, license issued 9 Jan. 1845; executed 9 Jan. 1845.

William M. Finley to Elizabeth West, license issued 13 January 1845.

Jeremiah Smith to Elizabeth Bone, license issued 15 Jan. 1845.

Sebron Whitaker to Nancy Briggs, License issued 18 January 1845, executed 19 Jan. 1845 by Sml. Tate, J. P.

Elbert J. Hicks to Mariah C. Huston, license issued 22 Jan. 1845.(Note: Although there is no solemnization on the license, this was a marriage that was solemnized. Their son's obituary appeared in the Dickson County Herald, 7 Sept. 1934 and noted that J. B. (or S.) Hicks had died at his home Sunday after four strokes and that he was son of Elbert J. and Mariah Houston Hicks, pioneer family; he died in the house he was born in on Jones Creek. Elbert Jackson Hicks, born 6 May 1821, died 4 June 1886, is buried in the old Hicks Cemetery on Jones Creek, with a stone marking his grave.)

Daniel Glass to Rachael King, license issued 18 January 1845, executed __ Jan. 1845.

Joshua Petty to Fatha Kimbrough, license issued 19 Feb. 1845, executed 19 Feb. 1845 by L. Russell, J. P. (Note: One copyist used the spelling Fatha Kimbro.)

W. H. Evans to Catherine Boyd, license issued 6 June 1845, executed 6 June 1845, by O. L. V. Schmittou, J. P.

George Russell to Nancy Hampton, license issued 21 June 1845.

William Hall to Nancy Carroll, license issued 17 July 1845, executed 17 July 1845 by C. Rooker, L. E. M. E. Church.

H. D. Bails to Mary A. Grymes, license issued 17 July 1845.

Henry R. Johnson to Martha J. Beck, license issued 23 July 1845.

Pullen A. Dudley to Lucyanah Graham, license issued 31 July 1845.

William T. Patterson to Milly Comes, license issued 15 Sept. 1845.

Humphries Halliburton to Mary E. Humphries, license issued 20 Sept. 1845.

Joseph Parker to Jemima Lankford, license issued 23 Sept. 1845. (Note: One person read the groom's name as Joseph Perker. However, Joseph A. Parker with wife Jemima appear on 1850 census of Dickson County.)

Zachriah Batson to Arabella Turner, license issued 18 October 1845.

Isaac King to Nancy Willie, license issued 26 Feb. 1845, executed 26 Feb. 1845 by John Eubank, J. P. (Note: One person read these names as Isaiah King to Nancy Williams.)

James Brown to Mary Link, license issued 27 Feb. 1845, executed 27 Feb. 1845 by John Eubank, J. P.

Jesse Rieves to Anny England, license issued 10 March 1845, executed 13 March 1845 by Samuel Tate, J. P.

Jasper R. Ferguson to George Anne Ellis, license issued 7 April 1845.

John Walker to Anne Coleman, license issued 8 April 1845, executed 8 April 1845.

Joseph Burgess to Rebecca Mahan, license issued 19 April 1845, executed 21 April 1845 by J. C. Pullen, J. P.

George M. Evans to Lucinda Brazzell, license issued 30 April 1845, executed 1 May 1845 by James Thedford, J. P.

William L. Baker to Lucinda J. Johnson, license issued 12 May 1845, executed 15 May 1845 by William Hand, J. P.

Noah Cross to Nancy Van Rutledge, license issued 28 May 1845, executed 29 May 1845 by J. W. Hedge, J. P.

David Sellers to Margaret Brown, license issued 20 Oct. 1845.

Wilson J. Mathis to Sarah E. Roberts, license issued 30 Oct. 1845. (Note: This marriage was solemnized even though it is not recorded. They are buried in the Roberts Cemetery at Charlotte. His stone reads: Hon. W. J. Mathis, 26 June 1808 - 2 August 1893; hers reads Sarah F. Mathis, 1 July 1826 - 20 Jan. 1911. He was onetime member of the General Assembly of Tennessee.)

Hiram Sears to Parthena Glass, license issued 5 November 1845.

Thomas Jones to Sarah C. Adams, license issued 8 Nov. 1845, executed ___ Nov. 1845.

Willis W. Spears to Susan Mosely, license issued 9 November 1845, executed 9 Nov. 1845 by J. C. Anglin.

_____ K. Boyce to Martha A. Bowen, license issued 24 November 1845, executed 25 Nov. 1845 by John W. Ogden, M. G.

N. A. D. Bryant to Susan E. Joslin, license issued 24 November 1845.

Micajah Blackwell to Rebecca Crain, license issued 25 Nov. 1845. Executed by James G. Hinson, _____.

Barney Wallace to Susan Holly, license issued 29 November 1845.

Granville Carter to Martha Jones, license issued 9 December 1845.

Alfred H. Douglas to Marilla Wiles, license issued 16 Dec. 1845, executed 18 Dec. 1845 by C. Rooker, L. E. M. E. Church. (Note: One copyist reported her surname as Miles. The solemnization date looks like 18 Dec. 1846 also.)

Jefferson Fowler to Eliza Vanhook, license issued 7 Dec. 1845, executed 7 Dec. 1845 by Cyrus Murry, J. P.

Richard C _____ to Louisa Chapman, license issued 16 Dec. 1845. (Note: One copyist read his name as Richard Couen. Another thought the name Caroland.)

John Harris to Mary A. Baker, license issued 18 Dec. 1845, executed 18 Dec. 1845 by Samuel Tate, J. P.

Mathew J. Smith to Martha A. P. Berry, license issued 19 Dec. 1845.

Robert Nolin to Kissiah Sears, license issued 22 Dec. 1845, executed 23 Dec. 1845 by John Brown, J. P.

Millington M. Petty to Cynthia Myatt, license issued 25 December 1845; executed 25 Dec. 1845 by David Gray, M. G.

Thomas Owens to Tennessee A. Shadrick, license issued 16 Dec. 1845; executed 18 Dec. 1845 by William Garrett, J. P. (Note: The bride's surname is in question in our original copy from Mrs. Gambill. Her name might possibly have been Shadowen.)

Drury Williams to Elizabeth Russell, license issued 26 Dec. 1845, executed 29 Dec. 1845 by David Gray, M. G.

Thomas Murrell to Eliza Austin, license issued 27 Dec. 1845, executed 28 December 1845 by Samuel Tate, J. P.

N. P. Hagewood to Mary J. Carroll, license issued 29 Dec. 1845, executed 8 January 1846 by E. Bishop, M. G.

1846

Jeremiah Bull to Mary E. Horn, license issued 2 January 1846, executed 6 January 1846 by E. Bishop, M. G.

I. B. Taylor to Cecelia McCarver, license issued 2 Jan. 1846, executed.

William Davidson to Patsey Luther, license issued 2 January 1846, executed 4 January 1846 by J. C. Anglin, J. P.

Michael Berry to Nancy A. S. Nesbitt, license issued 7 January 1846, executed by L. R. Dennis, M. G.

Allen G. Crow to Nancy Adcock, license issued 8 January 1846, executed 8 January 1846 by J. C. Pullen, J. P.

Giles J. Oliver to Nancy C. Evans, license issued 10 January 1846, executed 11 January 1846 by E. Bishop, M. G.

Nathaniel L. Duff to Elizabeth Jane Sullivan, license issued 12 Jan. 1846

John W. Rhea to Sarah Myatt, license issued 20 January 1846. Executed. (Note: These names are in question.)

Carroll Greer to Martha A. Pendergrass, license issued 2 Feb. 1846.

John B. Dickson to Nancy L. Binkly, license issued 4 Feb. 1846, executed 5 Feb. 1846 by J. Moore, M. G.

George Chrisman to Malinda Smith, license issued 23 Feb. 1846.

Gabrael Petty to Elizabeth Wells, license issued 6 March 1846.

Charles Halliburton to Nancy Ragan, license issued 10 March 1846, executed 11 March 1846 by J. G. Hinson, J. P.

James Kimbrough to Nancy Chappell, license issued 18 March 1846.

John H. Owens to Nancy B. Gamble, license issued 6 April 1846, executed 8 April 1846 by J. Moore, M. G.

W. A. James to Mary J. Collier, license issued 9 April 1846.

David Walls (or Wells) to Martha Christy, license issued 11 April 1846.

Benjamin Waynick to Elizabeth Fleet, license issued 20 April 1846, executed 23 April 1846 by James Daniel, J. P.

M. H. Meek to Artemica Davidson, license issued 21 April 1846, executed 21 April 1846 by J. C. Anglin, J. P.

Anderson Tate to Mary Luther, license issued 25 April 1846, executed 26 April 1846 by J. C. Anglin, J. P.

George W. Suggs to Martha Reynolds, license issued 11 May 1846, executed 12 May 1846 by Edward Holly, J. P.

Benjamin B. Dunnegan to Elizabeth Adcock, license issued 15 May 1846.

Moses Rhodes to Sarah A. Adcock, license issued 16 May 1846 executed 17 May 1846 by J. C. Pullen, J. P.

David Jones to Elizabeth J. Daniel, license issued 19 May 1846, executed 20 May 1846 by E. Bishop, M. G.

Thornton Perry to Mahala Leathers, license issued 21 May 1846, executed 24 May 1846 by L. Russell, J. P.

Drury C. Jones to Priscilla Appleton, license issued 23 May 1846.

John T. Patterson to Olive C. Webster, license issued 27 May 1846, executed 27 May 1846 by Edward Holley, J. P.

John C. Parrish to Stacy Wiseman, license issued 27 June 1846. (Note: Groom's middle initial could also be G.)

Hopkins Lloyd to Elizabeth Hughs, license issued 27 June 1846.

John Jones to Eliza Whatly, license issued 29 June 1846.

Henry Paschal to Catherine Link, license issued 29 July 1846, executed 28 May 1846 by W. B. Ross, J. P. (Note: These dates are the way they appear in our original copy.)

James W. Evans to Rhoda Willy, license issued 1 August 1846.

James B. Hayes to Malinda Gunn, license issued 2 August 1846.

John Welker to Elizabeth S. Latham, license issued 3 August 1846.

John Bishop to Jane Morgan, license issued 10 August 1846.

Reuben Brown to Marguerite Cathey, license issued 22 August 1846.

William M. Patterson to Mary A. Lane, license issued 2 September 1846.

Jacob S. Law to Sarah J. Whatley, license issued 3 September 1846.

Henry King to Sary Brown, license issued 11 September 1846.

Caber Dien to Martha Gunter, license issued 16 September 1846.

A. A. Fussell to Menerva Dunnegan, license issued 20 September 1846.

William R. V. Schmittou to Martha Tilly, license issued 22 Sept. 1846.

Marton Garton to Catherine Carter, license issued 30 September 1846.

Joel D. Everett to Nancy A. Smith, license issued 6 October 1846.

John B. Shelton to Mary Jennings, license issued 12 October 1846.

Wayne Vanleer to Mary E. Mills, license issued 21 October 1846.

George Pentecost to Paralee Davis, license issued 22 October 1846. (Note: This marriage was solemnized as the couple appear on the 1850 census of Montgomery County. The groom had a first initial which could not be read on the original copy furnished us.)

John Edwards to Mariah (Maryah?) Annah Pentecost, license issued 25 October 1846.

James C. Hambrick to Elizabeth Hickerson, license issued 5 Nov. 1846.

Newton Dodson to Nancy Sugg, license issued 9 November 1846.

Jesse Hagewood to Sarah L. Bryson, license issued 16 November 1846.

Daniel W. Anderson to Lucy A. Tilley, license issued 20 November 1846.

Lewis (Louis?) L. Petty to Manias Dunnegan, license issued 26 Nov. 1846.

William S. Latham to Cardine P. Hill, license issued 2 December 1846. (Note: This marriage was solemnized and the couple appears together on the 1850 census of Montgomery County. The bride's name is Caroline according to the census and this is possibly correct even though all the people who have copied the Dickson County marriages show her name as Cardin or Cardine.)

Benjamin F. Wills to Mary J. Clemmons, license issued 4 December 1846.

G. W. Gunn to Ritha Brazzell, license issued 7 December 1846.

Frederick Hughs to Margaret B_____, license issued 7 December 1846. (Note: One copyist shows her name as Baldin, another Bouldin, and another Baldwin.)

Edward D. Holly to Antoinette Lewis, license issued 20 December 1846. (Note: This marriage was solemnized as they are living in same household on 1850 census of Dickson County.)

James R. Rye to Jane A. Burgie, license issued 21 December 1846.

Washington Hunter to Charlotte Duke, license issued _____. (Note: No date given in book. Marriage was recorded between Rye-Burgie license above and Daniel-Cooksey license following. Marriage was solemnized and they will be found on 1850 census of Dickson County as W. A. and Charlotty G. Hunter.)

J. Daniel to Phebe Anne Cooksey, license issued 29 December 1846. (Note: This marriage was solemnized and they appear on 1850 census of Dickson County as Jesse and Phoebe Daniel.)

Allston Myatt to Mary Sugg, license issued _____. (Note: no date. License appears after the Daniel-Cooksey marriage above in the book. Apparently this marriage was solemnized as they appear on 1850 census of Dickson County as Alston and Mary Myatt.)

George Hambrick to Margaret Hickerson, license issued 31 December 1846.

1847

William Humphries to Arrabella Halliburton license issued 21 Jan. 1847. (Note: Apparently this marriage was solemnized as they appear together on 1850 census of Dickson County.)

William Gray to Margaret Dunnegan, license issued 7 January 1847.

Mathew J. Hayle to Rebecca Bone, license issued 7 January 1847.

Gideon Davis to Lucy J. Clardy, license issued 10 January 1847.

W. W. Walker to Mary Willy, license issued 11 January 1847.

Thomas W. Halliburton to Martha E. Ragan, license issued 12 Jan. 1847. (Note: This marriage seems to have been solemnized as they appear on the 1850 census of Dickson County.)

John B. Austin to Fredonia Walker, license issued 12 Janaury 1847. (Note: This marriage seems to have been solemnized as they appear on the 1850 census of Dickson County.)

John W. Fussell to Mary Hammond, license issued 14 January 1847. (Note: This marriage seems to have been solemnized as they appear on the 1850 census of Dickson County.)

Isaac Hall to Angeline Flannery, license issued 26 January 1847. (Note: This marriage was solemnized as Isaac Hall and Adaline Hall appear on both the 1850 and 1860 census of Humphreys County. Their daughter Emma Hall married a Baker and was the mother of Claud Baker of Dickson County. Even though Angeline appears to be the name on the license, possibly Adaline is correct.)

Ezekiel Jordan to Rachael Seal, license issued 27 January 1847.

Manley J. Pendergrass to Mary Tidwell, license issued 1 Feb. 1847.
(Note: This marriage apparently was solemnized even though she appears alone as head of household and with small child on 1850 census.)

John Robbins to Mary E. Norris, license issued 13 February 1847.

William Hand to Letticia Hunter, license issued 17 February 1847.
(Note: This marriage appears to have been solemnized as they are listed on 1850 census of Dickson County.)

George Ragan to Sarah J. Robertson, license issued 22 Feb. 1847.
(Note: This marriage appears to have been solemnized as they are listed on 1850 census of Dickson County.)

William D. Balthrope to Dilly A. E. Slayden, license issued 22 Feb. 1847.
(Note: This marriage appears to have been solemnized as they are listed on 1850 census of Dickson County living in the Yellow Creek area.)

William T. Weakley to Sarah J. Speight, license issued 24 Feb. 1847.

Robert Carroll to Elizabeth Everett, license issued 24 February 1847.
(Note: This marriage appears to have been solemnized as they are listed on the 1850 census of Dickson County.)

Charles Warren to M. M. Smith, license issued 15 March 1847.

Jesse Edwards to Elizabeth Smith, license issued 31 March 1847.

Wesley Holland to Nancy Yates, license issued 6 April 1847.

William Etheredge to Mary Underwood, license issued 13 April 1847.
(Note: This marriage appears to have been solemnized as they are listed on the 1850 census of Dickson County.)

Samuel D. Bowen to Mary A. Jackson, license issued 5 May 1847.
(Note: This marriage appears to have been solemnized as they are listed on the 1850 census of Dickson County.)

John Berthell to Martha Ethredge, license issued, no date. (Note: This license appeared between. Bowen-Jackson above and Ellison-Brown below. One copyist found his name to be John Bethel.)

John Ellison to Eliza Brown, license issued 3 June 1847.

Mathew P. Hall to Sarah C. Jackson, license issued 23 June 1847. Executed 30 June 1847 by C. Rooker.

George C. Brown to Lucinda V. Austin, license issued 24 June 1847.

William Sanders to Susan Martin, license issued 15 July 1847.
(Note: This marriage appears to be one that was solemnized; refer to 1850 census of Dickson County.)

Ira Castelman to Indiana Sears, license issued 26 June 1847.
(Note: This marriage appears to have been solemnized as they are listed on 1850 census of Dickson County.)

James Hudson to Nancy Tate, license issued 19 July 1847. (Note: This marriage appears to have been solemnized as they appear on the 1850 census of Dickson County.)

James Lewis to Susan Parrott, license issued 27 July 1847; executed 27 July 1847 by James G. Hinson, J. P.

Hartwell Sinks to Elizabeth Russell, license issued 18 August 1847.
(Note: This marriage appears to have been solemnized as they appear on the 1850 census of Dickson County.)

James Carter to Susannah Morris, license issued 4 September 1847.

W. P. Ryan to Elizabeth Calaway, license issued 14 September 1847. (Note: One former copyist read the bride's name as Elizabeth Galaway.)

John C. Weaver to Caroline Lampley, license issued 14 September 1847.

Benjamin W. Swift to Olive Sinks, license issued 16 September 1847.

Perry A. Cephart to Christiana M. Charlton, license issued 27 July 1847 executed 27 July 1847 by C. Rooker, L. E. Methodist Church. (Note: One copyist read the dates as 22 September 1847 and 23 September 1847. The surname is correctly Kephart.)

John R. Cathey to Rebecca Spicer, license issued 30 September 1847.

Isaac Anderson to Martha Glass, license issued 7 October 1847. (Note: This marriage appears to have been solemnized as they are listed on the 1850 census of Dickson County.)

G. W. Gray to Elizabeth J. Jones, license issued 13 October 1847.

Elias Sanders to Mary Hedge, license issued 16 October 1847.

William Petty to Susan Deshazer, license issued 18 October 1847.

Benjamin W. Weems to Mary Vineyard, license issued 25 October 1847.

Lenard A. Waynick to Elizabeth J. Baily, license issued 11 November 1847; executed 11 November 1847 by James G. Hinson, J. P. (Note: The groom's first name has been given by some copyists as Senard Waynick.)

Henry A. Petty to Lucinda Gentry, license issued 19 November 1847; executed by John Brown, J. P.

James M. McCollum to Sarah A. Sanders, license issued 9 December 1847; executed 9 December 1847 by Samuel Tate, J. P.

Thomas Flannery to Nancy Thedford, license issued 13 December 1847; executed 13 December 1847 by Samuel Tate, J. P.

James B. Rooker to Jane A. Williams, license issued 15 December 1847; executed 15 December 1847 by W. B. Ross, J. P.

George W. C. Lovell to Elizabeth A. Hunter, license issued 16 Dec. 1847; executed 16 December 1847 by W. B. Ross, J. P.

E. M. Potts to Rebecca Meyer, license issued 30 December 1847; executed 30 December 1847 by James Thedford, J. P.

Josiah Bagett to Harriett A. Suggs, license issued 30 December 1847; executed 30 December 1847 by R. P. Halliburton, J. P.

1848

Isaiah King to Rebecca King, license issued 3 January 1848; executed 3 January 1848 by J. C. Anglin, J. P.

Amos King to Elizabeth Dunnegan, license issued 9 January 1848; executed 9 January 1848 by L. Russell, J. P.

Lewis Hedge to Elizabeth S. Petty, license issued 24 January 1848; executed 24 January 1848.

Hugh Burns to Sarah Jordan, license issued 27 January 1848, executed 27 January 1848 by O. L. V. Schmittou, J. P.

John Hughs to Rebecca Dunaway, license issued 3 Feb. 1848, executed 3 Feb. 1848 by James Daniel, J. P.

James Staley to Elizabeth Hudgins, license issued 5 February 1848, executed 6 February 1848 by Allen Nesbitt.

Samuel A. Bigg to Martha Carr, license issued 3 February 1848, executed by John Brown, J. P.

John Porter to Zilpah Tidwell, license issued 2 February 1848, executed by John Brown, J. P.

John R. Brown to Sarah N. Norris, license issued 23 February 1848, executed 23 February by W. B. Ross, J. P.

Jacob Myers to Martha A. Eades (or Eddes), license issued 2 March 1848, executed 2 March 1848 by John Brown, J. P.

William P. Lankford to M. Davidson, license issued 2 March 1848, executed 2 March 1848 by John Brown, J. P.

John H. Caldwell to Donna M. Christian, license issued 5 March 1848, executed 5 March 1848 by Allen Nesbitt, J. P.

Thomas Ladd to R. Jane Baker, license issued 12 March 1848, executed 12 March 1848 by David Gray.

Thomas Clark to Elizabeth Hampton, license issued 22 March 1848, executed 22 March 1848 by William Garrett, J. P.

Jesse Stelley to Aney Jordan, license issued 24 March 1848, executed 24 March 1848 by R. P. Halliburton, J. P.

Thomas Alsbrook to Tennessee Owens, license issued 13 April 1848, executed 13 April 1848 by C. Grymes, J. P.

James H. Hall to Louisiana T. Richardson, license issued 13 April 1848, executed 16 April 1848.

Isaac Hailey to Rosannah Gray, license issued 27 April 1848, executed 27 April 1848. (Note: One early copyist read the groom's name as Isaach Haley.)

James Ellis to Abba Proctor, license issued 27 April 1848, executed 27 April 1848 by C. Grymes, J. P.

J. G. Marshall to Mary T. Mosley, license issued 3 May 1848, executed 3 May 1848 by C. Rooker, L. E.

John D. Woodward to Hannah E. Brown, license issued 18 May 1848, executed 18 May 1848 by J. S. Paschall, J. P.

Benjamin F. Larkins to Martha Willy, license issued 18 June 1848, executed 18 June 1848 by W. S. Coleman, J. P.

John B. Walton to Nancy Jordan, license issued 30 June 1848, executed 30 June 1848 by O. L. V. Schmittou, J. P.

Solomon McCauly to Elizabeth G. Paschall, license issued 2 July 1848, executed by C. Grymes, J. P.

Cyrus Chichester to Jane Mallory, license issued 5 July 1848, executed 5 July 1848 by Allen Nesbitt, J. P.

John R. Vanhook to Harriet A. Coleman, license issued 13 July 1848, executed 15 (or 13) July 1848 by James Daniel, J. P.

G. W. Choate to Mary Jane Gibbs, license issued 8 July 1848, executed ___July 1848 by William H____, J. P.

George T. Harris to Lucinda A. Walker, license issued 13 July 1848, executed 13 July 1848 by J. Paschall, J. P.

Simon Deloach to Ginnett Biter, license issued 13 July 1848, executed 13 July 1848 by W. S. Coleman, J. P.

L. S. Paschall to Martha F. Duke, license issued 13 July 1848, executed 13 July 1848 by C. Grymes, J. P.

Edward Caldwell to Elizabeth J. Durard, license issued 23 July 1848, executed 23 July 1848 by J. Hardin, J. P.

Harvey Dunaway to Tresa Bateman, license issued 30 July 1848, executed 30 July 1848 by O. L. V. Schmittou, J. P.

John M. Stringfellow to Sarah Jane Carroll, license issued 1 August 1848, executed 1 August 1848 by William Johnson, J. P.

Joshua Proctor to Martha Owens, license issued 3 August 1848, executed 3 August 1848 by C. Grymes, J. P.

W. G. Estes to Margaret Austin, license issued 6 August 1848, executed 6 August 1848 by A. V. Hicks, J. P.

Benjamin J. Mosier to Martha Jordan, license issued 14 August 1848, executed 14 August 1848 by O. L. V. Schmittou, J. P.

James James to Palitha N. Walker, license issued 24 August 1848, executed 28 August 1848 by A. V. Hicks, J. P.

A. W. Stroud to Mary Jane McLaughlin, license issued 31 August 1848, executed 31 August 1848 by J. Paschall, J. P. (Note: Other copyists have read the groom's name as both A. V. and A. B. However, our copy had A. W. which agrees with his listing on the 1850 census of Dickson County.)

James B. Stokes to Harriett A. Potts, license issued 3 September 1848, executed 3 September 1848 by O. L. V. Schmittou, J. P.

William Underwood to Nancy Dunaway, license issued 7 September 1848, executed 7 September 1848 by James Daniel, J. P.

James Stringfellow to Susan Carroll, license issued 21 September 1848, executed 21 September 1848 by William Johnson, J. P.

Wilson M. Sarrett to Catherine Miller, license issued 20 September 1848, executed by Samuel Tate, J. P.

John Hampton to E. A. Buchanan, license issued 25 September 1848, executed 25 September 1848 by C. Grymes, J. P.

John Carson to Hester A. Palmer, license issued 8 October 1848, executed by J. Hardin, J. P., 8 October 1848.

Thornton Hendricks to Amanda M. Smith, license issued 8 October 1848, executed 8 October 1848 by J. Hardin, J. P.

William C. Dotson to Nancy E. Hudson, license issued 8 October 1848, executed 8 October by William Hill.

W. D. Mitchell to Martha E. Barrow, license issued 26 October 1848, executed 26 October 1848 by O. L. V. Schmittou, J. P.

Andrew Cunningham to Bedy White, license issued 9 November 1848, executed 9 November 1848 by John Brown, J. P.

1849

John G. Reynolds to Frances Hand, license issued 22 March 1849, executed by J. P. Paschall, J. P.

William Beard to Paralee Clark, license issued 1 May 1849, executed 1 May 1849 by C. Grymes, J. P.

W. A. Wagoner to Elizabeth Ellis, license issued 3 May 1849, executed 3 May 1849 by J. T. Wagoner.

This concludes the marriage records copied from Dickson County Marriage Book 1838-1849 as copied by the late Mildred Sullivan Gambill of Waverly. These were given to the compiler by Mrs. Gambill in 1963. All the marriages were checked with previous compilations, especially those appearing in "35,000 Tennessee Marriage Records and Bonds, 1783-1870", edited by the Rev. Silas Emmett Lucas, Jr. and Mrs. Ella Lee Sheffield, published by Southern Historical Press, Easley, South Carolina in 1981. This book had been compiled from the marriages in the card file at the Tennessee State Library and Archives. Any differences are noted.

MISCELLANEOUS MARRIAGE NOTES

Jackson Brim married Mary Jane Boyd according to family records, and this gives the correct spelling of the surname to the marriage found on page 35 of this book.

Halliburton family records also indicate the following marriages for that family:

Martin Turner Halliburton married 24 November 1837 Eleanor Jane Toler

George Ragan to Sally Jane Robeson, 22 February 1847

James Rogers to Theny Bateman, 1847

Reuben P. Halliburton married 17 April 1825 in Dickson County to Cynthia McMurry, daughter of Thomas McMurry.
(Note: For these marriages I have no documentation other than "Family Records" sent to the compiler.)

III

DICKSON COUNTY WILLS

1804 - 1856

(The following are abstracted notes from Dickson County wills recorded in Will Book 1, sometimes called Will Book A, covering the years from 1804 to 1856. These were taken from the microfilm of this book by Jill Garrett and the microfilm was obtained from the Tennessee State Library and Archives, Nashville, Tennessee.)

JOSEPH DICKSON will - pages 1 through 3
Wife Jane, son Hugh, son David, son Molton, son Joseph...three youngest sons, Abner, Robert, and William...granddaughters Lucy, Jane Pearsale; niece Elizabeth Dickson, daughter of James Dickson of North Carolina; daughter Ann; son Michael to get mourning suit. Executors: Michael Dickson, Hugh Dickson, and David Dickson.
Signed 27 Dec. 1803.
Witnesses, D. Stewart, John Stewart, James Stewart.

WILLIAM STONE will - page 4
Son Hardeman Stone; daughter Dorcus; grandson Mumsford Smith, son of Bartholomew and Dorcus Smith; son John H. Stone; daughter Susanna; daughter Dolly; sons Marble Stone and Solomon Stone; wife Elizabeth; son William; wife and Bartholomew Smith to be executors.
Signed 26 April 1805.
Witnesses, James Foster, Thomas Hardeman, James Martin.

DAVID D. HUGHES will - page 5
Body to be buried; wife Mary; "my surviving children". John Nesbitt and Robert Nesbitt to be executors.
Signed 24 September 1804
Witnesses, Thomas Simpson, Isaiah Choate.

MOSES SMITH will - page 6
Wife Susanna; executors, Susanna Smith, Bartholomew Smith, William Stone.
Signed 11 July 1805.
Witnesses, John Davis, James Robertson.

MOSES MEEK will - page 7
Son Joshua; son Moses; wife Margaret, will written by Adam Meek, Knox County, Tennessee; daughters Elizabeth and Agness; daughter Jennet Genier; son-in-law James Martin. Executors, wife Margaret and James Martin.
Signed 5 November 1807

EDWARD FRANCES of Dickson County, will - page 9
Wife, dear and loving. Sons John and Gideon...land on south side of creek where David Howell now lives and on north side where "I now live"; till Gideon arrives at age of 21; neighbors, Henry Rape and Johnathan Johnson to be executors.
Signed 17 March 1812
Witnesses, James D. Sharp, Robert Stringfellow

SARAH MOLTON will - page 11
Granddaughter Sarah Ann Jane Molton, daughter of my son Abraham Molton; son Michael; daughters Jane Stewart and Patience Pearsall; daughter Elizabeth Simpson and her husband John Simpson; son-in-law Jeremiah Pearsall. Michael Molton and Jeremiah Pearsall to be executors.
Signed 14 July 1812
Witnesses, Edward Pearsall, Daniel H. Williams

WILLIAM NORRIS of Dickson County, will - page 11
Wife Jane. Educate my children. Son Robert to get blacksmith tools and 181 gallon still. Son John to get land on east side of Yellow

Creek known as the Puckett (or Pickett) place; deceased daughter Jane Maxwell and her son Jess when he becomes 18 and her daughter Jane when she is 14; son Ezekiah to get land on both sides of Yellow Creek including mill and mill seat and plantation known as the Holland place. Daugh-er Nancy Dillehay. When daughter Ellinor Norris becomes of age. Son William Norris to get plantation where "I now live"; and son William should "nurse brother John"; son Jesse to get one half land on Yellow Creek; daughter Betsy Norris; son-in-law Nathan Dillehay and sons Robert and Ezekiah Norris to be executors.
Recorded 10 Feb. 1820
Witnesses, Jno. Humphreys, Edward Swanson, Isaiah Moore

HOWELL ADAMS, Esq., will - page 16
"After being mortally wounded at the Battle of Muckfaw"...mentions all my children that is not married...wife Nancy...son William...son Hodge. Sworn to before Cuthbert Hudson and Jesse G. Christian, 10 Feb. 1814.

GABRIEL OVERTON will - page 17
Wife Elizabeth...three children, Robert, Elizabeth and Moses...child my wife is pregnant with.
Signed 21 September 1814
Witnesses, Cuthbert Hudson, James Hanna

LEVIN DICKSON (DIXON) of Dickson County, will - page 17
Wife Abigail; her brother David Parker...my youngest son when he reaches 18 years...if my mother dies before my wife...friend Daniel Parker and wife executors.
Signed 12 March 1815, LOVIN DICKSON
Witnesses, Daniel Hogan, William Hodges

REUBEN JONES will - page 18
Wife Ester...five children, John, Thomas, Elizabeth, Nancy, Sealum, and child my wife is pregnant with...executors to be wife and Joseph Manner.
Signed 24 January 1815
Witnesses, Cuthbert Hudson and Hugh Lewis

SAMUEL JOHNSTON (JOHNSON) will - pages 19 and 20
Wife Polly...three sons, William, Dunkin, and James...50 acres on head of White Oak Creek of Tennessee River..."all my children".
Signed 25 March 1816
Recorded 7 January 1817
Witnesses, William Gunn (or Givin) and John Epperson

JAMES McCLELLAND of Dickson County, will - pages 20 and 21
Wife Jane...son Frances...daughter Agness...youngest son Thomas when he becomes of age...my four sons...son William, son John, son Thomas... executors to be Thomas Bullion with wife Jane McClelland.
Signed 20 August 1818
Recorded April 1819
Witnesses, John West and Sally (X) West

DAVID McADOO will - page 22
Wife Margaret...son John to get one dollar...son Samuel to get part of land granted to James Ives...daughter Jane McClelland to get 80 acres... daughter Sarah Burkett...son David to get plantation on which I now live including water mill when he comes of age...mentions daughter Mary McAdoo when she becomes of age. Executors, Margaret McAdoo and David McAdoo.
Signed 6 Feb. 1815
Recorded March 1817
Witnesses, Samuel McAdoo and Thomas (x) Burkett

THOMAS RICHARDSON will - pages 24-26
Wife Winnefred...son Thomas J., daughter Frances...daughter Elizabeth Tatom...daughter Margaret Blount...executor to be wife Winnefred Richardson. Signed Thomas (X) Richardson
Witnesses, John Willey, John Mabin, Abram Caldwell
(See next page for note)

(Note: Humphreys County Deed Book E, page 577 has an entry for Winneford Richardson of Dickson County, who is deeding to "my daughter Sally Walker and her seven children, Betsy Jane, Winney, Marnerva, Nancy Ann, Isaac, James and Prillee Viena of Humphreys County," January 1833. This may possible be the same Winnefred Richardson of this will.)

CLAUDIAS DAVID L will - pages 26-27
To Jacob Johnston, son of Isaac, on his arrival at 21...my wife Elizabeth David L to receive Cave Spring tact of land.
No date.
Witnesses, Thomas Hunter, Jenet Copeland, Davy S. Whitmill.
(Note: This man's surname is intriguing. People have marked through the records in the Dickson County courthouse giving his surname as Davidson, Davidel, David-el, and David L. The name appears to be David L in this book.)

REAVES ADAMS of Dickson County, will - pages 28-29
Wife Sarah...all my children...son Howell Collen Adams when he is 20... children: Cinthy, Lillah, Sarah, Benjamin Johnson, William Thomas, and Howell Callier.
Signed 21 August 1810
Witnesses, John Humphreys, John Davidson, John Luke

JOHN BUGG of Dickson County, will - pages 29-31
Wife Elizabeth Bugg...son Willis Bugg...daughter Chanie Bugg...son Samuel...daughter Elizabeth...son Allen...daughter Mary Wall to get 75 cents...daughter Tennessee Loveache to get 25 cents...daughter Winefred Hicks to get 25 cents...daughter Sally Richardson to get 25 cents... son Jeremiah Bugg to get 25 cents...daughter Dorcas Bugg to get 25 cents ...William Bugg, son, to get 25 cents...son Henry Bugg to get 25 cents.. son Stiles Bugg to get 25 cents. Executors, Reuben Gunn and Charlie Hedges.
Signed 27 June 1809
Recorded 2 March 1821
Witnesses, William Gunn, Isaac Huges, Lewis Evans

JAMES DUNNEGAN of Dickson County, will - pages 31-32
Oldest son John...second son William...three younger sons Charles, James and Andrew...40-acre tract bought from Wyatt Fussell...son Charles to support his younger brothers and sisters, viz, Elizabeth, Ailsey, Matilda, Susannah, during their infancy. Executor, William Edwards, Sr. of Dickson County.
Signed 30 September 1818
Recorded October 1818
Witnesses, Calvin W. Eason, Joseph J. Eason, Solomon Graham

SOLOMON RYE of Dickson County, will - page 33
"Beloved son Solomon, son William, daughter Sarah B., my three surviving children"...heirs of my beloved daughter Martha Weaver...granddaughter Dorcas Weaver, daughter of Martha Weaver. Executors to be children.
Signed 15 August 1818
Recorded January 1819
Witnesses, George Bowen, William Given (Gunn?), Sterling Dillihay

WILLIAM HUDSON of Dickson County, will - page 34
Beloved wife Taffincous...son Baker...daughter Elizabeth Marsh...son William...daughter Polly F. Russell...daughter Taffinous Eason...son Thomas C...daughter Carry M...daughter Nancy Hodgins...daughter Judith J. Hudson...daughter Rebecca B. Hudson...my ten children's interest in suit against heirs of William Baker, deceased, in Mecklenburg County, North Carolina. Wife and William to be executors.
Signed 23 January 1821
Recorded April 1821
Witnesses, John Scott, Richardson Tatom, Solomon Graham

JOHN A. BAKER of Dickson County, will - page 38
Wife Jane...six children, Nelly, Sally, John, Patsey, Benjamin, and Nancy Baker...my daughter Margaret Evans...daughter Polly Hedges... daughter Betsy England...daughter Jane Evans...daughter Ann Tatom...

son Absalom Baker.
Signed 3 May 1820
Recorded 17 April 1821
Witnesses, John Wright, George Brazzell, James McKee

SETH B. JORDAN will - page 39
Wife Brittannia W...land on north side of Leatherwood Creek and east side of Yellow Creek...three sons, John Augustus, George West and Robert West; daughter Mary to be paid out of sale of plantation in North Carolina...had property in Beufort and Hyde counties, North Carolina...my brother George W. Jordan of Hyde County, North Carolina, to be executor. Robert West to be executor in Dickson County.
Signed at Mount Vernon on Yellow Creek 14 April 1822
Recorded 18 July 1822

JOHN HALL of Dickson County, pages 40-42
Sons, Joseph W., John, Jesse, David, Joshua, Berrmon, Wesley...daughters Martha, Elizabeth M. Susanna...wife Susanna...mentions "my wife's widowhood"...mentions my five youngest children...wife and son Jesse Hall to be executors.
Signed 17 May 1822
Recorded 18 January 1823
Witnesses, William Morrison, Martha Douglass, and Mark Reynolds

JOSHUA JAMES of Dickson County - page 44
Wife Aby...children: William, Thomas, Amos, Joshua, Jamay, Aby Tucker, Elijah, Jr. (son of my son Elijah), Enoch and Sally.
Signed 24 July 1820
Recorded March 1823
Witnesses, Archibald Pullen, John Stafford, George (x) Powell

JAMES GOODRICH of Dickson County, will - pages 45-46
Wife Dorothy...land on Yellow Creek...daughters Mary Rushing, Rebecca Hill, Sarah Bonds, Ellinor Hooper, Elizabeth Stanfield, Nancy Sturdivant; sons George Jackson Goodrich and William H. Goodrich...daughter Dorothy when she becomes 21 or is married...daughter Patsey when she becomes 21 or is married...sons James and John...daughters Charlotte and Alice... my mother to be maintained...my seven youngest children: William H. Dorothy, Patsey, James, Charlotte, Alice, and John. Wife Dorothy and friend Alexander Dickson to be executors.
Signed 29 August 1818
Recorded January 1824
Witnesses, Darrel Y. Harris, Robert P. Harris

JORDEN RICHARDSON of Greenville Co., Va., will - page 49
Daughter Rebecca Mason, wife of William Mason...daughter Frances Jackson, wife of Coleman Jackson...daughter Annie E. Marable, wife of Henry Marable...son Stith Richardson...daughter Amey Richardson...land owned in Brunswick County...daughter Sally when she becomes 21...all my children: Reb, Frances, Amey, Nancy E., Sally and Stith...daughter Polly...beloved wife...Mary Richardson, relict of my father William Richardson, deceased; wife Eliza and son Stith to be executors and son-in-law William Mason.
Signed 7 June 1800
Recorded July 1824
Page 53 - Granville County, Va. Thomas Spencer and Benjamin Maclin, justices of peace, examined Edmund Mason and Edwin Gailey witnesses to will of Jorden Richardson; mentions also Julia, a slave of Amey Richardson.

JOHN HUMPHREYS of Dickson County, will - pages 54-59
Son John Howard Humphreys to get negro Dorcus...daughter Clarida, who married Amos Reynolds, "she dieing and having left no issue" one dollar to Amos Reynolds in right of his marriage with my daughter Sophia, whom he left in a state of pregnancy with her third child and has remained from her ever since and therefore I consider him is not entitled to any more"...son Horatio to get Waynick and negro girl Chance and my survey instruments...son-in-law John T. Patterson to get negro Glaster and his daughter Polly White Patterson, my granddaughter, the red cambrick

(John Humphreys will, continued)
curtains in same of her dear deceased mother, my daughter...son-in-law
Edward Holley...daughter Sophia (her male children that she now has or
may have as well as two she had by Amos Reynolds and those she had or
may have since she married Edward Holly) the land and branch whereon I
now live...daughter Jenisha Brown to get $1.25...grandson John Humphreys
Brown and Asa Madison Brown and their father Asa A. Brown, give them
the negro which their father, Asa A. Brown "feloniously steal, take, and
carry her away from me". Son Stokely Humphreys: do not think it safe
to gift him with any land and negro property"...I give to all my children that I now have or may have...grandson Clinton Reynolds, John
Severe Reynolds, and Carolina Reynolds...100 acres of land in North
Carolina...my daughter Jenira received on her first marriage...directs
"my children bury me on the north side of my dear wife's grave and have
a small neat tomb erected over our graves out of rock and arched over
and made white with good lime mortar" and the expense of this is to be
met from the sale of Peggy, with friend Howard W. Turner as supervisor.
Executors: Horatio Humphreys, John T. Patterson and Edward Holly.
Signed 16 Sept. 1826
Proven January 1827
Witnesses, Robert Whittedge, B. B. Carbon, Daniel Billings
Ordered to be recorded in Book A, pages 69-73

EPHRAIM BREEDING will - page 60
All to wife Mary.
Signed 18 Feb. 1824
Proved January 1827, ordered recorded in Book A, pages 73-74
Witnesses, Robert Duke and Charlotte (x) Duke

ADAM WILSON of Dickson County, will - pages 60, 61, 62, No. 31
Will written 9 August 1822...beloved wife Margaret Wilson, 200 acres...
son Joseph Wilson to get 60 acres bought from John Lewis...son John to
get 60 acres...son James to get stud horse and 1/2 of wife's land...
daughters Margaret and Nancy...daughter Lucretia (or Lucrenia?) when
she becomes of age...Joseph and John Wilson to be executors.
Proved April 1824
Witnesses, Alexander Dickson, Chancey Desinport (Davenport?)

EBENEZER KELLy of Dickson County, will - page 63 No. 32
Wife Rachel...beloved nephew Nathan Foster of Kentucky.
Signed Ebenezer (x) Kelly
Proved July 1827
Witnesses, Thomas Richardson, Joseph Willey, Polly Willey

JOHN TURNER of Dickson County, will - page 64, No. 33
Wife Elizabeth to get plantation whereon I now live...all my children...
son Samuel, son William, son Howard.
Signed 28 June 1820
Proved January 1824
Witnesses, Jesse May, Willis Norsworthy, John (x) Dunning

LUCY HUDSON of Dickson County, will - page 65, No. 34
Son Cuthbert Hudson...daughter Susan Hudson...son Christopher Hudson
(Note: one place the name Christopher had been marked out and Cuthbert
written above it).
Signed 15 March 1825
Proven July 1825
Signed Lucy (x) Hudson
Witnesses, David Gray, Minor Bibb, Edward Tidwell

STEPHEN THOMAS of Dickson County, will - page 65, No. 35
My two sons John C. Thomas and William Thomas...wife Mary Thomas...
Signed 20 August 1824
Proved July term 1825
Witnesses, D. McAdoo and Robert Livingston

JOSEPH DAVIDSON of Dickson County - page 68, No. 36
Wife Elizabeth...son Aquilla when he is 21...equal division of property
"amongst my children"...brother John Davidson and brother-in-law Aquilla

(Will of Joseph Davidson, continued)
Tidwell to be execturo.
Signed 6 November 1820
Proved 26 April 1827
Witnesses, Mickins Carr, Edmund Tidwell, Sally Grigory

MOSES EASLEY of Dickson County, will - pages 69-70, No. 37
Wife Emaline...until daughter Eliza O. (or Eliza C.) becomes of age...
son James V. Easley to get land on little Hurricane Creek and son
John H. Easley land on Duck River...my three children...Reuben Comes
(or Comer) to see to the sale of land.
Signed 27 March 1824
Proved July 1824 term
Recorded 27 April 1827
Witnesses, Joel Massey, Michael Light, William H. Namett. (Note: This
last surname in question. Neblett?)

JOHN W. BAKER of Dickson County, will - page 71, No. 38
Verbal will: William Baker and John Humphreys acting for Rebecca Baker,
widow of John Baker, deceased...William Baker visited John W. Baker a
few days before he died and he said he had sold his land to Doctor
Francis V. Schmittou...my wife and children...my wife Beckah.
The statement of William Baker was signed 11 April 1823.
Recorded 27 April 1827

BARNABAS L. BLEDSOE of Dickson County, will - page 73 (?) No. 39
Wife Rebina Bledsoe...son Giles J. Bledsoe...rest of my sons...children,
Ann Holley, Hamor Hilley (Note: This name in question), Elizabeth Rae,
Agnes Rae, Elizabeth Wallace, Nancy Halliburton, Barney L. Bledsoe,
Pinkney T. Bledsoe, Drucilla Whitehead, Unity Jarnigan.
Signed December 1821
Recorded 27 April 1827
Witnesses, William Reynolds, William Lewis

ANN MARSH of Dickson County, will - page 74, No. 40
Son Gilbert Marsh...grandson Mineyard March...granddaughter Faney Shew-
maker. (Note: Both Marsh and March seemed to be the spelling.)
Signed, Ann (x) March 10 January 1822
Brought to court April 1825
Recorded 27 April 1827
Witnesses, William Hudson, Richard Evans

AMOS JAMES of Dickson County, will - pages 74-75, No. 41
The undersigned were with Amos James on his deathbed and he asked that
land be given to his son Joshua James and that property to widow to rear
her children. Signed by Enoch James and Abah (x--her mark) James
4 July 1825.
Recorded 27 April 1827

WILLIAM GILBERT of Dickson County, will - page 75, No. 42
Wife Nicy...son Henry Madison Gilbert when he is 21...son Thomas...son
Nathan when he becomes 21...son Maliel (?) Gilbert...daughter Temperance
Gilbert ...son James Monroe Gilbert...son William Gilbert...lands on
west side of Jones Creek...mentions the mill seat.
Signed 18 January 1827
Brought to January 1828 term of court
Recorded 15 July 1828
Witnesses, William Armstrong, Henry R. Ligget, Richard Cocke

MARTIN LOFTIS of Dickson County, will - page 78, No. 43
Wife Fereba...son William Loftis his lifetime and then to William's
three children, William, Samuel M., and Cinthia...son-in-law Andrew
Beard...daughter Pheba V., daughter Rella E., son Milton. Executor:
Josiah Thornton.
Written 6 January 285
Witnesses, Esther Thornton, Joseph McCrary, Reuben Thornton, Josiah
Thornton
    In 1826 a lawsuit when executors and William Loftis and
    Elisha Smith disputed the will. In 1827 the jury to hear

(Will of Martin Loftis, continued)
the lawsuit included: Thomas C. Smith, William Fentress, William Adams, Mumford Smith, Richard Murrell, James W. McCammon, Ashlum (Ashburn?) Vanhook, Absalom Baker, William Gunn, Jesse Alexander, Nehemiah Scott, and John Weakley. They found the will should be recorded.
(Note: The name Martin Loftis also appeared to be Milton Loftis at one place.)

JOHN REYNOLDS of Dickson County, will - pages 80-81, No. 44
Will of John Reynolds, Sr., mentions wife Susannah, "my plantation", land on which George Martin lived on, my two children...when son Thomas becomes of age...daughter Nancy. Also mentions "my first wife's children": John and Mark Reynolds, Charlotte Livingston, Polly Wilson, Gilly McMurry, and William Reynolds--they have already received from me. My friend Thomas Batson of Montgomery County and wife to be executors. Signed 6 July 1825.
Lawsuit: Susannah Reynolds vs Francis V. Schmittou, William T. Reynolds, and Mark Reynolds.
Jury: James M. Ross, Moses T. White, Samuel Mitchel, Matthew Crumpler, Raifred Crumpler, John T. (or P.) Williams, William Turner, Woodrow Daniel, William King, Benjamin Sanders, Thomas Brown, and Daniel Moore. They found the will to be the will of John Reynolds and recorded 30 January 1830.

RICHARD D. SANSOM will - page 83, No. 45
Wife Barbara...executors to sell tract of land on Town Creek...property divided among children when they come of age...brothers David N. Sansom and William C. Sansom and my uncle Henry A. C. Napier to be executors... later wife Barbara added as executrix.
Witnesses, Thomas K. Hardy (Handy?), Benjamin C. Robertson
Witnesses to codicil, B. N. Carter, A. W. Hicks
Will proved 10 July 1828
Recorded 10 September 1828
(Note: The son David N. Sansom name could also be Dorrel N. Sansom.)

JOHN R. CATHEY will - page 85, No. 46
Wife Peggy...son Archy...son Joshua...four youngest sons, David (or Daniel?), Samuel, Martin and John...daughters Jane and Dolly...son George ...daughter May, wife of William G. Austin...Mumford Smith and wife to be executors.
Signed 10 July 1827 by John R. Cathey
Witness, Jno. Forsythe

WILLIAM GARRETT, SENR. will - page 86, No. 47
Wife Sary, later found as Sarah in will...two minor children, William and Sary...rest of my children have received...William Garrett and wife Sary to be executors.
Signed 3 July 1828
Recorded 30 January 1830
Witnesses, Jacob Evans, W. Kerragin, Henry B. Koen

JOSEPH HALL will - page 87, No. 48
Daughter Nancy...grandson Henry Hall...Henry Hall to be executor.
Signed 22 February 1828
Recorded 13 February 1830
Witnesses, Robert Moore, Robert Whitwell
(Note: This will was very dim on the film.)

GEORGE ROSS will - page 88, No. 49
Son James M. Ross...grandson George R. Craft...granddaughter Sally West.. granddaughter Harriet Outlaw...granddaughter Marguerite Outlaw...grandson James Craft...daughter Mary Drake...granddaughter Sally Perry... granddaughter Lucy Eaton...grandson George Drake...granddaughter Permelia Williams...grandson James Drake....granddaughter Sally Bacon...land on which Jesse Craft lives in Montgomery County...the children of my daughter Margaret Craft...the children of my daughter Jane Bacon...James M. Ross, George R. Craft and John H. Marable to be executors.
Signed 18 October 1828   (continued on next page)

(Will of George Ross, continued)
Recorded 20 February 1830
Witnesses, George T. Cooksey, Robert Baxter, Daniel Moore

ENOCH JAMES will - page 90, No. 50
Wife and Archibald Pullen to be executors...my child...
Signed 25 August 1830
Proved January 1831
Recorded 18 February 1832
Witnesses, James Carter, John Stafford

ELIZABETH WALKER will - page 91, No. 51
My five living children, John B. Walker, Sarah R. Walker, Margaret R. Williams, May S. Walker and Nancy V. Gilbert...my deceased daughter Barbary H. Crews' son, Vance (or Vanning) S. Crews...Elizabeth T. Crews and Sarah Ann B. Crews, daughters of my daughter Barbara, when they reach 21...John B. Walker to be executor.
Signed 17 December 1828
Proved July 1830
Recorded 18 February 1832
Witnesses, Abram Caldwell, William Keragen

MOSES FUSSELL will - page 93, No. 52
Wife Lucy...heirs of my eldest son Wyatt Fussell...daughter Elizabeth Horner and after her decease to George Wyatt Horner...son William Fussell ...daughters Sally Horner, Lucy Horner (widow of James Horner) and Patsey Dunnegan.
Signed Moses (x) Fussell on 15 Dec. 1830
Proved April 1831
Recorded 18 February 1832
Executors, Mickens Carr and William Fussell
Witnesses, Eli Crow, John Dunnegan, Elizabeth Crow

DANIEL WILLIAMS will - page 94, No. 53
Having 12 children...my married children: Daniel H., Thos., Joseph, Christian Scott, Mary Killebrew, Cassander Napier, Susannah Norsworthy, Jennetta Napier, Benjamin, and Henry B. H...my son Richard Nixon Williams to have land on west side of Yellow Creek...son James Williams...son Joseph Williams, executor.
Signed 5 October 1830
Proved October 1831
Recorded 18 February 1832
Witnesses, James (x) Brown, John W. Scott, William Scott

THOMAS DRUMMOND will - pages 95-96, No. 54
My children to have equal shares...son Zacheus Drummond...son Thomas Drummond...daughter Elizabeth Shropshire...daughter Patience Ragan... daughter Peggy Rye...youngest son James M. Dummond...son William Drummond ...my wife to have title...wife Peggy.
Signed 30 March 1831 Thomas (x) Drummond
Proved October 1832
Recorded 1 November 1832
Witnesses, John Montgomery, Richard Waugh

JOHN JONES will - page 96, No. 55
Gives to Thomas Jefferson Jones...my next oldest sons Josiah Jones, Joshua Jones, John Jones, Jr., William Jones, James Madison Jones...wife Jane.
Signed 23 April 1832
Proved January 1833
Recorded 12 Feb. 1833
Witnesses, Joshua White, Simon Myers, William Morris

ELIZABETH RICHARDSON will - page 97, No. 56
Daughter Polly...grandson Jordan W. Richardson...Jordan M. Richardson, son of my son Stith...granddaughter Rebecca A., daughter of son Stith Richardson...my grandchildren Jordan W. A., Hartwell Henry Richardson, Rebecca Ann Richardson, Edward Richardson, Mary A. Richardson, Thomas E.
(continued on next page)

(Will of Elizabeth Richardson, continued)
Richardson, and _____ Richardson, sons and daughters of my son Stith...
granddaughter Elizabeth Jackson, daughter of Doctor Coleman Jackson...
Signed 4 October 1832
Proved January 1833
Recorded 12 February 1833
Witnesses, John H. Marable, Joseph Kimble

RANSOM ELLIS will - page 100, No. 57
Wife Nancy W. Ellis...my youngest child is twenty-one...my wife and children...my brother Thomas (?) Ellis...my worthy friend Willie Balthrop and brother Thomas to be executors.
First brought to court October 1832
Proved April term 1833
Recorded 17 April 1833
Witnesses, Stith Richardson, John Dye

GEORGE DAVIDSON will - page 101, No. 58
Land granted to me by state of Tennessee...son George Davidson...wife Elizabeth...daughter Jane Clark, wife of Richardson L. Clark.
Signed 10 July 1823
Recorded 12 November 1833
Witnesses, James Teas, Matthew Gilmore, James Gilmore

DAVID PASSMORE will - page 103, No. 59
Daughter Mary Reader, land on waters of Four Mile...daughter Elizabeth Black, land on headwaters of Four Mile and land on Beaverdam Creek...grandson William Black, son of Elizabeth Black, land in Hickman County on Blue Buck Creek of Duck River...my two daughters Mary Reader and Elizabeth Black...James Hicks, William Gentry to be executors.
Signed 20 February 1834
Recorded 7 April 1834
Witnesses, Davidson Cruick (?), John L. Hicks

LEBIUS RICHARDSON will - page 104, No. 60
Will written 20 February 1839...wife Frankey...my two youngest children to be schooled...my two youngest sons John and Stephen Dailey Richardson...my son Thomas...my son Lebbius Wilkins Richardson...my daughter Eliza Tatum to get land at head of Rockey Creek...son James Joy...daughter Polly Koon...son John.
Recorded 7 October 1833
Witnesses, John B. Walker, Allen Nesbitt

RICHARD CLAIBORNE NAPIER will - page 106, No. 61
My store houses on Union and College Streets, Nashville...my two tracts of land on Harpeth River "where my family have lately resided"...tract of land in Robertson Bend of Cumberland River in Davidson County where Hannah Napier now lives...my two youngest children Leroy W. and Charlotte Mary Napier, each to get $9,000...my wife Charlotte...my shotgun in possession of Thomas Overton...my rifle gun which James R. Napier used for a number of years...son James R. Napier's children to get $9,000 "which I advanced to their father during his lifetime" also a tract of land which I bought of their father on Nails Creek on the waters of Turnbull...son Madison C. Napier...money to be paid annually to Hannah Napier while she remains widow of my son James R. Napier...the five children of my son James R. Napier...my estate in five shares: my wife, Leroy, Charlotte, Madison, and James R...Peyton Robinson and Benjamin Sharp, Junr., to be executors.
Signed 7 March 1834
Proved April 1834
Recorded 21 July 1834

LEONARD PINEGAR will - page 111, No. 62
Wife Susannah...son Joseph...balance to be divided between my children.
Signed 12 February 1835
Recorded 16 September 1835
Witnesses, William Pinegar, David Gray

JAMES HOLLAND will - page 112, No. 63
Son Hardy Holland to get tract of land where he now lives...my second daughter Sally, a single woman...my second son Mark...my granddaughter Patsy Brier (?) and grandson John if they will stay with Sally...my daughters Delila and Mary, my first and third daughters.
Signed 12 Feb. 1835
Proved April 1835 court
Recorded 16 September 1835
Witnesses, Charles W. Brown, Isaac Fleming

JOHN CHOATE will - page 114, No. 65
My beloved wife Eleanor Choate...son John H. Choate...all of my children ...sons Peter Choate and Squire J. Choate...my old plantation and old tract...east section has a cave spring.
Signed 19 August 1834, John (x) Choate
Proved January 1835
Witnesses, William S. Coleman, Luke Matlock, John H. Choate

JOHN WILLEY will - page 115, No. 66
Wife Polly...daughter Polly...son John...son Washington...daughter Elizabeth...all my children...brother William Willey and my wife Polly to be executors.
Signed 18 August 1823
Proved October 1835
Witnesses, Lebius W. Richardson, Allen Nesbitt, A. Caldwell

JOHN JOHNSON will - page 116, No. 67
My beloved wife Amy...three youngest sons Thomas M., Joel S., and Stephen B. Johnson...daughter Patsey...daughter Cholaty...all my children: Polly Hudson, Patsey, John, William, Charloty, Thomas, Joel, and Stephen.
Signed 17 August 1835, John Johnson, Sr.
Proved October 1835
Witnesses, Charles W. Brown, Benjamin Hiland

PETER GOODWIN will - pages 118-119, No. 68
Wife Sally...my five youngest children, Lucy, William, Peter, Sal, and John...Thomas Murrell and George W. Tatum, executors.
Signed 29 November 1834, Peter (x) Goodwin
Proved January 1836
Witnesses, James Thedford, George W. Tatum

JOHN TUCKER will - page 119, No. 69
Children: James M., Jane, Lewis, William C., Mary Ann and Louise C. Tucker.
Signed 15 August 1835
Proved October 1835
Witnesses, William Gentry, James Hicks

WILLIAM BRASHER will - page 120, No. 70
Nephew William B. Simmons...to Lovy Council...to Minerva Malegin... brother-in-law Jacob Evans.
Signed 12 October 1832
Proved January 1836
Witnesses, William Shelton, William E. Slayden

WILLIAM MORRISON will - page 120, No. 71
"Buried on farm where I now live by the side of my daughter Charity Nolen"...my wife Rachel Morrison...daughter Betsy...granddaughter Betty Melinda Nolen...daughter Elizabeth "has been a dutiful child"...the whole of my children...son William...daughter Rachel Patterson...grandchildren William and Polly Patterson...but do not allow to Robert and Rachel Patterson a single one cent more...daughter Mary Weakley... "the children of Robert and Peggy Dickson not to receive a single division"...daughter Peggy Dickson...daughter Jane Reynolds, wife of Solomon Reynolds...Solomon Reynolds to get horse only on good behaviour...if daughter Jane has surviving children...if Solomon Reynolds dies then Jane can share with other children; children: Mary Weakley, Betsey Malinda Nolen in place of her mother Charity, heirs of Robert and

(Will of William Morrison, continued)
Peggy Dickson: Joseph Morrison Dickson, Robert Patton Dickson, Rachel
Ann Elizabeth Dickson, are entitled to mother's share; Elizabeth
Morrison, William Morrison, Jr., Rachel Patterson. My daughter Jane
Reynolds being left out but if she outlives her husband...Executors,
Robert West and George W. Jordan.
Signed 25 July 1835
Proved October 1835 term
Witnesses, Thomas McMurry, H. W. Turner

HOWELL FREEMAN will - page 126, No. 72
Wife Hannah...my six children: Buncels (Runcels?), Williams, Jeramiah
Freeman, Polly Burton (wife of Ambrose Burton), Martha Self (wife of
Abraham Self), Elizabeth Massey (wife of John Massie).
Signed 15 October 1835
Proved June 1836
Witnesses, Stith Richardson, John Hinson

DAVID WILEY will - page 127, No. 73
Brother Jonathan Wiley's son Gaston Wiley...brother Ebenezer's son
Louson Wiley...brother Ebenezer's youngest son Adderson Jasper Wiley...
brother Ebenezer's son Jesse Wiley...to stay with my father. David
Frasher to be executor.
Signed 29 December 1836
Witnesses, Josiah Thornton, Elizabeth (x) Myatt

THOMAS MATTHEWS will - page 128, No. 74
Wife Emilla...daughter Lollea...son Andrew Jackson Matthews...son George
T. Matthews...wife and friend George T. Cooksey to be executors...
Signed 28 April 1834
Proved April 1835
Recorded 16 September 1835
Witnesses, William Shelton, Creel Shelton

GEORGE TUBB will - page 129, No. 75
Sons Richard Tubb, Nathan Tubb, James Tubb...daughters Elizabeth Coleman
and Martha Middleton...note on William Gilbert...grandsons Daniel Tubb
and George Tubb...grandchildren: Pheba Cooksey's children, Isaac Tubb's
children, Mary Davidson's children, Cary Nolen's children...son
Nathan Tubb and W. S. Coleman to be executors.
Signed 17 October 1836
Witnesses, Daniel Leech, James Loggins

JOHN ANGLIN will - page 130, No. 76
In the name of God Amen I John Anglin on the State of Tennessee and
County of Dickson being weak in body but of sound and perfect mind and
memory, blessed be Almighty God for the same do make and publish this my
last Will and Testament in manner and form following, that is to say
First I give and bequeath unto my beloved wife Elizabeth Anglin the land
and possessions where I now live; also my negro woman Phebe and negro
boy William Henry. Also all my horses and cattle and all my other stock,
household and kitchen furniture and farming tools, my just debts first
to be paid, to hold during her widowhood then to be divided as follows.
I do give and bequeath to my four sons, Cornelius, William, Aaron and
George Anglin the sum of one dollar each. I also give and bequeath to
my two daughters Nancy and Margaret a new saddle each, daughter Sally
C. Anglin my negro woman Phebe. I also give and bequeath to my son
John C. Anglin my negro boy William Henry, and if said Phebe should have
any more children to be equally divided between my two youngest children, Sally C. Anglin and John C. Anglin, and lastly as to all the rest
residue and remainder of my personal estate goods and chattels of what
kind and nature soever I give and bequeath the said to my said youngest
children Sally C. Anglin and John C. Anglin. I hereby appoint Jacob
Tucker and Elizabeth Anglin my wife my sole Executors to this my last
will and testament, hereby revoking all former wills by me made. In
witnesses whereof I have hereunto set my hand and seal the fifth of
March in the year of our Lord 1828. Signed John (x) Anglin.
Witnesses, Archibald Ponder, Nicholas Dudley, Willis Dudley
(This will in full was contributed by Mrs. Dudley W. Layne.)

CHARLES THOMPSON will - page 131, No. 77
Wife Mary...my beloved helpless children, Nancy Sally, John, and Charles
...son James...to support them in their helpless situation and final
disease...
Signed January 1824
Witnesses, Ester E. Williams, Daniel H. Williams

BURRELL MYATT will - page 132, No. 78
Wife Polly...slaves mentioned...son Eldridge to have all my land on the
west side of my spring branch where I now live...Polly Myatt to be
executor.
Signed 2 August 1838
Witnesses, Kinderick Myatt, Daniel D. (x) George

J. BEV HUGHES will - page 133, No. 79
To my affectionate mother...among my brothers and sisters, Martha B.
Ragland, William Granville Hughes, Edwina Madison Hughes, Nancy Newton
Hughes, Lemuel Horace Hughes...my father to have my horse and bridle.
No date for signing.
Witnesses, J. R. Hudson, William T. Carter

MARY VARRELL, widow, will - pages 33-34, No. 80
Nephew Nathan Gilbert...nephew William Gilbert...niece Rosanna Gilbert..
niece Tempy Edwards...my adopted niece Rosanna Gilbert...my nephews and
nieces children of my brother William Gilbert, Nichols Gilbert, and
James Gilbert...brother William Gilbert, deceased...nephews Nathan and
Maliel (?) Gilbert to be executors.
Signed 6 March 1831 by Mary (x) Varrell
Witnesses, Caleb Evans, Mary (x) Suiter

SAMUEL JAMES will - pages 134-135, No. 81
Son James...daughter Polly...daughter Phamata for her kind attention to
me...John Cunningham to be executor.
Signed 20 May 1838
Recorded 8 February 1839
Witnesses, W. Hand, Aley (x-her mark) Williams

JAMES TIDWELL will - page 135, No. 82
Wife Mary...divided among Rebecca Lamp**ley**, Francis Tidwell's heirs,
John Tidwell, Mary Spencer's children (James, Daniel, and William...son
John K. Tidwell and Jacob Lampley to be executors.
Signed 22 August 1839
Recorded 29 October 1839
Witnesses, John B. Carr, Ruffin Perry

ANN WHITWELL will - page 136, No. 83
To Blount M. Bell and James Finly, to get the slaves...slaves were con-
veyed by John J. Bell to Ann Whitwell...grandson John P. Bell, son of
John J. Bell and my daughter Nancy K. Bell...grandson Montgomery Bell,
son of John J. and Nancy S. Bell...granddaughter Marceannia Bell,
daughter of John J. and Nancy S. Bell..the minor children of John J. and
Nancy Bell...my 8 grandchildren, children of Nancy S. Bell and John J.
Bell, Blount Bell, Elizabeth West Finley, Mary Ann Bell, Jane P. Bell,
John P. Bell, Thomas Drue Bell, Marceanna Bell, Montgomery Bell.
Signed 27 August 1839
Recorded 4 November 1839
Witnesses, J. R. Hudson, Elizabeth J. Richardson

JOHN DAVIDSON, SENR., will - page 139 No. 84
My beloved wife Violet...sons Henry, Joseph, James, William, David, John,
Elijah...daughters Sarah, Matilda, Peggy, Mary.
Signed 3 September 1839
Recorded 10 December 1839
Witnesses, B. B. Tidwell, John Porter

JAMES CUNNINGHAM will - page 141, No. 85
Wife Sarah...brother Thomas Cunningham...brothers and sisters John Cunningham, Nathaniel Cunningham, William Cunningham, Ann Patterson, Elizabeth Carroll, Mary Wilson, Amy Hogwood, Nancy Hamilton.   (Continued)

(Will of James Cunningham, continued)
Signed 5 December 1839
Recorded 11 January 1840
Witnesses, Thomas Poyner, Jas. Daniel, Elijah W. Cunningham

JAMES WHITE will - pages 141-142, No. 86
Two sons John and James S. White...wife Polly...son Crage White...to Charles White, Chapman White, Nancy McLaughlin, Polly Ann Hail, Sally Harms, Martha White, Mahala White.
(Note: surname Harms could be Harris.)
Signed 25 September 1838
Witnesses, E. Harns, William Harns, Jr.

WILLIAM HOGINS will - page 142, No. 87
To son Morgan H. Hogins, the Eason tract "bounded by William (Walker) Hogins, deceased" and to Eleanor Hogins his sister...to minor child of William W. Hogins, part of survey in name of Morgan Hood...to son Abram C. Hogins...my daughter Eleanor Phillips...my daughter Sally Clay also to get a bed her grandmother gave her...my daughter Polly to get Matilda and her child and Prince...my daughter Betsy to get Jane and Mary her two youngest children...my part of Poke Rool to Christopher C. Hudson. (Note: This will was not clear on my microfilm and those interested in this will should refer to an original copy.)
Signed 16 September 1840
Recorded 5 November 1840
Witnesses, D. Gray, A. D. Hogins

JOHN NESBITT will - page 145, No. 88
Youngest son Allen...rest of children, Thomas, John, Robert, and daughter Fanny Walker.
Signed 2 August 1838
Recorded June 1841
Witnesses, A. Caldwell, Thos. McNeilly

DANIEL TAYLOR will - page 146, No. 89
Wife Mary Ann...wife and Claiborne Taylor to be executors.
Signed 28 April 1841
Record 27 June 1841
Witnesses, Benajah Gentry, Mark Harns (or Harris)

HENRY LEEK will - pages 147-8, No. 90
Of Northampton County, N. C....to Elizabeth Leek land in the Rulian Swamp...to Nancy Sikes, wife of John Sikes...to Josiah Leek the blacksmith tools...to grandchildren of my deceased sister Mary...to Benjamin Young and grandchildren of Mary Young, deceased...slaves left to me by my brother Randolph Leek, deceased...my cousin Minah Leek...if Levina Sikes, daughter of John, lives to attain age of eighteen to have lands on the west side of Wrichan Swamp.
Signed 1 November 1832
Proved in Northampton County and recorded 22 June 1833
Recorded Stewart County, Tennessee, 13 October 1841
Recorded in Dickson County 2 November 1841
Witnesses, Davis Bryan, John Bryan

JOSHUA WHITE will - page 149, No. 91
Wife Martha...sons David and Benjamin...other children: Elizabeth, James, Nancy, Jesse, Roney and Daniel when they reach eighteen...wife and Owen Sullivan to be the executors.
Signed 5 October 1841
Recorded 10 becember 1841
Witnesses, Benajah Gentry, John Porter

WILLIAM WILEY will - pages 141-142, No. 92
Wife Ann...son-in-law Isaac Griffin...son Josiah...son Jesse...son Jonathan's heirs...daughter Elizabeth Myatt...son Ebenezer's heirs... grandson Eli Wiley...grandson Jesse Wiley...granddaughter Dosea Ann Griffin...granddaughter Eliza Jean Griffin. Executor to be David Gray.
Signed 21 May 1839
Recorded February 1842   Witnesses, J. Thornton, Nancy (x) Landrith

WILLIAM HIGHTOWER will - page 153, No. 93
Mentions's mother support...children of my illegitimate daughter Mary, wife of Willis Jackson...sister Polly Kirk, wife of William Kirk. Willis Jackson appointed executor.
Signed 29 November 1840
Recorded 8 August 1842
Witnesses, J. Voorhies, Jacob A. Karnes

HENDERSON ADCOCK will - page 154, No. 94
Wife Dolly M.
Signed 12 September 1842
Recorded 5 December 1842
Witnesses, David Gray, Matthew (x) Myatt

JACOB EVANS will - pages 155-156, No. 95
Wife Mary.
Recorded May 1842.
Witnesses, Allen (x) Hunter, C. A. Baker

MOSES STREET will - page 156, No. 96
Wife Ailsey...two eldest sons Techonias (?) Street and David Street... son Jackonias (Note: This may be the same as the eldest son, whose name was impossible to decipher on the film)...son Abram...son Moses...daughter Joanna Williams...daughter Susan Self...
Recorded 8 July 1843
Witnesses, C. C. Dodson, Jeremiah (x) Thompson

MARY BALTHROP will - page 58, No. 97
Son Wilie (or Willis).
Signed 4 Feb. 1837
Recorded 8 July 1843
Witnesses, James Daniel, H. M. Slayden

JAMES JOSLIN will - page 159, No. 98
One-fourth to daughter Jaretha Caroline Cochran...one fourth to Matilda Ann Boyd, wife of James H. Boyd...one fourth to daughter Elizabeth Jane Joslin...one fourth to daughter Mary Margaret Joslin...when my youngest daughter comes of age...John R. Hudson and John W. Napier to be executors.
Signed 23 July 1843
Recorded 8 September 1843
Witnesses, Jesse W. Bartee, J. W. Napier

JANE GOODRICH will - pages 160-161, No. 99
To Norman T. Baker land where Armstrong Baker now lives...to Felix G. Baker...to Cave J. Baker...to Mary Ann Baker...to Argain (?) Baker.
Signed 23 August 1843
Recorded 9 September 1843
Witnesses, G. W. Tatom, Samuel Bugg

MINOR BIBB will - page 162 No. 100
My four children, Sarah M. Jackson, Susan Stewart, John M. Bibb, and Elizabeth Bibb...was in partnership with John M. Bibb and Minor B. Hayes in distillery in Hickman County...purchased land in Hickman County from Samuel S. Porter on which there is a grist mill...beloved wife and son to be executors.
Signed 16 January 1844
Recorded 18 March 1844
Witnesses, John C. Collier, John Brown, Wiley Davis

JOHN BREWER will - page 165, No. 101
Wife Susan...to each of the children...my daughters Sarah Elizabeth and Mary Ann.
Signed 7 June 1844
Recorded 13 July 1844
Witnesses, J. R. Hudson, John H. Stone

ROBERT DUKE will - page 167, No. 102
Wife Charlotte...son Green W. Duke...lands on mouth of Harpeth to (continued on next page)

(Will of Robert Duke, continued)
Charlotte Road...grandson William S. Baker, lands on Harpeth River...
daughter Mary P. G. Duke married William Baker.
Signed 11 September 1838
Recorded 4 March 1845
Witnesses, Caleb Rooker, Joseph Morris

SHADRICK BELL will - page 169, No. 103
Daughter Mary Ross...sons Shadrick and Elisha...son Thomas Bell land on the east side of Bear Branch of Cumberland River...mentions Pond Branch and my saw and grist mills...daughter Nancy Williams, wife of Wesley A. Williams...the children of my daughter Nancy...daughter Elizabeth W. Coldwell...grandson Joseph A. Dickson.
Signed 7 June 1846
Recorded 4 November 1846
Witnesses, James Finly, John P. Bell, W. B. Smith

ANN WILEY will - pages 171-172, No. 104
My children...daughter Elizabeth Myatt.
Signed 14 August 1842
Recorded 28 January 1847
Witnesses, David Gray, Fanning Yates

THO. GENTRY will - page 172, No. 105
Wife Anney...son Anderson to get land where he now lives...son Benijah to get land on Pine River in District 2...daughter Jane, consort of Thomas Brown, to get land in District 4 beginning at Bell's Oar Road where it crosses Franklin Road where Columbia Road intersects the Franklin Road...daughter Lucinda..."that all of my children that I have not given any property"...mentions Eliza Jane...son-in-law Mark Harris.
Signed Thomas Gentry, 29 Sept. 1846
Recorded 1 March 1847
Witnesses, V. F. Bell, Matthew L. Gentry

ROBERT NESBITT will - page 175, No. 106
Body to be buried at Allen Nesbitt's in Dickson County...son Robert... pay Menajah Bills for medical aid...nephew Allen Nesbitt to take son Robert under his cared and build him a comfortable cabin...a slave was designated for care and support of Robert his lifetime...after son Robert's death to be equally divided among my children...son Samuel to be executor.
Signed 2 Feb. 1844
Recorded 25 July 1847
Witnesses, Robert McNeilly, John M. Larkins

HARTWELL M. SLAYDEN will - pages 177-178, No. 107
My children...my companion Jane...my daughters.
Signed 10 July 1846
Recorded 26 July 1847
Witnesses, John Mays, Jr., Samuel Adams

MARY ANN BELL will - page 178, No. 108
Brother Montgomery Bell...sister Jane...my other brothers and sisters... my father John J. Bell...my brother Thomas Drue Bell to be executor.
Signed at the mouth of Harpeth River 5 February 1847, M. A. Bell
Proved 1 March 1847
Recorded 26 July 1847
Witnesses, B. C. Duke, H. C. Larkins

ISIAH TIDWELL will - pages 180-181, No. 109
Wife Rebecker...each of my nine daughters...son-in-law John Porter to be executor.
Signed 12 March 1848
Proved April 1848
Recorded 1 June 1848
Witnesses, D. C. Chamberlain, William E. (x) Pendergrass

JAMES M. DODSON will - pages 181-182, No. 110
Wife Susan if she remains a widow...my children...brothers-in-law

(Will of James M. Dodson, continued)
Samuel Farmer and Nicholas P. Hardeman to be executors.
Signed 24 February 1847 James M. Dotson
Proved March 1847 term
Recorded 5 April 1847, 2 June 1848

E. W. NAPIER will - pages 183 and following, No. 111
Being weak and infirm in body and of advanced age...emancipates July, my seamstress, and her five children, Fanny, William Carroll, James Monroe, Tho. Benton, and Andrew Jackson...Fanny's children Leroy Lott, Malissa Lott, Margaret Arabella Lott, Judia Adonia Lott, and Mary Jane Lott... Lizza or Elizabeth, my cook (a yellow girl)...Amanuel, a forgeman and his wife Creecy...Jack, a mulatto, and his youngest child Emmaline... Tom Keys, my waggoner and overlooker, and wife Eady...Charity my old female cook...Sam Dillahunt, my good and faithful old servant...also my little house servant Simon, about 9 years...Daniel an old man who has been a teamster a number of years and his brother Jim Brown...Perry a man of advanced age, a coaling ground hand, many of the servants are of advanced age and have with faithfulness aided me in making what property and money I have and those yellow female servants have with vigilance and fidelity taken care of my property both by day and night both in Alabama and Tennessee, particularly in Alabama, watching and putting out fire placed in it to consume it by incendiaries and I do also hereby emancipate and set a liberty a yellow boy named Solomon, about 6, son of a mulatto girl Angeline, to be put under the care and charge of Judy and Lizzy until he is 21...The emancipation of these slaves has been the result of my deliveration for years passed which I this day bring to a close...request the earnest and direct attention of my friends Benjamin C. Robertson and Robert McNeilly to be executors.

To Charlotte Napier, widow of my brother Richard C. Napier...to her son Madison C. Napier and her youngest son Leroy Napier and to the female child of James R. Napier and his youngest son Richard C. Napier and his oldest son Blunt R. Napier...

To Martha Gould, wife of James Gould...to Elizabeth Gilbert, wife of Thomas Gilbert...to heirs of body of Martha Garret, wife of Phenius Garret...

To Jesse Beck, son of Jesse and Judy Beck, $200...to David C., Andrew J., and John T. Beck, the three youngest sons of Jesse and Judy Beck...to William J. Beck, eldest son of Jesse and Judy Beck...Martha Jane Johnson, daughter of Jesse Beck and wife Judy...to Lucy Ann Edwards, daughter of Jesse and Judy Beck, land on which David Record built a cabin and lived a while...

To Fountain Lester and wife Sarah Ann......to Richard Thompson and wife Lucy Ann...to Benjamin C. Robertson and wife Ann and their five surviving children, Martha D., Edward A., Christopher W., John H., and Benjamin J. Robertson...to Mary Eliza Wilson, an orphan girl at this time living with William H. and John W. Napier on Barton's Creek, $300...

To William J. Therman and wife Elizabeth and their daughter July Ann...to Richard, John, William, and James Therman, sons of William and Elizabeth Therman...to Carter or Dock, youngest son of William J. and Elizabeth Therman...

To James Thedford and wife during their natural life, a tract of land where James Thedford now lives, and negro Peggy, late wife of Bob, deceased, whose occupation at the present to rake leaves in the coaling ...mentions land adjoining Montgomery Bell's mother...

To my friend Robert McNeily...to his oldest son James Hugh McNeilly, an infant child to be delivered to him as soon as it can be taken from breast of the mother...to the female children of John and Eliza Yateman (Note: the names of children were left blank)...to P. S. Jones my negro Louanna, 22, daughter of London and wife Jane, deceased, and Eliza, 32, whom I bought in Alabama of a man by name of Only and a gray horse at this time working at the Mt. Etna furnace which I bought (continued)

(Will of E. W. Napier, continued)
of Dr. J. R. Hudson...

To Tarleton F. Moore a negro Kiah, 22, if he remains in the service of my estate...to James M. Holt a negro Burrell and wife Francis, a yellow woman, if he remains in service of my estate...

To brother John W. Napier, his daughter Araminta, who has intermarried with Dr. John R. Hudson...to my nephew William H. Napier (several negroes, occupation were given)...to John B. Carpenter and wife Mary, my niece and daughter of my deceased brother Thomas...to my kind faithful and worthy nephew William C. Napier, one of my brother Thomas's sons, all iron property, personal and real estate that I purchased of Napier & Catron and of Judge Catron on Shoals Creek, Chief Creek and Brush Creek.

To Benjamin Stones and wife Mary, daughter of my deceased brother Henry A. C. Napier...to heirs of Samuel B. Lee and wife Amanda, daughter of my brother John W. Napier...all my real and personal property in Davidson, Dickson, and Hickman counties to be sold and to be equally divided between the lawful heirs of my brother Henry A. C. Napier, except Benjamin Stones and wife Mary, and lawful heirs of Dr. John R. Hudson and wife Araminta, daughter of my brother John W. Napier...

Desires executors to protect emancipated slaves and to put them in possession of all my household and kitchen items, to be divided among them...set aside $50 per annum for Simon for his schooling and later when he commences his trade to give him $500...if any emancipated slave choses to live in Davidson County, then executors are to take slave and put him on the block in the town of Charlotte and to be sold and the money divided the remaining emancipated slaves...

Executors to be William C. Napier of Hickman County, Robert McNeilly Benjamin C. Robertson and William H. Napier of Dickson County.
Signed 12 June 1848, E. W. Napier
Witnesses, Thos. McNeilly, Thos. Overton

Codicil emancipates others and he gives to Judy the farm on Richland Creek in Davidson County...directs to be sold to the highest bidder the White Bluff Forge and negroes, the old Turnbull forge and sell negroes belonging to the forge...sell Piney Furnace, land and negroes...and sell Mt. Etna Furnace, all land and negroes.
Signed 22 July 1848
R. M. McNeilly, Tarlton F. Moore, witnesses.

Another codicil added with T. F. Moore and Joseph Groves, witnesses.

Another codicil added 6 August 1848 with Robert McNeilly and Jesse Beck as witnesses. (Will ended on page 198 and was recorded 22 Aug. 1848.)

BUCKNER HARRIS will - page 198, No. 112
Wife Lucy...my children...when youngest child becomes of age.
Signed 28 August 1847
Proved October 1847
Recorded 3 August 1848
Witnesses, Warren Jordan, Burrell Jackson

ARCHIBALD PULLEN will - page 199, No. 113
Wife Polly...son James C. Pullen, land on Nails Creek purchased from E. Bishop...son Nelson B. Pullen, land on Tumbling Creek in Humphreys County...son William C. Pullen land on Tumbling Creek, Humphreys County ...daughter Sophia B. McNeally...son John A. Pullen, land where I now live...land on Nails Creek deeded by David Passmore.
Signed 9 July 1842, Signed A. Pullen
Proved October 1847
Recorded 24 March 1848
Witnesses, Isaac Hill, William Thompson

JOHN SANDERS will - page 201, No. 114
To Squire J. Choat, Samuel W. Sanders, Marshall Larkins, and James McCollum, my negroes and land where James McCollum now lives...wife Susan ...the raising of the minor children.
Signed 26 November 1848, John (x) Sanders
Proved January 1849
Recorded February 1849
Witnesses, W. S. Coleman, D. C. Chamberlain

ANDREW WORK will - page 202, No. 115
Wife Catherine, land on which I now live...land on Charlotte Road, Piney River...children: Samuel, Andrew, Robert John F., Mary Dudley, Nancy Phipps, Jane Ezzell, and Rebecca Gordan. (Note: Her surname could be Gorday) A. C. Hogan to be executor.
Signed 9 January 1850
Proved June 1850
Recorded 5 July 1850
Witnesses, Tho. Hulme, William Green

RICHARD PRICHARD will - page 203, No. 116
Brother Cary Prichard...my share of uncle John Prichard's estate of Montgomery County.
Signed 18 December 1847
Proved 6 March 1848
Recorded 5 April 1848
Witnesses, Warren Jourdan, Susan Prichard

ROBERT F. BIBB will - page 207, No. 117
Wife Nancy...all my children...sons James, Minor, and John G. Bibb... a horse lost in the Florida war by son John G. Bibb, should the government ever pay.
Signed February 1846
Proved August 1850
Recorded September 1850
Witnesses, Jesse Beck, Oliver Spicer, Joseph F. White

THOMAS D. BELL will - page 208, No. 118
Memorandum of will and wishes...sister Marceanna...brother Montgomery... sister Elizabeth...nephew Thomas Finley...Silvester Finley to be the executor.
Proved October 1850
Recorded December 1850
Witnesses, W. S. Graves, C. C. Cobb

EPPS JACKSON will - page 210, No. 119
Executors to be Thomas Overton, James G. Jackson, Samuel D. Bowen... lands at Hurricane in Humphreys County...wife Sarah...my youngest children...estate to be divided into 11 parts...children, "the first set": Adaline Oliphant, James G. Jackson, Wm. M. Jackson, Mary Ann Bowen, Epsey Ann Jackson, Ribhard P. Jackson, Van J. Jackson...my present wife Sarah and her children, Robert, John, and Sarah, infants.
Signed 6 May 1850
Proved September 1850
Recorded 5 October 1850

JOHN BROWN will - page 212-213, No. 120
Wife Martha...son James...son Solomon's heirs...all my children.
Signed John (x) Brown, Senr., 25 March 1845
Codicil, Feb. 1849
Witnesses, Wiley Davis, Henry Garton
Codicil witnesses, H. R. Richardson, Gideon Davis

CHRISTOPHER STRONG will - page 214, No. 121
Directs to be "decently buried in my family graveyard"...wife Rosannah ...heirs of my daughter Martha Dickson...got in deed to me from Molten Dickson...to John and Reas Bowen the farm where I now live that I bought at their father's sale on Jones Creek...to Priscilla Dickson, B and Egbert Raworth, land in Haywood County...my great-grandsons Charles Betts and Joseph Dickson...land in Henry County (continued)...

(Will of Christopher Strong, continued)
directs if great-grandson "becomes minister in Apostate Reformed
Church"...number of books left...some slaves to be sent to Liberia...
mentions heirs of my three daughters, Martha Dickson, Jane Farrar, and
Sarah Bowen...all my grandchildren except Christopher Bowen...to the
three Raworth children...wife, John Montgomery, Christopher W. Dickson,
Christopher S. Bowen and Robert McNeilly to be executors.
Signed 16 November 1849
Proved December 1850
Recorded 20 December 1850
Witnesses, Robert McNeilly, John McNeilly

ELIZABETH GLEAVES will - page 224, No. 222
Daughter Isabella...son Ezekiel S. Gleaves...grandchildren: heirs of my
daughter Emalin Binkley, Parile Elise and Araminta Morris (Note: no
commas in listing), and my grandson William D. Gleaves.
Signed 28 Jan. 1851 (Note: Date in question)
Proved July 1851
Recorded 20 July 1850 (Note: This entry was very faded on film.)
Witnesses, Gardner Green, P. W. Simpkins

JOSEPH GROVES will - page 225, No. 223
One-third to daughter Mary Francis...one-third to son John Groves...one-
third to Step-daughter Lydia Ann Williams. Lydia to be executrix.
Signed 30 April 1851
proved July 1851
Recorded July 1851
Witnesses, U. T. Stuart, W. Coldwell

WILLIAM GARRETT will - page 226, No. 224
Wife Sarah...divided among the children...daughter Martha Ann Garrett...
Signed 3 July 1851
Proved August 1851
Recorded 12 August 1851
Witnesses, William H. Sensing, J. M. Larkins
Executors, B. H. Collier, Tho. McNeilly

RICHARD B. HINTON will - page 229, No. 225
Sisters Elizabeth Boyd Hinton and Rachael Adaline Hinton...father John
J. Hinton to be executor.
Signed 20 October 1851
Proved November 1851
Recorded 15 November 1851
Witnesses, B. C. Robertson, Washington Hunter

ROBERT WEST will - page 230
Wife Nancy...land on Yellow Creek which was granted by North Carolina to
Robert Heaton...brother George West...two sons Robert J. and Isaac D.
West...my five children, Louisa McClure, Robert J. West, Isaac D. West,
Martha J. Stacker, Sally C. West...mentions wife's estate which was de-
vised to her by Isaac Dortch, deceased, and what may be coming to her at
death of her mother, Mrs. Martha Dortch...land on Cumberland River below
the mouth of Yellow Creek which was purchased from the trustees of the
University of North Carolina...grandchildren, John Minor and Charles
Minor, children of daughter...tract of land where Robert McClure now
lives in Montgomery County...the Furnace and Forge to my wife...Isaac
is to get the family Bible. Executors to be: Quintus C. Atkinson of
Mississippi, Jesse C. Ingram of Dover, Burrell B. Corban of Sailors
Rest, and John C. Collier of Charlotte and two sons Robert J. and Isaac
D. West.
Signed 18 July 1850
Proved November 1850
Recorded November 1850
Witnesses, A. A. Brown, Nathan Nesbitt, Lewis T. Hughes, N. C. Parrish,
O. Nesbitt

WILLIAM PORTER will - page 237
Wife Matilda...my four youngest children, Mary E., William M., Samuel M.,
and Matilda S. Porter...son J. W...daughters Elizabeth Harvey (continued)

(Will of William Porter, continued)
Sarah Harvey, and Nancy Sullivan--I believe their full share which comes by my first wife, their mother...wife and B. B. Hall to be executors.
Signed 14 September 1849
Proved May 1851
Recorded November 1851
Witnesses, A. V. Nicks, N. M. Hall, James C. Pullen

GUSTAVUS RAPE will - page 239
Wife Barbra Rape, tract of land I purchased from H. J. Binkley...my ten children: Henry, Jacob, Peter, John, and the children of Daniel Rape, the child of my daughter Mary Funderbunk, daughter Elizabeth Nowles, my daughter Milly Hanks, daughter Frankey Evins, and daughter Nanvy Thomas. My grandchildren David and Emaline Bruns (?).
Signed 3 July 1848, Gustavus (x) Rape
Proved March 1852
Recorded 24 April 1852
Witnesses, William D. Speight, G. W. Scott
Executors, William Johnson, Benjamin C. Robertson

WILLIS WILLY will - page 241, No. 229
Beloved wife Pilly, also to be executor...daughter Martha Larkins...oldest son John W. Willy (also an executor)...second son Michael B. Willy, and my youngest son Willis Carroll Willy; two daughters Martha and Mary.
Signed 16 October 1850
Proved June 1852
Recorded 4 August 1852
Witnesses, Robert McNeilly, Thomas K. Grigsby

MOSES PARKER will - page 244, No. 230
Wife Hannah...son John...son Daniel...daughter Hulda May...daughter Kizziah Garton...son William.
Signed 15 July 1852, Moses (x) Parker
Proved June 1852 (Note: Date in question)
Recorded 11 September 1852
Witnesses, David Gray, Francis Vanlandingham

McKINDREE GARDNER SENSING will - page 245, No. 231
"...to be buried on farm where now lie by side of my beloved daughter Margaret Ann Sensing"...wife Drewsillar B. Sensing...my three children, John Henry, Polly Wilding Sensing, and Wiley Powel Sensing...Allen Nesbitt and William B. Bell, executors.
Signed 1847
Proved October 1852
Recorded 7 October 1852
Witnesses, E. Hickerson, Gilford Mills

WILLIAM E. PENDERGRASS will - page 246, No. 232
Wife Rilly...my several children...son Van Buren...son William E., youngest child and daughter Sarah Elizabeth...son John Harvey...my other living children. William S. White to be executor.
Signed 21 August 1852
Proved October 1852
Recorded 8 October 1852
Witnesses, William Dunagan, John (x) Jourdan

RUBEN WHITE will - page 248, No. 233
Wife Mary B. White...when youngest child comes of age...my niece Elizabeth Garton...brother W. S. White.
Signed August 1852
Proved October 1852
Recorded October 1852
Witnesses, John D. Mitchell, N. R. Emery

ABRAHAM J. AUSTIN will - page 251, No. 234
Daughter Elizabeth Jane Seals...wife Martha.
Signed 18 September 1852   (continued)

(Will of Abraham J. Austin, continued)
Proved November 1852
Recorded 5 November 1852
Witnesses, O. S. V. Schmittou, Sellman Edwards

WILLIAM D. SPEIGHT will - page 252, No. 235
Wife Emily C...my three children, Allis U., Paradise and William D, tract of land near old Brick Kiln on the River near the Lucas' Old Coal Pit... 50 acres on Harpeth.
Signed 9 June 1852
Proved November 1852
Recorded __?__ November 1852
Wtinesses, Washington Hunter, William Johnson

GEORGE MITCHELL - page 254, No. 236
Wife Martha...son John D. Mitchell...two sons Benjamin Franklin and Ballard...son Minor...daughter Sarah Mead to remain single until after death of her mother...daughter Mary B. White...has already given to children Josephus, Minor, Adeline, John D., and Asenatha.
Signed 30 May 1852
Proved November 1852
Recorded 6 November 1852
Witnesses, M. B. Stuart, W. S. White, Z. T. Garton
(Note: This will was hard to read on the film.)

JOAB HARDIN will - page 257, No. 237
Left money to Charlotte F&AM Lodge 97...and also to the Buena Vista Division of the Sons of Temperance of Dickson County...wife Minerva J. Hardin ...daughter Sarah Ann Hardin...saddlers shop in Charlotte and several town lots in Charlotte...daughter Lorena W. Hardin...daughter Faustine B. Hardin, land near mouther of Johnsons Creek on Cumberland River...E. E. Larkins, guardian of Sarah Ann...Daniel Leech, guardian of two youngest, Lorena and Faustina...to Delila Porch, wife of Henry S. Porch, $20 a year for 10 years...books, maps and charts to Sarah A...my three children... Thomas McNeilly and E. E. Larkins, executors.
Signed 26 June 1852
Recorded and proved December 1852
Witnesses, J. W. Dickson, W. W. Fussell, Allen Nesbitt

JOHN B. CARR, will - page 261, No. 238
Wife Susanna...son William H. Carr...son-in-law Samuel A. Bibb...son and son-in-law to be executors.
Signed 1 February 1852
Proved April 1853
Recorded April 1853
Witnesses, Thos. G. Taylor, James Taylor

ARCHIBALD SKELTON will - page 262, No. 239
Wife Sarah...son Abner B...daughter Mariah Allen...granddaughter Sarah Elizabeth Alfred Skelton...daughter Malissa P. Cunningham, the two Walker tracts; also mentions her husband Nathaniel Cunningham...grandson John M. Skelton...grandson John H. Bartee then to his brother Jasper B. Bartee... grandson Jasper B. Bartee.
Signed 12 August 1850
Proved June 1853
Recorded 18 June 1853
Witnesses, Jasper B. Bartee, C. Grymes, Andrew Jackson Brim

ALEXANDER WILKINS will - page 265, No. 240
Eldest son N. F. Wilkins, land on Walker's spring branch near old Kirk tract...wife Sarah M. Wilkins.
Signed 26 May 1853
Proved July 1853
Recorded 5 July 1853
Witnesses, Robert A. Wilkins, James M. Kirk

ELIZABETH VICK will - page 267, No. 241
Negroes to Daniel Leech...to Abner Shelton...to Henry Hickerson.
Signed 22 May 1840   (continued)

(Will of Elizabeth Vick, continued)
Proved June 1853
Recorded 5 July 1853
Witnesses, George T. Cooksey, William Rook

BENJAMIN TIDWELL will - No. 242, page 268
Wife Lucinda...eldest son Moses Harvey Tidwell, brother Silas.
Signed 16 May 1853
Proved August 1853
Recorded 18 August 1853
Witnesses, Moses Tidwell, John Brown

SAMUEL ADAMS will - page 269, No. 243
Wife Sarah H. Adams.
Signed 18 September 1852
Proved May 1854
Recorded 13 May 1854
Witnesses, W. A. Moody, Hugh McClurkan

BARTHOLOMEW SMITH will - page 271
Daughter Comfert T. Hudson...son Jackson Smith...daughter Nancy A. Everett...son William B. Smith...son Gray W. Smith...son Madison H. Smith...daughter Tennessee Eliott..sums to John H. Marable, Cuthbert Hudson and William Morrison...son Williamson E. Smith...wife Dorothy... wife, son Jackson Smith and friend Thomas Murrell to be executors.
Signed 25 December 1849
Proved October 1854
Recorded June 1855
Witnesses, Thomas Murrell, Jr., Thomas Flanary

WILLIAM MATLOCK will - page 245, No. 275
Wife Miriah...tract of land deeded to me by Elizabeth Acoff...my youngest children to be educated...all my children...wife and Thomas Mcneilly to be executors.
Signed 1 September 1854
Proved November 1854
Recorded 11 June 1855
Witnesses, Robert McNeilly, Benjamin Corlew

THOMAS ARMSTRONG will - page 277, No. 246
Three minor sons, Joseph M., George W., and Samuel...son John...daughter Susan Ann Forehand, land on north side of Bell's Metal Road... daughter Jane Clark, wife of George W. Clark...support of my wife... children of my daughter Lucy Ballard, wife of Theophilius Ballard... friend John P. Gafford and Wilson J. Mathis to be executors...children of my son James, deceased.
Signed 17 January 1855
Proved March 1855
Recorded 11 June 1855
Witnesses, John C. Collier, John P. Gafford

ABRAM CALDWELL will - page 281, No. 247
Wife Nancy...the old tract brought of Belius Richardson (or Lebius)... tract bought of Sims Tycer...my blacksmith tools...daughter Polly... daughter Emaline...daughter Delphia Jane Larkins...daughter Eliza Guthrey...sons Thomas Montgomery, Orville Bradly, Abram Ballard, and John Campbell Crawford Caldwell....land at the head of Rockey Creek...tract on the stage road.
Signed 19 November 1853
Proved March 1855
Recorded June 1855
Witnesses, Allen Nesbitt, M. T. Berry

WINNEFORD RICHARDSON will - page 283, No. 248
Daughter Sally Walker...granddaughter Elizabeth Jane Walker...Emily Hulissa and Sarah Berry, children of my granddaughter Nancy Berry...to John H. and Rufus C. Lain 50 acres adjoining John H. Wiley at the headwaters of Barton's Creek, and if they died, should go to their half-brothers and sisters...granddaughter Vienna Walker...(continued)

(Will of Winneford Richardson, continued)
grandson Thomas R. Coleman...Thomas McNeilly to be executor.
Signed 5 June 1853
Proved May 1855
Recorded 12 June 1855
Witnesses, Tho. C. Morris, Tho. McNeilly, Mary McNeilly

JOHN S. MARTIN will - page 286, No. 249
"Body decently buried in our family graveyard"..."my turnpike road"...
beloved wife Minerva...my children...Thomas McNeilly and Robert McNeilly, executors.
Signed 15 July 1855
Proved August 1855
Recorded 9 September 1855
Witnesses, G. W. Larkins, Joseph Larkins

ELIZABETH WALKER will - page 288, No. 250
...now in low state of health...son-in-law James James 50 acres where he now lives; this was land granted to me by State of Tennessee in 1847
...John V. Walker, son, to be executor....Martin Harbard shall have my colt and saddle when he comes of age provided he continues to live with my son John V. Walker...daughter Martha T. Walker...granddaughter Martha C. Reynolds...my children: Brunnetta J. Wook (Work?), Cynthia A. Cook, J. V. Walker, Martha Walker, T. N. James...the rest of my children having left me many years ago.
Signed 2 August 1855
Proved September 1855
Recorded 5 September 1855
Witnesses, Tho. McNeilly, Mary James

JEREMIAH NESBITT will - page 290, No. 251
Beloved wife to have land whereon I now live known as the Dickson tract
...sons Joseph, William A., Robert S., and Andrew F. Nesbitt...mentions the Balthrop tract...son John C. to receive one half of tract where I now live...daughters Nancy W. Nesbitt, Margaret Nesbitt, Catherine M. Nesbitt, Betsy Ann Nesbitt, and Martha Nesbitt...my two daughters by my first wife, Sally and Betsy...my two grandchildren, John Nesbitt and Betsy Nesbitt to receive their mother's portion...son Andrew F. Nesbitt to be executor.
Signed 9 August 1841
Proved September 1855
Recorded 5 September 1855
Witnesses, James Daniel, William R. Blount

JACOB LAMPLEY will - page 293, No. 252
Wife Rebecca...land whereon I now reside...raising my children...each of my sons and daughters...wife, son John T. and William C. Lampley to be executors.
Signed 4 January 1842
Witnesses, Miles Hutchison, Mark Harris
Codicil mentions daughters Nancy and Zilphia Lampley
Codicil signed 25 December 1855
Codicil witnesses, Joseph Lampley, William Hammon
Proved October 1855
Recorded 29 February 1856

JESSE WOODWARD of Davidson County, will - page 295, No. 253
Wife Elizabeth to receive everything...brother Benjamin Woodward to be executor.
Signed 14 November 1856
Witnesses, Michael D. Gill, Robert Hill
Proved 5 March 1856
    It was noted that Michael D. Gill has removed from state but his handwriting was proved by Warren Jourdan, S. B. Davidson, and Isaac Ivy.
    Recorded 6 March 1856
    Then George B. Woodward, William Woodward, and William Waynen Harriet Woodward, A. Woodward, state that the nuncupative will of Jesse Woodward, deceased, was made on the 31 January 1856
continued

(Will of Jesse Woodward, continued)
    in their presence and was made in the house of his brother Benjamin where he was surprised by sickness...in this will he wished his nephew John D. Woodward to have stock and at his death to go to John's son Jesse...wife Sarah was to have negroes...and that his brother Benjamin was to have all the rest of his estate.
Recorded 10 Feb. 1856, 6 March 1856

ELEANOR SHELTON will - page 298, No. 255
Son William H. Shelton...daughter Mary Harris...grandchildren, Sarah Agnes Jordan, Lydia Ellison, Hugh Ellison, Eleanor Kellam, William H. Kellam, Susan Kellam, Lucy Kellam and Isabella Kellam, children of my daughter Lucy Kellam. Executors to be Walter Jourdan, William Harris.
Signed 10 December 1853
Proved April 1856
Recorded 10 April 1856
Witnesses, Jesse Jordan, J. G. Lovell

    This concludes Will Book 1 or Will Book A, Dickson County Wills.

***

    Although we are working on the next will book of Dickson County, Will Book Volume B, covering 1849 through 1907, the project is still incomplete.

    Some of the wills listed in this book will be for: William Adams, Lewis Hedge, Robert L. Dunaway, Charles Dunnegan, Sarah M. Jackson, Susannah Crisman, H. S. Sugg, Willie Balthrop, George A. Bowen, Mary Earle, John A. Hedge, Samuel Lawrence, John P. Jordan.

    A survey of the wills appearing in the next will book, being recorded in 1909, shows wills for Roena Bradford, W. B. McFarland, Spencer T. Hunt (who wrote his will in 1843 and died not long afterward), C. D. Wills, Sr., Z. J. Graham, Thomas Baker, L. F. Harris, J. B. Holley, Martha C. V. Schmittou, William H. Sensing, Dr. Charles Morgan, Thomas Murrell, John H. Work, D. A. Rowell, J. O. Hooper, E. M. Cullum, J. A. Gilmore, Robert Martin, F. F. Tidwell, J. C. Foster, and others.

IV

DICKSON COUNTY ADMINISTRATOR SETTLEMENTS

1823 - 1841

These settlements were abstracted from microfilm of the book entitled "Dickson County Administrator Settlements, April 1823 to June 1841" and the reel was owned and loaned by Mrs. Bruce Tatum, Lyles, Tennessee. Some of the entries are for earlier settlements, and many entries were not dated. These are only brief abstracts but an attempt was made to copy any family information appearing in the records.

BENJAMIN COX - page 1
Inventory of estate of Benjamin Cox, deceased; mentions negro Jo and "payment to get one canoe seat in pursuit of negro Jo"; Jo "absented himself from the administrator." An allowance was made to the widow April 1824. (Notes due estate were listed but not copied.)

BENJAMIN COX - page 2
Account of sale of Benjamin Cox. Buyers included:

Benjamin Crews	Christopher Roberstson	John Carington
Washington Hunter	John Lucus	Andrew Moak
John Edwards	William Taylor	John Gibbs
Henry Richardson	Thos. Collier	Burrell Hamlet
William Richardson	Winnefred Cox	Alexander Hunter
Thomas Cox	Sterling Brewer	Esom Breading
Robert Noland	Benjamin Cox	Edward Raworth
Abner Driver	Cindarella Cox	Robert Jakes
Albert Speight	Allen Lucas	Shadrach Bell
Robert F. Williams	David Moser (?)	Adonijah Edwards
Thomas Edwards	Robert T. Hightower	John Brewer
Matthias Crumpler	Jesse Speight	Seburn Crews
Joseph Morris	Benjamin Andrews	William Turner
Thomas Bell (Box?)	Isaac Harris	Jacob Hunter
W_____ L. Dawson	William Carrington	James Fuqua
Joseph L. Hunter	William Thomas	Peter Ralph
Robert Fambrought	Noah Sugg	Robert Weakley
Charles P. Jones	Montgomery Bell	John Knight
George Reynolds	Hiram Anderson	James Gilburn
John Swinney	M. C. C. Robertson	John Exum
Robert Simpson	William Davidson	Francis Newsom
Wilkins Whitfield	Archibald Carington	Isaac Smith
Matthew Lea	William Brown	Ealum Anderson
James Russell	William Alison	Jesse Garland
John Carington, Sr.	Giles Jones	Robert Duke

(Ended on page 10)

SETH B. JORDAN - pages 11, 12, 13
Inventory of estate of Seth B. Jordan, deceased; Robert West, executor; mentions list of notes left in care of George W. Jordan (not copied); hire of negroes given and provision made for widow and family. (Ended on page 16. Widow's name and family members not given.)

WILLIAM B. WEST - pages 17-21
Account of sale of William B. West; buyers included Elizabeth West, who purchased most of the household items, William H. West, James West, Richard D. Sanson, Henry H. Marable, Moreland Merick, William Rushing, William S. Murrell.

JAMES GOODRICH - pages 21-23
Inventory of James Goodrich. Inventory of loaned property, loaned by James Goodrich to his wife Dorothy, inventory taken 19 Nov. 1823; the negroes owned by estate were named and were to be divided among William H. Goodrich, Dorothy Goodrich, Patsy Goodrich, James Goodrich, Charlotte Goodrich, Allen Goodrich, and John Goodrich. Dorothy Goodrich and Alexander Dickson were administrators of estate. (Buyers at the sale were not copied for this work.)

CUTHBERT HUDSON - pages 24-26
Inventory of estate of Cuthbert Hudson, deceased, and Account of Sale of buyers. Names mentioned were Benjamin Grimmitt, William Goodwin, William Gentry, Baker Hudson, Spencer T. Hunt (one of the administrators), Lucy Hudson (widow), provision made for her 23 Feb. 1822. Among the buyers at the sale were David Passmore, William Fortner, Archibald Pullin, Lemuel Russell, Jacob Pucket, Josiah Grimmitt, John Pendergrass, William Austin, Oran D. Hogan.

JORDAN RICHARDSON - pages 27-33
Inventory of estate of Jordan Richardson, taken 15 July 1823; negroes were owned by estate and names given; Stith Richardson was administrator; Elizabeth Richardson was one of buyers as were Hartwell Bass, John Turner, Basey G. Ragan. Settlement was made.

BURGESS HARRIS - pages 33-37
Inventory of estate of Burgess Harris, deceased, made 26 Jan. 1816. Also account of sale given, Thomas Lofton being one of buyers. Isaac Harris hired some of the negroes owned by the estate; Sterling Brewer was administrator. A Year's Provision for Jane Harris, widow, and family was signed 30 Jan. 1816. Thomas Williams was guardian of minor children, who were not identified by name.

AARON VANHOOK - pages 38-39
Account of sale of Aaron Vanhook, deceased. Lucy Vanhook purchased most of household furniture; other buyers included Richard Tatum, Robert Vanhook, Amander Vanhook, Drury Adkins; Lucy Vanhook and Henry H. Marable were administrators and filed report July 1824. Negro hire was also included. Year's provision made for "widow and children".

JOHN WEST - pages 39-40
Account of sale of property of John West, deceased; Sary West purchased much household items; other buyers included: Samuel West, John C. West, John Tatum, Pleasant Hart, George Tatum, Wilkins Tatum, Zaccheus Drummond, Sally West. Filed January 1827 by Samuel West and Sally West, administrators.

JOSHUA JAMES - page 41
Inventory of estate of Joshua James, deceased; estate included two negroes; filed July 1821 by Enoch Gideon and Elijah James, Jr. Also a return of the property sold on 29 Sept. 1821 by Amos James and Enoch James.

ELIZABETH WALKER - pages 41-43
Account of the estate of Elizabeth Walker, deceased, sold by George H. Walker and Jacob Walker, administrators on 6 Jan. 1825.

ISAAC JOHNSON - pages 43-44
Inventory of estate of Isaac Johnson, deceased, and account of sale by W. L. Dawson, administrator, filed 1 April 1822.

LUCY HUDSON - page 44
Inventory of estate of Lucy Hudson, deceased, filed Oct. 1825 by William Hogan, administrator. Account of sale also included. Mentions sale of negroes. Ended on page 46.

JAMES KIRK - pages 47-50
Inventory of estate of James Kirk, deceased, by James H. Davie, one of the administrators, 7 July 1825. "J. L. Kirk is dead." At the sale some of the buyers were William Kirk, Goodwin Kirk, Jesse L. Kirk, James M. Kirk, Graves Ragan, Thomas Drummonds. Widow's allowance was made 6 May 1825.

JOHN KELLY - pages 51-54
Inventory of estate of John Kelly, deceased, filed 5 Jan. 1823; buyers included Susannah Kelly (most of household items), John Kelly, Eli Crow. Susannah Kelly and George Smith were administrators, filed April 1823. Other buyers at sale included Solomon Milam, Thomas Graves, Harrison Fussell.

JOHN KELLY - page 55
Year's provision for widow and family of John Kelly made 15 Jan. 1823.

EBENEZER KELLY - pages 55-57
Inventory of estate of Ebenezer Kelly, deceased; mentions articles reserved for the widow; Nathan Foster, executor; gives account of sale and among the buyers were Thomas and Willis Willey, filed July 1825. (Note, widow's name not given.)

WYATT PARRISH - pages 57-59
Inventory of estate of Wyatt Parrish, deceased, 16 Sept. 1823, filed Oct. 1823 by Huel Parrish, administrator. Eleanor Parrish bought one bed, furniture and other items. Buyers included Chancery Davenport, Hollaway N. Merrill, Jane Norris. Year's provision for Widow Parrish, filed Jan. 1824.

LARKIN DAWSON - pages 60-61
Inventory of estate of Larkin Dawson, deceased, filed Oct. 1823 by J. J. Williams, administrator. Mentions the mercantile business of Larkin Dawson with Thomas Deadrick surviving partner.

JOHN PARROTT - pages 61-63
Account of sale of estate of John Parrott, deceased; Lettuce Parrott purchased most of household items. Other buyers were Samuel Turner, Mark Reynolds, John Turner, Samuel Self (administrator), Abraham Self, Ashburn Vanhook, George Turner, William S. Murrell, Aaron Vanhook, Robert Vamhook, filed 14 Oct. 1820. Also mentions support of widow allowed.

ROBERT ROGERS - pages 64-65
Inventory of estate of Robert Rogers, deceased. Buyers were Widow Rogers, E. Rogers, James Almon, Alexander Dickson, Jesse Rogers, William B. West, and was signed by Elizabeth (x) Rogers, administratrix. Mentions that one negro owned by estate was hired to the widow for 1816, 1817, 1818, 1819, and 1820.

ELISHA SMITH - pages 66-67
Inventory of estate of Elisha Smith, deceased, filed 5 Oct. 1818, West Wood was administrator. Buyers: Polly Smith, Sarah Smith, Edward Smith, Thomas Smith, Eleanor Parrish, James Smith. Also filed July 1819.

WILLIAM HIGHTOWER - pages 67-68
Inventory of estate of William Hightower, deceased; Caty and George Hightower were administrators; negroes hired and sale given. Among the buyers were James Hightower, Robert T. Hightower, William Hightower, Elias W. Napier. Negro Barry was hired to Vanleer. One negro was sold 28 Dec. 1820--only date mentioned in entry.

WILLIAM READ - page 69
Inventory of estate of William Read, deceased, by James Read, admr. Additional inventory made. Year's provision for Rebecca Read and family was made 23 Jan. 1816.

LEWIS BERRY - pages 72-73
Inventory of estate of Lewis Berry, deceased, by James King, admr. Account of sale given. Susanna Berry got most of household items. No date. Other buyers included Green Holland, Miles Boswell, Angus McLean.

ROSSER BROWN - pages 74-76
Account of sale of estate of Rosser Brown, deceased. Rachel Brown bought much household goods; other buyers were Spencer Brown, John B. Brown, Robert H. Brown. Elizabeth Morris also bought many items at sale. William F. Brown was administrator, filed July 1820.

MILLS EASON - pages 77-79
Inventory of estate of Mills Eason by Bethery Eason, admr., and account of sale. Estate owned negroes and 352½ acres. Sale was held Feb. 1815 and the buyers included Joseph J. Eason, James Eason, Elisha Gunn, Pleasant Irby, Rogal Ferguson (bought one negro woman), Calvin W. Eason, Carter F. Eason. Recorded April 1816. Bethina Eason, admr.

JAMES KING - pages 79-80
Inventory of estate of James King, deceased by Isabella King, admr., signed 1 Jan. 1820. Account of sale given. Buyers included Burrel R. Butler, Jacob Rasbery, Jesse May, John King, Samuel King. Another account of sale recorded 1 April 1820.

LEWIS EVANS - pages 80-83
Inventory of estate of Lewis Evans, deceased, filed April 1821. At the sale Peggy Evans purchased most of the items. Other buyers includded Thomas Flanary, George Evans, Sr., Rosamond P. Scott. Provision was made for widow. John A. Baker and Peggy Baker, admrs. (Note: The name Peggy Evans possibly should be listed instead of Peggy Baker; this may be mistake on my part.)

GEORGE WRIGHT, SR. - pages 84-85
Inventory of estate of George Wright, Sr., deceased, and sale. Buyers included John Wright, Willis Walker, William Tatum, John Tatum, and Nancy Wright. Filed Oct. 1817.

BENJAMIN BEDFORD - pages 86, 87.
Inventory of Benjamin Bedford, deceased, by Charles Winstead, administrator; he owned 42 acres on east fork of Yellow Creek and 100 acres on Cave Branch; served 6 months in militia; owned negroes, named; no date.

POWELL SINKS - pages 88, 89
Account of sale of estate of Powell Sinks, deceased. Filed April 1826. Buyers included Powell Sinks, admr., Elizabeth Sinks, Zachariah Sinks, Henry Sinks, Eleanor Parrish, Joseph Austin, Howard W. Turner, John Adams.

JOHN DICKSON - pages 90-93
Account of sale of estate of John Dickson, deceased, filed 6 Jan. 1823 by Robert Hugh and Joseph Dickson, admrs. Buyers: Joseph Dickson, Alexander Dickson, Robert Dickson, James W. Dickson, Adam Dickson, Hugh Dickson, Margaret Cowan (purchased much), Drury Adkins, Eleanor Parrish, William Morrison, Bnj. Cummins, Francis Balthrop, Levi Anderson, Joseph Handlin. Hire of negroes also given.

DRURY PRICE - page 95
Account of sale of estate of Drury Price, deceased, filed Oct. 1824. Provision for widow and family made 20 April 1824. Buyers at the sale: Sarah Price (purchased most of household items), Jesse Pully, James Price, Asia Price, John Adams, Drury Adkins, George West, John Turner, Randolph Harris, Sterling May, N. Hooper, Silvester Adams. (Ended on page 96.)

A. ROSE - page 94
Account of sale of estate of A. Rose, deceased, filed April 1823 by Aaron Vanhook, admr. Buyers: Horatio Humphreys, John Hinson, Polly Rose (many items), Emily Rose, Martin H. Burton, F. V. Schmittou, Wyatt Parrish and others.

R. E. COMER - pages 97, 98
Account of sale of estate of R. E. Comer, deceased, filed Jan. 1825 by William Johnson and E. A. Comer, admrs. Buyers: E. A. Comer (most of household items), Benjamin Easley, William Massie, William Armour, Mark M. Comer, R. E. Southerland.

JOHN TURNER - pages 98-100
Account of sale of estate of John Turner, deceased, filed April 1825. Buyers: E. Turner, Richd. Turner, Jno Adams, William D. Turner, A. Self, Berry Valentine, Horatio Humphries, M. Reynolds, H. W. Turner, Lucy Vanhook, M. Halliburton, Samuel Turner, Tho. Adams, Sil Adams, Samuel Adams, D. Taylor, Huel Parrish, Elisha Turner, George Adams, Jesse Norris.

JOEL SHROPSHIRE - pages 100-102
Inventory of estate of Joel Shropshire, deceased; account of sale. Polly Shropshire purchased many items; other buyers included Asa

Grissom, Thomas Nesbitt. No date. Polly Shropshire and Richard Batson, admrs.

THOMAS DAVIDSON - page 103
Inventory of estate of Thomas Davidson, deceased. Sarah (x) Davidson, adminstratrix. No date. Account of sale given.

ROBERT NORRIS - pages 104, 105
Inventory of estate of Robert Norris, deceased, Susannah Norris, admx. Also account of sale and some buyers were William Norris, Michael Molton, William Peacock, Ezekiel Norris and Eli Hubbard. Year's provision for widow was made 27 April 1816.

MARY AN HOPPER - pages 106-108
Inventory of estate of Mary An Hopper, deceased, filed 6 Jan. 1823. Also account of sale of Mary An Hopper. Buyers included William Brasher Edward Watts, Arthur Powers, John Reynolds, David Austin Barny Cliff. (Note: Deceased's name was given as Mary An all through this entry.)

HENRY GRIMES - page 110
Account of sale of estate of Henry Grimes, deceased. Buyers included Katharine Grimes, John Grimes, Thomas McRone, John Grimes, Jacob Grimes, Noble Morrison, John Giffin. Filed July 1825, John Grimes, admr. Provision for the widow was made April 1824.

REBECCA COUNCILE - pages 113, 114
Inventory of estate of Rebecca Councile, deceased, filed Oct. 1825 by Aquilla Council, admr. Buyers: Patsy Council, Lisa Council, Willis Council, James Council, H. W. Turner, Gipson Mills, Reuben P. H. Burton, William Hollingsworth, Henry W. Hinson, W. D. H. Burton, Samuel Turner. (Note: Council and Councile were both found in this entry.)

LEVI TIDWELL - pages 114, 115
Inventory of estate of Levi Tidwell, deceased, with Nancy (x) Tidwell and James Tidwell as admrs. Filed July 1823 and later Jan. 1825. Mentions widow's dowry. Buyers, Edward Tidwell, Nancy Corey, Nancy Tidwell, George Sullivant, Stephen Grigory, W. Gentry, Celina Tidwell.

JOHN LARKINS - pages 116, 117
Account of sale of John Larkins, deceased. (Note: The word deceased had been marked out and another written over it, but could not read.) Buyers included Robert Larkins, John Larkins, Joseph Larkins, Gabe Joslin. 13 May 1825. Signed by James Larkins, guardian.

PALATIRA SEALS - pages 117, 118
Account of sale of estate of Palatira Seals, deceased, filed April 1825. Buyers: Peter Seals, William T. Reynolds, William McMurry, John Seals, H. H. Burton, William E. Slayden, Thomas Jernigan.

WM. HUDSON - page 118
Inventory of estate of Wm. Hudson, deceased, by Wm. Hudson, Tho. C. Hudson. 13 negroes owned and names given. No date.

JOHN NESBITT - page 119
Inventory of estate of John Nesbitt, deceased, filed April 1825. Also the account of sale given. Buyers: Margaret Nesbitt, William Evans, Susan Evans and others.

ADELINE COMER - page 119
Widow's allowance for Adeline Comer filed July 1826.

JAMES McLELLAND - page 120
Inventory of estate of James McLelland, deceased. No date.

THO. RICHARDSON - page 120
Inventory of estate of Tho. Richardson, deceased. No date. Negroes owned by estate were named.

ROBERT WEST - page 121
Account of sale of estate of Robert West, deceased. Buyers included

George West and James West, filed April 1826.

MOSES EASLEY - pages 121, 122
Account of sale of estate of Moses Easley, deceased. R. E. Comer was executor. Buyers included Amy Easley, Elizabeth Easley, Nimrod Hooper, Drury Taylor, James Hooper, Hardy Sparks, M. McMillan; R. E. Comer, executor. Filed Oct. 1824.

JOHN BURGESS - page 122
Account of sale of estate of John Burgess, deceased. Among the buyers were Elijah Woode, Polly Burgess (bought most of items), Jesse Parker, Absalom Tribble. No date.

RICHD. NAPIER, SENR. - page 123
Inventory of estate of Richd. Napier, Senr., deceased, filed 6 Oct. 1823. Negroes owned given.

JOHN HAYS - page 123
Account of negro hire of estate of John Hays, deceased, filed April 1826, signed Alexr. Dickson.

CHESLA O. COLE - page 124
Account of sale of Chesla O. Cole, deceased, filed 7 Nov. 1826.

B. L. BLEDSOE - page 125
Inventory of estate of B. L. Bledsoe, deceased, filed April 1825 by Will B. Turley, administrator.

JOHN HALL - pages 125, 126
Inventory of estate of John Hall, deceased, signed by Susanna Hall and Jesse Hall, filed 2 April 1823. Estate included negro slaves.

DEMPSY ROBERTS - page 127
Inventory of Dempsy Roberts, deceased. Among the buyers were Veny Roberts, Benjamin Grimmitt, Jacob Pucket and David Passmore was the administrator. No date.

JOHN A. BAKER - page 128
Account of sale of estate of John A. Baker, deceased, made by John Taylor, 25 Sept. 1820. (Note: the date could be 1826--hard to tell.)

JAMES DUNNAGAN - page 129
Inventory of estate of James Dunnagan, deceased, by William Edwards and Charles Dunnagan, made 3 Jan. 1811.

ROBERT MELTON - page 129
Inventory of estate of Robert Melton, deceased, filed 5 April 1819 and signed by Absalom Tribble. Buyers: Massy Melton, James Melton, Nathaniel Simpson, Hannah Vinson, Jacob Rushing, John Melton. Also filed 7 Oct. 1817 by A. Tribble.

HOWELL ADAMS - page 131
Inventory of Howell Adams, deceased, by Nancy Adams, William Adams, Hodge Adams, admrs. No date.

REEVES ADAMS - page 132
Inventory of Reeves Adams, no date.

EDWARD TAYLOR - pages 133, 134
Inventory of estate of Edward Taylor, deceased by James Taylor, admr. No date. Lockey Taylor bought most. Benjamin Pearsall was one of buyers.

RICHARD JOHNSON - pages 134-136
Account of sale of Richard Johnson, deceased. No date.

WILLIAM SUGG - pages 136, 137
Inventory of estate of William Sugg, deceased; owned 222 acres on Harpeth; account of sale; taken by Nancy Sugg. No date.

AARON LAWS - page 137
Inventory of estate of Aaron Laws, deceased, made by Pheraby Laws (later Feraby Laws), administrator. Her securities were Stewart Pipkin, John Brown. No date.

Z. HOPPER - page 138
Inventory of estate of Z. Hopper, deceased, and account of sale; Mary Hopper was the buyer of most items; Mary An Hopper, admr. No date. (Note: in this same entry the deceased also given as D. Hopper.)

GEORGE WRIGHT, JR. - pages 139-141
Inventory of estate of George Wright, Jr., deceased, and account of sale. No date. Nancy Wright, John Wright, admrs.

GABRIEL OVERTON - page 142
Inventory of estate of Gabriel Overton, deceased. Estate included one negro slave. This inventory ended with the words "Amen". No date.

MOSES PARKER - page 142
Inventory of estate of Moses Parker, deceased. No date. Estate included 6 months service in the late regiment.

WILLIAM JONES - pages 142-3
Inventory of estate of William Jones, deceased and account of sale. No date.

GEORGE SHELTON - pages 144, 145
Inventory of estate of George Shelton, deceased, by James Shelton, administrator. Also account of sale. No date.

JOHN ARNOLD - pages 146, 147
Inventory of estate of John Arnold, deceased. Certification listed: "I certify that John Arnold, deceased, served in my company of horse troop from 28 Sept. 1814 until 23 Dec. 1814," signed Joseph Williams, Captain. Aron Arnold, administrator. Account of sale also recorded and buyers included Wyatt Arnold, Sally Ozment, Ezra Arnold, Ephrm Arnold. No date.

THOMAS ARNOLD - page 147
Account of sale of estate of Thomas Arnold, deceased. No date.

EDWARD J. SMITH - page 148
Inventory of estate of Edward J. Smith, deceased, returned 4 July 1816, signed 2 October 1815. Account of sale given. William Adams and Sealy Smith were the administrators of estate.

J. GOODRICH - page 149
Settlement with Dorothy Goodrich and A. Dickson, executors of J. Goodrich, deceased. Jan. 1826.

ROBERT ROGERS - page 150
State of estate of Robert Rogers, deceased. William Ragan, husband of the former widow of Robert Rogers, deceased, and Nallison (?) Ragan, guardian for the orphans of Robert Rogers. Elizabeth Rogers was the administrator. Signed 10 Dec. 1824. Estate paid for the clothing, boarding, and tuition of 7 children from 1815 to 1824.

HUEL PARRISH - page 151
Settlement with Huel Parrish, administrator of Wyatt Parrish, deceased, signed July 1826.

DRURY PRICE - page 151
Settlement with Thomas May, admr., and Sally Price, admx., of Drury Price deceased, filed July 1826. Paid Sally McDerman (McLennan?) for herself and guardian for her children Joshua Price, Thomas Price, and Willis A. Price.

C. HUDSON - pages 152-155
Settlement with Spencer T. Hunt, administrator for C. Hudson, deceased, 12 Sept. 1825.

JOHN DICKSON - page 156
Settlement with administrators of John Dickson, deceased. The administrators were Robert, Hugh, and Joseph Dickson.

JOSHUA JAMES - page 156
Settled with administrator of Joshua James, deceased. Enoch James was administrator, filed April 1825.

ISAAC JOHNSON - page 156
Settlement made with Willis A. Dawson, administrator of Isaac Johnson, deceased, April 1824.

LEVY TIDWELL - page 157
James and Nancy Tidwell, admrs. of Levy Tidwell, deceased, filed May 1825. Paid widow her year's dowry.

THOMAS SWIFT - page 157
Settlement made with estate of Thomas Swift, deceased, April 1827.

JOHN PARROTT - page 157
Settled with administrator of John Parrott, deceased, 2 April 1827.

CANY WIGGIN - page 158
Settled with Washington Hunter, administrator of Cany Wiggin (or Carry Wiggin), deceased, 20 June 1824.

RICHARD JOHNSON - page 158
Settled with administrator of Richard Johnson, deceased, 17 March 1825.

ROBERT WEST - page 158
Settled with D. Irvin, administrator of Robert West, deceased, filed 1823.

RICHARD NAPIER - page 159
Settlement with E. W. Napier, administrator of Richard Napier, deceased, filed July 1824.

LEWIS BERRY - page 159
Settled with administrator of Lewis Berry, deceased, Oct. term 1823.

SETH B. JORDAN - page 159
Settlement made with executors of Seth B. Jordan, deceased, on 5 July 1824.

WILLIAM REAVACE - page 160
Partition of land and negroes belonging to William Reavace, deceased, made and filed July 1824.

ELIZABETH WALKER - page 160
George Walker, admr. of Elizabeth Walker, deceased, returned the amount of the sale and filed 4 July 1823.

BENJA. CREWS - page 161
Account of sale of estate of Benja. Crews, deceased. Buyers at sale included Peter M. Crews, Lucinda (or Lucrecia) Crews, John Crews, William Simms, George Hightower, Priscilla Loggins, Polly Sims, John Grimes; mentions Seburn Crews. Filed Oct. 1826.

HENRY GRIMES, SR. - page 163
John and Katharine Grimes, return account of estate of Henry Grimes, Sr. deceased, filed Oct. 1826. He had notes on George Ginger and George Gallison.

ROBERT NORRIS - page 163
Settled with Susannah Norris, admr. of Robert Norris, deceased, filed July 1827.

THOMAS A. YOUNG - page 164
Inventory of property of Thomas A. Young, deceased; included $50 U. S. money supposed and pronounced counterfeit. Sale reported 13 July 1827

and included many items, including "three sheets partly worn and of little worth." Augustin Thompson was administrator and filed his report July 1827.

EBENEZER KELLY - page 165
Nathan Foster, executor in account with estate of Ebenezer Kelly, deceased, account rendered 12 May 1826. Paid Dr. James H. Brewer, Dr. A. Roberts and paid Mrs. Rachel Kelly.

JOHN REYNOLDS - pages 165, 166
Inventory of personal property of John Reynolds, deceased, taken 30 August 1827 and signed Susannah (x) Reynolds, executor.

GEORGE WEST - page 166
Inventory made by James West, administrator of George West, deceased, on 15 July 1826, filed Oct. 1827. He owned 246 acres on both sides of Yellow Creek, negro slaves were owned by estate. Sale held 28 Sept. 1836.

MARTIN LOFTIS - page 167
Inventory of personal estate of Martin Loftis, deceased, by J. Thornton and Pheraby Loftis, executors. Oct. 1827.

JOHN REYNOLDS - page 168
Amount of sale of estate of John Reynolds, deceased, sold 25 Sept. 1827. Among the buyers were William Reynolds, Howard W. Turner, William Morrison, Alfred Russell, Susannah Reynolds, John Rogers. Filed Jan. 1828.

JAMES GOODRICH - page 169, 170
Settlement with Alexander Dickson and Dolly Goodrich, executors of James Goodrich, deceased, made 29 Nov. 1827. Notes due the estate included one in Washington County, Alabama, in James Taggert's hands for collection.

DANIEL HARRIS - page 170
Sale of estate of Daniel Harris, deceased, sold on 19 Jan. 1828 by Minor Bibb.

R. E. COMER - page 170
Settlement with William Johnson, administrator of R. E. Comer, deceased, executor of Moses Easley, deceased. Filed April 1828.

EDWARD MURFRE - pages 170, 171
List of property belonging to estate of Edward Murfre, deceased, sold 23 Jan. 1828. Buyers included Elizabeth Murfree, Polly Murfree (who bought most of household things), John Adams, admr. Filed April 1828.

MARTIN LOFTIS - page 172
Account of sale of estate of Martin Loftis, deceased, 12 Oct. 1827, with Joseph Thornton as executor. Buyers were Thornton, Archibald Ponder, and William McCord.

BEAL GOODWIN - page 172
No property found belonging to Beal Goodwin, deceased, 7 April 1828, signed R. H. McCollum, administrator.

LEVI TIDWELL - page 172
Sold two tracts of estate of Levi Tidwell, deceased, on 19 Nov. 1826, signed James Tidwell, admr. Settlement ordered and filed Jan. 1828.

JOHN HAYS - page 173
Negroes divided belonging to estate of John Hays, deceased, and it was divided between his heirs: Archie Hays heirs, James Hays heirs, Ruther Archer, Esther McKinley and Mary Bryant's heirs. Made Oct. 1827, filed April 1828.

STEPHEN THOMAS - pages 173-176
Inventory and account of sale of estate of Stephen Thomas, deceased,

21 April 1828. Many buyers, but not copied. Returned 19 July 1828.

JOHN HALL - pages 177, 178
Inventory of property of John Hall, deceased, as taken by the executor of the will. Notes and several negroes owned. Executors were Susannah Hall and Jesse Hall, filed July 1828.

RALEIGH TANN or RALEIGH FANN - page 179
Account of sale of estate of Raleigh Tann or Raleigh Fann, deceased, 17 April 1828, filed July 1828. William Dunnagan, administrator.

ALEXR. ROSE (ROSS?) - page 179
Settled with D. H. Williams and B. Sturdivant, administrators of Alexr. Rose (Ross?), deceased. Paid Mrs. Rose. (Note: Faded entry.)

MARY ANN HOPPER - page 180
Settled with John Hodges, adminstrator of Mary Ann Hopper, deceased, 26 July 1827.

WYATT PARRISH - page 180
Settlement with Huel Parrish, administrator of Wyatt Parrish, deceased, filed July 1828, mentions payment to Ellenor Parrish.

THOMAS A. YOUNG - page 180
Settlement with Augustin Thompson, administrator of Thomas A. Young, deceased, filed Oct. 1828.

STEPHEN THOMAS - page 181
Settled with William Rye, administrator of Stephen Thomas, deceased, with will annexed, Oct. 1828.

BENJA. CREWS - p. 181
Settled with George Hightower, administrator of Benja. Crews, deceased, filed Oct. 1828.

BENJAMIN ANDREWS - page 181
Inventory of estate of Benjamin Andrews, deceased, filed Oct. 1828, signed Ednonijah Edwards and Agusta Andrews, administrators.

WILLIAM GARRET - page 182
Inventory of estate of William Garret, deceased, filed Oct. 1828.

HUDSON JOHNSON - pages 182-185
Account of sale of estate of Hudson Johnson, sold 26 April 1828, division given; made by Polly Shropshire.

GEORGE WEST - page 186
Last settlement on estate of George West, deceased, 1 July 1829.

JOSEPH DAVIDSON - pages 189-191
Inventory of property of Joseph Davidson, deceased; taken 3 Oct. 1829; included one negro, signed John Davidson, Aquilla Tidwell.

JOSEPH HALL - page 188
Inventory of property that Joseph Hall, deceased, left the children of Henry Hall, deceased, signed Robert Whitsett, administrator, 7 Jan. 1830.

LUCY HUDSON - page 188
Amount of sale of estate of Lucy Hudson, deceased, 13 August 1825. Settled with William Hogins, administrator of estate of Lucy Hudson, deceased, 5 January 1830. Ended on page 189.

JOSEPH DAVIDSON - pages 189-191
Account of sale of property of Joseph Davidson, deceased, sold 30 Oct. 1829. Among the buyers were Stephen Wetherford, Archibald Ponder, Abner Ventress, Aquilla Tidwell, Silas Tidwell.

JESSEE CRAFT - pages 191, 192
Account of sale of estate of Jessee Craft, deceased, by George Craft,

administrator. Had note on Samuel Craft, insolvent; among the buyers was a G. R. Craft, filed Jan. 1830.

RICHARD D. SANSOM - page 192
List of property came to hand of William C. Sansom, one of the executors of Richard D. Sansom, deceased. Filed April 1830. Account of assets came to hand of Henry A. C. Napier, one of the executors of Richard D. Sansom, deceased, filed April 1830.

M. WELLS - page 194
List of debts of estate of M. Wells (Webb?) 8 April 1830 by W. B. Young, administrator.

PARISH LANKFORD - page 194
Account of sale of Parish Lankford, deceased, sold 5 July 1829 by John Lankford, administrator. Filed April 1830.

GEORGE ROSS - pages 195-198
Inventory of estate of George Ross, deceased, taken 5 November 1829; several negroes owned by estate are named; mentions George Gallion and Thomas T. Watson. Signed also by James M. Ross, executor. Account of the sale held on 15 and 16 Dec. 1830; Mary Drake was among the buyers and bought a great many items.

HUDSON JOHNSON - pages 198, 199
Settlement with John Johnson, administrator of Hudson Johnson, deceased. Paid for "the hunting of William French 12 days in western district." Filed July 1830.

ROLLY FANN - page 199
Settlement filed July 1830 by William Dunnagan, administrator of Rolly Fann (or Fan), deceased.

MRS. McADOO - pates 199, 200
Mrs. McAdoo memorandum of articles sold at sale 24 April 1830. Buyers included John McAdoo, William McAdoo, Martha McAdoo.

RICHARD D. SANSOM - pate 201
Account of Henry A. C. Napier, one of executors of Richard D. Sansom, deceased. Paid Barbara Sansom. Negroes were owned by the estate. Filed July 1830.

WILLIAM GILBERT - page 201
Settled with George W. Hiland and James Baxter; met at house of Nancy Gilbert (also given as Nicy Gilbert) and find the legatees received and receipted agreeable to the will of William Gilbert, deceased, 24 June 1830.

MOSES COLEMAN - page 202
Inventory of estate of Moses Coleman, deceased, by William S. Coleman, made 8 Oct. 1830.

JAMES WILSON - page 202
Inventory of James Wilson, deceased, by R. Livingstone, administrator, filed October 1830.

ISAAC DAVIS - pages 202, 203
Account of the estate of Isaac Davis, deceased, by John Brewer, filed October 1830.

THOMAS DAVIDSON - page 203
Sarah Davidson settlement as administrator of Thomas Davidson, deceased, filed October 1830. The heirs to the estate were Sarah Davidson, James Davidson, John W. Thomas, Jesse Davidson, Abraham Davidson.

ELIZABETH WALKER - page 204
Inventory of Elizabeth Walker, deceased, filed January 1830 by John B. Walker, executor. Buyers were Nathaniel Cunningham, Benjamin Williams, John Daniel, William Carroll, James Hightower, William Sims, William Ward, John K. Walker, Thomas Cunningham, Thos. Gilbert, James Drake,

John McColy, John W. Napier, James Tapley.

WILLIAM HOUSTON - pages 204, 205
Inventory of William Houston, deceased, rendered by Nelson and John McClelland, administrators, made 3 Jan. 1831. Account of sale given, but no buyers' names were recorded.

JOSEPH HALL - page 206
Settled with Robert Whitwell, executor of Joseph Hall, deceased, 3 Jan. 1831, filed July 1831.

JESSEE STROUD - page 206
Inventory of Jessee Stroud, deceased, filed January 1831.

ENOCH JAMES - page 207
Inventory of Enoch James, deceased, filed January 1831.

SAMUEL PETTY - page 207
Account of sale of Samuel Petty, deceased. Buyers included Peggy Petty, Johnathan Petty, James M. (H?) Petty, Jesse Hugo, Joseph Eason, John McCommak, Alexander Chisenhall, James Hutson, George Davidson, Morgan Hood, Ambrose Petty, Tilman Pery, Gabriel Petty, Benjamin B. Dunnagan, Alfred Edwards. Filed April 1831.

ENOS JAMES - page 208
Amount of sale of Enos James, deceased, sold November 1828, signed 8 March 1831 by Howel Parish, administrator. Also another one on page 209, only the administrator is given as Huel Parish. (Note: We believe Huel is the correct name as the name Huel has been handed down in the Parrish line.)

STEPHEN THOMAS - page 208
Settled with William Rye, administrator of Stephen Thomas, deceased, on July 1831.

LEVIN DICKSON - page 209
Sale of Levin Dickson, deceased; Daniel Parker, executor, sold the negro Stephen on 8 August 1831.

JOHN REYNOLDS - page 210
Settled with Susannah Reynolds, executor of John Reynolds, deceased, January term 1831.

DANIEL HARRIS - page 210
Settled with Miner Bibb, administrator of Daniel Harris, deceased. Bibb made settlement 4 July 1831.

GEORGE LIGHT - pages 211, 212
Inventory and account of sale of George Light, deceased on 29 July 183_. Buyers:
George Tilly, Jas. Choat, Z. Drummond, Richard Cocke, Simon Deloach, George Kelly, J. A. Bowen, Joseph Choat, Luke Matlock, Hartwell Weaver, B. G. Ragan, H. J. Shropshire, Peter Cooke, Thomas Hudson, John A. Bullock, Peter Light, William Willy, Jas. Cook, J. R. Drake, Louis Ticer, Thomas McClellan, John Shropshire. Jos. (or Jas.) Choat, administrator.

ALSEY SPEIGHT - pages 212, 213
Inventory and account of sale of Alsey Speight, deceased, 15 April 1831 by Jesse M. Speight, administrator. Many notes listed. Estate included a negro man and a fiddle as well as other items.

WILLIS JACKSON - page 214
Inventory of 1831of Willis Jackson, deceased, taken 2 January 1832 by Mary (x) Jackson, administratrix.

JOSEPH HALL - page 214
Settlement made with Robert Whitwell, admr. of Joseph Hall, deceased, on 25 Jan. 1832.

ROBERT MARTIN - page 215
Inventory of Robert Martin, deceased; many notes but not copied; made by John S. Martin, administrator, filed January 1832. Year's provision made for widow and family.

DANIEL WILLIAMS - page 216
Inventory and account of sale of Daniel Williams, deceased, on __Feb. 1831. Jesse Williams, executor, filed Jan. 1832.

NAPOLIAN B. WEST - page 217
Inventory of Napolian B. West, deceased, sold by David Irvin, administrator, on 28 Dec. 1831. Negroes were sold to James Nolen, James West, John Outlaw. Filed January 1832.

SAMUEL PETTY - page 217
Settled with Johnathan Petty, administrator of Samuel Petty, deceased, filed January 1832.

GEORGE J. GOODRICH - page 218
Return of notes due estate of George J. Goodrich, deceased, by William B. Young, administrator, filed April 1832. Many notes included.

NAPOLEON WEST - page 219
Settled with David Irwin, administrator of Napoleon West, deceased, filed April 1832. John H. Marable medical bill mentioned. Many vouchers listed.

ROBERT MARTIN - page 220
Additional account of sale of Robert Martin, deceased, filed April 1832; many items were sold to Mary D. Martin. John L. Martin, administrator.

ELIZABETH D. FULCHER - page 220
Settlement with Jesse Beck, agent for Elizabeth D. Fulcher & Co., filed April 1832. She was the administratrix of John J. Fulcher, deceased. Daniel Crawford was guardian for heirs. Signed 5 April 1832.

LEVIN DICKSON - page 221
Settlement with Daniel Parker, executor of Levin Dickson, deceased, filed April 1832. Commissioners signed 8 August 1831, Archibald Preller (?) and Daniel Taylor.

BENJAMIN ANDREWS - page 221
Settlement with A. Edwards, administrator of Benjamin Andrews, deceased, March 1832. Signed 10 March 1832 by administrators Adonijah Edwards and Agness Andrews.

JESSE STROUD - page 222
Year's provision for Jane Stroud and her children. she was widow of Jesse Stroud, deceased. Signed 13 January 1831.

ALFORD EDWARDS - page 223
Year's provision for Sarah Edwards, late widow of Alford Edwards, deceased, filed July 1832, made 16 Jan. 1832.

ISAAC DAVIS - page 223
John Brown in account with estate of Isaac Davis, deceased, signed 2 July 1832. (Note: Page 224 was blank in this book.)

CUTHBERT HUDSON - page 225
Settlement with Spencer T. Hunt, administrator of Cuthbert Hudson, deceased, filed October 1832.

WILLIAM SHELBY - page 226
Account of sale of William Shelby, deceased, sold 21 August 1832. Buyers included Sally Shelby, George H. Walker, Sampson Black, John Starns, James Epperson, Isaac L. Shelby, John E. McNeely, William Johnson, William Morgan, John Edwards, James Briant. Year's provision for Sally Shelby and family, widow of William Shelby, was filed October 1832. (Note: Widow's provision was on page 227.)

JAMES GOODRICH - pages 228, 229
Settlement with Dorothy Goodrich, executrix of James Goodrich, deceased. List of vouchers recorded, but not copied as were the debts due the estate. Signed 8 January 1833.

CUTHBERT HUDSON - pages 229, 230
Settlement with Spencer T. Hunt, admr. of Cuthbert Hudson, deceased, signed 11 Jan. 1833.

ROBERT MARTIN - page 230
Account of sale of Robert Martin, deceased. Filed April 1832.*

THS. DRUMMONDS, JR. - pages 231, 232
Account of property of Ths. Drummonds, Jr., deceased, that was in his possession at his death on 17 July 1832; also account of sale was given and William Drummond was one of the buyers. Peggy (x) Drummond was the executor.

WILLIS JACKSON - page 232
Account of sale of Willis Jackson, deceased, 12 March 1832. (Note: This was a very faded entry.)

DANIEL WILLIAMS - page 233
Settlement with executors of Daniel Williams. (Note: This entry was faded and could not be deciphered.)

LUCY HUDSON - pages 234, 235
Settlement with William Hogins, admr. of Lucy Hudson, deceased. Estate was divided: 1/3 to Cuthbert Hudson; 1/3 to Christopher Hudson; 1/3 to heirs of Susan Hutson, and 1/8 of last 1/8 was due William B. Ross, 1/8 to Lemuel Russell, 1/8 to Owen D. Hogins, 1/8 to Edmund W. Gee, 1/8 to Spenter T. Hunt, 1/8 to Cuthbert Hudson, 1/8 to Christopher Hudson.

JOHN DICKSON - page 236
Settlement with Robert Dickson, administrator of John Dickson, deceased, 29 March 1833.

RANSOM ELLIS - page 236
Inventory of estate of Ransom Ellis, deceased, taken 25 June 1833; 13 negroes were owned by estate. Signed Willie Balthrop, executor.

MARTIN LOFTIS - page 237
Account of sale of Martin Loftis, deceased, filed October 1833. J. Thornton was executor. Among many buyers was Moses Langford.

ALSEY S. SPEIGHT - page 238
Settlement of Alsey S. Speight, deceased, by Jesse M. Speight, admr., filed July 1833.

WASHINGTON McMURRAY - page 239
Schedule of estate of Washington McMurray, deceased, made 2 July 1833, filed July 1833, by Thomas McMurray, administrator. Included notes on William McMurray, Esquire.

GEORGE LIGHT - pages 239, 240
Settlement with Joseph Choate, administrator of George Light, deceased, filed July 1833.

JOSEPH HALL - page 240
Account of sale of Joseph Hall, deceased, 2 October 1830.

ABEL SKELTON - page 240
Abel Skelton, deceased, inventory given in by Archibald Skelton, admr., filed Jan. 1834.

ROBERT MARTIN - page 241
Settlement with John L. Martin, admr. of Robert Martin, deceased, settlement order Oct. 1833, filed Jan. 1834.

---
*From this point most abstracts will be quite brief.

GEORGE DAVIDSON - page 241
Inventory of George Davidson, deceased, by Geo. Davidson, executor, filed Jan. 1834.

CUTHBERT HUDSON - page 242
Inventory filed April 1834 on Cuthbert Hudson, deceased, by Spenter T. Hunt, admr. Mentions amount received from Robert H. McCollum, admr. of Beal Goodwin, deceased.

ABEL SKELTON - page 242
Account of sale of Abel Skelton, deceased, by Archibald Skelton, admr., sold 25 Jan. 1834.

BEAL GOODWIN - page 242
Inventory of Beal Goodwin, deceased, by R. H. McCollum, filed Apr. 1834.

LEBUIS RICHARDSON - page 243
Account of sale of Lebius Richardson, deceased, by John Richardson, executor, filed Jan. 1834. Year's provision for widow and family was made on page 244. (Widow not named.) One of buyers was Mrs. R. Richardson.

PATTON S. McCOLLUM - pages 245, 246
Inventory and sale of Patton S. McCollum, deceased, done 26 Jan. 1835. Levi McCollum was one of the buyers. Year's provision made for Sarah P. McCollum, 26 Jan. 1835.

E. R. BAKER - pages 247, 248
List of property sold at sale of E. R. Baker on 25 Aug. 1834. One of buyers was Richmond Baker.

RICHARD N. WILLIAMS - page 248
Inventory of goods and chattels of Richard N. Williams, deceased, by Henry A. C. Napier, adminstrator, 1 Oct. 1834.

SAMUEL TATE - page 249
Year's provision for Eleanor Tate, widow of Samuel Tate, deceased; commissioners appointed July 1834 to make provision.

JOSEPH HALL - page 249
Settlement with Robert Whitwell, executor of Joseph Hall, deceased, made 5 Jan. 1835.

NAPOLEON B. WEST - page 250
Division of lands of Napoleon B. West, deceased, ordered Oct. 1833; division made between heirs and legatees, Lot 1, land on Yellow Creek to James West; Lot 2 to William H. West; Lot 3 to Mrs. Ellenor Irwin; Lot 4 to Mrs. Mary Ann Eliza Outlaw, made 14 Nov. 1833.

WILLIAM MORRIS - page 251
Sale of William Morris, deceased, 31 Oct. 1834. Susannah and John Morris were among the buyers.

CUTHBERT HUDSON - page 252
Settlement with Spencer T. Hunt, admr. of Cuthbert Hudson, deceased, 6 April 1835. Estate divided among: Lucy Hudson, wife of Cuthbert Hudson; Lemuel Russell and wife Elizabeth; William B. Ross and wife Martha; Orrin D. Hogan and wife Rebecca; Edmund Gee and wife Mary; John Hassell and wife Casy; Cuthbert Hudson; Susan D. Hudson; Christopher C. Hudson; Spencer T. Hunt and wife Mary also got part of estate.

NATHAN RAGAN - pages 253, 254
Inventory and sale of Nathan Ragan, deceased, 2 Feb. 1835, Elizabeth Ragan, administratrix. Buyers were given but not copied.

BURGESS HARRIS - pages 255, 256
Division of estate of Burgess Harris, deceased, 11 April 1834 between the heirs at law. Mentions land on Harpeth including place where Harris lived at the time of his death. Lot 1 to John Harris; Lot 2 to Jones Williams and wife's three children; Lot 3 to John Bradley and wife;

Lot 4 to Joseph Harris. One tract was divided into 5 lots and this went to Jesse Shearon and wife Ann, William Harris, Thomas Harris, Buckner Harris, and Burgess Harris; made 12 June 1834.

EPHRIM ELLIS - pages 248, 259
Inventory and account of sale of Ephrim Ellis, deceased, sold 28 July 1834. Sarah B. Ellis bought most of household items. Other buyers: Jerome B. Hinson, Martin Halliburton, Jesse Turner, Susannah Reynolds, Howard W. Turner, James G. Hinson, Michael T. Ellis, Thomas H. Hinson, Erasmus J. Ellis.

JESSE STROUD - page 260
Settlement with Jane Stroud, adminstratrix of Jesse Stroud, deceased, July 1834.

ALEXANDER MARTIN - pages 260, 261
Division. Agreement of Thomas Martin, and Bradley Martin; Lot No. 1 to Thomas Martin, land on middle fork of Barton's Creek; Lot 2 to Bradley Martin; both are joint heirs of Alexander Martin, deceased. Mentions their half-brother James Gee Thomas, deceased; both are of Dickson County. Sarah Thomas deeded land on 19 Jan. 1810 to said James Gee Thomas. Made 13 March 1832.

LEONARD PINEGAR - pages 262, 263
Schedule of property of Leonard Pinegar, deceased; had 625 acres and a negro girl Mary, age 14. Made 1 Jan. 1834 by Hardeman Stone, admr.

JOHN PICKET - pages 263, 264
Inventory and account of sale of John Picket, deceased; executors were Willis Collier and Rebecca Picket, 27 April 1835.

JORDAN A. BOWEN - page 266
Inventory and account of sale of Jordan A. Bowen, deceased, sold 22 Jan. 1835.

WILLIAM SHELBY - page 267
Settlement with administrators of William Shelby, deceased, 13 Dec. 1834 John King was administrator. Year's provision for Mrs. Shelby made.

JOSEPH HALL - page 269
Settlement with Robert Whitwell, administrator of Joseph Hall, deceased, and guardian of minor heirs of Henry Hall, deceased, 30 Jan. 1835.

NANCY SULLIVAN - page 269
Account of sale of property of Nancy Sullivan, deceased, on 1 July 1834; 14 slaves owned and sold. Owen Sullivan, Elley Sullivan, George Sullivan, Zachariah Sullivan and John Sullivan were among the buyers.

EPHRAIM ELLIS - page 270
Division of property of Ephraim Ellis, deceased, between Arthur J. Ellis, Mary M. Ellis, William D. O. Ellis, Erasmus J. Ellis, and Edward B. Ellis, 18 Oct. 1834.

ALFORD EDWARDS - page 271
Sale of property of Alford Edwards, deceased, 11 Jan.1832. Sally Edwards was one of buyers. Gabral Petty, admr. Settlement 5 Jan. 1835.

PARRISH LANKFORD - page 273
Sale of estate of Parrish Lankford, deceased, 25 July 1829; settlement 1 Oct. 1833, John Lankford, administrator.

GEORGE ROSS - pages 276-278
Sale and settlement of estate of George Ross, deceased, by James M. Ross, executor. Accounts listed through 1835.

JOHN JOHNSON - pages 279-285
Account of sale of John Johnson, deceased, sold 30 and 31 Oct. 1835. Lots were drawn on negroes and these went to William Johnson, John Johnson, Thomas Johnson, Charlotte Williams, Polly Lane, Joel S. Johnson, Stephen B. Johnson, Hutson Johnson, and Patsey Johnson.

MATHEW GLEAVES - pages 286-288
Inventory of Mathew Gleaves, deceased, by Elizabeth Gleaves, administrator, in 1835. List of sale also given and buyers included the widow and Emily Gleaves.

WILLIAM MORRISON - pages 289-293
Inventory of William Morrison, deceased; sale held 3 Oct. 1835. Number of books in estate as well as negro slaves, sold 3 Nov. 1835. Buyers included Callum Rogers, James S. Powers, Halliburton, Ellis, Parchment, Turner, William J. Knight (got slaves Milly and Elizabeth her child), Elizabeth Morrison and William Morrison.

JOHN KENNEDY - pages 294, 295
Account of sale of John Kennedy, deceased; John Kennedy a minor heir of John Kennedy, deceased. H. Stone, administrator. Mrs. Margaret Kennedy is mentioned but no relationship given. Settlement made 26 Oct. 1835.

DANIEL WILLIAMS - page 295
Settlement made on estate of Daniel Williams, deceased.

NATHAN DILLEHAY - pages 296-304
Inventory and account of sale of Nathan Dillehay, deceased, sold 3 Jan. 1836. Nancy Dillehay purchased many items; other buyers included Callum Rogers, John Norsworthy, Fountain Lester, and others. Many notes and accounts not copied.

ABEL SHELTON - page 305
Settlement made 30 April 1836 on estate of Abel Shelton, deceased.

ELIJAH BAKER - page 305
Settlement made with Alexander Campbell, administrator of Elijah Baker, deceased. No date.

AUSTIN RICHARDSON - page 305
Year's provision for widow and family of Austin Richardson made 29 Jan. 1836. (Note: His name also given as Augustin Richardson in this entry.)

SARAH HEWSTON - page 306
Inventory of Sarah Hewston, deceased, filed April 1836.

WILLIAM HUSTON - page 307
Inventory and account of sale of William Huston, deceased, 31 May 1836.

BENJAMIN HARDWICK - page 308
Sale of Benjamin Hardwick, deceased. Elizabeth Hardwick, administratrix. One of buyers included J. P. Hardwick. 2 March 1836.

GEORGE ROSS - page 309
Settlement with James M. Ross, executor of George Ross, deceased, 1 May 1836.

MAN BRASIER - pages 310-313
Inventory of estate of Man Brasier, deceased. (Note: His name is in question.)

G. BLOCKLEY - pages 314, 315
Inventory of G. Blockley, deceased. Sale also included in book but not copied for this work. No date. Wilkins Tatum was one of buyers.

NATHAN DILLEHAY - page 316
Year's provision for Nancy Dillehay, widow of Nathan Dillehay, Aug.1836.

ROBERT COLLIER - page 316
Inventory of estate of Robert Collier, deceased. Thomas W. Collier was administrator. No date.

HOWELL FREEMAN - page 317
Year's provision made for Hannah Freeman, widow of Howell Freeman, on 2 July 1836.

NANCY SULLIVAN - page 318
Account settlement of Nancy Sullivan, deceased, made 3 Oct. 1836 by administrators George Sullivan and Simon Miers.

WILLIAM H. DORCH - pages 319, 320
Account of sale of property belonging to William H. Dorch, deceased. Isaack Dorch was a buyer. Most of the buyers at this sale seemed to live at Charlotte, Tennessee.

THOMAS MASSIE - pages 326-331
List of notes belonging to estate of Thomas Massie, deceased. No date-- appears to be sometime in 1830s.

HOWELL FREEMAN - pages 332-336
Inventory of estate of HOWELL FREEMAN, deceased; sale held 6 Oct. 1835. Abraham Self, administrator.

HILLORY MORRIS - page 337
Inventory of estate of Hillory Morris, deceased, sold 1 Dec. 1836; Susan Morris was one of buyers.

GEORGE TUBB - pages 338-347
Sale of property of George Tubb, made 29 and 30 Nov. 1836, filed 9 Dec. 1836.

THOMAS MASSIE - pages 348, 349
Settlement made with Absolum Massie, administrator of estate of Thomas Massie, deceased, Dec. 1836.

DAVID PASSMORE - page 350
Amount of sale of David Passmore, deceased, by William Gentry and James Hicks, executors, Jan. 1837.

FIELD FARRAR - pages 351-359
Inventory and account of sale of property of Field Farrar, deceased, by John Montgomery, administrator, signed 29 Jan. 1837.

ABNER HUDGINS - page 360
Account of sale of Abner Hudgins, deceased, sold 17 Dec. 1836 by Miles Long, administrator. William Hudgins was one of buyers at sale.

FRANCES TIDWELL - page 361
Account of sale of Frances Tidwell, deceased, returned Feb. 1837 by Daniel Spencer, administrator.

MUMFORD SMITH - pages 362, 363
List of property sold by administrator of Mumford Smith, deceased, by Jackson Smith and G. W. Tatum, administrators. No date.

BERRYMAN TAILOR - page 364
Inventory of estate of Berryman Tailor, deceased, sold 21 Jan. 1837 by Lockey Tailor, administrator. (Note: The first name could be Benjamin.)

THOMAS MATHEWS - page 365
Settlement with George T. Cooksey, executor of Thomas Mathews, deceased, 4 March 1837.

PATTEN S. McCOLLUM - pages 365, 366
Settlement with Levi McCollum, administrator of Patten S. McCollum, deceased.

JESSE RAGAN - page 366
Settlement with Hewel Parrish, administrator of Jesse Ragan, deceased, 22 March 1837.

RICHARD N. WILLIAMS - page 367
Settlement with H. A. Napier, administrator of Richard N. Williams 3 April 1837.

JOHN HUDSON - pages 367, 368
Inventory and account of sale of estate of John Hudson, deceased, by William Hudson, administrator. Buyers included Mary Hudson, Nancy Hudson, Brinkley George. No date.

AUSTIN RICHARDSON - pages 369-372
Account of sale of Austin Richardson, deceased, sol 29 and 30 January 1836 by Winiford Richardson, administratrix.

NANCY SULLIVAN - page 372
Settlement with George Sullivan, administrator of Nancy Sullivan, deceased. No date.

WILLIAM MORRIS - page 373
Settlement with John Sellers, administrator of William Morris, deceased, 1 July 1837.

E. B. ELLIS - page 373
List of estate of E. B. Ellis, deceased, by W. D. Ellis, administrator, 1 January 1836.

JORDAN BOWEN - page 374
Settlement with estate of Jordan Bowen, deceased, by Archabald Pullen, administrator, 14 Aug. 1837.

WILLIAM MORRISON - pages 375, 376
Settlement with H. W. Turner and Thomas McMurray, administrators, of William Morrison, deceased, 4 Dec. 1837.

JOSEPH LARKINS - page 376
Year's provision for Mrs. Catherine Larkins, wife of Joseph Larkins, deceased. No date.

MATHEW GLEAVES - pages 378, 379
Settlement with Elizabeth Gleaves, administrator of Mathew Gleaves, deceased; to divide the negroes owned by the estate. Commissioners to settle were appointed Sept. 1837. Heirs were Thomas Ellis, David Mobley (or Mahley or Weakley?), William Gleaves, Henry Binkly, Elizabeth Gleaves, Gilford Morris.

JOHN TUCKER - page 379
Settlement with John M. Tucker and John Hinds, executors of John Tucker, deceased, 2 Dec. 1837.

FRANCIS TIDWELL - page 379
Daniel Spencer and Huldy Tidwell, administrators of Francis Tidwell, deceased, report amount of sale of estate. No date.

HOWELL FREEMAN - pages 380-383
Settlement with administrator of Howell Freeman, deceased, 20 Jan.1838. (Note: pages 381 and 382 were blank in this book.)

JOSEPH LARKINS - pages 383-385
Inventory and account of sale of Joseph Larkins, deceased. No date. Margaret Drummonds was a buyer at the sale.

ELISHA PASCHELL - page 386
Account of sale of Elisha Paschell, deceased, 15 Jan. 1838. Buyers included Middy Pashell, Elizabeth Paschell, E. A. Paschell, Nancy Paschell, and Ramey (?) Paschell.

JAMES MARTIN - pages 387, 388
List of property sold at residence of James Martin, deceased, 24 Feb. 1838. Rachel Martin bought many household items. John L. Martin was also a buyer at the sale.

NATHAN DILLEHAY - page 389
Settled with Howard W. Turner and John Adams, administrators of Nathan Dillehay, 3 March 1838.

EZEKIEL SMITH - pages 390-193
List of property at sale of Ezekiel Smith, deceased, 14 Sept. 1837.
Abner Smith, administrator. (Note: This was a faded entry.)

JOHN HUDSON - page 394
Settlement made with William Hudson, administrator of John Hudson, deceeased, 24 Feb. 1838.

STEPHEN ELEAZER - pages 394-400
Inventory and amount of property of Stephen Eleazer, deceased, 27 Oct. 183_. Among buyers, Sarah Eleazer (most of the household items).
Settlement made 30 March 1838 with Minor Bibb, administrator.

NATHAN DILLEHAY - page 401
Division of estate of Nathan Dillehay, deceased, reported 16 March 1838.
Lot 1 to Nancy Dillehay, Lot 2 to Robert Dillehay, Lot 3 to Alfred
Dillehay, Lot 4 to Nancy Dillehay, Jr., Lot 5 to Philemon (or Phelissan)
Dillehay.

JOHN DUNAGAN - page 401
Inventory of estate of John Dunagan, deceased. No date.

GUSTAVUS BLOCKLEY - page 402
Report of James Choat, administrator of estate of Gustavus Blockley,
deceased, 25 June 1838. Heirs at law were Lucretia Blockley and
Thadeus Blockley.

AUSTIN RICHARDSON - page 403
Report of Wineford Richardson, administrator of Austin Richardson, deceased. No date.

GEORGE C. PETTY - page 404
Inventory and account of sale of George C. Petty, deceased, 24 Oct.1838.
Buyers included Jonathan Petty, Gabriel Petty, John A. Petty, Sollomon
Petty, James D. Petty, Haywood Horner, George Adcock, John Adcock,
William G. Deshazer.

WINEFORD RICHARDSON - page number left blank
Account of sale of property belonging to Wineford Richardson, sold
20 Jan. 1838. Ended on page 406.

JOHN NEWMAN - page 406
Year's allowance for Francis Newman, widow of John Newman, deceased, no
date. Page 407 has account of sale of property of John Newman sold at
his residence 22 Aug. 1838 by Henry Newman, administrator.

ROBERT STUART - page 408
List of property sold belonging to Robert Stuart, deceased, 23 August
1838. Mrs. Stuart and Gustavus Rape were among the buyers.

GEORGE TUBB - pages 408, 409
Report by Nathan Tubb and William S. Coleman, executors of George Tubb;
paid heirs of Isaac Tubb, paid Philip Nolen, guardian for his children;
paid Philip Cooksey's heirs, paid George, Pernelia and Susan Davidson
balance due them as agreement made by the heirs of George Tubb. 1838.

BENJAMIN HARDWICK - pages 410, 411
Estate of Benjamin Hardwick, deceased, 1838. Elizabeth Hardwick was
administratrix.

FIELD FARRAR - pate 412
Additional inventory and account of sale of Field Farrar, deceased, with
the hire of negroes given. No date. John Montgomery, administratrix.

JOHN PICKET - page 413
Settlement made with administrator of John Picket, deceased. No date.

HILERY MORRIS - pages 414-418
Settlement with John Morris, administrator of estate of Hilery Morris,
deceased, made 22 Nov. 1838. Estate included numerous notes and many

receipts. Among the receipts: M. W. Farrar received her share, G. W. Smith received his wife's share, N. C. Tailor received his wife's share, and J. Voorhies received his wife's share. End on page 419.

ROBERT WEAKLEY - pages 419-422
Account of the sale of property of Robert Weakley, deceased, 17 Nov.1838.

WILLIS NORSWORTHY - pages 422-431
Account of sale of property of Willis Norsworthy, deceased, sold 25 and 26 Oct. 1838. William Norsworthy was a buyer. Many buyers listed, many notes and accounts. John Norsworthy also a buyer as were Sally C. Scott and John N. Scott.

ABNER HUDGINS - page 431
Settlement made with Miles Long, administrator of Abner Hudgins, deceased, 10 Jan. 1839.

GEORGE ROSS - pages 432, 433
Account of James M. Ross, executor of George Ross, deceased, from 1835. Settlement made 18 January 1839.

CALEB EVANS - page 434
Inventory of estate of Caleb Evans, deceased, J. W. Napier, administrator. (Note: This entry was dim on the microfilm.)

GEORGE C. PETTY - pages 434, 435
Settled with administrators of George C. Petty, deceased.

WILLIAM BALTHROP - page 435
Inventory of estate of William Balthrop, deceased, made 3 June 1839.

WILLIS NORSWORTHY - pages 436-439
Supplemental inventory of Willis Norsworthy. (Note: This entry was dim and even page numbers are in question.)

STEPHEN ELEAZOR - pages 437-439
Stephen Eleazor, deceased. (Note: Dim entry.)

MARY YARRELL - page 440
List of property of Mary Yarrell's property sold 5 Octobet 1838, by Nathan Gilbert, executor.

MILLINGTON J. LANE - page 441
Year's support June 1839 for widow of M. J. Lane. List of property sold of Millington J. Lane, 28 June 1839. Wineford Lane bought most of the items. Wineford Richardson was also a buyer at the sale. M. Berry was the administrator. Account of this settlement ended on page 445.

TAPLEY BINUM - page 445
List of property of Tapley Binum sold 25 August 1839.

J. JONES - page 446
List of property, notes and accounts of J. Jones, deceased, by Washington Hunter, administrator. Bellville mentioned as he owned a lot in Bellville.

JOHN DAVIDSON - page 446
List of property sold of John Davidson, deceased, by his executor Elijah Davidson.

ELISHA PASCHELL - page 447
Settlement made with Gilford Paschell, administrator of Elisha Paschell, deceased. Estate was to be divided into 8 parts, division not given.

MUMFORD SMITH - page 448
Mumford Smith, deceased, settled with George W. Tatum and Jackson Smith, administrators, 6 August 1839.

GEROME DODSON - page 449
Inventory and account of sale of Gerome Dodson, deceased, by William

Dodson, administrator, November 1839.

JAMES TIDWELL - pages 449, 450
List of property of James Tidwell made by executors 29 Oct. 1839.

JANE NORRIS - pages 450, 451
Inventory of estate of Jane Norris, deceased. Among the buyers were Nancy Norris, W. W. Norris, A. A. Brown. William C. Ellis was the administrator. No date.

ALFRED SKELTON - pages 451, 452
List of property sold by Abner B. Skelton, administrator of Alfred Skelton, deceased, 30 Jan. 1840. Mary Skelton was one of buyers. He had notes on the Alabama and Mississippi Railroad Company.

AMANDA HICKMAN - page 453
Inventory of goods and chattles, rights and credits of the estate of Amanda Hickman, deceased. Ro. C. Whittock, administrator. Gives the hire of negroes owned by the estate. Report taken 28 March 1837 to 28 Sept. 1838.

WILLIS NORSWORTHY - page 454
Supplemental inventory of Willis Norsworthy.

JAMES CUNNINGHAM - page 454
List of property sold by John Cunningham, executor of James Cunningham, 21 Jan. 1840. Report continues through page 457.

WILLIS NORSWORTHY - pages 458, 459
Silvester Adams, administrator of Willis Norsworthy, deceased, in account with estate, gives sale of negroes, 29 August 1840.

MILLINGTON J. LANE - page 460
Settlement with Michel Berry, administrator of Millington J. Lane, decceased, made 20 October 1840. Gives dowry for widow. Had note on Thomas Lane.

JOHN FORD - pages 460, 461
Sold at Public Auction the estate of John Ford on 24 October 1840. Martha Ford bought much of estate. Other buyers included D. S. Step, John Step, Isaac Grove, William Cain. D. S. Ford was administrator.

JANE BAKER - pages 462, 463
Inventory of perishable property of Jane Baker, deceased, October 1840. Buyers included Benjamin Baker, the administrator, Nancy Baker, John Baker, Madison Dunagan, Anderson England, Miles England, Stanford Dunagan, Washington England, Sharp Dunagan.

WINEFORD RICHARDSON - pages 463, 464
Settlement with Squire Richardson, administrator of Wineford Richardson, deceased, settlement made 22 August 1840.

JOHN LARKINS - pages 464, 465
Inventory of perishable property of John Larkins, deceased, no date.

WILLIAM W. HOGINS - pages 466-470
Account of sale of perishable property of William W. Hogins, deceased, 26 November 1840. Long account.

RICHARD MURRELL - pages 470, 472
List of estate of Richard Murrell, deceased, by G. W. Tatum, administrator, 5 December 1840.

C. GRYMES - page 472
Sale of property of C. Grymes, deceased, by John Grymes, administrator, November 1839.

WILLIAM GENTRY - page 472
Year's provision for widow of William Gentry, deceased, ordered April 1840. Estate of William Gentry ended on page 475.

C. GRYMES - page 476
Sale of property void of estate of C. Grymes, deceased, 3 Nov. 1839.

MILLINGTON J. LANE - page 476
Settled with Michael Berry, administrator of Millington J. Lane, deceased; made 26 October 1840.

JAMES MARTIN - pages 476, 477
Rachel Martin, administratrix of estate of James Martin, deceased, makes a return.

JAS. D. SCOTT - pages 477, 478
John G. Hill, guardian of William D., John W., and Mary S. and Parthenia Scott, minor children of Jas. D. Scott, makes return to court. Sarah C. Scott was the former guardian. The Scott estate was divided into 4 parts. Made 1 March 1841.

JOSEPH MORRIS - pages 478-484
Account of sale of property of Joseph Morris, deceased, at his late residence, 10 Dec. 1840. Buyers included John T. Morris, And. T. Morris. Mentions Andrew Stewart was administrator of Lucy G. Morris, 1 March 1841.

LUCY G. MORRIS - pages 487-491
Estate of Lucy G. Morris sold 13 Feb. 1841.

RICHARD MURRELL - page 491
October 1840, year's provision made for the family of Richard Murrell, deceased, for Susannah, Kisiah, and Mary, the daughters. Made 24 Oct. 1840.

JANE BAKER - page 492
Inventory of perishable property of Jane Baker, deceased, returned 22 March 1841. Ended on page 493.

ROBERT H. BROWN - page 493
Inventory of the personal estate of Robert H. Brown, deceased, 5 April 1841 by Jeramiah Hambrick, administrator.

JOSEPH LARKINS - page 494
Inventory of estate of Joseph Larkins, deceased, filed 5 April 1841.

WM. BAKER - pages 494-496
Year's support for widow and family of Wm. Baker, deceased, made 20 March 1841. Gives account of sale of property, Elizabeth Baker purchased most of the items.

EZEKIEL SMITH - page 497
Abner Smith, administrator of estate of Ezekiel Smith, deceased, gives hire of negroes belonging to estate; also notes and credits. Abner Smith was the guardian of the heirs. The amount came to hand 1 Sept. 1839.

WILLIAM BALTHROP - page 498
Hewell Parrish and Martin Halliburton, administrators of estate of William Balthrop, deceased, who left a will. Signed 16 Feb. 1836 by his heirs at law: Thomas W. Shearon, Edward Pearsall, Willie Norsworthy, Frances Balthrop, Thomas Ellis, W. W. Balthrop, Willie Balthrop, and Mary Davis by attorney William Shearon. Settlement made 15 April 1841.

JOHN NEWMAN - page 499
Henry Newman, administrator of John Newman, deceased, makes return, settlement made final 17 April 1841.

B. TAYLOR - page 500
Settlement made with Lockey Taylor, administrator of B. Taylor.

DAVID WILEY - page 500
David Frasher, executor of last will of David Wiley, settled. Mentions

that William Wiley, father of David Wiley, with whom David Wiley had resided. Settlement made and statement sworn to 26 April 1841.

JOSEPH LARKINS - page 501
Catharine Larkins, administratrix of estate of Joseph Larkins, makes a return to court. Estate was divided between Catharine Larkins, Howe C. Larkins, James M. Larkins, Laura Ann Larkins, Elzr. Newton Larkins, heirs at law, 5 in number. Made 7 Nov. 1839. Settlement made 16 April 1841. Account of settlement made 16 April 1861 and ended on page 502.

THO. J. JONES - page 502
List of property belonging to Tho. J. Jones, deceased, disposed of by Wa. Hunter, administrator, mentions that Jones had an interest in a Bolivar engine. Signed 3 May 1841.

JOHN BEV. HUGHES - pages 502, 503
Inventory of property belonging to John Bev. Hughes, deceased; mentions judgment in Smith County; property is divided between his brothers and sisters according to his will. He had no property in Smith County, signed 8 June 1841 by Smith County clerk.

HENDERSON JOSLIN - pages 503, 504
List of property of Henderson Joslin, deceased, 1841. Buyers included Gabriel Joslin, Patsy Joslin. Filed 7 June 1841 by Patsy (x) Joslin. Year's provision for widow and children of Henderson Joslin, June 1841.

_____ - page 505
List of property sold at our sale 28 Dec. 1841. All purchased by Beedy White. Property was given to widow to lay off year's support. (Note: This might possibly refer to following entry.

WILLIAM WHITE - page 507
Property of William White, deceased, listed and to be sold 4 May 1841.

JACOB SANDERSON - pages 508-512
Sale of property of Jacob Sanderson, deceased, 17 December 1840. Buyers included Emelia Sanderson, Robert Sanderson, David Record, James Sanderson, Miley Sanderson, Emily Sanderson. Returned 10 June 1841. Year's support for Milly Sanderson, widow, made 16 March 1841.

JOHN DUNNIGAN - pages 512, 513
Elisha Gunn, administrator of estate of John Dunnigan, deceased; Gunn's house burned 17 Jan. 1840 and he lost his papers; mentions the widow of the deceased. Mentions the amount in the hands of the administrator as of 6 March 1839. Settlement was made 8 May 1841.

JOHN ANGLIN - page 513
Inventory of estate of John Anglin by Elizabeth Anglin and John C. Anglin. Negroes were owned by the estate. Made 10 January 1841.

CHARLES THOMPSON - pages 514-516
Inventory of estate of Charles Thompson, deceased, made by James Thompson, executor, signed 3 May 1841.

THOMAS J. JONES - pages 516, 517
Washington Hunter, administrator of Thomas J. Jones, makes report on the expenses of getting the engine of S. Boat Bolivar out of the river; mentions the purchase of the Steamboat Bolivar.

GEORGE SMITH - pages 517-525
Account of sale of the property of George Smith, deceased, by Thomas J. Kelly, administrator, 17 March 1841. Many notes and accounts listed. He had partnership with Thomas W. Shearon at Paris, Tennessee. Settled the partnership of Jacob Voorhies and George Smith at Charlotte from 8 Sept. 1834, when partnership began. Signed 1 Sept. 1840 by Jacob Voorhies. Account of estate was returned 11 June 1841.

This ends this book of Dickson County administrators' settlements.

V

DICKSON COUNTY VITAL STATISTICS

1908 - 1912

These death records were copied from a reel of Dickson County Vital Statistics microfilm in the Tennessee State Library and Archives and are for the deaths of people over the age of 40--with a few exceptions. As will be noted in this list, a few deaths are for prior to the time period covered.

MYATT, Morgan, 42, died 10 May 1902, la grippe, married, born in Dickson County.

BRADFORD, Roena, 89, died 13 Feb. 1909 of old age, born in North Carolina, married. (Note: Her will is recorded in Dickson County.)

PENDAGRASS, William, 61, died May 1902, suicide, born in Dickson County, married.

MARTHA YATES, 56, died 6 October 1908 of heart disease, born in Dickson County, married.

FULTZ, Susan M., 81, single, died 6 April 1909 by accident, teacher, born in Ohio.

TIDWELL, M. E., 38, female, died 22 Jan. 1909 of consumption, married, born in Georgia.

ANDERSON, Mary H., 55, died 28 October 1908 of cancer, married, born in Dickson County.

RICHARDSON, R. J., 59, died 6 June 1909 of kidney disease, married, born in Dickson County.

HALL, Frank, 70, died 21 March 1909 of kidney disease, married, born in Dickson County.

ADCOCK, C. G., age 44, death date not given, died of kidney disease, married, born in Dickson County, lived District 2.

YOUNG, Sam, 40, died 22 July 1908 of fever, married, born in Cheatham County, lived in District 2.

FULGHAM, Martha, 91, died 9 March 1909, suicide, married, born in Davidson County.

COULTER, J. A., 73, died 4 March 1909 of stomach touble, married, born in Pennsylvania.

PENDAGRASS, 71, died 12 May 1902 from fall. (Compare with the one above. Name is also William Pendagrass.)

JAMISON, I. C., female, 57, died 5 January 1908 of meningitis, died in Dickson County, born in Dickson County, married.

McFARLAND, W. B., 82, died 4 June 1908 of old age, single, died in Dickson County, born in Pennsylvania.

EASLY, William, 80, died 23 December 1908 of old age in Dickson County, born in Dickson County, single.

SUTTON, J. R., 92, died 12 July 1908 of old age in Dickson County, born in Kentucky, married.

DAVIDSON, M. V., 56, died 27 June 1909 of heart failure in Dickson County, born in Tennessee, married.

SANFORD, Hester, 67, died 20 Feb. 1909 of cancer in Dickson County, born in Kentucky, married.

CLARK, J. C., 92, died 23 April 1909 of old age in Dickson County, born in Dickson County, widowed.

RYAN, D., 45, married, died 28 October 1908 in Dickson County of pneumonia, born in Huston. (Note: This might mean Houston Co., Tenn.)

WALTHOUR, J. R., 78, died 6 May 1909 of old age in Dickson County, born in Pennsylvania, married.

HURT, B. F., 48, married, died 7 July 1908 in Dickson County of consumption, born in Dickson County.

OAKLEY, Elizabeth, 70, widow, died 18 March 1909 in Dickson County, born in Dickson County.

ROBERTS, Alice, 55, died 15 May 1909, married, died in Dickson County of meningitis, born in Dickson County.

LINSY, Jackson, 64, married, died 24 August 1908 of cancer in Dickson County, born in Dickson County.

AVERETT, Walter, 75, died Sept. 1908, dropped dead, died at Cumberland Furnace, born at Cumberland Furnace, married.

BISHOP, Eliza, 79, single, died 20 June 1909 of tumor at Cumberland Furnace, born in Arkansas.

GRAY, W. M., 86, died 6 April 1909, widowed, died in Dickson County of cancer, born in Williamson County.

RABURN, Green, 80, died 28 June 1908 of old age at Stayton, born in Dickson County, married.

STARK, Florence, 42, died 23 Feb. 1902 of heart disease at Cumberland Furnace, married, born at Charlotte.

HUGHES, Martha, 92, died 10 April 1902 of old age at Stayton; born Houston County, widow.

MATHIS, John, 70, died 15 Nov. 1908 of old age at Hamble; born in Dickson County, single.

SUTTON, Ransard, 65, died March 1909 of pneumonia at Clarksville; born Dickson County, married.

BAKER, Tom, 62, died 30 Jan. 1909 of fever at Betsy Town; born Dickson County, married.

SCRUGS, M., 50, died Dec. 1908 of pneumonia at Betsy Town; born Mississippi, married.

McGOWEN, John, 54, died 5 Oct. 1908 of lung disease in Dickson County, born Bedford County, married, minister.

OAKLEY, William, 88, died 3 Oct. 1908 of old age in Dickson County, born Maury County, married, justice of the peace.

PARROTT, Alice, 48, marriaged, died 8 Nov. 1909 of cancer in Dickson County, born in Dickson County.

TAYLOR, Berry, 72, died 15 Jan. 1909 in Dickson County of old age; born Dickson County, married.

LATIMER, L. E., 70, died 14 Dec. 1908 at Tennessee City of heart disease, birthplace unknown, widowed.

McELHINEY, Lizzie, 71, died 15 June 1909 of heart disease, born in Pennsylvania, married.

District 2, 1910 deaths:

PENDAGRASS, Martha, 57, died 20 Jan. 1910 of consumption in Dickson County, born in Tennessee, married.

District 3, 1910 deaths:

SPENCER, Daniel, 52, died 1 April 1910, cause of death not given, born in Tennessee, died in Dickson County.

STUART, J. R., 63, married, died 16 Dec. 1909 at Burns of consumption; born at Burns.

GARTON, Sallie, 54, married, died 20 Dec. 1909 of consumption; born and died at Burns.

LARKINS, R. A., 40, married, died 9 Sept. 1909 of indigestion at Burns; born at Charlotte.

JENKINS, Alsey, 54, married, female, died 8 Sept. 1909, of "hiliaumers" in Dickson County at Burns; born in Bedford County.

TIPTON, S. J., 69, married, died 30 April 1910 in Dickson County of consumption; born in Roan County.

SYLVIS, Levi, 76, single, died 16 March 1910 in Dickson County of a diseased foot, born in Pennsylvania.

SCHMITTOU, M. C., female, 82, single, died 12 May 1910 in Dickson County of old age, born in Dickson County.

PORTER, J. K., 72, married, died 18 Dec. 1909 in Dickson County of old age, born in Bedford County.

WOLF, R. E., 43, married, died 2 Nov. 1909 in Nashville of appendicitis; born in Missouri.

COLLIER, M. E., 49, married, died 1 Dec. 1909 in Tennessee of paralysis; born in Dickson County.

HOOPER, W. M., 66, married, died 3 May 1910 in Dickson County of Bright's disease; born in Davidson County.

BRUCE, D., 74, married, died 1 March 1910 in Dickson County of consumption, born in Tennessee.

DODSON, R., 43, single, died 28 Jan. 1910 in Dickson County, born in Dickson County.

KELSY, William, 84, married, died 10 June 1910 in Dickson County of cancer, born in Georgia.

BAKER, Jane, 60, married, died 2 August 1909 at Colesburg, died of consumption, born in Tennessee.

DUGAN, Emaline, 70, single, died 28 Jan. 1910 in Dickson County of consumption, born in Pennsylvania.

GARSE, E., 72, married, died 1 Dec. 1909, of heart failure in Dickson County, born in New York.

BURGIE, Mrs. M. E., 85, <u>single</u>, died 4 Sept. 1909 in Dickson County of consumption; born in Montgomery County.

BANOCHET, C., 70, married, died 3 April 1910 in Dickson County of fever, born in Pennsylvania.

LARKINS, Mrs. F. K., 73, married, died 28 Nov. 1909 in Dickson County of bowel trouble, born in Davidson County.

WOLF, El<u>o</u>sie, 43, married, died 6 Nov. 1909 of appendicitis in Nashville, born in Dickson County.

JUSTICE, T. L., 92, married, died 2 Sept. 1909 in Dickson County of gall stone, born in Virginia.

CARNELL, Ira, 43, married, died 22 June 1910 in Dickson County of consumption, born at Port Royal.

MIXON, Dora, 40, married, died 1 Dec. 1909 in Dickson County of cancer, born in Montgomery County.

MILLER, Louise E., 70, single, died 6 May 1910 in Dickson County of lagrippe, born in Dickson County.

ELDER, Dilly, 59, married, died June 1909 in Dickson County of rheumatism, born in Dickson County.

HAWK, Zilla, 44, married, died 15 June 1910 in Dickson County of heart disease, born in Pennsylvania.

WILSON, Lizzie, 65, married, died <u>6</u> Oct. 1909 in Dickson County of pneumonia, born in Dickson County.

SHERWOOD, David, 83, married, died 17 June 1910 in Dickson County of old age, born in Virginia.

FOWLKES, Bettie, 54, married, died 5 April 1910 in Dickson County of consumption, born in Tennessee.

ADAMS, Jane, 76, married, died 16 Dec. 1909 in Dickson County of fever, born in Tennessee.

EDWARDS, Dillie R., 54, married, died 15 Sept. 1909 in Dickson County, born in Tennessee.

McCORMICK, T. M., 64, married, died 12 Oct. 1909 in Dickson County of dropsy, born in Dickson County.

MARTIN, R., male, married, 78, died 17 Jan. 1910 in Dickson County of kidney trouble, born in Dickson County.

DONEGAN, N. R., 45, married, died 26 Sept. 1910 in Dickson County of consumption, born in Dickson County.

SPRINGER, W. D., 53, married, died 17 June 1911 in Dickson County of gunshot, born in Dickson County.

CALL, C. F., 42, single, died 11 Jan. 1911 in Dickson County of pneumonia, born in Ohio.

CHADWICK, J. A., 65, single, died 14 Feb. 1911 in Dickson County of cancer, born in North Carolina.

UNDERHILL, G. W., 65, married, died 8 Sept. 1910 in Dickson County of consumption, born in North Carolina.

LUTHER, Mrs. Amanda, 67, married, died 23 Feb. 1911 at Burns of heart failure, born at Burns.

McCLURE, Mrs. Delila, 88, married, died 4 March 1911 at Burns of old age, born in Pennsylvania.

BROWN, Mrs. Lucinda, 45, married, died 12 March 1911 at Burns of consumption, born at Burns.

DAVIDSON, Mrs. Sallie, 90, married, died 23 June 1911 at Burns of old age, born in South Carolina.

HALL, J. M., Jr., single, 51, died 26 Sept. 1910 in Dickson County of consumption; born in Dickson County.

MILLER, V. A., female, 65, single, died 28 Aug. 1910 in Dickson County of dropsy, born in Dickson County.

McCLURE, J. E., 56, married, died 10 Dec. 1910 in Dickson County of heart disease, born in Kentucky.

EDWARDS, Lucy, single, 89, died 3 August 1910 in Dickson County of old age, born in Dickson County.

CULLUM, E. M., 71, male, died 10 Feb. 1911 in Dickson County of cancer, born in Cheatham County.

ANDREWS, E. G., 83, male, died 20 May 1911 in Dickson County of old age, born in Williamson County. Married.

MILLER, Cora, 43, married, died 3 Aug. 1910 in Dickson County of consumption, born in Dickson County.

TURNER, W. T., 41, married, died 3 March 1911 in Dickson County of heart disease, born in Dickson County.

STROUD, A. W., 49, married, died 4 August 1910 in Davidson County of consumption, born in Cheatham County.

MURRELL, T. J., 86, single, died 22 Nov. 1910 in Dickson County of old age, born in Dickson County.*

MARSH, Emiline, 70, single, died 19 Nov. 1910 in Dickson County of old age, born in Hickman County.

MATHIS, Sarah, 85, married, died 20 Jan. 1911 in Dickson County of old age, born at Charlotte.

HOOPER, J. O., 66, married, died 1 Feb. 1911 in Dickson County of consumption, born in Davidson County.

FERRILL, Mary C., 60, married, died 30 April 1911 in Dickson County of paralysis, born in Davidson County.

LANE, Thomas, 77, married, died 15 Sept. 1910 in Dickson County of old age, born in Dickson County.

STALEY, Elizabeth, 76, married, died 10 May 1911 in Dickson County of pneumonia, born in Dickson County.

CHOATE, James, 69, married, died 5 Sept. 1911 in Dickson County of fever, born in Dickson County.

SANDERS, John, 71, married, died 2 May 1911 in Dickson County of heart trouble, born in Dickson County.

---

*The marital status is always given as found on these records, even though at times it is believed it might be incorrect. It was impossible to determine if "single" was meant at the time of death only.

SANDERS, Martha, 60, married, died 4 July 1910 in Dickson County of flux, born in Dickson County.

BUTLER, Aaron, 67, married, died 21 October 1910 in Dickson County of blood poisoning, born in Dickson County.

WHITNEY, John, 70, married, died 20 May 1911 in Dickson County of old age, born in Dickson County.

LARKINS, Allie, male, 44, single, died 10 July 1910 in Dickson County of consumption, born in Dickson County.

ANDREWS, P. H., 58, married, died 19 June 1911 in Dickson County of consumption, born in Dickson County.

RODGERS, B. F., 55, married, died 14 Nov. 1910 in Dickson County of Bright's disease, born in Dickson County.

HATLEY, Mildred M., 61, married, died 22 Aug. 1910 in Dickson County of consumption, born in Cheatham County.

HATLEY, Rye, 70, married, died 25 Jan. 1911 in Dickson County of kidney trouble, born in Dickson County.

MULLINS, G. W., 78, married, died 2 Dec. 1910 in Dickson County of consumption, born in Rutherford County.

BAGWELL, J. M., 84, married, died 20 May 1911 in Dickson County of kidney trouble, born in Montgomery County.

McNICHOLS, Mrs. Ann, 90, single, died 4 Dec. 1910 in Dickson County of heart trouble, born in North Carolina.

SENSING, William, 80, single, died 10 Aug. 1910 in Dickson County of old age, born in Dickson County.

JUSTICE, Jane, 66, married, died 17 Nov. 1911 in Dickson County of pneumonia, born in Dickson County.

MITCHELL, Henrietta, 57, married, died 28 Jan. 1911 in Dickson County of consumption, born in Lake County.

SIMPKINS, Lizzie May, 52, married, died 16 Jan. 1911 in Dickson County of pneumonia, born in Dickson County.

PROCTOR, Mrs. Amanda, 74, single, died 11 June 1911 in Dickson County of uremic poisoning, born in Dickson County.

ELEAZER, John P., 79, married, died 2 Jan. 1911 in Dickson County of old age, born in Dickson County.

HAND, G. W., 50, married, died 21 Aug. 1910 in Dickson County of heart disease, born in Dickson County.

JACKSON, Martha Ann, 76, married, died 9 March 1911 in Dickson County of old age, born in Dickson County.

HUGHES, Martha, 83, married, died 3 May 1911 in Dickson County of old age, born in Dickson County.

LEE, Mrs. Mat, 60, married, died 19 Sept. 1910 in Dickson County of nervousness, born in Dickson County.

WILLIAMS, Louis, 75, married, died 13 April 1911 in Dickson County of heart disease, born in Ohio.

DANIEL, Elizabeth, 83, married, died 14 June 1911 in Dickson County of old age, born in Dickson County.

BENTLY, Sally, 63, married, died 11 Feb. 1911 in Dickson County of consumption, born in Illinois.

HOLLIS, Joseph, 79, married, died 12 March 1911 in Dickson County of dropsy, born in Dickson County.

POWELL, Dilly Ann, 79, married, died 15 Dec. 1911 in Dickson County of cancer, born in Dickson County.

CLARK, Mary, 43, married, died 3 Feb. 1911 in Dickson County of consumption, born in Montgomery County.

FOSTER, Augustus, 61, married, died 24 April 1911 in Dickson County of dropsy, born in Dickson County.

ELDER, Dilly, 55, married, died 1 July 1910 in Dickson County of consumption, born in Dickson County.

BLACK, Robert, 19, single, died 3 August 1910, killed by automobile, died in Dickson County, born in Dickson County.

SUGG, Polly, 78, married, died 21 Dec. 1910 in Dickson County of paralysis, born in Dickson County.

GILMORE, Mrs. J. A., 77, single, died 13 March 1911 in Dickson County of pneumonia, born in Dickson County.

BROWNING, C., male, 84, single, died 17 Feb. 1911 in Dickson County of old age, born in North Carolina.

DUGGER, Mary, 76, married, died 22 Nov. 1910 in Dickson County of dropsy born in Dickson County.

ADAMS, Martha, 80, single, died 30 April 1911 at Danville of old age, born at Danville.

WARD, Freda, 76, married, died 30 June 1911 in Dickson County of heart trouble, born in Alabama. (Note: Her first name could be Tuda.)

ETHERIGE, Mary, 67, single, died 8 April 1911 of consumption in Dickson County, born in Tennessee.

DONEGAN, J. W., 82, married, died 7 Dec. 1911 in Dickson County of pneumonia, born in Dickson County.

MANLY, S. A., 81, married, died 16 August 1911 in Dickson County of stomach and kidney disease, born in Tennessee.

SMITH, James, 68, married, died 21 June 1912 in Dickson County of bowel trouble, born in Montgomery County.

CORY, G. S., 75, married, died 12 April 1912 in Dickson County of paralysis, born in Dickson County.

CALL, Robert P., 67, married, died 6 May 1912 in Dickson County of heart disease, born Scioto County, Ohio.

BRAZELL, Emaline, 73, married, died 1 Feb. 1912 in Dickson County of paralysis, born in Dickson County.

REGISTER, T. S., 66, married, died in Dickson County 15 May 1912 of dropsy, born in Dickson County.

WHITE, R. F., 60, married, died in Dickson County 4 Oct. 1911, accident, born in Dickson County.

SPENCER, H. A., 76, married, died 11 May 1912 in Dickson County of Bright's disease, born in Dickson County.

HUTCHISON, F. C., 62, married, died 14 Oct. 1911 in Dickson County of typhoid fever, born in Hickman County.

BROWN, Susan, 64, married, died 19 August 1911 in Dickson County of consumption, born in Davidson County.

LANKFORD, T. P., 82, married, died 12 March 1912 in Dickson County of dropsy, born in Dickson County.

HUTCHISON, Mrs. Minta, 57, married, died 17 April 1912 of consumption in Dickson County, born in Dickson County.

REEDER, Eliza, 86, married, died 19 July 1911 of kidney trouble in Dickson County, born in Dickson County.

MITCHELL, J. D., 84, single, died 19 Dec. 1911 in Dickson County of pneumonia, born in Dickson County.

MEEK, Mrs. Susie, 48, married, died 12 March 1912 in Dickson County of consumption, born in Dickson County.

LARKINS, Mary, 67, married, died 19 Sept. 1911 at Colesburg of fever, born in Dickson County.

WATSON, A. W., 45, married, died 19 Sept. 1911 in Dickson County at Colesburg of juandice, born in Dickson County.

BATES, S. C., 75, married, died 20 April 1912 in Dickson County of pneumonia, born in Hickman County.

NEWHOUSE, Lonnda, female, 59, married, died 14 Sept. 1911 in Dickson County of blood poisoning, born in Ohio.

LARKINS, T. B., 73, married, died 10 Oct. 1911 in Dickson County, hurt by a wagon, born in Dickson County.

SIZEMORE, S. A., 79, single, died 1 April 1912 in Dickson County of old age, born in Dickson County.

McNEAL, J. R., 67, married, died 5 Dec. 1911 in Dickson County of nervous prostration, born in Lawrence County.

SAGER, Susan, 97, single, died 30 June 1912 in Dickson County of old age, born in Pennsylvania.

SANDERS, Martha, 60, married, died 4 July 1911 in Dickson County of flux, born in Dickson County.

COPELAND, John, 70, married, died 19 Oct. 1911 at the Poor House in Dickson County of old age; born in Dickson County.

DOTSON, J. C., 73, single, died 2 October 1911 at Charlotte of paralysis born in Dickson County.

SUTHERLAND, W. H., 70, married, died April 1912 at Charlotte of consumption, born in Dickson County.

WILLEY, John, 68, single, died 20 April 1912 at Charlotte of consumption, born in Dickson County.

HOWELL, Ros, male, 56, married, died 5 Oct. 1911 at White Bluff of locomotion of nerves, born at White Bluff.

CROW, Mrs. Eliza, 59, married, died 29 Jan. 1912 in Dickson County of pneumonia, born in Dickson County.

WICKS, Amos, 86, male, married, died 23 June 1912 in Dickson County of old age, born in Ohio.

JACKSON, Sallie, 41, married, died 23 Jan. 1912 in Dickson County of miscarriage, born in Dickson County.

JOHNSON, John J., 86, single, died 16 May 1912 in Dickson County of pneumonia, born in Hickman County.

POTTS, W. D., 40, married, died 5 Feb. 1912 in Dickson County of abcess of the brain, born in Dickson County.

BAKER, Claud G., 78, single, died 21 April 1912 in Dickson County of acute indigestion, born in Dickson County.

MILLER, Fred, 48, married, died 3 March 1912 in Dickson County of consumption, born in Dickson County.

CARVER, Neil, 79, married, died 1 Feb. 1912 in Dickson County of Bright's disease, born in Dickson County.

CARVER, Jane, 73, married, died 17 April 1912 in Dickson County of consumption, born in Dickson County.

WEAVER, Dave, 65, married, died 2 May 1912 in Dickson County of pneumonia, born in Wilson County.

TURNER, Maggie, 68, married, died 12 June 1912 in Dickson County of paralysis, born in Alabama.

AVERETTE, Alice, 52, married, died 5 April 1912 in Dickson County of cancer, born in Humphreys County.

CHOATE, Patia, 43, died 31 October 1911 in Dickson County of cancer of the stomach, born in Humphreys County.

1880 MORTALITY SCHEDULE

(These mortality schedules were transcribed by T. P. Hughes, Jr., Memphis, Tennessee, were originally published in the 1973 issue of "The River Counties" and repeated here in slightly different form. Mr. Hughes transcribed these from Microcopy T-655, Reel 28.)

1st Civil District, taken by N. R. Sugg, enumerator:

BAKER, J. W., 23, born in Tennessee, parents born in Tennessee, died September of meningitis.

SMITH, E. L., 2, male, born in Tennessee, parents born in Tennessee, died in April of typhoid fever.

BRINKES, D. R., 33, male, married, born in Tennessee, parents born in Tennessee, died in February of pneumonia.

SAYGER, Fred, 10 months, male, born in Tennessee, parents born in Tennessee, died in April of diabetes.

LANE, Rufus, 7, male, born in Tennessee, parents born in Tennessee, died in November of "diarrheah".

FOWLKS, E. A., 54, male, married, born in Virginia, parents born in Virginia, died in June of dropsy.

TATAM, M. E., 72, female, married, born in Tennessee, parents born in Georgia, died October, typhoid fever.

THORNTON, W. E., 1, male, born in Tennessee, parents born in Tennessee, died August of cholera infantum.

1880 Mortalities, continued:

CARR, T. J., 2, male, born in Tennessee, parents born in Tennessee, died September of "chorrhea infam."

BROWN, D. R., 2, male, born in Tennessee, parents born in Tennessee, died July of brain trouble.

WHITE, Mary B., 42, female, born in Tennessee, father born in Tennessee, mother born in Virginia, died in March of pneumonia.

HUTCHISON, no name, 7 months, male, born in Tennessee, parents born in Tennessee, died in September of croup.

MYERS, William, 55, married, born in Tennessee, parents born in Tennessee, died January of "Emsuhtion".

FORUEN, John T., 48, married, born in Tennessee, parents born in Tennessee, died in July of malarial fever.

SPENCER, Z. C., 23, female, born in Tennessee, parents born in Tennessee, died in February of consumption.

SPENCER, Celia, 4, female, born in Tennessee, parents born in Tennessee, died in August of "Enlessetic".

DUNNAGAN, M., 75, female, married, born in Tennessee, parents born in Tennessee, died in February of pneumonia.

UNDERHILL, Lorra, 35, female, married, born in Tennessee, parents born in North Carolina, died in May of consumption.

LUMPLEY, S. G., 2, female, born in Tennessee, parents born in Tennessee, died in May of diarrhea. (Note: The surname is possibly Lampley.)

2nd Civil District, T. M. Binkley, Jr., enumerator:

TANNER, Mary A., 4 months, born in Tennessee, father born in South Carolina, mother born in North Carolina, died in September of "cholrea infanton".

DUNNAGAN, Elizabeth, 96, female, widow, born in North Carolina, parents born in North Carolina, died in October of old age.

SUGG, John, 72, married, born in Tennessee, parents born in North Carolina, died in **March of** consumption.

HOLLAND, Wesley, 66, married, born in Georgia, father born in Georgia, mother born in South Carolina, died in July of consumption.

GLASS, Albert F., 9 months, born in Tennessee, parents born in Tennessee, died in February of croup.

Additions to Dickson County from Supplemental Schedule:

HARDAWAY, Mary A., 37, married, died in July, cause illegible.

CHAMY, Sarah, 51, widow, born in Tennessee, died in August of consumption.

BRYANT, J. P., 76, male, widowed, **born in** North Carolina, died in June of dropsy.

BAKER, Harriet, 34, married, born in Tennessee, died in July of consumption.

WOODDY, William, 68, born in Tennessee, died in May of "piritonitis."

CARVIN, William, age ?, married, born in Tennessee, died in May, cause of death not known.

1880 Mortality Schedule, continued:

4th Civil District, F. F. Tidwell, enumerator:

WILSON, Sarah, 78, married, born in North Carolina, father born in Ireland, mother born in North Carolina, died in March of "congestive B."

HARMACK, Walter R., 5 days, born in Tennessee, father born in Pennsylvania, mother born in Tennessee, died in May of debility.

RICHARDSON, Louis, 1 year, born in Tennessee, father born in Tennessee, mother born in North Carolina, died in July of "enleseles."

BECK, Mary, 40, married, born in Tennessee, parents born in Tennessee, died in February of childbirth.

TIDWELL, Cora S., 1, born in Tennessee, parents born in Tennessee, died in June of croup.

MYATT'S infant, male, born in Tennessee, parents born in Tennessee, died in June "injury by forseps".

RICHARDSON, Lewis, 2, born in Tennessee, parents born in Tennessee, died in July of "cholera inf."

COX, William James, 1, born in Tennessee, parents born in Tennessee, died in December of convulsions.

TIDWELL, Isedore, 1, female, born in Tennessee, parents born in Tennessee, died in July of croup.

RICHDSON, infant, male, 2 days, born in Tennessee, parents born in Tennessee, died in August, unknown cause.

5th Civil District, L. L. Leach, Jr.:

SYVUS, Sarah, 28, single, born in Pennsylvania, parents born in Pennsylvania, died in March of consumption.

EWELL, William, 30, single, born in Tennessee, parents born in Tennessee died in May of consumption.

GAY, William, 70, married, born in North Carolina, parents born in North Carolina, died in April, unknown cause.

MORGAN, Dodson, 25, married, born in Tennessee, parents born in Virginia, died in January of consumption.

HUNSLEE, Bay, age not given, born in Tennessee, father born Kentucky, mother born Tennessee, died July, stillborn.

EWELL, H. L., 27, male, born in Tennessee, father born in Tennessee, mother born in Tennessee, died in June, disease of the heart.

CUTHERN, Gains F., 44, married, born in Tennessee, parents born in Tennessee, died in December of pneumonia.

WYNN, James, 2, born in Tennessee, parents born in Tennessee, died in February of malarial fever.

6th Civil District, T. H. Lee, enumerator:

DICKSON, _____, 1 day, female, born in Tennessee, parents born in Tennessee, died May, stillborn.

WILLIAMS, Baby, 3 months, male, born in Tennessee, parents born in Tennessee, died May congestion of bowels.

1880 Mortality Schedule, continued:

MAY, Thomtas, 1, male, born in Tennessee, parents born in Tennessee, died March "hydrocephalies".

McMILLIAN, Mary, 74, married, born in Pennsylvania, parents born in Pennsylvania, died in September of consumption.

OVERTON, Katie, 1, born in Tennessee, parents born in Tennessee, died July of worms.

HICKERSON, Sarah, 76, widow, born in Tennessee, parents born in North Carolina, died in March of "softening of Rsdn."

HENDERSON, Julia, 1, born in Tennessee, parents born in Tennessee, died August of diptheria.

HOOPER, B. D., 1, male, born in Tennessee, parents born in Tennessee, died September of cholera infan.

HARVEY, Oney, 1, male, born in Tennessee, parents born in Tennessee, died in May of congestion of brain.

CLARK, George, 62, married, born in Tennessee, parents born in Tennessee, died in November of consumption.

JACKSON, Elizabeth, 28, born in Tennessee, parents born in Tennessee, died in February of consumption.

CALDWELL, Melberry, 4 months, female, born in Tennessee, parents born in Tennessee, died in April of congestion of stomach.

BEST, Elizabeth, 76, widow, born in Pennsylvania, parents born in Pennsylvania, died in October of heart disease.

LESTLER, Tennessee, 40, female, married, born in Tennessee, parents born in Tennessee, died March of pneumonia.

GRYMES, Elizabeth, 30, married, born in Tennessee, parents born in Tennessee, died in April of consumption.

STORY, Anna, 3, born in Tennessee, parents born in Tennessee, died in July of scroffula.

GREEN, Jackson, 45, single, born in Tennessee, parents born in Tennessee, died in February of dropsy.

PRICE, Mary Ann, 21, died in May of consumption.

8th Civil District, William H. Corlew, enumerator:

BROWN, Lular, 2, female, born in Tennessee, parents born in Tennessee, died November, "burnt".

GENSING, Authur, 1, male, born in Tennessee, parents born in Tennessee, died in November of meningitis. (Note: We believe the surname should be Sensing as this family lived in this neighborhood.)

GUTTON, Martha, 1, born in Tennessee, parents born in Tennessee, died in January of inflamation of brain.

BOWE, Eliza, 35, born in Tennessee, parents born in Tennessee, died in January of consumption.

CREECH, Lenorah, 7 months, born in Tennessee, parents born in Tennessee, died October of bold hives.

MONROE, Dollie E., 8 months, born in Tennessee, parents born in Tennessee, died in August of teething.

GROVES, Albert, 18, born in Tennessee, parents born in Tennessee, died in January of "billious fever".

WILSON, John B., 6 days, born in Tennessee, parents born in Tennessee, died in December, unknown cause.

FREEMAN, Annie, 78, married, born in Virginia, parents born in Virginia, died in July of paralysis.

FREEMAN, John, 44, born in Tennessee, parents born in Virginia, died in November of bronchitis.

BROCK, Robert, 22, born in Ohio, father born in Virginia, mother born in Ohio, died November, "shot".

PARDUE, May, 1 month, born in Tennessee, parents born in Tennessee, died in August of chills.

PARDUE, Fannie, 1 month, born in Tennessee, parents born in Tennessee, died in September of chills.

7th Civil District, G. W. Brown, enumerator:

COLLIER, T. L., 70, born in Virginia, parents born in Virginia, died in April of typhoid fever.

_____, Elbert, 3 months, male, born in Tennessee, parents born in Tennessee, died in December of inflamation of brain.

MITCHELL, John, 33, died in July of malarial fever.

8th Enumerator District, W. C. Crunk, enumerator:

BULL, Eudora G., 1, born in Tennessee, parents born in Tennessee, died August of inflamation of bowel.

BAKER, Susan C., 50, married, born in Tennessee, father born in Virginia mother born in North Carolina, died in June apoplexy.

TURNER, Amanda, 1 month, born in Tennessee, parents born in Tennessee, died September fits.

SUGG, Caey J., 1 month, female, born in Tennessee, parents born in Tennessee, died March "Hydrocephlus".

RAINES, Mary S., 1 month, born in Tennessee, parents born in Tennessee, died September of jaundice.

WETHERFORD (stillborn), female, born in Tennessee, parents born in Tennessee, died in January, no cause known.

SLAYDEN, John J., 1, born in Tennessee, parents born in Tennessee, died in October, "infl. bowels".

POWELL (stillborn), male, born in Tennessee, parents born in Tennessee, died in February, no cause known.

STOKES, John, 86, born in North Carolina, parents born in South Carolina died July disease of the heart.

RIGGON, Margrit, 1, born in Tennessee, parents born in Tennessee, died in April of diphtheria.

HUTCHINSON, Marthy E., 7, born in Tennessee, father born in North Carolina, mother born in Tennessee, died in April of diphtheria.

HUTCHINSON, Stella S., 2, born in Tennessee, father born in North Carolina, mother born in Tennessee, died in April of diphtheria.

10th Civil District, James W. Oakley, enumerator:

1880 Mortality Schedule, continued:

GILMORE, Louie, 1 month, female, born in Tennessee, parents born in Tennessee, died in September of hives.

POPE, Phoebia, 66, born in North Carolina, parents born in North Carolina, died in January of paralysis.

BAKER, Susan, 2, born in Tennessee, parents born in Tennessee, died in October of worm fever.

FINCH, Peter, 74, born in Virginia, parents born in Virginia, died in March of dropsy.

HASLEY, Abraham, 85, born in Tennessee, parents born in Tennessee, died in August of old age. (Note: In early Dickson County records this surname is found as Hosley, Hostley, etc.)

BROWNING, Millicent, 48, born in Tennessee, father born in Kentucky, mother born in Tennessee, died in August of dropsy.

DICKSON, Henry, 12, born in Tennessee, parents born in Tennessee, died in October of congestive chill.

11th Civil District, Jesse Daniel, enumerator:

DANIEL, Elizabeth, 76, widow, born in Tennessee, parents born in North Carolina, died in November of old age.

NESBITT, John B., 20, born in Tennessee, parents born in Tennessee, died December of hemorrhage of lung.

BURGASS, Ann, 73, widow, born in North Carolina, parents born in North Carolina, died in October of old age.

DUGGER, Sterling, 82, married, born in Virginia, parents born in Virgiana, died in November of old age.

12th Civil District, Thos. K. Dickson, enumerator:

PRICE, Joseph E., 3 months, born in Tennessee, parents born in Tennessee, died in July of bold hives.

HOOPER. A. N., 2 months, female, born in Tennessee, parents born in Tennessee, died in July, unknown cause.

HOOPER, N. W., 3 months, female, born in Tennessee, parents born in Tennessee, died in August, unknown cause.

HOOPER, J. D., 8, male, born in Tennessee, parents born in Tennessee, died in February of congestion of brain.

OLINGER, Susie, 3, born in Pennsylvania, parents born in Pennsylvania, died April of fever.

LEE, Nancy J., 22, married, born in Tennessee, parents born Tennessee, died in March of "inflam. of Bowel".

GUSTON, Elizabeth, 77, birthplaces not known, died in January of pneumonia.

CREECH, Thomas, 35, birthplaces not given, died in March of syphillis.

JACKSON, Jane, 20, married, birthplaces not given, died in May of bowel "collulitis".

Addition to Dickson County by Physician Report:

HOSLEY, Abraham, 77, died June consumption.

1880 Mortality Schedule, continued:

CANTRELL, ____, stillborn, died in August.

HUGGINS, William, 50, died in October of "telanos".

SLAYDEN, Joseph, 3, died in August of fever.

RUTHERFORD, male, died in January, stillborn.

FRY, Martin, 65, died in October of "Phthesis Peel".

NEBLEBO, infant, 1, male, born in Tennessee, died in January of tuberculosis.

SWAN, Mary, 41, died in October of abortion.

NESBIT, Mrs., 50, died in July, tuberculosis.

NICKS, Emma, 1, born in Tennessee, died in September of dysentery.

CALDWELL, Reney, 78, female, died in July of dropsy.

ANDERSON, infant, 6 months, died July meningitis.

LOVEL'S infant, 1 month, female, died in August of skin disease.

ADAMS, Kitchen, 40, male, died October, neck broken.

LANKFORD, John, 83, died in April, unknown cause.

SEARS, Elizabeth, 88, died in May, disease of heart.

CREECH, Willie, 10 months, died in July; cause, "don't know".

End of 1880 Mortality Schedule of Dickson County.

DICKSON CUMBERLAND PRESBYTERIAN CHURCH DEATHS

The Dickson Cumberland Presbyterian Church was organized 29 Sept. 1899 and is still an active church. The following are death records copied from the Session Book of the church, in possession of Lula Belle Hopkins when copied.

```
Sallie Sizemore, died 1 April 1912
C. P. Deason, died 28 March 1914, age 56 years 3 months
J. E. Dickson, died 6 June 1915
N. C. Averitt, died 1954
B. J. Vineyard, died 6 November 1936
J. T. Wrenne, died 2 Sept. 1934
J. T. Littleton, died 22 Jan. 1934
Mrs. Frank Hopkins, died 21 June 1946
Snow Wrenne, died 23 July 1951
Mrs. J. T. Littleton, died 29 June 1940
Bixler Houston, no date
Tom Williams, no date
Mrs. A. D. Rudolph, died 2 June 1962
Billie Boyd Littleton, died 19 March 1950
```

VI

DICKSON COUNTY DEED RECORDS

These abstracted notes were made from Dickson County Deed Book A, covering the period March 1804 to February 1812. These were abstracted from microfilm of the original books and some of the pages were dim. It is always advisable to recheck any entry in which a researcher might be interested, either the original record or by ordering a reader-print of the desired pages from the Tennessee State Library and Archives. Faded ink on microfilm often creates optical illusions--the name Parker can look like Baker, Joslin might seem to be Allen, and James and Samuel as well as David and Daniel often are hard to tell apart.

Many of these deeds were recorded in Davidson, Montgomery, and Robertson counties before Dickson was created.

Some of these entries are on several pages, but usually we have only noted the first page of the entry in these abstracts.

DEED BOOK A

JAMES WATSON of Alexandria, Virginia, to
JOHN WARD of Roertson County, Tennessee   pages 1, 2
Conveys land in Robertson County on the west fork of Jones Creek, being part of 2560 acres granted by North Carolina to Robert Bell on 20 May 1793; mentions a small walnut in the Barrens; this deed had been registered first on 6 Feb. 1801 by Andrew Jackson, one of the judges of the superior court.
Made ___ Feb. 1801   Recorded 20 March 1804
Witness: J. Wharton

JOHN DICKSON of Cumberland County, N. C., to
HUDSON JOHNSON of Williamson County   page 5
Conveys land in Robertson County on the south side of the Cumberland River on both sides of the upper fork of Barton's Creek; mentions John Nisbett corner. Land was originally granted to William Cochran on 30 Nov. 1790 and deed by Cochran to Dickson.
Made 4 July 1803   Recorded 19 June 1804
Witnesses, Nicholas Seals, Robert Edmondson, John Foran

STATE OF NORTH CAROLINA to
JOHN EDGE   page 7
North Carolina granted land to Edge in the Mero District for his services as a private in the continental line; land was granted to Buckley Sutton, his assignee; land on Barton's Creek.
Made 22 Sept. 1797   Recorded 19 June 1804

NATHANIEL PERRY of Wilson County to
HENRY CANNON of Duplin County, N. C.   page 9
Conveys land in Montgomery County (formerly Tennessee County) which was originally granted to John Edge and assigned to Buckley Sutton.
Made 23 June 1801   Recorded 19 June 1804
Witness, David Cannon.

JAMES WATSON of Alexandria, Va., to
JOHN HORNER of Robertson County, TN   page 11
Conveys land on west fork of Jones Creek; mentions John Ward's northeast corner.
Made 1 August 1802   Registered 28 July 1804
Witnesses, Jno. Sommerville, J. Wharton

JOHN HORNER of Robertson County to
JOHN LOW of Robertson County   page 12
Conveys land on west fork of Jones Creek, land was originally granted by North Carolina to Robert Bell in 1793.
Made 17 June 1803   Registered 30 August 1804
Witnesses, Charles Walker, Lakin Walker

JOHN HORNER of Robertson County to
CHARLES WALKER of Robertson County   page 13
Conveys land on west fork of Jones Creek, originally granted by North
Carolina to Robert Bell.
Made 4 June 1803
Witnesses, John Low, Lakin Walker

SAMUEL SMITH and JAMES A. BUCHANAN of Baltimore, Maryland, to
WILLIAM NORRIS of Montgomery County   page 14
Convey 640 acres in Montgomery County on both sides of Yellow Creek,
31 miles below the Chickasaw Trace, was granted to James Glasgow,
assignee of Thomas Aims, heir of James Aims, by North Carolina.
Made 8 Feb. 1804   Registered 1 Sept. 1804
Witnesses, William Cocke, Anderson W. Dickson (proved by Wm. Dickson)

ROBERT DUNNING of Robertson County to
WILLIAM TEAS of Robertson County   page 15
Conveys land; mentions the northwest corner of tract that John Drury
conveyed by Duncan Stewart to Robert Dunning.
Made 14 July 1803   Registered 8 Sept. 1804
Witnesses, Jeremiah Nesbet, James Teas, Margery Dunning

ROBERT DUNNING of Robertson County to
WILLIAM MOORE of Robertson County   page 16
Conveys land on east side of Yellow Creek; mentions the tract of John
Drury.*
Made 15 July 1803   Registered 8 Sept. 1804
Witnesses, James Teas, Nathan Nesbitt, William Teas

WILLIAM DICKSON of Nashville
ROBERT JAMESON of Dickson County   page 17
Dickson conveys land on Yellow Creek, part of 147 acres granted to Edward Dickson and conveyed by Edward Dickson to William Dickson on 20 Aug.
1796. Mentions Daniel Williams' line.
Made 22 May 1804   Registered 8 Sept. 1804
Witnesses, Nathan Nesbitt, James Means (?)

WILLIAM DICKSON of Davidson County
JOHN JONES   page 18
Dickson conveys to Jones land on Yellow Creek, mentions John Drury's
corner and Robert Jamison's corner; land was originally granted to Edward Dickson and conveyed by him to William Dickson.
Made 22 May 1804   Registered 3 Sept. 1804

JAMES ROBERTSON
GEORGE TEAL, SR.   page 19
Teal gets land from Robertson, land in Robertson County on the head-
waters of Johnston's Creek and was granted to Charles Stuart by North
Carolina; mentions the southeast corner of Doctor Hugh Williamson.
Made 23 Jan. 1804   Registered 13 Sept. 1804
Witnesses, Henry Owings, William B. Robertson, Payton Robertson,
R. C. Napier

WILLIAM ALLEN of Richmond County, Georgia
JAMES BROWN of Warren County, Kentucky   page 20
Brown gets land from Allen in Robertson County on the west side of Yellow
Creek; mentions Middleton's west boundary line and the south bank of the
second fork of Yellow Creek.
Made 10 Oct. 1803   Registered 13 Sept. 1804
Witnesses, Thomas Stuart, John Shute

WILLIAM P. ANDERSON   page 21
Anderson gets quit claim deed for 640 acres from James Brown.
Made 3 Feb. 1804   Registered 13 Sept. 1804
Witness, Allen Brewer

---

*The spelling of the creek names, etc., will be as found in the deed
 records, even though we know Yellow Creek mentioned here is Yellow
 Creek.

DAVID WILSON of Sumner County
HUGH DICKSON of Dickson County   page 22
Dickson gets 150 acres from Wilson on the third west fork of Yallow
Creek; mentions the southwest corner of James Middleton. James Wilson
made deposition that Zacheus Wilson was the son of David Wilson.
Made 6 Dec. 1803   Registered 19 Dec. 1804
Witness, James Salmon

DANIEL HARKLEROAD of Dickson County
JACOB W. MILLER of Dickson County   page 23
Harkleroad conveys to Miller land on Barton's Creek.
Made 18 Feb. 1804   Registered 19 Dec. 1804
Witnesses, James Gilaspie, George Miller

JAMES WALKER of Dickson County
JACOB WEST MILLER of Dickson County   page 24
Walker conveys to Miller land on Barton's Creek.
Made 2 May 1804   Registered 19 Dec. 1804

ROBERT DUNNING of Robertson County
THOMAS BOLES of Robertson County   page 25
Dunning conveys land on west side of Yallow Creek; mentions Hugh McCarron
upper fence; tract was located in the name of John Drury.
Made 27 Oct. 1803   Registered 15 Jan. 1805.
Witnesses, Charles Teas, Eli Crow, Thomas Gray

BRYAN FARRIOR of Montgomery County
SAMUEL PARKER of Robertson County   page 26*
Farrior conveys land on both sides of Yallow Creek about the Chickasaw
Trace; mentions Daniel Williams' line.
Made 14 Oct. 1803   Registered 15 Jan. 1805
Witnesses, Charles Teas, John Holland, Bailey Hooper

JAMES ROBERTSON of Davidson County
THOMAS BATTSON of Davidson County   page 27
Robertson conveys land which had been conveyed to Robertson by Henry D.
Downs, land on Barton's Creek.
Made 17 Aug. 1804   Registered 16 Jan. 1805
Witnesses, Isaac Roberts, Solomon Ives

DANIEL ROSS of Davidson County
MONTGOMERY BELL of Dickson County   page 28
Ross conveys 520 acres on Barton's Creek, known by the name of "Barton's
premtion"; mentions Henry Downs northeast corner.
Made 26 Sept. 1804   Registered 22 Jan. 1805

JAMES ROBERTSON of Davidson County
SAMUEL WALKER of Montgomery County   page 29**
Robertson conveys to Walker land on the "iron cu fork" of Barton's
Creek near a spring near Walker's house.
Made 2 Nov. 1797   Registered 23 Jan. 1805

HEZEKIAH BARR of Dickson County
AARON JAMES of Dickson County   page 30
James gets land on Yallow Creek, part of a tract originally granted to
David Willson.
Made 12 March 1804   Registered 24 Jan. 1805
Witnesses, William Doack, Hugh Dickson

JOHN GRAY BLOUNT of Beauford County, NC
GEORGE CLARK of Dickson County   page 31
Blount conveys 640 acres to Clark
Made 24 July 1804   Registered 24 Jan. 1805
Witnesses, George Bell, John Larkin

---

*The Daniel Williams property is very easy to identify in 1982 as he is
 buried in a small cemetery beside the Yellow Creek Road.

**First mention of house and someone living in it in Dickson County!

JOHN MATCHETT of Duplin County, NC
JOEL HOBBS of Montgomery County　　　　　　　　page 32
Matchett conveys land in Montgomery County on the eastern branch of
Barton's Creek.
Made 12 March 1803　　　　　　　　　　　　Registered 25 Jan. 1805
Witnesses, R. C. Napier, Thomas Napier

JOEL HOBBS of Dickson County
JOHN GRIMES of Williamson County　　　　　　　page 33
Hobbs conveys to Grimes land on eastern branch of Barton's Creek.
Mentions James Dickson's corner.
Made 3 Sept. 1804　　　　　　　　　　　　Registered 25 Jan. 1805
Witnesses, R. C. Napier, James Davis

WILLIAM RUSSELL of Dickson County
BENJAMIN JOSLIN of Davidson County　　　　　　page 34
Russell conveys to Joslin land on the middle fork of Jones Creek; mentions Abraham Robinson's northwest corner.
Made 20 June 1804　　　　　　　　　　　　Registered 12 Mar. 1805
Witnesses, Jas. Martin, Joseph Linn

BENJAMIN JOSLIN of Davidson County
JOSEPH LINN of Dickson County　　　　　　　　page 35
Joslin conveys to Linn 100 acres.
Made 20 June 1804　　　　　　　　　　　　Registered 15 March 1805

JOHN CHILDRESS and wife ELIZABETH
ROBERT DRAKE of Dickson County　　　　　　　　page 36*
Robert Drake gets land on the east waters of Pine River of Duck River
from John Childress and wife Elizabeth Childress, formerly Elizabeth
Robertson; land is east of mouth of Spring Creek and was granted by
North Carolina in 1793 to Childress; mentions northeast corner of
Joshua Hadley. She signed her name as Betsy Childress.
Made 15 June 1804　　　　　　　　　　　　Registered 4 April 1805
Witnesses, Joseph Colman, J. A. Parker

CAPT. ROBERT BELL of Hillsborough, NC
JOHN BECK of Fayetteville, NC　　　　　　　　page 37
Bell conveys to Beck land on Jones Creek and Big Harpeth that was granted to Bell by North Carolina. Plat of land is drawn on page 39.
Made 21 July 1804　　　　　　　　　　　　Registered 4 June 1805
Witnesses, Colin Shaw, John E. Beck, Sam Goodwin, Cumberland Co., NC

WILLIAM CONNELL
WILLIAM P. ANDERSON　　　　　　　　　　　　page 40
Anderson gets 640 acres from William Connell, collector for the district;
Anderson was highest bidder for land on the first large fork on the west
side of Yellow Creek; mentions Middleton's boundary line.
Made 20 Jan. 1804　　　　　　　　　　　　Registered 22 June 1805
Witnesses, Robert Nelson, Joseph Robinson

STATE OF NORTH CAROLINA
WILLIAM RYAL　　　　　　　　　　　　　　　page 42
North Carolina granted 640 acres to William Ryal for signal bravery in
continental line; land in Davidson County on south side of Big Harpeth,
including the mouth of the sulphur fork of Jones Creek; mentions
Raiford Crumpler's northeast corner in Duncan Stewart's boundary line,
surveyed in 1795.
Made 6 June 1796　　　　　　　　　　　　Registered 29 June 1805

JASON THOMPSON of Davidson County
ELIZABETH EVANS of Davidson County　　　　　　page 43
Elizabeth Evans gets 150 acres on west fork of Jones Creek from Jason
Thompson of Davidson County; a dry branch is mentioned.
Made 1 Nov. 1804　　　　　　　　　　　　Registered 29 June 1805

---

*This land apparently is in Hickman County today. Hickman County was
 formed 1807 from part of Dickson County.

REP (or RESS) BREWER of Robertson County
STARLING BREWER of Robertson County   page 43
Starling Brewer gets negro Sam, age 20, for $400 from Rep Brewer.
Made 9 Oct. 1802   Registered 15 March 1805
Witness, Christian T. Easton

DAVID ROSS of Dickson County
LEMUAL HARVEY of Montgomery County   page 44
David (or Daniel) Ross gets land on the south fork of the east fork of
Yallow Creek from Harvey.
Made 15 March 1805   Registered 6 June 1805
Witness, Stephen Murphrey

JOHN LARKINS, SR., of Dickson County
JOHN LARKINS, JR.,   page 45
John Larkins, Sr., conveys to John Larkins, Jr., 250 acres on Joneses
Creek. Another entry on page 46 for 250 acres with James Douglass
as witness, made 18 March 1805.
Made 18 March 1805   Registered 6 July 1805

JOSEPH ERWIN of Davidson County
THOMAS RIGHT and THOMAS MARTIN of Dickson Co.   page 47
Right and Martin get 250 acres from Erwin; land was granted by North
Carolina to John Larkin, begins at a white oak on the Chickasaw Trace.
Made 28 Jan. 1805   Registered 7 Aug. 1805
Witnesses, William Miller and John Nichols

JAMES ROBERTSON of Davidson County
WILLIAM MILLER of Davidson County   page 48
Miller gets land on west fork of Jones Creek from Robertson; mentions
Thomas Thompson's south boundary line.
Made 13 July 1804   Registered 7 Aug. 1805
Witnesses, William Millar, Junr., Isaac Patton

WILLIAM CONNELL
JAMES DOUGLASS   page 49
James Douglass, assignee of Daniel Ross, gets land from William Connell,
collector for the district; land was sold for 1799 taxes; mentions the
old corner of Thomas McQuiston and the dwelling houses.
Made 6 Nov. 1804   Registered 22 Aug. 1805
Witnesses, Charlotte Connell, R. Weakley

HAYDON WELLS and LEM HARVEY of Montgomery County
JOHN H. BURTON of Dickson County   page 51*
Burton of Dickson County gets 50 acres from Haydon Wells and Lem Harvey.
Made 8 May 1805   Registered 2 Nov. 1805
Witness, John Clift.

MARTIN ARMSTRONG OF Davidson County
JOHN LANGHAM of Davidson County   page 52
Langham gets 235 acres from Martin Armstrong, land in Montgomery County
on both sides of Harpeth River beginning at John Court's west boundary.
Made 24 Jan. 1805   Registered 23 Nov. 1805
Witnesses, Wm. German, Nathaniel McCrearey

WILLIAM GIFFIN of Dickson County
JOHN BROWN of Dickson County   page 53
Giffin conveys to Brown 100 acres on Barton's Creek; land was conveyed
to Giffin from James Robertson.
Made 17 June 1805   Registered 7 Dec. 1805

WILLIAM RUSSELL
ABRAHAM ROBERTSON   page 53
Russell conveys 75 acres to Robertson.
Made 3 Sept. 1805   Registered 7 Dec. 1805
Witness, George Horner

---

*John H. Burton of this entry is John Halliburton, brother of Martin
 Halliburton who was an ancestor of compiler. Name often given Burton.

DANIEL HYLTON of Smith County, Tenn.
WILLIAM P. ANDERSON of Davidson Co., Tenn.   page 54
Hylton conveys to Anderson 250 acres at head of Guice's Creek and on
Winters (or Werters) Branch of Yellow Creek; mentions the west corner
of Robert Searcy and George Walker's line.
Made 15 Nov. 1804   Registered 14 Dec. 1805
Witnesses, Tho. Crutcher, Robert Searcy
(Note: This land would be in Houston County today.)

THOMAS POLK   page 55
Polk, colonel in the North Carolina line gets land on Defeated Camp
Creek of Duck River on the side above the mouth of Pine River; mentions
Daniel Shaw's northeast corner and Allen Walker's line; surveyed
20 Dec. 1792.
Made 26 Dec. 1793   Registered 14 Dec. 1805
(Note: This land is in Hickman County today and will also be found
mentioned in Hickman County deed books. A plat of this land is also
found on page 56.)

GULLY MOORE et al
THOMAS HILL of Dickson County   page 57
Thomas Hill of Dickson County gets 50 acres from Gully Moore, Abner
Harris, executors, and Fanny Moore, executrix, of Jo. McCorkle, de-
ceased, land on Harpeth River; mentions Blount Whitmill's south bound-
ary line and Claudius David's southeast corner.
Made 2 March 1805   Registered 4 Dec. 1805
Witnesses, Stephen Corban, William Corban

THOMAS HAMBLETON of Guilford County, NC
ROBERT WEAKLEY, Davidson County   page 58
Hambleton conveys land on south side of Cumberland River on both sides
of Yellow Creek, two miles above the camp on the creek where Russell
Gower, Andrew (Anderson?) Lucas and James Russell hunted in 1784; land
was granted to Hambelton by State of North Carolina in 1790.
Made 13 Oct. 1800   Registered 28 Dec. 1805
Witness, William Tait

JOHN NICHOLS of Davidson County
ROBERT WEAKLEY of Davidson County   page 60
Nichols conveys to Weakley 640 acres in Montgomery County on Weakley's
Creek, a west fork of Barton's Creek; this land was a military warrant
to heirs of Isaac Hutson.
Made 25 May 1802   Registered 28 Dec. 1805
Witnesses, R. Searcy, R. M. McGavock

SAMUEL HOGG and JOHN B. HOGG
ROBERT WEAKLEY   page 62
Samuel Hogg and John B. Hogg, legatees of Thomas Hogg, deceased, con-
vey 174 acres in Dixon County (formerly Tennessee County) to Robert
Weakley; land was devised by Thomas Hogg at his death to his brother
Samuel Hogg; land on both sides of Yellow Creek; mentions Thomas
Hamilton's southeast corner.
Made 21 Nov. 1805   Registered 28 Dec. 1805
Witnesses, Thos. Mitchell, Thos. Talbot

THOMAS PENEL of Dickson County
PETER GOODWIN of Dickson County   page 64
Penel conveys land on Jones Creek to Goodwin; mentions the west side of
James Benell.
Made 23 Feb. 1805   Registered 28 Dec. 1805

WILLIAM PATERSON ANDERSON of Davidson County
ADAM WILSON of Dickson County   page 65
Anderson conveys to Wilson 320 acres of land on both sides of old Town
fork of Yellow Creek, including the farm and houses now in use and
occupancy of said Willson. Land was granted to William Allen and con-
veyed to James Brown and by Brown to Anderson.
Made 20 Nov. 1804   Registered 28 Dec. 1805
Witnesses, Thomas Carns, John Lewis

WILLIAM P. ANDERSON of Davidson County
THOMAS CARNS of Dickson County   page 66
Anderson conveys to Carns 320 acres on both sides of old Town fork of
Yellow Creek, part of 640 acres granted William Allen by North Carolina.
Made 20 Nov. 1804   Registered 28 Dec. 1805
Witness, John Lewis

STARLING BREWER of Dickson County
DANIEL ROSS of Davidson County   page 67
Brewer conveys land on south bank of Harpeth River to Ross; mentions
Henry Highland's northeast corner. Land was originally granted to
Thomas Moloy, assignee of Joseph Board (?).
Made 25 July 1804   Registered 28 Dec. 1805
Witnesses, Burgess Harris, Charles Parker

WILLIAM STONE of Robertson County
MOSES SMITH of Robertson County   page 68
Stone conveys 136 acres to Smith on west fork of Jones Creek.
Made 31 Jan. 1803   Registered 28 Dec. 1805
Witnesses, R. C. Napier, Bartholomew Smith

NATHAN NESBITT
JEREMIAH NESBITT of Dickson County   page 69
Nathan Nesbitt conveys to Jeremiah Nesbitt land on both sides of main
Yellow Creek, originally granted to James Dickson and conveyed by him
to Nathan Nesbitt in 1802.
Made 29 July 1805   Registered 24 Feb. 1806
Witness, S. Hasley

NATHAN NESBITT of Dickson County
JOHN TURNER   page 70
Nathan Nesbitt conveys to Turner land on both sides of main Yellow
Creek, originally granted to James Dickson and deed 1802 to Nathan
Nesbitt; mentions Teases north boundary line.
Made 12 Aug. 1805   Registered 24 Feb. 1806
Witnesses, William Teas, James Teas, Charles Teas

JAMES DICKSON of Duplin Co., NC
NATHAN NESBITT of Montgomery County   page 71
Dickson conveys land to Nesbitt on both sides of Yellow Creek; mentions
Teas's north boundary line.
Made 16 Dec. 1802   Registered 24 Feb. 1806
Witnesses, Ed McGowen, Michael Dickson, John McGowen

JOHN LOWE and JOHN WARD of Robertson County
ISAAC WALKER of Montgomery County   page 72
Lowe and Ward convey to Walker land on west fork of Jones Creek, part
of land granted Robert Bell by State of North Carolina; mentions Charles
Walker's northeast corner.
Made 12 Dec. 1803   Registered 24 Feb. 1806
Witnesses, Charles Walker, Jeremiah Walker

THOMAS BOLES of Dickson County
SAMUEL ELIOT of Wilson County   page 73
Boles (also found as Bowls) conveys land to Eliot on west side of
Yellow Creek; land was conveyed by Col. Duncan Stewart, by his power of
attorney, to Robert Dunning and from Dunning to Boles.
Made 22 Aug. 1805   Registered 24 Feb. 1806
Witnesses, Preston Nooner, Starling Dillehay, John Humphries

BENNET SEARCY of Davidson County
PATRICK LYON of Davidson County   page 74
Searcy conveys land on south side of Cumberland River including the
mouth of Johnsons Creek about 4 miles below mouth of Harpeth River;
originally conveyed by heirs of John Rice to Bennet Searcy in 1796.
Made 3 June 1805   Registered 24 Feb. 1806
Witness, John Dickinson

JOHN TURNER of Dickson County
NATHAN NESBITT of Dickson County   page 75
John Turner conveys to Nathan Nesbitt a negro man named Bill, age 22 on September 22 next. Turner describes the negro as "born and raised mine".
Made 4 August 1805   Registered 24 Feb. 1806
Witnesses, William Teas, Charles Teas, James Teas
(Note: The phrase "born and raised mine" meant the slave had been born into Turner's ownership and had not been purchased from another.)

JOHN JONES of Montgomery County
GEORGE TEAL, SR.   page 76
Jones conveys 160 acres to Teal on headwaters of Johnston's Creek, this being 1/4 part of tract granted to Charles Stuart by State of North Carolina in 1797.
Made 25 Oct. 1805   Registered 24 Mar. 1806
Witnesses, Jesse S. Ross, Robert Wright, William B. Ross

JOHN LARKINS, JR.
DAVID McADOW   page 77
Larkins conveys to McAdow land on four mile branch of Joneses Creek; mentions the south boundary line on which John Larkins now lives; a large hollow which leads out from the low ground; the east side of branch of four-mile on which David McAdow lives; mentions the tract granted by North Carolina to John Larkins, Sr.
Made 17 Dec. 1805   Registered 20 Apr. 1806

DANIEL HYLTON of Smith County
JOSEPH McKEEN (McKain) of Nashville
Hylton conveys to McKeen land on western waters of Yellow Creek, part of Hylton's 2560 grant as heir of his deceased father William Hylton; mentions George Walker's line.
Made 16 Nov. 1804   Registered 20 Apr. 1806
Witnesses, Alexr. Cragehead, Robert Searcy

JAMES ROBERTSON of Davidson County
ELIZABETH WALKER of Dickson County   page 79
Robertson conveys to Elizabeth Walker, widow of Vann Walker, 97½ acres; mentions Elizabeth Walker's spring.
Made 5 April 1805   Registered 20 Apr. 1806
Witnesses, James Gilaspie, John Paxton

SAMUEL WALKER
ELIZABETH WALKER of Dickson County   page 80
Samuel Walker conveys to Elizabeth Walker 5-3/4 acres on Barton's Creek mentions Elizabeth Walker's spring.
Made 6 April 1805   Registered 20 Apr. 1806
Witnesses, Jesse S. Ross, Simeon Walker

ELISHA ROBERTS of Warren County, KY
JOHN NESBITT of Dickson County   page 81
Roberts conveys to Nesbitt a negro Harry, age 18.
Made 18 Dec. 1805   Registered 20 May 1806
Witness, William Moore, Thomas Choat

SAMUEL ELIOT of Willson County
WILLIAM MOORE of Dickson County   page 81
Eliot conveys land to Moore "my interest in 100 acres".
Made 24 July 1805   Registered 20 May 1806
Witnesses, William Teas, James Teas

STEPHEN MURPHEY of Dickson County
JOHN HALL of Dickson County   page 82
Murphey conveys 100 acres on the south fork of the east fork of Yellow Creek.
Made 12 Dec. 1805   Registered 1 July 1806
Witnesses, John Snider, Sary (x--her mark) Clift

JOSEPH ERWIN of Davidson County
JAMES MARTIN of Dickson County   page 83
Erwin conveys 250 acres on west fork of Jones Creek, part of the John
Larkins grant.
Made 21 Nov. 1805   Registered 1 July 1806
Witnesses, John Hugh McNeilly, Robert McNairy

CHARLES JOHNSON of Dickson County
JAMES WHITE of Dickson County   page 84
Johnson conveys 100 acres on waters of Yellow Creek, mentions Johnson's
line.
Made 3 Jan. 1806   Registered 2 July 1806
Witnesses, Hardy Valentine, Benjamin Valentine

JAMES ROBERTSON of Davidson County
JAMES WALKER of Montgomery County   page 85
Robertson conveys 140 acres on Barton's Creek to Walker; mentions
Jonathan F. Robertson's and John Davises south boundary.
Made 16 Nov. 1802   Registered 2 July 1806

JOHN McCLISH of Dickson County
HENRY GRIMES of Dickson County   page 86
McClish conveys to Grimes land on Barton's Creek, joins Nathl Johnston
and Peter Renfroe.
Made 22 Feb. 1806   Registered 25 Sept. 1806
Witnesses, E. C. Napier, Peter Renfro

R. C. NAPIER of Dickson County
WILLIAM WARD of Dickson County
Napier conveys land on Barton's Creek to Ward.   page 87
Made 6 Dec. 1805   Registered 25 Sept. 1806
Witnesses, Robert Drake, James M. Ross

JAMES ROBERTSON of Davidson County
ADAM WILSON of Dickson County   page 89
Robertson conveys to Wilson land on both sides of Piney River; mentions
James Wyat's southwest corner, crosses the river and mentions Elijah
Robertson's northwest corner.
Made 21 Feb. 1806   Registered 25 Sept. 1806
Witnesses, John Davidson, Joseph Wood
Page 90 - Another conveyance for 640 acres on both sides of Piney River
including the mouth of Beaver Creek.
Made 20 Aug. 1805   Registered 26 Sept. 1806
Witnesses, R. C. Napier, Benjamin Wilson

JOSEPH GREER of Knox County
ADAM WILLSON of Dickson County   page 91
Greer conveys 640 acres on Pine River.
Made 4 Feb. 1806   Registered 26 Sept. 1806
Witnesses, Joseph Brown, James Willson

WILLIAM COLLINS of Knox County
WILLIAM BETTS of Davidson County   page 92
Collins conveys 640 acres in Montgomery County on south side of Cumber-
land River.
Made 2 Nov. 1802   Registered 26 Sept. 1806
Witnesses, Thomas Rose, John Mann

JOSEPH LIN of Dickson County
BENJAMIN BAKER of Dickson County   page 93
Lin conveys 100 acres.
Made 16 Aug. 1805   Registered 2 Oct. 1806
Witnesses, John Larkins, Jas. Martin

THOMAS BOLES of Dickson County
SAMUEL ELLIOT of Willson County   page 94
Boles conveys part of grant from North Carolina to John and Morgan
Drewry.
Made 20 Feb. 1806   Registered 2 Oct. 1806

Witnesses, William Teas, James Teas.

JOHN ROSS of Dickson County   page 95
John Ross of Dickson County conveys "to my son Jesse S. Ross" a negro woman and two boys.
Made 27 Feb. 1806   Registered 2 Oct. 1806
Witnesses, James M. Ross, George Ross

JOHN BURGAN of Dickson County
JOSEPH CALDWELL of Davidson County   page 96
Burgan conveys land on Barton's Creek; mentions Jacob Mers' corner.
Made 17 Oct. 1805   Registered 2 Oct. 1806
Witnesses, R. C. Napier, Charles Teas

STATE OF NORTH CAROLINA
NEHEMIAH PERRY   page 97
State of North Carolina grants land on the sulphur fork of Jones Creek to Nehemiah Perry, a fifer in the continental line. Land was assigned to Benjamin Fitz Randolph and mentions Benjamin Thomas' northwest corner.
Registered 5 Jan. 1807

STATE OF NORTH CAROLINA
JAMES NICHOLSON   page 98
State of North Carolina on 11 Nov. 1791 grants to James Nicholson, private, for his signal bravery on the continental line land on both sides of Barton's Creek; land was assigned to William Cochran. Land was registered in Montgomery County deeds also. Land at the time of the grant was in the "Territory of the United States of America South of the River Ohio, Tennessee County".
Registered 5 Jan. 1807

STATE OF NORTH CAROLINA
PETER JORDAN   page 99
State of North Carolina granted land to Peter Jordan, private in the continental line, on the upper fork of Barton's Creek; land was located in 1790; grant was made 30 Nov. 1790.
Registered 5 Jan. 1807

STATE OF NORTH CAROLINA
WILLIAM COCHRAN   page 100
State of North Carolina granted land to William Cochran, assignee of Allen Murdock, who was a private in the continental line 30 Nov. 1793. Land was on the upper fork of Barton's Creek.
Registered 5 Jan. 1807

STATE OF NORTH CAROLINA
JOHN HERLY   page 101
State of North Carolina granted land to John Herly, private in the continental line, on 30 May 1793, land was on a small branch on west side of west fork of Jones Creek.
Registered 26 Jan. 1807

WILLIAM KILLINGSWORTH of Halifax Co., NC
ROBERT WEAKLEY of Davidson County   page 101
William Killingsworth and his wife ___ Killingsworth, relict and legatee of Thomas Hogg, deceased, of Halifax County, North Carolina, convey land on both sides of Yellow Creek; Thomas Hogg deeded to his brother Samuel Hogg. Other legatees of Thomas Hogg were Samuel Hogg and John Baptist Hogg, sons of the deceased. Mentions Thomas Hambleton's southeast corner.
Made 20 Feb. 1806   Registered 27 Jan. 1807

HENRY FREELING of Roan Co., NC
JOHN PARKER of Dickson County   page 103
Freeling conveys land on Turnbull Creek; John Davis of Davidson County is "my lawful attorney".
Made 19 August 1806   Registered 27 May 1807

ALEXR. GREER of Carter County, Tenn.
ADAM WILLSON of Dickson County   page 104
Greer conveys to Willson 640 acres on both sides of Pine River.
Made 10 Feb. 1806   Registered 10 Mar. 1807
Witnesses, Thomas Talbot, John L. Talbot, Alexr. White, Joseph Greer,
W. Morow (?)

ADAM WILLSON, SENR., of Dickson County
JOHN WILLSON of Dickson County   page 105
Adam Willson, Senr., conveys to John Willson 100 acres on the west
side of Piney River; mentions James Wyet's southwest corner.
Made 23 Aug. 1806   Registered 10 March 1807
Witnesses, John Willson, William Willson, Ben Willson

ADAM WILLSON, SENR., of Dickson County
JOSEPH WILLSON of Dickson County   page 106
Adam Willson, Senr., conveys land on both sides of Piney River.
Made 23 Aug. 1806   Registered 10 March 1807
Witnesses, William Willson, Ben Willson

ADAM WILLSON, SENR., of Dickson County
JAMES WILLSON of Dickson County   page 107
Adam Wilson, Senr., conveys land to James Wilson on the east side of
Piney River.
Recorded 11 March 1807
Witnesses, William Willson, Benjamin Willson
(Note: Surname spelled both Wilson and Willson in these entries.)

JOHN MORRISETT and ABRAHAM ROBERTSON of Dickson County
BENJAMIN BAKER of Dickson County   page 108
Morrisett and Robertson convey 39 acres; mentions George Russell's
boundary line; Joslin's west boundary line; and the line between Willi-
am and George Russell.
Made 11 Aug. 1806   Recorded 11 Mar. 1807
Witnesses, Burgess Harris, William Morisett

JOHN LARKIN, JR., of Dickson County
ABSOLUM BAKER, JR., of Dickson County   page 109
Conveys land, mentions the original corner of John Larkins, Senr.,
grant.
Made 16 March 1806   Registered 11 Mar. 1807
Witnesses, John H. Stone, Polly (x--her mark) McKee

LEWIS RUSSEL of Dickson County
BENJAMIN JOSLIN of Davidson County   page 110
Russel conveys 100 acres to Joslin, part of tract granted to Charles
Stewart in 1796 where courthouse is now building, which is known by
CHARLOTTESVILLE by patent bearing date 6 June 1796 thereunto belonging
to my wife appertaining the said Benjamin Joslin.
Made 2 Sept. 1806   Registered 11 Mar. 1807
Witnesses, Jesse S. Ross, John Joslin

STATE OF NORTH CAROLINA
BENJAMIN MESSER   page 111
State of North Carolina grants 274 acres to Benjamin Messer, private
in the North Carolina line, land was on both sides of Piney River and
was assigned to Aaron Lambert.
Granted 1796

STATE OF NORTH CAROLINA
ARCHIBALD DAVIS   page 112
State of North Carolina grants 574 acres in 1796 to Archibald Davis,
private in North Carolina, land on both sides of Piney River.

STATE OF NORTH CAROLINA
BENJAMIN LUCAS   pages 113, 114
State of North Carolina grants 640 acres on Yellow Creek to Benjamin
Lucas, a private in North Carolina line on 16 Nov. 1790. Mentions
Mill Ramsey's southwest corner and assigned to Thomas Hogg.

JOSEPH TEAS of Dickson County
WILLIAM TEAS of Dickson County   page 114
Joseph Teas conveys to William Teas all claim to negroes "belonging to
the estate of my father Charles Teas, deceased". Several of the slaves
are named.
Made 9 Nov. 1806   Registered 8 April 1807
Witnesses, Thomas Gray, Robert Norris, Matthew Gilmore

STATE OF NORTH CAROLINA
TITUS WOOD   page 115
State of North Carolina grants 640 acres to heirs of Titus Wood and as-
signed to Elijah Robertson; land on both sides of Piney River.
Made 16 cec. 1791   Registered 27 April 1807

STATE OF NORTH CAROLINA
JOHN GAMBIER SCULL   page 116
State of North Carolina grants 1027 acres to John Gambier Scull.
Made 15 Dec. 1791   Registered 28 April 1807

STATE OF NORTH CAROLINA
GEORGE NORRIS   page 117
State of North Carolina grants land to George Norris, private in North
Carolina line, land assigned to Thomas Hogg; land on both sides of
Yellow Creek.
Made 16 Nov. 1790   Registered 28 April 1807

STATE OF NORTH CAROLINA
JOHN GUNN   page 118
State of North Carolina grants 1000 acres to John Gunn, private in
North Carolina line, land on west fork of Yellow Creek, mentions Samuel
Middleton's line and land is assigned to George Walker.
Registered 28 April 1807

STATE OF NORTH CAROLINA
RICHARD LEWIS   page 120
State of North Carolina grants 640 acres to Richard Lewis, private, land
on the sulphur fork of Jones Creek, land assigned to Charles Stewart;
mentions the northwest corner of Benjamin Thomas and northwest corner
of Duncan Stewart. Lewis was private in North Carolina line.
Made 26 June 1796   Registered 29 Apr. 1807

STATE OF NORTH CAROLINA
ROBERT MANN   page 119
State of North Carolina grants 640 acres on both sides of Yellow Creek
to Robert Mann, private in the North Carolina line; land was assigned to
Thomas Hogg.
Made 26 June 1796   Registered 29 Apr. 1807

STATE OF NORTH CAROLINA
GEORGE HOOK   page 121
State of North Carolina granted land to George Hook, private in North
Carolina line, land on east fork of Barton's Creek, about one mile below
the lower meat house made by Deason and Williams.
Made 20 May 1793

JOHN B. CHEATHAM, sheriff of Robertson County
RICHARD NAPIER of Dickson County   page 122
Cheatham, sheriff of Robertson County conveys 274 acres to Napier;
George Hook is reputed owner of land and land will be sold for non-
payment of taxes for 1803; land on east fork of Barton's Creek.
Made 14 April 1806
Witnesses, Thomas Johnson, E. W. Napier, George Lamb

RICHARD C. NAPIER
ELIAS NAPIER of Dickson County   page 124
Richard C. Napier conveys to Elias Napier 274 acres on the east fork of
Barton's Creek, being tract granted to George Hooks.
Made 16 April 1806   Registered 13 May 1807
Witnesses, George Lamb, Thomas Napier.
Another conveyance on page 126 has another entry from John B. Cheatham

for 96 acres to Richard Napier of Dickson County. Land was sold for
1803 taxes and John Dickson was the reputed owner.
Made 15 April 1805   Registered 13 May 1807

STATE OF NORTH CAROLINA
ROBERT GURTE   page 128
State of North Carolina to Robert Gurte, private in the North Carolina
line for 640 acres; Thomas Person was assignee of the land; land on
west bank of Pine River and mentions Joshua Hadley's northwest corner.
(Note: His name also spelled Robert Girt in same deed.)
Made 29 March 1794   Registered 25 June 1807

STATE OF NORTH CAROLINA
MARTIN ARMSTRONG   page 129
State of North Carolina to Martin Armstrong 10,000 acres on Robertson's
Creek of Duck River; mentioned a white oak on the old Indian trace
leading from Nashville to Tennessee River about 1 mile from Duck
River.
Made 7 May 1788   Registered 23 May 1807

STATE OF NORTH CAROLINA
JAMES MIDDLETON   page 130
State of North Carolina to James Middleton, heir at law of Samuel
Middleton, deceased, who was sergeant in North Carolina line; land on
both sides of Yellow Creek.
Made 20 May 1793   Registered 26 May 1807

STATE OF NORTH CAROLINA
DOCTOR HUGH WILLIAMSON   page 131
State of North Carolina grants land to Doctor Hugh Williamson, surgeon
in North Carolina line, land on east fork of Barton's Creek, 4,800
acres.
Made 27 April 1793   Registered 26 May 1807

STATE OF NORTH CAROLINA
ROBERT LANIER   page 132
State of North Carolina grants 640 acres to Robert Lanier, who paid for
it in pounds; land was "on Tennessee River six miles below where the
southernmost line of state strikes the river including Con Bluff".
Land was surveyed by Thomas Hickman.
Made 8 June 1797   Registered 26 May 1807

STATE OF NORTH CAROLINA
JOHN HARE   page 133
State of North Carolina grants 640 acres on Pine River to John Hare,
private in North Carolina line; mentions Aaron Lambert's line.
Made 20 Dec. 1792   Registered 26 May 1807

STATE OF NORTH CAROLINA
DANIEL MOTT   page 134
State of North Carolina granted land to Daniel Mott, private in North
Carolina line on 4 Jan. 1792; Edward Dickson was the assignee of Mott's
heirs; land is on south side of Cumberland River on both sides of Chick-
asaw Trace and the first east fork of Yellow Creek; mentions Daniel
William's line.
Registered 28 May 1807

STATE OF NORTH CAROLINA
LOTT WATSON   page 135
State of North Carolina granted land, 640 acres, to Lott Watson, private
in North Carolina line, land on Jones Creek, Davidson County, and assig-
ned to Benjamin Herndon.
Made 20 May 1793   Registered 26 May 1807

STATE OF NORTH CAROLINA
JAMES FAFAN   page 136
State of North Carolina granted 274 acres to James Fafan, private in
North Carolina line, land on largest west fork of Yellow Creek of about
the Chickasaw Trace; land was assigned to Joseph Kemp.
Made 14 Sept. 1797   Registered 26 May 1807

STATE OF NORTH CAROLINA
EPHRAIM BRADSHAW   page 137
State of North Carolina granted 640 acres to Ephraim Bradshaw, private
in North Carolina line, land on headwaters of Johnston's Creek, mentions the south corner of Dr. Hugh Williamson; land was assigned to
Charles Stewart.
Made 14 Sept. 1797   Registered 26 May 1807

STATE OF NORTH CAROLINA
MARTIN BLACK   page 138
State of North Carolina granted 274 acres to Martin Black, private in
North Carolina line, land on the largest west fork of Yellow Creek that
puts in about the Chickasaw Trace; land was assigned to George Ward;
land was surveyed 12 Aug. 1797 by D. Stuart, Charles Stewart, John
Simpson.
Made 4 Sept. 1797   Registered 26 May 1807

STATE OF NORTH CAROLINA
ISAAC RALSTON   page 139
State of North Carolina granted 1240 acres to Isaac Ralston, a lieutenant in continental line; William Blount was assignee of Isaac Ralston;
land was on north side of Tennessee River on Marks Creek.
Made 14 March 1786   Registered 26 May 1807
(Note: This land is now in Humphreys County.)

STATE OF NORTH CAROLINA
WILLIAM CAPPS   page 139
State of North Carolina granted 640 acres to William Capps, who served
in North Carolina line; land on east side of Tennessee River below
Marks Creek; assigned to John Gray Blount and Thomas Blount.
Made 14 March 1786   Registered 26 May 1807

STATE OF NORTH CAROLINA
WILLIAM SMITH   page 140
State of North Carolina granted 640 acres to William Smith, private in
North Carolina line; land was assigned to John Allen; land in Davidson
County on east fork of Buffalow Creek running into the Tennessee River
on the north side.
Made 7 March 1786   Registered 26 May 1807

STATE OF NORTH CAROLINA
THOMAS TAUNT   page 140
State of North Carolina granted 640 acres to Thomas Taunt, land in
Davidson County on Blount's Creek of Tennessee River; mentions Henry
Johnson's corner.
Made 7 March 1786   Registered 26 May 1807

STATE OF NORTH CAROLINA
THOMAS BLOUNT   page 141
State of North Carolina granted 274 acres to Thomas Blount, late a soldier of North Carolina, for his services, and he deeded this to John
Gray and Thomas Blount of Beaufort County, North Carolina.

DANIEL HICKS
LEWIS HICKS   page 144
Daniel Hicks conveys land to Lewis Hicks; land is in Tennessee County
on the southeast fork of Barton's Creek.
Made 13 May 1799   Registered 27 May 1807
Witness, Abner Hicks

JOSEPH HADDER   page 145
Joseph Hadder received military warrant for 640 acres; land was
assigned to William Caswell, 27 May 1807. (Note: This transaction needs
to be rechecked by those interested in these people.)

ISAM MATTHEWS
THOMAS MATHEWS   page 146
Isam Matthews conveys to Thomas Mathews of Dickson County; Isam Matthews
was of Montgomery County; conveys filey colt, 24 Jan. 1807.

STATE OF NORTH CAROLINA
WILLIAM TEMPLE   page 147
State of North Carolina grants 1900 acres to William Temple, colonel in
North Carolina line, land then assigned to John Johnston; land on east
fork of Pine River including a spring creek.
Made 20 Dec. 1791   Registered 7 May 1807

STATE OF NORTH CAROLINA
ANDREW ROWELL   page 148
State of North Carolina grants 640 acres to Andrew Rowell, private in
North Carolina line; land assigned to John Johnston; land was on the
east fork of Pine River.
Made 20 Dec. 1791   Registered ____

R. C. NAPIER of Dickson County
JACOB W. MILLER of Dickson County   page 149
Napier conveys to Miller land on Barton's Creek.
Made 3 Oct. 1806   Registered 27 May 1807
Witnesses, Rogal Ferguson, ___Hamilton

STATE OF NORTH CAROLINA
JOHN KING   page 150
State of North Carolina granted 457 acres to John King on east fork of
Duck River, Lick Branch, Davidson County.
Made __March 1793   Registered 25 May 1807

STATE OF NORTH CAROLINA
ALLEN WALKER   page 150
State of North Carolina granted 1000 acres to Allen Walker, assignee of
William Walker, land on both sides of Duck River about 7 miles above
the mouth of Pine River; mentions southeast corner of Daniel Shaw.
Recorded 27 May 1807

JESSE CRAFT of Dickson County
GEORGE WEST of Montgomery County   page 151
Craft deeds 320 acres to West; land on main Yellow Creek, above a spring
and camp known by name of Samuel Martin's hunting camp. .
Made 6 June 1806   Registered 2 May 1807
Witnesses, W. Clements, Frederick Hyre

WILLIAM NORRIS of Dickson County
MICHAEL DICKSON of Dickson County   page 152
Norris conveys 440 acres to Dickson; land on both sides of Yellow Creek
about 3½ miles below the Chickasaw Trace; land was granted to John Glasgow.
Made 19 June 1804   Registered 28 May 1807
Witnesses, Nathan Nesbit, David Robinson

ARCHIBALD McMILLAN of Cumberland County, NC
MICHAEL DICKSON of Dickson County   page 153
McMillan deeds 1127 acres to Dickson; land on Blue Creek of Duck River;
granted by North Carolina to John Gambier Scull and by Scull to McMillan in April 1806.
Made Dec. 1806   Registered 29 May 1807
Witnesses, P. R. Booker, Henry Minor

STATE OF NORTH CAROLINA
DAVID SLOAN   page 154
State of North Carolina granted land to David Sloan, private in North
Carolina line; land on second large fork on west side of Yellow Creek
near a large spring; mentions John Nelson's northwest corner; land was
assigned to Joseph Grayham.
Made 10 May 1793   Recorded 20 May 1807

STATE OF NORTH CAROLINA
MOSES HEZEND   page 155
State of North Carolina granted 640 acres to Moses Hezend, private in
North Carolina line, land lying on Meat Camp on Barton's Creek; surveyed for Moses Hubard on 14 July 1784; mentions Robert Calahan's line.
Granted 15 Sept. 1787   Registered 28 May 1807

(Note: Name given as both Hezend and Hubard in this entry.)

STATE OF NORTH CAROLINA
FREDERICK BECK   page 157
State of North Carolina grants to Frederick Beck, sergeant in North Carolina line land on both sides of Duck River; mentions Matthew Brandon's corner; land was assigned to David Wootson.
Made 22 Feb. 1795   Registered 25 May 1807

STATE OF NORTH CAROLINA
JOSEPH DANIEL and GEORGE BROWN   page 158
State of North Carolina grants to Joseph Daniel and George Brown, heirs of James Brown, deceased, assignee of John Myers, private in continental line; land on Pine River of Duck River; mentions Aaron Lambert's line. (Note: This entry not clear in our notes; could be Joseph, Daniel and George Brown.)
Made 31 Dec. 1793   Registered 28 May 1807

EZEKIEL NORRIS, JR., of Dickson County
NATHAN RAGAN of Dickson County   page 158
Norris conveys to Ragan land on east side of Yellow Creek, mentions the "dividing line of the orphans land"; part of tract granted by North Carolina to William Davis.
Made 3 Dec. 1805   Registered 29 May 1807
Witnesses, John Humphries, Nathan Dillehay, John Maxwell

JOHN McCLISH of Dickson County
DAVID HOGAN of Dickson County   page 159
McClish conveys to Hogan a negro girl Becky, aged 11 to 12 years.
Made 9 April 1807   Registered 27 July 1807
Witnesses, John Nisbet, George Kyes

EZEKIEL NORRIS
WILLIAM NORRIS   page 160
Ezekiel Norris conveys 190 acres to William Norris, father of Ezekiel Norris, for love and affection for father; land on Yellow Creek including the mill and a place called the Picket place; mentions mouth of the dry bottom and Robert Norris's corner; part of grant to Colonel William Davis originally.
Made 20 Dec. 1805   Registered 29 May 1807
Witnesses, Robert Norris, John Maxwell, John Humphries

STATE OF NORTH CAROLINA
CHRISTOPHER FOLK   page 161
State of North Carolina grants 640 acres to Christopher Folk, private, on the upper fork of Barton's Creek, 3/4 mile from Barton's Meat Camp; James Robertson was assignee of Christopher Folk.
Made 7 March 1796   Registered 25 May 1807

JAMES ROBERTSON of Davidson County
WILLIAM GIFFIN of Robertson County   page 162
Robertson conveys to Giffin land on east fork of Barton's Creek; mentions Nathaniel Johnston's southwest corner.
Made 2 ___ 1802   Registered 30 May 1807

WILLIAM GIFFIN of Dickson County
SIMON HOLT of Dickson County   page 163
Giffin conveys 100 acres to Simon Holt; land on Barton's Creek; mentions Zachariah Walker's northeast corner.
Made 25 Oct. 1806   Registered 30 May 1807
Witnesses, Andrew Giffin, George Gallion

THOMAS McQUISTON, SR., of Guilford County, NC
CHARLES BARNES of Davidson County   page 164
McQuiston conveys to Barnes 320 acres on the lick fork of Jones Creek.
Made 23 Aug. 1797   Registered 31 May 1807
Witnesses, Benjamin McQuistian, John Erwin, John Blair

JOHN NICHOLS of Davidson County
ABRAM CALDWELL of Hawkins County   (continued)

Nichols conveys 400 acres to Caldwell; land on east fork of Barton's Creek.
Made 20 April 1805   Registered 27 July 1807
Witnesses, A. Campbell, Joseph Park

WILLIAM NELSON of Dickson County
ROBERT DRAKE of Dickson County   page 165
Nelson conveys Lot 26 in town of Charlotte to Robert Drake; 1/2 acre lot; bounded on west by West Street.
Made 24 March 1807   Registered 27 July 1807
Witnesses, David Dickson, Molton Dickson

JOHN LOCK of Dickson County
DAVID and MOLTON DICKSON of Dickson County   page 167
Lock conveys to David and Molton Dickson mares, colt, bull, pewter dishes, and other items.
Made 10 April 1807   Registered 29 July 1807

WILLIAM RICHARDSON DAVIE of Halifax Co., NC
JOHN McCAULEY   page 168
William Richardson Davie of Halifax Co., NC, conveys 1200 acres to John McCauley of "the village nigh university in Orange Co., NC," land on middle fork of Barton's Creek, commonly called the Indian fork.
Made 16 April 1804   Registered 29 July 1807
Witnesses, G. Henderson, James McCauley

JAMES ROBERTSON of Davidson County
ALEXANDER GRAY of Davidson County   page 169
Robertson conveys to Gray land on Duck River part of grant to one Oliver.
Made 5 July 1806   Registered 7 August 1807
Witnesses, Robert Weakley, R. Hewitt, Gillium Harris, Thomas Childress

THOMAS CRAWFORD of Dickson County
WILLIAM HALE   page 171
Crawford conveys to Hale "my occupancy piece of land" on Hitt(?) Creek, a fork of Piney River.
Made 2 July 1807   Registered 18 Aug. 1807
Witnesses, John Low, Robert Dean

JAMES McCANN
GARRETT LANE   page 171
McCann conveys to Lane "my occupant right" on Piney River adjoining the Wyatt tract.
Made 25 July 1807   Registered 18 Aug. 1807
Witnesses, John Low, Robert Dean

HARMON HENSLEY
JOHN SPENCER   page 172
Hensley conveys to Spencer 200 acres on the sulphur fork of Jones Creek.
Made 28 July 1807
Witnesses, Charles Barens, David Hughes

WILLIAM CASWELL of Lenoir Co., NC
JEREMIAH PEARSALL of Dickson County   page 173
Caswell conveys to Pearsall land on both sides of main Yellow Creek, crosses the creek three times; mentions Col. William Davis' south boundary line.
Made 18 June 1806   Registered 23 Sept. 1807
Witnesses, Michael Dickson, Joseph Dickson

PATRICK LYONS of Davidson County
DAVID McGRAW of Montgomery County   page 174
Lyons conveys to McGraw 274 acres of land on and including the mouth of Johnson Creek, about 4 miles below mouth of Harpeth River.
Made 22 Sept. 1806   Registered 24 Sept. 1807

LEMUEL HARVEY of Montgomery County
BENJAMIN ADAMS of Dickson County   page 175
Harvey conveys to Adams 41 acres on the south fork of the east fork of Yellow Creek.
Made 15 Feb. 1806   Registered 24 Sept. 1807
Witnesses, Jonathan Adenge, Peter Phillips, Alexr. Mitchell

THOMAS MARTIN of Dickson County
THOMAS WRIGHT of Dickson County
Martin conveys land on west fork of Jones Creek.
Made 3 Dec. 1806   Registered 26 Sept. 1807
Witnesses, W. Miller, Jr., John Spencer

DANIEL ROSS of Davidson County
JOHN McELROY of Davidson County   page 177
Ross conveys land to McElroy on east side of Harpeth River, paid by Thomas Napier in behalf of John McElroy, part of 640 premption of Thomas Holley, assignee of Joseph Baird's heirs.
Made 20 June 1806   Registered 26 Sept. 1807
Witnesses, Elias Napier, George Lamb

JOHN BECK of Davidson County
GEORGE ROSS of Dickson County   page 178
Beck conveys to Ross land on Joneses Creek, being part of grant to Robert Bell for military services.
Made 29 Jan. 1807
Witnesses, P. W. Humphries, William Stone

STATE OF NORTH CAROLINA
THOMAS PERSONS   page 179
(Note: This entry very dim and hard to read.) State of North Carolina to Thomas Persons, assignee of Asa Thomas, private in continental line, 220 acres on Bushes Meat Camp fork of Piney River.
Made 29 March 1794   Registered 30 Sept. 1807

COMMISSIONERS OF CHARLOTTE
JOHN KIMBRELL   page 180
Sterling Brewer, George Clark, John Davidson, Robert Dunning, commissioners for the town of Charlotte, convey 4 lots in Charlotte to John Kimbrell.
Made 22 April 1807   Registered 26 Oct. 1807

JOHN BECK of Davidson County
ISAAC WEST of Dickson County   page 181
Beck conveys land on Jones Creek to West.
Made 29 Jan. 1807   Registered 26 Oct. 1807

THOMAS ARCHER of Dickson County
JAMES ARCHER of Dickson County   page 182
Thomas Archer conveys to James Archer tract where Thomas Archer now lives.
Made 1 April 1807   Registered 7 Oct. 1807
Witnesses, John Archer, Thomas Racher
(Note: This entry quite dim on film.)

ORDER   page 184
Ordered to be registered 640 acres. Jan. 1807 William Tait prosecuted in Davidson County for sheriff to take lands of Elijah Robertson in Dickson County at time of death; mentions land on Pine River; John Childress the younger was a bidder; David Hogan, sheriff of Dickson County conveys to Childress; order to be recorded Oct. 1807.

WILLIAM FORSYTHE of Logan Co., KY
JOHN LARKINS, SR., of Dickson County   page 187
William Forsythe of Logan Co., KY, attorney for John Thompson of Cumberland County, Pa., conveys land to John Larkins, Sr., of Dickson County; land on Jones Creek.
Made 10 June 1807   Registered 25 Jan. 1808
Witness, James McClurkan

STATE OF NORTH CAROLINA
HOWELL ADAMS   page 188
State of North Carolina conveys 320 acres to Howell Adams, assignee of
George Nevills, land on middle fork of Bartons Creek.
Made 1 Dec. 1801   Registered 16 Feb. 1808

DECREE   page 189
Decree of John Reed vs Jeremiah Section (also Sexton); Sexton had a
military warrant and Reed gets land; mentions the Mero District in Nov.
1807.
Registered 2 Feb. 1808

BENJAMIN JOSLIN of Davidson County
JOHN EACUFF of Dickson County   page 190
Joslin conveys 640 acres to John Eacuff, part of tract where courthouse
is now building which is known as CHARLOTTESVILLE by patent 6 June 1796.
Made 27 March 1807   Registered 16 Feb. 1808
Witnesses, Joseph Wingate, William N. Akin (Allen?)

JAMES ROBERTSON of Davidson County
JOHN BURGAN of Montgomery County   page 191
Robertson conveys 192 acres on Barton's Creek.
Made 16 Nov. 1802   Registered 16 Feb. 1808

STATE OF NORTH CAROLINA
JAMES WEST GREEN   page 192
State of North Carolina grants 4800 acres to James West Green, sergeant
in North Carolina line, mentions George Nash's south boundary. (Note:
This was possibly registered Feb. 1808, but date not given.)

WILLIAM TEAS of Dickson County
STERLING MAY of Dickson County   page 193
Teas conveys land on Yellow Creek.
Made 30 Sept. 1805   Registered 31 March 1808
Witnesses, Starling Dillehay, Robert Dunning

THOMAS WRIGHT and THOMAS MARTIN of Dickson County
WILLIAM MILLER of Dickson County   page 194
Wright and Martin convey land on west fork of Jones Creek to Miller.
Made 3 Dec. 1806   Registered 31 March 1808

COMMISSIONERS
WILLIAM MILLER   page 195
Sterling Brewer and Robert Dunning, commissioners of Charlotte, convey
two lots in Charlotte to William Miller.
Made 27 April 1807 (Date in question)   Registered 31 Mar. 1808

WILLIAM DICKSON, JR., of Dickson County
MATTHEW McCLURKAN of Dickson County   page 196
William Dickson, Jr., conveys 640 acres to Matthew McClurkan; land on
Jones Creek. (Note: Acreage is in question; hard to read.)
Made 30 Nov. 1807   Registered 31 March 1808
Witnesses, John McClurkan, Matthew Gaston

JOHN DAVIS of Davidson County
MARGARET MEEK of Dickson County   page 197
John Davis conveys to Margaret Meek, relict of Moses Meek of Dickson
County, 400 acres on Jones Creek; mentions Crumpler's line; Duncan
Stuart's line.
Made 20 Dec. 1807   Registered 2 April 1808
Witnesses, Thomas Wright, James Martin, William Miller, Jr.

MOSES FERGUSON of Dickson County
JOHN LINDLEY of Dickson County   page 198
Ferguson conveys land on Barton's Creek; mentions Nathaniel Johnston's
spring branch.
Made 7 May 1808   Registered 2 April 1808
Witnesses (names were illegible on film)

JAMES MARTIN
MARGARET MEEK   page 199
James Martin conveys land on Jones Creek to Margaret Meek, relict of
Moses Meek.
Made 28 Dec. 1807   Registered 2 April 1808
Witnesses, William Miller, Jr., Josiah Meek, Moses Meek

WILLIAM MILLER
MOSES MEEK   page 200
Miller conveys land on west fork of Jones Creek to Moses Meek.
Made 5 March 1807   Registered 2 April 1808
Witnesses, William Miller, Jr., Silas (?) R. Miller

WILLIAM PEACOCK of Stewart County
NATHAN NESBIT   page 200
Peacock conveys slave to Nesbit, 20 ____1807
Registered 2 April 1808
(Note: This was all that could be deciphered on the film.)

JOHN BECK of Davidson County
REES PORTER of Davidson County   page 201
Conveys land on Jones Creek.
Made 23 July 1807
Witnesses, J. B. Reynolds, Wm. Smith

JAMES MIDDLETON of Duplin County, NC
JAMES DICKSON and DAVID SLOAN of Duplin County   page 202
Middleton conveys land on both sides of Yellow Creek for 200 pounds.
Made 15 Dec. 1795
Witnesses, Michael Dickson, ____Sloan

ROBERT DUNNING of Dickson County
STERLING MAY of Dickson County   page 203
Dunning conveys land on Yellow Creek; mentions William Norris's line
and William Moore's corner.
Made 18 Dec. 1805   Registered 10 Aug. 1808
Witnesses, William Moore, Starling Dillehay

DAVID FAUSTER of Dickson County
JOHN ALSTON of Dickson County   page 204
Fauster conveys negro girl Rachel, age 15.
Made 13 Aug. 1807
Witnesses Allen Williams, Henry Haynes

JOHN ALSTON of Dickson County
DAVID FOSTER of Dickson County   page 204
Alston conveys to Foster a negro woman.
Made 13 Aug. 1807
Witnesses, Allen Williams, Henry Haynes

WILLIAM SULLIVANT of Montgomery County
WILLIAM READ of Dickson County   page 205
Sullivant conveys land on middle fork of Barton's Creek to Read.
Made 24 July 1807   Registered 4 April 1808
Witnesses, H. G. Humphries, William Parker, Jesse Sullavant

JASON THOMPSON of Davidson County
FRANCES BROWN of Dickson County   page 206
Thompson conveys land on west fork of Barton's Creek.
Made 22 May 1807   Registered 6 April 1808
Witnesses, John B. Brown, David Brown

THOMAS ARCHER of Dickson County
JOHN H. ARCHER of Dickson County   page 207
Thomas Archer conveys land where Thomas Archer now lives on the dry fork
of Yellow Creek to John H. Archer, son of Thomas Archer.
Made 1 April 1807   Registered 4 April 1808
Witnesses, James Archer, Thomas Archer

JOSIAH SHIP of Dickson County
WILLIAM GRIFFIN of Dickson County   page 209
Ship conveys land on main east fork of Turnbull Creek.
Made 10 Jan. 1807   Registered 5 April 1808
Witnesses, John Parker, Joshua McConnel

MICHAEL DICKSON and JANE DICKSON of Dickson County
JAMES GOODRICH   page 210
Michael Dickson and Jane Dickson convey to Goodrich land on both sides
of Yellow Creek, 1/2 mile below the Chickasaw Trace.
Made 5 May 1807   Registered 5 April 1808
Witnesses, Mumford Harris, Claiborn Harris

SAMUEL PARKER of Dickson County
JOHN WALKER of Dickson County   page 211
Samuel Parker conveys 50 acres on north side of Yellow Creek to John
Walker; this was a location in the name of Mary Rogers, heiress of
William Rogers and conveyed by Mary Rogers to Bryant Farrice and by him
to Samuel Parker.
Made 16 Aug. 1805   Registered 7 April 1808
Witnesses, Huse Roberson, Nathl Mcarry

STEPHEN CHILDRESS of Williamson County
JAMES GOODRICH of Dickson County   page 212
Childress conveys 731½ acres to James Goodrich on both sides of Yellow
Creek.
Made 20 May 1807   Registered 4 April 1808
Witnesses, Claiborn Harris, Samuel Strong

SAMUEL PARKER of Dickson County
JOHN HOLLAND of Dickson County   page 213
Parker conveys to Holland land on both sides of Yellow Creek a location
in the name of Mary Rogers, heiress of William Rogers and conveyed by
Mary Rogers to Bryant Farrice and by him to Samuel Parker.
Made 10 Jan. 1805   Registered 4 April 1808
Witnesses, Charles Teas, Caswell Matlock

ABSALOM BAKER, JR., of Dickson County
JOHN LARKINS, JR.   page 214
Baker conveys 33 acres to Larkins; land on Jones Creek.
Made March 1807   Registered 7 April 1808
Witnesses, John B. Brown, Benjamin Clark

JOHN WOOD of Dickson County
WILLIAM JOSLIN of Dickson County   page 215
Wood conveys negro Plato to William Joslin of Dickson.
Made 7 July 1807   Registered 6 April 1808
Witnesses, William Wilson, William Phillips

JOHN COOK, sheriff of Montgomery County
WILLIAM OUTLAW of Montgomery County   page 215
Cook conveys land for taxes; mentioned the line of John Ramsey, heir of
Mills Ramsey; land on east side of Yellow Creek.
Made 1 June 1807   Registered 7 April 1808

WILLIAM DOAKE of Dickson County
JOHN DICKSON of Dickson County   page 217
Doake conveys land on both sides of Yellow Creek to Dickson.
Made 11 June 1806   Registered 8 April 1808
Witnesses, John Humphries, W. Morrison

STATE OF NORTH CAROLINA
WILLIS SMITH   page 218
State of North Carolina grants 640 acres to Willis Smith, private, on
the Bushes meat house fork of Pine River including the Bushes meat
house.
Made 27 Jan. 1794   Registered 12 April 1808

COMMISSIONERS
ANDERSON CHEATHAM   page 219
Sterling Brewer, Robert Dunning, George Clark, and John Davidson, com-
missioners, convey two lots in Charlotte to Anderson Cheatham of Robert-
son County.
Made 28 April 1807   Registered 6 June 1808

DAVID DICKSON and MOLTON DICKSON of Dickson County
JOHN LOCKE   page 220
David Dickson and Molton Dickson convey to Locke a bull, cows, and other
property.
Made 13 Feb. 1808   Registered 6 June 1808
Witnesses, James Craig, ____Wingate

JAMES McCLELLAND of Dickson County
JOHN WEST of Dickson County   pages, 221,222,223
McClelland conveys to West.
Made 2 Jan. 1808   Registered 7 June 1808
Witnesses, Isaac West, Jr., Francis McClelland
Witnesses to second entry, John West, Frances McClelland

JOHN DICKSON of Cumberland County, NC
CHARLES JOHNSON of Bladen County, NC   page 225
Dickson for 300 pounds in North Carolina currency conveys land on both
sides of first east fork of Yellow Creek above where the Chickasaw Trace
crosses creek; mentions Edward Dickson's southeast corner; Daniel
Williams' line.
Made 3 Feb. 1798   Registered 7 June 1808
Witnesses, Henry Davis, Martha Houston, Hardy Valentine, Benjamin
Valentine, Edward Dickson

COMMISSIONERS
JAMES LARKINS   page 228
Commissioners of Charlotte conveyed Lots 39 and 48 in Charlotte to James
Larkins.
Made 11 April 1808   Registered 8 June 1808

RICHARD COCKE of Dickson County
THOMAS BATTSON of Dickson County   page 229
Cocke conveys land on Barton's Creek.
Made 10 Aug. 1807   Registered 8 June 1808
Witnesses, Ebenezer Kelly, Wm. Willy
(Page 230 another transaction when Cocke deeds land to Ebenezer Kelly
on Barton's Creek, 248 acres, made 12 Aug. 1807, registered 8 June
1808 with Thomas Battson, Richard Battson as witnesses.)

JAMES FENTRESS of Montgomery County
WILLIAMSON PLANT of Davidson County   page 231
Fentress conveys 192 acres to Plant on both sides of the first west fork
of Yellow Creek below the Chickasaw Trace; mentions Sterling May's line;
Fentress bought this land in 1797.
Made 19 Dec. 1807   Registered 5 Dec. 1808
Witnesses, John Plant, William Plant, Jesse May

HEZEKIAH BARR of Dickson County
HUGH DICKSON of Dickson County   page 232
Barr conveys 143 acres to Dickson.
Made 4 Dec. 1807   Registered 5 Dec. 1808
Witnesses, Claiborn Harris, Aaron James

OLIVER SMITH of Pittsylvania Co., NC
NATHAN WILLIAMS of Davidson County   page 234
Smith conveys to Williams 640 acres on Jones Creek of Big Harpeth.
Made 1 July 1806   Registered 5 Dec. 1808
Witnesses, William Barrow, Absolum Page

MOLTON DICKSON of Dickson County
FIELD FARRAR   page 235
Dickson conveys to Farrar two bay horses.
Made 27 June 1806   Registered 5 Dec. 1808

BENJAMIN JOSLIN of Davidson County
DAVID HOGAN of Dickson County   page 237
Joslin conveys to David Hogan a negro boy.
Made 16 April 1808   Registered 5 Dec. 1808
Witnesses, John Skinner, John Cimbord

DAVID DICKSON and MOLTON DICKSON of Dickson County
WILLIAM MOORE of Dickson County   page 238
The Dicksons convey land in Charlotte on Dickson Street on the north
bank of Town Creek.
Made 12 July 1808   Registered 5 Dec. 1808
Witnesses, D. Christian, Michael Molton

HARDY FREEMAN of Bertie Co., NC
MILLS RAYMOR of Bertie Co., NC   page 239
Hardy Freeman, executor of the will of John Ramsey, deceased, conveys
land on Yellow Creek; mentions Israel Hamond's southwest corner.
Made 13 May 1806   Registered 13 July 1808
Witnesses, Sim. Walker, M. Holley, Joseph Henney, Jno. Sessoms

MILES RAYMOR of Bertie Co., NC
WILLIAM PARROTT HARDY of Bertie Co., NC   page 242
Raymor conveys land on Yellow Creek to William Parrott Hardy; mentions
Israel Hammond's southwest corner.
Made __May 1807   Registered 5 Dec. 1808
(Note: This entry should be rechecked for those interested in this line.)

HARDY MURPHREE of Williamson County
HOWELL ADAMS of Dickson County   page 245
Murphree conveys land on the southwest side of Big Harpeth to Adams.
Made 29 April 1808   Registered 5 Dec. 1808
Witnesses, Robert Finney, David Dickson, John Odil, Robert Drake,
S. Brewer

WILLIAM JOHNSON of Duplin Co., NC
DAVID SLOAN of Duplin Co., NC   pages 246, 247
Johnson conveys land on Yellow Creek above the Chickasaw Trace.
Made 30 Jan. 1796   Registered 6 Dec. 1808
Witnesses, Gibson Sloan, William Rigby, Jr.

JOHN HOLLAND of Dickson County
GEORGE HUMBLE of Barren Co., Ky   page 249
Holland conveys 590 acres to Humble, land on main Yellow Creek about
the Chicksaw Trace; 50 acres of this land was conveyed to John Walker
by Samuel Parker, the original owner.
Made 8 Sept. 1807   Registered 7 Dec. 1808
Witnesses, David Dickson, A. McMillin, Edwd. Pearsall

WILLIAM SULLIVANT, SR., of Montgomery County
GEORGE CLARK of Dickson County   page 250
Sullivant conveys 60 acres; mentions the northwest corner of Richard C.
Napier's Forge Tract.
Made 13 July 1808   Registered 7 Dec. 1808
Witnesses, J. Walker, Jas. Walker, Joseph Walker

WILLIAM T. LEWIS of Davidson County
MARK HALY of Dickson County   page 253
Lewis conveys 31½ acres to Haly on west bank of Yellow Creek, originally
granted to Lewis on a military warrant and conveyed to Stephen Childress.
Made 24 Feb. 1808   Registered 7 Dec. 1808
Witnesses, Lewis Powers, John Lewis, John Northan

RAIFORD CRUMPLER of Dickson County
MATHEW CRUMPLER of Dickson County   page 255
Raiford Crumpler conveys land on southwest side of Big Harpeth on a
branch of Jones Creek.
Made 10 Oct. 1808   Registered 10 Dec. 1808
Witnesses, John Larkins, James Larkins

ELI TIDWELL of Dickson County
WILLIAM WHITE of Dickson County   page 257
Tidwell conveys to White land on first fork of Turnbull Creek; mentions
Allen's south boundary line.
Made 5 Oct. 1808   Registered 10 Dec. 1808
Witness, Eli Tidwell

THOMAS HILL of Dickson County
LARKIN DAWSON of Davidson County   page 258
Hill conveys to Dawson land on Cumberland and Harpeth Rivers in fork of
said rivers.
Made 6 Sept. 1807   Registered 10 Dec. 1808
Witnesses, Geo. Edwards, William Caldwell, C. Davidle

HOWEL TATUM, DOCTOR MORGAN BROWN, JOHN BAKER of Mero District
WILLIAM OUTLAW of Mero District   page 260
Tatum, Brown, and Baker convey to Outlaw 640 acres; this land was grant-
ed to John Ramsey, heir of Mills Ramsey and bounded by a tract owned by
Jesse Craft.
Made 19 Jan. 1805   Registered 28 Dec. 1808
Witnesses, Robert Searcy, Willie Blount, Nimrod Crosswell

SAMUEL HOGG and JOHN BAPTIST HOGG of Wilson County, TN
ROBERT WEAKLEY of Davidson County, TN   page 262
Samuel Hogg and John Baptist Hogg convey to Weakley 174 acres on both
sides of Yellow Creek; mentions Thomas Hamilton's southeast corner.
Made 1 June 1807   Registered 20 Dec. 1808
Witnesses, Samuel Weakley, Jr., John Gordon, Jr., Samuel McBride,
Thomas Claiborne, John E. Beck, Robert Drake

WILLIAM KILLINGSWORTH and Elizabeth, his wife of Halifax County, NC
SAMUEL HOGG of Wilson County, TN   pages 264, 267, 268
Killingsworth and wife convey to Samuel Hogg land in Williamson, Robert-
son and Montgomery counties; mentions her late husband Thomas Hogg.
Made 24 Sept. 1805   Registered _____
Witnesses, John B. Hogg, Isaac Harris

RICHARD ALLEN of Dickson County
SAMUEL ELIOT   page 266
Allen conveys to Eliot a negro Toney.
Made 14 Dec. 1808   Registered 11 Jan. 1809
Witnesses, John Humphreys, _____(illegible)

STATE OF NORTH CAROLINA
WILLIAM ROGERS   page 267
State of North Carolina grants to William Rogers, private in North Caro-
lina line, land on both sides of Yellow Creek, above the Chickasaw Trace
mentions Daniel Williams' upper line.
Made 1792   Registered 12 Jan. 1809

COMMISSIONERS OF CHARLOTTE
ALLEN THOMPSON   page 269
Commissioners of Charlotte convey to Allen Thompson Lot 8 on Robertson
Street and Lot 33, bounded by West Street and Spring Street.
Made 17 April 1807   Registered 23 Jan. 1809
Witnesses, Robert Drake, Carter Acuff

NATHANIEL JOHNSON of Dickson County
PETER RENFRO of Dickson County   page___(should be 272)
Johnson conveys to Renfro land on Barton's Creek.
Made 26 Nov. 1808   Registered 22 Jan. 1809
Witnesses, Jesse Brown, James Sims

MARGARET MEEK of Dickson County
MOSES MEEK of Dickson County   pages 273, 274
Margaret Meek conveys 200 acres to Moses Meek; land on Jones Creek, men-
tions the southeast corner of Isaiah Meeks.
Made 14 Jan. 1808   Registered 25 Jan. 1809
Witnesses, William Stone, Thomas Wright
Second one is conveyance for 200 acres to Josiah Meek on Barton's Creek.

DAVID DICKSON of Dickson County
JOHN NESBITT of Dickson County   page 276
Dickson conveys to Nesbitt a negro Sam.
Made 22 April 1808   Registered 11 March 1809
Witness, Abner Dickson

ROBERT WEAKLEY of Davidson County
WILLIAM DOKE of Bedford County, TN   page 277
Weakley conveys to Doke 25 acres on Yellow Creek, part of 640 acres
granted to Thomas Hamilton.
Made 22 Oct. 1808   Registered 11 April 1809
Witnesses, William Smith, Thomas Claiborn, William Caldwell

ROBERT WEAKLEY of Davidson County
WILLIAM DRAKE of Dickson County   page 278
Weakley conveys to Drake land on Yellow Creek.
Made 10 May 1806   Registered 11 April 1809
Witnesses, John Hall, Samuel Weakley, William Smith, Thomas Claiborn

JOHN TURNER of Dickson County
SAMUEL ELLIOTT of Williamson County   page 280
Turner conveys to Elliott a negro boy Armstead, age 12, "born and
raised mine".
Made 28 Feb. 1809   Registered 1 May 1809
Witnesses, R. Nesbitt, Jeremiah Nesbitt

JEREMIAH PEARSALL of Dickson County
JEREMIAH NESBITT of Dickson County   page 281
Pearsall conveys to Nesbitt a negro, Tobey, age 10.
Made __Oct. 1808   Registered 4 May 1809
Witnesses, N. Nesbitt, William Turner

MARGARET MEEK
WILLIAM MILLER of Dickson County   page 282
Meek conveys to Miller a negro, Dick, age 10.
Made _____   Registered 10 May 1809
Witnesses, Silas Miller, Thomas Wright

BENJAMIN BRACKETT of Smith County
DANIEL PARKER of Sumner County   page 283
Brackett conveys to Parker land on south side of Big Harpeth.
Made 8 Oct. 1807   Registered 10 May 1809
Witnesses, William Stuart, Jr., Francis Weathered, Thomas Header, Jr.

STATE OF TENNESSEE
WILLIAM STONE   page 285
State of Tennessee conveys to William Stone, assignee of John Waddle and
John McMillan, 130 acres on a branch of Jones Creek, a tract belonging
to heirs of William Stone, deceased. Signed 1 June 1810.
Made 25 July 1807   Registered 17 Dec. 1811

JAMES ROBERTSON of Davidson County
JAMES DUNNAGAN of Dickson County   page 288
Robertson conveys to Dunnagan 100 acres on the west fork of Pine River,
crossing Indian Camp Branch.
Made 22 Nov. 1808   Registered 25 May 1809
Witnesses, William Totty, R. Weakley, William Smith, Richard C. Napier

LEWIS RUSSELL of Dickson County
JOHN BAKER of Dickson County   page 290
Russell conveys to Baker land on west side of Pine River.
Made 30 Dec. 1808   Registered 25 May 1809
Witnesses, John Scott, John A. Baker

JEREMIAH WALKER of Dickson County
WILLIAM COX of Dickson County   page 291
Walker conveys to Cox a negro Abraham, age 22.
Made 17 March 1809   Registered 6 July 1809
Witnesses, David Hogan, David Dickson

JAMES JONES of Dickson County
DAVID McGRAW of Montgomery County   page 292
Jones conveys to McGraw a negro Jenny.
Made 1 Feb. 1808   Registered 6 July 1809
Witnesses, William McDaniel, Clemnt. McDaniel

WILLIAM DOAKE of Bedford County, TN
JOHN DICKSON of Dickson County   page 293
Doake conveys to Dickson land on both sides of Yellow Creek, part of
the original Thomas Hamilton tract.
Made 17 Jan. 1809   Registered 6 July 1809
Witnesses, Adam Willson, Robert Dickson

(Note: page 294 of this book was dim and illegible on the microfilm.)

DANIEL WILLIAMS of Sampson County, NC
ROBERT MERFRE of New Hanover County   page 295
Williams conveys to Merfre 640 acres on the south side of Big Harpeth
on the waters of Turnbull Creek.
Made 20 Aug. 1808   Registered 12 July 1809
Witnesses, E. Herrin, Gabriel Herrin, Joseph Williams, George Tennel,
Joseph Meredith

STATE OF TENNESSEE
JESSE S. ROSS   page 297
State of Tennessee conveys to Ross, assignee of John Waddle and John
McMillan, land on the west fork of Pine River.
Made 25 July 1807   Registered 12 July 1809

STATE OF NORTH CAROLINA
ALEXANDER NELSON   page 298
State of North Carolina conveys to Nelson, assignee of John Curry, a
private in North CArolina line, 640 acres on Yellow Creek; mentions the
south boundary line of Miles Ramsey.
Made 27 April 1793   Registered 3 Aug. 1809

JOHN H. ARCHER of Dickson County
ROBERT McNARY   page 299
Archer conveys to McNary three negroes.
Made 3 Nov. 1808   Registered 3 Oct. 1809
Witness, John Stevens

HOWELL ADAMS of Dickson County
JAMES TEAL   page 299
Adams conveys to Teal 205 acres on the middle fork of Barton's Creek;
mentions the Still House branch and William Giffin's line.
Made 11 Jan. 1809   Registered Jan. 1809
Witnesses, Joel Shropshire, Joseph Brown, Samuel Hosley

JAMES ROBERTSON of Davidson County
WILLIAM T. LEWIS of Davidson County   page 301
Robertson conveys to Lewis 640 acres on the Harpeth, including the Big
Clay Lick at which place Lewis is now sinking for salt water; mentions
Provine's south boundary line.
Made 18 Nov. 1802   Registered 11 Oct. 1809
Witnesses, Thomas Hickman, B. J. Bradford, Joseph McKean

STATE OF TENNESSEE
WILLIAM PAFFORD   page 302
Tennessee grants land to Pafford for military service; land in District
1, Range 19, land on both sides of White Oak Creek, was granted 5 Oct.
1808; William Hill was assignee; Edward Gwin's southeast corner.
Made 1 May 1784   Registered 5 Sept. 1809

STATE OF TENNESSEE
JOHN PARKER, SR.   page 305
State of Tennessee conveys to Parker, assignee of Robert Hays, who
entered it 5 Nov. 1808, 640 acres on Turnbull Creek; mentions Joseph
Voss's south boundary line.
Made 20 Feb. 1809   Registered 27 Dec. 1809

STATE OF TENNESSEE
JOHN PARKER   page 306
State of Tennessee conveys to John Parker land on Turnbull Creek, entered 20 Aug. 1809; mentions the west boundary line of Lewis Lodge's heirs.
Registered 28 Dec. 1809

THOMAS HILL of Dickson County
LARKIN DAWSON of Davidson County   page 308
Hill conveys to Dawson land on Harpeth River.
Made 12 Sept. 1807   Registered ___
Witnesses, C. David L, G. Edwards, William Caldwell

THOMAS BETHNY of Robertson County
DRURY CHRISTIAN of Robertson County   page 309
Bethny's power of attorney to obtain a grant of 320 acres on both sides of Big Harpeth.
Made 3 March 1803
Witnesses, S. Brewer, Jacob Bethny, Matthew Bethny, Edward Lucas

DAVID HOGAN, sheriff of Dickson County
JOHN SPENCER of Dickson County   pages 310-312
Hogan conveys 640 acres belonging to Thomas Hamilton on both sides of Yellow Creek, about 4 miles above the camp where Russell Gower, Anderson Lucas, and James Russell hunted in 1784; sold for taxes.
Made 4 July 1809   Registered ___July 1809
Witnesses, Michael Molton, Molton Dickson

BENJAMIN JOSLIN of Davidson County
WILLIAM PEACOCK of Dickson County   page 313
Joslin conveys Lot 14 in Charlotte to Peacock.
Made 11 April 1809   Registered April 1809
Witnesses, Francis S. Ellis, Edward Pearsall

DAVID HOGAN, former sheriff of Dickson County
CHRISTOPHER STRONG   page 314
Hogan as sheriff sold Lot 11 in Charlotte to Strong; this was part of lands and tentements of William Germain, who owned them and owed John Nisbett and William Mahan.
Made 11 July 18___   Registered 2 Jan. 1810
Witnesses, W. V. Akin, James Larkins

ISAAC HUNTER of Dickson County
GABRIEL ALLEN of Dickson County   page 315
Hunter conveys to Allen a negro named Alston.
Registered July term 1809
Witnesses, D. Christian, Cornelius McGraw

JOHN IRVIN of Tennessee
DAVID IRVIN of Tennessee   page 316
John Irvin conveys land to David Irvin; mentions Col. Barton's west boundary line crossing Barton's Creek.
Made 24 June 1809   Registered ___
Witnesses, Joseph Walker, Jacob W. Miller

SAMUEL ELIOT of Wilson County
RICHARD ALLEN of Dickson County   pages 317-318*
Eliot conveys 512 acres to Allen for $1536 in silver dollars; land on both sides of Yellow Creek, beginning on the west bank of the creek below the mouth of the Great Cave, 26 poles on above a great spring; mentions the former Edward Dickson corner, east boundary line of John Drury, being upper part of 640 acres granted Morgan Drury by North Carolina and conveyed to Eliot.
Made 14 Dec. 1808   Registered 2 Jan. 1810
Witnesses, John Humphries, James Goodrich, N. Nesbitt

---

*The Great Cave mentioned in this conveyance is believed to be the one known as Ruskin Cave in Dickson County today. This was the site in later years of the Ruskin Colony.

CASWELL MATLOCK of Dickson County
THOMAS HOLLAND of Dickson County   page 318
Matlock conveys to Holland a negro girl.
Made 18 July 1800 in 33rd year of Independence
Witnesses, Nathan Nesbitt, Robert Jameson

JAMES WALKER of Dickson County
SIMON HOLT WALKER of Dickson County   page 319
James Walker conveys to Simon Holt Walker 100 acres on Barton's Creek;
mentions Jacob W. Miller's line.
Made 10 Jan. 1809

TIMOTHY ANDERSON of Montgomery County
WILLIAM BAKER of Dickson County   page 320
Anderson conveys to Baker 320 acres on both side of the Leatherwood
Fork of Yellow Creek and on both sides of Rattle Snake Branch, once
Thomas McMurry's corner; mentions William Halliburton's line; being
part of tract granted to Timothy Anderson.
Made 3 Feb. 1809
Witnesses, Francis Baker, Samuel (or James) Perry

COMMISSIONERS OF CHARLOTTE
WILLIAM MOORE of Dickson County   page 321
Commissioners convey to Moore a lot in Charlotte.
Made 11 July 1809   Registered 11 Jan. 1810

JOHN BROWN of Dickson County
WILLIAM MORRIS of Dickson County   page 322
Brown conveys 100 acres to Morris; land on Barton's Creek and mentions
William Giffin.
Made 11 April 1809   Registered Apr. 1809

(Note: Page 323 was dim and could not be deciphered.)

CHARLES STEWART of Montgomery County
COMMISSIONERS OF CHARLOTTE   page 324*
Stewart conveys to the commissioners of Charlotte 50 acres on both
sides of the north____of Jones Creek, including the Cave Spring.
Made 12 Dec. 1808   Registered 4 Jan. 1810
Witnesses, J. B. Reynolds,_____(illegible)

COMMISSIONERS OF CHARLOTTE
JAMES CRAIG   page 325
(Note: This entry was faded on the microfilm but possibly can be read
in the original book.)
Made 12 April 1809   Registered 4 Jan. 1810
Witness, John Humphries

JOHN HOBBS
BENJAMIN BRACKETT   page 326
Power of attorney. (Note: This is another faded entry. Page 327 is
not in the book--either gone or the pages have been numbered incorrect-
ly. The next page number is 336.)

JOHN GRAY BLOUNT of Beaufort Co., NC, and
THOMAS BLOUNT of Edgecombe Co., NC   page 336
Conveys land on Turnbull Creek to John George Riner of Dickson County.
Made 2 Sept. 1809   Registered 5 Feb. 1810

STATE OF TENNESSEE
JOSEPH VOSS   page 338
Joseph Voss receives 640 acres on west fork of Turnbull Creek for his
military service to North Carolina; made 19 Mar. 1784, registered
26 Feb. 1810.

---
*This transaction is for land on which Charlotte, the county seat, is
located. For further information an account may be found in "A History
of Dickson County", by Robert E. Corlew, published by Dickson County
Historical Society and Tennessee Historical Commission in 1956.

REESE PORTER of Christian County, KY
ISAAC WEST, SR., of Dickson County   page 339
Porter conveys 220 acres to West on Jones Creek, adjoins the tract
whereon Isaac West now lives.
Made 20 June 1808   Registered 5 Apr. 1810
Witnesses, Elijah Threlkeld, Anderson West

STATE OF NORTH CAROLINA
JOHN WILSON   page 340
State of North Carolina grants to John Wilson, assignee of Barnebas
Barnes, private in the Continental Line, land in Davidson County on
Yellow Creek, 4miles or 5 miles below the Chickasaw Trace.
Made 20 May 1793   Registered 12 Apr. 1810

STATE OF NORTH CAROLINA
JOHN WILSON   page 341
State of North Carolina grants to John Wilson, assignee of Enoch King,
private in the North Carolina line, land in Davidson County on Yellow
Creek.
Made 20 May 1793   Registered 12 Apr.1810

COMMISSIONERS OF CHARLOTTE
JAMES MARTIN OF Dickson County   page 342
Commissioners convey a lot in Charlotte to Martin.
Made 27 April 1807   Registered 30 Apr.1810

COMMISSIONERS OF CHARLOTTE
THOMAS PANNELL   page 343
Commissioners convey part of lot in Charlotte to Pannell.
Made 11 Oct. 1807

COMMISSIONERS OF CHARLOTTE
JOHN McCLISH   page 344
Commissioners convey to McClish a lot, Lot 5, on Humphreys Street in
Charlotte.
Made 12 July 1807   Registered 30 Apr.1810

DAVID McGRAW of Dickson County
ISAIAH HAMBLETON   page 345
McGraw conveys negro named Jack.
Made 1 Sept. 1809   Registered 30 Apr.1810
Witnesses, H. Ragland, Betsy Burgan

_____McNAIRY
JOSEPH DICKSON   page 345
(Note: faded entry; conveyed feather bed and other items.)
Witness, William Cook

DAVID HOGAN, former sheriff of Dickson County
ROBERT DRAKE   page 346
Conveys land on the west side of Johnston Creek, the first creek that
runs into the Cumberland below the mouth of Harpeth River. Sheriff was
selling the lands of Samuel Jackson.
Made 3 July 1809   Registered 20 May 1810
Witnesses, William Peacock, John Nesbitt, Christopher Strong

JOHN McCLISH of Dickson County
PETER RENFRO   pages 347-348
McClish conveys to Renfro (also found as Rentfro) horses, cattle, and
other items which was the property willed to Jane McClish, now Jane
Rentfro, wife of Peter Rentfro, by William McClish, Jane's former hus-
band; it was willed to her for her natural life and then to John
McClish.
Made 14 Feb. 1810   Registered 30 June 1810
Witnesses, Mearian Lewis, John Grimes

JOHN McCLISH of Dickson County
PETER RENTFRO   page 348
McClish conveys to Rentfro a parcel of negroes, who were willed to
Jane McClish, now wife of Peter Rentfro, by William McClish, deceased,

her former husband.
Made 13 Feb. 1810   Registered _____
Witnesses, William Morris, ____ R. Drake
Signed 30 June 1810
(Note: Davidson County, TN, marriages show William McClish to Jennie
Johnston, license issued 10 Nov. 1794.)

DAVID WALLACE of Dickson County
WILLIAM HODGES of Dickson County
Wallace conveys land to William Hodges; land on a branch of the Leather-
wood Fork of Yellow Creek.
Made 16 Dec. 1809   Registered 9 Nov. 1810
Witnesses, Selman Edwards, John Hodges

JOHN DAVIS of Davidson County
CHRISTOPHER STRONG of Dickson County   page 350
Davis conveys to Strong 50 acres on Jones Creek, mentions the north
boundary line of 640 acres which Strong purchased from Mathew Brooks
and was granted by North Carolina to John Davis in 1796.
Made 30 Oct. 1809   Registered 10 Nov. 1810
Witnesses, Hugh McNeilly, Field Farrar

MATTHEW McCLURKAN of Dickson County
CHRISTOPHER STRONG of Dickson County   page 351
McClurkan conveys to Strong 48 acres on both sides of the main Joneses
Creek.
Made 9 Nov. 1809   Registered 10 Nov. 1810
Witnesses, Hugh McNeilly, Field Farrar

GEORGE ROSS of Dickson County
GEORGE GALLION of Dickson County   page 352
Ross conveys to Gallion 100 acres on Barton's Creek; mentions the south-
east corner of land where Ross lives and the mouth of Johnston's spring
branch where it empties into Barton's Creek and Moses Ferguson's west
boundary line.
Made 16 Oct. 1809   Registered 10 Nov. 1810
Witnesses, Mary Ross, Robert Drake

COMMISSIONERS OF CHARLOTTE
HUGH McNEILLY   page 355
Commissioners convey Lot 26 in Charlotte to McNeilly; lot on Clarksville
Street.
Made 27 April 1807   Registered 10 Nov. 1810

MOSES MEEK of Dickson County
THOMAS MARTIN   page 354 (a repeat)
Meek conveys to Martin land on Jones Creek, part of a tract granted to
John P. Crabtree; mentions the mouth of the sulphur fork above the
Town Creek.
Made 11 April 1809   Registered 10 Nov. 1810
Witnesses, James Martin, Silas H. Miller

DANIEL PARKER of Sumner County
CALEB DICKINSON of Dickson County   page 357
Parker conveys to Dickinson 50 acres on main Turnbull Creek, part of
640 acres surveyed for James Rail.
Made 14 Nov. 1809   Registered 10 Nov. 1810
Witnesses, Minor Bibb, George Powel, John Dining

DANIEL PARKER, JR., of Sumner County
GEORGE POWELL of Dickson County   page 356
Parker conveys to Powell 150 acres on the east side of Big Turnbull
Creek, part of tract granted to James Royal.
Made 14 Nov. 1809   Registered 10 Nov. 1810
Witnesses, Minor Bibb, Caleb Dickison, John Dinning

JAMES McCLELLAND of Dickson County
FRANCIS McCLELLAND of Dickson County   page 357
James McClelland conveys to Francis McClelland land.
Made 5 March 1810   Registered 10 Nov. 1810

Witnesses, William Miller, Jr., Thomas Pannell

JAMES ROBERTSON, JR., of Dickson County
WILLIAM EDWARDS of Dickson County   page 358
Robertson conveys to Edwards 100 acres on Russell's Fork of Pine River;
Jesse Edwards gave his premption to William Edwards.
Made 1 Aug. 1809   Registered 10 Nov. 1810
Witnesses, John Edwards, William Hudson

JOHN PARKER, SR., of Dickson County
MINOR BIBB   page 359
Parker conveys land on Parker's Creek.
Made 8 Dec. 1809   Registered 12 Nov. 1810
Witnesses, Caleb Dickison, George Powell

ABRAM CALDWELL of Dickson County
LABIUS RICHARDSON of Dickson County   page 362
Caldwell conveys 200 acres on Barton's Creek.
Made 17 Jan. 1809   Registered 12 Nov. 1810
Witnesses, Joel Shropshire, Hudson Johnson, Thomas Richardson
(Note: The pages jump from 359 to 362 in this book.)

WILLIAM BAKER of Dickson County
WILLIAM HALLIBURTON of Dickson County   page 363
Baker conveys 20 acres on Leatherwood Creek to Halliburton.
Made 2 April 1802   Registered 12 Nov. 1810
Witnesses, Martin Halliburton, Samuel Self

WILLIAM TATUM of Dickson County
WILLIAM CATES of Dickson County   page 364
Tatum conveys land to Cates on both sides of Yellow Creek being part of
100 acres located in the name of Lewis Powers and conveyed to Tatum.
Made 3 March 1810   Registered 12 Nov. 1810
Witnesses, John H. Stone, Stephen Tatom

STERLING BREWER of Dickson County
PAUL ABNEY of Dickson County   page 365
Brewer conveys to Abney 112 acres on the dividing ridge between the
Cumberland River and Harpeth River on both sides of the road leading
from David L ferry to Charlotte, about 4 miles from the ferry, inclu-
ding the head spring of Town Creek.
Made 18 Aug. 1810   Registered 13 Dec. 1810
Witnesses, William Handlin, Wilson McKinney

ROBERT WEAKLEY of Davidson County
WILLIAM B. WEST of Dickson County   page 366
Weakley conveys to West 602 acres on both sides of Yellow Creek on the
east side; mentions the east corner of Thomas Hamilton's grant, John
Dickson's line, the north bank of Raccoon Creek and the northwest cor-
ner of Samuel Middleton's grant.
Made 30 Aug. 1808   Registered 13 Nov. 1810
Witnesses, John Hays, James West

ISAAC HUNTER et al
DAVID McGRAW   page 367
Isaac Hunter, Alexander Hunter, James Jones, John Jones, Patsey Jones,
Polly Jones, Burrell Jones, and Giles Jones to David McGraw a negro
girl, Ginny.
Made 13 Oct. 1809   Registered 13 Nov. 1810
Witnesses, Cornelius McGraw, John Jones

DAVID McGRAW of Dickson County
JAMES WILLSON of Robertson County   page 368
McGraw conveys to Willson 270 acres of land at the mouth of Johnson's
Creek, 4 miles below the mouth of Harpeth River; land was granted to
John Rice, assignee of John Jones in 1784.
Made 26 Dec. 1809   Registered 13 Nov. 1810
Witnesses, H. Ragland, T. Y. Hundly, James Wilson, Jr.

PETER RENTFRO of Dickson County
HENRY GRIMES of Dickson County   page 369
Rentfro conveys to Grimes land on Barton's Creek, the place where Peter
Rentfro now lives.
Made 7 June 1810   Registered 14 Nov. 1810
Witnesses, R. Drake, John McClish, Benjamin Crews, John Benham

JAMES ROBERTSON of Davidson County
THOMAS MATHEWS of Dickson County   page 370
Robertson conveys to Mathews 100 acres on Barton's Creek; mentions
Stephen Ward's northeast corner.
Made 24 Aug. 1810   Registered 14 Nov. 1810
Witnesses, R. Drake, Robert Nesbitt, R. C. Napier, John Grymes

PETER RENTFRO and JANE RENTFRO of Murry Co., Tenn.
JOHN McCLISH of Dickson County   page 371
Peter Rentfro and Jane Rentfro, formerly Jane McClish, of Murry Co.,
Tennessee, convey to John McClish of Dickson County land on Barton's
Creek, mentions the northwest corner of 160 acres owned by Henry Grimes
Sr. (Note: Murry County is Maury County.)
Made 11 Sept. 1810   Registered 4 Nov. 1810

SAMUEL HARRIS and ALEXANDER PROVINE
ISAAC HARRIS of Dickson County   page 372
Samuel Harris and Alexander Provine, attorney for the legatees of
John Provine, of Wilson County, convey land on Harpeth River to Harris,
part of tract North Carolina granted to John Provine.
Made 15 Aug. 1809   Registered 14 Nov. 1810

JOHN PARKER of Hickman County
AARON LAWS of Dickson County   page 373
Parker conveys to Laws land on Haley's Creek.
Made 25 March 1809   Registered 19 Nov. 1810
Signed by Richard Eaton, acting justice of peace
Witnesses, Stewart Pipkin, Samuel Taylor, Daniel Taylor

JAMES DICKSON of Duplin County, NC
ALEXANDER DICKSON of Dickson County, Tenn. page 374
James Dickson conveys to Alexander Dickson for love and affection for
son Alexander Dickson, one-half of the military grant to James Middle-
ton and conveyed by Middleton to James Dickson and David Sloan; land
on Yellow Creek and includes the Old Indian Town; crosses old Town
Creek.
Made 7 March 1810   Registered 17 Nov. 1810
Witnesses, Jeremiah Pearsall, Molton Dickson

JOHN RABOURN of Dickson County
DANIEL PARKER of Dickson County   page 375
Rabourn conveys 25 acres to Parker; mentions John Davis' northwest
corner.
Made 15 June 1810   Registered 17 Nov. 1810
Witnesses, Calep Dickinson, Minor Bibb, Jesse Christian

JAMES McCALLISTER, SR., of Hickman County
JAMES McCALLISTER, JR.   page 376
McCallister, Sr., conveys to McCallister, Jr., a negro Julie, age 4.
Made 1 Oct. 1810   Registered 17 Nov. 1810
Witnesses, Charles Gilbert, Peter Gilbert

JAMES DICKSON of Duplin Co., NC
ALEXANDER DICKSON of Dickson County   page 377
James Dickson to son Alexander Dickson a negro Adam.
Made 17 April 1810   Registered 19 Nov. 1810
Witnesses, Molton Dickson, Jeremiah Pearsall

JOHN PARKER of Dickson County
STEWART PIPKIN of Dickson County   page 378
Parker conveys to Pipkin land on Turnbull Creek.
Made 9 Dec. 1809   Registered 19 Nov. 1810
Witnesses, Samuel Taylor, Aaron Laws, Daniel Taylor

STEPHEN WARD of Dickson County
THOMAS MATTHEWS of Dickson County   page 379
Ward conveys to Thomas Matthews.
Made 22 July 1809   Registered 19 Nov. 1810
Witnesses, James Trotter, Simon Miers

JOHN PARKER of Hickman County
SAMUEL TAYLOR of Dickson County   page 380
Parker conveys to Taylor 115 acres.
Made 25 March 1809   Registered 19 Nov. 1810
Witnesses, Aaron Laws, Samuel Taylor, Steward Pipkin

STATE OF TENNESSEE
JOHN WADDLE and JOHN McMILLAN   page 381
(Note--dim entry.) State of Tennessee conveys land on Cedar Creek to
Waddle and McMillan.
Made 25 July 1807   Registered July 1811

JOHN GRAY BLOUNT of Beaufort County, NC
JAMES STEELE   page 382
John Gray Blount of Beaufort County, NC, and Thomas Blount of Edgecombe
County, NC, convey to Steele 220 acres on west fork of Jones Creek.
Made 4 Sept. 1809   Registered 6 Mar. 1811
Witnesses, John Cocke, J. B. Reynolds

WILLIAM SHEPHERD of Orange County, NC
GENERAL JAMES ROBERTSON   page 384
Shepherd conveys to Robertson land on the east fork of Barton's Creek.
Made 1 Sept. 1809   Registered 6 March 1811
Witnesses, Thomas Claiborne, William Smith
Henry Shepherd was attorney for William Shepherd

JOHN DICKSON of Cumberland County, NC   page 383   (or 385)
EDMOND TAYLOR
Dickson conveys to Taylor land on the north of the east fork of Yellow
Creek; mentions John Drury's line. (Note: dim entry.)
Made--date illegible   Registered 1 June 1811
Witnesses, Daniel Williams, Nehemiah Scott

THOMAS CROSSNOE
JESSE STROUD   page 387
Crossnoe conveys to Stroud land on Beaver Dam Creek and Turnbull Creek,
originally granted to heirs of James Royal.
Registered 20 June 1811
Witnesses, Samuel McAdoo, George Powell

JAMES ROBERTSON of Davidson County
WILLIAM GILMOUR of Halifax County, NC   pages 389-391
Robertson conveys to Gilmour land near head of Barton's Creek.
Made 1 Aug. 1809   Registered 21 June 1811
Witnesses, Robert Searcy, A. Foster

STATE OF TENNESSEE
JAMES WADDLE and JOHN McMILLAN   page 392
State of Tennessee conveys to Waddle and McMillan 100 acres.
Made 1 June 1811   Registered 21 June 1811

FRANCIS BROWN
JOHN HALL   page 393
Brown conveys to Hall 72 acres on Jones Creek; mentions the old line of
Frances Brown; Francis Brown reserves one acre to his son Isaac Brown,
including the spring of Isaac Brown.
Made 15 Feb. ____   Registered 21 June 1811
Witnesses, John B. Brown, Matthew Crumpler

HAYDON WELLS of Mississippi Territory
BENJAMIN ADAMS of Montgomery County   page 395
Wells conveys to Adams land on the east fork of Yellow Creek, mentions
John Lee's, formerly John Burton's, boundary line.
Made 26 Aug. 1810   Registered 21 June 1811

Wells was living on the Biggey River in Mississippi Territory.
Witnesses, Drury Oliver, Thomas Simmons

JOHN GEORGE RAINER of Hickman County
JOHN GILBERT of Dickson County   page 396
Rainer conveys to Gilbert land on the west bank of main Turnbull Creek.
Made 7 Aug. 1810   Registered 21 June 1811
Witnesses, James Arnold, Benjamin Gilbert

SAMUEL ELIOT of Wilson County
JOHN ADAMS of Dickson County   page 397
Eliot conveys to Adams land which begins at two sycamores below the Great Cave on the west bank of Yellow Creek, was originally granted by North Carolina to Morgan Drury and later John Drury for military service.
Made 31 Dec. 1810   Registered 22 June 1811
Witnesses, John Turner, Samuel Turner, Elisha Turner

MARTIN WELLS of Dickson County
JAMES FENTRESS   page 398
Wells conveys to Fentress a negro.
Made 15 Jan. 1810   Registered 22 June 1811
Witnesses, Absolom Fentress, Thomas Simmons

JOHN GILBERT
CHARLES GILBERT   page 399
(Note: This entry impossible to read on microfilm.)
Made 8 Aug. 1810   Registered 22 June 1811

JESSE STROUD of Dickson County
GEORGE POWELL of Dickson County   page 400
Stroud conveys to Powell. (Note: Could not read transaction.)
Made 21 Nov. 1810   Registered 22 June 1811

CHARLES GILBERT
BENJAMIN GILBERT   page 401
Made 8 Aug. 1810

WILLIAM W. REYNOLDS
JOHN HALL   page 402
Transaction mentions William Morrison's line and the mouth of John Reynolds spring and John Reynolds line above the old school house.
Registered 22 June 1811
Witnesses, ____Williams, ____Self, ____Snyth

JAMES McCLELLAN
IRA ADDISON MEEK   page 403
This entry, faded, mentions land on Jones Creek.
Made 2 Dec. 1809   Registered 24 June 1811
Witnesses, Nancy McClelland, Elbert Threlkeld

HAYDEN WELLS of Mississippi Territory
BENJAMIN ADAMS of Montgomery County   page 404
Made 6 Aug. 1810   Registered 24 June 1811

(Note: The next several pages in Book A were quite faded and dim. One on page 405 could not be deciphered at all. Page 406 had a transaction from William Miller, Sr., and Benjamin Walker, Sr., about land on Jones Creek, made 1810, registered 1811.)

JOHN CARPENTER of Williamson County
LEVIN DICKSON of Dickson County   page 407
Carpenter conveys to Dickson 30 acres on the west branch of Turnbull's Creek; mentions William Russell's corner.
Made 11 Dec. 1810   Registered 25 June 1811
Witnesses, Field Farrar, Cuthbert Hudson

ROBERT McNAIRY of Giles County, TN   page 408
Robert McNairy of Giles County, TN, for good will and affection for my grandson Robert Dickson, son of David Dickson of Dickson County, conveys

some negroes.
Made 24 Nov. 1810   Registered 25 June 1811
Witnesses, James Larkins, Jonathan Ozment

JOHN HOLLAND of Dickson County
WILLIAM STONE   page 408
Holland (Note: surname in question) conveys to Stone hogs, feather-
beds, pots, bowls, etc.
Made Nov. 1810
Witnesses, Marable Stone, John Hanna
(Note: There was another bill of sale on this page which could not be
read on the microfilm.)

SOLOMON BRADSHAW   page 410
Bradshaw prosecuted a certain writ of venetiore expones for sheriff to
sell 50 acres on Jones Creek against a certain ___Davis.
Made 1 Oct. 1810   Registered 28 June 1811

WILLIAM SULLIVANT of Montgomery County
JAMES READ of Dickson County   page 412
Sullivant conveys to Read land on Barton's Creek, adjoins William Read
and John McCauley.
Made 5 Oct. 1808   Registered 29 June 1811

ABNER DICKSON of Dickson County
JOHN LARKINS, SR.   page 413
Dickson mortgaged negro Reddick.
Made 17 Jan. 1811   Registered 28 June 1811

STATE OF TENNESSEE
WILLIAM T. LEWIS   page 414
State of Tennessee conveyed to Lewis land on Hurricane Creek.
Made 12 Dec. 1807

STATE OF TENNESSEE
SPILSBY TRIBBLE   page 415
State of Tennessee conveys to Tribble, assignee of William T. Lewis,
land on Hurricane Creek of Duck River.
Made 12 Dec. 1807   Registered 26 Aug. 1811

STATE OF NORTH CAROLINA
PETER DINNICK   page 418
State of North Carolina granted 360 acres in Tennessee County to
Peter Dinnick, sergeant in Continental Line; William T. Lewis was the
assignee.

DAVID McGRAW of Dickson County
RACHEL McGRAW   page 418
David McGraw conveys to daughter Rachel McGraw a negro Viney, age 7, as
part of her legacy.
Made 1 Sept. 1809   Registered 12 Oct. 1811
Witnesses, Betsy Burgan, Henry Ragland

DAVID McGRAW of Dickson County
ISAAC McGRAW   page 418
David McGraw conveys to son Isaac McGraw a negro Daniel, age 9, as
part of his legacy.
Made 1 Sept. 1809   Registered 12 Oct. 1811
Witnesses, Betsy Burgan, Henry Ragland

DAVID McGRAW of Dickson County
JUDY McGRAW   page 419
David McGraw conveys to daughter Judy McGraw a negro girl Ferriby,
age 10, as part of her legacy.
Made 1 Sept. 1809   Registered 12 Oct. 1811
Witnesses, H. Ragland, Betsy Burgan

STATE OF NORTH CAROLINA
HEZEKIAH BARNES   page 419
State of North Carolina granted to Hezekiah Barnes, private, 157 acres

on both sides of Yellow Creek; mentions Col. William Davis' line.
Made 4 Jan. 1792   Registered 6 Dec. 1811

STATE OF TENNESSEE
JOHN WADDLE and JOHN McMILLAN   page 419
State of Tennessee conveyed 50 acres on both sides of Cedar Creek to
Waddle and McMillan; mentions Stephen Horsley's line.
Made 27 July 1807

STATE OF TENNESSEE
HOWELL TATUM and JOHN PERMOTE WIGGIN   page 421
State of Tennessee conveyed land on Garner's Creek of Pine River of
Duck River; mentions Henry Wirt's north boundary line.
Made 13 Oct. 1808   Registered 7 Dec. 1811

WILLIAM DICKSON of Davidson County
JOSEPH DICKSON of Orange County, NC   page 423
William Dickson conveys 640 acres on the east fork of Barton's Creek.
Made 19 April 1811   Registered 16 Dec. 1811
Witnesses, Edward Richardson, John Brahan
(Note: This William Dickson is quite possibly the one for whom Dickson
County was named.)

RICHD. D. DUNN of Davidson County
WILLIAM DICKSON   page 424
Dunn conveys to Dickson land on Barton's Creek.
Made April 1807
Witnesses, R. Searcy, Nathan Ewing, Jno. L. Ewing

STATE OF TENNESSEE
HENRY WIRT   page 426
State of Tennessee conveys to Henry Wirt, assignee of Thomas Molloy,
land on Garner's Creek, mentions the upper side of a trace leading from
George Evans to the head of Tumbling Creek.
Made 27 Jan. 1808   Registered 17 Dec. 1811

DANIEL WILLIAMS
THOMAS WILLIAMS   page 427
Daniel Williams conveys to Thomas Williams 175 acres on both sides of
Yellow Creek including "improvement"; begins at the southeast corner of
tract granted me by North Carolina in 1792 to the west side of the Cave
Hill.
Made 22 Feb. 1811   Registered 22 Feb. 1811
Witnesses, Dan H. Williams, Nehemiah Scott

DANIEL WILLIAMS
DANIEL HICKS WILLIAMS   page 428
Daniel Williams conveys to Daniel Hicks Williams 284 acres on Yellow
Creek.
Made 22 Feb. 1811   Registered 2 Jan. 1812
Witnesses, Nehemiah Scott, Thomas Williams

DANIEL WILLIAMS
JOSEPH WILLIAMS   page 429
Daniel Williams conveys to son Joseph Williams 312 acres; mentions
Nehemiah Scott's northeast corner, crossing the dry bottom.
Made 29 June 1811   Registered 2 Jan. 1812
Witnesses, Daniel H. Williams, Nehemiah Scott

DANIEL WILLIAMS
NEHEMIAH SCOTT   page 430
Daniel Williams conveys to Scott land on west side of Yellow Creek, part
of my grant for military service.
Made 22 Feb. 1811   Registered 2 Jan. 1812
Witnesses, Daniel H. Williams, Thomas Williams

WILLIAM WARD of Dickson County
JOHN HARRIS of Dickson County   page 431
Ward conveys to Harris land on Barton's Creek; mentions Daniel Hicks'
southeast corner.

Made 1 Dec. 1810   Registered 3 Jan. 1812
Witnesses, James Watson, Nelson McDowell, James Hightower

HEDON WELLS of Mississippi Territory
JOHN HALL of Dickson County   page 433
Wells conveys to Hall land on south fork of the east fork of Yellow
Creek.
Made 25 Aug. 1810   Registered 3 Jan. 1812
Witnesses, Jacob Henson, William Reynolds, Amos Reynolds, John Boon

EDWARD PEARSALL, sheriff of Dickson County
JOHN NESBITT of Dickson County   page 434
Pearsall conveys to Nesbitt 101 acres. In 1809 the lands of William
Cochran were sold for 1808 taxes; mentions Thomas Simpson's northwest
corner and joining Nesbitt's 39 acre tract.
Made 2 Oct. 1810   Registered 3 Jan. 1812

BENJAMIN JOSLIN
JOHN MORRISETT   page 436
Joslin conveys to Morrisett 228 acres on Joneses Creek, land was
granted to Andrew Cowsert, assignee of Jeremiah Doxy.
Made 15 March 1811   Registered 3 Jan. 1812
Witness, F. Farrar

EZEKIEL NORRIS of Hickman County
JAMES GOODRICH of Dickson County   page 437
Norris conveys to Goodrich 120 acres, mentions the southeast corner of
James Goodrich's tract that he got from Stephen Childress.
Made 16 Aug. 1811   Registered 3 Feb. 1812
Witnesses, Michael Molton, Joseph Wilson

WILLIAM MORRISON of Dickson County
JOHN HALL of Dickson County   page 439
Morrison conveys to Hall land on the Rainy Camp Branch of the Leather-
wood Fork of Yellow Creek.
Made 11 Jan. 1811   Registered 3 Feb. 1812
Witnesses, Joseph W. Hall, Thomas Morrison

HENRY GRIMES, SR., of Dickson County
JOHN GRIMES of Dickson County   page 441
Henry Grimes, Sr., conveys to John Grimes land on Barton's Creek.
Made 22 March 1811   Registered 3 Feb. 1812
Witnesses, Abner Brown, Issac G. Grimes

JOHN McCLISH of Dickson County
JOHN GRIMES   page 442
McClish conveys to Grimes land on Barton's Creek.
Made 22 March 1811   Registered 3 Feb. 1812
Witnesses, Abner Brown, Isaac G. Grimes

ALLEN THOMPSON of Davidson County
BARNA H. FLINN   ___
Thompson conveys to Flinn Lot 33 in Charlotte.
Made 8 Oct. 1811   Registered _____
(Note: This page was not numbered, possibly page 443)

WILLIAM MOORE of Dickson County
JESSE LUMSDEN of Dickson County   page 44_ (?)
Moore conveys to Lumsden 100 acres on east fork of Yellow Creek; men-
tions John Drury's line; Drury sold to Duncan Stewart; Duncan Stewart
sold to Robert Dunning; mentions junction of the Otter Branch.
Made 5 April 1810   Registered 3 Feb. 1812
Witnesses, Richard Waugh, Andrew Hamilton

JOHN MORRISETTE of Dickson County
THOMAS MURRELL, SR., of Dickson County   page 447
Morrisette conveys to Murrell 150 acres on Jones Creek; land was ori-
ginally granted to William Russell.
Made 3 April 1810   Registered 3 Feb. 1812
Witnesses, William B. Ross, Samuel Russell

EZEKIEL NORRIS of Hickman County
JAMES GOODRICH of Dickson County   pages 448-449
Norris conveys to Goodrich 40 acres; mentions the southwest corner of
land from Michael and Jane Dickson to James Goodrich; Davis' west
boundary line; goes east with line of Stephen Childress.
Made 16 Aug. 1811   Registered 3 Feb. 1812
Witnesses, Michael Molton, Joseph Willson

SAMUEL TAYLOR of Dickson County
AARON LAWS of Dickson County   page 450
Taylor conveys to Laws 12 acres.
Made 11 Jan. 1811   Registered 3 Feb. 1812
Witnesses, Howel Adams, Minor Bibb, Cuthbert Hudson

THOMAS PATTON of Dickson County
WILLIAM STONE and JOHN MOODY of Dickson Co.   page 451
Patton conveys to Stone and Moody a negro named Monday, age 17.
Made 15 Aug. 1811   Registered 3 Feb. 1812
Witnesses, Andrew Elliott, John Hanna, George Brazzell

ROBERT DUKE of Davidson County
ANDREW CALDWELL   page 452
Duke conveys to Caldwell negro named Winny, age 2.
Made___1810   Registered 3 Feb. 1812
Witnesses, Sarry Boyte, William Dunn, William Caldwell

HAYDEN WELLS of Montgomery County
WILLIAM B. ROSS of Hickman County   page 453
Wells conveys to Ross land on south fork of east fork of Yellow Creek;
mentions Benjamin Adams on the north and on the east land was bounded by
John Hall.
Made 5 Nov. 1810   Registered 3 Feb. 1812
Witnesses, Matthew Morgan, Charles W. Teas

DAVID ROSS
WILLIAM B. ROSS   page 454
David Ross conveys to William B. Ross "my right in the estate of John
Ross, deceased".
Made 8 Jan. 1810   Registered 6 Feb. 1812
Witnesses, David Hogan, William Hudson

STATE OF TENNESSEE
STERLING BREWER   page 455
State of Tennessee conveys to Sterling Brewer, assignee of James Suchars
granted to Suchars for military service, land on the road that leads
from Davidell's ferry on the Cumberland River, 4 miles from the ferry,
including head spring of lower Town Creek that empties into Harpeth
River.
Made 28 June 1809   Registered 19 Feb. 1812

STATE OF TENNESSEE
STERLING BREWER   page 456
State of Tennessee conveys to Brewer, assignee of James Suchars, land on
Jones Creek, 1½ mile from mouth.
Made 20 June 1809   Registered 19 Feb. 1812

JAMES STEELE of Dickson County
AUGUSTINE RICHARDSON of Dickson County   page 457
Steele conveys to Richardson 15-3/4 acres on Joneses Creek.
Made 30 March 1811   Registered 19 Feb. 1812
Witnesses, William Stone, John Hanna

JAMES ROBERTSON of Davidson County
MONTGOMERY BELL of Dickson County   page 459
Robertson conveys to Bell for $1920, 1/2 of three tracts on the Iron ore
fork of Barton's Creek, the one adjoining M. Bell's furnace tract.
Made 10 Oct. 1811   Registered 19 Feb. 1812
Witnesses, R. C. Napier, John Waters

RICHARD NAPIER of Dickson County
RICHARD NAPIER CLAIBORNE LAMB   page 460
Richard Napier conveys to grandson Richard Napier Claiborne Lamb, son
of George Lamb by my daughter Polley, now 4 years old, a negro Moriah,
age 12.
Made 15 April 1808   Registered 20 Feb. 1812
Witness, Roger Shackelford

JAMES ROBERTSON of Davidson County
ELLIS TYCER of Dickson County   page 460
Robertson conveys to Tycer 170 acres on headwaters of Barton's Creek;
mentions Tycer's southeast corner.
Made 19 Oct. 1811   Registered 20 April 1812
Witnesses, Richard C. Napier, John Carick

JOHN MORRISETTE of Dickson County
THOMAS MURRELL, SR.   page 462
Morrisette conveys 50 acres on Jones Creek, originally granted to
Ancdrew Cowsert.
Made 7 Oct. 1810   Registered 20 Feb. 1812

JOHN MORRISETTE of Dickson County
WILLIAM STONE   page 463
John Morrisette conveys to son-in-law William Stone 178 acres on Joneses
Creek below William Russell's, deceased, tract; also a negro Peggy,
tools, and other items.
Made 1 Oct. 1811   Registered 20 Feb. 1812
Witness, Richard Waugh

JAMES ROBERTSON of Davidson County
RICHARD CLAIBORNE NAPIER of Dickson County   page 464
Robertson conveys to Napier 2 tracts on Barton's Creek; mentions Thomas
Matthews southeast corner and Stephen Ward's corner and Weakley's
Ferry.
Made___1811   Registered 20 Feb. 1812
Witnesses, Isaac David and John Reeves

WILLIAM BRASHER of Dickson County
JACOB EVINS of Dickson County   page 465
Brasher conveys to Evins a mare, featherbed, cattle, and other items.
Made 5 Oct. 1811   Registered 20 Feb. 1812
Witnesses, John Davidson, Robert Simmons

ABRAHAM ROBERTSON of Dickson County
BENJAMIN JOSLIN of Davidson County   page 466
Robertson, administrator of William Russell, deceased, of Dickson
County conveys 170 acres to Joslin.
Made 7 Jan. 1812   Registered 20 Feb. 1812
Witnesses, William Stone, Augustine Richardson

This concludes the abstracted notes from Dickson County
Deed Book A.

DEED BOOK B

This book, also abstracted from the microfilm, covers the period February 1812 to March 1816.

EDWIN GWIN of Sumner County to
THOMAS HENDRIX of Dickson County   page 3
100 acres.
Made 2 Sept. 1811   Registered 24 February 1812
Witnesses: William Anderson, John Hendrix

JAMES ROBERTSON of Davidson County to
MOSES PARKER of Dickson County   pages 6 and 7
Robertson conveys 100 acres on the east fork of Turnbull Creek, including a spring...mentions a small creek above Joseph Shp's and a mile up creek from the mouth beginning at a sappling in the barrns...the cave spring branch was originally entered by John Childress...mentions the line between Moses Parker and Edward Smith.
Made 17 Jan. 1810   Registered 24 Feb. 1812

JAMES MARTIN of Dickson County to
WILLIAM MILLER   page 10
Conveys land on the west fork of Jones Creek, mentions it being northwest corner of Margaret Hicks.
Made 9 October 1809

JAMES ROBERTSON of Davidson County to
BARTHOLOMEW SMITH of Dickson County   no page
Conveys land on Russell's fork of Jones Creek.
Made 3 September 1811

JAMES McCLELEND of Dickson County to
THOMAS PANNEL of Dickson County   page number was torn--maybe 19?
Conveys land on Jones Creek, including improvements and also all the estate.
Made 23 March 1807   Registered 24 Feb. 1812
Witnesses, Silas H. Miller, Isaac West

SIMON HOLT of Dickson County to
ELIZABETH WALKER and MARY CLARK of Dickson County   pages 12, 13
Conveys 100 acres on Barton's Creek.
Made 16 Oct. 1809   Registered 28 Feb. 1812
Witnesses, Richard Tubb, Joseph Walker

WILLIAM GIFFIN of Dickson County to
ROBERT SIMMONS   pages 13, 14
Conveys 130 acres on the middle fork of Barton's Creek, beginning at oak on the stillhouse hollow..mentions the west boundary line of the Howel Adams grant.
Made 11 July 1809
Witnesses, William Brasher, James Seals

JOSIAH SUGG of Davidson County to
CHARLES CAMPBELL of Dickson County   page 15
Conveys 64 acres on the west side of Harpeth River one mile above mouth at Campbell's spring branch.
Made 26 Sept. 1806
Witnesses, William Caldwell, Barnebese Allen

CALEB DICKSON of Davidson County to
JOSHUA JAMES of Davidson County   pages 17, 18
Conveys 50 acres, part of 640 acre survey of James Rail, land on Turnbull Creek.
Made 30 July 1811   Registered 29 Feb. 1812
Witnesses, Cutburd Hudson, John George Raines, George Powell

EDWARD PEARSELL, sheriff of Dickson County to
JOHN McNAIRY, BENNET SEARCY of Davidson County   pages 18-24
John McNairy got judgment agains John Cole Montflorence for two tracts in Dickson County, 1000 acres each...land was on Weakley's Creek, a

west fork of Barton's Creek on the south side of the Cumberland River below Harpeth River. This was part originally granted to Benjamin Reeves, a sergeant in the continental line of North Carolina.
Made 25 January 1811   Registered 8 April 1812

CHARLES KOLB of Jackson County, Georgia, to
WILLIAM PEACOCK   pages 24, 25
Conveys negro man, Monday, age 18, now confined in Dickson County jail.
Made 15 August 1811
Witnesses, William Martin, Mill. (or Will.) Stone

JAMES READ, ESQUIRE, high sheriff of Dickson County to
ANDREW HAMILTON   page 26
Conveys 140 acres; land did belong to John Thompson and was sold 1810 by Edward Pearsall, then high sheriff...land was on a fork of Jones Creek..mentions Thomas Thompson's corner.
Made 22 December 1811   Registered 23 June 1812
Witnesses, Richard Waugh, John Spencer

ANDREW HAMILTON to
JOHN LARKIN, SR.   page 29
Conveys 140 acres on Jones Creek
Made 1 January 1812   Registered 23 June 1812
Witnesses, John Larkins, John Read

WILLIE BLOUNT, GOVERNOR OF TENNESSEE to
SAMUEL VANCE   page 31
Governor conveys 100 acres to Samuel Vance, assignee of John Gray Blount; land was on north fork of middle prong of Barton's Creek, adjoining Howel Adams.
Made 22 April 1809

EDWARD PEARSALL, High Sheriff of Dickson County, to
ELIZABETH HAYES of Dickson County   pages 33-35
Conveys 40 acres on Yellow Creek by virtue of execution in Stewart County to dispose of land of Thomas Hayes, deceased. Elizabeth Hayes was the administratrix of James Hayes, deceased. Land was on south side of Cumberland River on Yellow Creek...mentions southwest corner of Israel Harmon.
Made 11 October 1810
Witnesses, David Dickson, Abner Dickson

MONTGOMERY BELL of Dickson County to
EDWARD LEACH   pages 36, 37
Gives bond for $10,000..mentions 1000 acres of the Williamson tract.
Made 15 February 1812   Registered 24 July 1812
Witness, John J. Bell

MATTHEW McCLURKAN of Franklin County, Indiana Territory, to
JAMES McCLURKAN   page 37
Gives power of attorney to convey to Hugh McNeelly, Robert Harper, and John Evans.
Made 1 July 1811   Registered 24 July 1812

BENJAMIN ANDREWS of Dickson County, to
DRURY CHRISTIAN   page 39
Conveys one negro woman.
Made 8 July 1812   Registered 24 July 1812
Witnesses, David Hogan, William Speight

JOHN ASHE DAVIS of Hanover County, N. C., to
MICHAEL MOLTON of Dickson County   pages 40, 41
Conveys 416 acres on both sides of Yellow Creek...mentions Jeremiah Pearsall's corner...land above the mouth of Shoulder Strap Branch... part of tract conveyed by North Carolina to William Davis to which John Ashe Davis was heir to half.
Made 24 Feb. 1812   Registered 24 July 1812
Witnesses, James Dickson, David Dickson

NATHAN WILLIAMS of Davidson County to
JOHN TUBB of Dickson County   page 42
Conveys 640 acres on south side of Big Harpeth on Jones Creek, 3 miles
above its mouth.
Made 23 Dec. 1811
Witnesses, Benjamin Barton, John Sanders, William Sanders

SILAS TOMPKINS of Davidson County to
JAMES NORRIS of said county   page 43
Conveys 100 acres on waters of Turnbull Creek at the mouth of the Barren
Fork running to the mouth of the big branch.
Made 1 January 1811   Registered 24 July 1812
Witnesses, Benjamin Norris, William Turman

JOHN CARROTHERS to
THOMAS ROPER   page 44
Conveys negroes.
Made 6 July 1812   Registered 27 July 1812
Witnesses, Field Farrar, Drury Christian

STATE OF NORTH CAROLINA to
JAMES LEWIS, SR.   page 45
Conveys 112 acres; land on the wolf branch of Jones Creek, entered 1809,
now to William J. Morrisette. The conveyance also signed by Governor
of Tennessee 1812.
Made 27 Dec. 1787   Registered 26 July 1812

THOMAS ROPER to
JOHN CARUTHERS, JR   page 46
Conveys 330 acres at head of Leatherwood Creek, mentions corner of a
tract conveyed by Thomas Roper to John McAdoo, Jr.
Made 3 June 1812   Registered 26 July 1812
Witnesses, David McAdow, William Caruthers

ISAAC WEST, SR. to
ANDERSON WEST   page 47
Conveys 230 acres on west fork of Jones Creek.
Made 1 April 1812   Registered 26 July 1812
Witnesses, Elijah Threlkeld, Richard Murrell

SILAS TOMPKINS of Dickson County to
JOSEPH LAMPLEY   page 48
Conveys land on east side of Turnbull Creek, goes west to Beaverdam
Fork.
Made 10 August 1811   Registered 26 July 1812
Witnesses, Jacob Purkins, Ebben Perkins

WILLIAM ROPER of Smith County to
THOMAS ROPER   page 50
Conveys 330 acres, part of the 640 acres that William Roper bought of
John Smith.
Made 31 August 1811   Registered 26 July 1812
Witnesses, Johnathan Johnson, William Loving, John Brown

EDMOND GREGGORY of Chowan County, N. C., to
SILAS TOMPKINS of Williamson County   page 51
Conveys land on the east fork of Turnbull Creek, land was granted by
North Carolina to Frederick Hargett, assignee of Joseph Card.
Made 14 October 1809   Registered 27 July 1812
Witnesses, Thomas Talbott, Isaac Tompkins

SILAS TOMPKINS of Dickson County to
JACOB PERKINS   page 53
Conveys land on the east side of Turnbull Creek.
Made 10 August 1811   Registered 27 July 1812
Witnesses, Joseph Lampley, Ebben Perkins

DAVID HOGAN to
ZEBEEDEE HICKS   pages 55, 56
continued

Conveys 142 acres in District 1, mentions northeast corner of William Nalls, crosses 4-mile creek of Jones Creek, and excluding the plantation where Zebeedee Hicks now lives.
Made 5 May 1812   Registered 28 July 1812
Witnesses, William Nall, Thomas Nall

JAMES HOLT of Montgomery County to
BURGES WALL of Dickson County   page 57
Conveys land on middle fork of Barton's Creek.
Made __Sept. 1811   Registered 28 July 1812
Witnesses, James Read, William Read

ROBERT DUNNING, JOHN DAVIDSON, GEORGE CLARK
Commissioners of Charlotte to
STERLING BREWER   page 58
Convey Lot 28, bounded by Dunning Street on the north and Dickson Street on the west.
Made 13 July 1809   Registered 28 July 1812

ELIZABETH HAYS, JOHN HAYS, ROBERT HAYS AND ARTHUR SCOTT to
ROBERT WEST   page 59
Conveyance mentions Israel Harmon's southwest corner
Made 1 July 1812   Registered 28 July 1812

FIELD FARRAR to
JOHN EVINS   page 61
Conveys negro girl Easter.
Made 7 May 1812   Registered 28 July 1812
Witnesses, Thomas Wright, James Read

MONTGOMERY BELL   page 62
Montgomery Bell on the first Monday April 1810 prosecuted two writs to sell one house and lott in town of Fayetteville with advantages of Ferry, it being the lott where Robert Weakley now lives. (Note: This town was in Dickson County and possibly did not become a reality and is not to be confused with a town of the same name in Lincoln County, TN.)
Registerd 15 Sept. 1812
Witnesses, John Read, David Dickson

SILVESTER ADAMS of Humphreys County to
WILLIAM D. TURNER of Dickson County   page 65
Conveys land in District 1 on the west fork of Yellow Creek...mentions Thomas Archer's line crosses said fork.
Made 17 March 1812   Registered 15 Sept. 1812
Witnesses, Samuel Hostley, Samuel Turner

CALEB DICKERSON to
JOSHUA JAMES   page 67, 68
Conveys 25 acres.
Made 30 July 1811   Registered 17 Sept. 1812
Witnesses, Cut B. Hudson, George Powell, John George Rainer

WILLIAM PERSONS and THOMAS PERSONS of Warren Co., N.C., to
JAMES WATSON of Davidson County   page 68
Conveys 100 acres of land, originally granted by North Carolina to Thomas Persons, assignee of Samuel Tucker; grant was deeded to following: James Watson, 100 acres, Gabriel Overton, 260 acres, John Dunnagan, 200 acres, William Dunnagan, 100 acres, James Dunnagan, 40 acres.
Made 12 March 1812   Registered 17 Sept. 1812
Witnesses, B. B. Stewart, Millington Easley

WILLIAM. PERSONS and THOMAS PERSONS of Warren Co., N.C., to
JOHN DUNNAGAN   page 72-74
Same entry as one before.
Made 12 March 1812   Registered 17 Sept. 1812
Witnesses, B. G. Stewart, James Dunnagan
(Note: pages 79, 82, in this book have same entry for Gabriel Overton and William Dunnagan.)

STATE OF TENNESSEE to
JOHN SIMPSON   page 86
Conveys 320 acres for military service performed for North Acrolina;
land assigned to Obediah Roberts...land in District 1 on Hurricane
Creek (formerly Camp Creek) of Duck River below the Chickasaw Trace.
Reqistered 19 July 1812
(Note: another entry on page 87.)

STATE OF NORTH CAROLINA grant   page 89
No. 2185 for 640 acres on Barton's Creek for the signal bravery and
personal zeal of WALKER McFARLAND, a private in line; this land was
assigned to Chamerlain Hudson.
Made 13 May 1796   Registered 21 Sept. 1812

FRANCIS BROWN, SR., to
AUGUSTIN RICHARDSON   page 90
Conveys land on Jones Creek, being part of tract where said Brown
now lives...mentions southeast corner of Benjamin Joslin.
Made 6 April 1812   Registered 22 Sept. 1812
Witnesses, William Stone, SamuelRussell

BENJAMIN FITS RANDOLPH of Bladen County, N. C. to
ROBERT LITLE   page 93
Power of attorney.
Made 5 August 1812
Witness, J. Wright, James Smith

ARCHIBALD McMILLAN of Cumberland County, N. C., to
ROBERT LYTLE of Bladen County, N. C.   page 94
Power of attorney about land in Tennessee granted, No. 1855, and en-
tered in the name of Benjamin Mills and Isaac Bledsoe.
Made 17 August 1812
Witnesses, Daniel McMillan of Moore Co., N. C., Neel McKeethen

WILLIAM MILLER of Dickson County to
OLIVER B. HAYES and WILLIAM SMITH of Davidson and Williamson Co. -p.96
Conveys lots 10 and 19 in Charlotte, located on West Street.
Made 5 October 1812   Registered 28 November 1812

STATE OF TENNESSEE to
ARCHIBALD MARTIN   page 98
Conveys 230 acres for being a private in battalion of troops raised by
North Carolina for the protection of inhabitants of Davidson County;
land was in District 1, Hurricane Creek of Duck River, surveyed 1808
by Dawsey Hudson; mentions Lewis Collins' improvement. Land goes to
Lewis Collins, who is entitled to the land.
Registered 12 Dec. 1812

STATE OF TENNESSEE to
JOHN DICKSON   page 99
Conveyed to John Dickson, assignee of Thomas Hickman...Thomas Hickman
entered the land in 1807...land was in District 1 on Bear Creek of
Yellow Creek...surveyed 1809...mentions the 6-mile tree.
Made 12 August 1809   Registered 18 Dec. 1812

STATE OF TENNESSEE to
LEWIS POWERS   page 100
This land was granted to John Bruce for his military service to the
State of North Carolina, dated 27 Dec. 1796, and granted to Lewis
Powers, assignee of John Bruce...land in District 1 on Otter Branch
of Yellow Creek, mentions northwest of John Dickson.
Made 13 Dec. 1809   Registered 18 Dec. 1812

STATE OF TENNESSEE to
LEWIS POWERS   page 102
This land was granted to John Bruce for his military service on 20 Dec.
1796...land on Yellow Creek...mentions the southeast stake in Stephen
Tatum's corner.
Made 13 Dec. 1809   Registered 18 Dec. 1812

STATE OF TENNESSEE to
JOHN DICKSON, assignee of Thomas Hickman   page 103
Made 12 Aug. 1809   Registered 20 Dec. 1812

STATE OF TENNESSEE to
JOHN DICKSON   page 104
This conveyance is much like the others, also another one on p. 106.

GEORGE WRIGHT and JOHN WRIGHT to
ALLEN BOWEN   pages 107, 108
Conveyed 50 acres on both sides of creek, part of land crosses the
Hickman and Dickson line. (Note: Entry very dim on microfilm.)
Made 12 Sept. 1811   Registered 29 Jan. 1813
Witnesses, Elijah Renshaw, George Smith

DAVID ROBERTSON of Williamson County to
JAMES TIDWELL of Dickson County   page 110
Conveys 100 acres of land on Haley's Branch.
Made 16 July 1812   Registered 29 Jan. 1813
Witnesses, Cuthbert Hudson, Isaiah Tidwell

THOMAS MARTIN to
CHRISTOPHER STRONG   page 111
Conveys land on Jones Creek, part of 640 acres granted to John P. Crab-
tree...land goes up creek to mouth of Sulphur Fork above the Town Fork;
mentions Moses Meek southeast corner and John Davises line.
Made 1 January 1813   Registered 29 Januaey 1813
Witnesses, William Peacock, Thomas Wright

ROBERT DUNNING of Hickman County to
SAMUEL KING of Dickson County   page 113
Conveys land on Hurricane Creek of Duck River.
Made 20 June 1812   Registered 1 Feb. 1813
Witnesses, James King, James Alexander

POWER OF ATTORNEY   pages 115, 116
John Blackfan, one of heirs of William Blackfan, late of township of
Salisbury in county of Bucks in Pennsylvania, appoint brother Jesse
Blackfan of Philadelphia, power of attorney to receive my interest and
sell my land in Davidson County, Tennessee, near Cumberland River.
Made 3 May 1811   Registered 2 Feb. 1813
Witnesses, Abraham Dodson, A. B. Jones

BENJAMIN ANDREWS to
DRURY CHRISTIAN   page 117
Conveys cows, calves, horse, beds, etc.
Made 27 Nov. 1812   Registered 2 Feb. 1813
Witnesses, James Jones, Giles Jones

SOLOMON STONE of Dickson County to
MARBLE STONE and WILLIAM STONE   page 118
Conveys my interest in the tract whereon my mother now lives, being
one-third of 360 acres, my interest in stock belonging to my father's
estate before and since his death.
Made 22 Oct. 1810   Registered 2 Feb. 1813
Witnesses, Hardeman Stone, John Hannah

DRURY CHRISTIAN to
JOHN REYNOLDS and others   page 119
Conveys to John Reynolds, Richard Epps, William Brasher, John Shelton,
as trustees of Baptist Church on the middle fork of Barton's Creek 1½
acres on the north side of the middle fork for purpose of building a
Baptist meeting house for the promulgation of the Gospel of Jesus
Christ.
Made 5 December 1812   Registered 2 February 1813

JAMES ROBERTSON of Davidson County to
JOHN TATOM of Dickson County
Conveys land on west fork of Pine River east of Lewis Russell's south-
west corner. (continued)

Made 19 July 1809 Registered 4 Feb. 1813
Witnesses, Millington Easley, William Stone

POWER OF ATTORNEY   pages 122, 123, 124
Thomas Blackfan, one of heirs of William Blackfan, late of Salisbury, Bucks County, Pennsylvania, yeoman, deceased, gives power of attorney to my brother Jesse Blackfan of Philadelphia to received any sums, lands situate in Davidson County, Tennessee, by last will of William Blackfan.
Made 28 Feb. 1811   Registered 11 April 1812
                                     Davidson County
                                     Registered 5 Feb. 1813 in
                                     Dickson County

WILLIAM OUTLAW of Stewart County to
JOHN ALLEN of Montgomery County   page 125
Conveys land. (Note: This entry very faded on microfilm.)
Made 10 Sept. 1811   Registered 5 Feb. 1813
Witnesses, Robert West, William Morrison

STATE OF TENNESSEE to
GEORGE LEWIS   page 126
State of Tennessee grants 60 acres to George Lewis, assignee, for the military services of George Tippet of North Carolina, land in District 1 18th Range, 5th Section, on both sides of Childress Creek, surveyed in 1807.
Made 12 Dec. 1796   Registered 15 Feb. 1813

STATE OF TENNESSEE to
GEORGE TIPPIT of North Carolina   page 128
Grants land on Childress Creek in Dickson County.
Made 20 August 1808   Registered 15 Feb. 1813

JOHN GRAY BLOUNT, by Willie Blount his agent, of Beauford, N. C., to
AUGUSTINE RICHARDSON   page 129
Conveys land on west fork of Jones Creek.
Made 30 Sept. 1812   Registered 18 Feb. 1813

CARTER ACUFF to
ELIAS W. NAPIER   page 131
Conveys 103 acres and all his title and claim of tract of land whereon Elizabeth Acuff now lives.
Made 7 Dec. 1812   Registered 22 Feb. 1813
Witnesses, John Reads, C. Robertson

ROBERT DRAKE to
JOHN STEWART   page 132
Conveys 80 acres on Johnson's Creek, beginning where the waggon road crosses, leading from R. C. Nappier's furnace to Nashville.
Made 6 June 1811   Registered 22 Feb. 1813
Witnesses, R. C. Napier, Wm. R. B. Clements

WILLIAM OUTLAW of Stewart County to
JOSEPH KIMBLE of Montgomery County   page 133
Conveys 224 acres on main Yellow Creek, part of tract granted to John Ramsey, heir of Miles Ramsey, adjoining Israel Harmon's grant, now Robert West.
Made 10 Sept. 1811   Registered 28 Feb. 1813
Witnesses, William Morrison, Robert West

STATE OF TENNESSEE to
WILLIAM SKINNER   page 135
Conveyed to Jesse Ragan, assignee of heirs of William Skinner; land was from North Carolina to Skinner...land in District 1, mentions Hosley's Branch of Yellow Creek, including the improvements...surveyed 1809.
Made 20 Nov. 1807   Registered 3 March 1813

DAVID CALDWELL to
WILLIAM MOORE   page 136
Conveys 50 acres...mentions that William Moore, whereon he now lives.
Made 2 Jan.1812   Registered 13 March 1813

Witnesses, Francis S. Ellis, C. Robertson

ISAAC WEST, SR. to
SAMUEL SPARKS   page 137
Conveys land on Jones Creek.
Made 18 Sept. 1812   Registered 13 March 1813
Witnesses, James McGee, William McClelland

LEWIS BOND of Halifax Co., N. C., to
WHERRIOT LEWIS of Wilkerson County, Ga.   pages 138-140
Power of attorney to Lewis to received from Claudius David L of
Dickson County what Claudius David L has received of Abraham Whitehead
of Montgomery County, as agent for me.
Made 6 March 1813   Registered 7 May 1813
(Note: The surname is found as David L in this entry.)
Witnesses, John Passmore, R. A. Jackson

ANDREW HAMILTON to
CHARLES BARNES   page 140
Conveys one-half of Lots 31 and 41 in Charlotte.
Made 26 Oct. 1812   Registered 7 May 1813
Witnesses, John Read, Eliakim Raymond

WILLIAM MILLER to
THOMAS WRIGHT   page 142
Conveys land on west fork of Jones Creek...mentions James McClelland's
south boundary.
Made 28 November 1806   Registered 19 June 1813
Witnesses, William Miller, Jr., Thomas Martin

WILLIAM CURRY of Dickson County to
JOHN GWIN of Sumner County   page 143
Conveys land on the furnace fork of Barton's Creek, being a quit claim
deed as said land has been conveyed by John Gwin and others to William
Curry and now in dispute with Phillip and Camel.
Made 28 Sept. 1812   Registered 19 June 1813
Witnesses, Edward Gwin, Benjamin Alley

WILLIAM MILLER, SR., to
WILLIAM MILLER, JR.   page 145
Conveys land on west fork of Jones Creek...mentions Thomas Wright's
southeast corner.
Made 27 August 1812   Registered 19 June 1813
Witnesses, William Bullion, Thomas Bullion

ROBERT DUNNING of Hickman County to
JAMES KING of Dickson County   page 146
Conveys land on Hurricane Creek of Duck River.
Made 13 July 1812   Registered 10 June 1813
Witnesses, S. King, James Alexander

BENJAMIN BAKER to
GILBERT MARSH   page 148
Conveys 39 acres to Gilbert Marsh...mentions Joslin's west boundary line
and also Lewis and George Russell's lines.
Made 14 Sept. 1812   Registered 30 June 1813
Witnesses, James L. Scott, Joel Marsh, John Baker

CORNELIUS McGRAW to
ELISHA DICKSON   page 151
Conveys land on first branch below Harpeth...mentions William Caldwell's
northwest corner.
Made 21 Dec. 1810   Registered __July 1813
Witnesses, Benjamin Weakley, C. David L, R. Weakley, Jno. S. Whitmill

ROBERT ORMSBY of New Hanover County, N. C., to
ABSALOM FENTRESS of New Hanover County, N. C. page 153
Deeds negroes Sarah and her two children.
Made_____   Registered 1 July 1813

JOHN BROWN of Montgomery County to
EDWARD WATTS of Dickson County   page 154
Conveys 85 acres on Wallace's Branch, a branch of the Leatherwood Fork
of Yellow Creek...mentions William Hodge's southwest corner and John
Reynolds' line.
Made 7 April 1813   Registered 2 July 1813

BENJAMIN BAKER to
GILBERT MARSH   page 155
Conveys 100 acres, mentions Joslin's southwest corner.
Made 14 Sept. 1812   Registered 3 July 1813
Witnesses, Joel Marsh, John Baker

WILLIAM B. ROSS of Hickman County to
WILLIAM SHELTON, JR. of Dickson County   page 157
Conveys 81-3/4 acres on south fork of east fork of Yellow Creek, land
originally granted to Hayden Wells.
Made 16 Jan. 1813   Registered 3 July 1813
Witnesses, Benjamin Adams, John Gray

JOURDAN STROUD to
BENJAMIN GILBERT   page 159
Conveys land on Turnbull Creek...mentions John Morand's west boundary
line.
Made 2 March 1813   Registered 3 July 1813
Witnesses, William Robinson, Peter Gilbert

JAMES TIDWELL to
JOHN SILVERS   page 160
Conveys 100 acres on Haley's fork.
Made 6 Jan. 1813   Registered 16 July 1813
Witnesses, Knott Tidwell, Richard Robertson

DAVID WALLACE to
JOHN BROWN   page 162
Conveys 50 acres on a branch of Leatherwood fork of Yellow Creek, land
on both sides of branch.
Made 16 Dec. 1809   Registered 19 July 1813
Witnesses, Selman Edwards, John Hodges

JAMES KING
Deed of Gift   pages 163, 164
James King for natural love and affection for my children, Catren, John,
James, Robert, Alexander, William, Nancy and Patrick King and wife
Nancy, conveys all my property and 100 acres on the dry fork of Barton's
Creek adjoining Jesse Jarnegan's land. (Note: This conveyance is
signed James King, but in the wording of the entry his name is also
given as Samuel King and it was registered in name of Samuel King. Wife
Nancy refers to the wife of the conveyor.)
Made 5 Jan. 1813   Registered 20 July 1813
Witnesses, David Robinson, Patrick Woods, James Woods, Robert Simmons,
Samuel Robison.

JOHN HUNTER to
JOHN PLANT and BENJAMIN JAMES   page 165
Conveys 60 acres on west side of Yellow Creek...mentions Samuel Elliot's
west boundary line, formerly Morgan Drury's, including Harmas (Thomas?)
Torbet's improvement in the dry hollow.
Made 7 Jan. 1812   Registered 20 July 1813
Witnesses, William Plant, Charles Thompson, William Mills

WILLIAM NORRIS and JANE NORRIS to
DREWRY PRICE   pages 167-169
Convey 100 acres on west bank of Yellow Creek...mentions James Goodrich's
corner. (Note: She signed her name as Jane--her mark--Norris.)
Made 15 Dec. 1812   Registered 20 July 1813
Witnesses, Edward Pearsall, Nathan Nesbett, Thomas Williams.
(Note: pages 168-9 have another identical deed for these people.)

ABRAHAM ROBERTSON et al to
CHARLES HODGE   page 170
Abraham Robertson, one of the administrators of William Russell, deceased, and Charity Morrisett, the other administrator, convey 99 acres on Jones Creek, part of 320 acres granted to heirs of William Russell, deceased...mentions Benjamin Joslin's southwest corner.
Made 6 April 1812   Registered 27 July 1813
Witnesses, William Stone, Jesse Russell

DREWRY CHRISTIAN, Sheriff, to
BENJAMIN WEAKLEY of Montgomery County page 172
Conveys 640 acres...sheriff was directed to sell goods in 1805 as sheriff of Stewart and Montgomery counties as well as well property of William Wickoff in Dickson County as Robert Nelson had recovered against William Wickoff, Junr...land was on south side of Cumberland River between Yellow and Gues Creeks...began 1 mile east of Gues Creek...land was granted to William Wickoff on 23 Feb. 1793.
Made 8 July 1813   Registered 27 July 1813

WILLIAM B. ROSS of Hickman County to
GEORGE TUBB of Dickson County   page 175
Conveys 200 acres on Johnston's Creek on the south side of the Cumberland River...mentions Doctor Hugh Williamson's east line crosses the creek.
Made 19 March 1812   Registered 29 July 1813
Witnesses, William Hudson, James Dunagan

RICHARD COCK to
EBENEZER KELLY   page 177
Conveys 140 acres on Barton's Creek.
Made 6 April 1812   Registered 2 August 1813
Witnesses, Thomas Batson, Goodman Traywick

STATE OF NORTH CAROLINA to
JOHN BROWN   page 179
Granted 640 acres on the second large fork on the west side of Yellow Creek to John Brown, private, for signal bravery in continental line; granted to Archibald Allen, assignee of John Brown...adjoins the entries of James Middleton and John Nelson. (Note: plat of land appears on page 181.)
Made May 1793   Registered 11 August 1813

THOMAS BATSON of Montgomery County to
RICHARD COCKE   pages 182, 183
Conveys land on Barton's Creek.
Made 24 Jan. 1812   Registered 11 August 1813
Witnesses, Richard Batson, Griffin Mills

LEWIS RUSSELL of Hickman County to
WILLIAM HUDSON of Dickson County   page 183
Conveys land on west fork of Pine River...mentions northeast corner of James Tatum, George Russell's line, and John Scott's line.
Made 30 Dec. 1811   Registered 14 July 1813
Witnesses, Jesse Russell, William Hudson, Jr.

ROBERT LYTLE to
WILLIAM B. ROSS and DAVID HOGAN   page 186
Robert Lytle, attorney for Benjamin Fitz Randolph, conveys land on the headwaters of Jones Creek, the sulphur fork...mentions Charles Stewart's west boundary line.
Made 12 Oct. 1812   Registered 14 Aug. 1813
Witnesses, Cuthbert and William Hudson

JOHN MAXWELL to
KEDAR BRYAN of Sampson County, N. C. page 188
Power of attorney made Duplin County, N. C., from John Maxwell, executor of estate of James Dickson, deceased, esquire, of Duplin Co., N. C., to Kedar Bryan of Sampson County, N. C. Edward Pearsall was chairman of Dickson County court, April 1813.
Made 20 April 1813   Registered 11 Sept. 1813

DANIEL PARKER, JR., of Sumner County to
MINOR BIBB of Dickson County   page 189
Conveys 25 acres in District 1, Turnbull Creek.
Made 11 May 1811   Registered 16 Sept. 1813
Witnesses, Levin Dixon, Isaah Tidwell

STATE OF TENNESSEE to
HUGH NICHOLS   pages 191, 192
Tennessee granted land for services performed by William Clark on
24 April 1785...he got 75 acres in Dickson County on Johnson Creek
beginning at George Teal, Sr.'s northwest corner and running to a dry
hollow...mentions Dr. Hugh Williamson's south boundary line. "We
Hugh and Sarah Nichols and heirs sign over to Edward Teal all right to
this 75 acres forever."
Registered 16 Sept. 1813
Witness, David Crawford

JEREMIAH PEARSALL, planter, to
EDWARD PEARSALL, his son   pages 193, 194
Conveys 260 acres in love and affection...land on both sides of Yellow
Creek and the dry creek of Horsley's Branch near Sam Horsley's.
Made 5 Jan. 1813   Registered 16 Sept. 1813
Witnesses, S. Brewer, Jno. Humphreys

JOHN DAVIS of Davidson County to
CHRISTOPHER STRONG of Dickson County   pages 195, 196
Conveys land on Jones Creek, about 1 mile below Strong's mill.
Made 3 July 1813   Registered 16 Sept. 1813
Witnesses, Sophia W. Davis, (other witness name illegible)

HUGH NICHOLS of Mulingburgh Co., Kentucky, to
EDWARD TEAL of Dickson County   page 197
Conveys land at head of Johnson Creek...mentions George Teal, Sr.'s
northwest corner.
Made 6 Sept. 1813   Registered 16 Sept. 1813
Witnesses, J. Wingate, I. Walker

RICHARD ALLEN of Humphreys County to
SOLOMON RYE of Dickson County   page 199
Conveys land on east side of Yellow Creek "below the mouth of Great
Cave"; 26 poles below a great spring being lower part of 640 acres
granted to Morgan Drewry by North Carolina.
Made 29 May 1813   Registered 23 Sept. 1813
Witnesses, Thomas Williams, James Goodrich, Charles Thompson

RICHARD ALLEN of Humphreys County to
JAMES GOODRICH of Dickson County   page 201
Conveys 160 acres on both sides of Yellow Creek, beginning on west bank
of creek below the mouth of a Great Cave and 26 poles above a great
spring...mentions Charles Thompson's corner...this being the middle
tract of 512 acres deeded from Elliott to Allen.
Made 29 May 1813   Registered 23 Sept. 1813
Witnesses, Solomon Rye, Charles Thompson, Thomas Williams

WILLIAM WALKER of Hickman County to
ANDY BEAVERS of Dickson County   page 203
Conveys 82½ acres in District 1 on Jones Creek...mentions John Choat's
northeast corner.
Made 1 May 1813   Registered 23 Sept. 1813
Witnesses, Anderson West, Elijah Threlkeld

GEORGE EVANS of Dickson County to
SAMUEL TUBBS   page 205
Conveys land in District 1 on west fork of Pine River of Duck River.
Made 16 Nov. 1812   Registered 26 Sept. 1813
Witnesses, William Hudson, Jr., James Tabor, Russell Tabor

GEORGE EVANS to
SAMUEL TUBB   page 207
Conveys land in District 1 on west fork of Pine River. (continued)

Made 16 Nov. 1812   Registered 26 Sept. 1813
Witnesses, William Hudson, Jr., James Tabor, Russell Tabor

LEWIS POWERS of Humphreys County to
JESSE LUMSDEN of Dickson County   page 209
Conveys 100 acres on the Otter Branch of Yellow Creek...mentions John
Dickson's northwest corner.
Made 7 Feb. 1810   Registered 26 Sept. 1813
Witnesses, Hardy Valentine, William Tatum

WILLIAM LOVING of Smith County to
SUSANNA BURKETT   page 210
Conveys 150 acres on the head branches of Leatherwood Creek, part of
640-acre tract that John T. Smith sold to William Roper.
Made 21 Dec. 1812   Registered 26 Sept. 1813
Witnesses, Roger Gillison, Ephraim Burkett

RICHARD ALLEN of Dickson County to
CHARLES THOMPSON of Dickson County   page 212
Conveys land on both sides of Yellow Creek, beginning at the mouth of
the upper east fork of Yellow Creek...mentions Edward Dickson to John
Jones' line...part of Morgan Drury's 640-acre tract granted by North
Carolina.
Made 26 Oct. 1811   Registered 27 Sept. 1813
Witnesses, Solomon Rye, Jesse Lumsden

GEORGE MITCHELL to
JOSEPH MELUGIN   page 214
Conveys 56 acres on middle fork of Yellow Creek on west side of creek...
mentions William Read's line, John McCawley's line...Gee Bradley's line,
and the mouth of Joseph Melugen's spring dam (or drain).
Made 29 Oct. 1812   Registered 28 Sept. 1813
Witness, Alex. Martin

CHRISTOPHER STRONG to
MARTHA DICKSON, wife of Molton Dickson page 216
Strong conveys to daughter Martha Dickson, wife of Molton Dickson, "to
have use of negroes...intent to reserve title to myself and so will not
be misunderstood..." "At my death slaves shall become property of
children of Molton Dickson and said wife."
Made 10 April 1813   Registered 28 Sept. 1813

JOSEPH DAVIDSON of Montgomery County to
WILLIAM SHORES, SENR., Dickson County   page 217
Conveys 63 acres on Haley's Branch.
Made 13 July 1812   Registered 28 Sept. 1813
Witnesses, Cuthbert Hudson, William Hudson

RUEBIN SHORES to
CUTHBERT HUDSON   page 220
Conveys 32 acres on Haley's Creek.
Made 17 Nov. 1812   Registered 28 Sept. 1813
Witnesses, William Hudson, William McClendon

JOSEPH DAVIDSON of Montgomery County to
CUTHBERT HUDSON of Dickson County   page 222
Conveys 68 acres on west fork of Haley's Creek.
Made 13 July 1812   Registered 13 Oct. 1813
Witnesses, William Hudson, Junr., William Hudson

WILLIAM SHORES, SENR. of Dickson County to
EDMUND TIDWELL   page 223
Conveys land on Parker's fork of Turnbull Creek, part of Joseph David-
son tract...mentions Col. Murphree's north boundary line.
Made 21 June 1813   Registered 13 Oct. 1813

ICHABOD WATKINS of Humphreys County to
JAMES DICKSON, planter, of Dickson County   page 225
Bill of sale for negro Judy.
Made 7 May 1812   Registered 29 Oct. 1813 (cont'd)

Witnesses, Andrew Smith, Joseph Dickson

GABRIEL ALLEN of Dickson County to
WILLIAM SPEIGHT of Dickson County   page 226
Conveys 128 acres on Pigeon Creek and west side of Harpeth River, two miles above the mouth.
Made 11 Feb. 1811   Registered 30 Oct. 1813
Witnesses, S. Brewer, Edward Kellom

GABRIEL ALLEN of Dickson County to
WILLIAM SPEIGHT   page 228
Conveys 20 acres on Big Harpeth River, begins at the mouth of Pigeon Creek on the west bank of Harpeth.
Made 11 Feb. 1811   Registered 30 Oct. 1813
Witnesses, S. Brewer, Edward Kellom

JOHN JONES, SENR. of Dickson County to
JOHN JONES, JUNR.   page 230
Conveys land on south bank of main Turnbull Creek.
Made 24 Oct. 1812   Registered 3 Nov. 1813
Witnesses, Jno. Stafford, Joshua James

WILLIAM B. ROSS of Hickman County to
THOMAS M. OLIVER of Dickson County   page 231
Conveys land on Johnston's Creek of Cumberland River.
Made 6 Feb. 1813   Registered 3 Nov. 1813
Witnesses, Thomas Pannell, Drury Christian

ISAAC HARRIS to
BURGESS HARRIS   page 233
Isaac Harris conveys 70 acres on Harpeth River to Burgess Harris, trustee of Martha Williams of Dickson County and children.
Made 27 Oct. 1812   Registered 9 Nov. 1813
Witnesses, James Williams, R. Williams

LEWIS RUSSELL of Hickman County to
JAMES TATUM of Dickson County   pages 234, 235
Conveys land on west fork of Pine River near the mouth of a branch at lower end of the tract Russell sold to William Hudson.
Made 6 Sept. 1813   Registered 9 Nov. 1813
Witnesses, William Hudson, Jr., William Hudson, Sr., Baker Hudson

JOHN JOSLIN of Davidson County to
JOHN CRAIG of Dickson County   page 236
Conveys land on east fork of Blue Creek of Duck River...mentions the southwest corner of Thomas Hendricks.
Made 18 Sept. 1813   Registered 12 Nov. 1813
Witnesses, William Shelby, Robert Canon

WILLIAM STONE to
JOHN MORRISETT   pages 237, 238
William Stone gives interest by heirship to all land of William Russell, deceased...land on Jones Creek...heirs: James Robertson and James Tubb, Jr...John Morrisett buys the land. (Note: The meaning of this entry is unclear and should be rechecked by those interested in this line.)
Made 1 May 1813   Registered 15 Nov. 1813

WILLIAM STONE & heirs of William Russell, deceased   page 239
Land mentioned was on Jones Creek. Heirs: Willis Russell, Thomas Russell, Jesse Russell, Abraham Robertson, Lemuel Russell.
Made 10 Feb. 1813   Registered 15 Nov. 1813
Witnesses, Barth. Smith, James Luckett, Thomas Murrell, Richard Murrell

THOMAS PATTON to
CHARLES ROBB of Jackson Co., Ga.   pages 242, 242
Conveys negro boy Monday.
Made 9 Oct. 1800   Registered 29 Jan. 1814
Witnesses, Peter Robbs, Martin Robbs

STATE OF NORTH CAROLINA to
JONAS RICKLE   page 242
Grants 228 acres on Harpeth River, Davidson County, for services in or land was on continental line...John Mann was assignee of Jonas Rickle. Plat appears on page 244. (Note: Entry not clear.)
Made 22 Dec. 1797   Registered 30 Jan. 1814

STATE OF TENNESSEE to
JOHN WADDLE and JOHN McMILLAN   page 245
Grants 100 acres on Yellow Creek, Sylvester Adams is assignee of John McMillan...mentions east of Thomas Archer's line.
Made 29 Aug. 1808   Registered 31 Jan. 1814

STATE OF TENNESSEE to
JOHN REYNOLDS, assignee   page 246
Land was originally granted for military service by Smith Child by North Carolina on 14 Feb. 1797...land is in District 1 on both sides of Wallace's Branch of Leatherwood Creek...mentions Thomas McMurry's line.
Made 5 August 1809   Registered 31 Jan. 1814

STATE OF TENNESSEE to
JOHN REYNOLDS, assignee   page 247
Land was originally granted for military service of William Jarman of North Carolina on 12 Dec. 1796...291 acres on both sides of Yellow Creek on Wallace Branch.
Made 25 Aug. 1809   Registered 31 Jan. 1814

AARON LAMBERT of Wilson County to
MILLS EASON of Dickson County   page 248
Conveys land on west side of Pine River, part of 2000 acres granted by North Carolina to Aaron Lambert...mentions Morgan Hood's line.
Made 18 Dec. 1813   Registered 31 Jan. 1814
Witnesses, Carter T. Eason, Joseph Eason

JAMES READ, High Sheriff of Dickson County to
WILLIAM D. TURNER of Dickson County   page 250
Conveys 53 acres on west side of Yellow Creek, formerly Syl. Adams corner in Thomas Archer's south boundary line...part of tract granted Samuel Perry and levied on at instance of Thomas Gray.
Made 7 Sept. 1813   Registered 5 Feb. 1814
Witnesses, John Humphries, John L. McRae

JAMES REED, High Sheriff of Dickson County to
WILLIAM D. TURNER   page 252
Land on west side of Yellow Creek on both sides of Norrises branch. Signed Drury Christian, sheriff. (Note: This entry very much like the one before.)
Made 5 Jan. 1813   Registered 2 Feb. 1814
Witnesses, Michael Molton, William Stone

THOMAS MATTHEWS of Dickson County to
RICHARD HOWARD of Dickson County   page 254
Conveys 71 acres on middle fork of Barton's Creek...mentions G. Bradley line, northeast corner of George Mitchell, and Doctor Green's south boundary line.
Made 7 Sept. 1812   Registered 2 Feb. 1814
Witnesses, George Clark, Thomas Clift

JOHN GILBERT of Dickson County to
JOHN TUCKER JNR   page 255
Conveys land on main Turnbull Creek, up southwest fork of a branch.
Made 13 Feb. 1812   Registered 2 Feb. 1814
Witnesses, Peter Gilbert, John Stafford

WILLIAM MILLER, SR., of Dickson County to
DANIEL COLEMAN   page 257
Conveys land on west fork of Jones Creek...mentions northwest corner of Margaret Meeke's, Martin's north bounday line, southeast corner of Thomas Wright. (Continued)

Made 6 Nov. 1813　　　　　　　　　　　　　　　Registered 3 Feb. 1814
Witnesses, Silas Miller, Moses Meek

WILLIAM MILLER of Franklin, Indianna Territory　page 259
William Miller appoints by power of attorney his father William Miller to sell land on Jones Creek in Dickson County; land was conveyed to William Miller, Jr., by father; also one tract conveyed to him by James Martin.
Made 25 Oct. 1813　　　　　　　　　　　　　　　Registered 3 Feb. 1814
Witnesses, Frances McWilliams, Moses Meek

ALEXANDER DICKSON of Dickson County
WILLIAM B. WEST of Dickson County　　　　　page 260
Dickson conveys to West 500 acres on both sides of Yellow Creek, crossing Old Town Creek, being one-half of 1000 acres granted to James Middleton by North Carolina and conveyed to Alexander Dickson.
Made 31 Dec. 1813　　　　　　　　　　　　　　　Registered 3 Feb. 1814
Witnesses, Robert Dickson, John Humphries

JOHN VINEYARD of Dickson County
JOEL SHROPSHIRE of Dickson County　　　　　page 262
Vineyard conveys to Shropshire land in District 1 on the sulphur lick fork of Jones Creek.
Made 5 Nov. 1813　　　　　　　　　　　　　　　Registered 3 Feb. 1814
Witnesses, A. Caldwell, Jeremiah Pearsall

MARBLE STONE and WILLIAM STONE
ELIZABETH STONE　　　　　　　　　　　　　　　page 264
Marble Stone and William Stone convey to mother Elizabeth Stone; "our mother Elizabeth Stone shall remove herself and negroes from Williamson County and make it her settled home with either of us...give quit claim to our interest in negroes by our father's will..." Brother John H. Stone, one negro; mentions sister Dolly Stone, sister Susanna Hardeman and her husband Peter Hardeman.
Made 19 Aug. 1812　　　　　　　　　　　　　　　Registered 3 Feb. 1814
Witness, Jesse S. Ross

ABRAHAM ROBERTSON of Dickson County
LEVEN DICKSON of Dickson County　　　　　　page 265
Abraham Robertson, administrator of William Russell, deceased, conveys 320 acres to Dickson; land on Turnbull Creek.
Made 19 March 1812　　　　　　　　　　　　　　Registered 3 Feb. 1814
Witnesses, Cuthbert Hudson, David Hogan

JAMES ROBERTSON of Davidson County
ZACHARIAH WALKER, SENR., of Dickson County　　page 206 (Note page no.)
Robertson conveys to Walker land on Barton's Creek; mentions the northeast corner of Elizabeth Walker and the west boundary of William Gibbins.
Made 9 Jan. 1812　　　　　　　　　　　　　　　Registered 12 Feb. 1814.
Witnesses, R. C. Napier, Simon Walker

EDWARD GWIN of Sumner County
JACOB TOLAND　　　　　　　　　　　　　　　　page 208 (Note page no.)
Gwin conveys to Toland land on the south fork of Blue Creek.
Made 8 Nov. 1811　　　　　　　　　　　　　　　Registered 10 Mar. 1814
Witnesses, Isaac Toland, Jacob Toland, Jnr.

STATE OF TENNESSEE
MARTIN HALLIBURTON　　　　　　　　　　　　　page 270
Martin Halliburton, assignee, gets land in District 1, Leatherwood Creek; land was originally for the military service of William Clerk of North Carolina, granted 24 April 1785; mentions the northeast corner of Martin Halliburton's occupant claim, including Halliburton's improvement as of 1811.
Made 1 Jan. 1812　　　　　　　　　　　　　　　Registered 21 Mar. 1814

WILLIAM PEACOCK of Davidson County
FRANCIS S.ELLIS　　　　　　　　　　　　　　　page 271
Peacock conveys Lot 14 in Charlotte to Francis S. Ellis.

Made 8 March 1810   Registered 21 Mar. 1814
Witnesses, Robert A. Scott, Field Farrar

MOSES MEEK
JOHN EVANS   page 273
Meek conveys to Evans land on Jones Creek, mentions the southeast line
of Raiford Crumpler and southwest corner of Christopher Strong.
Made 24 Feb. 1814   Registered 25 Mar. 1814
Witnesses, Reece Bowen, Silas Miller

STATE OF NORTH CAROLINA   page 274
North Carolina conveys land on Barton's Creek; land was granted to
William Combs, private in North Carolina line and registered in Halifax
County; property was assigned to Charles Campbell, then to Samuel
Barton of Davidson County
Made 4 Jan. 1792   Registered 23 Apr. 1814

EZEKIEL NORRIS of Hickman County
NATHAN DILLAHAY of Dickson County   page 276
Norris conveys to Dillahay land on both sides of Bear Creek of Yellow
Creek.
Made 9 Jan. 1813   Registered 2 May 1814
Witnesses, William Norris, Samuel Turner

WILLIAM GATTIS
RICHARD   (Note: All given in entry)   page 278
Gattis conveys 48 acres on Yellow Creek, crosses the Troft Branch of
Yellow Creek. (Note: This could be Broft Branch also.) Also mentions
the Troft Shole; mentions a dry hollow that runs down to Tatom's house.
Made 3 Jan. 1814   Registered 2 May 1814
Witnesses, Reece Bowen, John Nesbitt

JAMES MARTIN
THOMAS PANNELL   page 280
Martin conveys one-half of Lot 6 in Charlotte to Pannell.
Made 4 April 1814   Registered 3 May 1814

ISAAC WEST, JR.
JOHN WEST   page 281
Isaac West, Jr., conveys to John West land, mentions James McClelland's
line, including plantation where Isaac West, Jr., now lives.
Made 14 Jan. 1813   Registered 3 May 1814
Witnesses, Anderson West, Samuel Sparks

ELIZABETH STONE and WILLIAM STONE of Dickson Co.
ISAAC WEST, Jr.   page 284
Elizabeth Stone and William Stone convey to West land on Jones Creek,
beginning corner of tract conveyed to William Stone, Senr., by Samuel
Thompson of North Carolina.
Made 16 July 1813   Registered 3 May 1814
Witnesses, Samuel Sparks, Anderson West

JOHN CRAIG of Humphreys County
JOHN HENDRICKS of Dickson County   page 285
Craig conveys to Hendricks 40 acres in District 1 on Jones Creek, land
goes north from a pen built by one Roper for the purpose of catching
wild horses.
Made 9 Sept. 1812   Registered 4 May 1814
Witnesses, Thomas Hendricks, Jno. Stafford

THOMAS GRAY
JOHN LEWIS   page 287
Gray conveys to Lewis land on Cedar Creek, a fork of Yellow Creek;
mentions Stephen Horsley's line.
Made 17 Feb. 1814   Registered 6 May 1814
Witnesses, James Goodrich, Nathan Nesbitt, John Woods

JESSE S. ROSS
JOSEPH EASON   page 289
Ross conveys to Eason land on the west fork of Pine River of Duck River;

mentions Aaron Lambert's northwest corner and mentions the low grounds of Pine River.
Made 15 Feb. 1814   Registered 7 May 1814
Witnesses, Carter T. Eason, Joseph Eason, Junr.

JOSEPH EASON
SUSANNA ROSS   page 290
Joseph Eason to daughter Susanna Ross, wife of Jesse S. Ross, one negro girl Hannah.
Made 15 Feb. 1814   Registered 7 May 1814
Witnesses, Carter T. Eason, Joseph Eason

THOMAS HENDRICKS of Dickson County
JOHN CRAIG of Humphreys County   page 291
Hendricks conveys to Craig land on Blue Creek of Duck River.
Made 16 Feb. 1813   Registered 7 May 1814
Witness, James Killpatrick

MARGARET MEEK and MOSES MEEK
WILLIAM BULLION   page 292
Margaret Meek and Moses Meek convey to Bullion 60 acres on the west fork of Jones Creek, mentions the southwest corner of William Stone.
Made 26 Feb. 1814   Registered 7 May 1814
Witnesses, Thomas Wright, Elijah Threlkeld

JAMES McCLURKAN of Franklin Co., Indiana Territory
ROBERT HARPER of Dickson County   page 294
James McClurkan of Franklin County, Indiana Territory, attorney in fact for Matthew McClurkan of Franklin County, Indiana Territory, conveys 100 acres to Robert Harper; land on west side of Jones Creek, originally granted by North Carolina to James Dickson and from him to William Dickson and from William Dickson conveyed to Matthew McClurkan, begins at mouth of Cave Branch and goes down creek to Major Strong's line.
Made 19 Oct. 1811   Registered 10 June 1814
Witnesses, F. Farrar, John Evans

HOWELL ADAMS and JOHN HUDDLESTON
RICHARD EATON   page 296
Adams and Huddleston convey to Eaton 260 acres on Beaver Creek, this is tract where Huddleston now lives; mentions southwest corner of Howell Adams survey.
Made 1 Feb. 1810   Registered 26 July 1814
Witnesses, Cuthbert Hudson, John Raiburn, James McCallister, David Hogan

JANE NORRIS and WILLIAM NORRIS of Dickson County
HUGH DICKSON   page 297
Jane and William Norris convey to Dickson a negro Rachel.
Made 22 March 1814   Registered 1 Aug. 1814
Witnesses, Shaderick Tribble, Drew Price

JESSE LUMSDEN
AARON VANHOOK   page 299
Lumsden conveys to Vanhook land on the Otter Branch of Yellow Creek; mentions the northwest corner of John Dickson.
Made 1 Aug. 1810   Registered 1 Aug. 1814
Witness, Samuel Turner

ANDREW CAROTHERS of Hickman County
MICAJAH BUSBY of Dickson County   page 300
Carothers conveys to Busby 30 acres on Yellow Creek, 8 poles "from the cabbin where said Carothers lived when said entry was made"; mentions a deep bottom branch.
Made 24 Dec. 1813   Registered 2 Aug. 1814
Witnesses, Mills Busby, Levi Anderson

THOMAS BLOUNT WHITMILL   page 302
Thomas Blount Witmill, late of Halifax County, deceased, by will left negroes to daughter Elizabeth West Whitmill, left several negroes and if she dies without lawful heir begotten of her body to return;

Elizabeth has married Claudius David L and has removed to Tennessee.
Thomas W. Whitmill and Drew S. Whitmill are two lawful heirs of the
deceased and her brothers deed their right to the estate.
Made 1 Oct. 1813   Registered 2 Aug. 1814
Witnesses, Shaderick Bell, William Caldwell
(Note: In this entry the unusual surname is written Claudius David'L.)

STEPHEN WARD
THOMAS MATTHEWS   page 303
Ward conveys to Matthews 25 acres.
Made 18 June 1814   Registered 2 Aug. 1814
Witnesses, William Hand, James Matthews

THOMAS MATTHEWS
STEPHEN WARD   page 304
Matthews conveys to Ward.
Made 8 June 1814   Registered 3 Aug. 1814
Witnesses, William Hand, James Matthews

WILLIAM NORRIS
BENJAMIN STURDIVANT   page 306
Norris conveys to Sturdivant 3 acres on the east side of main Yellow
Creek, mentions the southeast corner of William Norris.
Made 20 Aug. 1813   Registered 3 Aug. 1814
Witnesses, James Dickson, Robert Dickson

MICHAEL MOLTON of Dickson County
BENJAMIN STURDIVANT   page 308
Molton conveys to Sturdivant 100 acres.
Made 3 Dec. 1812   Registered 4 Aug. 1814
Witnesses, Edward Pearsall, James Goodrich

THOMAS HARRIS of Iredell County, NC
ENOS JAMES of Dickson County   page 310
Harris conveys 250 acres to James, the same deeded to Harris by David
Willson, being part of 1000 acres granted by North Carolina to David
Willson; mentions Col. William Davis' line.
Made 29 June 1814   Registered 6 Aug. 1814
Witnesses, Michael Molton, James Goodrich

WILLIAM D. TURNER of Dickson County
MICHAEL KIME of Dickson County   page 311
Turner conveys 53 acres to King on the west side of Yellow Creek on a
branch of Yellow Creek; mentions Thomas Archer's south boundary line,
a hickory formerly Syl. Adams corner in Thomas Archer's south boundary
line being tract of land granted by state to Samuel Perry and sold by
sheriff of Dickson County to William D. Turner.
Made 14 Aug. 1813   Registered 6 Aug. 1814
Witnesses, Samuel Hosley, James Brown

JAMES PATTERSON
ELEANOR PARRISH   page 313
Patterson conveys 50 acres to Parrish on the west fork of Yellow Creek;
mentions the southwest corner of Sylvester Adams and Andrew Carothers
line. (Note: Eleanor Parrish is referred to as "he" and "his" in this
entry. This agrees to some county court records in which Eleanor
Parrish is mentioned as "he".)
Made 1 Jan. 1814   Registered 8 Aug. 1814
Witnesses, William D. Turner, Wiatt Parrish

DRURY CHRISTIAN
SELMAN EDWARDS   page 315
Christian conveys to Edwards 148 acres on the middle fork of Barton's
Creek; mentions Montgomery Bell's west boundary line and James Seals
north line, all except 1½ acres deed by Drury Christian where the
Babtist meeting house now stands.
Made 4 July 1814   Registered 9 Aug. 1814
Witness, Thomas Simpson

JAMES WILLSON of Robertson County
THOMAS BRODIE of Montgomery County   page 317
Willson conveys to Brodie 274 acres on the south side of Cumberland
River, including the mouth of Johnson's Creek, 4 miles below the mouth
of Harpeth River.
Made 26 April 1814   Registered 10 Aug. 1814
Witnesses, Edm. Taylor, Jas. Jno. Williams, James W. Moody

FRANCIS McCLELLAND of Dickson County
JAMES VINCENT of Dickson County   page 318
McClelland conveys to Vincent part of James McClelland's original tract.
Made 3 March 1814   Registered 10 Aug. 1814
Witnesses, William Miller, Elijah Renshaw

THOMAS WRIGHT
MARBLE STONE   page 320
Wright conveys to Stone 145 acres on the west fork of Jones Creek.
Made 5 Feb. 1814   Registered 11 Aug. 1814
Witnesses, John H. Stone, J. McAdoo

DRURY CHRISTIAN, sheriff of Dickson County
STEPHEN TATOM   page 321
Christian conveys to Tatom 40 acres by writ of fiere facias, order of
sale issued by Montgomery County Feb. 1814 to direct sheriff to sell
all lands of heirs of Spilsby Tribble, deceased, to settle damages re-
covered by Goodman Traywick and wife Nancy against heirs in Montgomery
County; Spilsby Tribble had warrant for 2000 acres. Land was butted by
Stephen Tatom's upper tract.
Made 4 July 1814   Registered 12 Aug. 1814
Witnesses, Cyprian Farrar, Marble Stone

DRURY CHRISTIAN, sheriff
HENRY WEST   page 324
Christian conveys land to West, land on Garner's Creek, mentions Henry
Wert's south boundary line. (Note: practically the same entry as the
one before.)
Made 4 July 1814
Witnesses, Cyprian Farrar, Marble Stone

THOMAS PATTON of Jackson County, Georgia
JOHN KINNEY   pages 326-329
Patton conveys to Kinney a negro boy, Monday, a negro girl, Ailey, and
other items.
Made 8 May 1807   Registered 1 Sept. 1814
Witness, Eldridge Hargrove

JOHN KINNEY of Jackson County, Georgia
WILLIAM STONE of Dickson County   page 329
Kinney conveys to Stone the negro, Monday.
Made 7 Feb. 1814   Registered 1 Sept. 1814
Witness, P. Rodgers

GEORGE EVANS of Dickson County
SAMUEL TUBB of Dickson County   page 332
Evans conveys to Tubb 30 acres on the west fork of Pine River, District
No. 1.
Made 6 Nov. 1812   Registered 5 Sept. 1814
Witnesses, William Hudson, Rusel Tabor, James Taber

STATE OF TENNESSEE
WILLIAM CLARKE   page 335
State of Tennessee conveys 35 acres to Clarke on both sides of Wallace
Branch of Leatherwood Fork of Yellow Creek, District 1, was granted to
Clarke for his service to North Carolina, granted 24 April 1785.
Mentions David Wallace's west boundary line and John Reynolds line.
Made 4 April 1812   Registered 27 Oct. 1814

JOHN GRAVETT of Dickson County
JOSEPH WINGATE of Dickson County   page 337
John Gravett binds until Joseph Wingate his two sons Henry Gravett and

William Gravett to live in manner of apprentices or servants until they are 21 and the learn the hatting business; Wingate is to give them 18 months schooling and furnishing washing, lodging, and apparel. Henry is about 12 years old and William is about 6 years old.
Made 10 Sept. 1814   Registered 12 Dec. 1814
Witnesses, Cyprian Farrar, T. B. Young, Isaac Spear

JOHN GRAVETT
JOSEPH WINGATE, hatter   page 338
Gravett gives his power of attorney to Wingate.
Made 10 Sept. 1814   Registered 12 Nov. 1814
Witnesses, Dr. Caldwell, Cyprian Farrar, T. B. Young

ROGAL FERGUSON of Humphreys County
FELIX ALLEN of Dickson County   page 340
Ferguson conveys to Allen negro Lucy and her increase.
Made 6 Oct. 1814   Registered 23 Nov. 1814

JOHN BRAHAN and Mary, his wife
SHADERICK BELL of Dickson County   pages 341-343
John Brahan and Mary, his wife, of Madison County, Mississippi Territory, convey to Bell 530 acres on the south side of Cumberland River, 1½ mile below mouth of Big Harpeth; mentions Blount Whitmill's northwest corner, Harnett Rice's line, above the mouth of Johnson Creek. Mary Brahan is also referred to as Polly Brahan in this entry.
Made 3 Sept. 1813   Registered 24 Nov. 1814
Witnesses, Joseph Coleman, R. Weakley

STEPHEN HOSTLEY of Dickson County
WILLIAM PARKER of Dickson County   page 344
Hostley conveys to Parker 20 acres on Cedar Creek; mentions Barnes' line and including William Parker's improvement.
Made __Oct. 1814   Registered 24 Nov. 1814
Witnesses, Edward Pearsall, N. Hardy

WILLIAM MOORE of Livingston County, KY
JOHN STRAHAN & CO. of Dickson County   page 346
Moore conveys 50 acres near Charlotte to Strahan & Co., mentions a redbud near the corner of Dickson Street on the north bank of Town Creek.
Made 25 July 1814   Registered 24 Nov. 1814
Witnesses, Reece Bowen, Molton Dickson

WILLIAM MOORE of Livingston County, KY
JOHN STRAHAN & CO. of Dickson County   page 347
Moore conveys a lot in the commons of town of Charlotte to Strahan.
Made 25 July 1814   Registered 25 Nov. 1814
Witnesses, Reece Bowen, Molton Dickson

ENOS JAMES of Dickson County
HOWELL PARRISH of Dickson County   page 349
James conveys to Parrish 240 acres, part of David Willson's 1000 acres granted by North Carolina.
Registered 3 Dec. 1814
Witnesses, James Dickson, J. Willson

WILLIAM COLWELL of Dickson County
ANDREW COLWELL of same   page 351
Colwell conveys to Andrew Colwell land on Harpeth River, mentions old line of Hardick's. (Note: Name found as William Caldwell and Andrew Caldwell in same entry.)
Made 4 July 1814   Registered 3 Dec. 1814

STATE OF NORTH CAROLINA
AARON LAMBERT   page 353
North Carolina conveys to Aaron Lambert, assignee of Micahel Quin, land on both sides of Pine River, including mouth of Bushes Meat House, a fork of said river.
Made 4 Jan. 1793   Registered 10 Dec. 1814

STATE OF NORTH CAROLINA
JOHN HAYS   page 354
North Carolina conveys to John Hays, assignee of Anderson Nolly, a
private in North Carolina line, land on Yellow Creek; mentions Howell
Tatum's northwest corner.
Made 20 May 1793   Registered 21 Dec. 1814

STATE OF TENNESSEE   page 355
State of Tennessee conveys 50 acres which North Carolina granted to
Alemelick Howell for his military service in the North Carolina line on
22 Dec. 1796; land in District 1 on the west fork of Pine River.
(Note: The name is also given as Abelnelick Howell.)
Made 1 July 1809   Registered 24 Dec. 1814

STATE OF TENNESSEE
SAMUEL JACKSON   page 356
State of Tennessee conveys to Samuel Jackson land in District 1 on the
west fork of Pine River; was granted to Morgan Hood, 14 June 1808;
mentions Aaron Lambert's northwest corner and Jesse S. Ross's south
boundary line.
Made 14 May 1803   Registered 26 Dec. 1814

WILLIAM BROWN of Dickson County
WILLIAM ALLEN of Williamson County   page 358
Brown conveys to Allen 120 acres in District 1, land on Beaverdam Creek
of Turnbull Creek, adjoins Cuthbert Hudson northeast corner.
Made 15 Feb. 1811   Registered 6 Feb. 1815
Witnesses, Benjamin Gilbert, Richard Eaton

JOHN PARKER of Dickson County
THOMAS GENTRY   page 360
Parker conveys to Gentry 85 acres; mentions Eaton's north boundary line.
Made 25 Sept. 1809   Registered 6 Feb. 1815
Witnesses, Cuthbert Hudson, Minor Bibb

THOMAS CHOATE of Dickson County
EDMOND HOWARD   page 361
Choate conveys to Howard land on Jones Creek on the sulphur lick fork
of Jones Creek, mentions southwest corner of Charles Barnes, formerly
Thomas McQuistion.
Made 16 Feb. 1814   Registered 11 Feb. 1815
Witnesses, Christopher Connelley, John Read

WILLIAM BAKER of Dickson County
JOHN BAKER   page 363
William Baker conveys to John Baker land on the Leatherwood fork of
Yellow Creek
Made 18 Feb. 1814   Registered 4 Feb. 1815
Witnesses, John Humphries, Edward Watts

JESSE BLACKFAN
SILAS HARRIS   page 365
Blackfan conveys to Harris 640 acres on both sides of the Harpeth, 4
miles above its mouth, adjoining John Coart's south boundary line, near
the lower point of an island. Jesse Blackfan signed for himself and as
attorney for the rest of the heirs.
Made 22 Sept. 1812   Registered 4 Feb. 1815
Witnesses, Burgess Harris, William Harris

EDWARD WATTS
JOHN BAKER   page 367
Watts conveys to Baker land on the Leatherwood fork of Yellow Creek,
including where John Baker now lives; mentions William Hodge's west
corner and the fence which divides Watts' peach orchard from the field
where Baker now lives.
Made 18 Feb. 1814   Registered 6 Feb. 1815
Witnesses, John Humphries, William Baker

C. STUMP of Davidson County
FELIX ALLEN of Davidson County   page 369
Stump conveys 211½ acres to Allen on each side of Harpeth River near
Jones Creek; mentions Henry Hyland's northwest corner.
Made 5 Sept. 1814   Registered 7 Feb. 1815
Witnesses, Philip Shute, Richard H. Berry, Horatio Humphreys, Erin
Smith

RICHARD EATON of Illinois territory
ISAAC SELLARS of Dickson County   page 370
Eaton conveys 240 acres to Sellars on the beaverdam fork of Turnbull
Creek; mentions southwest corner of Howel Adams tract.
Made 27 July 1814   Registered 16 Feb. 1815
Witnesses, David Hogan, A. Hogan

WILLIAM H. BURTON of Humphreys County
GEORGE DARBY of Dickson County   pages 372-373
William H. Burton conveys 140 acres to Darby, land on Leatherwood Creek;
mentions west boundary line of Timothy Anderson, William Baker's south
boundary line, Thomas McMurray's south boundary line, including the
plantation where George Darby now lives on the cave spring fork of
Leatherwood.
Made 1 Sept. 1813   Registered 16 Feb. 1815
Witnesses, John W. Baker, William L. Baker

JOHN REYNOLDS
WILLIAM MORRISON, executor of Thomas McMurray, deceased   page 374
Reynolds conveys 3½ acres to Morrison, executor of Thomas McMurray, de-
ceased. McMurray entered in contract with John Reynolds in his life-
time; mentions fork of Wallace's branch of Leatherwood fork of Yellow
Creek and a high bluff in John Reynolds south boundary line.
Made_____   Registered 16 Feb. 1815
Witnesses, George Darby, William Baker

CHARLES GILBERT of Dickson County
DANIEL BAREFIELD   page 376
Gilbert conveys to Barefield land on the waters of main Turnbull Creek,
mentions the dividing line between Benjamin Gilbert; mentions the west
branch below the mill.
Made 10 Dec. 1813   Registered 17 Feb. 1815
Witnesses, John Stafford, John Spradling

ASA SHUTE of Davidson County
JESSE EPPERSON of Dickson County   page 377
Shute conveys to Epperson land on the east fork of Hurricane Creek of
Duck River entered in the name of Spilsby Tribble; mentions Jesse
Epperson's west boundary line.
Made 25 Oct. 1814   Registered 17 Feb. 1815
Witnesses, William Caruthers, L. B. Matlock

THOMAS PANNELL
WILLIAM MILLER   page 379
Pannell conveys land on Jones Creek to Miller; mentions the northeast
corner of Francis McClelland.
Made 4 April 1814   Registered 17 Feb. 1815
Witnesses, Marble Stone, John Nesbitt

JOSEPH EASON
CALVIN W. EASON   page 381
Joseph Eason conveys to Calvin W. Eason land on Pine River.
Made 11 Nov. 1814   Registered 17 Feb. 1815
Witnesses, James Dunnagan, John Dunnagan

JESSE EPPERSON
JOHN YOUNG   page 384
Epperson conveys to Young land on the east fork of Hurricane Creek of
Duck River.
Made 12 Nov. 1814   Registered 17 Feb. 1815
Witnesses, Daniel Williams, Thomas Williams

JANE THOMAS
BURGESS HARRIS   page 386
Jane Thomas, all and singular, deed of gift to Burgess Harris "for love
and affection I have for my beloved friend Burgess Harris of Dickson
County" conveys two negroes.
Made 3 June 1813   Registered 18 Feb. 1815
Witnesses, Jno. Brewer, Sally Brewer

JOHN REYNOLDS,SR., of Dickson County
JOHN REYNOLDS, JR., of Dickson County   page 387
John Reynolds, Sr., to John Reynolds, Jr., 86 acres for "natural love
and affection"; land on west side of leatherwood fork of Yellow Creek.
Made 4 Feb. 1814   Registered 18 Feb. 1815
Witnesses, John Humphries, Joseph Bunch

STATE OF TENNESSEE
JESSE EPPERSON   page 389
State of Tennessee conveys to Jesse Epperson, assignee of Daniel
Williams, land near head of east fork of Hurricane Creek of Duck River.
Made 27 Sept. 1814   Registered 18 Feb. 1815

CURTIS HOOKS of Maury County
JOHN LARKINS, SR., of Dickson County   page 390
Hooks conveys negro Jim, age 15, to Larkins.
Made 20 Dec. 1814   Registered 18 Feb. 1815
Witnesses, Joseph Larkins, Robert Larkins

JOHN HAYS of Chatham County, NC
JOHN H. ARCHER   page 392
Hays gives power of attorney to friend John H. Archer "in consequence
of relationship he bears to me"; also gives him part of land.
Made 2 Sept. 1812   Registered 20 Feb. 1815
Witnesses, Edwin Wood, A. Serin, Jo. Davis

EDWARD MACGOWAN of Bladen County, NC
WILLIAM PEACOCK of Dickson County   page 393
MacGowan gives power of attorney to Peacock to dispose of 600 acres on
Barton's Creek.
Made 2 May 1814   Registered 20 Feb. 1815
Witnesses, Thomas Brown, James Smith, Isaac Wright of Bladen County,NC

FRANCIS BROWN of Dickson County
JOHN B. BROWN of Dickson County   page 395
Francis Brown conveys to John B. Brown land on west fork of Jones Creek,
mentions northwest corner of John Larkins.
Made 11 July 1814   Registered 20 Feb. 1815
Witnesses, Spencer Brown, John Hale

JOHN TATOM, SR.
WILLIAM TATOM   page 396
John Tatom, Sr., for "good will I bear to William Tatom, my lawful son"
land stock, land where I now reside, and furniture.
Made 2 Feb. 1815   Registered 20 Feb. 1815
Witnesses, William Wright, William Tattom

JAMES SEAL
SAMUEL MITCHELL   page 397
Seal conveys negro child, Jude, to Mitchell.
Made 2 July 1814   Registered 20 Feb. 1815
Witness, Thomas Mitchell

THOMAS PATTON of Jackson County, Georgia
JOHN KINNEY   page 398
Patton conveys negroes, hogs, and other property to Kinney.
Made 8 May 1807   Registered 7 Mar. 1815
Witness, Eldridge Hargrove

RICHARD NAPIER of Dickson County
GEORGE F. NAPIER   page 99
Richard Napier conveys to George F. Napier land on the Iron Fork of

including place settled by and known by the name of Kelly's place.
Made 15 Dec. 1808   Registered 7 March 1815
Witnesses, Fon Lester, Nathan P. Thompson

REUBEN BENTSON of Guilford County, NC
RICHARD NAPIER of Dickson County   page 401
Bentson conveys to Napier land on Jones Creek, 2 miles from mouth.
Made 10 Dec. 1812   Registered 16 March 1815
Witnesses, Noel Hamon, Sary (X-her mark) Ingram

RICHARD NAPIER of Dickson County
GEORGE F. NAPIER   page 404
Richard Napier conveys to George F. Napier land on Jones Creek, 2 miles
from mouth where it enters Harpeth River.
Made 13 Dec. 1814   Registered Jan. 1815
Witnesses, J. W. Napier, David Irvin

MILES RAYNER of Bertie County, NC
WILLIAM PARROTT HARDY of Bertie County, NC   page 406
Rayner conveys 640 acres on Yellow Creek, mentions Israel Hammond's
southwest corner; land was granted to John Ramsay, heir of Mills Ramsey.
Made 16 May 1807   Registered 5 June 1815

HARDY FREEMAN, executor
MILES RAYNOR   page 408
Hardy Freeman of Bertie County, NC, executor of will of John Ramsey, deceased, late of Bertie County, conveys to Miles Raynor land on Yellow Creek.
Made 13 May 1806   Registered 6 June 1815

JOHN McADOO
JOHN LARKINS   page 413
McAdoo conveys to Larkins land on the 4-mile fork of Jones Creek.
Made 3 March 1815   Registered 26 July 1815
Witnesses, Edward Houston, James Larkins

STATE OF TENNESSEE
EDWARD GWIN   page 415
State of Tennessee conveys to Edward Gwin land on the Furnace Fork of
Barton's Creek.
Made 25 March 1813   Registered 24 Aug. 1815

EDWARD SMITH of Dickson County
JOHN STAFFORD   page 417
Smith conveys to Stafford land on Beaverdam and Turnbull creeks, mentions Thomas Crossnoe's north boundary line.
Made 11 Sept. 1813   Registered 24 Aug. 1815
Witnesses, Minor Bibb, William Adams

JAMES TABOR of Dickson County
JAMES TATOM of Dickson County   page 419
Tabor conveys to Tatom 31¼ acres on the west fork of Pine River.
Made 9 Nov. 1814   Registered 24 Aug. 1815
Witnesses, none given in notes.

JESSE STROUD of Dickson County
JOHN STAFFORD   page 420
Stroud conveys to Stafford land on Beaver Dam and Turnbull creeks; mentions Parker's west boundary line and George Powel's corner.
Made 4 Sept. 1813   Registered 24 Aug. 1815
Witnesses, Minor Bibb, William Adams

PATRICK WOODS of Dickson County
EDWARD BRIMM of Rutherford County, TN   page 422
Woods conveys to Brimm 63 acres on the dry fork of Barton's Creek; mentions Jesse Jernigan's southwest corner.
Made 1 Sept. 1814   Registered 24 Aug. 1815
Witnesses, Alexr Howell, James Dickson, Mary (X-her mark) Gabill

JOHN PARKER of Robertson County
HENRY HARDIN of Dickson County   page 424
Parker conveys to Hardin land on the waters of Turnbull Creek where said
Hardin now lives; mentions Thomas Gentry's northwest corner and John
Brown's line.
Made 5 Sept. 1814   Registered 25 Aug. 1815
Witnesses, Levin Dixon, Minor Bibb

NATHAN NESBITT of Dickson County
JOHN MORROW of Williamson County   page 425
Nesbitt conveys to Morrow land on both sides of Yellow Creek; mentions
John Turner's northeast corner and Jeremiah Nesbitt's north line.
Made 7 March 1815   Registered 28 Aug. 1815
Witnesses, John Nesbitt, Elis Tiser, William B. Haddon

JOHN LARKINS, SENR.
JOHN McADOW, SENR.   page 427
Larkins conveys to McAdow land on the sulphur fork of Jones Creek, mentions Thomas Thompson's corner.
Made 6 Feb. 1815   Registered 28 Aug. 1815
Witnesses, John Larkins, Jr., James Larkins

HENRY HARDIN of Dickson County
MINOR BIBB   page 429
Hardin conveys to Bibb 70 acres on the north bank of Parkers Spring
Branch; mentions Parkers fork of Turnbull Creek.
Made 17 Sept. 1814   Registered 28 Aug. 1815
Witnesses, Thomas Gentry, Aaron Laws, Hardy Sandford

FELIX ALLEN of Dickson County
DRURY CHRISTIAN   page 430
Allen conveys to Christian land which runs due south to Harpeth River
and crosses the river.
Made 16 Jan. 1815   Registered 29 Aug. 1815
Witnesses, S. Brewer, William Lucas, John Brewer, Benjn. Andrews

JOHN SILVERS of Dickson County
JAMES TIDWELL   page 432
Silvers conveys land, the line crosses Haley's fork.
Made 7 Aug. 1813   Registered 29 Aug. 1815
Witnesses, Levin Dixon, James Robinson

JAMES ARNOLD
MICHAEL ROBINSON   page 433
Arnold conveys to Robinson land on the middle fork of Turnbull Creek.
Made 7 June 1815   Registered 29 Aug. 1815
Witnesses, William Hodges, James M. Parker

WILLIAM CALDWELL
WILLIAM SUGG   page 434-438
Caldwell conveys 222 acres to Sugg, land on Big Harpeth River including
a small island.
Made 10 Nov. 1814   Registered 30 Aug. 1815
Witnesses, Charles Campbell, Drury Christian

MARBLE STONE
JAMES ROBERTSON   page 435
Stone conveys 150 acres to Robertson, land on west fork of Jones Creek.
Mentions Francis McClennen's line.
Made 3 July 1815   Registered 29 Aug. 1815

DANIEL PARKER of Dickson County
CHARLES GILBERT of Dickson County   page 436
Parker conveys to Gilbert 420 acres on main Turnbull Creek; mentions
George Powel's corner.
Made 1 July 1815   Registered 29 Aug. 1815
Witnesses, John Stafford, Joshua James, George Powel

ANDERSON WEST
JAMES ROBERTSON   page 439 (continued)

West conveys to Robertson land on the west fork of Jones Creek, mentions the corner of Robert Bell's survey and Samuel Sparks' corner.
Made 1 June 1815   Registered 30 Aug. 1815

WILLIS JACKSON of Montgomery County
RICHARD C. NAPIER of Dickson County   page 441
Jackson conveys to Napier land in Montgomery County on the waters of Barton's Creek; mentions John Busby's north boundary line.
Made 7 March 1815   Registered 30 Aug. 1815
Witnesses, John Mockbee, Alexr. Martin, J. W. Dougherty

WILLIAM PEACOCK, attorney
RICHARD C. NAPIER   page 443
William Peacock, attorney for Edward McGowen, conveys to Napier land on Barton's Creek, mentions the dividing ridge between Barton and Johnsons Creek.
Made 8 March 1815   Registered 30 Aug. 1815

KEDAR BRYAN
RICHARD C. NAPIER   page 445
Kedar Bryan, attorney of executor of will of James Dickson, deceased, late of Duplin County, NC, conveys to Richard C. Napier, land on the southeast fork of Barton's Creek; the 640 acres granted to James Dickson by State of North Carolina as the assignee of John Dickson, who was the assignee of the heirs of Thomas Morrow; mentions dividing ridge between Barton's and Johnson's creeks; John Maxwell was the executor of the will of James Dickson.
Made 15 Sept. 1813   Registered 30 Aug. 1815
Witnesses, John Mockbee, C. Robertson

DANIEL PARKER
MINOR BIBB   page 447
Parker conveys to Bibb land on Turnbull Creek; mentions John Davis' north boundary line.
Made 3 July 1815   Registered 30 Aug. 1815
Witnesses, David Hogan, William Hodges

DRURY CHRISTIAN, Sheriff
JAMES GOODRITCH   page 449
Christian was ordered to sell lands, etc., of Robert Ormsby to settle a judgment recovered by William Pryor; also sell Derry, negro, age 9.
Made 3 June 1815   Registered 31 Aug. 1815

JESSE RUSSELL
JAMES L. SCOTT   page 450
Russell conveys to Scott 31 acres on Jones Creek; mentions John Morrisett southwest corner.
Made 3 July 1815   Registered 31 Aug. 1815

JAMES STEWART, attorney
THOMAS PANNELL of Dickson County   page 452
James Stewart, attorney for Charles Stewart of Wilkinson County, Mississippi Territory, conveys to Pannell land on the sulphur fork of Jones Creek, granted by North Carolina to Charles Stewart.
Made April 1815   Registered 31 Aug. 1815
Witnesses, William Reasons, Nolen Stewart, Tengnal Stewart

WILLIAM STONE
JOHN H. STONE   page 453
William Stone conveys to John H. Stone land on the west fork of Jones Creek.
Made 10 Sept. 1814   Registered 31 Aug. 1815
Witnesses, Peter Hardeman, Thomas Murrell, Jesse Russell

JOHN GEORGE RAINER of Dickson County
JOHN SPRADLIN   page 455
Rainer conveys to Spradlin land on main Turnbull Creek; mentions Thomas Crossnoe's line.
Made 1 July 1815   Registered 1 Sept. 1815
Witnesses, John Stafford, George Powell

JOHN GEORGE RAINER
GEORGE POWELL   page 457
Rainer conveys to Powell 6 acres on main Turnbull Creek.
Made 1 July 1815   Registered 15 Sept. 1815
Witnesses, John Stafford, Joshua James

THOMAS PATTON of Jackson County, Georgia
CHARLES ROBB of Jackson County, Georgia   page 459
Patton sold negro Monday to Robb.
Made 9 Oct. 1809   Registered 5 Sept. 1815
Witnesses, P. Kolb, Martin Kolb

JOHN CAROTHERS of Dickson County
LEONARD P. PILES of Davidson County   page 462
Carothers conveys to Piles 130 acres at the head of Leatherwood Creek
where John Carothers now lives (which he got from Thomas Roper); men-
tions John McAdoo's line.
Made 10 Feb. 1815   Registered 15 Sept. 1815
Witnesses, William France, John Richardson

SAMUEL BARTON
CHARLES CAMPBELL   page 464
Samuel Barton conveys 140 acres to Charles Campbell in behalf of his
son John Campbell, Charles Campbell and Amy, his wife; land on Barton's
Creek below Harpeth River; land was granted to Joseph Setgreave by a
military warrant.
Made 31 Oct. 1798   Registered 19 Nov. 1815
Witnesses, James McCutchan of Williamson County, Charles Campbell

CHARLES CAMPBELL of Williamson County
JAMES CAMPBELL of Williamson County   page 466
Charles Campbell conveys 500 acres to James Campbell; part of tract
granted to John Segraves, heir of Joseph Segrave, assignee of William
Combs, land originally granted by North Carolina; land on Barton's
Creek.
Made 26 Nov. 1808   Registered 22 Nov. 1815

SAMUEL BARTON of Smith County, TN
CHARLES CAMPBELL of Williamson County   page 468
Barton conveys to Campbell, land mentioned in previous entry.
Made 18 Nov. 1808   Registered 23 Nov. 1815

JAMES KNIGHTON of Hickman County
POLLY McCRORY of Dickson County   page 470
Knighton conveys 10 acres to Polly McCrory; land was on Dickson's
Branch of Turnbull Creek.
Made 20 Jan. 1815   Registered 24 Nov. 1815
Witnesses, Michael Robertson, Richard Robertson

ISAAC BROWN of Dickson County
SPENCER BROWN of Dickson County   page 471
Isaac Brown conveys to Spencer Brown land on a branch of Jones Creek;
mentions Francis Brown's south bounday line.
Made 27 May 1815   Registered 3 Dec. 1815
Witnesses, John Hale, John B. Brown

STEPHEN TATOM
LEWIS EVANS   page 473
Tatom conveys to Evans land on Garner's Creek; mentions north boundary
line of Allen Bowen's upper tract.
Made 23 Aug. 1814   Registered 3 Dec. 1815
Witnesses, John A. Baker, George Evans

STEPHEN TATOM
LEWIS EVANS   page 474
Tatom conveys to Evans 1 acre on west side of Garner's Creek.
Made 23 Aug. 1814   Registered 3 Dec. 1815
Witnesses, John A. Baker, George Evans

JOSEPH MANNING
THOMAS JONES   page 476
Manning conveys 50 acres to Jones, land on Cedar Creek, a fork of Yellow Creek.
Made 29 Sept. 1815   Registered 4 Dec. 1815

STEWART PIPKINS of Dickson County
AARON LAWS of Dickson County   page 477
Pipkins conveys to Laws 3 acres on Parker's Creek; mentions the mouth of Laws's Spring Branch, including dwelling house of said Laws.
Made 8 Sept. 1814   Registered 4 Dec. 1815
Witnesses, Cuthbert Hudson, Levin Dickson, Henry Worly

WILLIAM B. ROSS of Hickman County
ALEXANDER DAVIDSON of Dickson County   page 478
Ross conveys to Davidson 50 acres on east fork of Pine River, 30 poles from house Gabriel Overton formerly lived in on west side of Overton's spring branch.
Made 2 Oct. 1815   Registered 5 Dec. 1815
Witnesses, George Tubb, John Grymes

THOMAS JOHNSON
JOSEPH LARKINS   page 480
Johnson conveys to Larkins 10 acres; mortgage on land.
Made 1 Sept. 1815   Registered 6 Dec. 1815
Witnesses, John Larkins, Robert Larkins

JOHN CARUTHERS
PHEBY BALDWIN   page 481
Caruthers conveys to Pheby Baldwin 40 acres on the headwaters of Leatherwood Creek; part of it "crossing Nashville Road".
Made 13 Feb. 1815   Registered 6 Dec. 1815
Witnesses, John Richardson, William France

HOUSTON WILLIAS
WILLIAM T. PATTERSON   page 483
Willias conveys to Patterson a negro named Sally. (Note: Houston Willias also appears as Augustan Willias in this entry.)
Made 13 July 1814   Registered 7 Dec. 1815
Witnesses, James Robertson, J. W. Kirk

STARLING MAY
JESSE MAY   page 484
Starling May conveys to Jesse May 100 acres on both sides of Yellow Creek, part of tract William Teas conveyed to Starling May.
Made 16 June 1814   Registered 7 Dec. 1815
Witnesses, Jeremiah Nesbitt, John May, Edmond Taylor

JOEL SHROPSHIRE
RICHARD BATSON   page 486
Shropshire conveys to Batson 100 acres in District 1, on Sulphur Fork of Jones Creek.
Made 1 Feb. 1815   Registered 10 Dec. 1815

JOSEPH J. EASON
CALVIN W. EASON   page 489
Joseph J. Eason "for love and affection I have for son Calvin W. Eason" conveys three negroes.
Made 3 Oct. 1815   Registered 11 Dec. 1815
Witnesses, William Stone, James Douglas

JOHN DAVIS of Davidson County
JOHN EVANS of Dickson County   page 489
Davis conveys to Evans 15 acres on the sulphur fork of Jones Creek; land was granted to Davis by State of North Carolina.
Made 3 Oct. 1814   Registered 11 Dec. 1815

EZEKIEL NORRIS
JESSE NORRIS   page 491
Ezekiel Norris conveys 250 acres to Jesse Norris, land was on both

sides of Bear Creek, a branch of Yellow Creek; conveys "for the natural love he hath for his brother Jesse Norris"; mentions Nathan Dillihay's northeast corner, the dividing line between Ezekiel Norris and John Ashe Davis, Nathan Ragan, Jr., corner; part of tract granted by North Carolina to Col. William Davis for military service.
Made 27 Aug. 1815   Registered 12 Dec. 1815
Witnesses, Edward Pearsall, Jeremiah Gray

DAVID DICKSON and MOLTON DICKSON
CHRISTOPHER STRONG   page 494
The Dicksons convey to Strong lots in Charlotte.
Made 6 June 1808   Registered 13 Dec. 1815
Witnesses, John Read, Edward Pearsall

JOSEPH EASON, SR.
JOSEPH EASON, JR.   page 495
Joseph Eason, Sr., conveys to Joseph Eason, Jr., land on the west fork of Pine River; mentions the southwest corner of Jesse S. Ross.
Made 16 Aug. 1815   Registered 16 Dec. 1815
Witnesses, Thomas Whitwill, Carter T. Eason

ROBERT MADON
NATHAN NESBITT   page 497
Madon conveys to Nesbitt the negro Chloe and child.
Made 17 March 1815   Registered 15 Dec. 1815
Witnesses, John Morrow, William B. Hadden

SAMUEL ORTEN
THOMAS GENTRY   page 498
Orten conveys to Gentry 25 acres on Haley's Creek; mentions John Parker west boundary line, including plantation where Orten now lives.
Made 21 July 1812   Registered 15 Dec. 1815
Witnesses, Cuthbert Hudson, William Hudson, William Adams

SAMUEL TAYLOR
STUART PIPKIN   page 500
Taylor conveys to Pipkin 100 acres; mentions the line between Samuel Taylor and Aaron Laws.
Made 2 April 1812   Registered 15 Dec. 1815
Witnesses, John Brown, Joseph Nale

WILLIAM McLENDON
CALEB HIGGENBOTTOM   page 501
McLendon conveys to Higgenbottom 68 acres on both sides of Haley's Creek mentions Cuthbert Hudson's northeast corner and Daniel Parker's northwest corner.
Made 20 Jan. 1813   Registered 20 Dec. 1815
Witnesses, W. Higgenbotham, Jesse G. Christian

STUARD PIPKIN
JOHN BROWN   page 503
Pipkin conveys to Brown land on Nail's Branch; mentions the line to Haley's Creek and John Parker's east boundary line.
Made 22 June 1812   Registered 20 Dec. 1815
Witnesses, Hixum Casey, Thomas Brown

WILLIAM WHITE
JEREMIAH SELEVANT   page 505
White conveys to Selevant (Note: Possibly Sullivan is correct) 300 acres on both sides of Turnbull Creek; mentions Jiles Thompson's corner. (Note: This entry was quite dim on microfilm.)
Made 6 Feb. 1815   Registered 22 Dec. 1815
Witnesses, Simon Miers, Isaiah B_____

JESSE NORRIS
EXEKIEL NORRIS   page 506
Jesse Norris conveys to Ezekiel Norris 190 acres on the west side of _____ Creek; mentions Robert Norris former _____(?); mentions Col. William Davis grant; land was deeded to Ezekiel Norris and by him to William Norris; mentions "my father William Norris."

Made 27 Aug. 1815   Registered 27 Dec. 1815
Witnesses, Jeremiah Gray, Edward Pearsall

STATE OF TENNESSEE
JAMES SIMMONS   page 508
Tennessee conveys to Simmons land on both sides of Cedar Creek; this
land was granted by North Carolina to Hack Cee by a military grant for
his military service.
Made 20 March 1809   Registered 22 Feb. 1816

WILLIAM PARKER
JAMES SIMMONS   page 509
Parker conveys to Simmons a negro girl Anne, age 3.
Made 13 Oct. 1814   Registered 22 Feb. 1816
Witnesses, Nathan Nesbitt, James Young, Edward Smith

STATE OF TENNESSEE
WILLIAM NAWL   page 510
State of Tennessee conveys to William Nawl, assignee of Isham Ferguson,
land on the north side of 4 Mile Creek of Jones Creek; land was granted
to Isham Ferguson on 22 Dec. 1796 for his military service; entered as
an occupant claim.
Made 28 March 1810   Registered 1 March 1816

STATE OF TENNESSEE
JOHN DICKSON   page 511
State of Tennessee conveys to John Dickson 25 acres on Racoon Creek of
Yellow Creek, land mentions "below a spring under a bluff".
Made 25 Feb. 1812   Registered 1 March 1816

SAMUEL McADOW
RICHARD CLAIBORNE NAPIER   page 513
McAdoww conveys two tracts to Napier on the 4 Mile Fork of Jones Creek.
Made 27 Nov. 1815   Registered 1 March 1816
Witnesses, B. D. Wills, Archd McHenry

JOHN GRYMES
RICHARD C. NAPIER   page 515
Grymes conveys to Napier land on the waters of Jonathan's Creek; men-
tions William Morrison's southeast corner and James Dickson's corner
and the south boundary of a tract granted to Daniel Hicks.
Made 24 Jan. 1814   Registered 8 March 1816
Witnesses, John Mockbee, George Tubb

MATTHEW McCLURKAN
HUGH McNAIRY   page 517
Matthew McClurkan, by his attorney James McClurkan, conveys to McNairy
300 acres on the east side of main Jones Creek, part of James Dickson's
North Carolina grant; mentions to lines of Christopher Strong and John
Larkins.
Made 29 June 1815   Registered 11 March 1816
Witnesses, Daniel Coleman, William Bullion, James Martin

ISAAC HARRIS
JOHN GARNER   page 519
Harris conveys to Garner 30 acres on Big Harpeth; mentions Henry Hyland
southwest corner.
Made 30 Dec. 1815   Registered 11 March 1816
Witnesses, James Hatfield, William P. Hatfield

ANDREW SMITH
DREWRY ADKINS   page 521
Smith conveys to Adkins land on Bear Creek.
Made 17 May 1815   Registered 12 Mar. 1816
Witnesses, Selman Edwards, James Dickson

ISAAC SELLARS
ELIJAH JONES   page 522
Sellars conveys to Jones 100 acres on Beaverdam Fork of Turnbull
Creek, part of tract originally granted Hardy Murphree.

Made 29 Nov. 1815   Registered 12 March 1816
Witnesses, Cuthbert Hudson, William Gentry

JAMES L. SCOTT
JESSE RUSSELL   page 524
Scott conveys to Russell 31 acres on Jones Creek where James Robertson
formerly lived; mentions John Morrisett's southwest corner of occupant
entry.
Made 2 Jan. 1816   Registered 18 Mar. 1816
Witnesses, William Hudson, Jr., William Russell

WILLIAM FLACK of Rutherford County, NC
WILLIAM MORRISON   page 525
William Flack for "natural love and affection of my beloved sister
Agness McMurray, deceased, of Dickson County, grant to William Morrison,
executor of last will of Thomas McMurray, deceased, for heirs ot Thomas
and Agnes McMurray, deceased, a negro Esther, age 40, for family use un-
til youngest child Washington McMurray comes of age."
Made 17 Nov. 1815   Registered 18 March 1816
Witnesses, Henry E. Williams, Robert McMurray

JAMES SEALS
JOHN SEALS   page 526
James Seals conveys to John Seals 40 acres on the middle fork of Bartons
Creek; mentions Simmons north boundary line.
Made 9 Dec. 1815   Registered 19 March 1816
Witnesses, Selman Edwards, William Seals

JESSE NORRIS
WIATT PARRISH   page 527
Norris conveys to Parrish land on Bear Creek of Yellow Creek; mentions
Nathan Dillehay's corner.
Made 20 Sept. 1815   Registered 19 Mar. 1816
Witnesses, Robert Jamison, Howell Parrish, Thomas Williams

JESSE NORRIS
WILLIAM HOOPER   page 529
Norris conveys to Hooper 125 acres on Bear Creek of Yellow Creek; men-
tions Wiatt Parrish's corner, the dividing line between Ezekiel Norris
and John A. Davis, Nathan Dillehay's corner.
Made 1 Jan. 1816   Registered 19 Mar. 1816
Witnesses, Eleaner Parish, Henry Story

DREWRY CHRISTIAN, Sheriff
SAMUEL NESBITT   page 531
Christian, sheriff, conveys to Nesbitt 50 acres; land belonged to
Benjamin Mills and was sold to satisfy judgment for taxes. Aaron Choate
was the highest bidder at the sale but transferred it to Samuel Nesbitt.
Mentions Thomas Choate's north boundary line.
Made 3 Jan. 1816   Registered 20 Mar. 1816

MARBLE STONE and ELIZABETH STONE
ISAAC WEST   page 534
They convey 160 acres to West; land on Jones Creek; mentions William
Stone's spring branch and where Marble and Elizabeth Stone now live to-
gether.
Made 24 March 1815   Registered 22 March 1816
Witnesses, Elijah Threlkeld, Samuel Sparks

ISAAC WEST, SR.
ANDERSON WEST   page 536
Isaac WEst, Sr., conveys to Anderson West a negro.
Made 19 March 1812   Registered 22 March 1816
Witnesses, Samuel Sparks, Elijah Threlkeld

EDMUND TAYLOR
STERLING MAY   pate 537
Taylor conveys to May land where Edmund Taylor now lives and which was
deeded to him by John Dickson in 1810.
Made 20 August 1814   Registered 22 Mar. 1816

Witnesses, Jesse May, Joshua Price

BENJAMIN JAMES
EDMOND TAYLOR   page 538
James conveys to Taylor 38 acres in the dry hollow of Yellow Creek.
Made 7 April 1815
Witnesses, John Adams, William Plant, William Crocket, Solomon Rye, Jr.

NOAH KELLEY
JOHN NALL   page 540
Kelley conveys to Nall 105 acres on Turnbull Creek.
Made 7 June 1813
Witnesses, William Nall, Andy Halford

    This ends Deed Book B.

VII

MILITARY RECORDS

From the earliest days of settlement, the men of Dickson County served in the state militia offering protection to the settlers in the frontier. But in 1812 they were called upon to fight when war began between the United States and Great Britain.

Three major causes contributed to this war: 1) British warships blockaded Napoleonic France and seized American trading ships, 2) British warships refused to recognize naturalized American sailors and seized and impressed thousands of them into British service; 3) Great Britain armed Indians who raided the U. S. western borders.

In 1813 a Creek Indian war party attacked Fort Mims, near Mobile, Alabama, massacring some 250 white men, women, and children. Tennessee's frontiersmen responded when a call for troops when out. Andrew Jackson received command of the Middle Tennessee contingent.

In a series of battles culminating with the decisive battle at Horseshoe Bend in Alabama, the strength of the Creek nation's warriors was broken, bringing to an end the Creek War. As the Creek War was fought during the War of 1812, veterans of this Indian war are considered soldiers in the War of 1812.

Many muster rolls and pay rolls for Tennessee's soldiers may be found in the Tennessee State Library and Archives. The following lists were copied from these rolls and pertain to men who served from Dickson County.

***

CAPTAIN MICHAEL MOLTON'S COMPANY

This group is often called the Natchez Expedition group as they were part of the Tennesseans who assembled at Franklin, Tennessee and marched overland to Natchez, Mississippi. Members of this company were:

Ephraim Arnold	John Hays	Benjamin Persel
Israel Arnold	Isaac Hill	Peter Phillips
Thomas Arnold	Richard Juster	William Powers
Charles Baker	Richard Justice	Shadrick Primm
John Bakers	Patrick Kelly	Samuel Richardson
Jesse Bays	Joseph Larkins	Richard Rushing
James L. Bell	Aaron Lewis (Laws?)	David Rushing
James Black	James Lewis	Elisha Simmons
John Boothe	John Lewis	James Simmons
John Cooper	Samuel Lewis	Andrew Smith
Alexander Dickson	John McHenry	Clarke Spencer
Hugh Dickson	Absolum Maddin	Howard W. Turner
William Evans	M. C. Molton	Jacob Vaughn
Isenias Haley	Samuel Morris	William Wingate
Andrew Hamilton	Jesse Norris	West Wood
Randolph Harris	Robert Norris	William Wright
Stephen Harris	Hewell Parrish	

The following obituary was found in the Huntsville Republican, Huntsville Alabama, 1 Sept. 1817 and was quoted in the Alabama Historical Quarterly, Winter 1944, pages 615, 616:

DEPARTED THIS LIFE on Sunday the 31st ult., at his residence in Meridianville in this county, Col. Michael Moulton in the 49th year of his age. After a tedious illness he was fondly indulging the flattering hope of returning health, when he was suddenly called from the state of mortal existence.

Col. Moulton was born in the county of Duplin, N.C.--he represented a county in that State in the Legislature several years. He afterwards removed and became a citizen of Tennessee. At the commencement of the great war with Great Britain, he flew with alarcity to the standard of his country; and continued his unremitting exertions in defence of our right, until the final and glorious conclusion of the struggle. He accompanied Gen. Jackson in the first descent of the Mississippi, as captain of a troop of cavalry from Tennessee; and also his expedition against the Southern Indians.

Afterwards, having been promoted to the command of a regiment of militia, he descended the river a second time under command of Gen. Carrol, and contributed by his services to "foil the last demonstration" of our enemy at New Orleans. Col. M. has left a wife and only daughter to lament his loss; they will find their best consolation in the sympathies of numerous acquaintances and friends, whose unfeigned sorrow will testify his worth.

His remains were attended to the grave by many of his friends and his Masonic brethren of this place, and interred with the ceremonies of their order. In the death of Col. M. society has lost a valuable and worthy member and his country a friend.

(Compiler's note: Michael Molton was sheriff of Dickson County, Tennessee, from 1808 to 1810. The name is spelled Molton on what remains of his son James Molton's tombstone in the Molton-Pearsall Cemetery on Yellow Creek in Dickson County. This son died in 1816 at the age of 17 years. Michael Molton was the son of Sarah Molton, whose will was recorded 1812 in Dickson County, but her tombstone shows she died 1811. Joseph Dickson, soldier of the American Revolution, and his wife Jane Molton are believed to be buried in unmarked graves in this same small cemetery. Many of the men in Molton company lived in the Yellow Creek area.)

***

CAPTAIN CUTHBERT HUDSON'S COMPANY

The following are the men who served under his company from 28 Sept. 1814 until 28 March 1815:

Cuthbert Hudson, Captain
Jesse S. Ross, 1st Lieutenant
William Adams, Second Lieutenant
Edward Smith, Third Lieutenant
Stuart Pipkins, Cornet
Thomas Adams, Sergeant
Mills Eason, Sergeant
Aaron Laws, Sergeant
John B. Walker, Sergeant
Carter B. Eason, Sergeant

John McCallister, corporal
Willis Walker, corporal
James Christian, corporal
William Austin, corporal
Pleasant Crews, corporal
David McAllister, corporal
Nicholas Baker, corporal
John Walker, trumpeter
Thomas Crossno, farrier

Privates

John Abner (Abney?)
Francis Brown
Eldridge Bowen
Allen Bowen
Thomas Brown
Empson Bishop
Russell Brock
Aaron Baldwin
Willie Davis
Isaac Brown
David Bunch
William Chambers
Hyram Dunagan
Moses Davis
John Davidson
Joseph Eason
Pleasant Irby
William Grimmitt

Benjamin **Gilbert**
John Gates
William Gates
John Holt
Henry Hunter
Thomas Hudson
Robert Hammond (?)
John Hammond
Jonathan Huddleston
Robert Hum____
Caleb Higgenbotham
Midd__ Higgenbotham
Francis Hutton
Reuben Jones
Elijah James
John Jones
Josiah Jones
Hugh Lewis

George Mitchell
John Marshall
Hugh McCrory
John McAlister
John Mitchell
John Mills
Edward Mills
John Malugan
James Malugan
James McKee
James Norris
Gabriel Overton
Wright Perkins
John Peake
Abraham Robinson
William Robinson
Joel Shelton
Jesse Stroud

William Stafford
Joel Smith
William Thomas
Benjamin Smith
George Shelton

Knott Tedford
William Tedford
Robert Tidwell
Quilla Tedford (Tidwell?)
John Wims

George Wright
Henry Worley
Joshua White
Medy White
William White

Deaths in Captain Hudson's company:
Edward Smith, died 23 Feb. 1815
Mills Eason died 23 Nov. 1814
Aaron Laws died 2 November 1815
John Abner (or Abney) died 23 Feb. 1815
Reuben Jones died 15 April 1815
Elijah James died 4 Feb. 1815
Josiah Jones died 25 Feb. 1815
Hugh Lewis died 14 Feb. 1815
Edward Mills, killed in battle 23 Dec. 1814
James Norris, died 12 Feb. 1815
Gabriel Overton, died 26 March 1815
George Shelton, died 21 January 1815
Knott Tedford, died 7 February 1815
George Wright, died 1 February 1815.

(Note: Many of these men lived in the Turnbull Creek and Beaverdam Creek area of Dickson County, near the Hickman County line.)

***

CAPTAIN DRURY ADKINS'S COMPANY

This company was in Colonel Richard C. Napier's regiment and served from 28 January 1814 until 10 May 1814. The muster roll was quite clear and easy to read, but the pay roll had some differences which will be noted in the following listing.

Drury Adkins, Captain
Samuel Story, First Lieutenant
Elisha Gunn, Ensign
David Fentress, Sergeant
John Pitchford, Sergeant
Andrew Nesbitt, Sergeant
   (His name is Nathan on pay roll)

John Hensly, Sergeant
Pleasant Heart
Robert P. Nesbitt
Leven Dickson
Allen Hunter

Privates

Charles Acuff
Hamilton Acuff
Elias Abney
Francis Kary
Benjamin Barton
Caleb Bright
Isaac Brown
Charles Butler
Joshua Butler
John Barton (James on pay roll)
Style Buggs
John Bradley
Peter Connelly
David Curry (Craig on pay roll)
Lewis Collins
John Cross
Edmond Campbell
John Cooper
Sandford Edwards
Enoch Edwards
John Forsythe
Abijah Gunn (Alisha on pay roll)
John Griggs
Peter Gilbert
Mark Holland
James Hanna

John Hodges
Robert Howel
Alexander Hunter
John Inman
Enos James
Amos James (appears on pay roll but not on the muster roll)
John King
Henry Kimbrell (name appears to be Nesbitt on pay roll)
William Light
William Lakeray (Lukeroy, possibly)
Enoch Lewis
John Lee
Gosham Lee
Alexander McGalughey
William McClelland
Michael McAdoo (McAdin?)
John Mitchell
John Moore (Mando on pay roll)
Edmund Milas (Miller on pay roll)
William Patteny (Patterson possibly)
Robert T. Patton (Richard on pay roll)
Alexander Petty (Alfred on pay roll)
William Ragan
James Robertson

Mark Reynolds (Amos W. on pay roll)
John Shehan
John Stewart
Claiborne Spiery
James Scott
John Tucker
William Tatum
Spier Boon (Brown on pay roll)

Robert Tidwell
Jacob Walker
Willis Willy
Robert Williams
Robert Ward (Thomas on pay roll)
Larkin Tate (Lakin?)

John Hensley was left sick at Fort Deposit on 28 February 1814.

***

CAPTAIN JOSEPH WILLIAMS'S COMPANY

This muster roll was for a company of Tennessee militia under the command of Joseph Williams, 1st Tennessee Militia, Dyer's Regiment, which served from September 1814 to March 1815.

Joseph Williams, Captain
Nehemiah Scott, Lieutenant
John May
Aaron Vanhook
William Varnal, cornet
Martin H. Burton
Charles Baker
Robert McClintock
John Plant
William Plant

William Allen
Howard W. Turner
William Turner
John Turner
John Rice
Nathan Nesbit
James Daniel
Robert Wilson
Thomas May
Henry Wayland

Privates

Thomas Arnold
John Arnold
Israel Arnold
Wyatt Arnold
Jacob Allen
John Adams
James Brown
William Bagley
Robert Busby
David Bunch
William Cottinham
John Curtis
Mitchell Childress
John Crage
Eli Crage
John Cooper
Lewis Collins
Ashburn Davy
James Douglas
John Davidson
James Davidson
Elijah Estes
Jeremiah Ethridge
Acres Etheridge
George Evans
Enoch Edwards
John Epperson
Joseph Edwards
William Gibson
Maliachie Garrett
George Humble
Green Holland
Stephen Harris
Dorrell Y. Harris
Thomas Hunter
James Hagler
Charles Howard

Edward Howard
John H. Humphreys
Zachariah Hopper
Robert Howard
Isaiah Howard
John Hinsley
William Hodden
Robert Jamerson
Rubin Johnson
George Lewis
George Lasley
  ?   Lewis
Aaron Lewis (Laws?)
Robert Livingston
William Mills
William McMurry
James McMurry
James McMurtrey
John McMurtrey
Benjamin Matlock
Smyth Matlock
David McAdoo
John McAdoo
Andrew Moody
Samuel McKay
Jeremiah Massey
Jonathan May
Jobe Manor
James McKee
John McClain
James Melugin
George Mitchell
Joel Massey
William Morris (or William Norris)
Jesse Morris   (or Jesse Norris)
Willis Norsworthy
John Pickett

Richard Powell
Wyatt Parrish
Joshua Price
William Potter
John Pitchforce
Mark Reynolds
William T. Reynolds
Jonathan Rogers
Ashburn Self
Clark Spencer
Joel Shelton
George Shelton
William Suter
William Simpson
James Thompson
William Thompson
Edmond Taylor
Isaac Toland
William Valentine
Richard N. Williams
Hartwell Weaver
James Walker
Isaiah Watkins
William Watson
James Willis
Alex Wilson
John J. Wells
John Cottingham

Lewis, waiter to Lt. Scott

Deaths in Captain Joseph Williams's company:
William Plant died 1 March 1815
Thomas Arnold died 24 March 1814 (Also given as 25 March 1815)
John Arnold killed in action 23 December 1814 or 25 December 1814
James Brown died ___January 1815
Malachi Garrett died 20 March 1815
Zachariah Hopper died 16 November 1814
Robert Howard died of wounds in action 2 January 1815 (Name also given as Richard Howard on another roll)
James McMurtrey died 6 February 1815
William Watson died 25 March 1815

(Note: Many of the men on this roll lived in the Yellow Creek area.)

***

CAPTAIN EDWARD NEBLETT'S COMPANY

This company is a Montgomery County outfit, serving under Captain Edward Neblett in the Tennessee militia, Napier's regiment, and the roll was dated from 25 January 1814 to May 1814. There was also a pay roll for this company, but this was not copied. Several names of Dickson County residents appear on this roll and although for Montgomery County, this roll will be included here.

Edward Neblett, Captain
Benjamin Neblett, Lieutenant
James Caldwell, Ensign
William Night, Sergeant
William Loggins, Second Sergeant
William Good, Third Sergeant

John C. Thomas, 4th Sergeant
John Bumpass, Corporal
David Vaughan, Corporal
William Johnston, Corporal
Adam Brown, Corporal

Privates

James Agee
Balam Bull
Thompkins Bumpus
Robert Baker
Drury Bonds
Andrew Chriswell
Abija Clark
Andrew Davis
James Estep
James Hightower
William Hightower
Yelverton Hambrick
John Harman

Laban Holt
Eli Hubbard
Epps Jackson
Benjamin Kizer
Benjamin Lewis
William Martin
Gibson Mills
Ambrose Martin
Henry Mosely
Joseph Morgan
William Nuson
George Outlaw
Abijah Heath

Burgess Walls
Rubin Oglesby
John Patter
Jesse Pierce
Benjamin Rye
Solomon Rye
James Smith
Allen Sorry
Jeffry Syms
Josiah Smith
John Thacker
Robert Way
Philmore Whitworth

***

CAPTAIN FRANCIS S. ELLIS'S COMPANY

This company was in service from November 1814 until May 1815. (Another roll says in service from 13 Nov. 1814 to 31 Dec. 1814.) Many names on this roll were quite difficult to decipher. Those interested in any names on this list should recheck with rolls in the Tennessee State Library and Archives.

Francis S. Ellis, Captain
Peter Hardeman, First Lieutenant
Jesse Russell, Second Lieutenant
Thomas Swift, Third Lieutenant
George Shelton, Ensign
John B. Brown, First Sergeant
William T. Patterson, Second Sgt.
Andrew Hambleton, Third Sergeant
William Freeman, 4th Sergeant
Robert Rogers, Fifth Sergeant

Absalom Swift, Corporal
Wilson Blanet (Blounton), Corporal
Willis L. Dawson, Corporal
Benjamin Crews, Corporal
John Lowder, Corporal
John Walker, Corporal
Willis Bugg, Fifer

Privates

- Elkanah Anderson, died 14 Jan. 1815
- John Anderson, died 10 Feb. 1815
- Felix Allen
- Elisha Arnold
- James Appleton
- Joseph Boyd (James Baker on the second roll)
- James Barfield (substitute for William Freeman)
- Samuel Bugg
- Charles Brown, deceased 9 Feb. 1815
- William B. Barton, died 13 Feb.1815
- John B. Barber
- Benjamin Bedford
- Henry Blalock
- Ephraim Burkett
- Joseph Brown (Boren? Barnes?), died 1 March 1815
- William W. Coleman
- John Crews (substitute for Benjamin Crews)
- Andrew Cooksey
- Francis Cary
- Robert Chance (substitute for Simmons S. Walker)
- Robert Doty
- Simon DeLoach
- Thomas Dunnagan
- James Dicus
- Thomas Davidson, deceased 29 Feb. 1815
- Jesse Epperson
- Lewis Evans
- Anderson England
- Robert Farris
- James Dyer (substitute for John Walker)
- John Farris
- Wyett Fussell (Name appears to be Willis Fussell on second roll)
- Gideon France (or Frane or Frame)
- John Forsythe
- John Gilpon (or Gippen or Giffen)
- Charles Gunn
- Austin Gresham
- Washington Hunter
- Robert Horner
- Henry Hall
- William Hubs (or Hubbles)
- Bain Hubs (or Hubbles)
- John Hicks
- Thomas Johnston
- Thomas James (could be Jones)
- John W. Leigh
- Isaiah Mathas
- John Murry
- James Mathas
- James B. Matlock (name is given as Charles B. Matlock on a second roll of this company.)
- David McClanahan
- Joel Mash
- John Manners
- Ephraim Perkins
- Benjamin Renshaw
- Elijah Renshaw
- Robert Roberts
- Robert Simmons
- James Sims, died 2 March 1815
- Henry Story
- Thomas Turner
- Edward Swan, died 12 Mar. 1815 (Surname in question)
- William Suggs, died 9 March 1815
- Rosamund Seat
- Thomas Whitwell
- John West
- John Watkins
- Joseph Walker
- Simpson S. Walker
- Adam, a negro waiter to Captain Ellis

Deathdate of Thomas Davidson is also found as 30 January 1815 in these records.

* * *

MILITIA INFANTRY DETACHMENT

This roll was a pay roll for a detachment of militia infantry under Lt. Col. R. C. Napier and commanded by _____; the only date that could be read was 22 May 1812.

- David Hogan, Second Major
- Francis Ellis, Captain
- William Moore, Lieutenant
- David Shropshire, Ensign
- William Miller, Sergeant
- Marbel Stone, Sergeant
- Andrew Hamilton, Sergeant
- Thomas Nesbitt, Corporal
- John Adams, Corporal

Privates

- William Shelby
- Robert Maran
- Elisha Gunn
- Lawson Gunn
- William Thomas
- William Cox
- Jeremiah Nesbitt
- Eleanor Parrish
- Mark Holloway
- William Crews
- John H_____
- Achilles Walker
- Benjamin Walker
- Alexander Nalls
- Thomas May

William Gunn
Larkin Tait
Thomas Hudson
Reuben Nalls
Eseb___Graham
John Tatum
William Tatum
James E____
Nathan Nesbitt
John Pitchford
Richard Barn (?)
John Shyster
Matthew Campbell
Joseph Nesbitt
Simon Deloach
Andrew Smith
John McAdoo
John Nesbitt
Thomas Williams
Robert Nesbitt
Allen Taylor

Jeremiah Gray
Sampson Bowles
Thomas Hunter
George Evans
William Clark
Edward Taylor
Allen Howard
Robert Larkins
John Hanna
Charles Reeves
Clark Spivy
James McKee
William Adams
Nehemiah Scott
Robert Scott
Robert Bowles
Robert Jamison
Aaron Hancock
G___Humble
John Robertson
Thomas Wright

Francis McClelland
John Lewis
Moses Meek
William McClelland
James Walker
Edom Walker
Lewis Ream
Samuel Sellers
Thomas Hadrick
Wm. H. Roberts
Samuel Martin
William Giffin
Andrew Giffin
Lewis Berry
____Shelley (Shelby)
John Baker
William Adams
John Spencer
Lewis Shehan
Cato Acuff (or
   Carter Acuff)

***

MISCELLANEOUS WAR of 1812 NOTES

The Clarion, newspaper published in Nashville, TN, 4 Oct 1814:
Men who deserted or mutinied on 20th and 21st Sept. 1814 from Dickson County were John Reed, John Benham, Isaac Wallace, Thomas Graves, Elisha Arnold.

The Clarion, dated 4 Oct. 1814:
On 20 Sept. 1814 deserted from Fort Jackson from Capt. Ebenezer Kilpatrick's company, James Arnold of Dickson County.

The Clarion, dated 11 Oct. 1814:
Charged with mutiny and desertion: Edward Pickett of Dickson County.

***

FIRST SEMINOLE WAR SOLDIERS

The following men from Dickson County were found as soldiers in the First Seminole War from Dickson County. Their records are in the Tennessee State Library and Archives. They enlisted 31 Jan. 1818 at Camp Blount and were discharged 30 June 1818. Only names and place of residence were copied for this list. Other information given included, rank, company, regiment, etc. They served in a company headed by Captain James L. Bell.

Hansellow Acuff from the lower part of Dickson County
Williams Allen from the lower part of Dickson County
James R. Bandolf from the lower part of Dickson County
Cuthbert Bell from the lower part of Dickson County
James Blanks from the lower part of Dickson County
Elijah Boyte from the lower part of Dickson County
Crawford Bradford from the lower part of Dickson County
Hella (or Hills) Bradford from the lower part of Dickson County.
John Bullian from the lower part of Dickson County
Thomas Bullian from the lower part of Dickson County
John Cook from the lower part of Dickson County
George Cooley from the lower part of Dickson County
Richard Cooley from the lower part of Dickson County
John Crane from the lower part of Dickson County
William Cross from the lower part of Dickson County
Robert Dickson from the lower part of Dickson County
John G. Dillehay from the lower part of Dickson County
Calvin W. Eason from the lower part of Dickson County
Thomas Edwards from the lower part of Dickson County
James Enlow from the lower part of Dickson County

Wyatt Epps from the lower part of Dickson County
David Fentress from the lower part of Dickson County
John Ghehan from the lower part of Dickson County
Beal Goodwin (or Goodman) from the lower part of Dickson County
Peter Goodwin from the lower part of Dickson County
Thomas Haley from the lower part of Dickson County
Jesse Hall from the lower part of Dickson County
John Hays from the lower part of Dickson County
James Hesbitt (or Nesbitt) from the lower part of Dickson County
William Hightower from the lower part of Dickson County
JOhn James from the lower part of Dickson County
William Joslin from the lower part of Dickson County
James M. Kirk from the lower part of Dickson County
Amos Lewis from the lower part of Dickson County
Daniel Logan from the lower part of Dickson County
John Luke from the lower part of Dickson County
John McClelland from the lower part of Dickson County
Rezdon Mackbee from the lower part of Dickson County
Isaac Manley from the lower part of Dickson County
Gideon Miller from the lower part of Dickson County
James M. Miller from the lower part of Dickson County
Samuel Offten from the lower part of Dickson County
James Napier from the lower part of Dickson County
Drury Oliver from the lower part of Dickson County
Howel Parish from the lower part of Dickson County
Thomas Randolf from the lower part of Dickson County
James B. Randolf from the lower part of Dickson County
Isam L. Roy (or Ray) from the lower part of Dickson County
Samuel Richardson from the lower part of Dickson County
Charles P. Robertson from the lower part of Dickson County
James Thomas from the lower part of Dickson County
John Thompson from the lower part of Dickson County
William Webster from the lower part of Dickson County
James West from the lower part of Dickson County
William West from the lower part of Dickson County
Charles B. Wilcox from the lower part of Dickson County
Caleb Williams from the lower part of Dickson County
Wayne N. Wilcox from the lower part of Dickson County
Allison Williams from the lower part of Dickson County

***

MISCELLANEOUS SOLDIERS

In 1976 a list of War of 1812 soldiers was published in the Dickson Free Press. It is believed this list was possibly from Goodspeed's History of the county.

"The soldiers furnished by Dickson County to the war of 1812 were as follows: John B. Walker, Thomas Edwards, David McAdoo, William James, Benjamin Swift, Daniel Williams, James Bell, Thomas Williams, James Daniels, Thomas Gilbert, William Porter, John Jones, John Hall, John Tilley, William Dodson, James Hightower, Obediah Spradlin, Abraham Heath Simon DeLoach, Jesse Beck, Francis Hunter, Drury Atkins, A. Etherage, Isaac Hill, David Bibb, Allen Bowen, Richard Watkins, Isaac Heath, Aaron Parrish, Willis Willey, Thomas Nesbitt, Richard Batson, Lawson Gunn, Anderson England, and Edward Niblack."

***

FLORIDA WAR

In 1976 a list of men who fought in the Florida War of 1836 in Capt. James Tatum's company was published in the Dickson Free Press. It is believed this list was possibly from Goodspeed's History of Dickson County. These men were given as:

Alexander Jones, Moses Street, Abraham Street, Allen Nesbitt, Mortimer Edwards, Joseph Parrish, William Tatom, James Hudgins, James Young, Hudson Shropshire, John Links, Washington Weems and William Young.

MEXICAN WAR

During the Bicentennial year, 1976, the following was published in the Dickson County Press and was possibly from Goodspeed's History of Dickson County:

"When the call was made for volunteers to serve in the Mexican War, in 1846, Dickson County responded promptly by raising two full companies, but before they could report at Nashville, Tenn., the quota was already full, and they were rejected. However, several members of the companies succeeded in getting into the service and served throughout the war. They were W. J. Mallory, James Hudgins, William Tate, John Owens, Bass Ferrell and John Morris."

***

CIVIL WAR

Dickson County was 1141 for secession to 72 against secession in 1861. The following companies for the Confederate Army were organized in the county:

    E. D. Baxter's Battery, the second organization
    Company C, 11th Tennessee Infantry
    Company E, 11th Tennessee Infantry
    Company K, 11th Tennessee Infantry
    Company B, 49th Tennessee Infantry
    Company D, 49th Tennessee Infantry
    Company A, 50th Tennessee Infantry

The following information was taken from J. B. Lindlsey's Military Annals and pertains only to men from Dickson County companies.

List of dead for Company C, 11th Tennessee Infantry:

BAKER, Stephen, died at Rome, Georgia, 30 April 1863
BALTHORPE, W. T., died 29 July 1861
CHESTER, C. B., killedd at Battle of Murfreesboro, 31 December 1862
CHESTER, J. A., killed accidentally in Atlanta, August 1864
COLLINS, Hazard, killed in Battle of Chickamauga, 19 September 1863
FITZGERALD, Edward, died 23 June 1861
FREEMAN, J. R., killed in Battle of New Hope Church, 27 May 1864
LATHAM, J. B., died 3 December 1863
McCLELLAND, J. R., killed in battle near Atlanta, 20 July 1864
McNEILLY, Hugh J., killed in battle near Atlanta, 22 July 1864
ROBERTSON, D. L., died 23 March 1863
SENSING, J. H., killed in Battle of Murfreesboro, 31 December 1862
STREET, F. M., died 20 July 1861
STREET, J. C., died 9 August 1861
STOCKELY, W. A., killed in Battle of Franklin, 30 November 1864

List of dead for Company E, 11th Tennessee Infantry:

ALISON, ____, killed in Battle of Missionary Ridge
BAKER, Robert, killed in Battle near Calhoun, Georgia
BAKER, W. L., killed in battle
DOUGHERTY, Martin, killed in Battle of Missionary Ridge
EUBANKS, E. G., killed in Battle of Franklin
HEATH, John, killed in Battle of Missionary Ridge
HUNTER, J. P., killed in Battle of Kennesaw Mountain
JACKSON, Epps, died at Normandy, Tennessee, January 1863
LARKINS, J. M., killed in Battle of New Hope Church, Georgia
MATHIS, Drew, killed in railroad collision
MUSGROVE, D., killed in Battle of Murfreesboro
NOLL, Rufus, transferred to cavalry and killed at Shiloh
O'CONNER, ____, killed at Battle of Missionary Ridge
RICHARDSON, M. T., killed at Battle of Jonesboro, Georgia
TAYLOR, Welton, died at Tunnel Hill, Georgia, September 1863
WALLS, John, killed at Battle of Murfreesboro
WILLIAMS, Stephen, killed at Battle of Kennesaw Mountain

List of dead for Company K, 11th Tennessee Infantry:

BROWN, Aaron, died at Camp Cheatham, Tennessee, 27 July 1861
BROWN, Wiley, died in prison
BRYANT, J. W., died 26 March 1863
BRAZZEL, John, died at Camp Cheatham 1861
CLIFTON, J. W., died in service 9 August 1861
CAPPS, Sterling, killed near New Hope Church, Georgia, 27 May 1864
CATHEY, Archie, died in hospital
CATHEY, W. J., died at Chattanooga, 3 April 1863
COX, S. A., died at Bean's Station, East Tennessee
COX, W. J., died 25 June 1861
CROW, M. B., died at Chattanooga, 3 April 1863
CAVIDSON, Calvin, died at Cumberland Gap, 17 April 1862
DAVIDSON, J. W., killed in Battle of Missionary Ridge
ESTES, Solomon, killed in Battle of Missionary Ridge
ETHERIDGE, William, killed in Battle of Jonesboro, Georgia
GALLOWAY, J. W., killed by his own men while in front of line near Cumberland Gap
GALLOWAY, Henry, died at Woodson's Cross Roads
GOODWIN, John, died in service, no date given
GENTRY, D. C., killed near New Hope Church, 27 May 1864
GREGG, J. C., killed in battle
HARRIS, William, died in service at Nashville, 17 Sept. 1861
HOUSE, John W., died in prison
JORDEN, Berry, killed in Battle at Chickamauga
LANKFORD, Lawrence, died in prison
LANKFORD, J. W. H., died at Cumberland Gap, 14 Feb. 1862
LANKFORD, Robert, died at Cumberland Gap
MANLY, Hugh, died at Camp Cheatham, 17 August 1861
MARSH, W. G., died at Camp Bheatham, 24 July 1861
RICHARDSON, B. W., died 1 August 1861
READER, J. L., died of wounds received at Battle of Franklin
STEWART, W. H., killed in Battle of Kennesaw Mountain
TIDWELL, Benjamin, died in hospital at Chattanooga
TIDWELL, C. M., died 16 April 1863
TIDWELL, Silas, killed in Battle of Jonesboro, Georgia
THOMAS, M. B., died in prison
WEEMS, G. W., died in hospital 10 November 1863

List of dead for Company B, 49th Tennessee:

CUNNINGHAM, A. J., died as prisoner of war
CUNNINGHAM, E. L., died 8 Jan. 1863
CLYMER, C. J., died as prisoner of war
FORD, W. D., died as prisoner of war
HAM, J. W., died as prisoner of war
HARRIS, J. T., died as prisoner of war
HARROD, M. G., died April 1863
LINDSAY, J. M., died 17 September 1863
LINK, Robert, died 7 September 1862
McCALL, John B., died 6 June 1862
SPRADLIN, A. O., died 14 March 1863
WILLIAMS, J. W., died March 1862
WHITE, W. H., died March 1863

List of dead for Company D, 49th Tennessee:

BROWN, J. H., died 16 March 1862
BURTON, W. H., died 25 February 1862
DANIEL, J. J., died
DUNNINGTON, T. J., died
FRASIER, N. C., died
FRASIER, M. H., died
GRANTUM, M., died
HOWARD, W. B., died
GARTIER, D. P., died
MANGLIN, E. B., died
NASH, J. W. R., died
SUGG, S. W., died 22 March 1863

List of dead for Company D, 49th Tennessee, continued:

SIGMORE, J. W., died 22 April 1862   (Note: Some believe this name should be correctly Sizemore)
SANDERS, H. W., died 20 March 1862
THOMPSON, J. M., died
THOMPSON, J. L., died 4 September 1863
THEDFORD, J. W. B., died 22 May 1862
WALKER, J. L., died 11 Feb. 1862
WILEY, J. K. P., died 8 September 1862
WALKER, R., died 30 March 1862
WALKER, J. N., died 16 April 1863

***

Confederate pensioners of Dickson County:

The following men served in the Confederate Army and drew pensions while living in Dickson County. Their pension applications are on file in the Tennessee State Library and Archives where copies of the complete pension application may be obtained.

J. I. J. Adams, 11th Infantry
Montgomery Adams
W. T. Adams, 11th Infantry
Thomas Benton Adcock
J. W. Adcock,, 11th Infantry
Martin V. Adcock, 11th Infantry
T. B. Adcock, 11th Infantry
John A. Albright, 10th Cavalry
Josiah Clifton Alspaugh, 11th Infan.
B. T. Andrews, 1st Heavy Artillery
George Wyatt Austin
Charles Van Buren Austin, 11th Inft.
H. G. Austin, Napier's Cavalry Bn.
George Washington Baker
Thomas Baker, 10th Cavalry
Wiley J. Baker, 11th Infantry
John T. Beck, Baxter's Company, Light Artillery
John R. Blackburn
W. H. Binkley, 11th Infantry
Thomas Bledsoe
B. F. Brown, Baxter's Company Light Arilltery
J. E. Brown, 48th Infantry
J. J. Brown, 11th Infantry
S. C. Brown, 22nd (Barteau's) Cav.
John Butler
William George D. Buttrey
John C. Buford, 3rd Ala. Infantry
J. D. Burney, 49th Infantry
Oscar Dunreth Caldwell, 49th Infant.
Thomas J. Carr, Baxter's Company, Light Artillery
Elias Newton Cathey, 11th Infantry
T. M. Childress, Cobbs Legion of Cavalry, Georgia
Burrel A. Clifton, 11th Infantry
James Kirby Clifton, 11th Infantry
George H. Cline, 8th N. C. Infantry
James Jackson Carroll
George Bryant Cavender
George W. Clark
Charles Elbert Climer
William Richard Cook
John Randolph Corlew
Willis Council
J. M. Collier, 3rd Cavalry
John Max Cowan
J. E. Craig, 10th Cavalry

J. P. Crutcher
E. G. Cullum, 18th Infantry
James Alford Curtis, 50th Infantry
Josiah Knox Davis
W. R. Deason, 49th Infantry
William Delonas, 19th Infantry
Edwin Dickerson, 23rd N. C. Infantry
William Hendry Dickson, 11th Infan.
John Dillard, Baxter's Company, Light Artillery
J. E. Dodson, 4th Cavalry
John W. Dotson, 3rd Cavalry, Forrest
John A. Doty, 49th Infantry
David Douglas
John Wesley Easley, 1st (Field's) Infantry
Jacob J. Elrod
S. G. Eleazor, 49th Infantry
George Epps, 11th Infantry
John Ethridge
G. G. Estes, 11th Cavalry (Holman)
Jerry M. Forsythe, 49th Infantry
John Estes Fortner
P. Frasher, 7th Kentucky Infantry
W. P. A. Frasher, Baxter's Company, Light Artillery
James L. Frierson, Cabell's BN, Georgia Artillery
Martin Garton
Moses Garton, 11th Infantry
F. M. Gary, 1st (Field's) Infantry
John F. Gatewood
R. M. Gibson, 10th (Demoss) Cavalry
J. D. Gill, 48th (Nixon's) Infantry
John William Gill
James W. Gillock, 6th Kentucky Mounted Infantry
George M. Godwin
J. P. Goodrich, 49th Infantry
P. S. Griffin, 48th Infantry
Thomas Kinley Grigsby
J. P. Grimes, 11th Infantry
A. J. Gunn, 1st (Field's) Infantry
E. T. Hagood, 14th Infantry
Ben Frank Hall, 11th Infantry
Joe A. Hall, 1st Heavy Artillery
Samuel Hammon, 11th Infantry
T. J. Harris, 11th Infantry
W. B. Hassell, 10th Cavalry

Confederate pensioners, continued:

N. G. Hatley, 1st Heavy Artillery
W. A. Hayes, 11th Infantry
H. H. Henderson, 11th Infantry
F. B. Henry, 24th Infantry
R. B. Herbison, 49th Infantry
Wilham Marion Hobbs
W. M. Hogins, 49th Infantry
J. Holley, 14th Infantry
J. O. Hooper, 50th Infantry
  (Full name, Jessie Owen Hooper)
A. Hooper
Simpson Homes Hooper
T. J. Hooper, Baxter's Company,
  Light Artillery
J. A. Hudspeth, 4th Infantry
F. M. Hugins, 11th Infantry
F. M. Hudgens
Robert Anderson Hudson
J. M. Huggins
J. V. Jackson, 2nd Woodward's
  Kentucky Cavalry
T. A. Jackson, 49th Infantry
T. G. Jarrett, 45th Infantry
J. M. Jennings, 14th Infantry
J. B. Johnson, 50th Infantry
J. T. Johnson, Forrest's Scouts
John Pinkerton Johnson
Willis R. Johnson, 44th Infantry
James T. Johnson, 11th Infantry
J. Y. Jones, 59th Infantry
  (Full name, James Yell Jones)
W. B. Joslin, Fisher's Company,
  Artillery
Thomas L. Justice, Harding
  Artillery
William T. Kelsey, 1st (Field's)
  Infantry
William Henry Lemastus, 10th Cavalry
A. J. Lampley, Baxter's Company,
  Light Artillery
Thomas Lane, 11th Infantry
Dillard H. Lankford, Baxter's
  Company, Light Artillery
J. H. Larkins, 11th Infantry
J. J. Larkins, 11th Cavalry
S. P. Larkins, 49th Infantry
  (Full name, Samuel Putnam)
J. B. Lawrence, 11th Infantry
James G. Lewis, Baxter's Company,
  Light Artillery
William Henry Harrison Linzey,
  11th Infantry
Alfred Long, 11th Infantry
W. H. Lowery, 5th Infantry
John A. Lunn, 17th Infantry
Samuel Brison McClurkan
B. T. McCaslin, Fisher's Company,
  Artillery
W. H. McCauley, 11th Infantry
Calvin McDonald McCord
Thomas Benton McElyea, 1st Field's
  Infantry
John R. McNeil, 48th Infantry
Thomas McNickols
D. M. Marsh, 1st Battalion of
  Heavy Artillery
John Shelby Martin
I. F. Martin, 10th Cavalry

Cave Johnson Martin
J. D. Martin, 10th Cavalry
J. T. Martin, 11th Infantry
Bennett Mason, 11th Infantry
W. J. Mathis
John T. Matthews, 11th Infantry
Lewis Matlock
A. B. Maxey, 14th Infantry
W. E. Mayfield, 49th Infantry
John A. Meador, 24th Infantry
Peter A. Miller, 49th Infantry
W. C. Miller, 6th Kentucky Cavalry
Ballard Mitchell
Frank B. Moore
Henry Allen Murray
William Jack Myatt, 49th Infantry
W. J. Myatt, 49th Infantry
Elisha J. D. Nall, 1st (Field's)
  Infantry
R. P. Neblett, 11th Infantry
James Wash Oakley
Curtis Alexander Oakley
William H. Orgain
James C. Oakley, 4th Infantry
W. P. Outlaw, 49th Infantry
H. B. Padgett, 1st (Field's)
  Infantry
J. J. Page, 51 Infantry
T. J. Parker, Baxter's Company,
  Light Artillery
G. H. Petty, 42nd Infantry
William Silons Porch, 11th Infantry
D. U. Putnam, 11th Cavalry
Horatio Clagett Primm
James Madison Rector, 10th Cavalry
J. H. L. Reeder, 11th Infantry
John Andrew Reeves
Dan Rice
William Turner Richardson
David Gay Robertson
Abson Seal
Archie Benton Sensing
Rufus Sizemore
James Montgomery Smith
Martin V. B. Smith
Robert A. Southerland, 49th Infantry
Wesley Speight, 15th Infantry
James Staley, 49th Infantry
Hiram A. Spencer, Baxter's Company,
  Light Artillery
A. H. Stacey, 8th Smith's Cavalry
H. W. Street, 11th Holman's Cavalry
John Minor Stuart, 11th Infantry
James Steele
Robert D. Steele
David G. Street
Thomas Jefferson Streetman
M. C. Summers
J. W. Redden, 11th Infantry
  (Full name, John Wiley Redden)
George W. Reynolds, 10th Cavalry
S. H. Reynolds, 10th Cavalry
John Riethmeir, 5th Infantry
William Roberts, 20th Infantry
John J. Sanders, 49th Infantry
Richard Sears, 8th Louisiana Inf.
Richard H. Seay, 23rd Va. Infantry
George W. Sensing, 49th Infantry

Confederate pensioners, continued:

I. N. Shannon, 9th Infantry
W. W. Smith, 18th Infantry
P. A. Span, 14th Infantry
J. M. Talley, 49th Infantry
William Henry Taylor
J. A. Thomas, 24th Battalion, Tennessee Sharpshooters
J. B. Thompson, Baxter's Company, Light Artillery
F. F. Tidwell, 11th Infantry
S. M. Tidwell, Baxter's Company, Light Artillery
Thomas S. Totty, 11th Infantry
Sylvanus Tratter, 14th Infantry
J. R. Venable, 6th Kentucky Infantry
C. T. Weems, 11th Infantry
John Welch, 11th Infantry
Wesley Welch, Baxter's Battery, Artillery
Daniel White, Baxter's Battery, Light Artillery
E. W. White, 26th Infantry
J. P. White, Baxter's Battery, Light Artillery
W. M. White, 11th Infantry
F. G. Williams, 11th Infantry
H. K. Williams, 49th Infantry
Thomas Williams, Harding's Light Artillery
G. W. Wimberly, 23rd Infantry
R. J. Work, 11th Infantry
L. D. Wright, 11th (Holman's) Cavalry
W. M. Wright, 10th Demoss Cavalry
J. F. Wyatt, 24th Tennessee Sharpshooters

(Note: This listing was compiled from the publication "Index to Tennessee Confederate Pension Applications" published by the Tennessee State Library and Archives, Nashville, Tennessee. Some of these men did not draw pensions but their widows did--however, in our listing we included the man's name and not the widow.)

***

Confederate Muster Roll:

The following was found in the Dickson County Herald, 6 November 1931:

"...Among the old papers found in the belongings of the late O. R. Leech, when disposal of the store's remnants were being made, which store Mr. Leech operated many years, was found a list of soldiers who were members of the Confederate company organized here in 1862. It is presumed that this company was reorganized at the time Captains Mallory and Tedford were disabled on account of sickness and affliction not occasioned by war. The list contains a few who deserted, etc., but their names will not be designated for publication. The list was evidently prepared by Captain Mallory, since he run a general store in the building in partnership with Dr. O. R. Leech, in which the soldier list was discovered." The quote herewith:

R. A. W. James, captain
W. D. Eleazer, second lieutenant
A. Y. Brown, first lieutenant
Thomas Lane, third lieutenant

Non-commissioned officers:
F. L. Fain, 1st orderly sergeant
W. G. Anderson, third orderly sergeant
Thomas Jackson, second orderly sergeant
Dick Gilbert, 4th orderly sergeant
Dick Taylor, 1st corporal, killed at Rockfall Ridge
John Heath, 2nd corporal, killed at Missionary Ridge
John Booker, 3rd corporal, leg shot off at Jonesboro
Pitts Hunter, killed on Kennesaw line

Private:
Thomas Atkinson, transferred to Company A
Pat Bail, transferred to Company B
J. A. Booker
Peter Burkhart, transferred to Company G
Robert Baker, killed at Eight Square House, 15 May 1864
W. H. Binkley
J. T. Binkley
Peter Burkhart, recruit at Shelbyville 1863
James Baxter, recruited, ditto
Cirus Chicester, relieved under conscript act
Wm. C. Crunk, wounded at Murfreesboro
Pat Conners, relieved under the conscript act
Martin Daugherty, transferred to Company G
Thomas Dooly, transferred to Co. G

Confederate Muster Roll, continued:

Rafe Eubank, killed at Franklin
Robert Eubank, recruited at Shelbyville, killed at Jonesboro, Georgia
Jesse Ford
Roger Flairty, transferred to Company G
Moses Garton
James Greer, transferred to Company H
J. Grimes
P. Grimes
Jesse Garland
W. G. Gafford
J. T. Gafford
Marcus Gorman, transferred to Company G
Pat Gorman, transferred to Company G
Frank Hannah
H. H. Henderson
F. M. Hudgens
Zack Hutton, relieved under the conscript act
Blurrel Heath
Eppes Jackson, died at Normandy January 1863
G. T. Jackson
J. V. Jackson, recruit at ShelbyVille or Readyville
M. Jordan
Thomas Joist, transferred to Company G
Martin King, ditto
Pat Kenedy, ditto
F. T. Kephart
W. R. H. Lindsey
Alfred Long
Joe Lawrence
Hol Lawrence
Dock Lawrence, recruit at Shelbyville 1863
James Larkins, killed at Newhope Church
J. H. Larkins, recruited from Company G
Drew Mathis, went to the 49th and got scalded to death in a collision
John Mathis
Thomas Mathis
William Marsh, relieved under the conscript act
David Musgrove
James McNeilly, transferred to Company G
A. M. McMahan
R. H. Napier
Rufus Nail, went to cavalry and got killed
N. Nall, went to cavalry and got killed at Shiloh
Joe Nesbitt, relieved under the conscript act
W. J. Osborn, transferred to Co. A
John Osburn, ditto
John O'Connell
J. M. Owen, recruit from Company G
Jesse Owen, ditto
J. T. Parker
Turner Richardson, got arm shot off at Jonesboro and died
S. M. Tolar
J. C. Parnell
A. J. Richardson, recruit at Shelbyville
Robert Scott
J. M. Stuart
H. E. Shacklett, transferred to Company K
F. G. Williams
Steven Williams, killed at Kennesaw
W. M. White
Jason Yates, relieved uner the conscript act

(Note: This company was Company E, 11th Tennessee Infantry.)

***

Confederate Soldiers of Dickson County:

The following is part of an unpublished manuscript on the Confederate soldiers of Dickson County. The listing is incomplete but appears as it was given to the compiler. Some of the information will be a repeat of other Confederate information given previously but is being presented in its complete form.

WILLIAM M. ADAMS - Company G, 12th Tennessee Regiment
Born 8 August 1843 in Roane County, Tennessee
Died 19 August 1921, buried Sil Adams Cemetery
Son of Nelson and Martha Mathis Adams
Married 15 January 1866 to Tennessee Dickson Daniel, born 15 Sept. 1847, died 31 December 1917.
Children:
1. Jesse R., born 1867, died 1895
2. Betty G., born 1871, died 1889
3. William W.
4. Joseph A.
5. Enola Ann
6. Emma A.
7. Mattie L.
8. Cora Hattie
9. Charley C., born 1883, d. 1917
10. Lewis Wade
11. James B., 1887-1887

W. T. ADAMS - service not determined
Dickson County Herald, 7 Jan. 1938, 21 Jan. 1938: Mrs. Laura Gray, 81, died Friday of last week; daughter of Jonas and Sara Gray; wife of W.T. Adams, Confederate soldier, who died nine years ago; buried Gray Cemetery at Glenwylde. She was born 5 June 1856, died 31 Dec. 1937.

THOMAS BENTON ADCOCK - Company K, 11 Infantry
Born 1841, died 1917, served under Frank Cheatham. He and his wife Sarah are buried in the Alf Richardson Cemetery, Dickson County.

*_____ALISON - Company E, 11th Tennessee
Killed in Battle of Missionary Ridge.

A. J. ALLEN - 1st Sgt., Company C, 11th Tennessee Infantry

JOSEPH ALSPAUGH - 2nd Sgt., Company K, 11th Tennessee Infantry

W. G. ANDERSON - 3rd Ord. Sgt., Company E, 11th Tennessee Infantry

J. W. ANGLIN - 4th Sgt., Company K, 11th Tennessee Infantry

THOMAS ATKINSON - Company E, 11th Tennessee Infantry
Transferred to Company A.

PAT BAIL (BAILY?) - Company E, 11th Tennessee Infantry
Transferred to Company B.

*ROBERT BAKER - Company E, 11th Tennessee Infantry
Killed at Eight Square House 15 May 1864. (Lindsley's Military Annals says killed in battle near Calhoun, Georgia.)

*STEPHEN BAKER - Company C, 11th Tennessee Infantry
Died at Rome, Georgia, 30 April 1863.

*W. L. BAKER - Company E, 11th Tennessee Infantry
Killed in battle.

*W. T. BALTHORPE - Company C, 11th Tennessee Infantry
Died 29 July 1861.

RILEY BEASLEY - Service not determined.
Confederate soldier captured several times during the war; lived at Tennessee City.

J. T. BINKLEY - Company E, 11th Tennessee Infantry

W. H. BINKLEY - Company E, 11th Tennessee Infantry

PRESS BISHOP - Gunsmith
Dickson County Herald, 8 Oct. 1937: He made guns for soldiers. He married Polly Weakley and they were the parents of four sons and two daughters.

JOHN BOOKER - 2nd corporal, Company E, 11th Tennessee Infantry
His leg was shot off at Jonesboro.

J. A. BOOKER - Company E, 11th Tennessee Infantry

ISAAC M. BOWERS - Captain, Major, Company K, 1st Kentucky Cavalry
Born 27 May 1835 Wilson County, Tennessee.
Died 24 May 1899, buried Charlotte Cemetery.
Married 1 Nov. 1865 Mrs. Mary C. Cayce, daughter of Thomas McNeilly of Charlotte; she was born 1838.
Children:
1. Maude married E. H. Stone of Cumberland Furnace
2. Julia married G. G. Cannon of Cumberland Furnace
3. Horace J.
4. Paul R., born 23 June 1879 at Charlotte, died 1933. He married Maggie Harris, daughter of Thomas W. Harris of Cumberland Furnace.
   (Continued on next page)

5. Mary married G. C. Dismukes
6. Minnie, born 1868, died 1870
Bowers was twice captured during the Civil War, once at the home of Mrs. Batson in Dickson County and was imprisoned at Clarksville. His son Paul in 1913 was the manager of the Warner Iron Company at Cumberland Furnace.

Dickson County Herald, 17 March 1939: "I. M. Bowers, a gallant scout of Forrest's command in the conflict between the North and the South, and who served as valiantly in peace and was for many years Clerk and Master of the Chancery Court, is interred beneath a beautiful pointed memorial."

*JOHN BRAZZEL - Company K, 11th Tennessee Infantry
Died 1861 at Camp Cheatham.

*AARON BROWN - Company K, 11th Tennessee Infantry
Died at Camp Cheatham 27 July 1861.

A. J. BROWN - 1st Lieutenant, Company E, 11th Tennessee Infantry
He was wounded and captured at Missionary Ridge and held to the end of the war. On some rolls his name appears to be A. Y. Brown.

BENJAMIN FRANKLIN BROWN - Baxter's Tennessee Artillery
Born 8 December 1841.
Died 21 March 1937, buried in family cemetery on Turnbull Creek.
Dickson County Herald, 26 March 1937: LAST SURVIVING CONFEDERATE VETERAN OF DICKSON COUNTY.--Lived 4 miles south of Burns, born in same place in which he died; married 22 Sept. 1861 to Louisiana Garton; enlisted in Baxter's Tennessee Artillery Regiment. A son was born in his absence; finally came home in 1865. His wife died 7 Dec. 1884. He married (2) Susan D. Campbell. He was also the last surviving member of Baxter's Artillery.

JAMES M. BROWN - 3rd Sgt., Company E, 11th Tennessee

*J. H. BROWN - Company D, 49th Tennessee
Died 16 March 1862.

*WILEY BROWN - Company K, 11th Tennessee Infantry
Died in prison.

J. R. BRYAN - Service not determined.
Born 12 August 1844 in Robertson County, Tennessee
Died 30 March 1902, buried Dickson Union Cemetery
Son of W. P. P. C. and Malinda Lenox Bryan
Married 5 April 1867 Anna M. Truby, born 1853, died 2 June 1900.
Children:
1. Maggie E.
2. Mattie M.
3. Robert T., born 1872 died 1900
4. Child, deceased in 1886
5. Child, deceased in 1886
No information on any other children.

*J. W. BRYANT - Company K, 11th Tennessee Infantry
Died 26 March 1863.

*S. M. BYRN - 1st Lieutenant, Company A, 24th Tennessee Sharpshooters
Born 16 Feb. 1820
Died 13 Feb. 1862. There is a tombstone for him in the West Simpson Cemetery on Blue Creek in Humphreys County. He was killed at Fort Donelson. According to one account, Lt. Byrn recruited and formed Maney's Battery but because of his lack of military experience and training the command was given to Frank Maney.

ABSALOM T. BUSSELLE - Confederate Soldier, service not determined.
Born 16 April 1838 Hawkins County, Tennessee
Died 8 (or 18) March 1910, buried Dickson Union Cemetery
(Continued on next page)

He was married 16 Oct. 1866. His wife Ella was born 1845, died 1922.

*GEORGE W. CARR - Baxter's Battery
Died 5 June 1863 of typhoid at Bean's Station. According to the Dickson County Herald, 2 July 1937, he was the son of John Bluford Carr and Susan Hamner whose "eldest son was killed in the war."

THOMAS J. CARR - Baxter's Company Tennessee Light Artillery
Born 23 August 1842
Died 20 December 1914, buried Dickson Union Cemetery
He was son of John Bluford Carr and his wife Susan Hamner. He enlisted 1 Dec. 1862. He married Tennessee Porter, born 1850, died 1936, also buried Dickson Union.

J. J. CARROLL - Service not determined.
He died 1923 in Dickson but was buried in the Willow Springs Primitive Baptist Church in Hickman County. He was 83 at his death and had come to Dickson from Hickman County.

*ARCHIE CATHEY - Company K, 11th Tennessee Infantry
Died in hospital.

*W. J. CATHEY - Company K, 11th Tennessee Infantry
Died 3 April 1863 at Chattanooga.

NEWTON CATHEY - Service not determined.
Born 18 August 1839
Died 11 July 1927, buried Stuart Cemetery
His obituary identified him as a Confederate soldier.

A. J. CHESTER - Company C, 11th Tennessee Infantry
On the rolls his name is often found as J. A. Chester.

*C. B. CHESTER - Company C, 11th Tennessee Infantry
Killed at Battle of Murfreesboro 31 December 1862. (Note: This man is believed to be the Claiborne Chester found on the 1850 Census of Dickson County.)

*J. A. CHESTER - Company C, 11th Tennessee Infantry
Killed accidentally at Atlanta August 1864.

CYRUS CHICHESTER - Company E, 11th Tennessee Infantry
Served as private and was relieved under conscript act. In 1850 he will be found as age 38, born in Pennsylvania, and was the jailor of Dickson County at the time. His wife Jane, age 25, was born in Virginia.

S. E. CHOATE - 4th Corporal, Company E, 11th Tennessee Infantry

JAMES MARION CHOATE - Confederate pensioner
Born 28 May 1842
Died 5 September 1910, buried Mt. Lebanon Methodist Church Cemetery.
Married 18 Dec. 1870 to Mary Duke, born 7 July 1850, died 22 Jan. 1916.

C. H. CLARK -16th Tennessee, CSA
Born 26 Feb. 1842
Died 27 April 1931 at Knoxville when hit by a street car and broke his hip. Although there is a stone for this man in Dickson Union Cemetery, he was buried at Spencer in Van Buren County, Tenn.

B. A. CLIFTON - Service not determined.
Born 18 January 1842
Died 5 July 1919, buried Dickson Union Cemetery
He married 25 August 1867 to Addie Bullock, also buried Dickson Union. His obituary noted he was a Confederate veteran.

*J. W. CLIFTON - Company K, 11th Tennessee Infantry
Died 9 August 1861 while in service.

*C. J. CLYMER - Company B, 49th Tennessee
Died as prisoner of war.

GEORGE H. CLINE - South Carolina troops
Born 9 Oct. 1844 in Concord, N. H.
Died 14 March 1931 in Dickson County, buried Dugan Cemetery
Married 20 April 1864 to Catherine Stewart; married (2) Mrs. Almira
White. He enlisted in Confederate Army in South Carolina in April 1863
and was wounded 20 April 1864 in battle of Plymouth, N. C. He married
his second wife in 1916. His wife Almira, born 27 Oct. 1849 in Allen
County, Indiana, died 15 Oct. 1932 and was taken to Greenwood Cemetery
in Zion, Illinois, for burial. (References: Dickson County Herald,
20 March 1931, 4 Nov. 1932, and Hickman County News, 20 March 1931.)

*STERLING CAPPS - Company K, 11th Tennessee
He was killed near New Hope, Georgia, 27 May 1864. Another source gives
death date as 22 July 1864.

*WILLIAM G. W. BUTTREY - Baxter's Battery
Died 5 Feb. 1864 of chronic disease at Covington, Georgia.

*W. H. BURTON - Company D, 49th Tennessee
Died 26 Feb. 1862.

CHRISTOPHER C. COLLIER - Company C, 49th Tennessee
He was son of John C. Collier and Mary Clements Collier.

*HAZARD COLLINS - Company C, 11th Tennessee Infantry
Killed in Battle of Chickamauga 19 Sept. 1863.

PAT CONNERS - Company E, 11th Tennessee Infantry
Relieved under the conscript act.

JEROME B. CORDING - Cpatain, Company D, 49th Tennessee Infantry
He was a Confederate pensioner. According to the Dickson Herald,
2 Feb. 1940, he was married to Sarah Bowen. However, according to
the Dickson Herald, 17 March 1939; Capt. J. B. Cording, a gallant
captain in the Confederate army in the Civil War...married Rosannah J.
Bowen, daughter of Reece Bowen and his wife Sarah Strong Browen...

CONFEDERATE VETERANS - As taken from Dickson Herald, 10 June 1932:
The following Confederate veterans are buried in Dickson Union Cemetery
and new markers have been placed at their graves:

W. M. Hogin	W. W. Smith
J. K. Davis	Dr. L. D. Wright
J. M. Talley	A. B. Williams
W. H. McCauley	Eugene Kelsey
F. F. Tidwell	Andrew Easley
John F. Alexnader	John Easley
F. A. Andrews	Bob Easley
John C. Buford	W. H. Lowery
B. A. Clifton	R. T. Work
Thomas Davidson	J. R. McNeil
J. E. Fussell	B. F. McCaslin
S. P. Larkins	J. T. Carr
J. T. Murrell	Green Davidson
W. H. Patterson	Rev. E. W. White
James Nall	I. N. Shannon
T. M. Childress	A. L. Dozier
Pete Miller	D. T. Pinkerton
James Lunn	John Brown
J. A. Thomas	

JOHN MAXWELL COWAN - Served in Confederate Army for 4 years.
He died 19 Dec. 1890.
He was wounded while in service and carried the ball in his jaw for
several months. He married Florence E. Turner, born 14 May 1853 in
Cool Spring, N. C., died 1938. They were the parents of 9 children.

*S. A. COX - Company K, 11th Tennessee Infantry
Died at Bean's Station in East Tennessee.

*W. J. COX - Company K, 11th Tennessee Infantry   (Continued)

Died 25 June 1861.

*_____CRAWFORD
Two brothers named Crawford were killed in service, one was killed at Perryville. No further information.

*M. B. CROW - Company K, 11th Tennessee Infantry
Died 3 April 1863 at Chattanooga.

WILLIAM C. CRUNK - Company E, 11th Tennessee Infantry
He was wounded at Murfreesboro.

*A. J. CUNNINGHAM - Company B, 49th Tennessee
He died as prisoner of war. He was born about 1835 and on the 1850 Census of Dickson County appears to be the son of Nathaniel and Malissa Cunningham.

*E. L. CUNNINGHAM - Company B, 49th Tennessee
Died 8 January 1863.

*J. J. DANIEL - Company D, 49th Tennessee
Died in service.

JOE DANIEL - Service not determined.

*CALVIN DAVIDSON - Company K, 11th Tennessee
Died 17 April 1862 at Cumberland Gap.

*J. W. DAVIDSON - Company K, 11th Tennessee
Killed in Battle of Missionary Ridge.

GREEN DAVIDSON - Service not determined.

J. K. DAVIS - Confederate soldier buried Dickson Union Cemetery
Born 26 May 1848
Died 13 Feb. 1899, buried Dickson Union.
He was one of the prime movers of the Bill Green UCV Camp at Dickson and served under General N. B. Forrest. He lived on West Walnut St., now owned by B. Foster.

THOMAS DAVIDSON - Service not determined.
Confederate soldier buried Dickson Union with "U.C.V. 1861-1865" at his grave.

NELSON DAVIS - Service not determined.
He lived at Cumberland Furnace and married Rebecca Harvey. They were the parents of 9 children.

*BEN W. DAWSON - Service not determined.
Born 5 July 1842
Died 30 November 1864, killed in Battle of Franklin, Tenn., buried in Leech Cemetery near Charlotte. His tombstone has the following: There is a tear for all who die, A mourner o'er the humblest grave, and nations swell the funeral cry and tryumphs weep above the grave. (His death in service is recorded on the tombstone.)

EDWIN HAYES DICKERSON - Service not determined.
Born 21 Feb. 1844
Died 12 July 1926, buried Williams Cemetery at White Bluff.
His wife Winnie Tate, born 1854, died 1934. Her obituary in Dickson Herald, 11 Jan. 1935, identified him as a Confederate soldier and said they were the parents of two children.

W. H. DICKSON - Service not determined.
Born 9 April 1836
Died 12 Dec. 1918 of influenza, buried Dickson Union Cemetery. His obituary identified him as a Confederate soldier. (Note: a note on his card from my family indicated "We knew this man and his family.")

J. A. DODSON - Company D, 49th Tennessee
Born 11 August 1837 in Halifax County, Virginia.
Son of William and Catherine Davis Dodson. He married Mary A. E.
Laird, who died 3 May 1879; married (2) Eliza C. Hopkins on 27 March
1884.

THOMAS DOTSON - 2nd Sgt., Company E, 11th Tennessee

THOMAS DOOLY - Company E, 11th Tennessee Infantry
Transferred to Company G.

MORDY JOHNSON DUKE - Confederate soldier
Born 28 Dec. 1840 Cannon County, Tenn.
Died 1937, buried Rock Church Cemetery.
His obituary in Dickson Herald, 26 Nov. 1937, says he came to Dickson
County after the Civil War; eldest son of Gideon and Betsy Ann Duke;
he fought for several months in Confederate Army and was at the Battle
of Murfreesboro; married Dovie Ewell, died 1883, and they had 5 children. He married (2) Pauline Hooper and had 4 children. His second
wife's obituary was published in Dickson Herald, 3 Feb. 1933, and
tells she was Mrs. Paulina Edwards Duke, born 1850, died 1933, buried
Rock Church Cemetery and she was married 1. Joe Groves, 2. Jep Hooper
and 3. M. J. Duke. She was survived by 5 children.

An earlier article in Dickson Herald, 22 July 1932: Uncle Maudie Duke
is now 91 years old; served in Baxter's Battalion for 23 months during
Civil War; was in Battle of Missionary Ridge; came home following the
Battle of Franklin.

ROBERT U. DUNLAP - Captain, Company D, 49th Tennessee Infantry

BOB EASLEY - Service not determined.
Buried in Dickson Union Cemetery and stone marked "U.C.V., 1861-1865."

STEPHEN GIBSON ELEAZER - Company B, 49th Infantry
Born 25 Sept. 1833 in Dickson County
Died 6 June 1908 and buried in family burying ground near Burns.
He married 5 May 1858 to Susan (or Susanna) O. Woodard, who died 1882.
He was the son of Stephen G. and Elizabeth Bibb Eleazer. He was taken
prisoner of war at Fort Donelson.
Children:
1. Benjamin F.   5. John D.
2. Sallie C.   6. William M.
3. Stephen G.   7. Elizabeth
4. George   8. Susie Ann

WILLIAM D. ELEAZER - 2nd Lieutenant, Company E, 11th Tennessee Infantry

GEORGE P. Y. EPPS - Company C, 11th Tennessee Infantry
He is buried at the Southerland Cemetery but no dates on stone.(D.1909)

*SOLOMON ESTES - Company K, 11th Tennessee Infantry
Killed in Battle of Missionary Ridge.

*WILLIAM ETHERIDGE - Company K, 11th Tennessee Infantry
Killed in Battle at Jonesboro, Georgia.

*RAFE EUBANK - Company E, 11th Tennessee Infantry
Killed at Battle of Franklin November 1864. (Lindsley's Annals gives
his name as R. G. Eubank.)

*ROBERT EUBANK - Company E., 11th Tennessee Infantry
Recruited at Shelbyville, killed at Jonesboro, Georgia.

R. D. EUBANK - Company D, 49th Tennessee Infantry
Born 14 March 1839 Dickson County
Son of John and Eliza Crumpler Eubank. He married 1860 to Lucinda
Corlew, who died 17 Sept. 1882.   Dickson County Herald, 5 July 1935
has obituary for Mrs. Josephine Donegan, 75, who died "in past week,
would have been 75 years old on August 10; widow of R. D. Eubank, Sr.,;

daughter of William and Emaline Donegan, reared on Jones Creek in Rock Church area. She was buried in the Corlew Cemetery by her husband.

He was the father of the following children Leona, Catherine, Ada B., and Richard D. Corlew. No information available on any other children.

F. L. FAIN - 1st Ord. Sgt., Company E, 11th Tennessee Infantry

*EDWARD FITZGERALD - Company C, 11th Tennessee Infantry
Died 23 June 1861.

ROGER FLAIRTY - Company E, 11th Tennessee Infantry
Transferred to Company G.

*JONATHAN FOSTER - Volunteer in a Hickman County company.
The following was found in the newspaper Clarksville Weekly Chronicle, 20 Dec. 1861: "Jonathan Foster, age 61, died in Clarksville last week; lives in Dickson County; volunteered last July in a company made up in Hickman County."

*HENRY GALLOWAY - Company K, 11th Tennessee Infantry
Died at Woodson's Cross Roads.

*J. W. GALLOWAY - Company K, 11th Tennessee Infantry
Killed by his own men while in front of line near Cumberland Gap.

JESSE GARLAND - Company E, 11th Tennessee Infantry

*D. P. GARTIER - Company D, 49th Tennessee Infantry
Died in service.

*D. C. GENTRY - Company K, 11th Tennessee Infantry
Killed New Hope, Georgia, 27 May 1864.

DICK GILBERT - 4th Ord. Sgt., Company E, 11th Tennessee Infantry

*HARRY GORDON - Company H, 11th Tennessee Infantry
Killed at New Hope, Georgia, 22 July 1864.

*JOHN GOODWIN - Company K, 11th Tennessee Infantry
Died in service.

MARCUS GORMAN - Company E, 11th Tennessee Infantry
Transferred to Company G.

PAT CORMAN - Company E, 11th Tennessee Infantry
Transferred to Company G.

*M. GRANTUM - Company D, 49th Tennessee Infantry
Died in service.

*WILLIAM R. GREEN - Captain, Company C, 11th Tennessee Infantry.
He was later promoted to major. Died as prisoner of war in 1864. The Bill Green Bivouac in Dickson County was named in his honor. The following note was found in the Nashville Banner, 6 May 1897: "The Confederate Veterans of Dickson have organized Bill Green camp with about 40 members."

JAMES GREER - Company E, 11th Tennessee Infantry

*J. C. GREGG - Company K, 11th Tennessee Infantry
Killed in battle.

J. T. GAFFORD - Company E, 11th Tennessee Infantry

W. G. GAFFORD - Company E, 11th Tennessee Infantry

THOMAS K. GRIGSBY - Company B, 49th Tennessee Infantry
Born 31 July 1822 in Madison County, Ala. (One source says born 1823.)
(Continued on next page)

Died 26 Dec. 1896, buried Charlotte Cemetery.
Son of Samuel and Dorcas Wyly Grigsby. Married 1846 to Sarah A. Priestley, born 1819, died 1871; married 1874 to Jane Hendreck, born 1841, died 1927, buried Leech Cemetery.
Children:
1. James P., born 4 July 1850, died 1 Oct. 1878 of yellow fever at Erin, Tenn.
2. Samuel W., born 26 Jan. 1852, married F. C. Hassell
3. William L., born 25 March 1854, died 24 May 1900, married Rosa McNeilly. He built the large house on Church Street, Dickson which was recently torn down.
4. Theodosia, died 25 May 1890, married D. S. Major
5. Kelly, born 1879, died 1883
6. Mabel, born 1882, died 1884
7. Thomas K., born 1874, died 1914
8. John W., died 1940 at 65, buried Elmwood Cemetery, Memphis
9. Harris, born 1884, died 1940

No information on any additional children.

JOHN P. GRIMES - Company E, 11th Tennessee Infantry

PRESTUS J. GRIMES - Company E, 11th Tennessee Infantry
His name will also be found as Preston J. Grimes; he was wounded at Chickamauga.

MARTIN GARTON - Confederate pensioner
Born 14 Jan. 1846, died 8 November 1907, Spencer Mill area, buried in Martin Garton Cemetery. His wife Lona, born 1859, died 1929, drew a pension on his service.

MOSES GARTON - 11th Infantry
Born 24 July 1842, died 19 April 1922, buried Martin Garton Cemetery.

JESSE FORD - Company E, 11th Tennessee Infantry
Official records show his name as Jesse M. Ford; born about 1834, the son of John and Sarah Ford.

*W. D. FORD - Company B, 49th Tennessee Infantry
Died as prisoner of war.

*M. H. FRASIER - Company K, 49th Tennessee Infantry. Official records give his name as M. H. Frashier, Company D, 49th Tennessee Infantry. He is believed to be Morgan H. Frazier, born about 1840, possibly the son of David and Elizabeth Frazier. Died in service.

*N. C. FRASIER - Company K, 49th Tennessee Infantry
He is believed to be Nicholas Frazier, possibly brother of Morgan Frazier. Died in service.

*J. R. FREEMAN - Company C, 11th Tennessee Infantry
Killed in Battle of New Hope Church, 27 May 1864.

*J. W. HAM - Company B, 49th Tennessee Infantry
Died as prisoner of war.

I. N. HANDLIN - Company C, 11th Tennessee Infantry

T. J. HANDLIN - Company C, 11th Tennessee Infantry

FRANK HANNAH - Company E, 11th Tennessee Infantry

*J. T. HARRIS - Company B, 49th Tennessee Infantry
Died as prisoner of war.

*WILLIAM HARRIS - Company K, 11th Tennessee Infantry
Died 17 Sept. 1861 at Nashville while in service.

*M. G. HARROD - Company B, 49th Tennessee Infantry
Died April 1863.

C. L. HAYES - Company F, 11th Infantry
Born 8 April 1837, died 28 March 1928, buried Thomason Cemetery (also Hayes Cemetery) near Vanleer.

BURREL HEATH - Company E, 11th Tennessee Infantry
The official records give his name as Burril J. Heath--sometimes on muster rolls he will be also found as B'lurrel Heath. He was born about 1839 and was the son of Abel and Delila Heath.

*JOHN HEATH - 2nd Corporal, Company E, 11th Tennessee Infantry
Killed at Missionary Ridge.

H. H. HENDERSON - Company E, 11th Tennessee Infantry

STANFORD HENDRIX - 3rd Lieutenant, Company C, 11th Tennessee Infantry

DR. J. T. HENSLEE - 7th Kentucky Volunteers
Born 5 May 1838, Kentucky; died 27 July 1895, buried Dickson Union. He was son of Joab Henslee and Nancy Justice; married 1870 to M. F. Lipe of Carroll County, Tenn., who died 1873; married (2) 1879 Dora M. Pickles, born 1858, died 1931.
Children:
1. Pitt, born 1871, died 1923.
2. Infant son born and died 1880
3. Floy
4. Iva Henslee Wynns
5. Vallie
No information on other children.

WILLIAM MILLINGTON HOGIN(S) - Company B, 49th Tennessee Infantry
Born 18 Dec. 1843, died 20 Sept. 1922, buried Dickson Union Cemetery. (His birthdate is given as 8 December 1841 in Hale and Merritt's history of Tennessee, book IV, page 1050.) He was the son of Abram and Sarah Easley Hogins. He was taken ill with typhoid at Fort Donelson and re-enlisted in the 11th Infantry but later returned to the 49th. He was shot in the right shoulder at Atlanta and was captured at Franklin. He married Susan Tidwell, daughter of Moses Tidwell, born 1848, died 1916, buried at Dickson Union.
Children:
1. A. F., born 1867, died 1919
2. Nannie L., married W. R. Leggit
3. Ella, married Dr. J. T. Sugg
4. W. W., born 1880, died 1950
5. Minnie, married T. C. Jordan
6. E. E.
7. Susan married J. M. Hooper
8. W. Ray
In 1904 he established a mercantile business in Dickson.

J. O. HOOPER - Fifer in Confederate Army
Born 10 Aug. 1845, died 1 Feb. 1911, buried in Charlotte Cemetery. His wife Mary G., born 1 Jan. 1842, died 26 Oct. 1862 is also buried there. Another wife Fannie L., born 1865, died 6 April 1935 is also buried in Charlotte Cemetery. When he died, his obituary noted he was survived by 5 sons.

*WILLIAM R. HOOPER - Baxter's Battery
Died 29 May 1863 at Bean's Station of typhoid fever.

*JOHN W. HOUSE - Company K, 11th Tennessee Infantry
Died in prison.

*W. B. HOWARD - Company D, 49th Tennessee Infantry
Died in service.

F. M. HUDGENS - Company E, 11th Tennessee Infantry

JAMES H. HUDGENS - Veteran of Mexican and Civil Wars
Born 2 April 1809, died 25 November 1888, buried Rock Church Cemetery. His wife Mary Jane, born 1826, died 1907, was a pensioner.

JAMES C. HUNT - Company C, 10th Tennessee Cavalry
Born 28 July 1839 at Clarksville, son of Solomon and Ann R. Hilliard Hunt, died 25 May 1922, buried Edgewood Cemetery. (Note: His birthdate on tombstone is 29 July 1839.) He married 17 Nov. 1859 to Serenia Parthenia Slayden, born 1839, died 1913.
Children:
1. William T., born 23 July 1860
2. Theodosia E., born 1861, died 1862
3. Robert B., born 1865, died 1870
4. Solomon E., born 5 Feb. 1867
5. Albert P., born 20 Aug. 1870, died 25 Jan. 1951
6. John Franklin, born 1872, died 1938
7. James Maurice, born 1875, died 1955. (Some accounts give his name as Morris. This listing of children made from tombstone records, obituaries, and his biography in Goodspeed's history.)
8. Noel Clarence
9. Hartwell Slayden, born 1877
No further information on his family available.

*PITTS HUNTER - Company E, 11th Tennessee Infantry
Killed on Kennesaw Line. (Lindsley's Annals says J. P. Hunter, killed at Kennesaw Mountain.)

ZACK HUTTON - Company E, 11th Tennessee Infantry
Relieved under the conscript act.

*EPPES JACKSON - Company E, 11th Tennessee Infantry
Died at Normandy January 1863.

G. T. JACKSON - Company E, 11th Tennessee Infantry

J. V. JACKSON - Company E, 11th Tennessee Infantry
Recruited for company at Readyville.

*RICHARD P. JACKSON - Baxter's Battery
Died 10 June 1863 at Bean's Station of typhoid fever.

THOMAS JACKSON - 2nd Ord. Sgt., Company E, 11th Tennessee Infantry

ROBERT A. W. JAMES - Captain, Company E, 11th Tennessee Infantry

JOHN J. JOHNSON - Company H, 11th Tennessee
He died 1912 at White Bluff, son of Granville M. Johnson, Sr. He had brother Jacob H. Johnson killed at Atlanta on 22 July 1864 and brother Granville killed at Chickamauga. He was born 27 Oct. 1826 and had also served in Mexican War. In 1846 enlisted in 1st Tennessee Regiment, Company A, Whitfield's Company of Hickory Guards and was at Vera Cruz.

THOMAS JOIST - Company E, 11th Tennessee Infantry
Transferred to Company G.

W. M. JONES - Company E, 11th Tennessee Infantry

*BERRY JORDAN - Company K, 11th Tennessee Infantry
Killed in Battle at Chickamauga.

M. JORDAN - Company E, 11th Tennessee Infantry

PAT KENEDY - Company E, 11th Tennessee Infantry
Transferred to Company G.

F. T. KEPHART - Company E, 11th Tennessee Infantry

JOE KIMBRO - Confederate soldier.
He lived to be 75 years old and married Serena King; they were the parents of 12 children, 9 boys, 3 girls. Information found in Dickson Herald, 3 Sept. 1937.

FENTRESS KING - Company E, 11th Tennessee Infantry
Transferred to Company G.

MARTIN KING - Company E, 11th Tennessee Infantry
Transferred to Company G.

W. M. KIRK - 2nd Lieutenant, Company E, 11th Tennessee Infantry.
The 1850 Census of Dickson County shows William M. Kirk, age 12, born in Tennessee, in household of Mary Kirk.

GEORGE WADE KNIGHT - Company B, 24th Tennessee Sharpshooters
Born 2 Feb. 1839 in Humphreys County, Tenn., died 17 Sept. 1893 in Houston County, Tenn., buried at Ben Brown Cemetery in Houston County. He married 12 Oct. 1856 in Humphreys County to Margaret Brown, born 1840. She died 1922 in Dickson, Tennessee and is buried in the Knight Cemetery in Houston County. He was the son of Wade Hampton Knight and Elizabeth Knight Knight. His brother J. Robert Knight, born 1840, died 1914, married Cynthia Thomas and Lou Hatcher and served in Company A, 24th Tennessee Sharpshooters. (J. Robert Knight lived for a time in Dickson County.)
Children of soldier:
1. Charles Nichols, born 1859, married Dora Nichols
2. Thomas Terry, born 1862, married Elizabeth Nichols
3. Laura Elizabeth, born 1866, died 1946, buried in Dickson Union Cemetery; married Frank Stephen Hopkins.
4. Robert Horace, born 1869, married Mollie Taylor
5. William Benjamin, born 1871, married Mollie McMillan
6. Johnnie, born 1876, died 1882

THOMAS LANE - 3rd Lieutenant, Company E, 11th Tennessee Infantry

*J. W. H. LANKFORD - Company K, 11th Tennessee
Died at Cumberland Gap 24 Feb. 1862.

*LAWRENCE LANKFORD - Company K, 11th Tennessee
Died in prison.

*ROBERT LANKFORD -
Died at Cumberland Gap.

*JAMES LARKINS - Company E, 11th Tennessee
Killed at Newhope Church. (Lindsley's Annals gives his name as J. M. Larkins.)

J. H. LARKINS - Company E, 11th Tennessee Infantry
Recruit from Company C.

JOSEPH HENRY LARKINS - 49th Tennessee Infantry
Born 12 April 1843, died 30 November 1905, buried in Leech Cemetery near Charlotte. He married Elizabeth Corlew, born 1842, died 1919, and they were the parents of 9 children. Hale & Merritt, V, page 1430 has: "At the outbreak of the Civil War, although but a lad, he enlisted in the 49th Regiment, Tenn., Infantry, in a company organized by Captain Green. He served in General Johnson's army, seeing much hard service, and at Bentonville, N. C., was severely wounded."

*J. B. LATHAM - Company C, 11th Tennessee Infantry
Died 3 December 1863.

DOCK LAWRENCE - Company E, 11th Tennessee Infantry
Recruit at Shelbyville, Tenn., 1863.

JOE LAWRENCE - Company E, 11th Tennessee Infantry

HOL LAWRENCE - Company E, 11th Tennessee Infantry

J. B. LAWRENCE - Service not determined.
Born 15 November 1833, died 28 March 1919, buried Jackson Chapel Cemetery. His stone reads "A brave soldier is buried here."

*J. M. LINDSAY - Company B, 49th Tennessee
Died 17 September 1863.

*ROBERT LINK - Company B, 49th Tennessee
Died 7 September 1862.

W. H. LINZY - Company E, 11th Tennessee Infantry
Born March 1841, died 7 June 1927, buried at Greenwood Methodist Church Cemetery. (On one roll his name is given as W. R. H. Lindsey. The name is spelled Linzy on his tombstone.)

ALFRED LONG - Company E, 11th Tennessee Infantry
He was born about 1840 and appears in the household of Miles and Josephine Long on 1850 Census of Dickson County.

*ROBERT B. LOVELL - Baxter's Battery
Died 13 April 1862 of tyhpoid in Knoxville hospital.

JOHN A. LUNN - 17th Regiment (We believed this should be James Lunn.)
Died 14 November 1926 at the age of 89 and was buried in Dickson Union Cemetery; born 1838 in Hickman County; married 1861 to Mollie White, who died 1875. He was wounded 5 times during the war and took part in 35 battles. He was buried by wife and son Terrell Lunn in Dickson Union according to the newspaper. This wife must have been his second wife as we found a stone for Callie Sparkman, born 15 Feb. 1858, died 15 Jan. 1919, and Terrell Lunn, born 1887, died 1943. We copied a stone for James Lunn, U.C.V., 1861=1865, which must be for him.

N. J. LUTHER - 2nd Corporal, Company K, 11th Tennessee Infantry
The 1850 Census of Dickson County shows Newton J. Luther, age 8, in the household of Travis and Lucy Luther.

WILLIAM J. MALLORY - Captain Company E, 11th Tennessee Infantry
Born 11 April 1828, died 8 Dec. 188_, buried in Charlotte Cemetery. The Dickson County Herald, 17 March 1939, identifies him as the son of Pleasant T. Mallory and that Captain Mallory "following the conflict was a store and saloon keeper in Charlotte for many years."

*E. B. MANGLIN - Company D, 49th Tennessee
Died in service.

*HUGH MANLY - Company K, 11th Tennessee Infantry
Died at Camp Cheatham 17 August 1861.

AQUILLA MARSH - 3rd Lieutenant, Company K, 11th Tennessee Infantry

THOMAS MARSH - Company E, 11th Tennessee Infantry

WILLIAM MARSH - Company E, 11th Tennessee Infantry
Relieved under the conscript act.

*W. G. MARSH - Company K, 11th Tennessee Infantry
Died at Camp Chase 24 July 1861.

JONES D. MARTIN - Company E, 10th Tennessee Cavalry
Born 13 July 1835 Dickson County, died about 1923, buried in Martin Cemetery, Eno Road, no marker. His father was sheriff of Dickson County before the Civil War. He married 8 April 1858 to Amanda England, died 18 May 1868; married (2) Dec. 1868 Matilda M. England, died 25 November 1910.
Children by first marriage:
1. Eunice A.
2. Edward F.
3. Hester L.
4. John E.

Children by second marriage:
1. Cora D.
2. William M.
3. Ludova J.
4. Samuel J. Tilden
5. Emily M.
(Some of the information on this man was furnished by Mrs. Alma Littleton of Dickson.)

*DREW MATHIS - Company E, 11th Tennessee
Went to 49th and was scalded to death in a collision.

*_____MATHIS
Name unknown. The Edwards Family Bible has a note about Mary Mathis: "Mary Mathis married first a Mathis, who died during the Civil War. They had one son."

JOHN MATHIS - Company E, 11th Tennessee Infantry

W. J. MATHIS - Company C, 11th Tennessee Infantry
Born 29 April 1837 at Charlotte, died 30 November 1924, buried in the Roberts Cemetery at Charlotte. He was the son of Wilson J. and Louisa Roberts Mathis; married 10 Sept. 1868 to Sarah E. Larkins. He also married Mrs. Nellie Bowen, widow of Billie Bowen. She died 25 Dec. 1937. She married William J. Mathis on 23 Dec. 1888.

LEWIS MATLOCK - Confederate soldier under Captain Gordon

WILLIAM MATTHEWS - Served in Home Guard
He married Mary Sensing.

MOSES MEEK - 2nd Lieutenant, Company K, 11th Tennessee Infantry
He is buried in Meek Cemetery south of Burns on the Riglea Farm.

CAPTAIN J. K. MILAM - Company F, 14th Arkansas
Born 1833 in Dickson County, died 10 July 1909 in Texas, married 1865 Blanche Green.

JOHN B. MONROE - Confederate soldier
Born 10 Feb. 1820 North Carolina, son of Johnson and Sallie Hanks Monroe. Married 1 March 1849 to Nancy Ann Luttrel. They were the parents of 11 children. He entered service under T. Grigsby, was captured at Fort Donelson and was in service a total of 18 months.

JAMES MARTIN MOODY - Company E, 10th Tennessee Cavalry
Born 8 June 1845 in Dickson County Tenn.
Died 4 January 1916, buried McEwen Cemetery. He was onetime county judge of Humphreys County. He was son of William and Charity E. Gardner Moody. He married 22 Dec. 1869 Maggie Blanks.

*JOHN MOORE - Baxter's Battery
Died 27 April 1863 at Tullahoma. Dickson County Herald, 19 Nov. 1937, says that John Moore, killed in war, also had brother J. B. Moore also who was killed. He married Lucy Redden and their children were:
1. W. Frank, born 20 Jan. 1856 Turkey Creek, married Molly Manley
2. John
3. James Moore of Lyles
4. Daughter married Charles Chappell
5. Daughter married Jimmy Kimbro

VIRGIL BURKE MOORE - 1st Lieutenant, Co. B, 50th Tennessee Infantry
Born 29 May 1839 near Cumberland City, Tenn.
Died 15 Oct. 1902 Houston County, Tenn. Married 7 July 1865 to Barbara Frances Rowland, born 23 Jan. 1845 Montgomery County, died 18 July 1931 at Nashville, Tennessee. He was son of William and Mary Moore.
Children:
1. Mary Elizabeth, born 10 October 1866, died 5 Feb. 1945, married John William Powers. She and her husband were buried in Dickson Union Cemetery.
2. Robert E., born about 1875
3. Virgil Burke, Jr., born about 1872
4. Son, deceased by 1908
5. William, born about 1869
6. Daughter, deceased by 1908
7. Ira, born about 1886

GEORGE H. MORTON - 1st Battalion Tennessee Cavalry, Colonel
Born 10 October 1836 in Haddington, Scotland
Son of Thomas D. and Marguerite Morton; came to United States at the age of 15. He was wounded six times while in service and rose from private to lieutenant-colonel. Married 1 May 1866 Dora Donelson. In 1886 they were the parents of 7 children.

*DAVID MUSGROVE - Company E, 11th Tennessee Infantry
Killed in Battle of Murfreesboro. He was born about 1836 and according to 1850 Census of Dickson County appears to be the son of Obadiah and Ann Musgrove.

BRADLEY MYATT - Confederate soldier.
According to Dickson Herald, 30 July 1937, he married Sarah Russell and was the father of 4 daughters and 5 sons. His son Jones Albert Myatt, born 1856, died 1940, married Palestine Holland and Callie Cox, and he operated Myatt Drug Store in Dickson for many years. Sarah Russell Myatt died 17 July 1917 at the age of 82 years.

J. F. MYATT - Company C, 24th Tennessee Sharpshooters
Born 12 Jan. 1843, died 8 August 1928. Buried Martin Garton Cemetery.

_____MYATT - Confederate soldier
Dickson Herald, 12 Nov. 1937, tells of a Myatt, oldest son of Kendrick Myatt and his first wife Cynthy Loftis, who served 4 years in the Confederate Army. Name of soldier was not given in the article.

ROBERT M. McALISTER - Blacksmith under General Forrest
He lived on Mill Creek in Hickman County; born 10 Jan. 1838 in Somerset, Kentucky, died July 1932, buried Dickson Union Cemetery by his second wife, Millie Rogers, died 1928.

*JOHN B. McCALL - Company B, 49th Tennessee
Died 6 June 1862.

WILLIAM H. McCAULEY - Captain, Company C, 11th Tennessee Infantry
Born 13 October 1837
Died 1 August 1922, buried Dickson Union Cemetery.

*J. R. McCLELLAND - Company C, 11th Tennessee Infantry
Killed in Battle near Atlanta on 20 July 1864.

*JAMES McCRARY - Baxter's Battery
Died 7 June 1863 at Bean's Station of typhoid fever.

A. M. McMahan - Company E, 11th Tennessee Infantry
Born about 1843 and on the 1850 Census of Dickson County appears to be the son of G. W. and Minerva McMahan.

ROBERT H. McCLELLAND - Captain, Company B, 49th Tennessee Regiment

FELIX W. McNEILLY - Forrest's Troops, 28th Mississippi
Born 19 March 1843 in Charlotte.
Died 28 January 1924 in Miami, Florida.
His obituary in the Confederate Veteran, May 1924, page 187: Served under General Forrest and also in 28th Mississippi Regiment as sergeant; had brothers Thomas Lucien and Rev. James H. McNeilly, who were also Confederate soldiers; Thomas Lucien was killed at Franklin in attack on the ginhouse. Married 15 Oct. 1873 to Ella E. Bagwell of Montgomery County, who died 14 Oct. 1909." He was buried in Ashland City and his children were Mrs. Sam Chesnut, G. W. McNeilly and Charles M. McNeilly.

*HUGH J. McNEILLY - Company C, 11th Tennessee Regiment
The following was taken from the 83rd Illinoisan, published at Clarksville, Tenn., 26 May 1865: Hugh J. McNeilly, son of James McNeilly of Dickson County, member of Company C, 11th Tennessee Regiment, was mortally wounded by Minie ball in Battle near Atlanta on 22 July 1864."

JAMES McNEILLY - Company E, 11th Tennessee Infantry
Transferred to Company G.

*LUCIEN McNEILLY -
Killed in Battle of Franklin in 1864, son of Robert and Margaret Larkins McNeilly.

REV. JAMES HUGH McNEILLY - Company D, 49th Tennessee Infantry
Born 9 June 1838 Dickson County, died 28 Sept. 1922 Nashville, Presbyterian minister. He was son of Robert and Margaret Larkins McNeilly; married Mary Russell Weatherford, died 1914. In 1866 he was the minister of the First Presbyterian Church, Nashville. He wrote many articles for the magazine, Confederate Veteran. He was married 10 Oct. 1865. When his wife died April 1914, her obituary noted she was "engaged at the age of twelve." They were the parents of five children.

*RUFUS NAIL - Company E, 11th Tennessee Infantry
Note in Dickson Herald 6 Nov. 1931: Went to cavalry and got killed. Lindsley's Military Annals says "killed at Shiloh".
His name is also found as Rufus Noll.

*N. NALL - Company E, 11th Tennessee Infantry
"Went to cavalry and got killed at Shiloh." Lindsley's Military Annals notes his name as Nicholas Noll.

ROBERT HENRY NAPIER - Company E, 11th Tennessee Infantry
He was born about 1840 and in 1850 Census of Dickson County will be found in household of William H. and Mary J. Napier.

RICHARD S. NAPIER - Company B, 49th Tennessee Infantry, Surgeon
Born 17 August 1832.
Died 9 October 1881, buried in McAdoo Cemetery, Humphreys County. He was married (1) Bettie McAdoo, born 15 Nov. 1846, died 26 June 1873. He was also married to a W. Z. Russell. And there is a tombstone for Nancy J. Napier, wife of Dr. R. S. Napier, born 21 Aug. 1850, died 10 Feb. 1881. He was brother of Thomas Alonzo Napier. He had children: Alonzo, Henry, Mary, John, and possibly others.

*THOMAS ALONZO NAPIER - Colonel, 10th Cavalry Battalion
Born 2 October 1837 in Dickson County, killed 31 Dec. 1862 at Parker's Cross Roads, buried Wyly Cemetery in Waverly, Tenn. He married 1859 to Victoria A. Wyly. She was born 12 July 1839, died 22 August 1881; married as her second husband R. W. Cooley. The Waverly Bivouac was named in honor of Colonel Napier.
Children:
1. Clarence, born 25 Sept. 1860, died 27 Aug. 1861, buried Wyly Cemetery.
2. Thomas Alonzo, Jr., born 15 Nov. 1861, died 9 November 1868, buried Wyly Cemetery. He was wounded when a Nashville & Northwestern train ran off track, three miles west of Waverly.

*J. W. R. NASH - Company D, 49th Infantry

*ANDREW F. NESBITT - 1st Lieutenant
Born 1 Jan. 1820, died 26 March 1863, killed at Brentwood, buried in Sil Adams Cemetery on Yellow Creek. Married Nancy Dilleha, born 1825, died 1 Jan. 1866.
Children:
1. William T., born 1845, married Cornelia Moore White.
2. Jerry M., born 1848, died 1928, married Minerva J. Dickson, born 1855, died 1934.
No information on any other children.

JOE NESBITT - Company E, 11th Tennessee Infantry
Relieved under the conscript act

WILLIAM J. A. NESBITT - Company E, 11 Tennessee Cavalry; Company C, 11th Tennessee Infantry; born 14 Feb. 1840, died 2 April 1921, buried Sil Adams Cemetery. He was the eldest of 11 children. He married 31 Aug. 1868 to Sally Sligh, born 1842, died 1898.
Children:
1. Zudie Ellis, born 1874, died 1938, married Andrew J. Smith.
2. Reuell E.
3. Martha Susan, died 22 April 1884.
No information on any other children.

WILLIAM THOMAS NESBITT - Company E, 10th Tennessee Cavalry
Born 25 Oct. 1845, died 31 March 1923; son of Andrew F. and Nancy Dilleha Nesbitt; married 26 Dec. 1876 Mrs. Cornelia Moore White, born 1851, died 1927.

JOE M. NEWBERRY - In Confederate Army for 4 years
He was from Stewart County and his wife's name was Lou Martha. They were the parents of 13 children, including James Newberry, born 18 Sept. 1854 at Cumberland City. (Reference: Dickson Herald, 4 Feb. 1938.)

JAMES K. NICHOLS - Company C, 1st Tennessee Regiment
Born 9 March 1844 Cumberland County, Kentucky; died 14 Jan. 1923.

WILLIAM A. NICKS - Volunteer from Maury County
Born 1 Sept. 1841, died 1899. His second marriage was to Margaret Ann Martin. He had a son Frank by his first marriage and 10 children by his second marriage.

WILLIAM J. NORRIS - 10th Tennessee Cavalry
Born 27 Jan. 1844 Dickson County; son of William W. and Elizabeth Balthrop Norris. He was once postmaster of Cave Mills. He married 15 Oct. 1865 to Dollie Ann Thompson, born 1847.
Children:
1. William J.
2. Lillie Ann
3. Donie Alice
4. Minnie
5. Daisy
6. Milton
7. Mary
8. Jennie
No information on any other children.

JOSEPH NEBLETT - Mallory's Company, 11th Tennessee
He was 45 years old when he enlisted 1861 at Charlotte and served for one year. He died 1898 at the Confederate Soldier's Home.

TOLBERT FANNING NICKS - Company E, 1st Tennessee Infantry
Born 10 Feb. 1843 Lewis County; died 16 Jan. 1925 near Dickson, Tenn., married 1866 Melvina Corlew, born 1841, died 1881.

CURTIS A. OAKLEY, SR. - Forrest Cavalry, 10th Tennessee, 12th Kentucky
Born 1842, died 1914, buried in Leech Cemetery near Charlotte.

J. W. OAKLEY - Sergeant, Company F, 10th Tennessee Cavalry
Buried Leech Cemetery near Charlotte, no dates on his stone.

JAMES COLEMAN OAKLEY - Company H, 36th Tennessee Infantry
Born 18 Jan. 1843 Dickson County, Tenn., died 8 Sept. 1914, married Nancy Westmoreland, born 1842, died 1902.

JOHN O'CONNELL - Company E, 11th Tennessee Infantry

*_____ O'CONNER - Company E, 11th Tennessee Infantry
Killed in Battle at Missionary Ridge.

W. J. OSBORN - Company E, 11th Tennessee Infantry
Transferred to Company A.

JOHN OSBORN - Company E, 11th Tennessee Infantry
Transferred to Company A.

JESSE OWEN - Company E, 11th Tennessee Infantry
Recruit from Company A.

J. M. OWEN - Company E, 11th Tennessee Infantry

A. E. PARDUE - 2nd Tennessee Regiment
Born Cheap Hill, Cheatham County, Tenn. He enlisted in Confederate Army and was in the battles of Bull Run, Shiloh, Franklin, Perryville, Chickamauga, Atlanta, Missionary Ridge, Nashville, and many other skirmishes. He married 1871 Bettie Edwards of Dickson County. He was son of Oliver and Erilla Reeves Pardue.

J. T. PARKER - Company E, 11th Tennessee Infantry

T. J. PARKER - Confederate soldier
On 27 June 1920 a monument was unveiled to Homer Parker, who died of influenza during World War I. The newspaper account noted his father T. J. Parker was a Confederate veteran, his grandfather was a veteran of the Mexican War.

THOMAS PARKER - Baxter's Battery, Tennessee Light Artillery
This information is on his stone in the Parker Cemetery. He is possibly the T. J. Parker above as Homer Parker is also buried here.

J. C. PARNELL - Company E, 11th Tennessee Infantry

GILBERT HOLLAND PETTY - Company B, 42nd Tennessee Infantry
Born 2 Feb. 1841 at Dickson, Tenn., died 6 March 1927; married Adeline Dunnegan 28 Nov. 1866, born 22 May 1846, died 1904. He lived on Piney.

C. J. PHILLIPS - Service not determined
Born 28 April 1842, died 1 Sept. 1916 Dickson County; married 18 Jan. 1871 to Jane W. Matthews.

JOHN W. PHILLIPS - Company K, 11th Tennessee Infantry, 2nd Lieutenant

DAVID THOMAS PINKERTON - Company B, or F, 42nd Tennessee Infantry
Born 20 Nov. 1845 at Whitfield, Hickman County, Tenn., died 26 April 1929, Dickson County, buried Dickson Union Cemetery. He married (1) Rebecca Katherine Murphree and they had 8 children. He married (2) Mrs. Polka Weatherspoon, who died 1926.

THOMAS J. POWERS - Company E, 49th Tennessee Infantry
Born 1828 in Montgomery County, Tenn., died about 1906. He was said to have been married 3 times. He married 11 May 1856 in Montgomery County to Margaret Rogers; was son of James and Martha Powers. He drew a pension for his services.
Children:
1. James Calvin, born about 1862, married Mary Virginia Winters
2. Fagin, lived in Texas
3. Eudora, born 1859, married Isaac Smith
4. Martha, born 1860, died 1944, married David Powers, born 1863, died 1927.
5. John William, born 14 Feb. 1862, died 29 Nov. 1935, married Mary Elizabeth Moore. They are buried in Dickson Union Cemetery.
6. Harrison W., born 19 Feb. 1864, died 3 Aug. 1935, married Nannie Roland.
7. Nannie, born 1865, married William Cole.
8. Ollie, born 1867, died 1956, married Will Warren of Humphreys County, Tenn.
9. Katherine, born 1869, died 1920, married Louis W. Nesbitt.
10. Fredonia, born 1873, married Hunt Sommerville.
11. J. Thomas, born 5 Aug. 1874, died 3 Jan. 1947, married Annie Sanders.

*J. L. READER - Company K, 11th Tennessee
Died of wounds received in Battle of Franklin.

J.H.L. REEDER - Company K, 11th Tennessee Infantry
Born 1843, died 3 Dec. 1899, buried in Hall Cemetery at Burns. He was son of John Reeder and a Miss Hall. He was wounded three times during the war, participated in 31 skirmishes and 21 battles. He studied medicine after the war and in 1876 married Almira Ann Walp. They were parents of eight children:
1. Kate
2. Elzina (Eliza?)
3. Joseph E.
4. Edward
5. Elmer
6. Roma
7. Alma
8. John Ernest
Source: Hale & Merritt, History of Tennessee, page 1448.

REV. W. A. REYNOLDS - Confederate Soldier
His tombstone in Dickson Union Cemetery reads: Born 10 May 1841, died

19 November 1933, age 92 years 6 months, 19 days; joined conference 1874; was Confederate soldier, captured at Fort Donelson, 1861 Mason." His obituary: born 11 May 1841, Dickson County, married 16 June 1865 to Martha Ann Allbright. He was a minister for 60 years. Four daughters and two sons survive.

DANIEL RICE - 11th Tennessee Regiment
Born 12 Oct. 1838, died 11 March 1898, buried Rice Cemetery at Tennessee City. (Note: His biography in Goodspeed gives additional information on him.)

*B. W. RICHARDSON - Company K, 11th Tennessee
Died in service 1 August 1861.

ANDREW J. RICHARDSON - Company E, 11th Tennessee

*TURNER RICHARDSON - Company E, 11th Tennessee Infantry
His arm was shot off at Jonesboro, Georgia, and he died.

*M. T. RICHARDSON - Company E, 11th Tennessee Infantry
Killed at battle of Jonesboro, Georgia. (Believed to be the same as the one before.)

W. TURNER RICHARDSON - Company K, 11th Tennessee Infantry
Born 1843, died 1892, buried at Alf Richardson Cemetery.

W. M. ROBERTS - 2nd Lieutenant, Company C, 11th Tennessee Infantry

WILLIAM ROBERTS - Confederate soldier, service not determined
Died Sept. 1908 near Chatlotte at the age of 79 years.

*D. L. ROBERTSON - Company C, 11th Tennessee Infantry
Died in service 23 March 1863.

*JASPER ROCHELLE - Company H, 11th Tennessee Infantry
Killed New Hope Church, Georgia, 22 July 1864.

J. M. ROGERS - Company C, 11th Tennessee Infantry
He lost arm and leg at the Battle of Murfreesboro. He was later register of Montgomery County.

JOHN W. ROOKER - 2nd Corporal, Company E, 11th Tennessee Infantry

*WILLIAM W. RUSHING - Service not determined
He died March 1864 as prisoner of war in Nashville; originally from Bedford County, Tenn., in 1860 came to Dickson County. He married Susan M. Springer and they were parents of 6 boys and 5 girls. Reference: Dickson Herald, 29 Oct. 1937.

WILEY M. RUSSELL - 49th Tennessee Regiment
Born 20 March 1830 in Dickson County, son of Lemuel S. and Nancy Myatt Russell; married 4 Dec. 1850 to Serena P. Frasier. They had six children. He married (2) 1866 Sarah M. Sugg and they had six children.

*H. W. SANDERS - Company D, 49th Tennessee
Died 20 March 1862.

JOHN J. SANDERS - Company D, 49th Tennessee Infantry
Born 3 November 1839, died 2 May 1911 on Jones Creek; drew pension for his service; lived on Jones Creek.

M. F. SAUNDERS - Company E, 16th Regiment
Born 25 August 1837, died 17 July 1915, buried Tennessee City Cemetery. (Note: This entry may be in error; hard to tell from his tombstone about his service.)

ROBERT SCOTT - Company E, 11th Tennessee Infantry

RICHARD SEARS - 8th Louisiana Infantry
He drew a pension for his service in Dickson County.

*HIRAM SEARS - Baxter's Battery
Died 20 Jan. 1864 of chronic diarrhea in Catoosa Hospital at Griffin, Georgia.

RICHARD H. SEAY - 23rd Virginia Infantry
Drew pension for his services. Dickson County Herald, 27 Dec. 1935: "One morning after the battle of Chancellorville, I passed a wounded Yankee begging for water. After filling his canteen I carried it to him. He thanked me and said, 'Johnnie, you have whipped us and whipped us bad, but you had better have lost 10,000 men than the one you did.' (He was referring to the death of Stonewall Jackson.) I wondered later how he knew the General was wounded, for the news had not then reached us." Seay was captured at Spottsylvania Courthouse in 1864 and confined at Fort Delaware and got black scurvy in prison which made him a cripple. He was father of Charlie Seay of Dickson. Dickson County Herald, 27 Dec. 1935: Richard H. Seay, 95, died in Dallas, Texas, on 23 Dec. 1935 and buried there by his wife. He was born 22 July 1841 in Amelia County, Va., son of Armistead and Martha Seay. He married 5 April 1861 and entered Confederate Army shortly afterwards.

*J. H. SENSING - Company C, 11th Tennessee
Killed in Battle of Murfreesboro on 31 Dec. 1862.

GEORGE W. SENSING - 49th Infantry
He drew pension for his services.

ARCHIE BENTON SENSING - Confederate soldier.

H. E. SHACKLETT - Company E, 11th Tennessee

ISAAC N. SHANNON - Whitworth's Sharpshooters
He died April 1913 in Dickson County, age 79 years.

*J. W. SIGMORE - Company D, 49th Tennessee
Died 22 April 1862. (Many researchers believe this is Jones W. Sizemore instead of Sigmore, who was 8 years old in 1850.)

*RICHMOND (or RICHARD) BAKER SIZEMORE - Company G, 26th Mississippi
Born 1824 Dickson County; died in service 11 December 1864 at Choctaw County, Mississippi; married 1852 Elvira Parlee Greenlee. His widow later married his brother Green McFerrin Sizemore.

SALLIE SIZEMORE - Confederate nurse
Mrs. Sallie Nesbitt Sizemore, 78, died 1 April 1912; native of Dickson County, great-niece of Samuel McAdoo; married Dr. Rufus Hix Sizemore, born 1831, died 1879. She was 78 years 3 months 27 days at her death. (Dickson Herald, 19 April 1912.) Confederate soldiers were the pall-bearers at her funeral. "At one time she passed between the Union and Confederate lines while under fire, with a looking glass under her arm, playing the citizen of the neighborhood. At another time on hearing of the hunger of an almost starving rebel, she determined to get some pota-toes nearby and though the army on both sides were in battle array she passed somehow the pickets; got the potatoes, and returned, and was reprimanded by her husband for taking such risks. Her simple reply was, "I got the potatoes."

At another time at the point of a pistol, she forced a horse thief to put back her horse in the stable, warning him that to carry out his orders would result in his death. She was taken to Atlanta while the city was being shelled, but made her escape in a meat car. In a dif-ficulty between a Federal officer and her husband, she threw herself between them to save her husband from the drawn sword in the officer's hand. She defied the officer and called him a coward. She assisted her husband in dissecting, often standing in heaps of limbs all around her, she holding the tallow candle, the only light available, while her husband was amputating and otherwise attending the soldiers. (Dickson Herald, 19 April 1912.)

She is buried in Dickson Union Cemetery.

JAMES MORRIS SKELTON - Lieutenant, Company C, 11th Tennessee Infantry
Born 23 Dec. 1834, died 6 Nov. 1927, buried in family cemetery, one-time merchant on Yellow Creek; married 15 Feb. 1865 in Houston County to Lenora Shelton.

DR. JOHN D. SLAYDEN - Sgt., Company C, 11th Tennessee Infantry
Born 1841 Dickson County (Goodspeed says born 1843), died 1922 in Clarksville; son of Hartwell and Jane May Slayden. He was severely wounded in the wrist during the war. He married 1881 at Cumberland Furnace to Augustine Russell, born 1863 in Louisiana. Their daughter Adella was born 1882. No further information on any other children.

W. M. SLAYDEN - 3rd Lieutenant, Company C, 11th Tennessee Infantry
He was severely wounded during the war, but recovered.

AUSTIN WILLIS SMITH - Private, Major, 4th Tennessee Infantry
Born 4 October 1836 Davidson County, died 23 Sept. 1875 in Columbia, Tennessee, son of Winn B. Smith of Dickson County; Methodist minister; married 30 April 1863 to Rebecca Wylie; buried Rose Hill Cemetery in Columbia. His obituary said born 1836, but on his tombstone the date appears to be 1826.

W. W. SMITH - "Old Hickory", Confederate soldier
The first UDC Chaper, Old Hickory Chapter, was named for him. The following undated clipping, but from 1913 newspaper, is owned by Lula Belle Hopkins, Dickson, Tenn.: "In the summer of 1903, Mrs. John P. Hickman of Nashville wrote Steve Eleazer, a Dickson county hero of 1863, to get someone interested in the UDC work, and he turned it over to W. M. Hogin, another valiant soldier.

"A few ladies that were interested then gave the matter into the hands of W. W. Smith, known as "Old Hickory" or "Uncle Hickory". He perservered until he had gotten the names of 35 ladies and called a meeting at the Methodist Episcopal Church South in October 1903. A number of ladies were there, Mrs. J. F. Tilmon presiding, and organized Old Hickory Chapter, naming it for the promoter and Jackson.

"Charter members were: Mrs. Stonewall Drane, Mrs. Tom Turner, Mrs. Clayton Smith, Mrs. Bow Hooper, Mrs. Charles Badge, Jr., Miss Eddie Williams, Miss Mamie Davis, Miss Bertie Tidwell, Miss Esther Anthony. Mrs. Drane was president, Mrs. Badge was recording secretary, Mrs. Clayton Smith vice-president, Miss Anthony corresponding secretary, and Miss Eddie Williams was treasurer.

"Mrs. Drane was followed by Mrs. S. E. Hunt who served one month and resigned. She was followed by Mrs. Smith as president and served for seven years.

"Mrs. W. H. McMurry was the next president for a few months and Mrs. Eugene Payne succeeding her.

"In the ten years of organization, the Chapter has bestowed 50 crosses of honor on Confederate veterans. Officers in 1913 are: Mrs. Eugene Payne, president; Mrs. Badge, Jr., first vice president; Mrs. Clayton Smith, second vice president; Mrs. Claude Hooper, secretary; Mrs. Sarah Wishart, treasurer; Mrs. James Watson, reporter."

ROB A SOUTHERLAND - Confederate pensioner, 49th Tennessee Infantry
He died 18 August 1922 in Birmingham, Alabama, at the age of 83 years 8 months 1 day. He married 19 Feb. 1873 to Dona Harrell, daughter of John and Jeanetta Dotson Harrell and they were the parents of 8 children.

SOUTHERLAND BROTHERS
Five sons of John and Mary Ann Williams Southerland fought in the Civil War--3 in the Confederate Army and 2 in the Union Army.

WESLEY SPEIGHT - 50th Infantry
Born 14 October 1837, died 15 Jan. 1918, buried Mt. Liberty Cemetery; married August 1865 to Martha E. Andrews, who died 1872; married (2)

1875 to Alice Nicks.

*A. O. SPRADLIN - Company B, 49th Tennessee Infantry
Died 14 March 1862.

BOB STEELE - Service not determined.
Died December 1922 in Dickson County, buried Steele Cemetery on Garners Creek; age 79 at his death.

*W. H. STEWART - Company K, 11th Tennessee Infantry
Killed in Battle of Kennesaw Mountain.

*W. A. STOKELY - Company C, 11th Tennessee Infantry
Killed in Battle of Franklin 30 November 1864.

M. A. STOKEY - Company C, 11th Tennessee Infantry

ROBERT B. STONE - 50th Tennessee Infantry
Born 16 September 1837 at Cumberland Furnace, son of Hardiman Stone; married 1864 Sarah M. Jackson and they were the parents of five children. He married (2) Kate Richardson. He has three infant children buried in the Harris Cemetery at Sweet Home.

*F. M. STREET - Company C, 11th Tennessee Infantry
Died 20 July 1861.

*J. C. STREET - Company C, 11th Tennessee Infantry
Died 9 August 1861.

DAVID G. STREET - Service not determined.

H. W. STREET - 11th Holman's Cavalry; Confederate pensioner.

J. M. STUART - Company E, 11th Tennessee Infantry

NATHANIEL W. SUGG - Company H, 11th Tennessee Infantry

QUINTUS SUGG (or QUINTESS C. SUGG) - Company B, 14th Tennessee Infantry

*S. W. SUGG - Company D, 49th Tennessee Infantry
Died 22 March 1863.

*DICK TAYLOR - 1st Corporal, Company E, 11th Tennessee Infantry
Died at Rockfall Ridge.

JAMES M. TALLEY - 49th Tennessee Infantry
Born 25 Nov. 1838 Lewisburg, Tenn. (or 25 Oct. 1838), died 26 Feb.1919 and buried Dickson Union Cemetery. He was son of William Talley (born Virginia) and Lucy Birmingham (born in Marshall County). James M. also served in 17th Tennessee Regiment. He was captured at Fort Donelson. He and A. N. Thompson were the only two men out of 150 in Company D, 49th Tennessee, to answer the final roll call of the company. In 1868 he married Katie McCauley.
Children:
1. William M. Talley
2. Alice M. Talley married Clayton Smith
3. Bertha Talley married Thomas Turner
4. Gertrude Talley married W. H. Murrey
5. C. M. Talley
6. James M. Talley, Jr.

ED L. TATOM - 6th Wheeler's Cavalry; Confederate pensioner

*WELTON TAYLOR - Company E, 11th Tennessee Infantry
Died at Tunnel Hill, Georgia, Sept. 1863.

JONATHAN TAYLOR - Confederate soldier
Born in Virginia, married Mary Ann Hall, born in Virginia. He was "in Confederate Army until he died." (Reference, Dickson Herald, 14 Jan. 1938.)

WILLIAM HENRY TAYLOR - Company B, 49th Tennessee Regiment
Born 9 Jan. 1836 Davidson County, died 6 April 1887, buried in Leech Cemetery near Charlotte.

*JOSEPH R. TERRILL - Baxter's Battery
Died 28 May 1863 at Bean's Station of typhoid.

*J. W. B. THEDFORD - Company D, 49th Tennessee Regiment
Died 22 May 1862.

WILLIAM R. THEDFORD - Captain, Lieutenant Colonel, Co. K, 11th Infantry
He died soon after the war. His son J. R. "Dick" Thedford was killed in car wreck in 1933 at the age of 75. (Dickson Herald, 25 Aug. 1933.) No further information on his family available.

J. A. THOMAS - 24th Battalion Tennessee Sharpshooters
Born 4 April 1842 Humphreys County, died 30 Oct. 1926, buried Dickson Union; he drew pension for his services. His wives are buried in Dickson Union: Maggie S., born 1856, died 1877, and Catherine L. Easley, born 1858, died 1921.

H. C. THOMAS - Service not determined.

*M. B. THOMAS - Company K, 11th Tennessee Infantry
Died in prison. (Official muster rolls show Minor B. Thomas.)

A. N. THOMPSON - Company D, 49th Tennessee Regiment
He married Mary Hudgins and they were the parents of 9 children, 4 girls and 5 boys.

JAMES J. THOMPSON - 10th Tennessee Cavalry, 11th Tennessee Infantry
Born 13 July 1842 Dickson County, died 17 August 1901, buried in Thompson Cemetery, Yellow Creek.

*J. L. THOMPSON - Company D, 49th Tennessee
Died 4 September 1863.

*J. M. THOMPSON - Company D, 49th Tennessee
Died in service.

*LEWIS P. THOMPSON - Baxter's Battery
Died 27 May 1863 at Bean's Station of typhoid fever.

JAMES B. THOMPSON - Baxter's Company Tennessee Light Artillery
He is buried in the Thompson Cemetery, Sertoma Road, out from Burns, but no dates on his stone.

*BENJAMIN TIDWELL - Company K, 11th Tennessee Infantry
Died in hospital at Chattanooga.

*C. M. Tidwell - Company K, 11th Tennessee Infantry
Died 16 April 1863.

FRANKLIN FULTON TIDWELL - Captain, Company C, 11th Tennessee Infantry
Born 25 July 1840, died 20 Feb. 1911, buried Dickson Union. He drew pension for his services. Served in the Tennessee General Assembly. Married 1866 to Magdaline Knox Petty and they were the parents of 11 children.

JOSIAH TIDWELL - Company K, 11th Tennessee Infantry
Born 26 April 1838, died 19 March 1874, buried in White Cemetery off Spencer Mill Road.

*SILAS TIDWELL - Company K, 11th Tennessee Infantry
Died in Battle of Jonesboro, Georgia.

S. M. TOLAR - Company E, 11th Tennessee Infantry

THOMAS L. TOTTY - 11th Tennessee Infantry
He died 5 June 1919, age 89, lived on Yellow Creek.

SYLVANUS TRATTER - 14th Infantry
He drew pension for his services.

J. R. VENABLE - 6th Kentucky Infantry
He drew pension in Dickson County for his services.

SAMUEL VANHOOK - Service not determined.
He was reported to us a Confederate soldier, no further information.

E. V. WALKER - Service not determined
He married Minerva Houston and they were the parents of 3 sons and one daughter.

*J. L. WALKER - Company D, 49th Tennessee
Died 11 Feb. 1862.

*J. N. WALKER - Company D, 49th Tennessee
Died 16 April 1863.

*R. WALKER - Company D, 49th Tennessee
Died 30 March 1862.

SAMUEL THOMAS WALKER - Service not determined.
He is believed to be the S. T. Walker, born 13 March 1837, died 26 October 1893 buried in the Walker Cemetery near or in Vanleer.

*JOHN WALLS - Company E, 11th Tennessee
Killed at Battle of Murfreesboro.

A. D. WASH - 16th Infantry
Drew pension in Dickson County for his services.

GUY WASHINGTON - 3rd Arkansas Infantry
Drew pension in Dickson County for his services.

W. T. WEAKLEY - 11th Infantry
Drew pension in Dickson County for his services.

JOHN L. WEAVER - Service not determined.

C. T. WEEMS - 11th Tennessee Infantry
Drew pension in Dickson County for his services.

*G. W. WEEMS - Company K, 11th Tennessee Infantry
Died in hospital 10 November 1863.

JOHN WELCH - 11th Tennessee Infantry
Drew pension in Dickson County for his services. He is possibly identical with the soldier following.

JOHN S. WELCH - Confederate soldier
Born 7 Oct. 1832 (another source says 1842), died 18 August 1927, buried Martin Garton Cemetery. His wife Susanna was born 1848, died 1919 and also buried in same cemetery.

WESLEY WELCH - Baxter's Battery
He drew pension in Dickson County for his services.

FELIX EMPS WILLEY - Company D, 49th Tennessee Infantry
Born 3 August 1830 at White Bluff, died 28 Dec. 1897, buried in Hutton Cemetery. He married 1854 Delila Roberts, born 1836, died 1900, buried in Hutton Cemetery.

DANIEL WHITE - Baxter's Company Light Artillery
Born 1840, died 1925.

E. W. WHITE - 26th Infantry
Drew pension in Dickson County for his services.

JAMES P. WHITE - Baxter's Battery Tennessee Light Artillery
Born 23 Feb. 1844, died 6 Oct. 1925, buried in White Cemetery.

*W. H. WHITE - Company B, 49th Tennessee Infantry
Died March 1863.

COLONEL W. M. WHITE - Company K (or E), 11th Tennessee Infantry
He is buried in White Cemetery in Dickson County.

*J. K. P. WILEY - Company D, 49th Tennessee
Died 8 September 1862.

ORVILLE WILKINS - 1st Corporal, Company E, 11th Tennessee Infantry

A. B. WILLIAMS - 2nd Lieutenant, Company C, 11th Tennessee Infantry
Born 16 Sept. 1836, died 27 June 1913, buried Dickson Union Cemetery; he enlisted in 11th Tennessee in 1861 but later served with General Forrest; married 1856 to Mary Street, born 10 July 1837, died 9 Oct. 1912. They had 9 children. (Reference: Dickson Herald, 4 July 1913.)

F. G. WILLIAMS - Company E, 11th Tennessee Infantry

GEORGE COLEMAN WILLIAMS - Confederate pensioner
Born 31 Oct. 1846, died 9 March 1919, buried in Williams Cemetery on Yellow Creek; wife Allonie A., born 1852, died 1935.

HENRY KEPHART WILLIAMS - Company B, 49th Tennessee Infantry
Born 21 Oct. 1844 Dickson County, died 3 Jan. 1916, lived at White Oak Flats; married 1866 Sarah Jane Carroll, born 1849, died 1920. He drew pension in Dickson County.

*J. W. WILLIAMS - Company B, 49th Tennessee Infantry
Died March 1862.

*STEVEN WILLIAMS - Company E, 11th Tennessee Infantry
Killed at Kennesaw Mountain. (Lindsley's Annals gives his name as Stephen Williams.)

THOMAS W. WILLIAMS - Harding's Light Artillery

WILLIAM WESLEY WILSON - Service not determined.

G. W. WIMBERLY - 23rd Infantry
Born 1843, died 1926, buried Rock Church Cemetery. He drew pension for his services.

*WILLIAM WINFREY - Service not determined.
According to Dickson Herald, 15 Oct. 1937, he was "First man from Dickson County killed in battle." Official records show W. E. Winfrey, Company B, 49th Infantry.

ROBERT J. WORK - 11th Infantry
Born 8 August 1841, died 9 Aug. 1920, buried Dickson Union. He also served in the Tennessee General Assembly. His wife Lissa T. Bingham Work, born 1849, died 1926, is buried in Dickson Union.

JOHN FRANKLIN WRIGHT - Service not determined.

DR. L. D. WRIGHT - 11th Holman's Cavalry
Born 29 May 1847 (tombstone has 1848 on it), died 13 May 1920, buried Dickson Union Cemetery; married Nannie Craft, born 1861, died 1920.

W. M. WRIGHT - 10th Demoss Cavalry
Drew pension in Dickson County for his services.

WILLIAM WRIGHT - Service not determined.

J. F. WYATT - 24th Battaltion Tennessee Sharpshooters
He drew pension in Dickson County for his services.

WILLIAM A. WYATT - Service not determined.

THOMAS LUIS YARBROUGH - Service not determined.

JASON YATES - Company E, 11th Tennessee Infantry
Relieved under conscript act.

WILLIAM DILLARD POYNER - Capt. O. C. Alexander's Company, Cox's Regt. Born 27 April 1833 Dickson County, died 29 Jan. 1929 Memphis, married 1853 to Amanda Bumpass, died 1920.

> (This concludes the unfinished manuscript of Confederate soldiers of Dickson County. This was the initial list for a proposed project on Dickson County soldiers; the project has been discontinued.)

***

Union Soldiers of Dickson County:
Although no effort was made to compile a listing of Federal soldiers, who lived in Dickson County, the following were discovered in the course of this work:

JESSE ALLEN - Company D, 10th Tennessee Mounted Infantry
WILLIAM M. ANDERSON - Company K, 1st Kansas Light Artillery
J. A. BETZ - Company G, West Virginia Cavalry
GEORGE WASHINGTON BROWN - Company G, 3rd West Virginia Cavalry
THOMAS W. BURNS - 12th Tennessee Cavalry
ROBERT P. CALL
JAMES E. CHADEWICK
WILLIAM PENN CROWELL
WILLIAM W. HEATH
BOB B. HEATH
_____HEATH, son of Samuel and Julia Ann McCormick Heath, one of three Heath brothers in Union Army.

DR. GUSTIE AUGUSTUS FRIEUDENTHAL - Infantry for two years
J. W. JOHNSON (or I. W. Johnson)
JOHN McELHINEY - Company D, 2d West Virginia Cavalry
WILLIAM C. McELHINNEY - Company G, 78th Pennsylvania Infantry
M. V. LITTLE
LEVI SHAWL
MARTIN SMITH
JESSIE R. MOORE
JOHN OWENS, SR.

When J. W. Johnson, 69, died 1912, the pallbearers at his funeral were William Anderson, D. F. Daubenspeck, E. Marsh, L. Shawl, B. A. Newton, F. Curtis, J. R. Work and J. S. Bakley. All except J. R. Work were Federal Civil War soldiers, but Work had been a Confederate. (Dickson Herald, 1 March 1912.)

***

When James A. Betz (also spelled Betts) died in 1939, his obituary noted he was "the last remaining Union soldier in Dickson County."

***

DICKSON COUNTY CIVIL WAR SOLDIERS RECAP:

    FIRST SOLDIER KILLED IN BATTLE (CSA) - William Winfrey

    LAST SURVIVING CONFEDERATE SOLDIER - Benjamin F. Brown, d. 1937

    LAST SURVIVING UNION SOLDIER - James A. Betz, died 1939

UNION MEN

At least 72 men voted in June 1861 to remain in the Union. To identify Union loyalists the following items are included.

"A Voice from Dickson County"

(From Nashville Daily Union, 3 July 1862)
Among all the proceedings of the many Union meetings which have reached us from various Southern States, we do not recollect any which please us so well as the resolutions passed some ten days ago by a gathering of plain Tennessee farmers in Dickson County. They are sensible and practical. They are clear:

Union Meeting at Valley Spring Meeting House

We, the Union men of Dickson County, Tenn., met at Valley Springs Meeting House, June the 21st 1862 and adopted the following resolutions:
1. Resolved, that we believe it to be the imperative duty of the Federal Government to put down the present rebellion.
2. Resolved, that we believe it to be the duty of all loyal citizens to aid the Government in suppressing the said rebellion.
3. Resolved, that we are in favor of the leading rebels bearing the burden of the Federal war tax.
4. Resolved, that we are opposed to the election of any person to any office whatsoever, whose loyalty is doubted.
5. Resolved, that we recommend to our brother loyal men, throughout the state to hold similar meetings for the purpose of perpetuating the Government of the United States.

Resolved, that when it is made to appear by the loyal citizens of any neighborhood or section, that certain persons from said neighborhood, who are held as prisoners of war to the United States are loyal to the Government, they should be released and restored to their families and friends.

A. J. H. Croson, President
G. W. Smith, secretary

***

Southern Claims

The following people presented claims to the United States saying they had been loyal to the United States during the Civil War and were asking for payment for damages done to them by the Federal troops. In order for their claims to be heard, they had to take an oath that they had remained loyal to the Government. This list was taken from micorfilm "Consolidated Index of Claims, Records of Commissioners of Claims, Southern Claims Commission, 1871-1180," Microcopy No. 87, Roll 13, Georgraphical Lists of Claims, Volume 55, Record Group 56, General Records, Department of Treasury.

From Dickson County, Tennessee:

James Adams	George C. Dodson	Geo. Wash. Moore
A. J. Allen	James E. Gillilan	James Sloan
Milly Beaumond	James Howell	John R. Vanhook
James Choate	Geo. Hutcheson &	Joseph J. Williams
William Cox	Alexander Kerr	John Franklin Wright

***

CLAIMANTS

Claimants against the United States under the 4th of July Act, from Dickson County:

W. A. Browning, administrator of B. W. Browning	$100.00
Caroline Bowen	$125.00
John M. Hall, administrator of Meckins Carr	$165.00
P. O. Caldwell, administrator of A. B. Caldwell	$450.00

George C. Dotson	$ 22.25
John W. Dotson	$150.00
Marion Jackson	$145.00
Daniel R. Leech	$150.00
Thomas McNeilly	$ 32.00
Barley Taylor	$125.00
Lucinda Tidwell	$125.00

(This list was published in the Hickman Pioneer, 13 March 1887.)

***

Dickson County Public Meeting

(This account was published in the Nashville Daily Union 7 June 1865.) A public meeting was held in Dickson County at Hutton's Chapel on 3 June 1865 and R. L. V. Schmittou presided. Parson Hutton addressed the group. This was a meeting of citizens and paroled soldiers. Resolutions were made by A. P. Nicks, J. H. Cullum, John McKechnie, N. M. Hall and Charles S. Jones that they would aid and assist in restoring civil law and order in the county and that they regretted the assassination of President Lincoln and indorse the General Assembly of Tennessee in their act in regard to bushwhackers and horse-thieves, etc. Signed:

D. C. Jones	Robert Larkins	William Loften
M. Q. Young	William B. Brim	William Esters
R. H. Rose	B___McCaslin	H. J. Richardson
W. S. Winfred	L. W. Hutton	J. P. Gafford
Steve Eleazer	S. Cathey	John Hooper
John H. Hall	Josiah Wood	C. Larkins
Thomas Creech	Williamson Nall	Lovel Hooper
S. A. Thompson	B. T. Andrews	N. P. Nicks
W. H. Chappel	G. W. Gray	W. R. Daniel
William Creech	A. J. Brim	Jesse Garland
Esquire Richardson	William Lewis	B. C. Anderson
Cave Richardson	B. D. Dilliard	J. M. Smith
P. Andrews	H. A. Davidson	W. Taylor
J. Southerland	John Hall, Jr.	William Hall
J. M. Davidson	J. B. Hall, Sr.	J. H. Tanner
Crawford C. Beck	B. F. Hall	Joshua Cathey
Joseph Hall	W. C. Hall	Ed McCormack
Miner Eleazer	B. B. Hall	John Dillyard
	Z. D. Hutton	

***

GUERRILLAS AND BUSHWHACKERS

(The following is a chapter from an unpublished manuscript entitled "Guerrillas and Bushwhackers in Middle Tennessee during the Civil War" and is the chapter labeled "In Dickson County". The source for information is usually given in parenthesis at the end of each paragraph.)

A continuous fight was kept up in the county (Dickson) between the Federals and the guerrillas during the war, "and not a few lives were sacrificed as a result."

In 1865 William D. Willey was captured by the Federals, under the command of Lieutenant Donnehue, and shot as a guerrilla. The latter, it is supposed killed John Lindsey, a Federal sympathizer, during the same year, and in a short time thereafter Demps Dobson, a guerrilla, was captured by the Federals and taken about a mile north of Charlotte and shot. When friends of Dobson went after the body to give it a decent burial, they found in his hand a scrap of paper on which was written: "Shot in retaliation for the killing of John Lindsey."

M. Gilbert, a citizen of Charlotte, was also killed by the Federals.

In 1863, "Mr. Samuel Baker, a Union man of Dickson County, was arrested las stummer and confined in jail at Columbia. He broke jail and reached Nashville. His wife, who kept a little store at Charlotte, was robbed of everything she had both in property and money last winter by guerrillas. Her property, $800 worth, was discovered the other day by

Col. Scully of 1st Middle Tennessee in an outhouse of 'Squire Dunn, a prominent secessionist near Kingston Springs. Mr. Baker can recover his property upon application." (Nashville Daily Union, 7 Oct. 1863.)

In October 1863, Gustavus Good murdered George and James Heath of Dickson County. He was taken to Nashville in May 1865 to be tried by court martial. This newspaper also says: ""Gustavus Good was of Davidson County and he was under arrest for committing murder by shooting James and Joseph Heath, both Union men." It is known that some of the Heath men were devout Unionists in Dickson County. (Nashville Daily Union 16 May 1865, Nashville Daily Dispatch, 16 May 1865.)

Much damage was done to Charlotte, the county seat, in addition to "eating the citizens out of house and home." The records in the courthouse were mutilated and destroyed in an "inexcusable and wanton manner, and private business houses invaded and pillaged." (Goodspeed's History of Dickson County, page 936. However, more of the county records escaped destruction than this seems to indicate.)

In 1862, a party of about 60 Federal soldiers visited the county on a raid and a slight skirmish occurred between them and a band of guerrillas a few miles out from Charlotte. (Goodspeed, page 936.)

During the latter part of November 1863, a portion of two Federal regiments (numbering between 300 and 400) took possession of Charlotte. They were under the command of Major Kirwine and remained here until the middle of March 1864. They established headquarters in the courthouse and erected barracks all around the courtyard, calling the place "Camp Charlotte".

After the order to complete the Nashville and Northwestern Railroad, Federal troops were in the county to build the railroad and to guard the workers.

The Cumberland River forms the boundary of Dickson County for a short distance, and the main roads in the county leading to the river were often traveled by troops of both sides.

W. W. Lowe wrote General Rosecrans on 27 January 1863, "Forrest and Wheeler, 7,000 strong are near Charlotte, tending to above Clarksville and the Harpeth Shoals, the object being to watch for transports and decoy Colonel Bruce across so that Morgan can dash into Clarksville. A scouting party from my command captured some prisoners and teams loaded with meat for Forrest. Roads almost impassable." (Official Records of the War of the Rebellion, Volume 23, Series 1, Part 2, page 16. Hereinafter, designated O. R.)

On the same day, S. D. Bruce, commanding at Clarksville, was notified: "Rebels on the south side of river near Shoals, 5,000 strong with 8 pieces of artillery." Bruce remarked that "I keep strong pickets at Shoals...Rebel cavalry are on south side in view." (O. R., Volume 23, Part 2, page 16.)

Bruce, on the same date again, reported to Rosecrans: "Wheeler's and Forrest are between Charlotte and Shoals. The gunboat Lexington was up to the Shoals today. Had three cannonballs strike her...5th Iowa Cavalry captured a few of their wagons yesterday and carried them to Donelson." (O. R., Volume 23, Part 2, page 16.)

Rosecrans on 28 January 1863, informed Mitchell in Nashville that "Forrest is not at Harpeth. Some portion of his command maybe and perhaps under Napier..." However, T. A. Napier was dead at this time. (O. R., Volume 23, Series 1, Part 2, page 20.)

On 20 January 1863, the Nashville Daily Union reported: "Mary Crane burned by guerrillas at Betsy's Landing near the shoals. Crew captured and carried off, mate killed and two of crew wounded." The boat had stopped at this point to take on wood.

On 7 March 1863, Bruce at Clarksville reported to General Rosecrans: "The rebel force firing on boats at Shoals is Col. (L. S.) Ross's regiment. They have their headquarters at Kinderhook near Williamsport where Wheeler, Forrest, and Woodward are said to be. They are conscripting and stealing all the horses in the county. Many conscripts have come in, asking protection which I gave..." (O. R., Volume 23, Part 2, page 117.)

On 26 March 1863, Brigadier-General Robert B. Mitchell reported to J. A. Garfield, "Have just returned from near Harpeth and am satisfied the enemy is headed for the shoals in considerable force." (O. R., Volume 23, Part 2, page 175.)

Colonel William P. Boone returned from Harpeth Shoals on 6 April 1863 and reported no force there but that the Confederates "or the enemy" was camped two miles from river on Charlotte Road. He also reported that the gunboats shelled and burned Palmyra "last evening." (O. R., Volume 23, Part 2, page 212. Note: Palmyra is on Cumberland River in Montgomery County.)

The next day, S. D. Bruce wrote: "On Sunday 800 enemy (C.S.A.) with artillery were at Cumberland Furnace, 15 miles from Palmyra." (Ibid., pages 219-220.)

On 14 April 1863, Bruce wrote Garfield: that he had barricaded the ferry boat Excelsior with hay and used it as a gunboat and thus conveyed the fleet above the shoals with it...that he recovered the starboard gun from the wreck of the Slidell and dispersed a rebel band at the Shoals. He also reported he had captured several men belonging to Woodward's command. (Ibid, page 240.)

Six days later Bruce wrote "Woodward's 600 and two artillery left Van Lew's furnace Saturday midnight for Columbia, by way of Centerville." (Ibid., 258. Note: Woodward had possibly been encamped at Cumberland Furnace, built by Van Leer or Vanleer, not Van Lew.)

On May 22, 1863, Judge Jackson shot James May. The Nashville Daily Union wrote on August 22, 1863:

> "The findings and decision of the military commission is the case of Judge Jackson, who was arraigned for shooting James May in Dickson County, Tenn., on May 22, 1863, have been approved of by General Rosecrans and returned to Col. Bruce, with orders to have the sentence carried into effect.
>
> Since this trial Jackson has been in very feeble health, and for the past month has been a patient at the Post Hospital. He was brought down from the hospital on Tuesday and the sentence read to him. It is: "And the commission do sentence him, Judge Jackson, to be confined to the penitentiary of the State of Tennessee, and kept at hard labor for the term of two years."
>
> The following is the endorsement: "The finding and sentence of the Commission are approved. The commanding officer at Clarksville will forward the prisoner with a copy of this order to Nashville, by Command of Maj. Gen. Rosecrans."
>
> The Judge is still feeble and his steps are slow and tottering. His face is careworn and pale, showing that repentance is inflicting a terrible punishment. When his sentence was read to him on Tuesday, the old man bowed his head and wept like a child."

The sentence on Judge Jackson was possibly not carried out because an unnamed Confederate soldier made the following diary entry:

> November 19, 1863--Was sent with another comrade to scout the country for cattle for provisions. We had a bag of gold nuggets to pay for them; was caught by enemy skirmishers, who took what cattle we had. We buried the gold, and after close

questioning were turned loose, spent the night at a friendly preacher's house, who promised again to give us lodging when we returned for the gold. His name was Rev. Judge Jackson, Charlotte, Tenn. (Dickson County Herald, 24 October 1919.)

The soldier also wrote: "The gold was buried under the Southeast corner of Jackson's Chapel." This gold was found in 1919 and returned to the soldiers who had buried in in 1863.

Judge Jackson (apparently his name was Judge and not a title) is buried in the cemetery of Jackson's Chapel Methodist Church, located about 8 miles from Charlotte on Highway 49, leading to the Cumberland River. This small Methodist Church was named for Judge Jackson and the Jackson family, early settlers in this area of Dickson County. The inscription on his stone reads:

>JUDGE JACKSON
>Born 30 Jan. 1812
>Died 25 Jan. 1888
>Professed religion 7 Oct. 1837

Have been unable to find out the reason for the shooting, but possibly May was a Union man. There must have been a strong motive for the sometime Methodist minister, Jackson, to shoot May.

Nashville Daily Union, 23 Sept. 1863: "Detachments of F and C companies, 31st East Tennessee Cavalry went on scout in Dickson County last week, routed a party of Hawkins rebel cavalry, capturing nine privates and Captain Rowland of Hopkinsville, Kentucky, and Lt. Kerr and Lt. Jonnaul, formerly of Nashville."

Nashville Daily Union, 24 Dec. 1863: "Dr. Aaron Jones of Dickson County was convicted of being a rebel spy and sentenced to be hung has been pardoned by the President."

Nashville Daily Union, 6 Jan. 1864: "A statement made in the New York Times that a Tennessee guerrilla named "Jones" sentenced to be hung by court-martial has been turned loose by the President. We presume the statement refers to the case of Dr. Aaron James, who was sentenced to be hung upon the charge of being a guerrilla. After a careful examination of all the evidence by the President, he was satisfied that the man was not guilty and the sentence was disapproved."

Some Smith family records have this about Aaron James: "Aaron James, a lifelong resident of this state, began his career as a teacher, later studied medicine and for 52 years devoted his professional services to the young and old of Humphreys County. He death occurred at the advanced dage of eighty-six. He served as a surgeon in the Civil War, and was held in one of the northern prisons for six months." (His daughter Ida P. James married John Smith of Humphreys County, Tenn.)

Nashville Daily Union, 20 Sept. 1863: The Nashville and Northwestern railroad, 28 miles long, is being extended 4 miles beyond Kingston Springs in Dickson County; the road is graded from Kingston Springs to Waverly. From Waverly to Reynoldsburg the road is complete, 6 miles, and from Reynoldsburg to Hickman the road is graded for 40 miles. Stone for the bridge is ready.

A report on the railroad through Dickson County was made in January 1864:

THE NORTHWESTERN RAILROAD
The above-named road is a military railway under constructtion to run from this city (Nashville) west to the Tennessee River, striking the river at or near Reynoldsburg. It will not be finished, probably, much before spring.

It is not needed at any rate this winter, not so long as the Cumberland River will permit even the smallest boats to float. The siege of water at all seasons of the year will permit boats upon the Tennessee River to run between Paducah, Ky., and Florence, Ala. Thus supplies can be carried up the Tennessee to Reynoldsburg, and shipped by rail to Nashville on this new road. Its distance will be but 78 miles, while the Louisville and Nashville Railroad is 185.

The Northwestern Road will run through a barren country, and passes over but four streams, while the Louisville and Nashville Road requires an average of 12,000 men to protect its dozen of bridges, water tanks, and wood piles, and the country or at least, most portions of it along the road, is infested with guerrillas.

The track is laid upon the Northwestern Road, 32 miles from this city and 4 miles from Reynoldsburg, at the other end of the road, making 36 miles in all, or nearly half the road. The whole line is graded, and all but 16 miles is ready for the iron. General Gillem, the Adjutant General of the State, has military command of the road and has three negro regiments at work upon it.

The regiments doing guard duty are the 10th Tennessee Infantry, the 8th Iowa Cavalry, and the 1st Kentucky Battery. A considerable amount of railroad iron was received here yesterday, and portions of the Memphis and Clarksville roads will be torn up if a sufficiency of iron cannot be obtained otherwise. The benefits of this road when completed will be almost incalculable. (Nashville Daily Union, 10 Jan. 1864.)

Nashville Daily Union, 8 March 1864:

SUCCESSFUL SCOUT BY TENNESSEE CAVALRY
On Tuesday last, Capt. Higginbotham of the 4th Tennessee Cavalry, at the head of a portion of Companies A and B, numbering in all 42 men, made a reconnoissance to a place about 15 miles beyond Charlotte, capturing 22 rebel soldiers, a portion of a band which has been infesting the county for some time.

The facts, as related by Sergeant William Smith, are these: The advance of four men, led by the corporal, whose name our informant had forgotten, discovered, while passing over a hill, two persons at a distance, whom they supposed to be citizens, but they directed their horses toward them that they might not be mistaken. The guerrillas--for such they proved to be-- immediately commenced retreating towards a wood.

The advance was then halted and the alarm given, when our cavalry dashed down into the creek bottom, in the direction of the rebels, who fled promiscuously at our approach. They were not sufficiently fleet of foot, however, and 11 of their number were picked up in a chase of two miles, when further pursuit became impracticable. The whole band numbered, it is believed, from 40 to 60 men.

Nashville Daily Union, 12 April 1864:

NASHVILLE AND NORTHWESTERN RAILROAD.--A correspondent of the St. Louis Union writing on the line of this railroad says it is slowly though steadily approaching completion. The black regiments that have been grading it have nearly completed their work. The Missouri and Indiana mechanics and engineers have but to lay the "ties" and spike on the rails for 25 to 30 miles, and then the iron-horse will water in the Tennessee and from thence transport forage and produce to Knoxville and beyond; while on its way through Nashville, Murfreesboro, Bridgeport, Chattanooga, and other places, it can deposit its freight without unnecessary detention or trans-shipment.

A channel like this, opened at all seasons of the year, from the Ohio and the great Father of Waters, for all the wants of the army of the nation, is one of the great works performed in these troublous times. Like the builders of ancient Jerusalem surrounded by their enemies, our black and white soldiers have for months toiled with pick and shovel, with ax and saw, while their arms and ammunition have always been within their reach. The guerrillas and Forrest's marauders have been careful not to make any concentrated attack upon those hard-handed laborers.

Nashville Daily Union, 19 May 1864:

MURDER OF SOLDIERS.--Camp Gillem, Tenn., 19 May 1864. On Tuesday evening last, four men of Company E, 10th Reg. Tenn. Vol. Cavalry departed from this camp away with their arms and accoutrements. Lt. Gilbert B. Harvey and ten of the same company were soon afterwards sent out in pursuit of them.

The Lieutenant pursued them as far as Charlotte, and here stopped, permitting his men to procure all the liquor they desired, which was soon done, and the effects no less sooner visible.

A small dispute soon arose between the Lieutenant and one of his men, and the Lieutenant drew his revolver and shot him on the spot. An hour afterwards a similar quarrel arose between a brother of the deceased and a man of the party, when the man drew his pistol and killed the brother. Thus the lives of two brothers, noble and true-hearted soldiers, were sacrifieced by the poisonous venom.

An escort was sent out as soon as the facts were ascertained, and the lieutenant and party arrested and brought to camp, where they are now awaiting trial. Signed, truly yours, John Rodgers.
(Note: Gillem is now Tennessee City in Dickson County.)

Nashville Union, 21 May 1864:

SWORD PRESENTATION, Fort Gillam, Tenn., 20 May 1864.--It is a delightful thing to see officers and men in the service mutually and socially attached to each other. This is as it should be in every Regiment and in all Companies in the service.

Good officers make, in a majority of the cases, good privates and good privates make good officers. At vigorous prosecution of the war is essentially necessary, and to do this rightly, it will required good, faithful, and obedient privates, as well as good officers.

In token of the high appreciation of his goodness as an officer and gentleman, the non-commissioned officers and privates of Company I, 10th Tennessee Infantry, have by contribution purchased a sword and presented to their worthy Capt. M. L. Moore.

Capt. Moore received the sword, and assured the men in his company that no one could more highly appreciate such a token of respect than himself.

It is a nice thing to see officers and men work harmoniously together--then each other's true estimate is fully appreciated. The presentation of the sword to Capt. Moore could not have been more worthily bestowed. Such manifestations of respect and appreciation are worthy of publicity.
  F. R. S., one of the 10th Tennessee Infantry

In July 1864:

                         Camp 1st Paris Battery
                         Nashville & Northwestern Railroad
                         July 25, 1864

This morning there was a company of guerrillas, 5 miles from camp on Yellow Creek, supposed to be in command of some rebel colonel and citizens say to strike this railroad...70 to 100 estimated...persons pressed as guides of the party.

The foregoing letter was signed by Marcus D. Tenny, Captain, First Kansas Battery.

A report was made 25 October 1864:

"...The track repairers at Section 36 were taken prisoners by McNary's gang (variously estimated at from 15 to 40 men, while some place the number at exactly 23) on the night of the 17th, about 12 o'clock, and held till late on the following morning, and made by McNary to draw the spikes from a rail and removed the fastenings at its end so as to be loose.

"The gang then drew back from oberservation, and in this condition of affairs the first a.m. train passed safely by them, except that a shower of bullets was poured in, which wounded a surgeon, Hogle, Engineer E. Andrews, and killed a boy, who was cook and brakeman, dead on the bunk, where he happened to be lying.

"The second a. m. train came to the loose rail and ran off; the engineer and fireman were wounded. Everybody was stripped of whatever money, watches or valuables they had which pleased the fancy of the robbers.

"The locomotive was upset and slightly injured by cutting places with axes. One box-car was burned, but their efforts to burn the flat-cars loaded with iron, which composed the balance of the train were not successful, and these were slightly injured.

"The third train, loaded with sawed timber from Ayres' saw-mill at Section 29 ran up and was fired into. All hands jumped off and were robbed, except Engineer W. H. Stevens, who ran the train back to Section 32, White Bluffs, in safety.

"Meantime, the first train, Civil Conductor Charles White, arrived at Sneedville and Colonel Murphy, who was on board, had the telegrapher G. W. Leedon, send a dispatch to Lieutenant Orr at White Bluffs, to come on with his cavalry. The dispatch was promptly obeyed, and Lieutenant Orr arrived with 25 men twenty minutes after the gang had taken their departure, and, pursued them a short distance unsuccessfully; and his horses being tired and inferior he returned.

"A wrecking train was dispatched with hands from Gillem's Station, Section 51, to clear the road, and Lieutenant Cox, with a detachment of Company B, 100th U. S. Colored Infantry, and Capt. Frost, with a detachment from companies of the 12th U. S. Colored Infantry from Sullivan's Branch, were sent to Section 36, and the road made clear on the following morning, the 19th instant."
(O. R., Volume 39, Part 1, page 877. Note: Section 29 would be in Cheatham County today; Sneedville is now Dickson; Gillem's Station is now Tennessee City in Dickson County.)

This article continues:

"Again on the 21st instant, as the p.m. train for Johnsonville was passing Section 36 it was signaled by the section foreman, whose cook had informed him she had seen men tearing up the track. Capt. O. B. Simmons, military conductor, had the train stopped, and with his large train guard pursued the bushwhackers, whose numbers could not be ascertained, for a considerable distance, but as they were mounted the pursuit was unavailing.

"Civil Conductor Charles White fastened down the rail and the train passed on.

"Afterward the gang returned and burned the house and commissary of the section foreman, who lay in the bushes in sight. They also burned nearly all the negro and other dwellings along the railroad for two miles. Piles of wood at Sections 38 and 39 were burned, and various estimates placed the loss in wood at from 3,000 to 15,000 cords. The wood being in several ranks close to the road, many ties were burned at the ends, and the rails warped by the intense heat, so that the 3 o'clock train for Nashville could not pass.

"The telegraph operator at Sneedville called operator at White Bluffs, Section 32, and while calling the line was cut before getting an answer.

"Capt. J. W. Dickins, at Sneedville, went to the burning wood with part of his company and arrived in time to hear the retreating bushwhackers laughing and talking, but was not able at that time (11 o'clock night) to do anything and returned to Sneedville.

"On the 22d Military Conductor Capt. Van Skike, from Nashville, found out the condition of the road at Section 38 and 39, and took a detail up from White Bluffs and repaired the road as soon as possible so that trains ran through on the 23d of October.
Signed, William L. Clark, 1st Lieutenant, 12th U. S. Colored Infantry."

McNairy's Gang of these reports was led by Alexander Duval McNairy of Nashville. In 1906 Bromfield Ridley wrote of him: "Captain Alexander Duval McNairy, of Nashville, commanded a company of independent scouts between Cumberland and Tennessee rivers, 1862-1865, and was the terror of the Federal armies. His dashes were vigorous and his execution phenomenal."

Jerome Spence, writing in his History of Hickman County, wrote that in the winter of 1863 a troop of Federal cavalry was in District 7 of Hickman County, capturing Confederate soldiers who might be home on furloughs. They pretended, however, to really be there searching for the guerrilla bands of Henon Cross, Duval McNairy, and James McLaughlin.

Following a skirmish that day, 11 Federal cavalrymen went in pursuit of Duval McNairy, who left the main road and ascended a steep, rough point. When he reached the top, he turned and fired both barrels of his shotgun at his pursuers, wounding 10 out of 11 men. He, however, did not stop to learn the result of his fire. (Spence, page 219.)

There are many references to McNairy in the Official Records. He was said to have been a third lieutenant in Cross's company, but there is also record he was third lieutenant in Company B, 20th Infantry. (According to Part 1, "Tennesseans in the Civil War", Company B, 20th Infantry was known as "The Sewanee Rifles" and was formed of men who lived in Davidson County.)

He also appears in Nashville newspapers of the Civil War period:

Nashville Dispatch, Friday, 5 May 1865:
Duval McNairy and eight of his men were captured Wednesday by colored troops on Harpeth River near Northwestern Railroad. Entire gang were shot by negroes we are told.

Nashville Dispatch, 6 May 1865:
Rumor of the capture and execution of McNairy.

Nashville Dispatch, 17 May 1865:
Duvall McNairy surrendered at Franklin.

Nashville Dispatch, 18 May 1865:
McNairy, 8 officers, and 48 men surrendered...arms consisted of 20 inferior guns, some old pistols, and 10 poor horses...not all of his command surrendered; others fearing to risk the terms. Lt. Bracken received them, paroled them, and they are to go to their homes.

Nashville Daily Union, 18 May 1865:
Duval McNairy surrendered to Lt. Bracken, Provost Marshal General, at Franklin...surrender took place at house of Mr. Dean, 30 miles from Franklin...8 officers and 48 men surrendered.

Nashville Dispatch, 11 June 1865:
Louisville Journal...Col. Duval McNairy, Rebel guerrilla leader, who

came in two weeks ago and took oath has returned to his old quarters in vicinity of Columbia and Pulaski, and is busily engaged in reorganizing guerrilla bands. A plea is that the government or some representative promised them that no more Federal raiding parties should traverse that section...Vigorous measures are being taken to bring this guerrilla in.

Nashville Dispatch, 13 June 1865:
William H. NcNairy, father of Col. Duval McNairy, published a card in Sunday's Gazette emphatically denying that his son was re-organizing guerrilla bands.

Nashville Daily Union, 27 June 1865:
Mr. J. Norman of Williamson County was killed by the guerrillas, led by Duvall, a few days ago when at work in the field.

McNairy's activities even made the Northern newspapers. The following comes from the New York Times, 5 October 1864: "Numerous guerrilla bands operating around Athens, Ala.--one of these commanded by Duval McNairy."

***

McNairy's name lived on in Dickson County for many years. The following item was found in Columbia, Tenn., Herald, 8 Dec. 1893:

A Ghost by Daylight

The residents in and around Burn's Post Office in the county of Dickson, are greatly wrought up over the appearance in broad daylight of a mysterious visitor or apparition. The following is a statement made by a Mr. Terrell, who saw the strange spector, and it is reliably vouched for.

"I have visited the haunted spot and seen the ghost. The place where the apparition is most frequently seen is in a sag just beyond the noted McNairy's Cut, about a mile east of Burn's Station on the Nashville, Chattanooga & St. Louis Railroad. It was in the forenoon when I approached the spot, walking quietly, and concealed myself where I could have a good view of the headless mystery, should it materialize.

I had not long to wait until the apparition made its debut to my vision and I know I was not the least excited when I saw the ghost moving along the railroad track about 200 yards distant.

"It did not seem to move with any object in view, nor did it apparently make any progress in its travel, yet it looked to be moving all the time. It was in the form of a large, chuffy man, and it was plainly visible that the object had no head; aside from this it appeared a perfect man.

"Taking my tourist's glasses from my pocket, the headless monster was apparently brought within ten feet of me, as I beheld it moving aimlessly about--a man without a head.

"The bleeding neck appeared as if it had been severed with a sword, while the arteries and veins constantly blubbered and spurted blood-stained foam. I removed the glasses and the ghost was where I first saw it. I turned to flee, but hesitated, and then determined to go to it.

"As I approached, it neither came forward nor retreated, it vanished completely. I returned to my first place and saw it as before. Then several men came up the track, and I heard their story, unmixed with my own, and it corresponded with mine. They had seen the object also.

"I do not believe that any living mortal can explain the presence of the mysterious human body. McNairy Cut has been haunted for years. It was here that, during the late war, the noted bushwhacker, McNairy, committed many bloody deeds. Two trains collided here and the engineer named Johnson was caught between the engines and his body scalded and cut from his lower limbs, and lifted from the roasting pyre, only in time to die, by Dr. Anderson. It was here, also, that an unknown negro was murdered a short while ago.

"I confess I do not believe in ghosts, but it may be that away down in the silent depths of nature where mortality ceases and immortality begins there is a power that reflects back to mother earth the image of deeds that have angered and defied the just-loving God of the universe."

***

WORLD WAR I DEAD

A memorial marker in front of the Dickson County Public Library, 305 Hunt Street, has the following names of those who died during World War I inscribed:

McKinley Adams	Thomas C. Field	Athie Nesbitt
Richard Ashworth	Sam Virgil Goodman	Frank Oakley
Lucian Berry	Ellis Herbison	James Oakley
Lawrence Breeden	Pearlis Hooper	Grover Outlaw
William Luther Browning	Walter T. Hudgins	Philip Pack
Clyde T. Buckner	John Brady Hutton	William E. Peeler
Dorsey Buttrey	Hugh James	Dudley Shawl
James L. Carter	Charles L. Knott	John C. Sheley
William C. Carter	Justin Lyle	Olin D. Stuart
Jeff T. Carter	George K. McCollum	Ulysses Spicer
Samuel J. Clifton	Walter Manley	Aretus Taylor
Sam R. Dunnegan	Roy Martin	George L. Tidwell
Rawleigh Donaldson	William E. Martin	Mark Welch
Zuma England	Elijah Moore	Selkirk Woodard

WORLD WAR II DEAD

Carl Adams	Monroe Field	Oscar Martin
Curtis Adcock	Wesley B. Foster	William T. Miller
Fred W. Ashworth	Howard Franklin	Van J. Mitchell
William N. Baker	Austin Finch	Harry Murrell
Robert Bellar	Allie F. Gentry	James Osburn
James L. Black	John L. Gray	Andy L. Ostrander
Thomas Bone	James E. Hall	Randel Patey
Elmer Bradford	William R. Hood	Daniel C. Petty
Joe H. Brown	Johnny Paul Hood	Horace N. Seel Jr.
Robert E. Boaz	E. W. Hudson	Arnold Sensing
Archie Browning	Nelson Hopson	Benjamin Sensing
Frank Brunet	Woodrow W. Kelly	William E. Sizemore
Allen Buchanan	Dudley B. Lamastus	George Skeggs
Larry L. Burgess	Mike Lamb	Raymond Spahr
Newton Cannon	James D. Lankford	Roy L. Stinson
Charles T. Capps	John M. Larkins	Granville Stokes
Robert E. Daniel	James Y. Lowe	John Hugh Stokes
Nollie Dickson	Delbert G. Luther	Louie E. Story
James W. Edgin	John W. Luther	Clyde M. Taylor
Philip M. Edwards	Cecil R. McElhiney	Joe W. Tuggle
		Leamon Underwood
		Adrain F. Vetters
		Mack Walton

(Note: On some lists of Dickson County World War II dead the name of Landon C. Tidwell is given.)

KOREA

Mack Cavender	Herbert H. McClelland
Jesse Rook Cooksey	Billy Pardue
Robert M. Gerron	William Carlton Long
Clifford A. Llewellyn	

VIETNAM

James C. Alderidge
George W. Coone, Jr.
V. Eugene Davidson
Billy E. Lankford
Jimmy M. Logan

Wm. L. (Sonny) Marlin
Stephen L. Miles
Charles W. Smith
Benjamin S. Underhill
Jack Weaver

***

REVOLUTIONARY WAR SOLDIERS

A marker to Dickson County men, who served in the American Revolution, was dedicated 4 July 1976. The marker is on the courthouse lawn in Charlotte. The inscription reads:

In Memory Of
Soldiers Of The
American Revolution
Buried In Dickson County

Paul Abney, Va.
Gideon Carr, Va.
George Clark, N. C.
Benjamin Darrow, Conn.
George Davidson, S. C.
Joseph Dickson, N. C.
Sgt. Richard Eppes, Va.
Howell Freeman, N. C.
Abraham Hogins, N. C.
Morgan Hood, N. C.
William Hudson, Va.
Aaron James, Pa.
John Larkin, N. C.
John Mabin, N. C.
John Maybourn, S. C.
William Morrison, S. C.
Capt. Richard Napier, Va.
John Nesbitt, S. C.

Robert Nesbitt, S. C.
David Passmore, N. C.
Gustavus Rape, N. C.
John Reynolds, N. C.
William Reynolds, N. C.
Christopher Strong, S. C.
John Tatum, N. C.
William Tatum, N. C.
Charles Thompson, Va.
Edmond Tidwell, S. C.
George Tubb, S. C.
John Turner, N. C.
Isaac Walker, N. C.
Benjamin C. Waters, Va.
Lt. William Wiley, N. C.
Capt. Daniel Williams, N.C.
Ellis Tycer
Bartholomew Smith

Erected By
Gideon Carr Chapter DAR
1976
American Revolution Bicentennial

***

Some other soldiers of the American Revolution known to have lived in Dickson County included:

Charles Gilbert
Alexander Anderson
Williamson Plant
Caleb Mason
John Mitchell
Thomas Petty
John Tubb
Frederick Davis
Benjamin Daniel

VIII

CIRCUIT COURT MISCELLANY

The following genealogical abstracts were taken from circuit court minute books. Some of the entries appear to be really county court minutes but recorded in circuit court. Part of these books had no page numbers and the researcher, wishing to see the original entry, will have to look under the date. Some of the information may appear earlier in this book in the marriage section.

MADDEN, Minerva, versus Ephraim R. Madden, petition for divorce in Feb. 1839; she says he has abandoned her. (Circuit Minute Book A, page 9.)

HAFT, Mary Ann, petition for divorce from Jacob Haft; she charges they were married in 1833 and lived together until 30 May 1835 when Jacob deserted her. He has been gone for two years and has moved to parts unknown. They were married in Dickson County. (Circuit Minute Book A, pages 11, 12.)

FARRAR, Field, deceased; John Montgomery appointed administrator of his estate in 1839. (Circuit Court Minute Book A, page 25.) Jacob Voorhies and wife Margaret sue Martha W. Farrar and other heirs of Field Farrar, deceased. Farrar died Oct. 1836 and left widow Martha, and his heirs Margaret Voorhies, Jane Montgomery, wife of John Montgomery, Charles C. S. Farrar, Matilda Taylor, wife of Nicholas C. Taylor, and Elizabeth Smith, wife of Gray W. Smith. (Circuit Minute Book A, pages 64, 65.) Later Charles C. S. Farrar is found as Christopher C. S. Farrar.

HOUSTON, William, of Charlotte, departed this life in the winter of 1835; his brothers and sisters are his heirs and they are: Patsy Houston, Anne Houston, Isabella Houston, Nelson McClelland and wife Nelly (a sister), John McClelland and his wife Sally (a sister), and Emily and Minervy, infant heirs of Edward Houston, brother, heirs at law of William Houston, Jr., deceased. (Circuit Minute Book A, pages 38-43, Feb. 1839.)

PARKER, Martha, petition for divorce from John Parker, June 1839; she says they were married 1 Jan. 1835 and he stayed until 2d or 3d of August 1836, and has abandoned her over two years and has gone to parts unknown. (Circuit Minute Book A, pages 50, 5a.)

GRYMES, Missoniah, in June 1839 petitions for divorce from William Grymes; they were married Jan. 1822 in Dickson County and lived together until 2 Feb. 1837 when he abandoned her. William has removed to the state of Arkansas as she is informed. (Circuit Minute Book A, pages 51, 52.)

VANHOOK, Ashburn, laborer, charged with gambling on 18 Oct. 1838 at Maysville in Dickson County, entry dated June 1839. (Circuit Minute Book A, page 71.)

WINGATE, William H., a poor person of the county was paid a sum for his support by the county. (Circuit Court Minutes, April 1820, no pagination.)

HADDEN, William B., was paid $15 for keeping Elickim Raymond, a poor person of this county. (Circuit Court Minutes April 1820.)

ETHERIDGE, Willoughby, was appointed guardian of minor children of Phillip Etheridge, deceased, to wit: Sally, Nathan, Jackson, and Nancy Etheridge. He was also appointed administrator of the estate. (Dickson Circuit Court Minutes July 1820.)

ETHERIDGE, James, minor orphan of Philip Etheridge, deceased, to be bound until he is 21 years of age to Nathan Nesbit, Esquire. (Dickson Circuit Court Minutes July 1820.)

GIFFIN, William, deceased. On 5 April 1820, Samuel Nesbitt and wife sue the heirs of William Giffin for partition of 400 acres on which he lived at his death. Elinor Giffin petitions for her dower as the widow of William Giffin, deceased July 1820. John Giffin was appointed administrator of estate October 1820. (All from 1820 circuit minutes, no pagination.)

LUKROY, Isaac, sues Nelson McClelland and wife for slander on 5 April 1820. (Dickson Circuit Minutes April 1820.)

READ, William, deceased. On 2 Oct. 1820 the court ordered division of his estate and guardian to be appointed for his minor children. His widow Rebecca was to receive $25 for each of her five children. (Dickson Circuit Minutes, Oct. 1820.)

McMURRY, William, was appointed guardian of Sally and Washington McMurry, minor orphans. Robert McMurry was appointed guardian of Polly McMurry, minor orphan; James McMurry was appointed guardian of Sinthey McMurry, minor orphan. All entries were dated 2 Oct. 1820. (Circuit Minutes, Oct. 1820.)

BAKER, Richmond, was appointed guardian of Absalom Baker, minor child of Benjamin Baker, deceased, July 1820. (Circuit Minutes, July 1820.)

KING, William, minor, was ordered to be bound to C. Baughman July 1820. (Circuit Minutes, July 1820.)

WINGATE, William H., a poor person; court ordered for his support to be paid again. 2 Oct. 1820. (Circuit Minutes, 2 Oct. 1820.)

HUNTER, Joseph, appointed guardian of Susannah Hunter, minor child of Joseph Hunter. July 1818. (Circuit Minutes, July 1818.)

PARRISH, Eleanor, to be administrator of John H. Archer, deceased, in place of Eli Hubbard, deceased, former guardian. (Circuit Minutes July 1818.)

PARKER, Daniel, deceased. Sale of his estate returned to court and settlement ordered to be made with administrator of John McAdoo, deceased also. (Circuit Minutes, July 1818.)

DAVIDSON, Joseph, was charged by the state with bastardy on the body of Liddy Lane. He was found guilty and ordered to pay $20 annually for the child. (Circuit Minutes, July 1818.)

DOUGLAS, James, was appointed guardian of Teracy Bedford, minor of Benjamin Bedford, deceased. Clarke Spencer was the former guardian. (Circuit Minutes, July 1818.)

WRIGHT, George, deceased, court orders settlement to be made with his administrator, John Wright. (Circuit Minutes Oct. 1818.)

READ, William, deceased, court orders settlement to be made with his administrator, James Read. (Circuit Minutes Oct. 1818.)

JONES, William, deceased, court orders settlement to be made with his administrator. (Circuit Minutes Oct. 1818.)

TOMPKINS, Silas, was granted $10 for keeping his son, a poor person of this county. (Circuit Minutes Oct. 1818.)

STEWART, Alena, appointed administrator of estate of Peter B. Stewart, deceased. (Circuit Minutes Oct. 1818.)

TAYLOR, James, appointed administrator of estate of Edward Taylor, deceased. (Circuit Minutes July 1819.)

TIDWELL, Edmond, appointed guardian of Richard Tidwell. (Circuit Minutes, July 1819.)

PARKER, Daniel, gave his bond as administrator of Levin Dickson, deceased. (Circuit Minutes July 1819.)

WALKER, Sally, gave bond for support of a bastard child called Jerusha, begotten on her body by Oliver Vincent. (Circuit Minutes July 1819.)

LUCAS, John, appointed guardian to minor children of William Sugg, deceased: Noah, Josiah, Sally, Howell, Mary and Aquilla Sugg. (Circuit Minutes July 1819.)

BURTON, Ambrose H., Joseph J. Eason, and James Gunn were given license by the court to keep ordinaries at their dwelling houses. (Circuit Minutes July 1819.)

NAPIER, Elias W., charged with bastardy; fathered a child on body of Betsy Shelton. (Circuit Minutes July 1819.)

FUSSELL, John, charged with bastardy; fathered child on body of Lucinda Swinney. He gave bond for the support of the child. (Circuit Minutes July 1819.)

BLOUNT, Margaret, was charged by the court with bringing into the world a bastard child. (Circuit Minutes July 1819.)

JOSLIN, John, was placed under peace warrant to keep peace toward his wife Rebecca. (Circuit Minutes July 1819.)

RHOADS, James, charged with fathering a bastard child on the body of Nancy Acuff. (Circuit Minutes July 1819.)

TAYLOR, Edward, deceased; year's provision for widow and family of Edward Taylor allowed. (Circuit Minutes Oct. 1819.)

JAMES, William, deceased; settlement made with his administrators. (Circuit Minutes Oct. 1819.)

ROEBUCK, John; settlement made with administrator. (Circuit Minutes Oct. 1819.)

STAFFORD, Cealy, late widow of Edward Smith, deceased; court orders an examination of Cealy Stafford about land sold to Minor Bibb, Esquire. (Circuit Minutes Oct. 1819.)

ROGERS, James, appointed administrator of estate of Lewis Berry, deceased. (Circuit Minutes Oct. 1819.)

LARKINS, James, appointed guardian of John, Sally, and Matilda Daniel, and Betsy Hall, minor orphans. (Circuit Minutes Oct. 1819.)

BOOKER, Levicy, and Joseph Easom give bond about a bastard child which she has and which she refuses to declare. (Circuit Minutes Oct. 1819.)

IRBY, Pleasant, petitions court as one of the heirs of Aaron Lambert, deceased, for distributee share of estate. (Circuit Minutes Oct. 1819.)

KING, James, deceased; allowance made for his widow and family. (Circuit Minutes Oct. 1819.)

WALKER, Joseph, a poor person; court makes an allowance for his support. (Circuit Minutes Jan. 1820.)

TOMPKINS, Silas, has a son who is a poor person and court makes an allowance for his support. (Circuit Minutes Jan. 1820)

FRANCIS, Matthew, a poor person; court makes an allowance for his support. (Circuit Minutes Jan. 1820.)

WEST, William B., deceased, year's provision made for his widow and family. (Circuit Jan. 1820.)

EVINS, Lewis, deceased, year's provision made for widow and family. (Circuit Minutes Jan. 1820.)

DOUGLAS, James, makes report as guardian of Terasy Bedford. (Circuit Minutes Jan. 1820.)

LAMBERT, Aaron, deceased, division of his estate ordered to be filed. (Circuit Minutes Jan. 1820.)

EVINS, Peggy, is one of the administrators of Lewis Evans, deceased. (Circuit Minutes Jan. 1820.)

EVINS, George, is appointed guardian of William Doty, minor orphan of Robert Doty, deceased. (Circuit Minutes Jan. 1820.)

HARDY, Nehemiah, appointed guardian of Abraham, John, Jane, Polly and Nancy Howard, minor orphans of Richard Howard, deceased. (Circuit Minutes Jan. 1820.)

NIMO, Allen C., charged with fathering bastard on body of Elizabeth Butler. (Circuit Minutes Jan. 1820.)

BRIGHAM, Louisa, sues Elizabeth David L. for debt. (Circuit Minutes Jan. 1820.)

PEARSALL, Benjamin, appointed by court to settle with West Woods, the administrator of Elisha Smith, deceased. (Circuit Minutes 3 July 1820.)

WALLACE, David, settlement to be made with administrators of his estate. (Circuit Minutes 3 July 1820.)

SAUNDERSON, Jacob, vs Nancy Sullivan and Elisha Sullivan; petition for distributee share. (Circuit Minutes 7 July 1820.)

HIGHTOWER, William, deceased; court order to sell negroes belonging to the estate. (Circuit Minutes 2 Oct. 1820.)

TAYLOR, Edward, deceased; court orders a year's provision for his widow and family. (Circuit Minutes 2 Oct. 1820.)

KIRK, Young, paid $60 by court for keeping James Bradford, a poor person. (Circuit Minutes 2 Oct. 1820.)

GRIMMITT, Benjamin, appointed constable in Dickson County with Cuthbert Hudson and Stuart Pipkin as his sureties. (Circuit Minutes 2 Oct. 1820.)

ROBERTS, Dempsey, deceased; settlement made with his administrator, David Passmore. (Circuit Minutes 2 Oct. 1820.)

HIGHTOWER, William, appointed guardian of Martha and Polly Hightower, minor orphans. (Circuit Minutes 2 Oct. 1820.)

SELF, Samuel, ordered by court to administer on the credits of John Parrot. (Circuit Minutes Oct. 1820.)

BAKER, John A., last will and testament brought to court and proved on oaths of John Wright, George Brazeal and James McKee. (Circuit Minutes Oct. 1820.)

DUNIGAN, Charles, appointed to be administrator of James Dunigan. (Circuit Minutes Oct. 1820.)

HUDSON, Cuthbert, guardian of minor heirs of Moses Smith, deceased, sues Jesse Russell. (Circuit Minutes Oct. 1820.)

ROGERS, Elizabeth, administratrix of Robert Rogers, settlement made with her. (Circuit Minutes Jan. 1821.)

WILLIAMS, Garland, appointed administrator of goods and chattels of Alexander McDaniel. (Circuit Minutes Jan. 1821.)

PARROTT, John, deceased; provision for his widow and family was ordered by the court and the commissioners made their report. (Circuit Minutes Jan. 1821.)

PARNELL, John, a minor, bound to Robert Livingston to learn the hatting business. (Circuit Minutes Jan. 1821.)

HIGHTOWER, William, deceased; settled with his administrators George Hightower and Kitty Hightower. (Circuit Minutes April 1821.)

PAYNE, Pryor, a poor person, was allowed $90 by the court for support. (Circuit Minutes April 1821.)

RUMAN, Eliakiam, a poor person of county, and Labeus Richardson was allowed $30 for her support. (Circuit Minutes April 1821. Her name is in question.)

HUDSON, William, deceased; his will brought to court and Thomas Hudson qualified as the executor. (Circuit Minutes April 1821.)

ADAMS, Howell, deceased, administrator of his estate is allowed to sell personal property. (Circuit Minutes April 1821)

SMITH, Elisha, deceased; settlement was made with West Wood, administrator. (Circuit Minutes April 1821.)

WEST, Elizabeth, widow of William U. West; court orders her dower to be laid off. (Circuit Minutes April 1821.)

SMITH, Ezkil, departed this life in Dickson County about 1837, leaving Nancy (now married to Thomas C. Hale), Tennessee (now married to James D. Breckenridge), Frances, Newton, and Jasper Smith, his children and heirs; Frances, Newton, and Jasper are minors; ex parte of Thomas C. Hale and others, heirs at law of Ezekil Smith, deceased, Feb. 1849. (Dickson Circuit Minutes, Volume A, page 279.)

SCHMITTOU, Lavinia, versus Francis F. V. Schmittou, petition for divorce; they were married in 1844 and lived together 3½ months and he abandoned her. She is now dependent on the charity of her father. Filed Feb. 1849. (Circuit Minutes, Volume A, page 268.)

IX

DICKSON COUNTY GAZETTEER

The following will be a listing of towns, villages, and post offices found while doing research on Dickson County. Although this list will be far from complete, as there are many places "lost" in a county's history, this is a fairly complete list.

PLACES

ABIFF
This community is in the southeastern part of the county near the Hickman County line. A post office was established here in Feb. 1886 and Andrew Black was the postmaster. The railroad stop at this place was known as Brown's Station on the N&T Railroad. The post office has been discontinued. Mrs. Bruce Tatum of Lyles, Tenn., said she heard the unusual name came from a proposed fistfight--"I'm going to give him a biff".

ACORN HILL
This community is the area around Acorn Hill Church of Christ on the Jones Creek Road off Highway 70. Once there was an Acorn Hill School.

ADAMS CROSS ROADS
At one time there was a post office at this place, located on the Yellow Creek Road where the Edgewood road intersects, near old Danielsville.

ADENBURGH
This place was a post office in Dickson County in 1880. The location today is not known to the compiler.

ANTIOCH
This community is about two miles from Vanleer on the Charlotte Road; a church here, said to have burned, is now marked by an old cemetery.

BACKBONE RIDGE
This ridge is 1/2 mile off the Ashland City Highway.

BAKER SPRING, BAKER CAVE SPRING
A tubular spring issuing from the west bank of the East Fork of Piney River, about 300 yards south of the Centerville-Dickson Road, at the foot of the Center Avenue Hill in Dickson. The spring is now owned by the City of Dickson.

BAKER'S WORKS
This name was applied to the area which was the center of the charcoal burning activities, a section producing most of the charcoal used to fire the railroad engines on the line from Memphis to Nashville. It is between Burns and White Bluff, near the back entrance to the Montgomery Bell Park. The name appears as early 1870 when the place was described in the Nashville Republican Banner of 10 Dec. 1870 as being between "Burns and Smeedsville".

BAKER BRANCH
This is a small creek branch off West Piney named for early settlers in the area.

BALTHROP BRANCH
This is a branch of Yellow Creek named for early settlers.

BALTHROP HOLLOW
This is a hollow off Garner's Creek, south of Tennessee City.

BARTONS
This was a post office in Dickson County in 1833.

BARK SPRING
The location of this place is not known today. Dickson County Court Mintues for December 1804 indicate that William McMullin lived near Bark Spring.

BARTON'S CREEK
One of the main creeks in Dickson County, Hudson Johnson of North Carolina and Montgomery Bell of Pennsylvania are said to have settled on the creek in the 1790s. Early settlers here during the period between 1800 and 1805 were Col. Richard Napier, Robert Drake, Major John Davidson, Capt. Silmond Edwards, Col. John Nesbitt, Robert Nesbitt, Abraham Caldwell, John Willie, William Willie, William Slayden, and Epps Jackson.

BARTONVILLE
This was a post office in Dickson County in 1890 and C. Pres Wood was the postmaster. (Source, Maury Democrat, 23 Jan. 1890.)

BATSON'S STORE
This was a post office in District 10 in 1886.

BEAR CREEK
There are two creeks of this name in the county. One is located in the southern section and extends into Hickman County. Fraziers, Tuckers, Willeys, Luthers, Hollands, Hoods, and Russells were early settlers here.

The second is Bear Creek of Yellow Creek in the northwest part of the county. Nathan Dillehay, Andrew Smith, James Dickson, John Woods, Huling Robards, and Sam Morris were early settlers here.

BEATTY HOLLOW
This is a hollow off Garner's Creek.

BEAVERDAM CREEK
This creek is in the southeastern part of the county and during the period 1804-1806 the following people settled here: Howell Adams, Elias Lane, Thomas Davidson, Robert Simmons, Reuben Jones, John Stafford, Cuthbert Hudson, and others.

BEECH GROVE
This community existed about Beech Grove School on East Piney. The school was moved to Cedar Hill in 1920.

BEEFRANGE
In the northwest part of county near the Montgomery County line, this place will be mentioned early in Dickson County deeds. Apparently, the area took its name from the cattle turned loose to range here.

BELL HOLLOW
This place is also known as Cloverdale and is on the road leading from Vanleer to Cumberland Furnace. Cloverdale Academy flourished here at one time.

BELL MINE
This mine was on the south side of Bell Hollow, about 3½ miles southwest of Cumberland Furnace. In the spring of 1923 it was operated by Warner Iron Company.

BELLSBURGH
This community is on Highway 49 between Charlotte and the Cumberland River. Mt. Liberty Cumberland Presbyterian Church was organized here in the 1820s and is still an active church. In 1886 there was a post office at this place.

BELLVIEW, BELLEVIEW
On Jones Creek, this is the old name for Rock Church of Christ and was once a powder house or ammunition storage house. Bellview Furnace was built here in 1825 and ran until abandoned in 1834. Named for Montgomery Bell.

BETSYTOWN
On the Cumberland River, this was once a landing for the metal products of the Dickson County iron furnaces. Early records refer to it as Betts' Town or Betts' Landing. In 1899 L. G. Monroe ran a general merchandise store here. (Also found as Betsy Landing.)

BIG ROCK
The location of this place is not known. The Dickson Press of 30 Nov. 1882 described it: "A thriving little place with grist mill, saw mill, cotton gin, and carding factory as well as a corn and flouring mill." From the newspaper item, this place was in Dickson County.

BIG SPRINGS
This is the site of a Cumberland Presbyterian Church and burying ground near Charlotte, near the home of Glen and Betty Loggins in 1982.

BON AIR
Briefly, this was the name of Colesburg in Dickson County.

BON SYLVA
Today this place is known as Pomona. The Dickson Press of 4 Jan. 1883 noted, "The name of Bon Sylva went out with New Year." The name lasted less than a year, as the Dickson Press of 20 April 1882 announced "a new station on N&T Railroad, five miles from Dickson, and the highest station on the road."

BOWMAN'S CAVE
This cave is on the Sulphur Fork of Jones Creek.

BROWN'S STATION
This was a railroad station on N&T Railroad. About 1886 the place became known as Abiff.

BRUCE SPRING
Also known as the Lal Bruce Spring, this place is near West Piney and is about 1 mile off Highway 48.

BUCK SPRING
This is a perennial spring about 1 mile north of White Bluff.

BURNS, BURNS STATION   37029
According to one source this place was known as Grade 42 until about 1886 when it became Burns Station. Others say it was originally known as Halls Station. A Captain Burns was once encamped here and it is said Alfred Andrew McCaslin suggested the name Burns. In 1882 "Station" was dropped from the name according to another. In 1873 there was a post office here and by 1916 the town had a progressive newspaper, 5 merchants, 2 restaurants, 2 boarding houses, 2 sawmills, an ax handle factory, a stave mill, a grist mill, lime kiln, a school and 3 churches. Moses Tidwell is credited with building the town by some as he began building houses here shortly after the railroad was built by the Federal troops during the Civil War.

BUSHES MEAT HOUSE
The earliest deeds of Dickson County have several references to this place. Today its location is not known. It was somewhere on Piney.

CAVE MILLS
Ruskin Cave on Yellow Creek was once known as this.

CAVE SPRING
There are at least two places called this in Dickson County. One is off Big Barton's Creek near the Montgomery County line. Another is 3½ miles east of Slayden.

CEDAR CREEK
The early settlers along this creek during the period 1802-1804 were James Simmons, Joseph Manning, Thomas Jones, Capt. Matthew Gilmore, George Davidson, William Taylor, all from the Carolinas. Thomas Gray and William Parker of Kentucky also settled here. The first church

erected in Dickson County was built by the Primitive Baptists near the mouth of Cedar Creek in 1804 and the Rev. John Turner was the first minister.

CARROLL FURNACE
This iron furnace was on Barton's Creek, north of Charlotte and 4 miles south of Cumberland Furnace. It was rebuilt in 1853.

CEDAR HILL
This community took its name from an old school and was just off Highway 48. Possum Hollow is near here.

CENTER POINT
This community is said to have been near Slayden. No further information available.

CHARLOTTE   37036
Charlotte is the county seat of Dickson County. From early deeds it appears that the name Charlottesville was considered first, but the name was changed to Charlotte, being named for Charlotte Robertson of Nashville.

An old manuscript in the Tennessee State Library and Archives, one predating the Goodspeed's history of the county, has the following information about Charlotte: "First house was built by William Peacock in the west part of town, house built 1804, burned in 1850s; next house stood on southwest corner of public square and built in 1804 by John H. Hyde, built of logs.

"By 1815 Charlotte was a live business town. In 1806 the first store opened by John Spencer; Thomas Parnell was first hatter; Benoni Campbell was furniture and cabinetmaker. Elisha Williams operated the first blacksmith shop, 1805-1806. Early settlers here were William Peacock, Thomas Parnell, Elisha Williams, James Douglas, John H. Hyde, John Reed, Sterling Brewer, Ben Joslin, John Spencer, John Ellis, Marable Stone, Christian Robertson, Frank Ellis. In 1812 a tavern was operated here by Ben Joslin."

Early authorities seem to disagree about the first store in Charlotte as another gives John Holland, and still another John Spencer.

The following has been abstracted from the Dickson County Herald, 29 Sept. 1911: "The first county election held in Dickson County was on the first Thursday in June 1804. August 3, 1804, Robert Dunning, Sterling Brewer, John Davidson, Montgomery Bell, and George Clark were appointed commissioners to fix on the most central and suitable situation for the erection of the courthouse, prison and stock for Dickson County, whose duty it was to purchase 40 acres of land on the most reasonable terms, on some part of which the above buildings were to be erected.

"The commissioners were also authorized to lay off the said 40 acres into a town, to be called Charlotte, and to sell said town lots, and with the proceeds of such sales erect and pay to the courthouse, prison, and stocks, and should the money derived from such sales be insufficient to pay all costs in creating such buildings, the county court was authorized to levy a tax for such purchase.

"In 1808, Charles Stewart donated to Dickson County 50 acres of land for the location of the county site, which that year was surveyed into town lots and the county site being christened Charlotte. The courthouse was completed in 1812 at a cost of $1,100.

"In May 1830 Dickson County was visited by a very destructive hurricane. The courthouse and jail at Charlotte were demolished. The books and papers in the former building were scattered in every direction for miles and many of them entirely destroyed. Several large books were carried by the wind into Cheatham County, and afterward recovered. A man was in the second story of the courthouse when the storm occurred, and was completely buried in the rubbish, but escaped serious injury.

"The roof of the jail was carried 13 miles. Charlotte was damaged by this storm to the extent of about $30,000, and the balance of the county as much more.

"The new building, the same size, on the same location, and almost an exact model of the first courthouse, was rebuilt in 1832. Peter Seals was the first man sent to the penitentiary from Dickson County, being convicted of whipping his wife."

CHICKASAW TRACE
This was an old Indian trail through Dickson County and later the old stage road followed the same path. It crossed Yellow Creek near the place Daniel Williams settled and continued into Humphreys County, crossing Richland Creek. It will be found mentioned in 1803 also in Stewart County deeds, before Humphreys County was formed.

CHILDRESS BRANCH
This was a small branch of Yellow Creek.

CLAYLICK
This community is near White Bluff and is one of the oldest place names in Dickson County, being found in 1802 deeds as the Big Clay Lick.

CLOVERDALE
This was the name of a school operated by the Bell family three miles west of Cumberland Furnace. There was a post office here in 1880.

CLOVER VALLEY
Today the exact location of this place is not known, but in 1833 this was a post office in Dickson County.

COLESBURG, COLESBURGH
A post office was here at least as early as 1880 and by 1882 a Mrs. Moore was the postmaster. Originally the place was called Bon Air. (See Dickson County Press, 20 April 1882.) It has also been known as Gunthersville or Gunklesville briefly. According to the earliest histories, the first businessman here was W. H. Crutcher, who began selling general merchandise in 1863 and by 1879 he built a large building in which he operated a hotel. In 1870 J. C. Donnegan opened a store here but sold it to F. C. Willey. In 1886 J. D. Griffin was a leading merchant at this place.

COLLIER'S BEND
This bend in the Harpeth River, across from Harpeth Valley, is in the northeast part of the county. This name has been in use since at least 1832.

COX SPRING
The Cox family settled here and the spring at this point, now in Dickson, was named for them. At one time a cotton gin, a voting precinct, and a school house were here. Samuel W. Cox, born 1813 in S. C., settled here, today on Hummingbird Lane between Highway 70 and the Jones Creek Road.

CROSS ROADS
Sometimes Adams Cross Roads was known simply as Cross Roads.

CUMBERLAND FURNACE   37051
The village of Cumberland Furnace grew up about the iron furnace operation, first built by General James Robertson about 1793. Cannon balls used by Andrew Jackson's troops at the Battle of New Orleans were molded here under the supervision of Montgomery Bell, who took over the ironworks after Robertson.

About 1820 Anthony W. Vanleer purchased the furnace from Bell and it continued in operation until 15 February 1862 when Fort Donelson in Stewart County fell to the Federal troops. Cumberland Furnace became a temporary refuge for Confederate soldiers retreating before the Union Army's advance.

The furnace became active after the war and continued in operation until 1924 when the low price of iron made it unprofitable. In October 1937 the furnace was reopened and continued for a time.

The Vanleer interests were inherited by Vanleer's granddaughter Florence Kirkman, who married J. P. Drouillard. The Drouillard home still stands on a hill overlooking the town. (Refer also to page 333 of this book.)

The following 1942 clipping was found in one of our family's scrapbooks: "Following a four year shutdown of the historic plant, Cumberland Furnace resumed the manufacture of pig iron Sunday. The age-old iron works is now operated by the Cumberland Iron Company, headed by Roger Caldwell of Nashville, which purchased the plant in 1940 and began preparations months ago to reopen it. The plant is expected to give employment to approximately 250 people."

A second undated clipping is in the scrapbook. It is believed this clipping came from a 1953 paper:

"HILLSIDE SAID TO BE SMOULDERING AT OLD FURNACE SITE.--Old Hillside Furnace located at Cumberland Furnace, believed by the residents of the community to have been retired as an iron furnace over 150 years ago, mysteriously began smoldering underground a week ago and today has scorched vegetation over a wide area.

"The mysterious fire began about a week ago on a line on the property of Albert Phillips and Mrs. Dee Crowell.

"Witnesses said it began a week ago and covered an area the size of a bucket, but that today it was about 30 feet in diameter.

"It is said that a house burned in the stricken area in 1946 and the cause was never determined.

"Mrs. Phillips said she heard an explosion Wednesday of last week in her yard and investigated. That's when she discovered the smouldering hillside at her place.

"Residents are at a loss to explain the mystery, other than to reason the fire was caused from the underground smouldering from the furnace when it was in use 150 years ago.

"Visitors from all over this section have visited the spot during the past few days. One man was said to have been burned while walking across the area. Witnesses said that his shoes were burned...

"The furnace assumed the name of J. P. Drouillard Iron Company when Vanleer's granddaughter, wife of Capt. J. P. Drouillard, inherited the business. It so operated until 1889 when the Southern Iron Co., Nashville, acquired ownership and later it became the property of Joseph Warner of Nashville. He operated it until 1938 when business ceased."

DANIEL, DANIELSVILLE, DANIELTOWN
This community took its name from Jesse Daniels, early merchant here. Located on Yellow Creek, below Ruskin and Jewel Caves, there was a post office here in 1873. (There was also a community called Daniel in White Oak Flats area and G. M. Duke had a store here once. There is an old Daniel Cemetery there today.)

DEADMAN'S CURVE
This curve was in the road between Dickson and Colesburg and received its name from the many wrecks and deaths that happened at this spot.

DENT
This settlement was on the Mineral Branch Railroad. Another says Dent was about 1½ mile below the Mud Cut in Dry Hollow, northeast of Vanleer.

DICKSON   37055
The largest town in Dickson County was first known as Forty-Two because

it was located 42 miles from Nashville by railroad and was named this by the Federal Army who built the Nashville and Northwestern Railroad through here. The name was changed to Sneedville (some say Smeedville), then Dickson Station, and finally Dickson. Until 1973 the official name was the Town of Dickson, but in that year it became the City of Dickson.

The following was found in the Dickson County Herald, 17 March 1911:

"PEN PICTURE OF DICKSON THIRTY YEARS AGO.--Well does the writer remember how Dickson first appeared to him 30 years ago. There was then no side track north of the main line of the railroad, and a little depot was built at the rear of the present Citizens National Bank Building, where the platform ran up to the track.

"There was then a two-story frame hotel building on the vacant lot, now owned by the railroad next to the depot. Our esteemed townsman, J. A. Thomas, conducted a general merchandise business in a one-story frame building.

"While on the lot where Simon's corner building now stands was another saloon. While on the lot where W. A. Self has a grocery store was a frame building occupied by William and Henry Pickett for a store. W.J. Mathis was conducting a store on the old Mathis corner and A. Myatt had his business in the building now occupied by the Dickson Bakery.

"These were the only four stores in Dickson, except a Mr. McWilliams was Postmaster and sold a few drugs, where the Christian Livery stable now stands.

"Public school at that time was taught in the Lutheran Church and there was not a residence within several hundred feet of this building.

"The Centreville Branch Railroad then left the main branch of the N.and C. road about where the Dickson Ice Company now stands, the track ran off southward and in about 150 feet of the Lutheran Church, the road went out through Scuff Town by Willow Spring and struck the present line of the road near Pomona.

"The Southern Methodist Church was on South Main Street on the lot now occupied by the residence of Mr. W. J. Cummins. There was a brick yard just back of where Mr. C. M. Turner's office is now located. There was a log house on the corner of Main and College Streets, which had been occupied by the Federal soldiers during the war.

"There was no manufacturing interest at Dickson except a flouring mill owned and operated by the late Dr. T. F. McCreary, one half mile north of Dickson on the Charlotte road, near where John Woody now lives. There were no buildings then on McCreary Heights, none in West Dickson, none on Rickert Avenue, and none in the vicinity of Dickson College.

"Several years later the public school building then known as the Dickson Academy was erected just back of where Prof. S. E. Hunt now lives and was built jointly by the public school fund and the Masonic Lodge of this place. The Masons using the second floor for their lodge room.

"The first brick store house erected in Dickson was built by Tom and John Coleman and is now occupied by the Anderson Hardware Company.

"Mr. Will Conant published the first paper in Dickson, being the Dickson County Press. After a few months he moved his printing outfit to Charlotte and Mr. Sam Freeman then founded and published the Dickson Democrat.

"The part of Dickson now known as West Dickson was formerly owned by Mrs. Dikeman and was bought by Dr. C. M. Lovell and Mr. W. E. Cullum and laid off in town lots."

Abstracts of the newspaper Dickson Home Enterprise, dated 1893, published by R. H. Hicks, were used in the Dickson County Herald, dated

17 May 1940:

"FORTY-SIX YEARS AGO.--A beautiful pulpit has been placed in the First M. E. Church, the work and donation of Mr. Joseph Heatherinton. It is a handsome piece of workmanship, made of oak, ornamented with walnut panels and speaks much to the credit of the builder."

"Maude, the little daughter of J. T. Moore, is much improved and on the road to recovery...These windy days make it extremely dangerous for female pedestrains on the street...Work on the new railroad bridge has commenced in earnest and will be pushed rapidly...J. N. Hutton and son Comer attended the funeral of Mrs. Zack Drummonds at Waverly last Sunday...R. M. Hicks, junior editor, is vacationing at his grandmother's in the country. His latest advices are that he does not intend to return till fall.

"A K. of P. Lodge was organized here last Friday night and christened the W. A. Hopkins. That it is strong to membership is manifest by the fact that it took all night for each member to get his turn at "riding the goat."

"Born to Mr. and Mrs. J. B. Ballard on North Main Street, April 8, 1893, a son.

"We erred last week in the birth notice that a daughter was born to Mr. and Mrs. Portwood. Mr. Portwood informs us that the girl was a boy. Our treat to Mr. P.

"Mrs. Callie White is visiting her sister, Mrs. Mollie Hicks...The elegant new residence of Judge W. L. Grigsby will be completed the middle of this month and the family will take possession.

"Fresh bread every day at Scott & Wynns...Fresh meat at J. N. Hutton's.. Fine line of jewelry just opened at Henslee & Myatt...E. E. Miller will sell queensware at cost the next ten days...A large quantity of rice has been received by Ankeny & Brown and they are selling it at five cents per pound.

"All delinquent members of the Home Building & Loan are requested to be at a meeting Tuesday night...M. L. McCaul, president; J. L. Ankeny, secretary.

"Have a full line of coffins and trimmings and solicit orders from the citizens of Dickson and surrounding territory--J. Davis & Son, undertaker."

And from the Dickson County Herald, 17 November 1911:

"LAST EVIDENCE OF THIRTY YEARS AGO REMOVED.--One of the old landmarks of Dickson, the house of Aunt Dona Swanson, colored, on Church Street was torn down last week by the owner Dr. L. D. Wright.

"This marks the passing of the last evidence of Dickson 30 years ago. The old house which Aunt Dona, with her deceased husband, Uncle Jeff Swanson, have occupied for over 35 years, was built during the war, and at the time of its building there was no residence in Dickson east of Main Street, and there were only a few houses in town. When built, it was in the midst of the woods and for several winters Uncle Jeff cut the wood from trees within a few feet of his home.

"The building that stood in front of Aunt Dona's residence, which was also torn down, was the old calaboose, or jail, used by the corporation from 1870 to 1875. The house erected with lumber, three to four inches thick, was substantial enough to hold the strongest man safely between the walls.

"A proposition is now on foot for the Methodist Episcopal Church to buy the now vacant lot from Dr. Wright and build a handsome two story parsonage building on same."

DONEGAN'S CROSS ROADS
Just off Highway 70, this place is located near Dickson.

DONEGAN CROSSING
This was a railroad crossing on the NC&StL railroad, west of Pond.

DONEGAN SPRING
A spring located on Coon Creek of West Piney.

DRY HOLLOW
Dry Hollow branch is a branch of Furnace Creek. Some iron ore was once mined here and the road and branch run between Cumberland Furnace and Vanleer.

DULL
This place was once a post office and named for Ira Dull, who ran a saw-mill on Jones Creek. This place still has an identity and is out from Charlotte on the Ashland City Highway.

DUNN'S CHAPEL
This community grew up around a church. (See church section.)

EASTSIDE
Eastside is a community out from Burns on Highway 96. Once a school was located here.

EAST FORKS
This community in 1939 was near the Dickson-Montgomery County line.

EDGEWOOD
This community on Yellow Creek grew up about Edgewood Normal College, established here in 1885, disbanded in 1897. Lots were sold here in 1898 when it was believed a town might develop. (See Dickson County Press, 24 Nov. 1898.) For many years reunions of former students were held. In 1937 Alfred Hatcher was president of the alumni. (Dickson County Herald, 6 August 1937.)

EDNEY SWITCH
This railroad switch was on the Centerville Branch Railroad. The name first appears in the Hickman Pioneer, 20 Feb. 1885.

EGGVILLE
The location of this community is not known today, but it was active in 1892 newspapers. Not to be confused with an Eggville once a post office in Benton County, Tenn.

ELLIOTT
An area around Elliott School was often known as the Elliott community. The school had been known earlier as Murray School. This place, never more than a school-community, was on Barton's Creek.

ENGLAND BLUFF
This is the name given to a steep hill overlooking a creek branch at Eno.

ENO
Eno is a community that grew up around Eno Methodist Church. When a log church was built here about 1845, the people in the neighborhood brought logs for the church until the preacher shouted, "Enough! Enough!" In the 1880s the county newspapers spelled the name Enoe.

FALL BRANCH COALING
The location is not known. In 1882 it was reported to the local news-paper that a skillet full of gold had been found here.

FATTY BREAD BRANCH
This creek branch is near Stayton and said to be named for the type of bread made using animal fat and other ingredients. Early historians believed the name was a corruption of "batter bread", a bread loved by the Indians. They could not say "Batter bread" correctly and it often

came out "fatty bread" instead.

FAYETTEVILLE
This was an early community in Dickson County and the location cannot be determined today--but it is not to be confused with Fayetteville in Lincoln County. The name first appears in Dickson County records as early as 1805. In 1812 deeds reference is made to this place as where "Robert Weakley now lives." (See Deed Book B, page 62.)

FEW'S CHAPEL
Few's Chapel was an early Methodist Church on Garner's Creek, south of Tennessee City. Today the site is marked by a cemetery. The building, used jointly as a church and school, burned January 1939. Miss Margaret Brown was the last teacher and there were 23 pupils at the time of the fire.

FEWVILLE
This was a post office and store on Garner's Creek, operated by James "Judge" Few (born 1843, died 1930.) The mail was brought from Tennessee City by mule back.

FIELDER SPRING
This spring is on West Piney near the Wells Cemetery.

FORKS OF PINEY
Neighborhood in the area of Piney River, where the river becomes East Piney and West Piney.

FORTY-TWO
This was the first name for the town of Dickson; so named because the site was 42 miles by railroad from Nashville.

FROG POND
No information has been available on this place name, which is in District 15, southeast of Dull.

GALLION HILL
This hill bears the name of Captain George C. Gallion, who died 1853 at the age of 75, and is near Stayton.

GARNERS CREEK
Garners Creek was named for Colonel William Garner. There is disagreement in sources about why it was named for him. The first item comes from the Dickson County Herald, 20 Sept. 1911:

"There is only one instance on record where the life of a white man was taken by the Indians in this county. In 1809 the Indians were on a general raid, destroying much property. One band of them crossed Duck River and came into this county and raided the farm of Col. William Garner, killing him, driving away his stock, and taking his family captive. Garner's Creek took its name from Col. Garner."

The 29 Sept. 1911 issue of the same paper has the following:

"One of the readers of the Herald told us this week that Gen. Garner was drowned in Garner's Creek, instead of being killed by Indians. We cannot vouch for the correctness of either statement, except from history, as all information we may published in regard to the early history of Dickson County is secured by us from history."

GILLEM
Today this place is Tennessee City. The Dickson County Press of 7 Dec. 1882 describes the place: "We are surrounded by almost an unbroken forest, over the hills and faraway, and we get the benefit of the fresh, fragrant breezes that come from the vegetable world. This is the most beautiful place for a town I ever saw. In fact, for symnetery and natural beauties, Gillem is the eldorado of this county!!!"

GLENWYLDE
This community is in northwest Dickson County.

GRAB CREEK
This creek is southeast of Dickson.

GRASSY SPRINGS
No reliable information on this place has been available. It was a community around a Primitive Baptist Church, believed to be near or at Burns.

GREEN VALLEY
Green Valley was once a voting precinct on Yellow Creek in Dickson County about two or three miles above Jackson Forge. Living here in 1844 were W. S. Fentress, W. B. Young, W. E. Ellis, William A. Woody, H. McClurkan, and T. R. Gorin. (Source: Clarksville Jeffersonian, 3 August 1844.)

GREAT CAVE
Early deeds refer to the Great Cave, first name of Ruskin Cave.

GREENWOOD
Greenwood Methodist Church is on the Ashland City Highway out from Charlotte and the neighborhood is known as Greenwood from the church.

GRIFFIN TOWN
No reliable information on this place was available.

GRIMES ORE BANKS
This place was located near the headwaters of the east fork of Yellow Creek and Rainy Camp Creek, three miles northwest of Slayden. Ore obtained here was sent to Sailors Rest Furnace in Montgomery County. The Carroll Ore Banks were about one mile away.

GRYMES
In 1844 this was a voting precinct in Dickson County and noted for its political gatherings. The location is not known today. (Source: Clarksville Jeffersonian, 1 June 1844.)

GUNTHERSVILLE
Colesburg was once known as Gunthersville after an early settled, Mr. Gunther, about 1888. When a coal chute was built here later, the name was changed to Colesburg. (Source: Information supplied in Sept. 1971 by Leslie Nelson of California to Miss Lula Belle Hopkins.)

HAISLIP'S IRON WORKS, HASLIP'S IRON WORKS
The location of this place cannot be determined. Possibly it was the name of a furnace known by another name. It has been found mentioned as early as 1818. In 1820 a William Wall lived near this place.

HALL STATION
This was at one time the name for Burns.

HAMBLE
Hamble is a community in the north part of Dickson County. This was onetime a school-community.

HARPETH RIVER
This river originates in Rutherford County, flows through Williamson, Davidson, Cheatham and Dickson counties, empties into the Cumberland River below Ashland City. In 1763 the river was known as Fish Creek. Harpeth River is also a community name in Dickson County.

HARRIS HOLLOW
Neighborhood in the Sweet Home section of Dickson County named for an early family here. Sometimes called Lick Skillet.

HAZEL RIDGE
The location of this place cannot be determined. This was a post office in District 2 in 1886.

HEATH
This was a post office on Johnson Creek. In 1891 Lon M. Sensing was

the postmaster.

HELL'S HALF ACRE
A limestone cave near Fatty Bread Branch, near Slayden, once furnished water for whiskey making. People opposed to the whiskey industry named the place "Hell's Half Acre".

HICKORY GROVE
This was a school-community on the East Piney Road.

HILLCREST
Once a school, now a community, this place is off Highway 48.

HILLMAN'S LANDING
From old newspapers this appears to be another name for Betsytown.

HORTENSE
This was a village set up under the W. B. Leech Colonization group. William Mallory, colored, age 70, who died Dec. 1939, was one of the early settlers here. He joined the Hortense Baptist Church in 1895. (Source, Dickson County Herald, 12 Jan. 1940.) The town was dedicated 26 April 1913 and the first settlers were E. W. Washington, Dick Long, James Dickerson, and Foster Washington. The town was "organized by J. B. Mullins of Nashville two years ago for colored inhabitants." (From Nashville Banner, 25 April 1913.) The town was on the Mineral Branch railroad.

HORTENSE MINES
These mines were about one mile southeast of Hortense and considerable mining was done here at one time. Ore was obtained at intervals from 1879 but no important scale of mining was done until 1915. The mines operated until World War I, but were idle after 1920. Ore mined here was sent to Helen Furnace in Montgomery County. A spur track was built here and extended for a mile to a washer.

HUTTON'S CHAPEL
(Also found as Hutton's Station in 1864) The site of this place is marked only by a cemetery today and is two miles east of White Bluff on Highway 70. It was named for the Rev. H. M. Hutton, born 1793, died 1873. In 1883 a school was taught here by Miss Eunice Hutton. (Source: Dickson County Press, 28 June 1883.)

INDEPENDENCE
This post office in Dickson County was in operation until at least 1873, but the location is not known. The following item appeared in the Nashville Daily Gazette, 7 Oct. 1852: "Independence is a new post office established in Dickson County with T. Hayden as postmaster."

OLD INDIAN TOWN
This was on Yellow Creek and mentioned in the Dickson County deeds as early as 1810. The correct location was not available.

IRON HILL
The Hickman County Pioneer, 19 Nov. 1886: "A new works opened in Dickson County; vast quantities of ore in these lands." This was also a station on the Centerville Branch railroad and an iron ore washer here used ore obtained from Nails Creek mining. Even in 1982 the fields in this area are almost as red as blood from the iron ore still in the soil.

JACKSON CHAPEL
This is the area around Jackson Chapel Methodist Church, about 8 miles from Charlotte on Highway 49. The Reverend Judge Jackson was a leading citizen here about the time of the Civil War. The Duke family also settled here early as Denver Duke and his wife Abigail House came here in 1832 from North Carolina.

JASON CHAPEL
This is the area south of Tennessee City and took its name for a church and school. Named for Jason Brooks the first minister of a Methodist Church once here.

JEWEL CAVE
First known as Rogers Cave, this cave was discovered 1885 when Thomas Rogers and daughter Fannie Crawford crawled in the opening. It was also known as Stalactite Cave. (Source: Dickson County Herald, 18 Oct. 1937.) The Hickman Pioneer, issue of 22 Aug. 1886, reported this to its readers: "A large cave has been discovered on Yellow Creek in Dickson County at T. Rodger's spring."

JOHNSON CREEK
Early settlers along this creek were George Tubb of South Carolina, Charles Teal of Maryland and William Ward of Virginia. Hugh Nichols got 75 acres here quite early, land adjoining George Teale Sr.'s land. William B. Ross recorded his land here in 1812.

JONES CREEK
This is one of the major creeks in Dickson County. In the period 1801-1803, John and James Larkins, George Clark, William Cox, William Stone, Batholomew Smith, James Douglass, Christopher Strong, all from North Carolina, settled here. Goodspeed's history gives the following as early settlers: Reece Bowen, Molten Dickson, James Martin, James Steel, Eleazer Smith, from North Carolina; Robert Harper from Ireland; John Larkins and Field Farrar from South Carolina; Gabe Joslin from Nashville. William Stone ran a mill here as early as 1804. His grandson Mumford Smith is buried on Jones Creek near Acorn Hill Church.

When John Craig got land in District 1 on Jones Creek in 1810, his land ran "north from a pen built by one Rogers for the purpose of catching wild horses." (Tennessee Land Grants, Book E, page 17, Tennessee State Library and Archives.)

JONES CROSS ROADS
This location of this place is not known. This was a voting precinct and political meeting ground in the county in 1844. (Source: Clarksville Jeffersonian, 1 June 1844.)

LARKINS
This was a post office in Dickson County in District 3 in 1886.

LAUREL FURNACE
This furnace was originally built 1815 and rebuilt in 1854. It was owned and operated by Epps Jackson. The furnace grounds served as a muster field for Civil War soldiers. After the furnace was abandoned, a camp meeting pulpit was erected in the runout. Pig iron made here is said to have won first prize at an exposition in London in 1851. The site of this furnace is now in Montgomery Bell Park. A post office was here as early as 1833.

The following sketch was found in the Dickson County Herald, 23 June 1911:

"SOME INTERESTING FACTS.--One of the Herald's readers, Mr. John Jackson, who lives about six miles northeast of Dickson, was in town a few days ago and told us on the best authority that the negro whom we mentioned in a sketch on the history of the iron industry of Dickson County, as jumping into a burning furnace to escape a whipping at Cumberland Furnace, prior to the war, was the father of old Uncle Jeff Swanson, who is well remembered by many of the old citizens of Dickson. Uncle Jeff was the husband of Aunt Dona, who now lives near the Methodist Episcopal Church.

"Mr. Jackson had with him a large sample of very fine iron ore, which he had brought from the old ore mine, near his home where Laurel Furnace was operated by his father, Mr. Epps Jackson, before the Civil War.

"Mr. Epps Jackson was buried about 50 years ago, near Laurel Furnace, and the tombstone at his grave is both a wonder and work of art. The gravestone is of the kind most generally in use 50 years ago. It covers the entire grave, is about 8 feet long, 4 feet wide, and 4 feet high, on the top is a very fine specimen of superior carving, showing an old-fashioned hillside charcoal furnace, and as perfect and as well preserved as when last under the sculptor's chisel a half century ago. In a stone's throw of old Laurel Furnace site and the grave of Mr. Jackson is the spot where the Cumberland Presbyterian Church was first organized over a century ago."

The earlier sketch mentioned in the above account was in the Dickson County Herald, 9 June 1911:

"THE FIRST FURNACE IN MIDDLE TENNESSEE.--Before Tennessee was admitted as a state into the union, Dickson County was widely known as a great producer of iron. The first furnace built in Middle Tennessee was erected in Dickson County in 1793 by Gen. James Robertson, at or near the present site of Cumberland Furnace.

"Gen. Robertson was the same man who founded Nashville. After operating the furnace for several years, Gen. Robertson sold the property to Montgomery Bell. Cumberland Furnace is situated on Barton's Creek in the 8th district of the county and has been operated almost continuously since its erection 118 years ago.

"It is claimed that all the cannon balls used by General Jackson at the great battle of New Orleans where he defeated the English, were cast by slave labor at Cumberland Furnace and shipped in keel-boats down the river.

"For nearly 100 years prior to the building of the Mineral Branch railroad all iron made at Cumberland Furnace was hauled in wagons to the Cumberland River, a distance of 8 miles, and loaded on boats at the present landing at Betsy's Town.

"It is told on good authority that one of the negro slaves working at the furnace before the Civil War, to escape a whipping for having disobeyed some trivial order, ran and jumped into the burning furnace and was immediately burned to death.

"Worley Furnace, which was established by Dr. Napier in about 1820, was located about three miles southwest of Dickson and was run in full blast until 1874, when it was closed down until 1880, and was then operated for two more years, since which time it has been abandoned.

"In 1889 the Buffalo Iron Company built a railroad from Pond Switch to old Worley Furnace site, expecting to extensively operate large iron ore banks at that place, but after working some for several months, the mines were abandoned and the railroad track torn up.

"Furnaces were also operated before the Civil War at the following places in the county: Carroll Furnace and Bellview Furnace on Barton's Creek in the 6th district; Piney Furnace on Piney Creek in the 2nd district; Laurel Furnace on Jones Creek; Jackson Furnace on Beaver Dam, in the 4th district. Iron forges were erected at the same time and in conjunction with the furnaces as follows: Turnbull Creek, in the 10th district; Valley and Jones Creek Forge on Jones Creek, in the 6th district; Red House Forge on Jones Creek, and Steam Forge near Cumberland River in the 8th district.

"Both iron ore experts and geologists tell us that Dickson county is possessed with a rich deposit of iron ore almost general throughout the whole county."

LEATHERWOOD CREEK
This is a large creek in the northwest corner of the county, near Slayden. John Reynolds got 68 acres here in 1810 on the Wallace Branch of Leatherwood Creek.

LIMESTONE HOLLOW
This is a well known hollow on Garner's Creek.

MAYSVILLE
This was a post office in 1864 on Yellow Creek.

MARTHA'S CHAPEL
This community is on Highway 49 near the Houston County line and grew up around a Methodist Church here. The church was named for Martha Hinson, who gave the land.

MILLER HILL
Miller Hill is today a neighborhood on Highway 70.

MONTGOMERY BELL PARK
This is a state park, begun in the 1930s, at the site of old Laurel Furnace and the Birthplace of the Cumberland Presbyterian Church.

MOUTH OF HARPETH
This was a post office in Dickson County in 1880.

McFARLAND SPRING
This spring, about 3/4 miles northeast of Dickson, was formerly owned by the railroad. It furnished 150 gallons of water a minute.

McKEE
Today this is Vanleer. The Dickson Press of 21 May 1891 carried the following announcement: "The post office at McKee has been changed to Vanleer."

McNAIRY'S CUT
A cut through the earth along the railroad out from Burns and the place the so-called headless man was once seen.

NAILS CREEK
Nails Creek is a creek in the southern part of the county. In 1805 Reuben and William Shores, Joseph and Ben Nail, and Stewart Pipkins settled here.

NARROWS OF HARPETH
This site is now in Cheatham County, but once was in Dickson County. The following article was in the Nashville Union and American, 2 Aug. 1874:

"Mysterious footprints have been found on wall at Narrows of Harpeth when the late Montgomery Bell, pioneer iron manufacturer in Tennessee, pierced it with two tunnels, the first of which was completed the fourth of July 1818 and celebrated with a great festival and cost $8,000. It was unimproved until 1830 when Mr. Bell built a large forge with four large tilt hammers for making hammered iron about 1830 or 1831 he pierced the second tunnel about 60 yards south of the first; the second tunnel was 16 feet wide, 6 feet high, and cost $6,000. The property was willed to his nephew James Bell. Several human footprints may be seen imbedded in the rock--two pairs of children and one adult." (For those interested in this place, this is a long article in the newspaper and only portions were copied for this entry.)

NEW PORT
Newspaper accounts indicate this is a present day community in Dickson County.

PARDUE
In 1916 this was a community in Dickson County, the location cannot be determined today.

PARKERS CREEK
Early deeds refer to this creek as Parker's Fork of Turnbull Creek. John Parker, Sr., in 1810 received 640 acres on Parker's Fork, bounded by Joseph Vos's west boundary line. Early settlers were James Tidwell, Moses Parker, Isiah Tidwell, and Levin Dickson.

Moses Parker came here in 1804. "and all he had was two horses, a rifle, axe, handsaw, knive, wife, and four children." He was the father of 12 children and his tombstone in the Parker Cemetery reads: "Born 31 Oct. 1778, died 9 August 1852."

Moses Parker and John Parker of Elbert County, Georgia, received a passport in Georgia to "visit the Natchez Country" and they both came to Dickson County. Some family researchers believe Moses Parker was the nephew of Elder John Parker, Primitive Baptist minister. Elder John Parker was later killed in Texas in 1836 by Indians. His granddaughter Cynthia Ann Parker was captured by Indian in 1836 and spent 25 years in captivity; she was 9 years old when captured and married a Comanche Indian. Her son Quanah Parker was the last chief of his tribe.

PAYNE SPRING
This spring was named for Albert B. Payne, who owned 5,000 acres near Worley Furnace called Worley Wilds. He was killed in 1894 when his horse threw him from his buggy against a gatepost. This spring is the source of Dickson's water supply.

PIGEON ROOST
This is a branch or fork of Turnbull Creek and Cuthbert Hudson got land here in 1812.

PINEY RIVER
Sometimes called Piney Creek, originally known as Pine River, and usually referred to as Piney, this stream runs through Dickson County into Hickman County, emptying into Duck River in Hickman County. In 1800-1804 those who settled along the stream were Lawson and Elisha Gunn, Morgan Hood, Abraham Hogan, Thomas Petty, John Dunnagan, Joseph Eason, all from North Carolina. Goodspeed also includes the following as settlers: William Hogins from Virginia, Nicholas and Hutson Dudley, and Thomas Petty from North Carolina.

PINEY FURNACE
Authorities disagree about the location of this iron furnace. One says it was located south of Burns on Beaverdam Creek. A second one says it was on the headwaters of Piney River. The furnace was built 1832.

PLUNDERS CREEK
Only a short distance of the stream is in Dickson County and the creek is mostly identified with Hickman County. Plunder was the name of a settler's dog.

POMONA
In 1883 the village of Bon Sylva became Pomona. This community is on I-40.

POND, POND SWITCH
This was the start of the Mineral Branch railroad, leading into Montgomery County. It was once called Rapid City and Treswell, about 3 miles out from Dickson.

POND SPRING
This spring, formerly used as a water supply for the blast furnace, is one mile southwest of Cumberland Furnace.

PORTER
School-church community settled by John Porter. A school was conducted here in the 1830s.

PROMISED LAND, PROMISE LAND
This is a black settlement out from Charlotte, north of St. Paul's Presbyterian Church.

RAPID CITY
This was once the name for Pond.

RAINY CAMP
The name of a creek and a hollow near Slayden. A Methodist Church was established here in the 1850s. This name is found in some of the earliest deed records in Dickson County, and the creek is a branch of Leatherwood Creek. The old stage road from Clarksville to Waverly ran through this area and the old Franklin Waynick house on the stage road was used as a stage stop.

The following article on some stage coach routes was found in the Dickson County Herald, 21 July 1911:

OLD STAGE COACH ROUTES.--The old stage was a very large, old-fashioned vehicle with very large wheels, made to accommodate from 12 to 15 passengers. Passengers entered the inside of the stage by a door on each side.

One passenger usually sat with the driver, while there was room on top of the stage for the mail and for from four to six passengers. On the back end was a large platform built up from the bottom of leather which was known as the mail boot, which was large enough to hold the mail pouches of that date, and also six or eight trunks.

Stage stands, where the horses were kept and usually a post office, were located about 10 miles apart. The first stage stand out of Nashville was on Robertson's Hill, the second was at Tom Osborne's farm, on Harpeth River, near mouth of Dog Creek, the third at Charlotte, the fourth at Williamsville, on head of Yellow Creek, the fifth at Burl Spicer's store on head of Trace Creek, the sixth at Waverly, and the seventh just across the Tennessee River at Reynoldsburg, conducted by Jim Wiley, who for many years before the war, was the owner and manager of the stage route system.

Four horses were always used to draw the stage, except in winter time, when six and sometimes eight were driven. Horses were driven from one stage stand to the other where they were then quickly unhitched and fresh teams were sent on with the precious load in a gallop.

Mr. A. B. Williams tells us that for many years before the war the stage always left Nashville at 6 o'clock in the morning for the west, arriving at Williamsville, 48 miles distance, at one o'clock, where dinner was always awaiting. The stage from the west was scheduled to arrive in Nashville from Memphis each afternoon at 3:30.

At that time this was the only direct mail route between Nashville and Memphis. From Charlotte to Williamsville was 10 miles, and the time allowed the driver to make this distance was one hour and thirty minutes. In the winter time the roads got very bad, two horses were usually hitched to a vehicle of two wheels, known in that day as the mud box, which only carried the U. S. mail.

The old original stage road route through this county was surveyed and located about 200 years ago, and was at that time the most direct route between the capital of the state and the great cotton market on the bank of the Mississippi.

The pathfinders who recently traversed the three highways between Nashville and Memphis state that the old stage road route is 40 miles shorter than the route by way of Columbia and Lawrenceburg, and is 20 miles nearer than the Centerville route.

REDDEN SPRING
This spring is on Fielder Branch of West Piney.

RICHLAND FURNACE
The location of this iron furnace cannot be determined, but was listed in 1835 by Troost as a furnace in operation in Dickson County.

RICKERT'S SPRING
This spring, near Dickson, was once used by the NC&StL Railroad to furnish water to a tank in Dickson for the train engines.

ROBINSON'S CHAPEL
This church-community developed around a Methodist Church, built 1942 as a mission, and named for the Rev. E. U. Robinson, minister of the First Methodist Church in Dickson.

ROCK CHURCH
Church-community which grew up about Rock Church, three miles off

Highway 48. This is the oldest Church of Christ in the county.

ROCK SPRINGS
This is in the northeastern part of Dickson County on the road leading to Bloom Landing on Cumberland River.

RODGERSVILLE
East Dickson was known as Rodgersville or Rogersville in 1908.

ROGERS CAVE
This was the onetime name for Jewel Cave.

RUSKIN CAVE
This large cave on Yellow Creek was once known as the Great Cave and was once the site of a socialist colony and a school. Today it is a tourist attraction.

The following article was found in the Hickman Pioneer, 27 Sept. 1886:

"**Now as** it is just a week until the Baptist Association comes off on Tumbling Creek, it calls my mind back to the association on Yellow Creek in Dickson County 12 months ago, when on my return I had the pleasure of going into the mammoth cave of that creek.

"Near the mouth of the cave is standing a grist mill, which is run by the stream of water proceeding down the bluff from the cave. The entrance of the cave is about 25 yards wide from wall to wall, and some 40 feet to the ceiling overhead; immediately on your left as you go in the young folks have a dancing yard; with a beautiful stream of cold water running along in troughs by which the young man can water his partner by stooping down, handing her a dipper of water, and swinging off again in the dance. I supposed 30 feet long and 15 feet at the widest place, which I was informed was 72 feet down.

"Just back of this was a dirt floor, which was thrown up in little mounds about like there had been some Indians there. But I was informed by a man who lived there that that was where the neighbors had put up potatoes, turnips, apples, etc.

"I passed on gradually ascending until I came where I could reach the rock overhead, which was very smooth, and more names written with pencils, fire coals, and chalk than you could read in two days.

"But I still went on until the rock became so low that I could go no further. The cave still remained its full width or nearly so, it turned to my left and looked very dark and I thought I was about 200 yards in but when I came out and went to the store just by the cave, the storekeeper told me I had been 100 yards instead of 200.

"It was definitely the grandest thing that nature did for Yellow Creek. Signed, "B."

The following article is not dated nor is the author known, but it is believed to have been written by R. A. Freeman for the Dickson County Herald:

"Ruskin was first known as Cave Mills Cave, deriving its name from a large grist mill operated at this time in that section, and cave. This was the only grist mill at this time in that section and citizens brought their "turn of corn and wheat" to be ground to meal and flour, from all around.

"Some coming so far on horseback it took more than a day to make this trip and mail service at that time was by horseback star route, and other post offices of Edgewood, Danielsville, Ellis Mills and other communities down the Yellow Creek Valley. These communities are now served by rural routes out of Dickson, Sylvia, Vanleer, Erin, and Cumberland City.

"In 1896 this property belonging to Tom Rogers, an early settler, together with the adjoining farm lands, was sold to J. A. Wayland and E. W. Dodge and others, who established a Socialist colony and the post office was changed from Cave Mills to Ruskin.

"Quite a number of families moved here from the north and west and joined this colony, which was operated on the Socialistic theory--the managers, storekeepers, office clerks, farmers--in fact, all were to share equally.

"They operated a large commissary, one large kitchen and dining-room and all ate together and of the same food. They operated a large printing plant, publishing a Socialist paper, mailing thousands of copies to all parts of the United States and many foreign countries.

"This arrangement proved satisfactory for only a few years and about the year 1900 a large number of the members became dissatisfied and the colony was disbanded and the property disposed of."

The Tennessee Historical Commission erected a marker to be found on Highway 70 at Tennessee City:

> RUSKIN CAVE
> Near here, in the late 19th Century, disciples of John Ruskin, under J. A. Wayland, established a colony to practice Ruskin's socialistic teachings. In a short while it moved to Ruskin Cave, 8 miles N., where several buildings were erected. The colony soon failed; its buildings were used by a boys' school until 1917.

SALEM
A church-community which developed around a church on Williamson Branch of Yellow Creek. A school was here as early as 1844.

SALMON BRANCH
Today this is in Houston County, but Salmon Branch will be found mentioned many times in early Dickson County records.

SAM HOLLOW
This hollow off Garner's Creek on a road leading to Highway 48 was named for an old colored man who once lived there.

SCOTTSVILLE
According to the Dickson County Press, 19 Nov. 1891, this was the name for Scuff Town in 1891.

SCUFFTOWN
This is now East Dickson and has been known as Scufftown, Scottsville, and Rodgersville.

SIMMONS OLD PLACE
The location of this place cannot be determined today but in 1834 it was a voting place on Yellow Creek. (Source: Central Monitor, 6 Sept. 1834.)

SLAYDEN   37165
This town is located in the northwest part of Dickson County.

SLICK ROCK
The location of this place name is not known, but it is said to be a landmark in Yellow Creek.

SMITHVILLE
Location is not known, but this was a onetime post office in Dickson County and was discontinued by 1833.

SMYRNA
This was the first Methodist Church established in Dickson County, 1810. Today this is the Mount Lebanon neighborhood.

SNEEDSVILLE, SNEEDVILLE, SMEEDVILLE
This was the second name for the town of Dickson, originally known as Forty-Two. There is much disagreement about the name: Sneedsville or Smeedsville, or Sneedville or Smeedville. The earliest time the name was located in print by this researcher was in the newspaper Memphis Daily Avalanche, issue of 2 July 1869: "Sneedsville on the Nashville and Northwestern Railroad contained only a few shanties two years ago, but now has 1500 inhabitants."

SOULE'S CHAPEL
Church-community located on Big Horse Branch of Barton's Creek. A Methodist church was started here in 1830s. This community is now known as Glenwylde.

SPENCER'S MILL
Sam Spencer established a mill on Parker's Creek before the Civil War and it was operated continuously by him until his death in December 1895. Early settlers here were Mose and Jim Tidwell, Sam Hammons, Sam and High Spencer, D. Lankford, John Dillard, Jimmie Fowlkes, George Herron, Dr. Stuart, Rev. Jim Williams, John Jordan, Morg Hogin, Ben and William Brown, Joe Hutcheson, Till Lampley, Sam Bibb, Nathaniel Tomlin (or Tomlinson), and Moses Parker. (Source: manuscript entitled "Settlers of 30 Years Ago", copy in compiler's possession.)

STALACTITE CAVE
This was an early name for Jewel Cave.

STAYTON
The land at Stayton was once owned by the Hughes family. This village is in the 8th Civil District, formerly the 4th District, and the Old Metal Road ran through this place. The road led to Betsytown Landing on the river and large amounts of metal were hauled over the road from the Cumberland Iron Works.

STRINGTOWN
The Sweet Home community has been called this by some residents.

STRONG'S HILL
This is a steep hill near the county poor farm and was named for Christopher Strong, soldier of the American Revolution, who settled here early.

SULPHUR FORK, SULPHUR LICK
This is a fork of Barton's Creek and mentioned early in Dickson County land transactions.

SWAMP
This was a place name in Dickson County in 1892, location unknown. At that time S. Roberts had a store there.

SWEET HOME
This is a community on Barton's Creek and was named for a school once here, according to some authorities. It is between Cumberland Furnace and Charlotte.

SYLVIA   37176
This town is on the old Mineral Branch railroad line--the track has been removed but the road follows the old railroad bed. Settlement began in 1890s and it is about 5 miles west of Charlotte. By 1916 it had 100 inhabitants, a Methodist and Baptist Church, and lumbering was the chief occupation.

TAYLOR'S CROSS ROADS
This place was on the road leading from Sylvia to Vanleer, on the old Mineral Branch railroad line. An old Taylor home and cemetery are still at this place.

TAYLORTOWN
This is a community near White Bluff.

TENNESSEE CITY   37177
This place is 10 miles west of Dickson and was the stopping place for locomotives after the railroad was built during the Civil War. The first name for the place was Gillem, named for Brigadier General Alvan Gillem of the Union Army. The name lasted about 20 years. The Dickson County Press, 7 Dec. 1882, offers this about the place: "We are surrounded by almost an ubroken forest, over the hills and faraway, and we get the benefit of the fresh, fragrant breezes that come from the vegetable world. This is the most beautiful place for a town I ever saw. In fact, for symmetry and natural beauties Gillem is the eldorado of this county!"

THOMPSON CROSS ROADS
Charles Thompson, soldier of the American Revolution, was an early settler on Yellow Creek. The cross roads settlement here was named for him or his family.

TIDWELL SWITCH
This community grew up around the railroad switch on the Centerville Branch railroad.

TRESSWELL
This was a onetime name for Pond Switch.

TURKEY CREEK
This is a large creek in the southern part of the county. Early settlers here in the period 1800-1804 were John Redden, Sam Redden, Isaac Redden, Francis Jones and Nathan Nawls (or Nalls.)

TURNBULL
This was a onetime post office in Dickson County. An annoucement appeared in the Jackson Whig and Tribune, 21 Oct. 1871: "Turnbull is a new post office established in Dickson County."

TURNBULL CREEK
This creek is in the southern part of Dickson County. Early settlers here in the period 1805-1808 were Moses Parker, William White, John Garton, John Pendergrass, Samuel Sellars, Minor Bibb, all from North Carolina. Goodspeed's history gives the following as settlers: John Brown, Edmund Tidwell, Samuel Sellars, Minor Bibb, from South Carolina; Milton Johnson, William and Thomas Gentry and William Pullen from Virginia.

The name is said to have come from the day a party was crossing a deep ford in the creek. One man was riding a bull and was carried downstream and yelled, "Turn, bull. Turn, bull."

UNION HOLLOW
This hollow was named for a church-school and is on Yellow Creek.

VANLEER   37181
Once known as McKee, this town is in the western part of the county on the road leading to Erin. It was at one time on the Mineral Branch railroad line. It was named for the Vanleers, who were pioneers in the iron industry in Dickson County.

VANLEER'S LANDING
This landing was on the Cumberland River and may be the same as Hillmans Landing or Betsytown. Those interested in this place should refer to the Nashville Republican Banner, 5 Jan. 1870, 8 Jan. 1870, 24 Feb. 1871 for further information.)

WEST POINT
The location of this place cannot be determined today. In 1840 this was the place where Robert West lived in Dickson County. (Clarksville Gazette, 20 Feb. 1840.)

WHITE BLUFF, WHITE BLUFFS   37187
The name came from the white, chalk-life bluff on Turnbull Creek and was first called White Bluffs. The railroad called the place White Bluff

and in 1936 at the instigation of J. K. St. Clair, onetime postmaster, the town's official name became White Bluff. It was first incorporated in 1870. This charter lapsed and the town was incorporated 1907 with Ben Myatt as mayor. At that time the town marshall was B. F. Rodgers. Electricity came to the town in 1927 and the first hard surfaced highway, Highway 70, through White Bluff was completed in 1922.

The Farmers and Merchants Bank was organized in 1903. William James School was established in 1923 and named for Colonel William James, who gave the land for the school. He also donated $1,000 to get the school started.

The Highland Summer Club of White Bluff was organized in 1904 by Nashville families, wishing to spend their summers in the fresh air of the White Bluff area.

In 1898 a newspaper, White Bluff Star, was published here. (Abstracted from "Along the Way" by J. B. Worthy, undated clipping in family scrapbook.)

WHITE BLUFF FORGE
The name White Bluff was used first for a forge owned by Dr. Elias W. Napier, who died in 1848.

WHITE OAK FLATS
This is a community on the Ashland City highway out from Charlotte.

WILLIAMSVILLE
This was a onetime post office and stage stop on Yellow Creek, later known as the Coleman Williams place. Apparently, a post office was conducted here at least as early as 1856.

WORLEY FURNACE
This iron furnace, 2½ miles west of Dickson, was built in 1844 or 1847, and rebuilt in 1854. It was built by Montgomery Bell and named for James Worley, the first slave he purchased and his favorite slave. Today no one can give the exact location of the furnace site.

It was an extensive operation as shown in the advertisement for a sale in chancery court: FOR SALE.--To satisfy chancery decree; hot-blast charcoal furnace, store houses, managers and operatives houses, sidetrack, station house, machinery, mules, horses, wagons. (Nashville Republican Banner, 1 Nov. 1870.)

Another advertisement of interest was published in the Clarksville Jeffersonian, 23 Aug. 1845:

"REWARD OF $100.--Eloped from Worley Furnace on the 3d, two light colored men--Tom, age 21, and Joe, age 46. Two white women left the neighborhood at the same time and it is supposed that the boys are in their company. (Signed) Montgomery Bell."

The following historical marker was erected in Cheatham County in regard to Montgomery Bell:

> MONTGOMERY BELL
> Born in Pennsylvania in 1759, he came to Tennessee in 1802 from Lexington, Ky., where he had worked as a hatter and tanner. Here he developed several forges and furnaces. With success, he endowed the school in Nashville bearing his name; he was also a prominent turfman. He died April 1, 1855, and is buried about 3 miles northeast.

WOODS VALLEY
This is a community in the northwest part of the county out from Slayden. It was a post office in 1880. The name first appears in county records in 1820.

WORK SETTLEMENT
In 1884 this was a community in the southern part of Dickson County on Pine River.

YELLOW CREEK
In 1880 this was a post office, but it is believed it was over the line in Houston County.

YELLOW CREEK
A large creek in the western part of the county, one which eventually empties into the Cumberland River.

Early settlers in the period 1802-1804 were John Jordan, Edward Pickett, Jeremiah Nesbitt, Nathan Nesbitt, the Rev. John Turner, the Teas family, Williamson Plant, Charles Thompson, Austin Grissom, Jeremiah Pearsall, Robert West, Parry W. Humphreys, Daniel Williams--all from the Carolinas.

An old manuscript in the Tennessee State Library and Archives states the first school in Dickson County was established on Yellow Creek in 1804 by James Hicks, at the mouth of Bear Creek.

In 1804 Sterling May built a horse mill on Yellow Creek and he also built the first cotton gin in the county.

The first camp ground on Yellow Creek, 1808-1810, was near the Rev. James Goodrich's who with the Rev. Mills and others conducted services.

The Goodspeed list of early settlers contains the following men: George Turner, and John Adams from Virginia, John Lemastus from North Carolina, and Jerry Nesbitt from South Carolina.

In August 1836 there was a disastrous flood along Yellow Creek and its valley.

William Reynolds in 1810 got 103 acres on the Leatherwood Fork of Yellow Creek and his land calls included John's Spring Branch and "above old School House." In 1804 Stephen Murphy lived near the Yellow Creek School.

***

CHURCHES

A complete list of churches in Dickson County has never been compiled. The following will only be some of the churches found during the research for this volume.

ACORN HILL CHURCH OF CHRIST
This church is near White Bluff on the Jones Creek Road, off Highway 70. The present minister if Joe McGaw.

ANTIOCH CHURCH OF CHRIST
No information was available on this church.

ANTIOCH FREEWILL BAPTIST
No information was available on this church. It will be found mentioned in the Dickson County Press, 10 Aug. 1899.

ASSEMBLY OF LITTLE FLOCK PRIMITIVE BAPTIST
This church meets in the old Wynn home on the corner of Scott and High streets in Dickson. Elder E. S. Yates is the current pastor.

BAPTIST CHURCH
In 1812 this church was on the middle fork of Barton's Creek. At this time Drury Christian deeded 1½ acres "to build a meeting house". (Dickson County Deed Book B, page 119.) This may, or may not be, the Barton's Creek Church mentioned in Goodspeed's history in 1886.

BARTON'S CREEK PRIMITIVE BAPTIST CHURCH
The present minister of this church is Jacob Huff.

BEACH GROVE METHODIST CHURCH
This church was on Piney in District 2 and was active in 1886. No further information available. Note: The name was spelled Beach and not Beech.

BEAR CREEK FREEWILL BAPTIST CHURCH
This church is south of I-40 and west off Highway 46. In 1982 Wayne Lankford is the minister. The church, built in the early 1880s, was a Primitive Baptist Church at first. In 1919 the old building was torn down and moved 1/2 mile to a main road. The first service in the new building was in September 1920. By 1940 the older members of the church had died and there were not enough people attending services. In a few years the Freewill Baptists used the church and this congregation has been active since 1963. The church burned one Easter Sunday, but has since been rebuilt.

BETHEL BAPTIST CHURCH
This church was active in 1886 and was on Piney River. No further information available.

BETHEL CUMBERLAND PRESBYTERIAN CHURCH
This church was on Yellow Creek and was erected in the 1830s. It was still active in 1886, but no further information available.

BETHEL METHODIST CHURCH
Bethel Church is on Highway 49 not far from the Dickson-Cheatham lines. A sign at the church says "Built 1897".

BETHANY METHODIST CHURCH
This church was active in 1886 and was on the Harpeth River. Early ministers were the Rev. Michael Berry (who preached 62 consecutive years) James Sizemore, Henry Hutton and Caleb Rucker.

BETHLEHEM CUMBERLAND PRESBYTERIAN CHURCH
Built in the 1830s, this church was on Jones Creek near Burns. The congregation met in the old log school house called Bethlehem and it was known as Bethlehem congregation. In 1896 the Bethlehem congregation moved from Burns to the site of the Birthplace and adopted the name of the McAdoo Memorial Church.

BIBLE MISSIONARY BAPTIST CHURCH
This church is on the Ashland City Road and Donny Hutchenson is the present pastor.

BIG SPRINGS CUMBERLAND PRESBYTERIAN CHURCH
Although this is no longer an active church, the building still stands near Charlotte. The building and adjoining cemetery are still taken care of by relatives, neighbors, and friends.

BOWMANS CHAPEL UNITED METHODIST CHURCH
This church is on the corner of Walnut and Mulbery streets in Dickson and is a black congregation. The present minister is E. E. Buford and the congregation dates back over 90 years.

BOX HOUSE
Goodspeed's history refers to this building on Parkers Creek, circa 1886, and noted it was used by the Methodist Episcopal North and the Missionary Baptist congregations.

BROWN'S CHAPEL CHURCH OF CHRIST
James Allen is the present minister of this church on Porter Road in the Porter Road, Abiff, community.

BROWN'S CHAPEL METHODIST CHURCH
This church was flourishing in 1886 and was in old District 7 on Jones Creek.

BURNS CHURCH OF CHRIST
This building was erected in 1910. No further information available.

BURNS CHURCH OF GOD OF PROPHECY
Weldon Gulledge is the minister of the church in 1982.

BURNS PRIMITIVE BAPTIST CHURCH
The congregation was first known as the Grassy Springs Church and was built in 1808. It was flourishing in 1886. No further information available.

BURNS UNITED METHODIST CHURCH
Itinerant minister and circuit rider Lorenzo Dow is said to be the first Methodist minister to preach in this area, coming in 1820. When a church was started here Mrs. Sarah Davidson and Mr. and Mrs. William Austin, from Albemarle County, Virginia, were prime movers in the organization. The Austins contributed the major financial support to the building of the church and Mrs. Davidson donated the site and all the timber needed in the construction.

By 1850 the church had grown and another location was needed, one that would be more central for the members. The church was moved two miles north of the former location to a grove near Beaverdam Creek. The church became known as Marvin's Chapel. During the Civil War the church was inactive.

As the village of Burns grew, it seemed necessary for the church to be moved again, and this was done in September 1903. Ellis Felts is the present minister.

CALVARY BAPTIST CHURCH
This church is on old Highway 46 at the county line, Bon Aqua. Gene Hopkins is the present minister.

CAMP GROUND
The first camp ground in Dickson County was on Yellow Creek during the period 1808-1810, near the home of Rev. James Goodrich. Goddrich, along with Williams Mills and others, was a leading spirit of this group.

CARTER'S CHAPEL
This was reported to us as both a church and a school, but no further information was available.

CEDAR GROVE UNITED METHODIST CHURCH
This church is on Highway 46 at Vanleer and Tilford Cothain is the present minister.

CEDAR HILL INDEPENDENT MISSIONARY BAPTIST CHURCH
Houston Tidwell is the minister of this church at Vanleer.

CENTRAL CHURCH OF CHRIST
This church is one mile east of Charlotte and David Holder is the present minister.

CHRISTIAN CHURCH
This church organized in 1826 by natives of Dickson County and new citizens brought in by Montgomery Bell was organized in the home o William Talley.

CHURCH OF GOD OF PROPHECY
This church, built 1930, is on the Ashland City Road near Charlotte.

CHURCH OF GOD OF PROPHECY
This church is in Dickson and J. W. Jernigan is the minister.

CHURCH OF GOD OF PROPHECY OF WHITE BLUFF
This church is on Church Street at White Bluff and Rick Brenizer is the minister.

CHURCH OF JESUS CHRIST OF LATTER DAY SAINTS
This church is presently on Hiway 70 East at Dickson.

CHURCH OF CHRIST - WHITE BLUFF
Leonard Owens is the present minister of this congregation on Highway 70 at White Bluff.

CLAYLICK CHURCH OF GOD OF PROPHECY
Lynon Ward is the minister of this church. No further information was available.

CHARLOTTE CUMBERLAND PRESBYTERIAN CHURCH
This church is served by the minister of the Dickson Cumberland Presbyterian Church. The church is about one block from the courthouse in Charlotte and is one of the most historic buildings in the county.

In December 1837 the first Cumberland Presbyterian congregation was formed in Charlotte. There were 40 members and Christopher Dickson was one of the early elders. Miss Sally Walker was among the first to join the church on profession of faith.

Although a fund was started to build a church in 1837, there was not enough money until the mid-1850s when Leonard Lane Leech, Benjamin Corlew and Clark Larkins contributed most of the money necessary for a church to be built.

The following was taken from the Dickson Free Press, 16 May 1973, and was written by an unknown author:

"Bricks were said to have been manufactured within the town limits of Charlotte at a kiln owned by James Dickson. Carpenters were aided by slaves, of which both Leech and Corlew had an ample supply."

The church was still being built when the Civil War began. Following the fall of Fort Donelson early in 1862, Federal troops began appearing in the county and in November 1863 both the courthouse and the church were occupied. The church was used as a hospital.

In 1905 the United States government appropriated $1,800 to the church for the damages suffered during the war.

The church bell bears the name "A. Fulton, Pittsburgh, 1845" and was once the bell on a steamboat the "Sara Blader". "It is said that it can be heard for miles around."

CHARLOTTE METHODIST CHURCH
The year 1834 is given as when the Charlotte Methodist Church had its beginning in Dickson County with John L. Hill as the first minister. The first church was log with split log seats.

In 1877 the church was deeded property by E. E. Larkins. The trustees of the church were D. R. Leech, W. H. Neblett, James Steel, Robert Steel, Thomas Overton, T. H. W. James, and J. M. Bell. A new church was built in 1877 and Richard P. Gannaway was the minister.
During the period when John W. Gilbert was the minister, 1896-1899, the church was extensively remodeled and the building turned around.

In 1974 the Charlotte Church merged with Fagan's Chapel and a new one built between the old Charlotte Church and Fagan's Chapel. The handhewn oak pews from Fagan's Chapel and the pulpit from both churches were put in the new church.

Today the church is known as CHARLOTTE FAGAN'S CHAPEL and J. B. Pennington is the present minister.

COLESBURG CHURCH OF CHRIST
The church at Colesburg was built in 1948 and Dwight Nelson is the present minister.

COLORED CHURCHES
Goodspeed's history notes two colored churches were active in District 12 in 1886--one Baptist and one AME. No further information was available on these churches.

COUNTY LINE CHURCH OF CHRIST
Keith Pruitt is the present minister of this church on old Highway 46 at the Dickson-Hickman line.

CUMBERLAND FURNACE CHURCH OF CHRIST
Sam Brown is the present minister of this church on Highway 48.

CUMBERLAND FURNACE UNITED METHODIST CHURCH
The Rev. Charles Becher is the present minister of this church and also serves churches at Woods Valley, Martha's Chapel, Soule's Chapel, Vanleer.

This church was organized in 1911 by the Rev. W. M. Martin, Mrs. R. B. Stone, and others. There were 35 charter members and they first worshipped in a school near the Episcopal Church. The church building was erected in 1913-1914.

CUMBERLAND PRESBYTERIAN CHAPEL
This chapel in Montgomery Bell Park was built of Crab Orchard stone and was dedicated 18 June 1960. At the dedication Governor Buford Ellington gave greetings and the shrine's key was turned over to the moderator. Chaplains are provided through June, July, and August for services, attended by members from all churches.

CUMBERLAND PRESBYTERIAN CHURCH - BIRTHPLACE
An old manuscript in the Tennessee State Library and Archives, Tennessee Historical Society files, Box D1, No. 54-D, has the following sketch:

"It was in this county that the Cumberland Presbyterian Church had its origin as an independent church. The first step toward an organic form was the constitution of the Cumberland Presbytery by Rev. Messrs. Finis Ewing, Samuel King and Samuel McAdoo, at the house of the latter, seven miles southeast from Charlotte on Jones Creek, 4 Feb. 1810.

"'The old log house,' where these fathers of the church convened to organize the first Presbytery of this flourishing branch of the church militant has passed away; the wide spreading oak under which Mr. McAdoo poured out his soul in secret prayer before proceeding to the formation of the Presbytery, has also disappeared; and the 'family spring,' through neglect, has almost ceased to run; but the influence of that day's proceedings lives on--will live forever!

"...It has now (1880), 1283 ordained ministers; licentiates, 257; candidates, 201; Presbyteries, 110; Synods, 26; General Assembly, 1; and communicants, not less than 125,000. And yet it is but 70 years old!"

CUMBERLAND PRESBYTERIAN CHURCH
A church was built in 1830s on Johnson's Creek, about 5 miles northeast of Charlotte. No further information was available on this church.

DICKSON CHAPEL
Tommy Sesler is minister of this church, now meeting behind a downtown business. No further information available.

DICKSON MISSIONARY BAPTIST CHURCH
This church is at 101 McCreary Street and the Rev. Jack Huchel is the present minister.

DICKSON CUMBERLAND PRESBYTERIAN CHURCH
This church is at 501 West Fifth Street and the Rev. Dean Guye is the present minister. The present building was constructed in 1925.

The church was organized 29 Sept. 1899 in the home of Bettie Sheron and named the Dickson Memorial Church. The following article was printed in the Dickson Free Press, 4 April 1973, quoting an earlier article in the Dickson County Herald, with additional information added by Mrs. Mrs. Annie Lee Williams:

"According to an article in the souvenir edition of the Dickson County

Herald 'issued by the women of Dickson and devoted to the interest of the county' in the early 1900s, the Presbyterian Church in Dickson has had a checkered career.

"The congregation first worshipped in the Cumberland Presbyterian Church on Main Street. When the union question came up and the congregation lost this house, they went to the old U. P. house on Church St., where the residence of Robert Clements stood.

"That house was erected in the 1870s by the U. P. congregation. F. F. Thompson was their first pastor. The mortgage on the house was lifted by the Southern Presbyterians in 1891, when the house was turned over to them.

"For a number of years the Missionary Baptists shared the building with the Southern Presbyterians. The Sunday schools were conducted together but each had its own superintendent and had charge of the school alternately. Each school had its own literature and the Presbyterians went to one end of the building and the Baptists to the other.

"It was into this body of Southern Presbyterians that the U. S. A.'s or C. P.'s were received when they lost their first house of worship. They remained there until Robert Clement purchased the lot.

"The Southern Presbyterians had turned their property over to the U.S.A. and had made their own organization. Then the Congregation bought a lot on Main and Murrell Streets to build a modern building on. They worshipped in Miss Hord's studio over Wynns Brothers store until the building was finished in 1912. Reverend J. W. McDaniel and Reverend T. G. Henry and Reverend W. T. Salman were among the pastors.

"...Founders of the Cumberland Presbyterian Church left the Presbyterian Church over some differences in doctrine and organized a new one.

"Information was further secured from a record book furnished by Miss Lula Belle Hopkins, dated 1899-1929, kept by her mother, Mrs. Laura Knight Hopkins from 1929 until 1946. It is titled 'Session Minutes and Church Register of Dickson Memorial Congregation' and was published by the Cumberland Presbyterian Publishing House in 1897.

"The first minutes, dated Sept. 29, 1899, recorded in the home of Sister Bettie Sheron, stated that Reverend J. F. Lackey organized what was known as the Dickson Memorial Congregation Church. The following were present: Mrs. Bettie Sheron, Mrs. Bettie Heard, Mrs. Bettie Boone, Mrs. Sallie Sizemore, Mrs. Mary F. Buquo, Mrs. Kate W. English, Mrs. Letty Grandy, Miss Mary Agness Buquo, Mr. A. D. English, Mr. R. L. Buquo, Mr. G. W. Buquo, Mr. Tom Heard, Mr. Edward Buquo, Mr. H. C. Buquo, Mr. S. T. Larkins, Mrs. Marvin Jones and Mrs. Jane Clark.

"Mr. English was elected ruling elder and was confirmed by the laying on of hands. Elders Leech and Buquo were elected to attend the Charlotte Presbytery on Oct. 6, 1899.

"On January 6, 1900, the local congregation voted to call Reverend E.L. McWilliams to preach twice a month for $150 a year.

"On July 3, 1900, the elders voted to urge the members of the congregation to give to the causes of the church as God had prospered them. The only record of the August 6, 1900, meeting was 'prayer and praise rendered to God for his guidance and gracious keeping' because a quorum was not present to conduct business.

"Other names that began to appear in the record book were Reverend H. M. Gardner, S. Drane, Mrs. Annie McQuerter, C. H. Leftwich, Edgar Slaughter, D. S. Jett, Mrs. Lula Martin, Reverend W. C. Logan, Mrs. Minnie Neeley, W. T. Richardson, Claude Craig, W. H. Dickson.

"On October 28, 1903, the elders voted to discontinue the building of a memorial church and the presbytery accepted an invitation to meet with the Dickson congregation, then in December, it was agreed to begin building a church in 1904.

"In January 1913 Miss Mary Jett, Miss Lula Belle Hopkins, and Mrs. Monsie Wright were named on the music committee.* In October 1925, Missess Alice Thompson and Lillian Vineyard were nominated deaconesses.

"Miss Hopkins has in her possession a memorial pin, 'Centennial Anniversary, 80th General Assembly Cumberland Presbyterian Church, birthplace Feb. 4, 1810, Dickson, Tennessee, May 19, 1910.' The log building is pictured on the pin.

"Ministers of the Cumberland Church not already mentioned are Reverends J. B. Dwyer, H. H. Binkley, S. A. Sadler, F. T. Arterburn, W. A. Blades, A. W. Clinard, A. D. Sykes, Z. N. Clinard, C. P. Mayhew, M. C. Powers, Carl Davis, Edward Halliburton, Tom Hunter, A. D. Rudolph, Doug Phelps, Cordell Smith, Marvin Wilkins, Joe Snider, Dale Bilbrey, and the present (1973) minister Paul Shepard.

"...In 1907 the USA and Cumberland Presbyterian Church officials assembled and agreed to unite in Dickson. The church property on Main Street was turned over to the USA group and was occupied by the union until 1909 when the courts decided the building belonged to the Cumberland group."

E. E. Littleton (Bill) served as clerk of session for the Dickson Church from 1937 to 1963.

DUNN'S CHAPEL CHURCH OF CHRIST
This church is on Little Barton's Creek near Woods Valley. Shaw Caldwell is the minister.

EASTSIDE BAPTIST CHURCH
This church is between the Spencers Mill Road and Highway 96. The building was once East Side School. In 1982 Jack A. Stone is minister.

EDGEWOOD METHODIST CHURCH
This church on Yellow Creek, about 15 miles northeast of Dickson, is one of the oldest in the county, the area having been served by circuit riders since 1832.

ENO METHODIST CHURCH
The unusual name was given to the church and area when a church was being built in 1845. People brought logs for the building until the preacher shouted, "Enough! Enough!" In 1880 the name was being spelled Enoe in old newspapers. Wayne Epley is the present minister.

EPISCOPAL CHURCH
In 1914 the Episcopalians living in Dickson worshipped in the Presbyterian Church on the corner of Main and Murrell streets. This same year there were missions at McEwen and White Bluff. In the 1960s the Church of the Nativity was located at 306 High Street. In 1978 work was started to restructure the Episcopal Church in Dickson County as one church with two chapels under the title the Church of St. Michael and St. James, with one council and one priest. At that time there were about 80 Episcopalians in Dickson County. (Source: Highland Review, 7 Sept. 1978.) Refer also to the entry on St. James Episcopal Church, Cumberland Furnace.

FAGAN'S CHAPEL (METHODIST)
This church was on Barton's Creek and in 1974 merged with the Charlotte Methodist Church. The old building was sold to Erl and Ann Sensing for

---

*Lula Belle Hopkins is the compiler's aunt and as of spring 1982 she has been pianist (and onetime organist) for the Dickson Church for 76 years. She first began playing at an old pump organ in the church when she was 12 years old and is possibly the oldest continuous member of the church on the rolls.

a residence. The hand hewn oak pews from Fagan's Chapel and the chancel rails from the Charlotte Church and the pulpits from both churches were to be placed in the new church, located halfway between the old Charlotte Church and Fagan's Chapel.

The property for Fagan's Chapel was deeded by W. M. Lane to the trustees James W. Christian, W. H. Neblett, and J. H. Caldwell. The first church was a log structure and was named for Robert L. Fagan, the first minister.

FAIRVIEW BAPTIST CHURCH
Tommy Byrne is the present minister of this church on Nails Creek Road and Highway 46.

FAITH FREEWILL BAPTIST
The congregation of this church began in 1961 and Jay Davidson is the current minister. The building is over 100 years old and at one time this was a Methodist Church and the Colesburg School. The church is at Colesburg.

FEW'S CHAPEL (METHODIST)
This church was on Garner's Creek and the site is marked by an old cemetery today. The building was used jointly as a church and school and burned January 1939. Miss Margaret Brown was the last teacher here and there were 23 pupils at the time of the fire.

FIRST ASSEMBLY OF GOD
James T. Galligan is the minister of this church on Highway 70 West.

FIRST BAPTIST CHURCH, BURNS
Howard Atkins is the present minister of this church.

FIRST BAPTIST CHURCH, CHARLOTTE
Al Ground is the minister of this church.

FIRST BAPTIST CHURCH, DICKSON
Today this church is on the By-Pass, Highway 70 East and Rev. Dr. Don McCoy is the minister with the Rev. Micheal Schwartz in charge of education and music. This church was organized on 28 Feb. 1892 with seven members and was at one time located on the corner of East College and Church streets.

FIRST BAPTIST CHURCH, WHITE BLUFF
This church is on the Taylor Town Road.

FIRST CHRISTIAN CHURCH
Stephen Smith is the minister of this church on Highway 70 East.

FIRST CHURCH OF THE NAZARENE
Henderson Goins is the minister of this church at 103 East End Avenue. The church was started on North Main Street and never finished and built here later.

FIRST FREE WILL BAPTIST CHURCH
Ray Prince is the minister of this church on Highway 96.

FIRST PENTECOSTAL HOLINESS CHURCH
In 1976 this church was at 107 Spring Street, Dickson, and the Rev. Terry Steppee was minister. No further information available as to the present status or location.

FIRST PRESBYTERIAN CHURCH
Woodrow Richardson is the present minister of this church at 212 North Main Street. This building was completed in the spring of 1912 and cost $7,000.

The Cowan families were leaders in the organization of this church. Some of the ministers who have served this congregation have been: T. G. Henry, 1909-1911; J. W. McDaniel, 1911-1916; Herman Goff, 1916-1920; T. G. Henry, 1920-1921; Albert Keller, 1921-1923; Horace Cowan,

1923-1927; M. M. Crow, 1927-1934; R. O. Garden, 1935-1936; Herbert M. Houston, 1936-1941; Morris Hunt, 1941-1946; William H. Chaplin, 1949-1952; Charles Harvey, 1954-1955; Alex Stuart, 1955-1956; Herbert Catlin, 1956-1957; William David, 1957-1958; Robert Nicholson, 1959-1960; Charles G. Hosay, 1960-1961; Milton Wright, 1961-1963.

FIRST UNITED METHODIST CHURCH
Luke Fuqua is the minister of this church at 215 North Main Street in Dickson. The church today is the outgrowth of unification in 1939 of the First Methodist Episcopal and the Main Street Methodist Episcopal Church, South.

In 1867 a group of settlers from Pennsylvania organized a Methodist Church and located it on Church Street, 1½ blocks north of the railroad and this church was in operation until the unification.

The Methodist Episcopal Church, South, organized a church in 1872, located on Main Street two blocks south of the railroad. In 1892 when Dickson Normal College was established, a move was made to a new location near the school and was known as College Hill Methodist Episcopal Church, South. They continued to meet there until 1922 when a new church was built on North Main Street, the present site.

An old picture in our family scrapbook shows the men's class at the Methodist Church on Water Street. Some of the members in 1914 were: Tom Taylor, Joe B. Weems, Rev. John Durrett, W. R. Boute, Verge Miller, A. B. Kelly, W. C. Holt, Dr. W. J. Sugg, Jim Dean, Zorie Sensing, John Gossett, John Brown, H. Newt Williams, Ed Murchison, George Collins, Sr., Cecil Fentress, Tom Collier, John Sheley, L. E. Leech, Horace Self, Hickory Smith, J. A. Clement, George Mullins, J. T. Holley, Graham Robertson, Jack Taylor, Gardner Sensing, Lem Sensing, Marion Hurt, Earl Saeger, Dr. Frank Walker, John Dunn, George Jones.

FLORAL CUMBERLAND PRESBYTERIAN CHURCH
This church, no longer existing, was on Jones Creek near the old Peabody School, on a road that leaves the Ashland City Road near White Oak Flats. This church was torn down or fell down years ago and the lumber was used in the Charlotte Manse. The name of James F. Williams is the only one whose name has been turned in as a member of this church. (Source: The information on this church was given by Dr. Mary Baxter Cook, Mrs. Greer, and Mrs. Leora Lewis to Lula Belle Hopkins in 1982.)

FRIENDSHIP CHURCH OF CHRIST
This church on Fatty Branch was organized 1886 and the land was given by B. W. S. Nicks. Some early members of this church included the Nicks, Phillips, Speights, Stark, Smith, Scott, McCasland, and Monroe families. Early ministers included John, James, Gus, and Jasper Dunn of Murfreesboro.

FRIENDSHIP CHURCH
Old Friendship was on Coon Creek in front of the old Suggs farm and was torn down. It was moved to Eno where another and larger house was built. Later in the day the day the church was torn down Bill Springer was returning home on horseback and was shot, being killed. The man who shot him was sentenced to the penitentiary for life. Springer was killed 17 June 1911.

GILLILAND CHAPEL
No information on this church has been available, only the location is known. Today Oaklawn Cemetery (called in old newspapers the Gilliland Chapel Cemetery) is west of White Bluff, just of Highway 70.

GRACE CHAPEL UNITED PENTECOSTAL CHURCH
Clifford Reynolds is the minister of this church on Furnace Hollow Road.

GREENBRIER METHODIST CHURCH
This church was in operation in 1886 and was on Harpeth Road. No further information was available.

GREENWOOD METHODIST CHURCH
Horace Perkins is the minister of this church on Highway 48 out from Charlotte in District 4 of Dickson County. In 1976 a new church was built across the road from the old church. Originally this was a log church known as Walnut Grove School about 1854. Later a log meeting house was built and stood until 1899 when another was built.

The Rev. J. M. Heath, local preacher, is credited with the establishment of this church. In 1876 he donated land for the church.

HARDSIDE BAPTIST CHURCH
This church, flourishing in 1886, was somewhere on Barton's Creek. No further information was available.

HIGH POINT CHURCH OF CHRIST
Robert L. Manley is the minister of this church on Highway 96, between Dickson and Burns.

HILLVIEW BAPTIST CHURCH
This church is on 70 By-Pass West at Weaver Road and Earl Wilcher is the minister.

HORTENSE BAPTIST CHURCH
This church for blacks was in operation at least as early as 1895.

HUTTON'S CHAPEL
Today a cemetery marks the site of this church, 2 miles east of White Bluff on Highway 70. The church was named for the Rev. Henry M. Hutton, born 1793, died 1873, who is buried here.

INDEPENDENT FUNDAMENTAL MISSIONARY CHURCH
No further information available on this congregation.

JACKSON CHAPEL (METHODIST)
This church and cemetery are 8 miles from Charlotte on Highway 49. The church was active before the Civil War. No further information was available on this church.

JACKSON TEMPLE
This church is near Burns on Highway 96. No further information was available.

JASON CHAPEL (METHODIST)
This church was the first Methodist Church near Tennessee City and was built on Garner's Creek, being named for Jason Brooks, the first minister. It was a log building, built about 1886 and John McElhiney, Ned Fulks, Mr. Turner and others helped build the church.

The first church burned and in 1893 the congregation received 1-1/8 acres on which to build a new church. The land was purchased for $5.62 from W. M. Miller by Ed Moore, B. S. McElhiney and A. M. Gunn. This building was also used as a school. Later the church was torn down and moved further down Garner's Creek and is now being used by the Nazarenes.

JASON CHAPEL CHURCH OF THE NAZARENE
Refer to above entry.

JEHOVAH'S WITNESS
This building is on the corner of Lovell and Walnut streets in West Dickson and was built about 1965.

JOHNSON'S CHAPEL CUMBERLAND PRESBYTERIAN CHURCH
This was an early Cumberland Presbyterian Church in Dickson County, but the location and its history are not known.

JOHNSON CHAPEL IND. UNITED BRETHREN CHURCH
This church at White Bluff was named for the Rev. Thomas Andrew Johnson, who died in 1937 at the age of 82 years. At his death he had performed more funerals and marriages than anyone else in the county. The minister

today is John Arms.

LANDMARK BAPTIST CHURCH
This church was formerly Oak Grove School. In 1976 Jack Caldwell was the minister. The congregation is no longer active.

LIBERTY BAPTIST CHURCH
Carl Connley is the minister of this church at White Bluff.

LIBERTY METHODIST CHURCH
In 1886 there was a church of this name on Leatherwood Creek near Slayden. No further information available.

LIBERTY METHODIST CHURCH
This church is on Steel Road between Dickson and Charlotte. There is a large, active cemetery in the churchyard.

MAPLE GROVE MISSIONARY BAPTIST
This church is on the East Fork of Yellow Creek, about 3 miles from Sylvia. In 1975 the congregation was over 100 years old.

MARTHA'S CHAPEL (METHODIST)
This church was named for Martha Hinson (mother of the Reverends J. G. and Thomas H. Hinson), who gave the land. Early records of this church were destroyed by fire, but it is known the church was flourishing before 1856. The last church here was built about 1903.

MARVIN'S CHAPEL (METHODIST)
This church was organized in 1820 and named for Bishop E. E. Marvin and in 1903 moved to Burns. Today the site is marked by the cemetery known as Fulgum Cemetery, but the cemetery is really Marvin's Chapel Cemetery.

McADOO MEMORIAL CUMBERLAND PRESBYTERIAN CHURCH
The following information was taken from an article on this church written by Ruth Eleazer and published in the Dickson Free Press, 3 Sept. 1970:

"Between 1888 and 1890, people came from far and near and camped on the grounds around the McAdow home in the little valley four miles north of Burns, Tennessee. Revivals were held, and thus came the name of Camp Ground.

"On 5 Oct. 1890, in Burns, Tenn., the session met at the home of F. M. Porter at 5 o'clock p.m. with elders R. A. Johnston and A. N. Thompson. W. E. Jones was moderator. Other elders appointed were Ed Sager, Alfred Tucker and J. A. Dugan with H. N. Johnson as Deacon.

"Along about this time the congregation began meeting in the old log school house of Bethlehem and was called the Bethlehem congregation.

"In 1891 the first church was being built on the site of the church birthplace at Samuel McAdow's home. The architect was W. E. Smith of Nashville.

"During the years between 1890 and 1896 the Rev. W. M. Cooley was pastor, with members meeting in homes. On March 11, 1896, the congregation moved from Burns to the site of the birthplace of the Cumberland Presbyterian Church.

"On Aug. 29, 1901, with A. G. Castleman as moderator, the church met with the Rev. B. M. Taylor of Texas...A. N. Thompson, Jr., and V. J. Eleazer were elected elders, along with former elders, with V. J. Eleazer elected clerk of session. It was voted to adopt the name of the McAdow Memorial Church and a petition to be presented to the Presbytery. In 1901 Rev. S. T. Larkins was elector pastor of the new church.

"In 1907 the name of the church changed to McAdow Memorial...

"Over the years until 1939 the pastors were Rev. J. E. Powers, Rev. T.H. Padgett, Rev. W. N. Woodson, Rev. G. W. Philips, Rev. W. A. Blades, Rev. J. A. Dillard, and Rev. Z. N. Clinard.

"Rev. A. H. Sykes was pastor in 1939 when the old church disbanded for the reason that families moved away when the surrounding land became a park...

"After 1939 the old church building and manse were torn down and a log cabin representing the Samuel McAdow home was built on the site.

"The elders over the many years were John V. Jackson, R. A. Johnson, T. M. Porter, A. N. Thompson, V. J. Eleazer, A. N. Thompson, Jr., E. A. Sullivan, W. R. and J. H. Eleazer, Zula Eleazer, Ed Thompson, Edward Thompson, Jr., and J. H. Bryant.

"The deacons were T. O. Bedford, Miss Dora Gentry, W. R. Eleazer, Ed Thompson, Zula and Venessa Eleazer. Clerks of the session were T. M. Porter, V. J. Eleazer and Ruth Eleazer."

Dickson County newspapers in 1911 show that the original log cabin was being torn down.

McGAVOCK CHAPEL AME CHURCH
This church at Charlotte is for blacks and the Rev. W. R. Rogers is the minister.

McNAIRY HILL
This is a church for blacks and no further information was available.

METHODIST EPISCOPAL CHURCHES
Goodspeed's history of the county noted that churches of this denomination were on Yellow Creek, District 13, and on the Nashville, Chattanooga and St. Louis Railroad, District 13, in 1886. No further information was available. Also this year there were two churches on Beaverdam in District 5 in 1886. There was one for blacks in Dickson this year as well.

MIDWAY CHURCH OF CHRIST
This church is on Highway 49 out from Charlotte.

MILLER'S CHAPEL FREEWILL BAPTIST
Today James Black is the minister of this church. Hart Miller, who died in 1935 at the age of 75, was one of the founders of this church and his grave was the first one in the cemetery here. (Source: Dickson County Herald, 21 July 1939.)

MT. CARMEL METHODIST CHURCH
This church was built during the 1830s at the head of Barton's Creek and was still active in 1886. No further information available.

MT. HEBRON CHURCH OF CHRIST
This church is at Dull on Peabody Road, Highway 49, and Shaw Caldwell is the present minister. The church was founded in 1892 and land was deeded by Bud Dowden for a church and cemetery. Sunday School rooms, rest rooms, and other improvements have been added in recent years.

MT. LEBANON UNITED METHODIST CHURCH
Horace Perkins is the present minister of this church. Methodism in Dickson County began near this church at the old log church Smyrna, built 1810, 1/4 mile northeast of Mt. Lebanon. This building served for 40 years until W. S. Castleman gave two acres of land upon which a log church was built and the name changed to Mt. Lebanon. This second log building served for 29 years until destroyed by fire. Another log church was built and served until 1913 when the present church was built. The cornerstone was laid Nov. 1913 when W. L. Harwell was the minister. The cemetery here was started in 1904 when James M. Steele was buried. In 1910 James M. Choate was buried and they, with Thomas B. Sanders are three Confederate soldiers buried here. (From Marvin Choate's history, published in Free Press, 6 Sept. 1972.)

MT. LIBERTY CUMBERLAND PRESBYTERIAN CHURCH
This church was organized in the 1830s and is still an active congregation about 12 miles east of Charlotte. The Rev. Gideon Blackburn and the Rev. John L. Smith were some of the early ministers here. Today Mike Duke is the minister.

MT. OLIVE CHURCH OF CHRIST
Ted Kerley is the minister of this church at Cumberland Furnace on the Maple Valley Road.

MT. OLIVET NAZARENE CHURCH
No further information available about this church.

MT. SINAI BAPTIST CHURCH
The building was constructed in 1957 and is on West Rickert Avenue in Dickson. Earl Craig is the present minister.

MT. VIEW CUMBERLAND PRESBYTERIAN CHURCH
This church was active in 1886 and was between Bartons Creek and Bear Creek. No further information was available.

NEW HOPE CUMBERLAND PRESBYTERIAN CHURCH
This church was organized between 1810 and 1830 and was four miles west of Charlotte, at the head of the east prong of Bartons Creek. In 1886 the church was a log building. Mention has been found as late as 1899 about this church, but no further information was available.

METHODIST EPISCOPAL CHURCH NORTH
NORTHERN METHODIST CHURCH
This congregation organized in 1867 and the church was originally a box frame building, used during the week as a school. This building was replaced in 1892 with a brick building, remodeled into an office building in 1950. Charter members of this church were Dr. T. F. McCreary, R. W. McCombs, Henry Reep, William McFarland, James Lamb, Lewis Lightner, James Harnish and their families. The Rev. J. H. Derryberry was the first minister. The church ceased to be an active congregation when the Northern and Southern branches of the church united.

NOSEGAY
Today this is a cemetery out from White Bluff. The area around here took its name from this cemetery.

OAK AVENUE CHURCH OF CHRIST
The church was built in 1966 on Henslee Drive and Bill Ashworth is the current minister.

OAK GROVE FREEWILL BAPTIST
The church was established in 1901 and is on the Ashland City Highway in the Dull community. The land was given by Layton and Sallie Hughes Jackson and W. M. (Bill) Sensing gave $1.00 to make the transaction legal. Ronnie Smith is the present minister.

OAK GROVE UNITED METHODIST CHURCH
This church was flourishing in 1886 when the Goodspeed history of the county was written. The church is on Highway 48 South and Wayne Epley is the present minister.

OAK HILL PRESBYTERIAN CHURCH
Only one mention has been found of this church. In April 1893 J. B. Tidwell was to represent the church at presbytery. No further information has been available.

OLD SCHOOL PRESBYTERIAN
The church was on North Church Street and was active in 1886. The building has been torn down.

OPEN BIBLE PRAISE CENTER
Don Tyler is the pastor of this congregation, meeting at this writing in the Schrader U.A.W. Hall.

MT. LIBERTY CUMBERLAND PRESBYTERIAN CHURCH
This church was organized in the 1830s and is still an active congregation about 12 miles east of Charlotte. The Rev. Gideon Blackburn and the Rev. John L. Smith were some of the early ministers here. Today Mike Duke is the minister.

MT. OLIVE CHURCH OF CHRIST
Ted Kerley is the minister of this church at Cumberland Furnace on the Maple Valley Road.

MT. OLIVET NAZARENE CHURCH
No further information available about this church.

MT. SINAI BAPTIST CHURCH
The building was constructed in 1957 and is on West Rickert Avenue in Dickson. Earl Craig is the present minister.

MT. VIEW CUMBERLAND PRESBYTERIAN CHURCH
This church was active in 1886 and was between Bartons Creek and Bear Creek. No further information was available.

NEW HOPE CUMBERLAND PRESBYTERIAN CHURCH
This church was organized between 1810 and 1830 and was four miles west of Charlotte, at the head of the east prong of Bartons Creek. In 1886 the church was a log building. Mention has been found as late as 1899 about this church, but no further information was available.

METHODIST EPISCOPAL CHURCH NORTH
NORTHERN METHODIST CHURCH
This congregation organized in 1867 and the church was originally a box frame building, used during the week as a school. This building was replaced in 1892 with a brick building, remodeled into an office building in 1950. Charter members of this church were Dr. T. F. McCreary, R. W. McCombs, Henry Reep, William McFarland, James Lamb, Lewis Lightner, James Harnish and their families. The Rev. J. H. Derryberry was the first minister. The church ceased to be an active congregation when the Northern and Southern branches of the church united.

NOSEGAY
Today this is a cemetery out from White Bluff. The area around here took its name from this cemetery.

OAK AVENUE CHURCH OF CHRIST
The church was built in 1966 on Henslee Drive and Bill Ashworth is the current minister.

OAK GROVE FREEWILL BAPTIST
The church was established in 1901 and is on the Ashland City Highway in the Dull community. The land was given by Layton and Sallie Hughes Jackson and W. M. (Bill) Sensing gave $1.00 to make the transaction legal. Ronnie Smith is the present minister.

OAK GROVE UNITED METHODIST CHURCH
This church was flourishing in 1886 when the Goodspeed history of the county was written. The church is on Highway 48 South and Wayne Epley is the present minister.

OAK HILL PRESBYTERIAN CHURCH
Only one mention has been found of this church. In April 1893 J. B. Tidwell was to represent the church at presbytery. No further information has been available.

OLD SCHOOL PRESBYTERIAN
The church was on North Church Street and was active in 1886. The building has been torn down.

OPEN BIBLE PRAISE CENTER
Don Tyler is the pastor of this congregation, meeting at this writing in the Schrader U.A.W. Hall.

ROBINSON CHAPEL FREEWILL BAPTIST CHURCH
This church on Highway 48 on Mt. Sinai Road burned in 1971. It was originally built in 1942 as a Methodist church. In 1956 the Methodist congregation joined the Oak Grove Methodist Church and the building was sold to the Missionary Baptist Church and later to the Free Will Baptists. Jeff Lankford is the present minister.

ROCK CHURCH, CHURCH OF CHRIST
This stone house was built in 1826 by Montgomery Bell and it served as a storehouse for iron hollow-ware molded in his foundry nearby. In the same year a little Christian Church was organized in the home of William Talley. After the iron industry waned in 1856, the church bought the old warehouse to use it as a church. Located in a picturesque spot, the church is on Rock Church Road, 6 miles northeast of Dickson and 4 miles southwest of Charlotte. Bobby Boyd is the present minister.

ROCK SPRINGS FREEWILL BAPTIST CHURCH
Paul Sitton is the present minister of this church.

ST. CHRISTOPHER'S CATHOLIC CHURCH
St. Christopher's was built by Edward Henslee of Chicago, Illinois, a native of Dickson, in thanksgiving for the safe return of a son from World War II. In 1951 there were 10 families and by 1976 there were 140 families as parishioners. The church is at 713 West College Street in Dickson and the Rev. F. J. Crump, O.M.I, serves as priest.

ST. JAMES AME CHURCH
This church for blacks is at 110 West Rickert Avenue and Eddie Marshall is the present minister.

ST. JAMES EPISCOPAL CHURCH
This church at Cumberland Furnace has been placed on the National Register of Historic Buildings. The church was consecrated 13 Aug. 1882 and presented to the Episcopal Diocese of Tennessee by James P. and Florence Kirkman Drouillard.

ST. JAMES EPISCOPAL CHURCH
The church is at 306 West Walnut Street in Dickson and the Rev. Michael Moulden is the vicar.

ST. JOHN'S LUTHERAN CHURCH
This church was organized in 1872 and the Rev. E. M. Anthony was the first minister. The church was organized through the efforts of Mrs. Kate Sylvis. In 1876 they purchased the unfinished property of the Southern Presbyterians on Walnut Street and completed the building. Under the Rev. W. C. Barnett the church was finished. Although the congregation was never large in number, it was "composed of people noted for their loyalty to the distinctive doctrines and methods of the Reformation."

The church served for several years both as a church and school, with classes taught by Miss Kate Boggs, a returned missionary. The last regularly held service at St. John's was in December 1940 and there were only nine members at the time. The building remained vacant from 1942 until its demolition in 1955.

Some of the family names in the congregation were Badge, Donegan, Hanley, Helberg, McCreary, Shawl, and Sylvis.

The church stood on East Walnut Street and a house has been built on the lot today. There are still some who remember the cemetery about the church (the writer being one).

ST. JOHN'S UNITED METHODIST CHURCH
This is a colored congregation in Promised Land out from Charlotte.

ST. MARK'S METHODIST CHURCH
No information has been available about this church or its location. In 1891 the Rev. Klyce was the minister of the church according to the local newspaper.

ST. PAUL'S USA PRESBYTERIAN CHURCH
This church, near Charlotte, no longer has a congregation and the building and adjoining cemetery have been given to the Dickson County Historical Society.

SEVENTH DAY ADVENTIST
John Riggs is the present minister of this group at 101 McCrary Street.

SLAYDEN CHURCH OF GOD OF PROPHECY
No information has been available on this church at Slayden.

SLAYDEN MISSIONARY BAPTIST CHURCH
Howard Lee is the minister of this church in 1982.

SLAYDEN CHURCH OF CHRIST
No information has been available on this church.

SLAYDEN PRESBYTERIAN USA CHURCH
This church had its beginning 8 Dec. 1930. Approximately, 125 years ago this was a Methodist Church with the Masonic Hall on the upper floor and stood in Rainey Camp Hollow. The old building burned and was rebuilt in the village of Slayden. This building stood until 1941 when a new church was built.

SMYRNA CHURCH
This was the first Methodist Church in Dickson County. Refer also to the listing of Mt. Lebanon Church.

SOULE'S CHAPEL UNITED METHODIST CHURCH
Soule's Chapel was organized in 1851 in a community called Beefrange on Horse Branch of Barton's Creek. On 6 Oct. 1851 W. M. Mathis deeded to William Mathews, Randolph Mills, John Hinton, S. C. Whitsett, D. N. Mathew, Daniel Mills, trustees, land in District 8 of Dickson County. The upper room of a church here could be used for the meetings of the Planters Division No. 264 Sons of Temperance.

The church was almost burned during the Civil War when the Yankees gathered driftwood and piled it against the church preparing to burn the building. Only a call to report to their company saved the church.

The original church building was torn down in 1888 and rebuilt. This church burned 11 Sept. 1970 and a new church was built 1/2 mile from the old church. Today Paul Ford is minister of Soule's Chapel.

STONY POINT CUMBERLAND PRESBYTERIAN CHURCH
This church, flourishing in 1886, was on Williamson Creek or Williamson Branch. No further information was available about the church.

STONEY POINT FREE WILL BAPTIST CHURCH
This church is at Vanleer and the present minister is H. C. Beasley.

SUNDAY SCHOOL
A Sunday School was organized in Dickson in 1891 and the class met in the Bank Hall. This seems to have been the first Sunday School in the town. (Dickson County Press, 12 Nov. 1891.)

SWEET HOME CHURCH OF CHRIST
No information was available about this church in the Sweet Home community.

SYCAMORE UNITED METHODIST CHURCH
This church is near Pond on Sycamore Road. Wayne Epley is the present minister serving the congregation.

SYLVIA BAPTIST CHURCH
Lauren Atkins is the present minister of this church at Sylvia.

SYLVIA CHURCH OF CHRIST
No information was available about this church at Sylvia.

TAYLOR TOWN CHURCH OF CHRIST
This church is in Taylor Town community near White Bluff. No further information was available.

TENNESSEE CITY INDEPENDENT MISSIONARY BAPTIST CHURCH
Dave Coulter is the present minister of this church at Tennessee City.

TENNESSEE CITY UNITED METHODIST CHURCH
The first Methodist Church near Tennessee City was Jason's Chapel on Garner's Creek. A church was built at Tennessee City 1903 and dedicated on 12 June 1904. The present minister is Silas Decker.

TENT CHAPEL METHODIST
In 1892 and 1893 there was a place of worship known as Tent Chapel. No further information available, but apparently the congregation was a Dickson one. (Source: Dickson County Independent, 9 June 1892, 2 March 1893.)

TURNBULL BAPTIST CHURCH
This church was organized in 1806 on Turnbull Creek and was very active in the days of early settlement. The Parker family was long identified with the church.

UNION METHODIST EPISCOPAL CHURCH
This church was 1-1/2 miles from Ruskin Cave, 10 miles northeast of Dickson. It was organized in 1830 and by 1867 the membership totaled 85 people. The church is in Union Hollow on Yellow Creek.

UNITED PRESBYTERIAN CHURCH
This church was organized in 1871. In 1882 S. F. Thompson was the minister.

VALLEY SPRINGS MISSIONARY BAPTIST CHURCH
In 1886 this church was on Barton's Creek. No further information was available.

VANLEER BAPTIST CHURCH
Randy King is the present minister of this church.

VANLEER CHURCH OF CHRIST
The church is on Highway 49 and James Reynolds is the present minister.

VANLEER CUMBERLAND PRESBYTERIAN CHURCH
No information is available about this church, except that it was in existence in 1899, according to old newspapers.

VANLEER METHODIST CHURCH
The Vanleer Methodist Church was organized in 1893 by Rev. J. R. Holmes and there were 30 charter members. For a number of years the members worshipped in the Cumberland Presbyterian Church and later in the Baptist Church. The cornerstone to the church was laid in 1927 and the church was dedicated 1930.

WALNUT GROVE BAPTIST CHURCH
Harley Tidwell is the present member of this church. No further information available.

WALNUT STREET CHURCH OF CHRIST
The present building of this church was built in 1911. The church is on the corner of Center Avenue and Walnut Street. In June 1891 J. W. Grant of Nashville came to Dickson to hold a meeting in the hall above the old Dickson Bank and Trust Company. The meeting, lasting three weeks, adding 35 members to the group. A regular congregation was formed, containing 40 members.

Some of the charter members were Mrs. Beulinda Page, Rachel J. Haynes, the Dan Sager family, and a Mr. Stacey.

As early as 1880 the church was represented in Dickson by Mr. and Mrs. J. W. Shaw. Later the J. M. Talley family moved here.

Gynath Ford is the present minister of the church.

WATER STREET CHURCH OF CHRIST
This church, distinguished by an imposing tower, is in Charlotte and Robert Cullom is the present minister.

WATER VALLEY PRIMITIVE BAPTIST CHURCH
J. A. Adams was minister here in 1907. This church is three miles below Eno near Piney River.

WESLEY CHAPEL UNITED METHODIST CHURCH
This church is at the mouth of Cedar Creek and was organized in 1863. The first site was about one mile from the present location on the east side of Yellow Creek. The old church was sold many years ago and in 1954 the congregation used a school for the church. Today the minister is the Rev. Silas Decker.

WEST DICKSON CHURCH OF CHRIST
Zellie Ray Daniel is the present minister of this church on Dickson Avenue at 2nd Street in West Dickson.

WEST FIFTH STREET PRIMITIVE BAPTIST CHURCH
Elder Lynn Russell is the pastor of this church.

WESTVIEW BAPTIST - WHITE BLUFF
This church is on the Kingston Springs Road and no additional information was available.

WHITE BLUFF UNITED METHODIST CHURCH
Ellis Felts is the present minister of this church. In 1877 Alex Kerr and George Hutchenson sold a lot to W. C. Charlton, H. M. Carroll, Thomas Whitfield, M. W. Hooper and C. H. Yates as trustees for the White Bluff Methodist Church and it is believed the congregation had organized a year or so before this time.

The first church was rebuilt in 1902 and in 1926 was replaced by a new building. This was destroyed by a fire which struck the business district of White Bluff on 7 Jan. 1946. A new church was built shortly afterward.

WHITE BLUFF CUMBERLAND PRESBYTERIAN CHURCH
This church was listed in 1886 as being an active congregation in the county, but no further information is available.

WHITE OAK FLATT CHURCH OF GOD OF PROPHECY
William Crook is the minister of this church on Highway 49 north of Charlotte.

WILLIAMS CHAPEL (METHODIST)
This church is mentioned in 1937 newspapers as being an extinct church, in Dickson County. No further information is available.

WOODS VALLEY METHODIST CHURCH
This church on Little Bartons Creek was organized in 1892 and the land was donated by a Mr. Slayden, member of the Primitive Baptist Church.

WORLEY BAPTIST - WHITE BLUFF
This church is listed in the 1982 directory of Dickson County churches and located on the Kingston Springs Road.

WORLEY FURNACE MISSIONARY BAPTIST CHURCH
A church for blacks on Eno Road, this church is over 100 years old. No further information on its history is available.

WHITE BLUFF - ELIZABETH HOUSE
This was a mission of the Episcopal Church at White Bluff. Miss Kate Edmundson was in charge from 1922 until 1937. When she retired, the Church Army took over the operation. No further information available on when the mission ceased.

SCHOOLS

The following will be only a partial listing of schools that have been in Dickson County. A complete listing would probably never be complete as there have been numerous field schools and subscriptions started and discontinued through the years. The listing was mainly compiled from two master lists in the 1880s and in 1937. Many of these schools were conducted in churches and many have given their names temporarily or permanently to communities in the county. This list will possibly have some places not listed in the "Places" section of this work.

ACADEMY
Academy Street in Dickson takes its name from this old school In 1882 the school was described as a two story frame building of four rooms, situated in a grove of trees. At that time Professor J. E. Cole was the teacher. Also known as Dickson Academy.

ACORN HILL SCHOOL
This school was near White Bluff. In 1937 it was a one-teacher school with Edwin Charlton as teacher.

BAKER'S, BAKER SCHOOL
In 1883 this was described as a free school in District 1 with George Hudson as teacher. In 1937 this was a one-teacher school and Gertrude Borchert was the teacher.

BEECH GROVE SCHOOL
This school was built in 1904 or 1905 on East Piney, about one mile east of the forks of Piney. The first teacher was Johnny Fielder and the second was Willie Nelson. Other teachers included Mark Tidwell, Cave Tidwell, George Springer, Hubert Redden, George Crow, Hattie Cuniff, Millie Moore Springer, Clara Fielder Frazier, Clatie Donegan Odell, Mollie Spencer, Gracie Wilkins and Martie McCorpin. The school was moved to Cedar Hill in 1920. (This information came from Dickson Free Press, 27 March 1976 and an article written by Dewey Bowen.)

BELLSBURG SCHOOL
In 1937 this was a two-teacher school in Dickson County.

BELLVIEW SCHOOL
This school was on Jones Creek and also known as Rock Church. Virgie Larkins was one of the teachers at this school, in 1907.

BRUCE SCHOOL
This was a free school in District 1 in 1883. B. Baker was the teacher.

BURNS SCHOOL
The first school was 1/2 mile south of Burns near Beaverdam Creek and the teachers were Mrs. Ann Alspaugh and a Mr. Pippin. The public school was later in a frame building on the north side of the railroad, taught by A. L. M. Johnson in 1901. A subscription school was taught at Burns in 1901 by Mrs. Bert Tidwell Wyburn. A new school was built in 1902 and burned in April 1940. This was replaced by Sept. 1940. Carney Nicks and J. C. Erranton have served as principals of this school. In 1942 Aline Smith Stuart was elected principal--retiring in 1973 after 39 years at Burns School and 45 years teaching in Dickson County.

An old picture in our family scrapbook shows the following pupils at Burns School in 1901: Gilla Richardson, Katie Boone, Carl Thompson, J. L. Johnson, Kendrick Thompson, Jody Austin Betty Austin, Nannie Thompson, Blanche White, Floye Thompson, Narvie White, Clara Richardson, A. L. M. Johnson (was teacher), Beechie Carr, Ora Tidwell, Pearl Groves, Clara White, Docie Tidwell, Pet Spencer, Morton Richardson, Leonard Oliphant, Jim Richardson, Will Adcock, John Cunningham, Dave Saegar, Oscar Tidwell.

In 1919 the teachers at Burns School were Maude Tidwell, Clara Meek, and Leeta Meek. Pupils enrolled that year included: Ezra Hall, Grace Brown, Bert Bissenger, Randolph Adcock, Hassie Tidwell, Paul Tidwell, Minnie Hall, Thelma Thompson, Ruth Hogin, Willie Mai Beck, Arnold Gentry, Rodney Richardson, L. P. Johnson, Floyd Carney, Walter Ladd,

Eugene Wyatt, Claude Daniel, Authur Adcock, Irene White, Marie Austin, Jessie White, Eddie Adcock, Margaret Austin Howard Chandler, Ezra Richardson, Forrest Carney, Flora Cathey, Laura Jones, Emory Alspaugh, Jr., Virgil Myatt, Sammie Spencer, Hazel Anderson, Stella Vey Myatt, Maurice Oliphant, Alene Walp, Nettie Thompson, Allie Chandler, Christine Gentry, Pauline Johnson, Maybelle Thompson, Ora Hall, Roy Ladd, Lucille Oliphant, Grover Johnson, Paul McIntire, Mary Knox Mathis Claude Larkins, Otho White, Jewell Richardson, Billy McIntire, Malcolm Ladd, John Parcy Johnson, Seth Gentry, Buford Thomas, Grady Walp, and Clarence Loggins.

Others in school that year were Clara Estes, Maudie Cathey, Ross Mathis, Lexie Estes, Earl Gentry, Roy Baker, Hazel McCoy, Ham Carney, Evelyn Johnson, Lyndell Hall, Aline Thomas, Vudus Taylor, Elsie Mai Brown, Hazel Richardson, Dovie Loggins, Bessie McCoy, Ed Walp, Marie Garton, Nettie Garton, Wilma Garton, Christine Johnson, Myrtle Beck, Pearl Beck, and Florence McIntire.

The 1919 school enrollment also included Dimple Hogin, Gladys Tidwell, Rosie Daniel, Velma Carney, Ruth Chandler, Corinne Walp, several Johnson children, Edna Ruth Oliphant, Katherine Oliphant, Mildred Wyatt, Sue Mathis, Lorene Cathey, Elsie Estes, Evie Estes, Allie Estes, Pearl McCoy, some Bishop children, Earline Hall, Pearl Chandler, Lilburn Hogin, Lloyd Walp, Alvin Chandler, Paul Tidwell, Marion Adcock, Harris Stuart, Fuller Richardson, Edd Meek, Martha White, Horace Cathey, Theo Oliphant, Joe Alspaugh, Roscoe Holland, Percy Bear, Paul Turner Gentry, and several whose names were not remembered.

The only other picture in our family scrapbook is for the seventh grade at Burns Elementary School and was made in 1941 when Carney Nicks was the teacher. This class included: Roy Baker, Jr., Shirley Johnson, Billie June Johnson, Betty Lynn Mathis, Edith Mai Brown, Clyde Jones, Walter Bear, Loyd Daniel, Edith Myatt, Ann Hall, Lucille Chew, Dorothy Bell Hall, Oneida Stuart, Loyd Smith, Frances Walp, Dorothy Bishop, Joe Brown, Eddie Ray Tomlinson, Sarah Richardson, Aline Smith, Sammy Bishop, Richard Stuart, Edward Lynn Oliphant, Glynn Daniel, Howard Lankford, Mattie Ashworth, Jean Edney, June Edney, Billy Bishop, Frances Eleazer, Madaline Houston, and Betty Sue Hall.

CAMPBELL SCHOOL
One of the earliest schools in the county was taught by Alexander Campbell in the southwest part of the county near or at the forks of Piney.

CARTER'S CHAPEL SCHOOL
Miss Amy Simpson was the teacher of this school in 1898, and believed to be somewhere in the Mt. Lebanon community. Pupils at this school in 1898 were Henry Choate, John James, Martha James, Minnie Rithmier, Doss Choate, Floy Baker, Annie James, Essie James, Hugh James, Bessie James, Virgie James, Ed Choate, Vernie Choate, Linda Choate, Leslie Choate, Lester Choate, Hattie Choate, Sally Carter, Buck Baker, Will Matlock, Lula Matlock, Mimey Matlock, Elmer Brazzell, Della Brazzell, Talmadge Johnson, Walter Keel, Frank Carter, Will Carter, Jim Carter, Walter Carter, Essie Carter, Myrtle Bateman, and Essie Bateman.

CAVE SPRINGS SCHOOL
The location of this school is not known to the writer. In 1913 the following attended this school: Daniel Loggins, Douglas Crow, Margaret Walker, Lucile Ragan, Ruby Long, Ruby Matlock, Mary Loggins, Eddie Loggins, Henry Nicks, Albert Nicks, Lorena Loggins, Ruth Loggins, Allen Spann, Betty Loggins, Lloyd Ragan, Dee Nicks, Tenor Long, Tommy Greer, Roy Martin, Douglas Loggins, Parks Corlew, Mary Nicks, Vera Spann, Mabel Spann, Dee Walker, Dora Nicks, Minnie Spann, Dottie Spann, May Long, Sara Loggins, Lee Petty, Allene Matlock, Porter Nicks, and Leo Matlock.

CEDAR HILL SCHOOL
This school was in the Piney community and merged with other nearby schools to form Hillcrest school. This was a one-teacher school in 1937 and Willa Erranton was the teacher.

CHARLOTTE ACADEMY
This school was established by Jacob Voorhies about 1823. This may be

the same academy that was authorized in 1806 and whose trustees in 1807 were Michael Molton, Richard C. Napier, Christopher Strong, Molton Dickson, William Stone, Montgomery Bell, and Robert Jarman.

CHARLOTTE FEMALE ACADEMY
This school was in operation at Charlotte at least by 1840.

CHARLOTTE ACADEMY
This was a training school for girls and boys and E. G. Atlee was the proprietor in 1899. (Source: Dickson Free Press, 23 March 1899.)

CHARLOTTE SCHOOL (c)
In 1937 this was a one-teacher school for blacks and Juanita Horner was the teacher. A school for blacks was in Charlotte as early as 1887.

CHARLOTTE HIGH SCHOOL
This school was established 1919 by Professor W. L. Rochelle. (Source: Dickson County Herald, 20 March 1936.)

CLAYLICK SCHOOL
This was a one-teacher school in 1937 and Sadie Bibb was the teacher.

COLLIER'S BEND SCHOOL
This was a one-teacher school in 1937 and Mildred Ferrell was the teacher.

CENTER POINT SCHOOL
In 1937 this was a two-teacher school in the county.

COALING SCHOOL (c)
In 1937 this was a one-teacher school for blacks and M. E. Dansby was the teacher.

COLESBURG SCHOOL
In 1937 this was a two-teacher school. In our family scrapbook is a picture made 1934-1935 and shows the following were in school there that year: Will Corbitt, Jr., Forrest Bishop, James Bishop, Freeman Brown, Maurice Owens, Loyd Goodwin, Clinton Corbitt, Sonny Adcock, James Goodwin, Edward Goodgine, Gibson Goodine, J. R. Filson, Roy Chun, Bulah Brown, Hattie Bishop, Mary Helen England, Dorothy Corbitt, Mary Trollinger, Louise Dunnagan, Mildred Bishop, Lucille Bishop, Hazel Sanker, Edna Sue Sanker, Wilma Trollinger, Louise Dudley, Carl Goodwin, Katherine Bishop, Eldridge Bishop, Leland Depriest, Ruby Bishop, Duel Filson, Christine Goodgine, Elizabeth Trollinger, Glenn Anderson, Eulia Luther. (Note: Either Glenn Anderson or Elizabeth Trollinger was the teacher that year, but not made clear in our scrapbook picture.)

COLORED SCHOOL
In 1883 Ben Hall had a free school for colored pupils in District 1. In 1891 there was a colored school at Dickson on the Charlotte Road.

SCHOOL AT COX SPRING
At one time there was a school house located here, but no name has been turned in to us.

CLOVERDALE ACADEMY
This was a private school located at the Bell homeplace 3 miles west of Cumberland Furnace. The school was operated by the Bell family.

CUMBERLAND FURNACE SCHOOL
This was a two-teacher school in the county in 1937.

CUMBERLAND FURNACE SCHOOL (c)
This was a school for black pupils in 1937 and was a one-teacher school. Henry Nesbitt was the teacher that year.

DANIEL TOWN SCHOOL (c)
This was a one-teacher school for blacks in 1937 and Emmogene Springer was the teacher.

DEAN SCHOOL HOUSE
In 1899 this school was near or at Vanleer or Cumberland Furnace, as the Baptists at those places met here to organize a church.

DICKSON CENTRAL HIGH SCHOOL
This school was on Highway 70 East, College Street, and was where the old Dickson Normal was at one time. As a high school, it first opened in 1919. Today the only county high school is Dickson High School on Highway 48 North, the Charlotte Road, between Dickson and Charlotte.

DICKSON ACADEMY
According to the Dickson County Herald, dated 22 Nov. 1935, in the 1889s this school was under Johns and Osborne and was in a grove of trees at the rear of S. E. Hunt property on East College Street and was owned by the Masons. It served until Dickson Normal College was established 1890 by Wade & Loggins on the site later occupied by the high school. David J. Johns died in 1935 at the age of 74 years.

DICKSON NORMAL COLLEGE
The brick building was demolished in 1964. It was completed by Prof. W. T. Wade and Prof T. B. Loggins in the summer of 1892, following the establishment of the Dickson Normal College. The school had been established in a frame building on what was later known as the Cox property. From that time until the passage of the general education bill in 1909 the Dickson Normal College experienced great growth.

The faculty at the turn of the century included: W. J. Davies, Greek and mathematics; Professor Wade, Latin and natural sciences; Mrs. Lucia Wade, German and bookkeeping; Flavia Gaines, elocution and physical culture; A. C. Hughes, preparatory mathematics, history and geography; G. H. East, penmanship; J. L. Wyman, piano, organ and voice; Idella Ottenville, mandolin, violin, and guitar; Mrs. Lula Hughes, librarian; J. T. Fulghum, telegraphy; Mrs. Annie Garton, matron. There were about 700 pupils enrolled.

By 1906 Professor Loggins announced the school had 800 enrolled. Prizes and awards were given by local citizens: W. H. McMurray gave a ten dollar gold medal to the most outstanding student in writing and speech making; W. T. Rogers award a ten dollar prize to the best music pupil; and A. H. Leathers gave a similar award to the music student with the best all-round record.

Students honored during the preceding term had included Bessie Smith, Lucile Ridings, Donald Sensing, Arthur Miller, Lida Rogers, Dockie Shipp, Wilson Sharp, and others.

At the end of the 1911-1912 term, Professor Loggins turned the school over to E. B. Wilson, who operated it for several years. In 1913 the General Assembly passed a law requiring every county to maintain at least one high school. The property was purchased from Loggins for $16,500. The first four-year high school term opened in 1919 with W. M. Bratton as principal. Among the first pupils were Walter Erranton, Mary Allen, Frank Gatewood, Kate McMurray, Lipe Henslee, Albert Wilson, and James Bryan. (Source: Dickson County Herald, 28 May 1964.)

DICKSON TRAINING SCHOOL (c)
This school began in the 1920s and later became Hampton High School.

DICKSON NORTHERN ACADEMY
The Hickman Pioneer of 24 Sept. 1880 (published in Centerville) had the following: "Dickson Northern Academy is in full blast. Rev. William Huston is the principal with Rev. C. E. Evans, governor, and H. C. Neville as music teacher."

DISTRICT 3 SCHOOL
The following was found in the Hickman Pioneer, 1 Oct. 1886: "The time mentioned was the days of my youth and I flatter myself I was uncommonly well acquainted with those $15 school teachers and those good old sisters mentioned. The first school I ever went to was taught by Mr. Wm. H. Carr, who is now a resident of Centerville. I do not

remember what they gave him, but am confident he was not employed for his beauty.

Well, as I was quite young and the school crowded, I received but little attention, and therefore learned but little. And as I made such poor progress, father despaired of sending me to school, so I was kept at home until I was in my thirteenth year without even learning the alphabet. In the first of that year there was a gentleman named Jordan, who was raised in Maury County, moved to our neighborhood and got up a subscription school, near three miles from our place, and as father had taken quite a fancy to him and one of my brothers was going, he concluded to send me for a few days to see if I was really a block head, so the school commenced and I staid at home the first day for mother to make me a new dress to wear, the material being the genuine coperas and white, six and six checked.

Well, I donned my gaudy attire on the second morning and started for the academy, which consisted of a pile of rough logs, a slab floor and a fireplace nearly large enough to take in a fence rail, with chimney a little above the mouth; but as it was as good as most of the school houses of that day, we were proud to call it our school house.

My brother carried me in and introduced me and the teacher carried me through an examination and found I had not taken the first degree, although much larger than some of his pupils who was right smartly advanced.

He called the alphabet over and I followed suit and when done he bade me to take a seat by one of the girls on the seat near, who eyed my dress with great scrunity, and as soon as recess came said the reason I didn't come the day before was because I had to wait for that dress to be made, which was true, but I did not like to be told of it, and she said I was large as her mother and didn't know my ABCs, and wasn't I ashamed to be such a fool.

I didn't think school very pleasant just then, the children all teased me for not knowing anything, which seemed to renew my energy, and I strove with all my power and the teacher seemed to take an uncommon interest in me, and gave me words of encouragement every day, and he would say to those who were scoffing at me for not knowing anything that little as I knew I would soon be leading them, which was soon verified.

It was a four months term, and before it near expired I was standing at the head of the class, which did his heart good to see, for he could plainly see I was an underling among the scholars, and it did him good to see me get ahead of them.

Well, it closed in June, and I was reading in McGuffey's third reader and ciphering and studying grammar so father began to think I was not such a numbskull after all.

The district commissioners hired Professor Jordan to teach our free school at $20 per month, I think and we had a splendid school while it lasted, but the money soon gave out, but lasted as long as our house would give us comfortable entertainment.

On the following spring, Professor Jordan opened another four months session, and I attended every day and advanced rapidly, and I can say of a truth those were the happiest days of my life.

I had so many dear school companions, many who are now living, yet some have gone on that journey from whence the traveller ne'er returns, but I love to dwell upon their memory; they are all growing old, but they are young in my recollection.

Well, after our spring term expired, our commissioners began to see about the free school. My father was one, and he wanted to employ Mr. Jordan, but he wanted $25 a month and the other commissioners would not give that. So they concluded to hire a Mr. Vanlandingham, who proposed to teach for $15 per month. Father contended Mr. Jordan would be the cheapest after all, but they hired Vanlandingham, and he went to business. Well, it is useless to try to describe him, but I will endeavor to give a few outlines.

He was about six foot and a half, and the only time he thought it was necessary to bow to his pupils was when he had to bow to get in the low door. He would come in and fall down on the chair and lay his old hat down on the floor by him and then bow his head on his hands and sit until some of the boldest of the children would go up and begin to recite and if they wanted instruction on a word, they would punch him in the side nearly hard enough to dislocate a rib, he would rouse up and see after them, but as soon as the desired information was given, he would drop back in his old position.

We just read when we pleased and where we pleased, and done nothing when we pleased. Some of the girls brought their knitting work to school, and they would knit when they wished and chew sweet gum and eat apples and write love letters, and all went well.

And at noon all would play together and court and fight and quarrel, and all was well with the teacher; he was such a cheap teacher, those who had employed him thought it best to keep him if things did go a little slack.

I have seen the boys sit and thump gravels at him for hours, and he would scarcely ever rouse up. One day a boy who was the best thumper aimed to thump a gravel against the wall just behind him and missed and hit him on the forehead hard enought to make a big bump. He roused and rubbed his head and said, "Who's that?" and as no one thought it their business to tell; all was silent, and as he could get no answer, he rubbed his head a while longer and then dropped back in his old position.

And talk about haw seed! I have dropped a half pint of hazlenut shells down his back while reciting one lesson; while some was reading their paragraph, the rest would be eating hazlenuts and all would pass the shells to the one next to the teacher and they would drop them down his shirt collar, which I think must have been near a yard big. The only change you would see was a slight movement like a fly might have lighted on his neck.

I cannot tell why he was dilitory; it might have been laziness and he might have thought he was getting such little pay that it didn't matter. I knew we were doing no good but as father had opposed him, I would not complain, so the school lasted seven weeks before there was any complaint brought against him, but at least his employers concluded that a $15 teacher would not pay, and hastened to dismiss him.

But as all the teachers that was of consequence was employed, it fell to our lot to do without, but it would have taken a Samson to have straightened the kinks he had left, and we never had a good school again.

I always will oppose a $15 teacher. Better have none and keep one's children at home out of mischief. I am in favor of employing a good teacher if we have but one month of school a year, and never let's hire a teacher because he is cheap, and by such doing deprive our children of both education and good morals.

Now let us hear from someone else on the $15 teacher question, for I am sure there are others who have had the same experience and whenever I think of those bygones I am sure to appear (signed) JOVIAL.

P. S. I forgot to state that the above scenes transpired in the 3rd district of Dickson County."

DRY HOLLOW SCHOOL
In 1937 this was a one-teacher school and Lawrence Averitt was the teacher.

EAST SIDE
In 1937 this was a two-teacher school in Dickson County.

EBENEZER SCHOOL
The location of this school is not known but it was in Dickson County in 1887.

EDGEWOOD ACADEMY
EDGEWOOD NORMAL SCHOOL
This school was chartered 1885 and flourished until 1891 when the faculty was moved to Dickson Normal College. The citizens of Edgewood operated the school until the turn of the century when it merged with Ruskin Cave College.

ELLIOTT SCHOOL
This school was in operation at least by 1887, and possibly before. It was known earlier as Murry School and was on Barton's Creek. In 1895 Allie Byrn was the teacher and some of the people attending the school were Elliott Haynes, Lem Loggins, John Jackson, Wall Elliott, Wayne Harris, Nissie Harris, Maude Loggins, Nellie Nesbitt, Mamie Nesbitt, Lavenia Nesbitt, Lurline Haynes, Daisy Haynes, Ida Gilliam, Lee Gilliam, Mary Pentecost, Sue Pentecost, Dolly Pentecost, Hugh Nesbitt, and Will Luton.

ENO SCHOOL
This school was on the headwaters of West Piney and Tommy Fuqua was the last teacher in the old school in 1920. When a new school building was opened in 1921, he and Mittie Adcock were the teachers. In 1937 Eno was still a two-teacher school.

Pupils attending this school in 1913 included: Murry Tatum, Ellis Call, Corby Brazzell, Rufus Vineyard, Claude Sullivan, Huelett Moize, Wesley England, Ethel Call, Eddie Tatum, Annie Sullivan, Nora Harrell, Allie McElhiney, Gretchel McElhiney, Bessie Brazzell, Mary Hager, Elzilma Street, Rowena Street, Roxie Donegan, Doye Vineyard, Elmer England, Glover England, Lloyd Donegan, Walton Donegan, Diamond Donegan, Henry Herbison, Coleman Brazzell, Wesley Brazzell, Andrew Fuqua, Gladys Springer, Fordie Baker, Elton Brown, Addie Call, Myrtle Donegan, Lorene Roberts, Emmie Roberts, Pearl Herbison, Lillie Donegan, Clara Donegan, Earlie Russhin, Curlie Russhin, Bettie Hagar, Vester Hamilton, Clyde Hamilton, Corby Adcock, Wesley Tatum, Jessie Tatum, Arnold Donegan, Monroe Baker, Clarence England, Dee Fields, Hettie Hagar, Euell Donegan, Leona Donegan, Tommie Fuqua, Ethel Baker, Johnny Fielder, Linnie Fields, Jim Donegan, Rosa Donegan, Dewey Donegan, and Curtis Fields. The teacher in 1913 was Miss Millie Moore.

FAIRVIEW SCHOOL
Located on Jones Creek, as late as 1937 this was a two-teacher school. In 1907 the teacher was Claude Stroud and some of the pupils that year: Rosco Pardue, Clyde Fussell, Ben Walker, Dallas Nicks, Hugh Overton, Claude Wimberly, Felix Duke, Lottie Hooper, Alberta Reep, Paul Fussell, Jesse Bush, Verda Fussell, Marshall Nicks, Nellie Rockey, Hershel Hooper, Norman Fussell, Scott Walker, Tom Bush, Cam Estes, Clarence Nicks, Mary Fussell, Stanton Overton, Rosa Bishop, Lucy Fussell, Irene Walker, Emps Fussell, Mary Pardue, Forrest Fussell, Susie Bishop, Eddie Bishop, Ray Hooper, Scott Hooper, Florell Reep, Clayton Daniel, Mary Walker, Johnetta Rockey, Paul Lunn, Scott Hooper, Dimple Walker, Roland Reep, Kate Taylor, Myrtice Fussell, Nannie Bush, Carrie Shirley, Met Hooper, Eunice Daniel, Clara Walker, Oscar Fussell, Hardin Pardue, Mary Bush, Ennis Daniel, Grant Surgerner, Roy Fussell, Talmadge Taylor, Mabel Shirley, Loyd Pardue, Ludie Estes, Lucy Estes, Myrtle Lunn, Izora Taylor, and Hubert Ray.

FEW'S CHAPEL SCHOOL
This school appears as a free school in 1883 and in District 1 under R. L. Few. Pupils at this school in 1896 included: Carter Stewart, Zack Vineyard, Tom Few, Jessie Harris, Georgie Murrell, Myrtle Few, Herman Few, Wash Few, Fordie Martin, Sissy Duggan, Mary Ann Harris, Vickey Duggan, Rosaetta Murrell, George Duggan, Zackie Few, Walter Harris, Nellie Few, Emma Few, Annie Few, Lilly Cooper, Ella Baker,

Sam Martin, Betty Few, Jasper Few, Grover Spicer, Will Bruce, John Bruce, Lucy Vineyard, Myrtle Yates, Florence Vineyard, Lemmie Cooper, Allie Cooper, Nola Bruce, Hester Vineyard, Ella Bruce, Janie Stewart, Hattie Donegan, Debbie Vineyard, Nannie Fielder, Mood Vineyard, Amanda Few, and Wash Erranton. The teacher that year was Sally Work.

In 1913, according to a picture in our family scrapbook, pupils at the school were: Leamon Yates, Orland Few, J. C. Erranton, Joel Erranton, Floyd Vineyard, Eunice Ladd; Florence Vineyard, Joe Dotson Beasley, Earl Yates, Morrison Donegan, Lowell Few, Hardy Few, Geneva Ladd, Helen Hemmerly, Mabel Fielder, Bess Few, Epsia Petty, Henry Murrell, Buck Steward, Mick Murrell, Hulan Fielder, Floy Few, Girlie Beasley, Lester Petty, Buddy Vineyard, Leonard Petty, Francis Hemmerly, Lucille Vineyard, Oscar Few, Hubert Hudgins, Grace Few, Virgie Few, Lester Simmons, Lula Murrell, and the teacher was Miss Hollie Bryant, later Mrs. Clyde Hamilton.

By 1916 pupils at Few's Chapel School were: Floyd Few, Garner Harris, Burton Fielder, Dorris Harris, Alex Stewart, Doyle Yates, Bertie Crowder, Oliver Stewart, Conroy Hood, Altha Claire Fielder, Martin Fielder, Eunice Ladd, Earl Yates, Geraldine Harris, Lela Murrell, Lowell Few, Elsie Few, J. C. Erranton, Hurbert Hudgins, Grace Few, Virgil Few, Mable Fielder, Oscar Few, Bessie Few, Mick Murrell, Stella Crowder, Ivan Crowder, Orland Few, Henry Murrell, Thurman Hood, Hardy Few, Grover Luther (identified as the teacher on the class picture), Wesley Murrell, Thomas Stewart, Leamon Yates, Geneva Ladd, Hulan Fielder, Joel Erranton, and Pearl Stewart.

Pupils in 1917 were: Floyd Few, Garner Harris, Burton Fielder, Dorris Harris, Alex Stewart, Doyle Yates, Bertie Crowder, Oliver Stewart, Conroy Hood, Altha Claire Fielder, Martin Fielder, Eunice Ladd, Earl Yates, Geraldine Harris, Lela Murrell, Lowell Few, Elsie Few, J. C. Erranton, Herbert Hudgins, Grace Few, Virgil Few, Mable Fielder, Oscar Few, Mick Murrell, Bessie Few, Stella Crowder, Ivan Crowder, Orland Few, Henry Murrell, Thurman Hood, Hardy Few, Wesley Murrell, Thomas Stewart, Leamon Yates, Geneva Ladd, Hulan Fielder, Joel Erranton, and Pearl Stewart. The teacher that year was Grover Luther.

FIELDER'S SCHOOL
In 1883 this was a free school in District 1 and Mollie Dull was the teacher. This school was built on the Silas Fielder farm. James Scott from England was the first teacher.

FRAZIER SCHOOL
In 1937 this was a one-teacher school with Gladys Weems as teacher.

GARNER'S CREEK SCHOOL
In 1937 this was a one-teacher school with Artie Bowen as teacher.

GARRETT SCHOOL
This school was in the Greenwood community and was a one-teacher school. In 1937 Nellie Doty was the teacher. The school had grades 1 through 8 and there were usually 80 to 100 pupils. Teachers and pupils served as janitors at this school.

In 1924 pupils here included: Lee Doty, Lem Tolar, Tom Doty, Ellis Hayes, ___Reeves, Lonnie Garrett, Rons Spicer, William Proctor, ___Harris Melvin Hayes, Raymond Sensing, George Tolar, Helen Proctor, Mary Lee, Gwen Proctor, Lucille Tolar, Peggy Nicks, Ruby Fowler, Diane Garrett, Ruby Sensing, Valley Garrett, Sally Bell Sensing, Pearl Garrett, Dolly Sensing, Allen Hayes, Thornton Fowler, Bill Reeves, Ruby Spicer, Mary Daniel, Bertha Doty, Luther Wicks, James Doty, Edna Sensing, Nora Hayes, Clara Hayes, and Clyde Lee. The teacher was Miss Mary Loggins.

GILLEM SCHOOL
In 1882 the Dickson County Press announced that Mollie Bruce "has a school at Gillem." In 1883 it was called a free school in District 1 and Miss Bruce was still the teacher.

GLENWYLDE NORMAL SCHOOL
The Dickson County Press, 10 Aug. 1899, announced that H. G. Gilbert was principal of this school, now in its 6th year.

GLENWYLDE HIGH SCHOOL
The Dickson County Independent, 8 Oct. 1891, announced that this school on Horse Branch would open 17 Aug. 1891. Dr. W. H. Crouch was the president of the board and Rev. H. H. Marshall was principal. The school was two miles north of Cumberland Furnace.

By 1937 this was a two-teacher school called Glenwylde School.

In 1910 when Mrs. Billy White was teacher, the pupils included: Norman Freeman, Minor Hamilton, Lloyd Swift, Carl Hailey, Jesse Ferrell, Ira Crick, Grigsby Wall, Leonard Wall, Ernest Wall, George Ferrell, Wilson Wall, Fannie Allman, Alfred Nelson, Hershell Wall, Earl Hamilton, Judge Crockett, Edwin Smith, Arthur Wall, Izetta Smith, Frances White, Ivie Batson, Ralph White, Addie Nelson, Golden Davis, Avie Hailey, Ara Davis, Irene Wall, Celia Nelson, Hattie Freeman, Addie Freeman, Dolma Hamilton, Granville Yates, Ammon Wall, Buena Wall, Irene Swift, Ruth Matthews, Ruth Daniel, Alva Wall, Lilly Hamilton, Hattie Hailey, Pearl Wall, Tena Bishop, Carrie Hamilton, Mattie Nelson, Marvin Proctor, Carl Harris, Gilbert Freeman, Joe Hamilton, Louis Wall, Melvin Hailey, Emma Hailey, Novella Wall, Ellen Wall, Cyrns Neblett, Henreitti Jobe, Charlie Gray, Fronia Bishop, Brackin Osburn, Lavana Wall, Grady Wall, Clara Wall, Earl Smith, Maud Jobe, Guy Nelson, and Alma Wall. Professor W. A. White also taught at this school.

In 1937 the pupils in the 5th through 8th grades were: Louise Wall, Carl Davis, Warner Powers, Robert Tilley, Minnie Bentley, Cecil Freeman, Clifford Phillips, Ozell Baldwin, Opal Bentley, Rebecca Wall, Sara Sue Sensing, Edward Davis, John Dillard, Mack Gray, Jr., Edna Baldwin, Ethel Proctor and Billy Jackson. Miss Glen Loggins was the teacher of this group.

HAMBLE SCHOOL
By 1937 this was a one-teacher school with Mabel Speight as teacher. There is a 1908 picture of this school in our family scrapbook, but no names of pupils given.

HAMPTON HIGH SCHOOL (c)
The teachers of this school in 1937 were A. J. Hardy, S. C. Watkins, and Vance Kinnard.

HAND'S SCHOOL
This school was in District 8 and was burned in 1898. Will Walton, age 15, who lived near Betsytown, confessed to setting it afire. (Source: Dickson County paper, 24 Nov. 1898.)

HAPPY VALLEY SCHOOL
This school was once located about a mile from old Laurel Furnace.

HARPETH VALLEY SCHOOL
This was a one-teacher school in 1937 with Bertha Oakley as teacher.

HENDRICKS SCHOOL (c)
In 1937 this was a one-teacher school and Earsley Vanleer was the teacher. The colored settlement known as Hendricks was about this school.

HERBISON SCHOOL
This school in District 3 was a one-teacher school in 1937 and the teacher was Virginia Ray.

HICKORY GROVE SCHOOL
This school was on East Piney. In 1937 it was a one-teacher school and Mildred Twomey was the teacher. Originally the school was on what is now Cowan Road, but in 1906 was moved to the East Piney Road. Land for the school was donated by Vardie McCorpin. An article in our family scrapbook, by an unidentified author, has the following:

"Miss Hattie Cuniff taught the first school, a five month term. Some of the pupils were Claud McCorpin, Estell McCorpin, Mintie Weems Murphy, Callie Weems Vineyard, Bryant Weems, Era Fussell Crow, Mable Stephens, and Mike Cuniff. This little house was used every year through 1915.

Mr. Rollen Crow and Miss Bessie Beck taught the second year..."

Later teachers included: Mark Tidwell, Mrs. Bell Bryant, Miss Millie Moore, Miss Clara Walker, and Miss Clara White.

In 1916 a new school building was constructed. Joe Springer taught the first school in the new one, while he and his wife lived in the old one. Mildred Twomey was the last teacher and the school and grounds were turned over to John Stephens, who owned the farm from which it had been originally taken. Mr. McCorpin had stipulated that if this ever ceased to be a school it would revert to the original land.

In 1925 pupils at this school were: Keith Harbison, Evelyn Harbison, Onita Fielder, Thomas Wells, Doye Garton, Harden Fussell, Mildred Donegan, Lorene Garton, Albert Garton, Bessie McCorpin, Dorothy Greer, Catherine Fussell, Alma Fussell, Charlotte Greer, Daisy Tucker, Edna Fussell, William Bradford, Julian Fielder, Novie Donegan, Karen Greer, Eva Clifton, Ida Pearl Tucker, Lillian Bradford, John Fussell, Clara Mae Clifton, Evelyn McCorpin, Willie Erranton, Genevieve Donegan, Dell Greer, J. M. Donegan, Ed McCorpin, Malcolm Fussell, Luther Mangrum, Blake Urown, Bill Fussell, Sally Brown, Lou Dora Donegan. Joel Erranton was the teacher that year.

Pupils in 1932 were: Graham Donegan, Linward Parchment, Elmer Bradford, Albert Warren, Thomas Parchment, Elton Bradford, Elbert Ray Fussell, Helen Parchment, Edna Fussell, Velma Fussell, Lorene Garton, Lillian Vineyard, Albert Sager, Lucille Garton, Imogene Fussell, Frank Brannon, Wiley Tucker, Thelma Garton, Hazel Wiley, Mildred Donegan, Margaret Sager, Ida Pearl Tucker, Doy Garton, William Bradford, Howard Horner, and Buford Warren. The teacher that year was Mrs. Mollie Blake.

HIGH POINT SCHOOL
In 1937 this was a one-teacher school and Miss Beatrice Work was the teacher.

HILLCREST SCHOOL
This school was started 1936-1937 and included children from Plunders Creek, Oak Grove, Cedar Hill, Water Valley, and by 1941 Few's Chapel. Mrs. Joe Puckett Bowen named the school in a contest held at a school box supper. Miss Madge Hagood and Mrs. Agnes Mays were the first teachers at the school. Miss Mattie Boaz was the last teacher in 1960-1962. The building is now used as a community center and a voting precinct.

In 1937-38 the first class at Hillcrest School included: Donald Fielder, Charles Hood, James Donegan, James Harold Lucas, Billy Fielder, Clovis Adcock, Ewel Donegan, Lee Hood, Hershell Fielder, Frank LeComte, James Jones, Ward Kimbro, Junior Moore, Mary Lucas, Lucille LeComte, Ann Clifton, Jean Moore, Christine LeComte, June Donegan, Alice Donegan, Jimmy Clifton, Charles Bruce, Hazel Moore, Irene Wills, Billie Bruce, Louise Mathis, Josephine Whitson, Wilma Brown, James Robert Work, Margie Bruce, Mable Jones, Lorene Fielder, Louise LeComte, Jeanette Manley, Bessie Lu Fielder, Mary Brunette, Emma Jean Fielder, Marie Whitson, Jewel Moore, Opan Fielder, Woodrow Mathis, Myrtle Jones, Ann Donegan, Lynwood Parchment, Etta Bowen, Manis Adcock, Dollie Bell Kimbro, Carson Fielder, and Cecil Donegan. (Source: Dickson County Herald, 17 April 1975, quoting article by Mrs. Carlton Bowen. This also appeared in Dickson Free Press.)

HORTENSE SCHOOL (c)
This was a one-teacher school in 1937 and Alice Bomar was teacher.

HORSE COLLAR SCHOOL
Miss Serena Clark was the teacher of this school in 1887; the location is not known.

JACKSON CHAPEL SCHOOL
This school was on the Ashland City Road and in 1937 was a two-teacher school.

In 1912 the teacher was Mrs. Milbria Larkins Jackson and the pupils that year: Charlie Hamilton, Gilbert Connell, Herman Walker, Earnest Glasgow, John Robertson, Alvin Jackson, Maggie Connell Lovell, Horace Pickering, Rachel Walker James, Luna Hunter, Gurtie Hunter, Fostina Thatch, Virgie Jones Glasgow, Luna Pickering Watts, Beulah Glasgow Jones, Odell Jackson Larkins, Sherman Mitchell, Lillian Jackson, Ella Jones Lovell, Mary Connell DeLones, Maggie Jones Stacey, Zelmer Jones Choate, Dona Mitchell, Euvals Hunter Reed, Elvis Jones, Lance Hunter, David Robertson and Eckford Jones.

WILLIAM JAMES HIGH SCHOOL
This school at White Bluff opened 1923 on land given by Col. William James, whose grave is on the school grounds.

JASON SCHOOL
In 1937 this was a one-teacher school with Mrs. Mollie Brake as the teacher.

LAMPLEY SCHOOL
In 1937 this was a one-teacher school with Alice Bledsoe as teacher.

LIBERTY SCHOOL
This school is listed at least as early as 1887. In 1937 Mary E. Hutton was the teacher and it was a one-teacher school.

MAPLE GROVE SCHOOL
A one-teacher school in Dickson County in 1937, Mary Carroll was the teacher that year.

MAPLE VALLEY SCHOOL
In 1937 this was a one-teacher school and Katherine Nichols was the teacher.

MARIDA SCHOOL
This was a school is Dickson County in 1887, but no further information was available about it.

MARVIN'S CHAPEL SCHOOL
In the 1860s this was a school taught by Mrs. Liza Reeder.

MEEK SCHOOL
The site of this school is now the westbound lane of I-40, 3 miles east of Highway 46.

Miss Susie Hogin was the teacher in 1904 and the pupils included: Rachel Brown, Clara Meek, Homer Tidwell, Ida Garton, Leta Meek, John Dillard, Ruby Dillard, Paul Beck, Blanche Bissinger, Mary Brown, Edgar Beck, Thelma Buttrey, Johnnie Mai Tidwell, Myrtle Bissinger, Clayton Luther, Anna Brown, Clyde Brown, Vera Tidwell, Clude Brown, Beadie Brown, Tommie Brown, Elton Brown, Fate Brown, Mary Brown, Callie Bissinger, Corbitt Brown, Colista Borchert, Hinchey Beck, Cora Meek, Edgar Luther, Odie Brown, Connie Tidwell, Pearl Ridgeway, Turner Brown, Cordon Garton, Wade Brown, Sam Dillard, Vergie Bissinger, Allie Garton, Edgar Spencer, Emma Spencer, Iva Carr, Ray Hogin, Trula Brown, Arthur Tidwell, Bessie Beck, Eva Luther, Mark Welch, Ruth Brown, Eunice Meek, Thurman Brown, Susie Brown, Turner Brown, and Genie Brown.

Grover Luther was the teacher in 1913 and pupils that year were: Jack Holland, Hubert Thompson, Nolan Cathey, Clement Holland, Richard Dillard Marion Debusk, Glenn Anderson, Marvin Brown, Noel Brown, Harmon Tidwell, Tillman Brown, Emmett Brown, Vara Thompson, Lovine Gentry, Doye Brown, Clarice Smith, Vara Tidwell, Lera Totty, Bessie Garton, Alice Lankford, Jewel Holland, Lois Totty, Gladys Anderson, Cecil Brown, Thelma Gentry, Clara Buttrey, Iva Cathey, Lurline Lankford, Spencer Tidwell, Inez Thompson, Erline Gentry, Leo Cathey, Pauline Meek, Alice Tidwell, Adell Totty, Thelma Debusk, Cletus Meek, Blanche Luther, Clyde Brown, Nora

Wilkins, Claude Brown, Vera Tidwell, Tommy Brown, Ruby Dillard, Clarence Brown, Clemmie Ridgeway, Arthur Buttrey, Vally Luther, Victor Smith, Lucille Meek, Lynn Brown, Bessie Luther, Vegie Brown, Mamie Brown, Myrtle Bissinger, Lera Brown, Thomas Wilkins, Hassie Tidwell, Harland McCoy, Bessie Holland, Cuba Garton, Cordelia Smith, Estella Gentry, Jessie Garton, Dewey Brown, Jewell Smith, Homer Dillard, Alice Meek, Bennie Totty, and Needham Gentry.

MILLER'S CHAPEL SCHOOL
In 1937 this was a one-teacher school with Warren Cratty as teacher.

MOKSON FLOP SCHOOL (c)
This was a school in old District 1 on Plunders Creek and was built for the children of the seven colored families there. All the men had been slaves.

MT. CARMEL SCHOOL
This was a school in Dickson County in 1887, but no further information has been available.

MT. GOSSETT SCHOOL
This school was at Bon Aqua, but some pupils were from or later lived in Dickson County. Those attending this school in 1934-1935 were Billy Martin, Leroy Lane, Ronald Gossett, Thomas Morgan, Herbert Estes, Cecil Martin, Howard McDaniel, Arthur McDaniel, Buford Morgan, Ammon Stinson, Tommy Morgan, Marshall Martin, Billy Fitts, Chester Harbison, Artie McDaniel, Herbert Estes, Corrinne Stinson, J. W. Morgan, Ellis Tidwell, Barbara McDaniel, Hazel Tidwell, Jimmy McMahan, Ammon Rainey, Bill Rainey, Margaret Sue Booker, Evelyn Tidwell, Thelma Tidwell, Arlis Stinson, Lula Mae McDaniel, Mary Ruth Holt, Ruth Fitts, Elsie Morgan, Florence Beasley, Novalene Morgan, J. W. Stinson, Lillian Booker, Doye Tidwell, Walker Stinson, Diamond Tucker, Lorene McDaniel, Sterling Holt, George William Ledbetter, Margaret McDaniel, Marie Stinson, and Freda Mae Rainey. The teachers were Lavert Uselton and Miss Alma Gillespie.

MT. LEBANON SCHOOL
This school was in operation at least by 1887, and possibly before. Those attending this school in 1901 were: Edgar Martin, Herman Stewart, Oscar Oakley, Edd Lyles, Ben Greer, Clarence Brazzell, Arthur Richardson Marshall Larkins, Elmer Brazzell, Clyde Larkins, Virgil Choate, Lizzie Stewart, Fannie Hale, Faustina Greer, Kathleen Simpson, Mary Choate, Bertha Cratty, Della Brazzell, Irene Allen, Ora Larkins, Stella Walker, Emma Dotson, Florence Stewart, Jennie Greer, Stella Larkins, Ethel Choate Ola Choate, Bonnie Oakley, Ethel Hale, Effie Lindsey, Fred Brown, Albert Choate, Van Sanders, Minnie Brown, Evie Simpson, Lena Larkins Mary Cratty, Evie Choate, John Simpson, Earlie Greer, Walter Choate, Mark Brown, Zollie Martin, Marvin Choate, Carter Sanders, Bea Lyles, Nellie Lyles, Ida Richardson, Emma Richardson, Lee Richardson, Herman Allen, Wed Greer. The teacher that year was Miss Lizzie Steele.

In 1912 Marvin Choate was the teacher and the pupils were: Charlie Larkins, Ruby Hudson, Minerva Brown, Blanche Cratty, Robert Larkins, Burton Greer, Wed Greer, Gladys Allen, Elsie Hudson, Ruth Buttrey, Helen Brown, Zelma Allen, Ilma Cratty, Sam Buttrey, Paul Hudson, Claude Fussell, Alfred Buttrey, Howard Austin, Dausey Buttrey, Lee Walker, Docia Buttrey, Viola Walker, Mary Ferebee, Faustina Greer, Ilma Hudson, Ora Allen, Lloyd Fussell, Burnard Ferebee, and Clarence Cratty.

In 1937 this was a two-teacher school.

MT. SINAI SCHOOL
This school was on East Piney and in operation at least by 1898. By 1937 it was a one-teacher school and Lillian Vineyard was the teacher. The first school here was built of logs. Some of the early teachers have been Tom Weems, Agnes Work, Belle Bryant, Thad Register, Kitty McWilliams, Lou Moore, Hattie Cunniff, Clara White, J. B. Sugg, and Eva Brown.

In 1910 some of the pupils attending this school were: Loyd Frazier, Ernest Holland, Frank Redden, Ernest Kimbro, Clarence Bowen, Tom Wiley,

Carl Clifton, Paul Russell, Hubert Luther, Ruby Myatt, Ruby Clifton, Bonnie Frazier, Irene Work, Darlean Frazier, Arthur Clifton, Myrtle Holland, Claude Holland, Elvis Holland, Anval Frazier, Ramie Myatt, Percy Holland, Loyd Holland, Sallie Russell, Lee Holland, Ernest Redden, Edd Holland, Carl Sugg, Sim Kimbro, Bertie Clifton, Hubert Vineyard, Elijah Moore, Mary Holland, Lucy Dudley, Sarah Nelson, Docia Kimbro, Annie Clifton, Gurtha Dudley, Annie Holland, True and Ivan Vineyard, Herbert Garton, Hardy Holland, Percy Wiley, John Bowen, Guy Nelson, Mary Bowen, Joe Kimbro, Lizzie Moore, Willie Myatt, Mollie Rogers Yates, Maude Garton, Zollie Bowen, Ola Yates, Willie Dudley, Tina Dudley, Noah Clifton, Maude Kimbro, Noel Kimbro, Clara White, Rosa Holland. The teacher was Clara White Stephens.

Other teachers have included Noah Clifton, Grover Luther, Hollie Bryant, Maude Garton, Dan Fielder, Evie Fielder, Euzella Bissinger, Clara Weems, Vesta Register, Mattie Boaz, Louise Annis, Helen Burges, Lula Fussell, Mary Louise Larkins, and Belle Bryant. Roy Donegan also taught here.

Agnes Work, onetime teacher here, later Mrs. Agnes Shipp Clement was the first woman superintendent of schools in Tennessee, and possibly in the nation. She served from 1896 until 1898.

MT. ZION SCHOOL
This school was at one time on Turkey Creek, but no further information was available.

NAILS CREEK SCHOOL
Mrs. Mollie Tidwell Hooper was once a teacher in this school. The school was active in the 1880s. No further information available.

NEBLETT SCHOOL (c)
Ella Robins was the teacher of this school for blacks in 1887.

NEW HOPE SCHOOL
This school was in the Rock Springs community and still stands as a community center.

NEWPORT SCHOOL (c)
In 1937 this was a one-teacher school and Etta Mai Ransom was the teacher.

NICKS SCHOOL HOUSE
In 1882 this was a school in the Flat Gap neighborhood.

OAKDALE SCHOOL
This school near Vanleer was a one-teacher school in 1937 with Opal Dean was the teacher.

In 1917 pupils attending the school included: Eugene Hassel, Ray Berry, Claud Trotter, Olin Robertson, Leon Halliburton, Clyde Jones, Howard Jones, Almond Robertson, Sidney Waynick, Alvin Ferrel, Willie McGee Robinson, Forrest Waynick, ___Chandler, Ollen Robertson, Tunley Trotter, Myrtle Jones, Guy Robison, ___Edwards, Georgia Ragan, Madeline Hassel, Claborne Gilmore, Pauline Robertson, Ethel Jones, Elthia Ragan, Zelma Trotter, Ernest Jones, Nollie Berry, Birdie Ragan, Ada Coon, Katrine Gilmore, Valeria Ragan, Sammy Robison, Alvin Edwards, Clyde Allen, David Ferrel, Dan Edwards, Cordie Hassell, Floyd Hassell, Maggie Robertson, Bethel Collier, Vera Gilmore, Vera Collier, Amanda Waynick, and Maudie Deason.

OAK GROVE SCHOOL
This school was 10 miles south of Dickson on Highway 48 between Piney River and Garner's Creek. In 1937 it was a one-teacher school with Madge Hagood as teacher.

The first school was built of log and for a time a holiness group also used the building as a meeting house. In 1936 or shortly afterwards the school was consolidated with Water Valley School to form Hillcrest School. Madge Hagood, now Mrs. Daniel, was the last teacher here.

A picture in our family scrapbook shows the pupils here in 1920 and they were: Edd Betty, Paul Booker, Berry Wills, Roy Moore, J. D. Rains, Wilson Booker, Homer Moore, Gertrude Fielder, Joe Bowen, Harvel Sullivan, Gladis Booker, Tennessee Betty, Rosa Rains, Burton Fielder, Christine Bowen, Hallie Sullivan, Clatie Moore, Oda Rains, Zollie Moore, Carl Moore, Marson Donegan, Perry Sullivan, Wade Moore, Earl Wills, Hubert Moore, Dean Wills, Fred Wills, Earl Yates, Norman Moore, Christine Moore, Claude Fielder, Doyl Yates, Virgil Moore, Wade Moore, Alton Baker Willie Vineyard, Hulan Fielder, Leamon Yates, Grace Fielder, Martin Fielder, Augie Vineyard, Floyd Wills, Eddie Moore, Tinnie Pearl Fielder, and Elergy Betty. At that time Wade Wilson was the teacher.

OAK HILL SCHOOL
This was a school in 1887 and in that year a Sunday School was also formed here by James Corlew. In 1937 this was a one-teacher school and Elsie Hudson was the teacher.

OAKMONT SCHOOL
This school was on Bryant Avenue. The school burned 2 March 1941 and now a low rent housing project is on the property. S. E. Hunt has been credited with much of the success of getting this school started. For many years this was the leading school in Dickson.

The first school in Dickson was held in the Dickson courthouse on the site of the War Memorial building. Miss Lela Rice was the first grade teacher here. Then school was also held for a time in the Bryant house and Miss Gilbert was the second grade teacher there. But after a fire in the Bryant house, classes were once again held in the courthouse.

As one pupil of the time said recently, "We went to school all over town."

The name Oakmont for the school is said to have come from Mrs. W. P. Morrison because the school set in a grove of trees.

The following information was found in the cornerstone of the school: "Dickson, Tennessee, Sept. 16, 1915. This building was erected in 1912-13 and the cornerstone was left unfinished and open until above date when it was ordered closed by W. H. Walker, mayor, while the roof of the building was undergoing some repair work by L. B. Donnelly, brick mason, and Bert Parchman, helper. In the absence of the records that were intended to be sealed up in this vault, the present school enrollment is approximately 650, with Prof. W. P. Morrison, formerly of Centerville, the principal. Signed: W. H. Walker, Mayor of Dickson, term expired Oct. 1, 1915." The school cost $25,000 to build.

After the fire in 1941 classes were held in various churches and at the War Memorial Building while an addition was built to the school. Eight years later and after a second fire, Oakmont was condemned and a new school built on McLemore in 1949.

In 1917 before Dickson High School was started, Oakmont included high school work. Members of the May 1918 high school graduating class were: Louise Johnson, Curtis Sheely, Sammy Bryan, William Thompson, Rosanna Oakley, Iris Hopkins, Ione Larkins, Willie Collier, John Brown, Mary Walker, Gilbert Petty and Esta Jones.

In the scrapbook is a picture of the 1920-21 second grade class at Oakmont. The teacher was Miss Mable Mathis. Those in the class that year were: Paul Perry, James Corlew, Forrest Boone, Ida Mae Brown, Mildred Jones, Elizabeth Boone, Marjorie Austin, Lois Powers, Jane Taylor, Evelyn Fussell, Pauline Grant, Daisy Cowan, Dorothy Mae Larkins, Kris Gossett, Charles Chappell, Harry Bryan, J. W. Shawl, Juanita Locke, Tully Easley, Jim D. Rice, and Mary Alice Meadow.

The eighth grade graduates of Oakmont in 1937 were: Elton Clifton, Robert Lee, James Larkins, James Clark Mack, E. W. Alheight, Billy Hurt, Ray Buchanan, Glen Myatt, Charles Booker, Leburn Pierce, Hubert Gilmer, Thomas Bell, Will Morrison, Charles Kratchman, Bobby Meeks, Jack Duncan, Charles Wright, Orman Hailey, Kenneth Fielder, Billy Stewart, Betty Pack

Paul Larkins, Neil Fussell, Remellia Watts, Evelyn Bradford, Sara Deason, Sigma Fay Stinnett, Emma Jean Bachman, Wilma Larkins, Margaret Myatt, Mary Ann Leathers, Juanita Binkley, Betty Richards, Anna Belle Clement, Oneida Fuqua, Dorris Sue Caldwell, Louise Springer, Dorris Graybill, Margaret Hite Robinson, Donnie Mai Baxter, Sammie Hammons, Mary Jean Martin, Mary Ann Williams, Frances Buttrey, Louise Larkins, Henrietta Miller, Willie Mai Ritcherson, ___Tidwell, Mary Emma Baker, Carrol Tipton, Blanche Redden, Bruce Houston, Sherman Anderson, Verlie Donegan, Neil Buckner, Charles Grant, Jimmy Taylor, Lester Hampton, William Hurt, Marshall Fields, James Grant, Harris Few, Richard Orgain, Melvin Larkins. The principal that year was Tom T. Sugg and the class teacher was Carney Nicks.

The last Oakmont picture in our family scrapbook is for the eighth grade class in 1941 with Miss Willie G. McMillan as homeroom teacher. Those in the class included: Marie Herbison, Letha Fay Rushton, Juanita Powers, Alma Jean Weakley, Mary Alice Taylor, Harry England, Billy Joe Brake, Joe Billy Rainey, Bobby Saeger, Jack Mitchell, Ted Melton, Dan Andrews, Betty Adcock, Reba Nicks, Eloise Houston, Jean Smith, Frances Lane, Edith Jane Ladd, David Hurt, Gus Foster, Marie Work, Melba Booker, Juanita Harrell, Sue Rocky, R. D. Chandler, Bobby Mitchell, Walter Erranton, and several whose names were not recalled.

A list of principals of the school was published in the Dickson Free Press, 31 Jan. 1973: Miss Patterson, A. P. Whitlock, W. P. Morrison, V. L. Broyles, H. J. Bynum, Mr. Owen with J. J. Dugger as assistant, J. H. Bayer (superintendent of Dickson High and Oakmont), Joel D. Sugg, O. J. Seymour, John Hutchinson, Tom Sugg, Elizabeth Dunn, who had been principal 29 years in 1973.

Some of the teachers at Oakmont through the years were: Frank Frazier, Mrs. Frank Frazier, Miss Iva Allman, Mrs. H. J. Bynum, Miss Mintie Pounds Miss Donna Worley, Miss Jennie Harville, Miss Nora Dodd, Mrs. Vina Alspaugh, Miss Vera Miller, Miss Annie Laurie Dance, Miss Anita Smith, Miss Myrtle Vowell, Miss Flora Hobbs, Miss Herriges, Miss Hollie Perry, Mrs. Mollie Brake, Miss Annie Graves, Miss Ada Curtis, Mrs. Lura Holbrook, Miss Belle Bryant, Miss Mable Mathis, and Miss Eva Brazzell.

Later teachers recalled were Joel Erranton, Pearl Roth, Anne Heard, Aileen Tomlinson, Alene Stone, Willie G. McMillan, Hazel Halbrook, Dorothy McCaul, Maggie Williams, Thelma Davis, Mary Yancy, Allene Coleman, Aline Smith, Howard Ewing, Carney Nicks, Annie Lee Sugg.

Others have been: Annie Lee Helberg, Annabelle Taylor, Karene Larkins, Grace Hudson, Mable Miller, Mrs. Virginia Hayes, Marian McCaul, Ann Sugg, Hazel Youree, Lilah Pearl Blackwell, Mrs. Ida Nicks, J. C. Erranton, Mrs. G. P. Paulk, Ora Nicks, Izetta Smith, Elizabeth Dunn, Albeth Donegan, Irene Long, Mary Alyce Eubank, Exie English, Ella Tidwell, and Mary Leech.

OLD SCHOOL
This school was on Yellow Creek just above the mouth of Bear Creek and was said to be the first school in Dickson County, taught by James Hicks in 1804.

OPOSSUM COLLEGE
This school was in the Fourth District near Stuart Cemetery just off Highway 96. The origin of the unusual name was not available. In 1913 those attending this school were: Tinsley Spicer, Curdon Spicer, Bates Young, Willie Spicer, Percy Sullivan, Odell Sullivan, Birdie Gentry, Ordie Dillard, Basil Gentry, Clark Spicer, Percy Borchert, Harvey Borchert, Webster Johnston, Percy Sullivan, Carl Garton, Howell Beck, Lola Borchert, Leegie Deal, Armour Carter, Irene Gentry, Mamie Brown, Valerie Sullivan, Freddy Bissinger, Edna Jackson, Ora Jackson, Hettice Carter, Eulon Gentry, Clarence Buttrey, Winfred Borchert, Odie Gentry, Mark Brown, Lance Young, Carley Jackson, Emma Luther (teacher), Arlie Jackson, Lula Dillard, Cletis Spicer, Lynn Brown, Hubert Bissinger, Bessie Bissinger, Cordan Borchert, Lola Deal, Earl Sullivan, Maude Beck, Lora Deal, Virgil Jackson, Bessie Borchert, Irsle Sullivan and Nannie Borchert.

The 1937 list of schools and teachers shows a one-teacher school named O'College with Mary Hooper as teacher. Possibly this was a mistake in the newspaper and should be O'Possum College.

PEABODY SCHOOL
This school was in operation as early as 1887 and possibly before. It was in the Greenwood community. One who attended this school recalled the boys cut and brought in the firewood for the stove and that water was from a spring. All the pupils drank from one bucket and dipper. By 1937 this was a one-teacher school under Ella Mae Caldwell.

POND SCHOOL
This was one of the last of the county schools to close.

PORTER SCHOOL
This was a school in operation very early in the county. The school roster for 1839 and 1840 show the following were enrolled: John H. Perry Benjamin Hayes, Mary Tidwell, Wm. E. Pendergrass, Violet Davidson, E. Sears, Silas Tidwell, T. W. White, Moses Parker, Joshua White, Alf Brown, Ely Tidwell, Thomas Martin, Richard Garton, Benjamin Walker, Mark Garton, Solomon Marsh, William L. Walker, B. Tidwell, Martha V. Van, Ruffin Perry, G. Sullivan, John B. Carr, William Parker, Jacob Lampley, John McCashin, Martha Y. Vanlandingham, John Underhill, and James Underhill. The school was taught by John Porter.

PORTER SCHOOL
In 1937 this was a two-teacher school in the county and Iva Cathey and Evelyn Tidwell were the teachers.

POSSUM HOLLOW SCHOOL
This school was an early school in the first district of Dickson County. The land for the school was given by Jake Peeler and the school was off Highway 48 South on old Cedar Hill Road. Little John Donegan taught school here in 1830 according to Goodspeed's history of the county. Melvin Harris was a teacher here at a later period.

PROMISE LAND SCHOOL (c)
In 1937 this school for blacks was a two-teacher school with J. C. Dickson and Tommie Gilbert, teachers.

POTTS SCHOOL
Potts School was on Little Barton's Creek. In 1926 some of those attending this school were Emma Baker, Annie Potter, Ruby Smith, Eva Hayes, Kathleen Rawlston, Jeston Hayes, Cordis Hayes, Sally Hayes, Myrtle Phelps, Nettie Schmittou, Isabell Baker, Othie Schmittou, Caroline Hayes, Mildred Hayes, Clyde Schmittou, Blake Lilly, Orena Smith, Kattie Smith, and Vera Schmittou. Walter Weakley was the teacher that year.

ROCK CHURCH SCHOOL
This school was in operation in 1887, but no further information was available.

ROCKDALE SCHOOL
In 1937 with was a one-teacher school with Mrs. A. P. Jobe as teacher.

RUSKIN CAVE COLLEGE
This college began in 1904 and was an exclusive private-co-educational college, closing in the 1920s. It began as a music conservatory and later became Ruskin Cave College. According to our family scrapbook, "young men could not bestow a gift upon a young lady or even write to her unless the gift or letter had first been inspected by the president of the school. The ladies could not be on campus after sundown unless properly chaperoned, and none were to wear low-necked dresses or appear in classes on campus without hose."

RUSKIN CAVE SCHOOL
This school, 12 grades, opened in 1922 with L. A. Dickson as principal. Dickson died of measles in 1923 and the school closed in 1925.

SALEM SCHOOL
This was a school in Dickson County in 1844; location not available.

SCHOOL
Frank H. Artress once operated a school on Porter Road, about 1918. He was active in the Seventh Day Adventist Church. (July 1967 clipping.)

SCHOOL
A school was held at the courthouse in Dickson briefly. Iris Hopkins remembers attending the 6th and 7th grade at this location.

SEALS SCHOOL (SCROUGE OUT)
In 1937 this school on Yellow Creek was a one-teacher school with Helen Stokes as teacher.

SLAYDEN SCHOOL
In 1937 this was a three-teacher school in the village of Slayden.

SLYVIA SCHOOL
There was a school at Sylvia at least by 1899 when Maud Frey "started up a school at Sylvia." "Marion Keele, Baptist minister, and Lallie Adams, daughter of Nelson Adams married at Sylvia school house. (Dickson County Press, 23 March 1899.) By 1937 there was a county school here and it had three teachers on the faculty.

SPICER SCHOOL (c)
Willard Bowden was the teacher at this school in 1937.

STAYTON SCHOOL
In 1937 this was listed as a two-teacher school. As early as 1895 there was a school near Friendship Church of Christ and was torn down in 1900. There have been two schools by the name of Stayton, one in 1899, and one in 1940s. A PTA organized at this school in 1940 with Mrs. John D. Sensing as president. Another school was built here in 1943, and today the building is used for family reunions and other community activities.

STONY POINT SCHOOL
This school in 1940 had been in operation for 47 years. In 1937 this was a one-teacher school under Mary Cooksey.

STORY SCHOOL (c)
Pherson Lanier was the teacher at this school for blacks in 1887.

STREET'S SCHOOL
In 1883 this was listed as a free school in District 1 and Miss Mollie Sugg was the teacher.

SULPHUR SPRINGS SCHOOL
This school was on Barton's Creek. It was a school at least by 1907 and possibly earlier. In 1907 residents along Barton's Creek had the Sulphur Springs Brass Band and members were Orville Raymond, Walter Bateman, Billy Hickerson, Asa Hickerson, Buck Leech, Earl Leech, Billy White, Walker Ferrell, Po Caldwell, Allie Byrn, Clyde Speight, Ben Berry, Wall Elliott, Hermie Lane, Clyde Miller, Charlie Elliott, Clarence Ferrell, Dick Neblett, Willie Van Raymond, Arthur Berry, Harris Daniel, Lindsey Raymond, Johnny Frey and Alvin Dickson.

This school was three miles northwest of Charlotte. In 1922 William Byrn was the teacher and some of those attending school that year were: Polly Daniel, Margaret Sanders, Leona Story, Mary Julia Dickson, Edith Hooper, Faustina Daniel, Ethel Hamm, Edna Willey, Nellie Dee Raymond, Aline Berry, Orville Raymond, Jr., Thurman Dickson, Hick Loggins, Dennis Willey, William Daniel, Woodrow Hooper, Harris Greer Daniel, O'Neal Davis, Gene Hooper, Hooper Dickson, Leon David, Lester Hooper, Bernard Willey, Henry Story, Bruce Hooper, Curtis Hamm, Robert Burgess, and James Byrn.

SWEET HOME SCHOOL
In 1937 this was a one-teacher school with Decima Carroll, teacher.

SYCAMORE SCHOOL
In 1937 this was a one-teacher school with Lola Miller, teacher.

TATUM SCHOOL
This was found as a school in Dickson County, but no information has been available on it.

TAYLOR TOWN SCHOOL
In 1937 this was a one-teacher school with Vanessa Eleazer as teacher.

TENNESSEE CITY SCHOOL
In 1937 this was a one-teacher school. In 1932 Lillian Vineyard was the teacher for Grades 1 through 4 and those in these grades were Ruth Stevens, Rachel Ritchison, D. D. McElhiney, Charles Burgess, Ramey Vetter Myrtle Berryman, Mildred Campbell, Morel Johnson, Lavern Berryman, Leon Burgess, Robert Lane, J. D. Littleton, Boogie Lane, Laymon Vetter, Floyd Tummins, William Simons, Jackie Lane, Harvey Burgess.

In 1932 Ruth Loggins was the teacher for Grades 5 to 8 and those in this section included: Donald Campbell, Percy Corbin, Scott Stevens, Helen Luther, Wilbert Vetter, Lou Ella Lane, Stella Rachel Durham, Thelma Lane, Charles Wright, Adrain Vetter, Genevieve Hutcheson, Dimple Stevens, John Thomas Crickman, Helen Corbin, Albert Vetter, Junior Luther, Elvin Roach, Olene Littleton, Vera McElhiney, Pauline Durham, Maurine Johnson, Ruby Tummins, W. A. Durham, Edith Crickman, Derbert Kretchman, Loretta Luther, Gracie McElhiney, and Raymond Tummins.

THOMPSON SCHOOL
In 1937 this was a one-teacher school with Vella B. Adams, teacher.

TICK GROVE SCHOOL (THOMPSON CROSSING)
This was a school on Yellow Creek. No further information available.

TIDWELL SCHOOL
In 1937 this was a one-teacher school under Lela Brown. In 1934 pupils at this school included: Paul Cathey, Leamon Register, Bessie Luther, C. B. Palmer, Audie Garton, ___Palmer, Jimmie Register, Arnold Welch, Paul Garton, Hattie Welch, Freddie Luther, Edward Register, Otho Brown, Warren Kemp, Delbert Glass, Loretta Register, Ruby Garton, Mary Garton, Lucille Luther, Bill Luther, John Register, Cecil Luther, Bessie Cathey, Robert Luther, Gilbert Brown, Orville Brown, and Mary Hooper was the teacher.

TRACY ACADEMY
This was a school in Charlotte. In 1842 Valentine S. Allen deeded land to the school's trustees: John C. Collier, Theodore L. Collier, and William Balthrop. For many years this was the center of Dickson County education. In 1907 the school was conveyed to the county.

In 1908 Richard Heffington was a teacher and those who studied under him included: Charles Leech, Rook Roberts, Neut Gill, Shook Roberts, Corine Hicks, Marjoribanks Edgerton, Collier Cook, Rob Hicks, Shearon Frey, Alma Fielder, Lovey Fielder, Lorene Harris, Pauline Hickerson, Willie Gilbert McMillan, Lucy Hickerson, Nannie Frost, Geneva Frey, Hattie Staley, Mary Dickson, Daisy Bouldin, Ilma Hudson, Graham Edgerton, Ruth Harper, Edna Castleman, Althea Harper, Vera Adams, Myrtle Ferrell, and others.

TRESWELL SCHOOL
In 1937 this was a one-teacher school with Mrs. Dorris Harris as teacher. A PTA was organized here in 1940 and Loyd Donegan was the president.

UNION SCHOOL
This school was on Yellow Creek near Ruskin Cave and was destroyed by fire in 1939. The school continued operation in the church.

VANLEER SCHOOL
This school closed in 1955. Pupils attending this school in 1929 were: Billy Averitte, N. H. Eubanks, several Burgess children, __Deason, Buster Tibbs, ___Allman, Ruth May Jobe, Evelyn DeBusk, Imogene Deason, Leola Springer, Mary Lee Robertson, Granville Stokes, Leon Averitte, Bill Jobe,

Emmett Hamilton, Gertrude Schmittou, several Deason children, ___Powers, Margaret Leftwick, Lubie Dunn, Lawrence Averitte, Russell Lee, Roberta Houston, Estelle Fleet, Margie Burgess, Rosie Fleet, Imogene Stokes, Ida Mabel Hamilton, Cleo Trotter, Sally Houston, Warren Deason, Albert Stokes ___Turner, Helen Leftwick, Geneva Burgess, Mildred Walker, ___Murphy, Kenneth Robertson, Howard Jackson, Montine Deason, Etta Kate Wolfe, Kate Anna Jobe, Albert Deason, Cecil Lee, Katherine Dean, Olin Springer, Geneva Stokes, Jewell Robertson, Annie Mae Averitte, Laverne Trotter, Mildred Murphy, Alice Jane Cunningham, Anna Elizabeth Seals,___Turner, Carrie Stokes, Hazel Spradling, Hazel Dean, Julia Browning, Pauline Weakley, Hubert Murphy, Mildred Deason, Gordon Creech, Joe Cunningham, W. A. DeBusk, Lincoln, Miller, Leonard Wall, Walter Bell Jackson, Elvin Hamilton, Eugene Miller and Newton Cannon. The teacher that year was Minor Stuart.

WALNUT GROVE SCHOOL
In 1937 this was a one-teacher school with Annie Louise Miller, teacher.

WATER VALLEY SCHOOL
In 1897 Water Valley school was built on Piney, replacing White's school. In 1937 this was a one-teacher school with Agnes Holland as teacher. The last school held here was in 1936.

In 1915 those attending this school included: Carlton Bowen, Willie Vineyard, Claude Bowen, Homer Bowen, Ada Fielder, Alton Baker, Virgil Fielder, Velma Bowen, Loyd Bruce, Loyd Fielder, Clint Donegan, Willie Fielder, Augie Vineyard, Nannie Bruce, Linda Donegan, Clarence Bowen, Gina Vineyard, Ferbe Bowen, Mattie Donegan, McKinley Donegan, Fannie Bowen, Elmer Harrell and Joe Harrell. The teacher that year was Mrs. Bell Bryant.

Some other teachers here have included Mrs. Milbria Larkins Jackson from 1904-1905. Nora Tidwell was here in 1906. Others have been Sally Work, Mark Tidwell, Melvin Harris, Mrs. Carla Walker Larkins, Clara Donegan Work, Milas Fielder, Mrs. Clatie Donegan Odell, Maude Garton, Mrs. Lunora Moore Wills, Mrs. Artie Weems Bowen, Madge Hagewood, and Mrs. Agnes Holland Mays. (This list of teachers came from a Bicentennial article written by Dewey Bowen.)

WAYMAN ACADEMY (c)
This school for blacks was built in Dickson in 1891.

WESLEY CHAPEL SCHOOL
This school was on Cedar Creek near Yellow Creek. In 1937 it was a two-teacher school. In 1926-1927 Alice Bradford was the teacher and those who attended the school included: Lillie Huff, Sadie Dickson, Mattie Guthrie, Mildred Adams, Nannie Weaver, Annie Huff, Bertie Guthrie, Evie Waynick, Mollie Lyle, Clorene Huff, Altha Ellis, Bethel Waynick, Odell Adams, Laura Dickson, Fannie Dickson, Richard Lyle, Garfield Reynnolds, Ernest Ellis, Toby Lyle, Ray Ellis, Clifton Reynolds, Maurice Weaver, Roger Nesbitt, Alver Weaver, Jack McClurkan, Elgie Reynolds, and Garner Pa____.

WHITE BLUFF SCHOOL
In 1937 this was a three-teacher school. About the turn of the century it is said there was a "college" at White Bluff. William James High School in White Bluff had its beginnings in 1923. Land was deeded by Col. William James, retired, U. S. Army. He also gave $1,000 to help the school get started. He was born 1849 and died 1933, and his grave is on the school campus.

WHITE SCHOOL
This school was built in the old first district and was just above the forks of Piney. This is said to be the log school where Alexander Campbell taught. (Refer to Campbell School listing.)

Some of the people who attended this school during its history were: Lowry Bowen, Richard Bowen, William Bowen, James Bowen, Hickman Bowen, Robert Thomas Bowen, Buford Bowen, Agnes Bowen, Charles Bowen, Alvie Bowen, Houston Wills, and Melvin Harris.

WHITE SCHOOL
In 1937 this was a one-teacher school with Eulalia Luther as teacher. The school was on Turnbull Creek and in our family scrapbook is an undated picture of the pupils of the school. That unknown year the following were attending the school: Glenn White, Hubert Dillard, Dardy White, Tula White, Uda White, Etta White, Ruby Spencer, Ruby Herbison, A. D. Spicer, Earnest Olin Welch, Ada Welch, Bee Garton, J. B. White, Will Spicer, Cacy Garton, Essie White, Ruby Garton, Elizabeth Garton, Calley Garton, Alma Hutcherson, Burl Spicer, Clint Spencer, Olie Garton, Ellet Herbison, Alex Spicer, Archie Spicer, Burt Garton, Murt Hagan, Thurman Garton, Edgar Tidwell, Dixy Hutcherson, Vernon Garton, Eugene Spicer, and Erin Garton. The teacher that year was Ollie Tidwell.

WHITE OAK FLATS SCHOOL
In 1937 this was a one-teacher school with Ruth Sensing as teacher.

WILLIAMS CHAPEL SCHOOL
In 1937 this was a one-teacher school with Luella Pack as teacher.

WOODS VALLEY SCHOOL
In 1937 this was a two-teacher school at Woods Valley.

ZION SCHOOL (c)
In 1937 this was a one-teacher school taught by Lizzie Gleaves

> This concludes the school section of this work. There are many more schools in the history of Dickson County, but these are the only ones in our files to date. Additional information could not be obtained on some of the schools in this listing.

+++

MOST COMMON SURNAMES IN DICKSON COUNTY

By using census records, tombstone inscriptions, school and church records, and newspaper listings, the following appear to be the most common or frequently found surnames in Dickson County from 1804 to 1982:

1. Brown
2. Baker
3. Tidwell
4. Moore
5. Williams
6. Johnson
7. Jones
8. Smith
9. Myatt
10. Jackson
11. Martin
12. Hooper
13. Thompson
14. Miller

X

CHRONOLOGY

This section contains a listing of only some events or highlights in Dickson County history and does not claim to be a complete listing. These are only some of the events and were found while doing research on the county and its families.

Readers who wish to know more about the county are urged to read "A History of Dickson County" by Robert E. Corlew, reprinted in 1981 by the Dickson County Historical Society.

1780

Colonel John Donelson began the voyage on the flatboat Adventure down the Tennessee River and up the Cumberland in 1779 and reached the site now known as Nashville. James Robertson, "Father of Middle Tennessee," had also begun an overland trek to the Cumberland Settlements in 1779, returned to Watauga, and made return trip to the Cumberland area.

1784

Russell Gower, Anderson Lucas and James Russell hunted and camped on Yellow Creek in the future Dickson County. (Deed Book A, pages 310-312.)

1796

Tennessee admitted to the Union as the sixteenth state on June 1. Old Tennessee County was abolished to establish Robertson and Montgomery counties, and the name Tennessee was given to the state.

1803

The following was found in the Dickson County Herald, 29 Sept. 1911:

"Dickson County was named in honor of William Dickson of North Carolina, who was a United States surveyor. The county was surveyed out of, or from the territory of Robertson and Montgomery counties in 1803, by the following enactment:

"An act erecting part of Robertson and Montgomery counties into a separate and distinct county:

"Section 1. Be it enacted by the General Assembly of the State of Tennessee, that a new county by the name of DICKSON be and hereby is erected and established out of that part of Robertson and Montgomery, comprehended within the bounds following to it: Beginning on the south bank of the Cumberland River, where the line which separates the counties of Robertson and Davidson intersects the same, running thence down said river to a point half a mile below Fayetteville, thence southwardly to a line which shall intersect Barton's Creek, one half mile north of the forge; thence due west to a stake or point one mile east of the east boundary line of Stewart county, thence south to the southern boundary of this state, thence east with said southern boundary to the southwest corner of Williamson county as established by an act of the last session of General Assembly, entitled An Act to extend the jurisdiction and to ascertain the bounds of the counties therein mentioned," thence north with the east boundary line of the counties or Williamson and Dickson to the beginning."

"The above limits were materially reduced by an act of the Legislature passed on 3 Dec. 1807, which provided for the establishment of Hickman County out of the south part of Dickson, and again by an act creating Humphreys County, passed 19 Oct. 1809, and again in the erection of Cheatham County by an act passed 22 Feb. 1856, and still again by an act passed 23 Jan. 1871, which a portion of the county was taken in the formation of Houston County. The county at present contains 470 square miles.

"The first meeting of the county court in Dickson County was held 19 March 1804, at the residence of Col. Robert Nesbitt, a log structure three miles north of Charlotte.

"The first county election held in Dickson County was on the first Thursday in June 1804. August 3, 1804, Robert Dunning, Sterling Brewer, John Davidson, Montgomery Bell, and George Clark were appointed commissioners to fix on the most central and suitable situation for the erection of the courthouse, prison and stock for Dickson County, whose duty it was to purchased 40 acres of land on the most reasonable terms, on some part of which the above buildings were to be erected.

"The commissioners were also authorized to lay off the said 40 acres into a town, to be called Charlotte, and to sell said town lots, and with the proceeds of such sales erect and pay to the courthouse, prison, and stocks, and should the money derived from such sales be insufficient to pay all the costs in creating such buildings the county court was authorized to levy a tax for such purchase.

"In 1808, Charles Stewart donated to Dickson County 50 acres of land for the location of the county site, which that year was surveyed into town lots and the county site being christened Charlotte, the courthouse was completed in 1812 at a cost of $1,100."

The following entitled "Some Early History" was found in the Dickson County Herald, 20 Sept. 1911:

"The first land entries bear evidence of the presence of white men in Dickson County as early as 1786. These land grants were issued by the governors of North Carolina for service rendered in the Revolutionary War. The first land grant on record was to John Hogg for 640 acres.

"Among those who settled on Barton's creek prior to 1800 were Gen. James Robertson, who came from Nashville, John Nesbitt, from South Carolina, Abraham Caldwell, from Ireland; Richard Napier from Virginia, and Montgomery Bell from Pennsylvania.

"Those who settled about the same time on Jones Creek were Molton Dickson and James Steele, from North Carolina; John Larkins from South Carolina; and Gabe Joslin from Nashville.

"On Yellow Creek, same time, John Adams from Virginia, John Lamastus from North Carolina, Jerry Nesbitt from South Carolina. On Turnbull Creek, Edward Tidwell, John Brown, Minor Bibb from South Carolina.

"On Piney River, William Hogins from Virginia, Hutson Dudley and Thomas Petty from North Carolina. Daniel and Jacob Leech located near the present site of Charlotte. John Spencer, Anthony Vanleer, Epps Jackson, and James Fentress were some of the settlers that came to Dickson county between 1800 and 1810.

"Two blockhouses or forts were built for protection about 1800. These forts were rude, but strong, log houses with doors and windows made of puncheons, calculated to withstand both bullets and arrows, and were situated near Cumberland Furnace and the town of White Bluff.

"About 1810 the first public road was located or established from Nashville to Charlotte and then run westward to the Tennessee River.

"The first man licensed by the county court to keep a general store was John Holland, who, in 1806, opened a store in the county (the exact location of which cannot be ascertained) and sold dry goods, notions, groceries, and whisky. The first corn mill erected in Dickson County was on Jones Creek and built by Arter West about 1800. The building was a one-story log structure about 25 x 30 feet in dimensions and was water power.

""Still-houses were numerous from the very early days of the settlement until the breaking out of the Civil War. The distilleries were supplied with the old-fashioned copper worm. The beer would be run off one day, allowed to cool for a day, and then run through the worm again on the third day. The capacity of the average still was about one barrel per day. Pure whisky at that time sold for 25 cents to 40 cents per gallon.

"The first post office was established in Dickson County at Charlotte in 1806, Richard Waugh being postmaster."

1804

The following historical marker was erected on the highway out from Charlotte by the Tennessee Historical Commission:

> ROBERT NESBIT
> The former home of this pioneer is 0.2 miles north. Here, March 18 1804, the first County Court of Dickson County met with Lemuel Harvey presiding. Other members were Montgomery Bell, Richard Napier, Jesse Craft, William Doak, William Teas, Gabriel Allen, William Russell, and Sterling Brewer, with David Dickson, clerk.

Court minutes for the first year in Dickson County history are still in existence and have been microfilmed in recent years by the Tennessee State Library and Archives. These court minutes show that in 14 Dec. 1804, Isaac West, Sr., was given permission to keep an ordinary in his dwelling house.

1805

Thomas Batson was granted permission by the court to keep an ordinary at his dwelling house in June 1805.

1806

John Spencer was granted leave to keep an ordinary at his dwelling house in Sept. 1806. Thomas Martin was also allowed at the same time to keep an ordinary in his dwelling house at Charlotte.

1810

This year estray notices were published in the Clarksville newspaper, U. S. Herald, issue of 11 Aug. 1810: Edmund Howard, living on Town Creek in Dickson County, 1 mile from Charlotte, took up a bay mare; Thomas Martin on Jones Creek near Major Strong's took up a sorrel horse; William Morriss, living near Giffin's Mill, took up an iron gray mare; and Henry Williams of Cumberland Furance advertised he had a sorrel horse to stray in December 1809.

Court records show that David Hughes was charged with petit larceny and William Norris with assault and battery. Sophia Reynolds sued her husband Amos Reynolds for divorce this year.

1811

Carr Allen and Francis Martin were charged with assault and battery--and it appears they were fighting each other. Ezekiel Norris was also charged with assault and battery. as were Henry Hudson and William Abney this year.

1812

Alice Paxton sued her husband John Paxton for divorce; Polly Moulder sued Abraham Moulder for divorce; Alexander Sweeney sued his wife Nancy Sweeney for divorce; and Robert Madden sued wife Frances for divorce. Francis Hutton was charged with assault and battery.

In April Christopher Robertson, and Minor Bibb were permitted to keep ordinaries and William Parker was given permission to operate a house of entertainment. In July William Speight and William Ward were given permission to have ordinaries at their dwelling houses, and in October Joseph Wingate was also given permission.

William Pearce Humphrey, age 6, was bound to William Pearsall until he was 21 years and Elizabeth Pearce Humphreys was bound to Michael Molton.

1813
Nicholas Wilson and Christopher Wilson were arrested this year for having money molds in their possession. Richard Napier was charged with assault and battery and Peggy McHenry was charged with larceny.

1814
Elizabeth Goodwin sued Joseph and Sarah Alexander for slander this year and Elias W. Napier was charged with rape.

1818
A reward for $20 was offered by William Wall for the return of a runaway slave, Allen, 28, "belonging to William Wall living near Haslip's Iron Works." (Weekly Chronicle, Clarksville, 26 Aug. 1818.)

This year Nathan Nail and Henry A. L. Napier were charged with assault and battery. Joseph J. Eason was given permission to keep an ordinary. George F. Napier was admitted to practice law at the bar of Dickson County.

1820
Robert Cleghorn advertised he had a sorrel horse stolen from him. (Clarksville Gazette, 25 Nov. 1820.)

Estrays were taken up by William Turner at the mouth of Jones Creek and Levi Tidwell on Turnbull Creek. (Clarksville Gazette, 18 March 1820.) Elizabeth David on Turnbull, Sampson Bowls on Yellow Creek, William Tatom on the east fork of Yellow Creek, Charles Rever on Turnbull, and Joseph Eason and William Gentry also took up strays this year. (Clarksville Gazette, 22 July 1820.)

The census taken in 1820 is the first one for Dickson County that is available for researchers. The complete listing of this census was published in the genealogical magazine THE RIVER COUNTIES in 1972. The following will be a listing of the names from that census and will not include all the information given. This will be presented as a list of early settlers in Dickson County, and not as the complete census.

Oney Henry
Lovet Lockalier
Tobias Clark
John Frasure (Frazier)
Samuel Nesbitt
Benjamin Crews
Seburn Crews
Richard Jackson
Wm. B. Madden
George Hightower
John Choate
Alexander Hunter
William Hightower
Willie Underwood
Washington Hunter
Wilson Gilbert
Henry Highland
William M. Thomas
John Lokalus
Nancy Way (May?)
Wicoy Way
Allen C. Nimmo
William Turner
James Jones
Mabel Gilbert
John Harris
Benjamin Andrews
  (or Anderson)
Nicholas Baker
James W. Christian
Samuel Richardson
George Tubb
Phebe Cooksey

Nathan Tubb
Edward Lucas
Philip B. Noland
Drury Christian
Thomas Whitmill
Thomas Edwards
John Barthe (?)
Isaac Hunter
Adonijah Edwards
Isaac Tubb
Pleasant Crews
Casy Wiggins
William Hand
Mathew Gilmore
Mathew Crumpler
Isaac Johnson
Jacob Marsh
Daniel Leech
Richard Waugh
William Pearson
Thomas Noland
John Crews
William Lewis
David McAdoo
Thomas Drummond
Giles Jones
Micajah McGee
Elijah Jones
John H. Stone
Benjamin Clark
Jacob Walker
Edward Smith
John Northern

Thomas Jones
William Tippet
George Davidson
William Evans
Elisabeth Butler
Robert Shelton
William Taylor
Winnifred Richardson
John Walker
Richard Batson
John McAdoo
John W. Napier
Henry A. C. Napier
John H. Hyde
Nathan Nesbit
Francis S. Ellis
Andrew Hamilton
Thomas Pannell
Field Farrar
Sterling Brewer
James Nesbitt
Elisha Williams
William Light
David Shropshire
John C. Massie
Edward Houston
James McClanahan
Christopher Robertson
Robertson Dickson
Joseph F. Cloud
William Hendricks
Robert Jornegan
Polley Shropshire

Allen Howard	William Williams	Reece Bowen
John Lockney, Jr.	Benoni Crawford	John Humphreys
Hutson Johnson	Elias W. Napier	Anguish McCloud
Middleton Higinbottom	Edward Teale	James Vincent
William Willey, Sr.	John L. McRae	William Miller
Elliss Tycer	George Mitchell	John Larkin, Jr.
William Griffin(Giffin?)	Daniel Williams	John Hall
John Griffen	William B. Dodson	William Morreset
John B. Walker	Daniel H. Williams	Molton Dickson
Henry Grimes	Frederic Collins	Thomas Murrel, Jr.
Elizabeth Walker	Martha King	Samuel Fate (?)
George Clark	Absalom Tribble	Gilbert Marsh
Ezekiel Hickerson	Isabella King	Austin Richardson
Asa A. Brown	Jones Rogers	James Hudson
Thomas Mathews	Thomas Key	Bartholomew Smith
Daniel Moore	Jesse Tribble	Jesse Russell
William Hickerson	Jacob Rushing	William Stone
James M. Ross	William Armour	Rachel Brown
Joseph Rye	Robert Armour	Minor Bibb
Nehemiah Hardy	James Rogers	Sarah Bibb
Young W. Roland	Elias Rogers	Daniel Harris
John Dickson	Hutson Shropshire	Jesse De__
Ephraim Arnold	Jeremiah Nesbitt	Levi Tidwell
Enos James	Jesse Ragan	Thomas Stroud
Robert West	William May	Joseph King
Robert Dickson	John Adams	John Jones
Eleanor Parrish	Acheus Ethridge	Simon Myer
Donel Y. Harris	Joseph Williams	Joshua White
Stephen Harris	Nehemiah Scott	Amos James
Abraham Robertson	Ashburn Vanhook	Joshua Jones
Jonathan Brown	Lockey Taylor	James Larkins
Matthias Krane	William Balthrop	Jacob Pipkins
Thomas Ellis	Willie Balthrop	Edward Perkins
Aaron James	Laura Burns	Joseph Lampley
Susannah Norris	Joseph Rogers	David Passmore
Ambrose Burton	Charles Thompson	Benjamin Gilbert
(Halliburton is correct)	William Tatum, Sr.	William White
William Balthrop, Jr.	Stephen Hosley	William Morris
William Webb	William Tatum, Jr.	James Hicks
John Hays	John Parrot	John Tucker
Joseph Kimble	James Smith	Joseph Davidson
Wyatt Parrish	Benjamin Valentine	George Powell
Hugh Dickson	James Thompson	Cuthbert Hudson
Nathan Dillehay	Charles Boles	William Gentry
Ephraim Ellis	Sampson Boles	Young Kirk
John J. Coppage	John May	Thomas Gentry
John Hinson	James Taylor	Abraham Davidson
Randolph R. Harris	Ebenezer Whitehead	Silas Thompkins
John W. Leigh	Benjamin Pearsall	David Gray
Nathan Ragan	Tillis Collins	George Mitchell, Jr.
Jacob Hardy	David Robertson	John Stafford
William S. Murrell	Jesse May	Edmund Tidwell
Isaac Hill	Samuel Sparks	Ebon (?) Parker (Parkin)
Alexander Dickson	Ezra McAdoo	Benjamin Grimmett
William Anderson	Robert Nesbitt, Sr.	Moses Parker
Benjamin Sturdivant	John Nesbitt, Jr.	Jacob Puckett
Mark Reynolds	James Matlock	John Garton
Willis Norsworthy	James Douglass	William Austin
John Wilkerson	Willis Willey	Nancy Sullivan
James Goodrich	Abram Caldwell	George Sullivan
Amos Lewis	John Evans	Sherod Thompson
Robert Moding	Boshie Box	Nancy Adams
(Madden?)	Moses Fussell	James McCollister
Alex. Anderson	John S. Brown	Elmore Walker
John T. Wells	Christian Baugham	Richard Johnson
Daniel Tolar	John Wright	Edmund Tidwell, Sr.
Aaron Vanhook	Rafred Campler	Tilman Perry
Thomas Hudson	(Crumpler?)	David Bibb
Jesse L. Kirk	John Grimes	Daniel Underhill
Henry Hudson	Sandford Edwards	Stewart Pipkin

Richard Nalls	John Lukeroy, Sr.	Jesse Epperson
Austen Seaton	Hardin Charles	William Thomas
Archibald Pullin	Naoma Edward	Labeus Richardson
James Ferrell	Polly Chambers	Willie Myatt
Charles Gilbert	Luke Medlock	Larkin Tate
Willis Davis	Robert Whitwell	Mary Baker
George McCollister	John Nesbitt, Sr.	George Brazeal
Thomas Gray	Burgess Wall	John Baker
Isaiah Tidwell	Robert Vanhook	John (?) Rutledge
William Grimmett	John Larkins, Sr.	Elijah Ivey
Hudson Dudley	Joseph Larkins	Asa Epperson
Henry H. Marable	John Hall	John Larkins
Solomon Rye	Peter Gilbert	John Johnson
Robert Webb	Daniel Coleman	Michael Light
Drury Adkins	Samuel Russell	John Rickell (?)
James Daniel	John Cunningham	James Coromny (?)
Joseph Edwards	Hewell Parrish	Thomas Graves
Francis Balthrop	James Gunn	George Lewis
William Blake	James Hartley	Isaac West
John Allen	James Tatum	John Neeley
John Baker	Allen Bowen	Joseph Eason
David Fentress	William Hudson	James Kirk
John Wilson	Stephen Tatum	John B. Brown
John Turner, Jr.	John Tatum, Sr.	John Moore
Thomas Hunter	James Martin	William Hogins
Thomas Williams	William D. Turner	Delilah Fussell
Adam Wilson	Anderson England	Calvin W. Eason
Sterling May	Ebenezer Kelley	James Eason
William Morrison	Polly Sims	Joel Marsh
Sally Carroll	Shadrach Bell	Morgan Hood
Samuel Mitchell	Robert Duke	William Robertson
Pinkney T. Bledsoe	Asa Gresham	Abraham Hogins
Auzey Burgess	Rhoda Abney	George Light
John B. Adkinson	Elias Abney	Evans McAdoo
John Seals	Robert Jackson	James Thedford
Barney B. Bledsoe	Benjamin Bruce	Jane Lovelady
William Brasure	Nathan Nall	John Robertson
Rebecca Walker	Isaac Walker	Ephraim Roy
Edward Brame	Henry Goodrich	John Daniel
James McCauly	Robert Patterson	John Lewis
Jonathan Melugin	John Dunnigan	Drury Price
John Hodges	Armour King	Jane Norris
John Toler	Andrew Graham	Micajah Busby
Joseph Melugen	Andrew Flowers	Levi Anderson
Martin H. Burton (Halliburton)	Elisha Turner	Peggy Anderson
	Thomas Smith	William West
Abner Howell	Benjamin Blackburn	Elizabeth West
Josiah Davidson	Jane McClelland	Hugh Dickson, Jr.
William E. Haden	James Hunter	Nancy Walls
John Crane	George Evans	Thomas Simmons
John Coleman	Gaskey Hunter	Richard D. Simmons
John H. Humphreis	Charles Dunnigan	John Nichols
Alexander Rose	Joseph B. (?) Eason	Shepherd Lanerum
James Melugen	Larkin Dawson	Peter Tatum
William Hollandsworth	Jane Baker	Howell Freeman
Selman Edward	Marble Stone	William B. Freeman
James Shelton	John Willey	John T. Hutcheson
Thomas Jernigan	Samuel D. Austin	Moses Street
David Austin	Stiles Bugg	Jesse Turner, Jr.
Daniel Hickerson	John West	John R. Caskey
Robert Shelton	Holloway Morris	William Hedge
Jesse Cunningham	Isaac H. Lanier	John Uruce
Archibald Sensing	Eldridge Bowen	Margaret Evans
William Edwards	John Sowell	Henry Hall
George Ross	Robert Claghorn	Joseph Hall
Benedict Bacon	John Cames (?)	Nancy Hall
Mary Drake	John Moran	William Powers
Jacob Leech	William Bullick	Michael Page
John Ward	William Cox	Charles Gunn
John Nesbitt	David O. McAdoo	Delila Gray

Mark Bullard	William Ward	Hugh McNeiley
Samuel King	William Donnigan	Josiah Meek
William Johnson	Thomas Jurrell, Sr.	George Adams
Willoughby Etheridge	Richard Murrell	James M. Thomas
John Maben	Jesse Ellis	Michael Gafford
Howard W. Turner	George Southerland	John Bernard
Gavon Bone	Thomas Wilson	Ann Lucas
James Walker	Gabriel Shaddock	R. C. Napier
Spencer Brown	Eliza Ward	James R. Napier
John Gamble	A. W. Vanleer	Cyprian Farrar
John Reynolds	Jacob Forsythe	Epps Jackson
John Davis	Charles Mixon	Hugh Norris
Enoch Massey	John Gunn	Samuel Sellers
Elizabeth King	John McCormac	Nancy Stone
Samuel King	William Gunn	George Cathey
John Joslin	Elizabeth Shelton	Polly West
Kendrick Myatt	Thomas Simpson	Clabourn Spicer
William Ragan	Polly Gray	William Hall
William Baird	Margaret Blount	John Forsythe
William McMurry	Montgomery Bell	John Hand
Richard Cocks	Richard Napier, Sr.	Robert McCallum
Samuel Self	John C. Collier	Peter Goodwin
Abraham Self	William Wright	James Walker
George F. Napier	Thomas Bullion	James Watson
George Clark	Elizabeth Walker	Elizabeth Horner
Elizabeth Acuff	Robert Larkins	(Homer?)
Elisha Gunn	Joseph Nesbitt	Alexander Chizenhall
William France	Robert Nesbitt	Elizabeth Darr
Christopher Strong	James McKey	William Houston
John Wims	Willis Walker	Nelson McClelland
Thomas Collier	John Read	William Fussell
Archibald Slatton	Samuel Turner	James Horner (Homer)
John Scott	William Teague	Dr. James Walker
John Hendricks	William Rye	Edmond Howard
Willis Jackson	William Hooper	Babel Patterson
John Durell	Edward Pickett	John Skelton
Micajah Bennett	Robert Livingston	Sarah Anderson
William Gammell	Ebenezer Petty	Mary McClane
Pryor Pane	Alexander Brown	Samuel M. Garver
John S. Spencer	Burwell Etheridge	Hartwell Weaver
Thomas Mitchell		Robert Harper

(Some of these names were very hard to decipher on the census. This listing should be used as a guide and if a researcher finds a name in which he is interested, then this name should be re-checked on the census, found on microfilm in the Tennessee State Library and Archives.)

1821
Thomas Simpson was charged with larceny in Dickson County during this year.

1825
The following were charged with "riot" this year: Joel Marsh, Samuel Bugg, John Gunn, Laban Holt, Balaam Bull, Susanna Hall, Berryman Hall, David Hall, James Hold, John Tatum, and James Thedford. James McCauley was charged with stabbing and John Lain with perjury. William Abney was charged with murder, but the victim's name was not given in the circuit court minutes.

1826
Circuit court records show Francis V. Schmittou was charged with assault and battery this year and Jesse Gardner with larceny.

1830
A tornado struck Dickson County on May 30, 1830. The Dickson County Herald, 23 Feb. 1940 has the following: "The cyclone of 1830 demolished the courthouse and blew the whole town practically away, many of the court records being found soon after in Cheatham County, where they were

taken by the wind. The circuit court records suffered most from the devastation, there being many early record books missing from the Circuit Court Clerk's office, which were likely destroyed in the storm.

"Steps were taken immediately after the destructive storm had done its work to erect a new public building and by 1836 the county's affairs were being transacted in the new courthouse."

And from the Dickson County Herald, 29 Sept. 1911:
"In May 1830 Dickson County was visited by a very destructive hurricane. The courthouse and jail at Charlotte were demolished. The books and papers in the former building were scattered in every direction for miles and many of them entirely destroyed. Several large books were carried by the wind into Cheatham County, and afterward recovered. A man was in the second story of the courthouse when the storm occurred, and was completely buried in the rubble, but escaped serious injury.

"The roof of the jail was carried 13 miles. Charlotte was damaged by this storm to the extent of about $30,000, and the balance of the county as much more.

"A new building, the same size, on the same location, and almost an exact model of the first courthouse, was rebuilt in 1832. Peter Seals was the first man sent to the penitentiary from Dickson County, being convicted of whipping his wife."

1833

The post offices in Dickson County this year were: Barton's, Charlotte, Clover Valley, Green Valley, Laurel Furnace, Piney River, Tennessee Iron Works, and Smithville, which was discontinued.

The following article entitled HISTORY OF A MURDER was found in the Dickson County Herald, 6 October 1911:

"A bit of interesting history was enacted by the county court in 1833, which has few precedents in the State of Tennessee. It was as follows: on the 25th of November 1833, William C. Bird, a white man and a patrol, was assaulted by one Wiley, a slave, with a club and murdered. Wiley was soon afterward arrested and the county court convened in special session on the 19th day of December of the same year for the purpose of trying the slave on the charge of murder.

"The trial was by jury and lasted three days, a verdict of guilty being returned on the third day, fixing the penalty at death by hanging. The charge was read to the negro, and the day of his execution being set for December 28 following; he was remanded to jail.

"On the appointed day Wiley was taken from jail and placed in a cart and conveyed to the place of execution. The gallows had been erected the previous day at a point about half mile east of Charlotte, and was in the shape of two upright posts and a cross piece to which the rope was attached.

"Several thousand people gathered on the surrounding hillsides and climbed up into the neighboring trees to witness the hanging. Slaveowners took their slaves to see the negro hung, hoping thereby to give them a terrible lesson and warning. The cart bearing the doomed man was driven between the two uprights, the noose was placed around the slave's neck and the driver was instructed to 'drive up the cart' and the negro was jerked into eternity. An aged darkey preached a funeral sermon over the remains and delivered a solemn warning to his brethren.

"Until 1836 the county courts of the various counties of the state had jurisdiction in all matters, but by an act of the Legislature of 1836, circuit and chancery courts were created, giving to these courts criminal and equity jurisdiction and limiting the power of the county court to county affairs. The Supreme Court of the State of Tennessee held regular sessions in Charlotte during the years 1819 to 1821. The Supreme Court was then composed of three members, Judges Haywood, Emerson and Catron."

1838

"The oldest bell in the county, of which there is a record, is in the courthouse cupola. According to the minutes of the County Court, dated at April term 1838, Absalon Massey was allowed $35.75 for finishing carpeting the courthouse floor and hanging the bell.

"The courthouse bell was not cast for long distance volume, but has served well its purpose for a hundred years and more and will likely continue to ring out many more decades to herald the approach of solemn court sessions." (Dickson County Herald 23 Feb. 1940.)

1840

"The Whigs of Dickson County will have a barbecue at Charlotte next Thursday." (Announcement in newspaper Tennessee Telegraph, 19 Sept. 1840.)

The following is a list of heads of household as found on the 1840 Census of Dickson County. This transcription was made by T. P. Hughes, Jr., Memphis, Tennessee, and originally published in THE RIVER COUNTIES, October 1973. The listing, verified by Mrs. Jewel B. Standefer, was taken from Microfilm Roll 165.

Armstrong Baker
Green Tatom
Jackson Brazil
Samuel Bugg
William Creech
John K. Goodrich
Henry Goodrich
Edward Hunt
James Cox
Franklin F. Ball
Alvin Dunnigan
Washington T. Wimms
  (possibly Weems)
James K. Clifton
William B. Inman
Jonathan Johnson
James Tedford
William S. Dunnigan
George H. Horner
O'Kelly McGee
Henry Potts
Jesse Graham
John Dunnigan
Amelia Loyd
Patience Vineyard
Lemuel J. Russell
James Yates
Lemuel Bruce
Sarah Bruce
Spartan Bruce
Charles Timon
Sarah Bowen
Allen Bowen
Benjamin C. Waters
  (or Clearwaters)
Charles Dunnigan
Andrew Dunnigan
James Tatom
Archibald D. Hogins
Elisha Gunn
George Evans
James A. Sizemore
Absolem Baker
John Baker
Benjamin Baker
Nancy Baker
Washington England
Henderson Dunnigan

Margaret Brazil
Anderson England
Mary Dunnigan
George Brazil
John Rutledge
Thomas Watkins
John Watkins
Lawson Gunn
William Hedge
George W. Few
William Crittenden
Crawford Lovell
Thomas Flannary
Joel Erranton
Eklkanah Flannery
William Few
James Few
Franklin Craft
Isham West
Joseph George
Andrew Haley
Mary Monk
George Gray
William Gray
Asa Barbee
Liddy Dunnigan
Alexandria Wilkins
Nancy Bird
Andrew J. Myatt
John J. Clifton
William Dunnigan
Fanning Yates
Jethro Yates
Henry Harward
Jonathan Adcock
Henderson Adcock
David Gray
Francis Johnson
Stephen Adcock
Eldridge Myatt
Samuel King
Alford King
Richard Murrell
Burkett Murrell
Jessie Adcock
James Byron
William W. Hogins
Charles Hutson

Lucretia Horner
Madison Dunnigan
Reubin Thornton
William Hutson
Hezekiah Gray
Rosanah Gray
Willie Myatt
Jacob Petty
Isaac Haley
George W. Reddin
John H. Wright
Nathaniel Kimbro
Gabriel Petty
James D. Petty, Jr.
James D. Petty, Sr.
Jonathan Petty
Thomas Petty
Anderson King
John A. Petty
Henry Martin
William Kimbrel
Jacob Nelson
Robert Booker
Solomon Petty
Lucy Reddin
Susan Pinegar
Edward Terry
Reddick Myatt
Mary Myatt
William Pinegar
Brinkley George
Martha Holland
Josiah Willie
Allen Willie
Nancy Hutson
Elijah Humphreys
Henry Gosset
John Holland
David Frasher
Milton Loftin
Nathaniel Childress
Elizabeth Anglin
John Anglin
Sarah Blackburn
James Spears
Travis Luther
George Luther
Kindrick Myatt

Alsey Myatt
Garrison King
Gilford Cook
Delilah Gray
Joshua Cathey
Jessie Eastus
Daniel Cathey
Reubin Goodin
Sarah Goodin
Joseph Spicer
Archibald Cathey
Uriah Harnbrick
  (or Hambrick)
William G. Austin
Margaret Cathey
Gilbert Marsh
William Hogins
Ozzy Burgess
John Larkins
Robert H. McCollum
Albert Speight
Martin Halliburton
William Powers
Silmons Edwards
James Gilmore
Ashburn Vanhook
John Adams
Jacob Evans
Michael Berry
Willis Willey
John Byers
Stephen Horsley
  (or Hasley?)
James Daniel
Robert A. S. Nesbitt
John Grymes, Sr.
Cornelius Grymes
Green Jackson
James Hicks
Spilsby Cocke
Samuel Adams
David Waller
Robert Oakley
Murrell Myatt
William Hightower
George W. Larkins
George W. Hiland
James Oliver
James Givins
William W. Norris
William Dudley
Willis Cunningham
Israel McLaughlin
Alexr Campbell
Samuel C. Robertson
Gibson Taylor
William Matlock
Peter Choate
Minor Bibb
Benjamin F. Larkins
Burgess Harris
Thomas Rose
John N. Scott
Benjamin B. Hall
George Sullivan
William Austin
Absolem Massie
Samuel Tate
John Brewer
James Larkins

Benjamin Gray
James Bibb
Lewis Thompson
Harey Pinson
Jeremiah Harnbrick
  (or Hambrick)
Martha Houston
William Fuzzel
Henry Bullion
James Walker
Elizabeth Walker
Meckins Car
John Sanders
Berryman Walker
Benjamin Bowen
Henry Walker
William Willey
Edward Smith
Nelson McClelland
Willis Miller
Jeremiah G. Martin
Lewis Evans
John Murrell
Green H. Swisher
William Bullion
Yelvington Harnbrick
James A. Nesbitt
Wyatt Price
Eldridge N. Philips
Thomas Durin
John Galloway
Albert Joslin
Raford M. Crumpler
Cornelius Bagley
Stanford Hatley
David O. Reese
Reason B. Whatley
Benjamin Clark
Thomas Armstrong
Bartholomew Smith
William Cox
Henry Stone
Joel M. Hobs
Garret Hall
George W. Tatom
Thomas Murrell
Joseph Owen
Jeremiah Pearce
Elizabeth Bynum
Moses Pinson
Hiram Hambrick
Catherine Larkins
George Southerland
John Southerland
Christopher Strong
Flemming H. Fowler
Henry Southerland
Gabriel Joslin
William B. Joslin
William Hambrick
Caroline Dunnaway
Bartholomew Richardson
Benjamin Wells
John Marsh
Rachael Martin
John McClelland
John L. Martin
Charlotte Price
James Hall
Jta Christy (?)

Robert Williams
Henderson Joslin
Edward McCormick
Robert McNeilly
Daniel McCall
John Caldwell
John G. Crumpler
Allen Nesbitt
Thomas McNeilly
John Ladd
William Lane
William Hickerson
Henry Hickerson
Drury Sinks
Robert Nesbitt, Sr.
Nancy Nesbitt
Miles Long
John McAdoo
William Hudgins
Thomas Hudgins
Sarah Houston
James Ashworth
James Stanley
Thomas Nesbitt
Furney Toler
Ann Crumpler
William Long
Jonathan P. Hardwick
William B. Dotson
Madison Miller
William Marsh
Squire Richardson
Malachi Tidwell
William Porter
John Hall
James Pullin
John McCaslin
Reese Bowen
Lucy Lockilear
Willis Foster
Simon Deloach
Abel Heath
Granderson D. Neville
Daniel Leech
Mary Jackson
William Kirk
Margaret J. Steele
Daniel M. Shearing
Robert Livingston
Martha Dickson
William S. Coleman
James Cook
Pleasant T. Mallory
Margaret Drummonds
Travis E. Slayden
George Tilley
John Irby
Joseph Choate
Jackson Choate
Elenor Choate
Peter Light
Abner H. Ragan
William D. Willey
William Willey, Sr.
James D. Dickson
Winneford Richardson
Thomas Palmer
William S. Adamson
Wilson J. Mathis
Joseph Coffy

John Stokes	Henry Legitt	Robert Duke
William Carroll	Henry M. Gilbert	Shadrick Bell
Darius Collier	Jessee Woodward	Thomas Bell
Stephen Smith	Henry Kiphart	Robert Demery
John Matlock	Caleb Rooker	William Demry
John Eubanks	James W. Christian	Felix Robertson
Abraham Phillips	Jacob H. Reeder	Charles Robertson
Thomas W. Collier	Jane Stroud	George Robertson
Gilford G. Paschal	Jessee Beck	William Crewdson
Thomas Moore	Oliver Spicer	William Harid
Nancy Link	James M. Tucker	Keziah Harid
Thomas Bennet	John Luther	Mary James
William Gafford	Archibald Pullin	John Ford
Dabney Duke	James Carter	John M. Coley
James Loggins	Martin Garton	Jobe Doty
John Linzy	William White	George Groves
Alxr Paschal	Zachariah Garton	Anthony G. Carmion
Ezekial Hickerson	John Garton	John Weakley
William Garret	John Underhill	David Weakley
Samuel B. Alston	Joshua White	John Haywood
John Brown	Moses Parker	William Miller
Jane Bell	Isaah Tidwell	Isaac Groves
James Matlock	Daniel Spencer	Susannah Ford
Daniel Hickerson	William Hammonds	Daniel S. Ford
Willis Stroud	John B. Carr	Joseph T. Daniel
Matthew J. Crumpler	Joseph Jones	Susannah Swift
Thomas Edwards	Silas Tidwell	Carter Morris
Wilkins Corban	Richard Garton	William Barnes
James Choate	John H. Perry	Solomon Dannah
Abraham Baughman	John Langford	John Harris
James T. White	John Brown	James Hightower
Moses B. Street	John Morris	Missianianah Grymes
Thomas Overton	Willis Johnson	George Clark
William Richardson	Mark Harris	John W. Porter
William James	Alford Brown	David Burgis
James T. Kerley	Isaac Hill	Daniel Moore
Jacob Voorhies	Edmond Tidwell, Sr.	John Wilken
William Balthrop	Edmond Tidwell, Jr.	James Trotter
Volintine J. Allen	Jessie Crow	George Cooksey
James Finley	Willis Davis	Milly Matthews
Jonathan Ward	Jacob Puckett	John Gambles
John C. Collier	Aquilla Tidwell	William Lewis
Charles A. Wilkins	William Parker	Abner Skelton
William Dodson	Ruffin Perry	John Cunningham
Charles B. Taylor	Benajah Gentry	William Ward
Archibald Skelton	John Meek	James K. Morris
William McMurry	John Porter	Nathaniel Cunningham
Thos. Harnes	John Brown, Sr.	James Carooth
Susan Green	Moses Tidwell	George Gallion
William D. Sensing	Michael Tidwell	Belfield N. Carter
Archibald Sensing	Gideon Cunningham	John Stepp
Joseph Grymes	John Davidson	John Grymes
Joshua Claxgon	Franklin McCadin	William Griffin
Robert Newson	Vilet Davidson	Green Jackson
Thomas Mathews	Matthew Morris	Richard Jackson
Christopher H. Russell	Benjamin Tidwell	Gabrael Shadick
Pleasant Crews	Solomon Marsh	William Lyle
Seaborn Crews	Augustian Roberts	William Penticost
William J. Wilkison	Franklin M. Binkley	Robert Bibb
George Dunnivan	Alford P. Granger	Edward Sellars
Gabrael Andrews	Charles Baker	Marcus B. Stewart
Crosey Jones	David Alsbrook	Sarah Eleazer
Richard Smith	Abner Smith	Anderson Gentry
Matthew Crumpler	Patunel (Patience?) Hunter	Susan Johnson
Nicholas C. Taylor	Alxr. Hunter	James Glass
William Pinkston	John Jones	William L. Thompson
William Ward	James Hunter	Aaron Laws
George Purnell	William Mitchell	George Mitchell
William Clifton	John Vanderwater	Thomas Gentry
John Law	William H. Miles	Lucy Gentry

William T. Gentry	Nancy W. Ellis	Joseph Morris
Davidson Crunk	William S. Fentress	William M. Mitchell
Howell Davidson	Isaac Walker	Aquilla Everett
Sarah Davidson	Willis Walker	Burrel Hunter
John Thomas	Hozy Bennett	Benjn Sims
Benjamin Bryant	Spencer T. Hunt	Bennet Duke
John W. Coleman	Michael T. Ellis	Thomas Bryan
George Oakley	Willis E. Lewis	Epps Jackson
Benjamin Walker	Abner Adkins	Samuel Austin
William E. Pendergrass	Thomas Jarnagan	Henry A. C. Napier
Huldy Tidwell	Thomas Ellis	Cyrus Murry
Ely Tidwell	Thomas McMurry	Willey Balthrop
David Record	Abraham Self	Hartwell M. Slayden
Daniel Taylor	O. L. V. Schmittou	Charles Halliburton
Jacob Lampley	John G. Hill	John May
Joseph Lampley	William E. Ellis	Charles Nixon
Mary Tidwell	John Norsworthy	(Mixon?)
Owen Sullivan	Thomas J. Ragan	James C. Balthrop
Rebecca McClelland	James G. Herison	Isaac Bone
Miles Hutchison	John P. Dicks	Larra Burns
Jefferson Jones	William Baker	Daniel W. Martin
Susan Morris	Edward Rogers	Alford B. Norris
Jacob Sanderson	William J. Hays	Richard Brazil
Jane Jones	William D. Turner	William E. Slayden
Samuel Sellars	Allen Hunter	Jeremiah Street
Reubin White	Berryman R. Horsley	Robert Vanhook
David Castleman	Ellenor Spencer	Thomas C. Smith
William Pendergrass	Joseph Nesbitt	Benjn. Smith
John Garton, Jr.	Nancy Dillahay	Irwin Parrish
Henry Garton	Francis Fowler	Daniel H. Williams
Huldy Davis	William Adams	Callum Rogers
Christopher Meek	Frankey Newman	Jeremiah Nesbett
John Pendergrass	William Fleet	H. B. H. Williams
John R. Hudson	Isaac Hill	Robert Jenkins
Joseph Rye	Allen Hamlin	Walter Jenkins
Abram Caldwell	Nicholas H. Nichols	William Norsworthy
Charles Gunn	William Loyd	George G. Dotson
Madison Gunn	William H. Nichols	John Perigin
Ellis Tycer	William Irby	William S. Self
John W. Rogan (Ragan?)	Gelford Mills	William H. Napier
Sarah R. Walker	Syloira Loftin	Joel Rogers
Willoby Ethridge	Alexr. Brown	William Tatom
Thomas Willey	Burrell Jackson	William Lamaster
John F. Willey	Peter Jackson	William Norman
Mary Willey	Buckner Harris	Jeremiah Thompson
James Young	Joseph Hall	Henry Starnes
Jane Lovelady	Jessee Shelton	Rebecca Pickett
Thomas Jones	Plummer Williams	Mary Thompson
James Jones	Mark Robertson	John Jackson
Elisha Burgiss	John J. Bell	Jessee Norris
James Smith	Henry Whizzenhunt	James M. Albright
Woodson Daniel	John C. Carroll	Elinezer Whitehead
Locky Taylor	Henry J. Holand	(Ebenezer?)
Howell Underwood	George Raworth	Archius Ethridge
Benjamin R. Craige	Benjn. C. Robertson	Washington Irby
John Northern	Susan Richardson	Sarah Smith
George Davidson	Gustavus Rape	James Irby
David Robertson	Henry J. Binkley	Edward Balthrop
Abraham Horsely	William Johnson	Mary Murphy
(Hasley, Hosley?)	William Brummet	Thomas Cunningham
Solomon J. Reynolds	Silas Harris	Thomas Pines
John James	David Rutledge	John T. Turner
John S. Reynolds	John Speight	Stevison Archer
Lorenzy Burpoe	Washington Hunter	Isaac Morriset
William R. Blunt	Norflet Jordan	Alexander Jones
Thomas Balthrop	Winn B. Smith	John J. C. Stokey
William R. Hicks	Lewallen Shadowin	John Bishop
Edward Holley	David C. Weakley	Susan Norris
William B. Young	Elizabeth Gleaves	Cyrus J. Burns
Huel Parrish	Jessie M. Speight	Willis Underwood

Jeremiah Underwood	Robert Burton	Nathan Nesbitt
William J. Knight	George Lewis	William W. Goodridge
James W. Ragan	Daniel Toler	William Seay
David B. Street	Jane Maddin	James Goodridge
Moses Street	John T. Patterson	James B. White
Kindrick Ethridge	William Ragan	M. L. Lewis
Nancy James	Andrew A. Brown	Haney White
William Volentine	Robert Mickle	Thomas Dickson
Joseph Ethridge	William Jarnagan	Nancy J. Hankins
Willoby Ethridge	Downs Jemson	Zadock Potter
McIndry G. Sensing	John Dickson	Robert Patterson, Sr.
John B. Walker	Sarah James	Robert Patterson, Jr.
William B. Bell	Hugh Dickson	James R. Allen
Elizabeth Garret	William Morriset	Bryan Latham
William J. Baker	John Green	Nathaniel Conner
William T. Reynolds	James Hendricks	John E. Conner
Reuben Shadowen	Elizabeth Hendricks	Moses Conner
Isaac Parrish	Patrick H. Madden	Winney Mitchell
George W. Oliver	Ezekiah Linzy	William Shelton
Humphrey Halliburton	Prier H. Smith	Coleman Shelton
John Storey	William Pines	Joseph Payne
Rebecca Wallace	Drewry Adkins	George Shelton
Margaret Jones	Levi Baldin	Jessee Sinks
William Bone	Alexander Coppage	Absolem Swift
Thomas Martin	George Cox	William Patterson
James Bull	Francis Parrish	Gilbert T. Abernathy
Henry Garner	Elizabeth West	A. W. Vanleer
Oney Harvy	Memican Hunt	Henry Pratt
Elizabeth Harvy	Robert Bohannan	Thomas Hinson
James Lee	Solomon Rye	Sarah Bartee
Harman Christy	James Robertson	Benjn Summers
Burgess Wall	Daniel Thorn	Obediah Spradlin
James Dickson	Robert West	Elias W. Napier
Sarah Dowden		

Total population of Dickson County in 1840: 7,074
Signed 21 Oct. 1840, Robert McNeilly.

1842

Charlotte Lodge 97 F&AM was organized 2 Oct. 1842. Henry H. Guerin was worshipful master, Daniel Hillman, senior warden, W. H. Williams, junior warden. (Dickson County Herald, 19 Oct. 1967.)

In July 1842 William Kauffman was assassinated. This story belongs both to Dickson and Humphreys counties. The following was sent to the compiler in 1965 to be published:

KAUFFMAN ASSASSINATION

by

John A. Lehman

"The removal of the monument of Spencer T. Hunt from the NcEwen City Cemetery to its present site brings back to memory the assassination of William Kauffman.

"One July day, in the year 1842, William Kauffman left his recently married wife and started on his way from his home in Little Rock, Arkansas, to Nashville, Tennessee, to deposit his money in the Bank of Tennessee, one of the few banks in the country at that time.

"It was never known how much money he carried but it was supposed to be a large amount of gold and silver which he carried in a pair of saddle pockets; he also wore a large belt which showed evidence of having money in it.

"Kauffman rode a large black shiny horse; he was followed by a man named Stallcup. Kauffman's horse became lame near old Reynoldsburg on the Tennessee River. Upon inquiring for a blacksmith, he was directed to Wells Blake, who ran a shop nearby at the time. Mr. Blake, afterwards one of the largest landowners and stock raisers of this and Houston counties. He was the grandfather of the Bunnells and Rosses. Stallcup passed while Mr. Blake was shoeing the horse.

"Spencer T. Hunt ran a tavern on the old Stage Road, 1-1/2 miles north of McEwen and near where the Westbrook house now stands. This tavern was a noted stopping place for travelers as the stages changed horses here. Stallcup spent the night at Hunt's Tavern. There was very little ever known about him. He was supposed to be a gambler.

"Some thought Hunt also was a gambler and that they had met before. Stallcup left the next morning on his way east. That night Kauffman stopped at Hunt's to spend the night. It is not known if the Tavern kept a register but Kauffman, when informed that a man named Stallcup from the same state had spent the previous night before, stated that he knew this man and that they were from the same town.

"A maid by the name of Molly Noyswether (possibly Norsworthy), whose parents lived in Union Hollow some six miles east, worked at Hunt's Inn. According to her statement, after supper Kauffman being tired, retired early. Shortly after Mr. Hunt saddled his own horse, had a short conversation with his wife, and she begged him not to go, but her persuasions were in vain. Mrs. Hunt walked the floor all night, crying and wringing her hands. Mr. Hunt returned home shortly before daybreak next morning.

"After eating a hearty breakfast Kauffman proceded on the way little thinking that an assassin lying wait some four miles up the road with loaded rifle. About 100 yards from the Dickson-Humphreys County line, near the forks of the old stage and Jewel Cave road, there had been an old house and small clearing. The assassin was hid in a fence corner on the north side of the road and some 30 yards back.

"As Kauffman came by the assassin shot him off his horse and drug his body nearly 100 yards down a small hollow on the south side of the road and left it. Kauffman's horse came back to Hunt's about noon the same day, stopped at the gate and neighed.

"It was said Hunt went out and put the horse up without any words and made no inquiries of what became of Kauffman.

"At that time George Wright's father, Frank Wright, who lived where George now lives (George Wright is about 90 years old) on Yellow Creek, was the driver of one of the stage coaches and upon approaching the place where Kauffman was killed, he was attracted by buzzards.

"He stopped the stage coach and began to investigate and in a short while found Kauffman's remains some 80 or 100 yards south of the road.

"This country was thinly settled at that time. It was 4 miles west to the Hunt Inn and 2 miles east to where Mr. Frank Wright lived. Mr. Wright reported his find. Immediately the news spread over the neighborhood.

"George Dotson was teaching school at old Union schoolhouse in Union Hollow. Dotson was also a magistrate. Upon hearing the news he adjourned school and went to hold the inquest. Several witnesses were examined, among them Spencer T. Hunt, but very little was found out.

"The patching that was around the bullet that killed him was found. Mr. Kauffman was buried near the place where he was killed and his grave may be seen on the left of the forks of the road.

"Among those attending the inquest were Frank and Jennie Wright, Dempse Hooper and daughter Mary Lankford Hooper, Bill Hooper, Dave Winstead, Burrell Spicer, Richard Batson, Alex Coleman, James Williams, Christopher Hudson, Jake Street, Benjamin Adams, Henry Williams, Jerry Thompson, and John Adams. George Turner, a Primitive Baptist preacher, preached Kauffman's funeral.

"The night before Kauffman was murdered, Father Aloysus Oringo, the first Catholic Priest ever seen in these parts and who later was pastor of the

McEwen Catholic Church for 30 years, was on his way from Clarksville to Jackson. He rode a large black horse, and was stopped near the place Kauffman was killed and was questioned but he gave a reasonable account of himself and was let go unmolested. He always thought he was held up by the same parties who murdered Kauffman and that they thought at first he was Kauffman.

"Some time later Jim Ethridge, who lived near Higs Spring on a branch of Yellow Creek some three miles north of where Kauffman was killed, was seen in Charlotte, about 12 miles east. Jim displayed several pieces of gold but didn't seem to know the denomination of any of them.

"Suspicion soon arose. Jim was arrested and tried at Charlotte, the Dickson County seat. He stoutly maintained his innocence; the jury did not agree and the result was a mistrial, but later he was tired in Clarksville, and sentenced to the penitentiary for life.

"It developed at the trial that the night before Kauffman was killed, Jim Ethridge went to George Noyswether (Molly's father), who lived at that time in Union Hollow and borrowed a rifle. Noyswether swore that the bullet patching found where Kauffman was killed was the same used by him when he loaded the gun. It was mostly upon this evidence, and Ethridge not being able to explain where the gold came from, that convicted him.

"Several years after the Civil War, (Ethridge having died in the penitentiary) there was a man by the name of Isom Brazzel, who hailed from DeKalb County, who came to the vicinity and put up at Jim Williams (who was the father of our fellow townsman, G. L. Williams). Brazzell served in the penitentiary with Ethrdige and was his cellmate.

"Brazzell had a crude drawing given him by Ethridge, purporting to tell where he buried his portion of the money. He said it was about 150 yards back of his cabin and close to a white oak tree and he use to sit on his porch and play on his fiddle and see the tree; but at this time both the tree and cabin had vanished.

"Upon being shown about where Jim's cabin stood, he proceeded to dig as many others in time. Brazzell left in a short time and was never heard of in these parts. If he or any of the others ever found anything, it was never told.

"Since that time the grave was molested and left half open. Neighbors filled it up and piled some rocks on top of it. The neighbors in the early 1920's talked of putting an iron fence around it, but it was never done. Thus the end of William Kauffman.

"Now a word about Spencer T. Hunt.

"It was never known where Mr. Hunt hailed from, but the general consensus was he came from Virginia, and no one seemed to know about what year. He had large land holdings on Yellow Creek in Dickson County and owned a number of slaves. He purchased the land where the Inn stood from Richard Batson, who entered some land.

"As legend has it, he had the Inn built which was large and roomy. It was thought that he ran a high-class gambling house as prominent people from afar visited there. Andrew Jackson was seen there on several occasions, also lawyers, judges, legislators of the day, as well as many others, that did not stop at inns either above or below Hunt's Inn.

"As the finger of guilt and scorn rested on him, he seemed to suffer a nervous breakdown. His health having failed him, he proceeded to make his last will. The writer remembers his reading a copy to the will but it was blurred and parts could not be distinguished, but remembers he will John West, a boy whom he raised, one bay mare and one hundred dollars.

"He willed his wife Mary all the rest, to be hers as long as she lived. (I believe she died in the late 40's or the early 50's), and after her death it was to be placed in perpetual fund in the Bank of Tennessee. The interest was to go to the schools of Dickson and Humphreys counties, but in the 1820's it was forgotten by some of the authorities.

"In the 1930's, I asked my friend A. B. Simpson, who was then county superintendent, if they were still drawing. He said he understood there was a settlement made between the State and County and it had been settled; but upon investigation he found that it had been overlooked. And the State paid several hundred dollars back money to Humphreys County.

"Shorly after his death (Hunt's) they proceeded to have a sale. Burrell Spicer was sheriff at the time. Dave Winstead was the auctioneer. Among some of those present were Lankford, Jimmie, Billie, and Demps Hooper, John and George Dotson, Syl Adams, Cave and Mage Adams, Wells Blake, Frank Wright, Ned Pruitt, Wyley Turner, Richard Turner, George Turner, Ike Turner, Ned Bateman, John and Zeke Hatcher, Josh Curtis, Jerry Sheehan, Pat McEnroe, Michael May, Johnie McGuire, John Coleman, John Edwards, and Levi McCollum. There were 23 yoke of oxen sold and all the slaves, horses, and mules, among other things too numerous to mention.

"Gotten together over a period of 50 years by John A. Lehman. 'I am now in my 89th year,' signed John A. Lehman, 15 March 1965."

***

"This suspicion shadowed Mr. Hunt and his inn, which rapidly declined in popularity and was soon forced out of business. The money was never recovered and is reported by some to be buried near where the inn stood.

"A marble shaft was erected in 1887 to the memory of Spencer T. Hunt by Dickson and Humphreys counties in grateful appreciation of his bequest to the children of both of these counties. The money from the estate was collected after the death of his wife, Mary, sometime after 1848, and was invested in bonds of the state of Tennessee for the educational programs of the two counties.

"The memorial shaft was to be placed over Hunt's grave but the grave could not be located. The authorities then directed that the shaft be placed in the McEwen Protestant Cemetery. In 1939 the marble shaft was moved to its present site at the southern corner of a filling station, on the north side of U. S. Highway 70, where it can be seen today. The inscription reads:

                    Spencer T. Hunt
                   Died February 1844
     He who does most for the education of the
     masses serves his country best. As the
     preservation of our liberty depends upon
     the virtue and intelligence of its people."

(Source: A History of Humphreys County, Tennessee, by Jill Garrett, page 26, 1963 edition.)

Spencer T. Hunt's will was later recorded in Dickson County on 21 July 1909, page 4: Will of Spencer T. Hunt of Humphreys County...give to a young man raised by me, Reuben McQuerter...my track of land on Yellow Creek in Dickson County, 926 acres...beloved wife Mary...then gave to counties for educational purposes. His executors were Christopher C. Hudson of Dickson County and Burwell B. Spicer of Humphreys County. The will was signed 9 Dec. 1843 and the witnesses were Alex R. Coleman, William Hooper, David Winstead, Lankford K. Hooper. The will was originally recorded in Humphreys County Will Book E, page 630.

1843

On 4 Jan. 1843 and 16 Jan. 1843 earthquakes were felt in Davidson County and possibly in Dickson County.

March 1843 heavy snows blanketed Middle Tennessee and stayed for weeks. In some places 18 inches to 20 inches of snow were reported. In many places farm work was suspended.

1850
Henry Duke of Dickson County was sent to prison for murder. (Source: Appendix to House Journal for 1859-60, pages 248-249.)

1855
John Luther was sentenced to four years in prison for harboring slaves. Scarborough Penticost was acquitted of killing a Mr. Edwards.

1856
A slave insurrection scare in Middle Tennessee. (For further reading on this see Robert Corlew's "History of Dickson County.")

1857
Willis Johnson sentenced to six years for the murder of John Welsh.

Convicts from Dickson County in the state prison fro 1857-1858 were:
Willis Johnson, age 55, born in South Carolina, sentenced to six year for murder.
William Borum, came to prison in 1853 for horse stealing; he was sentenced for three years but was discharged and pardoned 1855.
John Luther, sent to prison in 1855, had received four years for harboring slaves; was discharged and pardoned 1855.
(Appendix to House Journal, 1857-1858.)

1859
P. H. Hamilton, age 21, from Dickson County, but born in Alabama, farmer, was sentenced to prison for three years and was in prison during the 1859 count. (Appendix to House Journal, 1859-1860, page 262.)

1860
Construction on Charlotte Cumberland Presbyterian Church was started this year.

1861
Dickson County voted 1141 for secession and 72 against.

"At the October term of the circuit court in 1861, John H. and W. J. H. Ross and D. A. Gallighy were convicted of murder to the first degree and sentenced to be hung. Their case was taken to the Supreme Court at Nashville and the prisoners were liberated by Federal soldiers when that city was captured during the war." (Dickson County Herald, 29 Sept. 1911.)

1862
Fort Donelson surrendered to Union forces in February 1862. The roar of guns could be heard in Dickson County.

1863
"Skirmish with guerrillas at Harpeth Shoals. The rebels afterwards retreated toward Charlotte and there was some sharp skirmishing." (Nashville Union and American, 14 January 1863.)

"Mary Crane (steamer) burned by guerrillas at Betsy's Landing near the Shoals. The crew was captured or carried off. The stamer had stopped to take on wood. US gunboat shelled the woods. The mate was killed and two wounded." (Nashville Daily Union, 18 Jan. 1863, 20 Jan. 1863.)

"The negroes, cooks, etc., on the steamboats captured near the shoals were butchered; rebels cut their throats." (Nashville Daily Union, 24 Jan. 1863.)

"The Nashville and Northwestern Railroad is now 28 miles and is being extended 4 miles beyond Kingston Springs in Dickson County; the road is graded from Kingston Springs to Waverly and from Waverly to Reynoldsburg is completed, a distance of 6 miles. Stone for the bridge ready to be put up. From Reynoldsburg to Hickman the road is graded, a distance of 40 miles." (Nashville Daily Union, 20 Sept. 1863.)

"A large body of bushwhackers have established their headquarters at Charlotte, Tenn., organizing themselves into a regular company and have begun to recuit a company." (Nashville Daily Union, 8 Oct. 1863.)

"The last three years of the Civil War there was no circuit or chancery courts held in Dickson County." (Dickson County Herald, 29 Sept. 1911.)

1864

General Lyon, CSA, is on the south side of the Cumberland River and intends to strike the railroad near Charlotte. (New York Times, 25 Oct. 1864.)

Guerrillas are extremely troublesome on Cumberland River and Northwestern Railroad. (New York Times, 1 Nov. 1864.)

1865

The railroad bridges between Nashville and Johnsonville are being repaired. (Nashville Daily Union, 28 Feb. 1865. For more on the Civil War period refer to the section on Guerrillas and Bushwhackers found earlier in this Dickson County Handbook.)

1866

Yellow Creek Lodge No. 317 was formed this year in March. A. J. Parrish was the worshipful master, W. H. Daniel, senior warden, J. J. Pickett, junior warden, Jesse Daniel, secretary, T. H. Hinson, treasurer, T. W. Nichols, senior deacon, James Smith, junior deacon, and Isaac Turner, tyler. Others who were members: A. J. Cooksey, A. A. Brown, J. T. Turner, R. S. Nesbitt, A. B. Skelton, S. R. Averitt, W. V. Turner, J.M. Skelton, E. Adkins, H. E. Pickett, P. P. Potter, and William Pickett.

"Petroleum has been struck on Jones Creek." (Memphis Avalanche, 1 Nov. 1866.)

A. W. Hawkins of Dickson County, is delegate to the black and tan convention in Philadelphia. (Memphis Avalanche, 18 Sept. 1866.)

Laborers are grading the railroad from Nashville to the Tennessee River. (Memphis Avalanche, 31 Oct. 1866.)

A. P. Nicks was the Freedmen's Bureau agent at Charlotte. (Tennessee Historical Quarterly, Spring 1966, page 56.)

1867

Methodist Church established in Dickson.

Dickson County has 585 registered voters. (Memphis Avalanche, 27 July 1867. At this time former Confederates could not register.)

"Oil was struck a week ago 7 miles from White Bluff near the Nashville and Northwestern line; running at last accounts at 12 barrels per day." (Memphis Avalanche, 19 June 1867.)

1868

Dickson was laid off, and platted, by C. Berringer of Alleghany City. It was called Sneedsville in honor of a civil engineer who located the first side tract here. (Nashville Tennessean, 16 Oct. 1942.)

Jeff Swanson, old negro, once belonged to Daniel Hillman, was brought down from Sneedsville yesterday and put in workhouse. He stole from Hillman. (Nashville Republican Banner, 4 March 1868.)

The newspapers of this time are full of immigration to Dickson County.

In November 1868 there was a train wreck three miles west of Waverly when the Nashville and Northwestern ran off the tracks. Among those injured was T. A. Napier, Jr., who died November 9. (Nashville Republican Banner, 10 Nov. 1868.)

1869

Dickson County claims against the government for loyal losses:
- U. S. Government $3,508.65
- C.S.A. $29,425.03

(Memphis Daily Appeal, 10 Jan. 1869.)

A Mr. Helm of Pennsylvania and five others have purchased farms in Dickson County for emigration. (Memphis Daily Appeal, 4 Feb. 1869.)

Fifty-three families from Pennsylvania have embarked on steamer for Tennessee, probably booked for Dickson County, which has a large Pennsylvania settlement. (Memphis Daily Appeal, 21 March 1869.)

Sneedsville on the Nashville and Northwestern Railroad contained only a few shanties two years ago; now has 1500 inhabitants. (Memphis Daily Appearl, 2 July 1869.)

John Groves, Proctor, and Ferguson, charged with murder of a negro in Dickson County, have been taken to Charlotte for trial. The murder took place last October. (Nashville Republican Banner, 3 Dec. 1868, 17 Feb. 1869.)

1870

Dickson was incorporated and now called Dickson. This charter was abandoned about 1883. (Nashville Tennessean, 16 Oct. 1942.)

In April the town was still being called Smeedsville. (Columbia Herald and Mail, 29 April 1870. Historians are still divided whether the town was called Smeedsville or Sneedsville. It is found both ways in the contemporary newspapers--but Sneedsville is generally accepted.)

1871

The Nashville and Northwestern Railroad was purchased by the Nashville and Chattanooga Railroad. (Columbia Herald, 13 Oct. 1871.)

1873

There was a cholera epidemic in adjoining Houston County this year.

"The Quarterly Court of Dickson County met at Charlotte last Monday. The question of the removal of the courthouse from Charlotte to Dickson was before the courts, and after arguments as to the legality of the election held on June 10 last, the court decided that the same was not legal and so the matter rests." (Nashville Union and American, 11 July 1873.)

Dickson County claimants for damages during the Civil War or for supplies taken or furnished by the following to the U. S. Army, all made oath that they were loyal adherents of the U. S. cause:

- James Adams, $150
- A. J. Allen, $75
- Milly Beaumont, $126
- James Choate, $875
- William Cox, $790
- George C. Dotson, $570
- James E. Gilliam, $570
- James Howell, $570
- George Hutcheson and Alexander Kerr, $4800
- George W. Moore, amount illegible
- James Sloan, $13,130
- John R. Vanhook, $144
- Joseph J. Williams, $300
- John F. Wright, $210

(Nashville Union and American, 24 Dec. 1873.)

1878

"Last Monday the Dickson County jail at Charlotte took fire and burned down." (Hickman Pioneer, published Centerville, 29 March 1878.)

1879

Track laying on the first 20 miles of the Nashville & Tuscaloosa Railroad is progressing. (Hickman Pioneer, 13 June 1879. Note: This line would be known as the Centerville Branch.)

1880

The first carload of iron ore was made on the 8th by the Nashville and Tuscaloosa railroad by L.S. Goodrich to be used in Worley Furnace. (Hickman Pioneer, 18 June 1880.)

Dickson is growing. There are 16 stores, 5 churches, 2 mills and one broom factory. The Hickman minstrels performed at the LutheranChurch, a nice brick building. (Hickman Pioneer 2 July 1880.)

On Tuesday the 13th at 8 p.m. an earth tremor felt. (Hickman Pioneer, 16 July 1880.)

The Dickson Normal Academy is in full blast with Rev. William Huston, principal; Rev. C. F. Evans, governor; and H. C. Neville, music teacher. (Hickman Pioneer 24 Sept. 1880.)

1881

"The last man convicted of murder in the first degree in Dickson County and sentencedto hang was Jack White, who lived a few miles south of Burns, and was convicted of the murder of William Clardy in 1881. White's death sentence was commuted by Gov. Hawkins to life imprisonment. White served 23 years in prison, but was given his freedom by pardon of the Governor two years ago. At present there are three convicts serving in the state pen from Dickson County." (Dickson County Herald, 6 Oct.1911)

Andrew Jackson White has been setenced to be hanged in Charlotte on August 26 for murdering P. Clardy. An appeal is probable. (Hickman Pioneer, 5 Aug. 1881.)

Andrew Jackson White, who murdered James T. Clardy near Charlotte in January was to have been hanged on 26th at Charlotte; he is 22; Clardy was bachelor 65 to 70 years old. The case has gone to the Supreme Court. (Erin Review, 10 Sept. 1881.)

Andrew Jackson White has been found guilty of murder of James Clardy by the Supreme Court and to be hanged April 28. Clardy was murdered the night of 25 Jan. 1881. The court recommended the governor commute sentence to life. (Hickman Pioneer, 17 March 1882.)

Local tradition about the Clardy murder says that White murdered Clardy with a poker. White, a simple-minded man, was spending the night with Clardy. He stole Clardy's horse and took it to Nashville to sell. He stood trial and was put in prison for life. He broke out once and went home. When the officers went for him, he was ploughing. He just unhitched the horse and went back peacefully. At one time he had served a longer prison term than anyone in the state.

"On Wednesday a fire broke out in a drug store in Dickson while many citizens were attending a funeral. A gravel train came long and the engineer cast water from the tender on the fire." (Erin Review, 17 Dec. 1881.)

PEN PICTURE OF DICKSON 30 YEARS AGO.--Well, does the writer remember how Dickson first appeared to him 30 years ago. There was then no side track north of the main line of the railroad, and a little depot was built at the rear of the present Citizens National Bank Building where the platform ran up to the track.

"There was then a two story frame hotel building on the vacant lot, now owned by the railroad next to the depot. Our esteemed townsman, J. A. Thomas, conducted a general merchandise business in a one-story frame building occupied by a saloon. Where Simon's corner building now stands was another saloon.

"While on the lot where W. A. Self has a grocery store was a frame building occupied by William and Henry Pickett for a store. W. J. Mathis was conducting a store on the old Mathis corner and A. Myatt had his business in the building now occupied by the Dickson Bakery. These were the only four stores in Dickson, except a Mr. McWilliams was post master and sold a few drugs, where the Christian Livery stable now stands.

"Public school at that time was taught in the Lutheran Church and there was not a residence within several hundred feet of this building.

"The Centerville Branch Railroad then left the main branch of the N and C road about where the Dickson Ice Company now stands, the track ran off southward and in about 150 feet of the Lutheran Church, the road went out through Scuff Town by Willow Spring and struck the present line of road near Pomona.

"The Southern Methodist Church was on South Main Street on the lot now occupied by the residence of Mr. W. J. Cummins. There was a brickyard just back of where Mr. C. M. Turner's office is now located. There was an old log house on the corner of Main and College Streets, which had been occupied by the Federal soldiers during the war.

"There was no manufacturing interest at Dickson except a flouring (or planing?) mill owned and operated by the late Dr. T. F. McCreary, one half mile north of Dickson on the Charlotte road, near where John Woody now lives. There were no buildings then on McCreary Heights, none in West Dickson, none on Rickert Avenue, and none in the vicinity of Dickson College.

"Several years later the public school building known then as the Dickson Academy was erected just back of where Prof. S. E. Hunt now lives and was built jointly by the public school fund and the Masonic Lodge of this place. The Masons using the second floor for their lodge room.

"The first brick store house erected in Dickson was built by Tom and John Coleman and is now occupied by the Anderson Hardware Company.

"Mr. Will Conant published the first paper in Dickson, being the Dickson County Press. After a few months he moved his printing outfit to Charlotte and Mr. Sam Freeman then founded and published the Dickson Democrat.

"The part of Dickson now known as West Dickson was formerly owned by Mrs. Dikeman and was bought by Dr. C. M. Lovell and Mr. W. E. Cullum, and laid off in town lots." (Dickson County Herald, 17 March 1911. No author's name was given to this sketch in the paper.)

1882

Dickson--100 new houses will be built in this place next year. Cumberland Furnace "blew out" last Saturday for repairs and will be in operation in about a month. (Hickman Pioneer, 13 Jan. 1882.)

A plat of Union Cemetery has been drawn up and lots numbered. Emma L. Harris sued W. T. Harrison for divorce. (Dickson County Press, 16 Feb. 1882.)

This year the overhead bridge was brought from Humphreys County and put up over the railroad. This bridge was pulled down in 1962.

John P. McFarland married Ella Chappell on Feb. 8. (Dickson County Press, 16 Feb. 1882.)

The six-year-old child of Phil Hogan (c) of Burns Station died last Monday from the effects of drinking a quart of gin which its mother had left within its reach while she "stepped out" to visit a neighbor. (Hickman Pioneer, 31 March 1882.)

The site for the new depot building at Dickson is the finest on the NC& StL railroad. (Dickson County Press, 23 March 1882.)

J. N. Alexander is the proprietor of the Alexander House in Dickson.

Corsica Mills is on the George Sinsabaugh property 1½ miles from Dickson on the narrow gauge railroad. (Dickson County Press, 23 March 1882.)

The railroad is finished to Graham in Hickman County, 26 miles from Dickson. Hall & Mentlo has begun operating spoke factory at Dickson. (Hickman Pioneer, 14 April 1882.)

The new depot will be an ornament for our town. Work is to begin on Monday. (Dickson County Press, 20 April 1882.)

A telephone line from Capt. Brown's residence to the depot will be erected in a few weeks. (Dickson County Press, 13 April 1882.)

Dickson Station in Dickson County has a new depot building just completed. (Erin Review, 3 June 1882.)

A telegraph line is being built between Dickson and Bon Aqua Springs. (Hickman Pioneer, 2 June 1882.)

New depot at Dickson is completed and the old one was torn down on Monday. (Hickman Pioneer, 16 June 1882.)

Twenty-five carloads of lumber for the new hotel at Bon Aqua have been shipped through Dickson; the telephone line between Dickson and Bon Aqua is to be in operation in June. (Dickson County Press, 13 April 1882.)

There are 6 churches in Dickson: Methodist Episcopal South, Methodist Episcopal, United Presbyterian, Lutheran and two colored. (Dickson County Press, 15 June 1882.)

Divorces filed by Doney McCaulley vs Henry McCaulley and Mary Bell vs Wilson Bell. (Dickson County Press, 31 Aug. 1882.)

J. T. Baker elected county court chairman. (Dickson County Press, 7 Sept. 1882.)

J. W. Clark is mayor of Dickson. Dr. W. A. Moody is building a house at Gillem. (Dickson County Press, 16 Nov. 1882.)

1883

The first church wedding held in Dickson when Ida Williams married Russell Spicer in May 1883.

J. W. Shaw was elected mayor of Dickson and J. B. Robinson, recorder. (Dickson County Press, 25 Jan. 1883.)

Old Mr. Cordie Vineyard is very low and there is no hope for his recovery. (Dickson County Press, 25 Jan. 1883.)

A silver communion service has been obtained for the Lutheran Church. (Dickson County Press, 18 Jan. 1883.)

The oldest people in District 1 are John Chester, 85; Lemuel Bruce, 85; Nelly England, 95; and London Springer (c), 100. (Dickson County Press, 15 Jan. 1883.) Old people in District 3 are John Ranie, 91; Mr. and Mrs. David Fraser, 80 and 77; Mr. and Mrs. Huttson, 70-ish. Old people also in District 3 this year were Mrs. T. Luther, 70; Mrs. Porter, 70; Mrs. Irwin, 61 and William Irwin, 65. (Dickson County Press, 17 May 1883.)

1884

The passenger train between Dickson and Centerville began to make regular trips on January 1. (Hickman Pioneer, 4 Jan. 1884.)

Dickson County is 1090 feet above sea level. On Janury 5 it was 8° below at Dickson and on January 6 it was 18° below.

Andrew Bunch petitioned for divorce from Julia Bunch and W. S. Fortner petitioned for divorce from L. C. Bunch. These were filed in January 1884.

Rollie Painter, adopted son of Elder Nicks of Dickson County, who attempted to kill Nicks some time ago, has been sentenced to penitentiary for 3 years. (Hickman Pioneer, 28 March 1884.)

War of 1812 pensioners in Dickson County were published in the Dickson County Press, 7 Feb. 1884:

    Dicey Austin, Burns, survivor, War of 1812
    Eleanor Gossett, Burns, widow of soldier
    Christian Borchet, Burns, suffers with chronic rheumatism
    Kinchen Mathis, Cave Mills, received gunshot wound in mouth during War of 1812
    Alexander Jones, Charlotte, gunshot wound in right arm during War of 1812
    Nancy Walker, Charlotte, widow of War of 1812 soldier
    Jane Evans, Charlotte, widow of War of 1812 soldier
    Amanda Hightower, Charlotte, widow of War of 1812 soldier
    Caroline Spradling, Charlotte, widow of War of 1812 soldier
    Mary A. Swift, Charlotte, widow of War of 1812 soldier
    Nancy Russell, Charlotte, widow of War of 1812 soldier
    Eveline D. Bell, Charlotte, widow of War of 1812 soldier
    Mary Lucas, Charlotte, widow of War of 1812 soldier
    Rebecca Jones, Charlotte, widow of War of 1812 soldier
    Sarah E. James, Charlotte, widow of War of 1812 soldier
    William Dodson, Charlotte, survivor, War of 1812 soldier
    Empson Bishop, Charlotte, survivor, War of 1812 soldier
    James Larkins, Charlotte, gunshot wound in right breast during War of 1812
    Elizabeth Denning, Cumberland Furnace, mother of War of 1812 soldier
    George D. Whittier, Cumberland Furnace, gunshot wound in right thigh during War of 1812
    Peter Oakley, Cumberland Furnace, gunshot wound in left foot, War of 1812
    Rachel Kimbro, Dickson
    John O. Harshman, Dickson, injury to right eye, War of 1812
    Nancy Gustin, White Bluff, dependent mother of War of 1812 soldier
    William Hagey, White Bluff, left arm amputated above elbow, War of 1812
    Elizabeth Pack, White Bluff, widow of War of 1812 soldier
    Elizabeth McCaslin, White Bluff, widow of War of 1812 soldier
    Charles L. Reynolds, White Bluff, disease of the eyes, War of 1812 soldier

1885

Parker's Creek in Dickson County was named for Moses Parker, who killed a bear and cut his name and 1808 in a tree at Bon Aqua. Tree blew down in storm on the 22d ult. (Hickman Pioneer, 5 Dec. 1885.)

Jewel Cave discovered when Thomas Rogers and daughter Fannie crawled in cave; first called Rogers Cave. (Dickson County Herald, 18 Oct. 1937.)

Edgewood Normal College established. (Dickson County Herald, 13 Aug. 1937.)

John Grace has been arrested in Nashville for killing Dan Price at White Bluff in March 1884. He has eluded arrest ever since. He said the killing was in self defense. (Hickman Pioneer, 3 July 1885. Some accounts give the victim's name as Dan Rice.)

1886

A large cave has been discovered on Yellow Creek in Dickson County at T. Rodger's spring. (Hickman Pioneer, 22 Aug. 1886.) (Note: It is not known if this were a late report to the newspaper, or if the cave were discovered in 1886 instead of 1885 as usually given.)

Distinct shock of earthquake felt August 31. It was centered around Charleston, S. C. (Hickman Pioneer, 3 Sept. 1886.)

1887

On May 25 George W. DeHaven's show and free menagerie was in Dickson; it featured clowns, tumblers, jugglers, and contortionists. (Hickman Pioneer, 20 May 1887.)

John Rickert, aged, married Mrs. Nancy Myers, widow, in District 3. (Dickson County Press, 30 June 1887.)

Dennis Grundy petitioned for a divorce from Viney Grundy. (Dickson County Press, 30 June 1887.)

The criminal docket for court included: Easter Bacon charged with murder and J. C. Donegan with embezzlement. John Ladd and Mat Hayes were to be tried for going armed. John Murphy and Fannie Cooksey were charged with lewdness. (Dickson County Press, 21 July 1887.)

An earthquake was felt last Monday night at 12 o'clock and lasted 6 seconds. (Hickman Pioneer, 5 Aug. 1887.)

1888

A new church is to be dedicated on the fourth Sunday at Beef Range. (The News, Houston County, 24 May 1888.)

According to an old undated clipping: "The first bank in Dickson was the Dickson Bank and Trust Company in 1888. It was located where Kelly Dry Cleaners is in 1966. Dr. C. M. Lovell was first president and others connected with the bank were J. R. Bryan, J. R. Sutton, Bob Boyt, W. H. McMurray, and Arthur Hopkins."

1889

John Hollins, living south of Dickson, has been arrested for selling illicit liquors. Deputy Marshal Pendergrass is under arrest for abducting a girl. (Maury Democrat, Columbia, TN, 5 Dec. 1889.)

Dr. J. G. Brake of Wood's Valley was killed by George F. Talley. Brake had treated Talley's daughter Ella, who claimed she was seduced by the doctor. (Maury Democrat, 5 Dec. 1889.) (An account of this affair is also found in the Dickson County Press, 5 Dec. 1889.)

1890

State Bank opened at Dickson last week. (Hickman Pioneer, 7 Nov. 1890.)

The construction on the Mineral Branch railroad from Clarksville has begun. (Maury Democrat, 7 Aug. 1890.)

1891

Rev. Henry Crocket of the Methodist Church at Dickson has suddenly and mysteriously disappeared. Some think foul play; some think there is a woman in the case. (Maury Democrat, 27 March 1891.)

Wayman Academy for negroes contract is to be let. This school will be under the AME in Dickson County. (Maury Democrat, 3 July 1891.)

Smith & Talley, publishers of the Dickson County Press, have moved the paper from Charlotte where it has been published for 6 years to Dickson.

Found in family scrapbook: "Arthur Hopkins has treated himself to a fine silver alto horn. It is solid silver finished and will be played by Mr. Hopkins in the Citizens Band of Dickson. This makes, in connection with those owned by W. J. Conant, R. H. Hicks and Mat Hopkins, a quartet of as fine instruments as can be purchased, and when their owners are behind them, there is music in the air." (The clipping was from the newspaper the Home Enterprise.)

1892

James Thomason of Vanleer was shot by Mr. Daniel, a railroad agent and telegraph operator there. Thomason was shot 4 or 5 times. There had been a feud for several months. Daniel escaped, took the train at Burns but was caughte before getting to White Bluff. It is rumored a mob has been organized at Vanleer to lynch Daniel. (Dickson County Press,

9 June 1892.)

The newspaper Dickson County Press was moved back to Charlotte to be published.

Braxton C. Linzy married Miss Florence Kephart on lower Jones Creek, Alf Watson married Etta Larkins. (Dickson County Press, 18 Feb. 1892.) A. J. Lampley married Molly Menders. (Dickson County Press, 14 July 1892.)

"Last Saturday James Wynn took double-bit axe and murdered his wife in bed. Her 12 year old daughter was next assaulted, severed her fingers, and crashed her brain, and it is thought she will die. He tried suicide but was lynched. The mob took him from sheriff near the old Spicer place two miles from Burns. The mob hanged him. Mrs. Wynn was widow Anderson before she married and was the mother of Will Anderson. (Dickson County Press, 28 July 1892, Thursday.)

"Wynn, wife murderer, was lynched by the people of Dickson, Tennessee." (Florence, Ala., Times, 6 Aug. 1892.)

1893

The newspaper Dickson Independent was being published this year at Charlotte.

A newspaper called the Dickson Home Enterprise was published by R. H. Hicks. The following comes from an 1893 issue:

"A beautiful pulpit has been placed in the First M. E. Church, the work and donation of Mr. Joseph Heatherington. It is a handsome piece of workmanship, made of oak, ornamented with walnut panels and speaks much to the credit of the builder.

"Maude, the little daughter of J. T. Moore, is much improved and on the road to recovery...Work on the new railroad bridge has commenced in earnest and will be pushed rapidly.

"A K. of P. Lodge was organized here last Friday night and christened the W. A. Hopkins. That it is strong to membership is manifest by the fact that it took all night for each member to get his turn at "riding the goat."

"Born to Mr. and Mrs. J. B. Ballard on North Main Street, 8 April 1893 a son...We erred last week in the birth notice that a daughter was born to Mr. and Mrs. Portwood. Mr. Portwood informs us that the girl was a boy. Our treat to Mr. P.

"The elegant new residence of Judge W. L. Grigsby will be completed the middle of this month and the family will take possession. (Note: This house was torn down in 1972.)

"Fresh bread every day at Scott & Wynns...Fresh meat at J. N. Hutton's ...Fine line of jewelry just opened at Henslee & Myatt...E. E. Miller will sell queensware at cost the next 10 days...A large quantity of rice has been received by Ankeny & Brown and they are selling it at five cents per pound...

"All delinquent members of the Home Building & Loan are requested to be at a meeting Tuesday night; M. L. McCaul, president, J. L. Ankeny, secretary..."

In Feb. 1893 the General Assembly House Bill 152 was introduced to change the line between Cheatham and Dickson counties, to include in Dickson County the "Horseshoe".

1894

Jim Bell (c) charged with killing a child was lynched and burned at Charlotte, Tenn., on Friday. (Columbia Herald, 13 July 1894.)

On last Saturday the first broad gauge train ran from Dickson to Mannie.

(Maury Democrat, 12 July 1894.)

1895

On 5 Oct. 1895 there was a $50,000 fire at Dickson and many prominent business houses were burned. (Columbia Herald, 18 Oct. 1895.)

1896

Ruskin Co-operative Colony is to build a town in Dickson County. (Columbia Herald, 6 March 1896.)

There was a jail break at Charlotte last week. (Columbia Herald, 24 Jan. 1896.)

1897

The Confederate veterans of Dickson County have organized the Bill Green Camp with 40 members. (Nashville Banner, 6 May 1897.)

Graham Egerton was arrested in Cincinnati. He was the defaulting tax attorney of Dickson County--some $2000 missing. He had wealthy relatives in England and it is thought he was trying to make his way to them. (Maury Democrat, 28 Jan. 1897.)

1898

The Dickson County court is to hold an election 1 Sept. 1898 about moving the county seat from Charlotte. (Columbia Herald, 8 Apr. 1898.)

The election in Dickson County defeated the movement to remove the county seat. (Columbia Herald, 9 Sept. 1898.)

County officials this year were: W. L. Grigsby, circuit court judge; J. T. Hudson, county court judge; I. M. Bowers, clerk and master; R. L. Leech, circuit court clerk; H. J. Larkins, county court clerk; J. W. Fielder, register; W. R. Hudson, sheriff; J. N. Parrotte, coroner; and T. R. Dickson, trustee.

The Ruskin Band and Dramatic Company are arranging to give an entertainment. Earnest A. Jones married the daughter of I. M. Nelson of White Bluffs. (Dickson County Press, 10 Nov. 1898.)

The newspaper Dickson County Press was revived and Volume 1, Number 1, published at Charlotte was dated 3 Nov. 1898. In this issue it was noted that the promoters of a long distance line from Charlotte to Dickson had all the poles cut and were distributing them along the line.

Wellington and Ewing Larkins on Saturday at Liberty got cut severely by John Dawson and James Powers, who were bound over to court. (Dickson County Press, 3 Nov. 1898.)

Marriages licenses issued and reported were for Stephen Adams of Yellow Creek to Mrs. Tenn Nelson of Piney; W. P. Parker to Nanna Henry, both of Jones Creek; G. M. Foster to N. E. Miller, both of near Slayden; J. D. Glover to Otie Simpson, both of Dickson; R. A. F____ to ____Payne, both of Dickson; A. J. Donegan to Dalie Fielder, both of Piney. G. T. Gibbons was married to Buena Gilbert of Charlotte, daughter of the Rev. Gilbert. (Dickson County Press, 24 Nov. 1898.)

Criminal court charges were placed against N. Bibb, carrying pistol; Pleas Lewis, profanity; Susie Lewis, carrying pistol; Ersher Larkins, violating the age of consent; F. Nicks, disturbing public worship; and Marshall Hall for housebreaking and larceny. (Dickson County Press, 24 Nov. 1898.)

1899

The corporation of Dickson was re-created 12 May 1899. (Dickson Free Press, 2 Jan. 1980, quoting "From Mile Post 42 to City of Dickson 1980" by Robert S. Clement. This series of articles on the history of the town of Dickson is recommended for those interested in further study of the town.)

Ruskin Cave Co-operative is to be sold. The Baptists at Vanleer and

Cumberland Furnace have organized at Dean School House. (Daily Leaf Chronicle, Clarksville, 8 July 1899.)

Marriage licenses issued and reported: M. H. Keele to Lottie Adams; W. G. Moody to Ada Donegan; M. B. Spencer to M. C. Welch; J. C. Shrom to Sophie Sanker; Berry Petty to Alice Scott; L. D. Sanders to Etta Hicks; and M. D. Buttrey to M. A. Spicer. Colored marriage licenses issued: Erskin Larkins to Clara Bibb; Robt Robinson to Francis Cheatham. (Dickson County Press, 23 March 1899.)

Criminal docket published: E. Van Fossen, false pretense; Johnnie Baker for house breaking and larceny; William Ricker, larceny; Elvin Adcock, disturbing public worship; Jim Meek for carrying knuckles; Jim Redden, carrying pistol; Marshall Hall, tippling; Robert and Lula Baker, tippling; Bud Smiley, larceny; William Austin, carrying pistol; Clint Ham, disturbing public worship; Willie Perdue, disturbing public worship; J. D. Murrell, carrying pistol; William Beasley, carrying pistol; and L. Meacham, tippling. (Dickson County Press, 23 March 1899.)

B. Petty married Alice Scott on March 18. L. D. Sanders married Etta Hicks on March 21. Henry Taylor married Bessie Marton in February. (Dickson County Press, 23 March 1899.)

Divorce petitions filed: Frank Smith vs Lizzie Smith; Nannie Daily vs D. A. Daily; and Mary Hicks vs James Ed Hicks. (Dickson County Press, 28 Oct. 1899.)

"It is said a Mormon Church will soon be organized near the head of the east fork of Yellow Creek in Dickson County; they only lack two or three of having enough." (Daily Leaf Chronicle, Clarksville, 29 Dec. 1899.)

There are five cases of typhoid at Sylvia. (Daily Leaf Chronicle, 20 Oct. 1899.)

The Dickson courthouse and jail are nearly complete. Circuit court was in session at Dickson this week and last week at Charlotte. (Daily Leaf Chronicle, 21 Nov. 1899.)

"New courthouse at Dickson is nearly completed and will be ready at the next term of court." (Maury Democrat, 13 July 1899.) (Note: This was an auxiliary courthouse and stood on the lot where the War Memorial building is today on Center Avenue. On 13 July 1928 the courthouse was being razed as it had been condemned. An article in 1928 paper noted "a great deal of brick and timber to be used in annex of Oakmont School.")

A purchase of 2000 acres, east of Dickson adjoining Bakers Works, was made for a colony of Northern people engaged in agriculture by Col. J. B. Killebrew, the immigration agent for the NC&StL railroad. (Daily Leaf Chronicle, 9 Nov. 1899.)

Telephone service began 19 June 1899 with 39 phones in Dickson. Frank Bright was the first night chief operator.

Bob Turner, age 2, was bound to T. C. H. Joslin. The court gave a year's support to Mrs. M. G. White (widow of John) and Mrs. Z. E. Daniel (widow of W. H.) of Edgewood. M. Hober was appointed administrator of his wife Sarah M. Hober. (Dickson County Press, 10 Aug. 1899.)

"A saloon is to be opened soon it is rumored." (Dickson County Press, 10 Aug. 1899.)

Marriage licenses issued: W. L. Weaver to Anna Browning; William Wills to Annie Hunter, M. G. Lowell to Ethel Emmers (?), R. W. Caldwell to Lulie Albert; S. C. Tidwell to M. E. Pendergrass. (Dickson County Press, 10 Aug. 1899.)

1900

The census takers for Dickson County will be: T. W. Weems, C. J. Tidwell, Martin Smith, A. G. Rickert, J. B. Robinson, J. H. Abercrombie,

C. H. Underhill, Melvin Harris, S. F. Bowker, M. G. Harris, W. M. Story, and W. W. Jordan. (Daily Herald, Columbia, TN, 25 April 1900.)

One of the bloodiest fights ever happened at a picnic at Pomona in Dickson County on Saturday between Estes, Greers, and Works, and fully 25 men participated with clubs, knives, and pistols used freely. Alex Estes was fatally cut in the neck; two Greer boys had their faces beaten beyond recognition. All have been arrested. (Daily Herald, 21 Aug. 1900.)

1901

The Ann Scott and Frank Rickert houses in Dickson burned March 3. (Daily Herald, 8 March 1901.)

Rev. W. H. Harton was arrested Sept. 24 for approaching too near election polls and obstructing sidewalks. Dickson voted $85,000 bond to secure waterworks and electric lights. There were 218 for and 41 against this. (Daily Herald, 26 Sept. 1901.)

J. R. Bryant of Dickson was married May 14 to his daughter-in-law Mrs. Cecil Bryant of Paducah. The marriage was not made known until a few days ago. (Daily Herald, 7 Oct. 1901.)

John Russell resisting arrest at Dickson for drunkenness bit off the entire forefinger of deputy policeman Bowers Hooper. (Daily Herald, 11 Nov. 1901.)

W. M. Swain, saloon keeper in Dickson, arrested 4 times Dec. 9 for violating law about the sale of whiskey. (Daily Herald, 11 Dec. 1901.)

An injunction has been issued to stop the bond issue for the waterworks and electric lights. (Daily Herald, 26 Nov. 1901.)

Mayor Slayden of Dickson was instructed to write J. A. Wayland, editor of Girard, Kansas, and invite him to Dickson with his publication. He was once editor of The Coming Nation at Ruskin. (Daily Herald, 2 Oct. 1901.)

On 20 August 1901 a span in the railroad bridge across the Tennessee River at Johnsonville was washed out. All traffic was suspended on the railroad until the bridge was replaced.

"The Verdict" was a newspaper published in Dickson County by Harry L. and Charles D. Bevan. The following information was taken from an issue dated 11 Oct. 1901:

"S. G. Holland went to Nashville Wednesday to see Buffalo Bill. He said he had not intended to go, but Buffalo Bill sent for him and he did not wish to disappoint the old fellow...Mrs. Charles Badge was among the passengers to Nashville Monday morning...Someone stole W. W. Walker's medicine case one evening early in the week, and about one o'clock in the night Officer Sheley found it sitting in the alley at the rear of the Red Star Store...

"Postmaster Scott, Mayor Slayden, J. J. Blackwell and L. M. Sensing were among those who took advantage of the cheap rates to Nashville Tuesday and we presume visited the horse show...Bow Hooper, J. T. Halbrook and Charley Hardin were all in Nashville Wednesday to see Buffalo Bill. Halbrook and Hardin say it was all they could do to keep Bow from following Buffalo Bill away...

"Shoes for sale by W. H. Walker...Mrs. Clayton Smith went.to Nashville Monday where she will spend the week in the wholesale millinery store getting posted up on styles...Call of Mrs. Dollie Smith for the latest things in millinery...Miss Lorena Bright has accepted the position as "Hello" girl at the Central office made vacant by the marriage of Miss Hattie Ethridge.

"A. M. Hartman's Cheap Grocery in Dickson...A pleasant and jolly party of ten were gathered at the home of Miss Belle Murrell Tuesday night. The party was composed of the following well known society people:

Hattie Davis, Sue Scott, Jessie Sanford, Maude Murrell and Belle Murrell, and Messrs. Clyde Buquo, Joseph Latimer, Delpho Sprague, Will Shepherd, and Ewell Williams...

"Night prowlers kept Ed Morrow's mind pretty well occupied Wednesday night. Ed is unable to tell the color of the fellows, as he n'er could get a good glimpse at them. We hope someone will gather them in soon as it is very uncomfortable to have them at large.

"Mrs. John Churchill is spending a few days in Nashville this week visiting her sister Mrs. Hearn...N. R. Sugg is erecting himself a new eight room house on his place south of town known as the "Goat Ranch". Mose Lucas, the well known Tennessee City carpenter and builder has the contract.

"Prof. W. M. Adcock of Burns was a Saturday visitor in Dickson. Prof. Adcock is a bright young educator and we always have a vacant seat for him when he calls in....

"The Myatt Drug Company carries a large stock of drugs, paints, oils, varnishes, etc...Fall and winter apparel at W. A. Barnett & Company...

"Charlotte news items: Hon. W. H. Leech, W. E. Cullum, S. E. Hunt, R. L. Leech, and H. C. Richardson represented the Dickson County Bar here Monday...Jim Eleazer came to town Monday and the freedom of the city was promptly extended to him on the condition he'd "yelp" one time...He wouldn't take us up...Dr. Charlesworth a few days ago removed another large piece of glass from the foot of Miss Mary Egerton and it is now thought a thorough cure will be affected. She has suffered from this injury several months...Esq. Henry Sesler of the Seventh tore himself away from his sawmill and attended strictly to his district's interest Monday...J. W. Fielder, our efficient register, has been confined to his home the past week with chills and fever...W. R. Hudson, who aspires to the position of county judge next August, is doing more active electioneering than all other aspirants for offices put together."

professional and businessmen advertising in this newspaper included: W. T. Crotzer, Henry C. Richardson, Lanier & Kannard, Clark & McFarland, Graham Egerton, W. E. Cullum, J. W. Grigsby, Morris & Morris, lawyers; Dr. G. A. Slayden, dentist; Charles I. Eccles, painter; W. B. Williams, justice of the peace.

1902

The first long distance call was made to Waverly this year.

Harry L. Bevan filed a libel suit for $50,000 at Dickson against Mrs. Cora C. Hicks, publisher of the Home Enterprise and R. H. Hicks, writer of certain articles detrimental to Mr. Bevan's character. (Daily Herald 14 Jan. 1902.)

Gas has been struck at 100 feet on Jones Creek near White Bluff while drilling for oil. (Daily Herald, 6 Jan. 1902.)

A. L. Scott has been appointed postmaster at Dickson. (Daily Herald, 10 Feb. 1902.)

Sam Jones, evangelist, was in Dickson Feb. 24 and delivered lecture at Centerville that day also. At Dickson he said, "I see you have had to give up your saloons at this place, but you have a sufficiency of other things to insure your safe arrival in hell." (Daily Herald, 26 Feb. 1902.)

White Bluff had a 15-inch snow; Tennessee City had 12 inches. (Daily Herald, 15 Feb. 1902.)

John W. Grigsby of Charlotte, while attempting to mount a horse, was thrown and leg broken. (Daily Herald, 28 Feb. 1902.)

1903

James Gilliam of Charlotte said to have a stream of oil running 6 feet be;ow the surface, 4 miles west of Charlotte. (Daily Herald, 27 Jan. 1903.)

First National Bank of Dickson chartered 19 August 1903. The bank's organizers were Pitt Henslee and J. A. Myatt. In later years Mr. Myatt often recalled he and Henslee decided to organize a bank in a meeting held under a peach tree. The original stockholders were S. E. Hunt, R. C. Howell, M. G. Nesbitt, W. M. Adams, F. O. Watts, S. G. Holland, C. M. Turner, H. B. Horner, J. G. Henslee, J. A. Myatt, L. M. Sensing, J. C. Foster, W. C. McLaughlin, J. R. McClelland, J. A. Turner, J. M. Allison, G. A. Slayden, Pitt Henslee, J. C. Cox, E. H. Stone, John T. Overby, W. H. Greer and J. W. Johnson.

1904

A new bank established at White Bluff with $20,000 capital stock. (Daily Herald, 15 Sept. 1904.)

Dickson is suffering from a water famine. Water is being hauled from a mile distant and selling for 15 to 20 cents a barrel. (Daily Herald, 16 Sept. 1904.)

Nearly a race riot: Trouble between a whie man and negroes at Hortense. Scott Stephens, storekeeper and Ann Neblett had dispute over an account. He flogged her. The store was subsequeantly surrounded by negroes and a posse of 40 to 50 men was needed to break up the crowd. (Daily Herald 19 Sept. 1904.)

A train wreck near White Bluff and one man was killed while two others were hurt. Six cars were demolished. George Davis the baggage master was killed. It was a rear-end collision. (Daily Herald, 3 Oct. 1904.)

The family of Jim Clifton of Dickson were poisoned. They became ill from eating souse. (Daily Herald, 23 Nov. 1904.)

The officers of the Dickson Bank and Trust Company were: W. B. Leech, president; C. M. Lovell, vice president; W. H. McMurry, cashier; board of directors, J. R. Sutton, C. M. Lovell, W. H. McMurry, J. R. Baker, W. B. Leech, J. Davis, W. H. Fletcher, E. George and Dan Joslin. The bank had $12,500 capital stock.

1905

The Cumberland Telephone Company's rates are prohibitive. The people in Dickson County are in revolt against the rates. (Daily Herald, 18 May 1905.)

"TERRIBLE TRAGEDY AT DICKSON.--July 8. A terrible tragedy was enacted here this morning. J. E. Fowler, a mechanic and musician, shot and fatally wounded Dr. E. W. Ridings, Dickson's foremost physician and surgeon, five shots been fired, all taking effect.

"The tragedy occurred on Main street in the heart of the city, where Fowler approached his victim just as he was passing from his office entrance to Main street, and said, 'You have ruined my home. You die like a dog.' With these remarks the shooting began.

"Dr. Ridings fell to the ground crying, 'I have been killed for nothing. I am an innocent man.'

"Fowler immediately gave himself up and was taken to some unknown place of safety, the authorities fearing mob violence. Fowler is believed to be insane and suffering a hallucination of the mind." (Columbia Herald 14 July 1905.)

Worst fire in Dickson's history hit November 24 on East Main Street to the depot and from Ab Myatt Drug Store to West Main. Only 12 businesses left on North Main Street. (Daily Herald, 25 Nov. 1905.)

North Dickson was hit by a tornado on December 28. It demolished the

J. Davis home. Two other houses were blown away and many barns and out-buildings damaged.

Thomas Edison visited Hickman County recently. He went by Clemore Pharmacy (owned by Claude Sizemore and W. A. Clement, Sr.) in Dickson to buy some materials and rode the Centerville Branch Railroad which ran from Dickson to Allen's Creek south of Hohenwald. C. M. Turner was the superintendent of the Centerville Branch and L. A. McCaul was the fireman on the run. (Nashville Tennesseean, 2 Oct. 1955.)

Electric lights were installed in Dickson this year. (Dickson County Herald, 18 Oct. 1937.)

Miss Nettie Hord was a music teacher in Dickson. Pupils who studied under her 1906-1907 were: Minnie Wynns, Hattie Buford, Lida Rogers, Lula Belle Hopkins, Emma Bell, Rainy Wood, Hester Palmer, Vallie Henslee Elsie Boone, Faye Bell, Agnes Buquo, Eddie Lee Boone, Ethel Moore, Lucy Wynns, Katie Bell Morris, Judson Palmer, Annie Few, Courtney Scott, Myra Bevans, Maggie Wilson, Hazel Gibbs, Iva Henslee, and Clara Bevans. (Names found on picture in family scrapbook.)

1907

"Dickson, Oct. 14.--Mrs. W. W. Rayburn of 173 Fain Street, Nashville, brought her 7 year old son here today to have Dr. L. D. Wright apply a madstone. The latter has two bites inflicted upon the child recently. Mrs. Rayburn said that the dog that bit her son was a strange one that came to her home. It attacked the child and inflicted a number of ugly wounds upon his leg. She said further that she had the dog killed, sent its head to an analytical chemist at Vanderbilt and that an analysis of the same proved that the animal was mad. Having been informed of a famous madstone which Dr. Wright has had for a number of years and its marvelous success in the prevention of rabies, she came with her little son to the doctor.

"Upon her arrival the stone was immediately prepared and applied. It clung tenaciously to the wounds when first applied but gradually relaxed the hold, till finally it ceased to adhere at all.

"This stone which came originally from the East Indies and has been handed down from generation to generation has been applied to many hundreds of mad dog bites and never yet has one of the victims thus treated ever developed the disease.

"Dr. Wright has applied it to some ninety-odd patients, many of them in Dickson County and were known to have been bitten by dogs that were raving mad and never has one of them developed the least symptoms of hydrophobia.

"Dr. Wright feels confident that the stone has furnished a safe and effective antidote to the child's wounds." (Hohenwald Chronicle, 17 Oct. 1907.)

Ruskin Real Estate Company of Ruskin recently incorporated with $20,000 capital stock and the purchase of the college and the cave. They will build an addition to the college and a concrete dam across Yellow Creek for water power for electricity. (Clifton Mirror, 7 June 1907.)

The Dickson County Herald was established November 1907 by W. L. Pinkerton of Hickman County and it was sold to Ralph A. Freeman and Pitt Henslee in 1910. Volume 1 Number 1 appeared on 15 Nov. 1907.

Peoples Bank established.

1909

A tornado struck at Dickson and Centerville in April 1909. (Some authorities say it happened in March. However, the only documentary evidence located has been for the one April 30 which killed several people in Hickman County.)

The balloon Indiana, winner of the great national balloon race, landed on the east fork of Yellow Creek near Choate and Hunt's store, 6 miles north of Dickson. (Daily Herald, Columbia, 10 June 1909.)

The entire family of Joseph Locke while visiting relatives were poisoned by eating ice cream. The flavor was blamed. (Daily Herald, 29 June 1909.)

Smith, who keeps a boarding house at Cumberland Furnace, shot and injured Mr. Holland of the L&N Friday night. Holland was a boarder. Smith met him at the door with a gun in hand. He has been charged with assault with intent to commit murder. (Daily Herald, 29 June 1909.)

Taylor Funeral Home was established by Tom, Marvin and Talmage Taylor.

1911

The Belle Meade deer herd has strayed to the wilds of Dickson County. Many have gone to the Tennessee River bottom. They were collected by General W. H. Jackson of Belle Meade. (Maury Democrat, 2 Feb. 1911.)

On 11 April 1911 J. M. Smith was the mayor of Dickson and J. W. Turner was the recorder. In November Charles I. Eccles became the recorder. The board of alderman were Joslin, Roth, F. S. Hopkins, J. A. Myatt, Johnson, C. A. Myatt and J. H. Christian. This board had also served in 1907 under W. T. Turner Mayor.

"LAST EVIDENCE OF 30 YEARS AGO REMOVED.--One of the old landmarks of Dickson, the house of Aunt Dona Swanson, colored, on Church Street was torn down last week by the owner Dr. L. D. Wright. This marks the passing of the last evidence of Dickson 30 years ago. The old house which Aunt Dona, with her deceased husband, Uncle Jeff Swanson, have occupied for over 35 years, was built during the war, and at the time of its building there was no residence in Dickson east of Main street, and there were only a few houses in town. When built, it was in the midst of the woods and for several winters Uncle Jeff cut the wood from trees within a few feet of his home. The building that stood in front of Aunt Dona's residence, which was also torn down, was the old calaboose or jail used by the corporation from 1870 to 1875. The house erected with lumber, three to four inches thick, and was substantial enough to hold the strongest men safely between the walls. A proposition is now on foot for the Methodist Episcopal Church to buy the now vacant lot from Dr. Wright and build a handsome two-story parsonage building on same." (Dickson County Herald, 17 Nov. 1911.)

The Dixie Theater, formerly Simon & Sons' Play House, is to be run by R. Simon and son of Clarksville. (Dickson County Herald 10 Dec. 1911.)

The log cabin of Samuel McAdoo was torn down this year.

1912

Ruskin Cave College is to build a new dormitory. One burned down last week. (Dickson County Herald, 1 March 1912.)

Presbyterian Church, USA, completed in the spring at a cost of $7,000.

In September 1912 Pitt Henslee was the Mayor of Dickson with Charles I. Eccles as recorder. The board of aldermen included: Joslin, Roth, F. S. Hopkins, J. A. Myatt, Johnson, C. A. Myatt, and J. H. Christian.

1913

Capt. C. M. Turner was the Mayor of Dickson and H. C. Thompson was the recorder. Aldermen were A. C. Hughes, H. L. Grigsby, R. A. Freeman, John M. Gossett, Dan Joslin, E. S. Payne, G. C. Redden and Orey Harris. The town marshall was John Sheley.

A. L. Scott was the postmaster at Dickson and F. L. Story was the postmaster at Sylvia.

Pitt Henslee was president of the First National Bank with S. G. Holland and J. A. Myatt, vice presidents, H. H. Self, cashier and S. G. Robertson, assistant cashier and H. L. Grigsby, assisant cashier. The bank's board of directors were J. S. Johnson, D. E. Beasley, Robert Clement, L. M. Sensing, J. A. Myatt, A. D. Clark, S. G. Holland, J. T. Patten, H. H. Self, S. G. Robertson, and Pitt Henslee.

Mrs. Ada Sorg Drouillard of New York sued for divorce from Capt. J. P. Drouillard, son of Lt. J. P. Drouillard. He met and married Florence Kirkman in Nashville and her aunt tried to prevent the marriage, carrying uniform in carpetbag they left Nashville. Lt. J. P. was at house when a Confederate soldier was hid in cellar three days. (Daily Herald 20 Oct. 1913.) (Refer also to page 246 of this book also.)

The Halbrook Hotel is to be completed the first of September. (Dickson County Herald, 18 July 1913.) (Note: from 1917 to 1920 this hotel was operated by Mrs. Belle S. Goad. Frank G. Clement, her grandson, was born here 2 June 1920. He was three times governor of Tennessee.)

Mag Hinson was charged by the police with keeping a bawdy house.

1914

This year one funeral in every 10 was a death from tuberculosis. From 1 Jan. 1914 to 15 August 1914 there were 53 deaths in Dickson County. In all 85 people died in Dickson County in 1914. The deaths for the year were tuberculosis, 15; cancer 2; paralysis, 1; stillborn, 10; burned, 1; chronic jaundice, 1; pneumonia, 3; nephritis, 1; typhoid, 1; diabetes, 3.

It was about this year Mrs. Frank Curry began a greenhouse in McCreary Heights--believed to be first greenhouse operation in county. This year O. V. Clark established the Coca Cola company.

1915

There were 76 deaths in Dickson County this year.

Curley Nickell, age 17, has been sent to Louisiana to the leper colony. His was the first case of leprosy ever discovered in Tennessee. (Maury Democrat, 10 June 1915.)

1916

Electricity 24 hours a day was started this year. It began when a lady in town bought an electric fan for a party and asked the mayor to run the electricity that afternoon. Soon after this the decision was made to have electricity on for 24 hours. (Dickson County Herald, 18 Oct. 1937.)

The officers and directors of the First National Bank this year were: Pitt Henslee, president; J. A. Myatt, S. G. Holland, H. L. Grigsby, S. G. Robertson, H. H. Self (first cashier), G. L. Pentecost, A. D. Clark, J. J. Patten, Jessie Allen, Robert Clement, L. M. Sensing, Dan E. Beasley. (From picture in family scrapbook.)

1917

Mrs. Dockie Shipp Weems's expression class this year included the following students: Ida Clement, Dolly Sugg, Nell Burgie, Winnie McLaughlin, Iris Hopkins, Louise Johnson, Elizabeth Eleazer, Martha Joslin, Emma Gatewood, and Mary Wheeler Murry. For many years Mrs. Weems conducted the Shipp School of Expression and its students took many prizes for public speaking through the years. Mrs. Weems died 1965.

Middle Tennessee was blanketed by a bad snow in December 1917.

1918

The first occurrence of influenza in the United States appeared in the spring of this year and the following epidemic of 1918-1919 is referred to as Spanish influenza. This was a worldwide event affecting some 200 million people and caused 20 million deaths. There were 25 million cases in the United States with about 500,000 deaths. The Dickson County papers are filled with deaths and illnesses at this time. Entire families were often stricken and often there were multiple deaths in the same household. Mrs. Florence Ann Buttrey died in November 1918 and one week later her daughter Ruth succumbed; they were buried in the same grave at Dickson Union Cemetery. Even the county's soldiers were hard hit during the epidemic. William Edward Peeler died while on the high seas. Young Mable Roth died in Dickson and was buried in her own yard as Dickson Union was expanded at this time. Iris Hopkins McClain recalls this period: "Between the service and the flu there was not a labor force to dig graves as fast as people died. In our own family my father had to shovel the dirt on his only son. The cemetery on the left (of the main entrance to the Dickson Union Cemetery) was opened in 1918 in the Roth's garden."

About this time she also wrote: "Camps sent the soldiers' bodies home in express carloads. The undertaker told you when the burials could be. You had no choice. Dickson went wild 11 Nov. 1918. Some of our boys did not get home for over a year."

1919

The influenza epidemic lasted well into this year. Some deaths for this time included: Perny Holland, his brother Hardie and a sister in January; Mike Welch, his son Odell, his daughter Ola, his brother Bates and Bates's wife in February; Ezra Lovell in January; Brown Doty, Henry Thomas, William Streetman, and Mrs. William Murphey.

In April 1919 the papers reported that Mrs. Evia Starns had died; she had been killed by her husband with a meat cleaver.

Charlotte High School was established by W. L. Rochelle. (Dickson County Herald, 20 March 1936.)

In September 1919 Dan Beasley of Dickson bought the Pinewood mansion and farm in Hickman County for $75,000. This farm included 900 acres. As a young man he had once worked here as a $6-a-month clerk.

1920

A library established by the Twentieth Century Club in the First Baptist Church on College Street.

1922

H. T. V. Miller became mayor of Dickson and served until 1930.

1923

In October of this year the earliest snow known in the county fell. (Dickson County Herald, 6 November 1936.)

1924

In the period 1924-1925 the first sewer line was laid in Dickson.

The Cigar Factory was built (closed 1930). Frank Hopkins did the plumbing on this building.

1927

Cheatham Bates, policeman in Dickson, was shot by Loyd Garton; he shot Garton in return. The shooting happened on the main street in Dickson. (Lewis County Herald, 27 January 1927.)

In July the concrete wall was started in front of Dickson Union Cemetery. The first bridges across Yellow Creek were built at the Adair Ford and Ruskin. During the winter months and rainy seasons, these fords had been most dangerous.

Pupils at Oakmont School this year included J. B. West, Wilson Long, Delbert Kretchman, Connie Fielder, Albert Vetters, Charles Wright, Scott Fielder, Leonard Dotson, Harden Lane, __Murrell, Lou Ella Land, __Dotson Alma Lane, Gladys Tipton, Dorothy Tipton, Westell McCord, Ruth Wallace, Johnny Hall, Harvey Ewing, Jr., Hallie Hall, Ruby Wallace, Evelyn Ewing, Willie Mai Tipton, Mildred Vetters, Elsie Tummins, Ruby Hall, Leamon Hall, Talmage Lane, Ezra Adkins, Mary Lane, Odie Lane, Delsie Hall, Mary McCord, Maggie Lee Wallace, Westell Vetters, Aubrey Baker, Eugene Lamay, Horace Luther, Maybelle Balthrop, Christine Crawford, Catherine McCord, Christelle Kretchman, Adell Wallace, Mable Adkins, Albert West, Ealic Ramey Reed, Thurman C. Wallace, Alonzo Balthrop, Randell West, and Donald Ritchison. The teachers were Mildred Twomey and Kathleen Harris. (Source: School picture in our family scrapbook. A few of the children could not be identified.)

Frank S. Hopkins died 14 May 1927. The following items were taken from the local papers at that time:

USEFUL CITIZEN PASSES TO THE GREAT BEYOND.--The untimely death of Frank S. Hopkins which occurred in a Nashville hospital late Saturday night, May 14th, is to be deeply deplored. He was taken to Nashville about 10 days previous to his death, where he underwent an operation for appendicitis, and it was thought he had a fair chance of recovery, when suddenly he took a turn for the worse and answered the final summons that comes to all. His remains were brought here Sunday morning and conveyed to the Hopkins new home on Centre Avenue, where funeral services were conducted Monday afternoon by Rev. A. W. Clinard, pastor of the Cumberland Presbyterian Church at Charlotte. The service at the grave was in charge of local Oddfellows, Mr. Hopkins being a member of Harmony Lodge, I.O.O.F.

"He was also a faithful member of the C. P. Church. He was identified in business here as a plumber, and was master of his profession. He will be greatly missed as a citizen and laborer of our city, as well as a devoted companion to his wife and children.

"Besides his wife he is survived by two daughters, Miss Lula Belle Hopkins and Mrs. Iris Powers. A son, Basil Hopkins, preceded his father to the grave several years ago. The bereaved ones have the tender sympathy of the community."

"RESOLUTION OF RESPECT.--Resolved that in the death of our brother, F.S. Hopkins, this Lodge has lost a worthy member, who will not only be missed, but was devoted and loyal to its every interest. We also extend our deepest sympathy to his family.

"Be it Further Resolved That these resolutions be spread upon the Minutes of the Lodge and that a page of records be dedicated to his memory and that a copy be furnished his family and also printed in the Dickson County Herald. Signed, G. L. Scott, B. B. Underhill, W. H. Walker."

"POND NEWS.--We take these means to extend our sympathy to Mrs. Frank Hopkins and family in their bereavement. Mr. Hopkins was a frequent visitor here at the home of Mr. and Mrs. Tom Williams to whom he was closely related, and who will miss his pleasant visits. To Mr. and Mrs. Williams I also extend my sympathy."

"CARD OF THANKS.--To those who have been with us in our bereavement and by kind words and kindly acts have tried to lessen our sorrow, we wish to extend our sincere thanks. We wish to especially thank friends for the beautiful floral offering. Signed, Mrs. Laura K. Hopkins, Miss Lula Belle Hopkins, Mrs. Iris Powers, Mrs. C. L. Wall."

1929

On 21 Feb. 1929 a 13-inch snow fell in Dickson. The Home Journal of 22 Feb. 1929 called this the worst snow in Middle Tennessee since 1917.

Slayden Phillips and son Tony, 19, were found guilty of assault with intent to murder. They attacked Professor W. L. Rochelle, principal of Charlotte High School last December. (Daily Herald, Columbia, TN, 11 May 1929.)

Lt. Edward L. Meadow was killed when his plane collided with another in Ohio. He was buried in Dickson. (Daily Herald, 20 May 1929.)

The old Brown Well on Jones Creek, drilled in 1866, caused great noise by roaring gas and water on the 24th. The gas and oil came out by pressure when men were drilling a well nearby. The drillers were Oscar Pinion and M. J. Duke. (Daily Herald, 26 July 1929.)

1931

Mrs. Martha Halliburton Averitt died this year at the age of 96. Her obituary noted she owned the first sewing machine in Dickson County.

1933

On 26 Nov. 1933 the Dickson County Public Library began, sponsored by the Twentieth Century Club. (Dickson County Herald, 26 Nov. 1937.)

Building of the Henry I. Siegel plant began, to be opened in 1934. This plant closed in December 1980.

1934

In October 1934 the Dickson County Public Library re-opened in War Memorial Building.

1935

"A LYNCHING.--Four brothers and a cousin took a negro from officers at White Bluff and killed him. The negro had allegedly insulted the wife of ____ and his brothers and cousin of White Bluff killed him. They lived just over the line in Cheatham County. She had stopped in a negro cafe for a beer and he made advances toward her and accosted her. The five men accused of the lynching were freed. The Judge told the jury: "I am astonished at your verdict. By your action you will make Cheatham County the dumping ground for lawlessness in the future."" (Dickson County Herald, 8 Nov. 1935, 15 Nov. 1935, 22 Nov. 1935.)

"Shirley Ann Palistrant, guest of Pauline and Ella Shrieber, was given a party Tuesday night. Those attending: Virginia and Betty Pack, Violetta Weems, Reba Clement, Dorothy Chappell, Rebecca and Mary Ann Williams, and Jill McClain of Florence, Alabama." (Dickson County Herald, 5 July 1935.)

1936

In January of this year an 8-inch snow fell.

The cornerstone of the post office was laid.

There were 77 elementary schools in Dickson County with 4,292 pupils and 126 teachers.

TVA power came to Dickson this year and it was the third city in the state to have it. The event was celebrated with a mile-long parade with Dr. H. A. Morgan, David Lilienthal, Governor Hill McAlister, Mayor Dan Beasley, and Frank Hall, city attorney in the parade. (Nashville Tennessean, 10 June 1936.)

1937

W. M. Leech was the county judge of Dickson County. (Dickson County Herald, 8 Jan. 1937.)

Miss Mary Elizabeth Easley, daughter of Elbert Easley, was chosen "Miss Dickson" and was to represent the county in a beauty contest. (Dickson County Herald, 22 Jan. 1937.)

History's greatest flood had devastated Kentucky and 250 flood refugees were at the fairgrounds in Dickson. (Dickson County Herald, 29 Jan. 1937.)

The remaining assets of the Citizens National Bank were sold. (Dickson County Herald, 12 Feb. 1937.)

Charlie Porter, while walking the tracks, was killed by a train at Pond. (Dickson County Herald, 19 Feb. 1937.)

A new standpipe was put into service, using water from Payne Spring. Superintendent W. H. Adcox was in charge. Hugh Reeves was appointed postmaster. He had been acting postmster for 10 months. Work on the new post office was progressing. Dan E. Beasley was mayor of Dickson. (Dickson County Herald, 5 Feb. 1937.)

On 18 March 1937 the President's Birthday Ball was held and it was considered the social event of the year. Vince Genovese's orchestra played for the occasion. (Dickson County Herald, 5 March 1937.)

Plans were announced about the development of Montgomery Bell Park. (Dickson County Herald, 12 March 1937.)

Benjamin Franklin Brown, the county's last Confederate soldier, died at the age of 95 years. (Dickson County Herald, 26 March 1937.)

The new book "Gone With the Wind" was given to the library as a gift from Mrs. Mary M. Whitemer. (Dickson County Herald, 26 March 1937.)

Sam T. Whited was elected mayor of White Bluff, succeeding O. A. Reeder. (Dickson County Herald, 2 April 1937.)

Final (and third) dividend was paid to the depositors of the Citizens National Bank. (Dickson County Herald, 16 April 1937.)

Divorces granted: Charles Weaver vs Mary Lee Weaver; Dewey Waynick vs Maude Waynick. (Dickson County Herald, 16 April 1937.)

Efforts to unionize Seigel plant were being made. (Dickson County Herald, 23 April 1947.)

Garland Pack was hurt in plane crash which took the lives of two passengers in Kentucky. He had been flying for three years from Sanker Field near Dickson. (Dickson County Herald, 7 May 1937.)

The new stadium at Hake Field was to be opened. This was a $5,000 project of the Lions Club. (Dickson County Herald, 4 June 1937.)

On June 27 the third annual reunion of students at Ruskin Cave College was held. (Dickson County Herald, 11 June 1937.)

A softball league was organized in Dickson. (Dickson County Herald, 2 July 1937.)

New post office "will be open next week on the old Dickson Tobacco Warehouse lot." It cost $65,000. (Dickson County Herald, 9 July 1937.)

Tom Hale, 71, was rescued from a 50-foot well. The well was an abandoned one and he fell in while blackberry picking, northwest of Tennessee City. (Dickson County Herald, 16 July 1937.)

The Community Players was organized and Mrs. Claude Hooper was the president. (Dickson County Herald, 24 Sept. 1937.)

Actor Charles Farrell ate at the Kopper Kettle Tea Room while coming through the county. (Dickson County Herald, 1 October 1937.)

Sheriff W. E. Hutton and his officers found a still near Belltown. They heard the playing of a harmonica and this led the officers to the site. Dickson County was described as having 620 square miles and 20,000 inhabitants. (Dickson County Herald, 22 October 1937.)

Will Allen Spann, 23, local boy, went to Hollywood to work at Warner Brothers. (Dickson County Herald, 26 November 1937.)

1938

Wayside Inn and Tourist Home burned. (Dickson County Herald, 8 April 1938.)

1939

A couple was found dead in a parked car. They had died of carbon monoxide poisoning. (Dickson County Herald, 13 Jan. 1939.)

Plaque to the war dead unveiled at the War Memorial Building. (Dickson County Herald, 2 June 1939.)

First dial phones in operation on 9 Sept. 1939; 752 customers.

1940

The population of Dickson was 3,512. (Nashville Tennessean, 16 Oct. 1942.)

Dr. B. F. Nesbitt, optometrist, installed air conditioning in his office. (Dickson County Herald, 19 July 1940.)

Estha Cole became the Home Superivisor in Dickson County. (Dickson County Herald, 30 August 1940.)

Dickson County National Guard, Company E, 117 Infantry, will "leave Monday to be gone for a year." They pitched tents in the wooded area at Wayside Inn while awaiting time to leave. (Dickson County Herald, 20 Sept. 1940.)

Victor Brown, recently called to preach, was scheduled to preach at the Baptist Church. (Dickson County Herald, 4 October 1940.)

On 16 Oct. 1940 men between the ages of 21-36 were to register for the draft. W. M. Harris was chairman of the county election committee, J. P. Owens was secretary and Harry Davis on committee. J. F. Crosby was to be instructor of the registration.

The Dickson Armory was built this year by the WPA under Vernon Rogers. It was constructed of stone and cost $48,000.

1941

The Japanese bombed Pearl Harbor on 7 December 1941.

Undated clippings: "Thomas Knight, 20, son of Mrs. T. D. Knight of Dickson, is in the battle zone. His mother stated that the last letter that she received from him was dated November 22. He is a sailor and was thought to be at Pearl Harbor during the attack on December 7. No word has been received from him, since his letter of November 22, his mother stated."

"A representative of The Herald was elated to receive an Air Mail special a few days ago from W. P. (Peediddle) Kelly, who enlisted in the U. S. Navy the first of last January and is now aboard the U. S. S. Gridley, his address being in care of the Postmaster, San Diego, Calif.

"Peediddle went into Naval service with Cannon Redden and Harvey Ewing, Jr., all three being sent to an Illinois training station near Chicago. Upon reaching the West Coast recently, the threesome were separated. In being assigned to the Gridley, Kelly said in his letter that he was afraid he would be 'all alone' insofar as there being anyone else from 'dear old Dickson' aboard. But lo! and behold! the first man he saw as he went aboard was Thomas Knight, Dickson boy.

"Each were agreeably surprised to see the other and to be on the same ship. Both boys were reported getting along fine, but they were seemingly worried, as Kelly stated in his letter they were having a tough time convincing some of their shipmates that there is a town in the U.S. by the name of Dickson and that Dickson is having a part in this man's war!

"Being loyal sons of the local commonwealth, we feel sure that they will carry their point on any question pertaining to the defense of their 'old home town.' But, boys, if there be any further argument as to whether or not Dickson and Dickson county is not in the war, well, we promise to come to the rescue by citing the skeptical that already nearly 500 young men from Dickson county are in some branch of service in defense of our country--which is rather a nice ratio, considering area and population."

1942

Industries in Dickson this year: Henry I. Seigel Company, Central Manufacturing Company, A. H. Leathers Hardwood Flooring Company, Cowan Lumber and Planing Mill, E. W. Stewart and Company, L. F. McCaslin and Company (Nashville Tennessean, 16 Oct. 1942.)

Charles Hartmann was manager of the Montgomery Bell Park project. The park covered 3,810 acres. A description of the property noted: "A building located a few hundred yards from the entrance is 150 years old. Slits in the wall show that it was used to fight Indians when they were in the area. Yankee bayonets, Minie balls and shell are still being found in neighborhood, as well as Indian relics." (Nashville Tennessean 13 March 1942.)

About Dickson: There is a 20-acre lake west of the city which gives the town an abundant water supply...there are 12 churches in the city, 9 are white and 3 are black...Schools are Oakmont Elementary School, Dickson Central High, and Hampton High School for negroes. Both the Dickson County War Memorial Building and the Dickson County Armory were erected under the sponsorship of the American Legion Post. The NYA Training School is one mile west. Civic clubs in the city are the Chamber of Commerce, Lions Club, Kiwanis Club, Lucian Berry American Legion and Auxiliary, Dickson Golf and Country Club, McDowell Music Club, Twentieth Century Club, Old Hickory Chapter UDC, Dickson Garden Club, Cotillion Club and the PTA. (Nashville Tennessean, 13 March 1942)

Justice William Loch Cook, 72, died 5 March 1942, member of the Tennessee Supreme Court. He was buried in the Collier Cemetery.

Arnold Sensing died 12 May 1942 in the Philippines. He had been taken prisoner by the Japanese at Corregidor and died in Japanese prison. James Shelton Lamb, Jr. (known as Mike) was also captured in the Philippines. He died 24 October 1944 as prisoner of war when a ship transporting prisoners was sunk.

In October 1942 the U. S. S. Hornet was sunk in the Solomons during the Battle of Santa Cruz. James B. Rumsey of Dickson was a crew member on this aircraft carrier and survived the sinking. He died in Dickson in 1979.

1943 - 1945

(This section will be taken from a scrapbook with information saved about these years and will be presented as found.)

Will F. Davis, died 14 April 1945 at the age of 88 years. He was undertaker and funeral director in Dickson for 50 years. He made the first hearse ever used in funerals in Dickson and made all of the coffins out of walnut by hand. He came here from Greenville, Pa. At the time he came Dickson was called Sneedsville and Main Street had only six frame buildings and a log hotel. The railroad trestle here was guarded then by the soldiers. (Dickson County Herald, 24 April 1968.)

A. G. (Abb) Rickert died 26 Feb. 1943 at the age of 85 in Illinois. He came to Tennessee in 1868, settling on a farm a short distance north of the business center of Dickson, the now railroad spring on Pump Street being about the center of the acreage. When he settled here, Dickson was then known as Sneedsville, its business section comprising only a box store and a double-log hotel. He helped establish the Peoples Ice Company, which later became Jenkins Ice Company. Rickert Avenue bears his name, being named for him and his family.

Cecil McElhiney was killed in action 16 October 1943. His plane was found in New Guinea.

Thomas Bone was killed in action 16 September 1943. He was a waist gunner on a Flying Fortress.

Billy M. Duncan was killed in action 22 January 1943 in North Africa. He was an aerial gunner on a B-25.

S/Sgt. Dudley B. Lamastus, 26, was killed in action on Leyte Island 21 Nov. 1944.

Joe H. Brown was killed in action 22 Dec. 1944 in Belgium.

Robert M. Bellar was killed in action Leyte on 22 Nov. 1944.

Edgar W. Hudson was missing in action in the Pacific on 13 August 1944 when the submarine Flier was sunk. He was later declared dead.

Curtis Adcock was killed in the sinking of the U. S. S. Langley.

Horace H. Self was killed in action 26 July 1944 while on a bombing mission over Austria. Roy Stinson was killed in action in France on 1 Oct. 1944. James D. Neely was killed in action in Italy on 19 July 1944.

Randall Patey was killed in action in France on 17 June 1944. Clifford Sensing died of wounds received in France on 14 Oct. 1944. John W. Luther was killed in action 29 June 1944 in Italy.

Oscar Lee Martin was killed in action 16 August 1944 in Italy. Van J. Mitchell was killed in action 10 August 1944 in France. Herbert Morris was killed in action on 1 Dec. 1944 in Germany.

The year 1944 had many accounts of men reported missing in action. The majority of these survived. Those reported included: Norman K. Schmittou, missing in Germany since 16 Dec. 1944; Arthur K. Bishop, missing in France, 13 Nov. 1944; Robert V. Davis, missing in Germany 21 Dec. 1944. George M. Chappell and Edward Riordan were reported missing action in Germany on 21 December 1944. James W. Bruce and Marlin H. Hawkins were missing in action in Germany on 16 December 1944.

In the Dickson County Herald, 22 July 1965, in an article by Herbert S. Tallent, entitled "Down Memory Lane" the following was printed:

"LOCAL SOLDIER EULOGIZED.--Appreciation for the deeds of heroism of a Dickson County soldier is expressed in a letter received by Archie Spicer of Burns, written by Cpl. John M. Cook, Jr., whose home address is Narcus, Texas, Rt. 1, being one among the 511 men recently liberated from a Jap prison camp at Luzon in the Philippines, and he gives most of the credit for the group's freedom to Mr. Spicer's son, Pfc. Buford K. Spicer.

"Quoting an excerpt from his letter: 'I take this privilege to show my appreciation toward your son, Pfc. Buford K. Spicer, for his heroic mission of coming 25 miles behind Jap lines and endangering his life to liberate us. It was one of the most wonderful feelings that I have had in my experience in the service to see the look of happiness on their faces after they got us back to the American lines out of the Japs' reach. They did everything in their power to make us happy and make us realize that we were free American boys again.'"

Bernard T. Corlew was killed in action 25 January 1945 on Luzon Island. He was a member of Company B, 118th Medical Battalion. Paul G. McClurkan, 44, was killed in action 23 Feb. 1945 in Germany. Elmer Bradford was killed in action on the Island of Luzon on 11 Feb. 1945.

Virgil M. Wallace, killed overseas, was buried 1948 in Dickson Union Cemetery. His parents Mr. and Mrs. William A. Wallace, formerly of Humphreys County, lived in the Pond community.

Newton E. Cannon was killed on Luzon Island on 21 March 1945. James Dalton (Lightning) Langford was killed in action in Germany on 13 Apr. 1945.

Louie E. Story, 27, was killed in Germany 16 October 1944. His parents lived in Sylvia. Warner Berry was reported missing in action in France in November 1944. William M. Spicer, wounded by a bullet in the neck while attacking with his infantry unit near St. Lo, France, is now recovering in an army hospital in England. (Dec. 1944 clipping.)

Capt. W. G. Pursley, 31, died 18 Feb. 1949 and was buried in Dickson Union. He became ill while serving in the Army of Occupation in Frankfort, Germany.

Listed as prisoners of war in May 1945: George M. Chappell, who made his escape. He had been held since December 1944. Marlin Hawkins was

was freed from prisoner of war camp May 1945.

James W. Edgin, 24, was killed in action in Germany on 17 Jan. 1945.

John Carlos Baker, age 10, was truly a "martyr from the civilian ranks of World War II, being a victim of electrocution as he was enthused in performing a patriotic deed for his county - that of collecting scrap metal in the all-out effort to aid Uncle Sam in winning the war. The accident occurred at 5:30 p.m., 7 Oct. 1942, at his parents home two miles of Dickson. Arriving home from Oakmont School where he was a pupil in the sixth grade, he had gone across the highway in the quest of scrap metal to aid in his school's scrap drive collection. He was given a large iron pipe that had been used in a cistern. Returning to his home with the pipe, he had reached the front yard where he accidently touched the pipe against a high tension wire above, the electric voltage killing him instantly."

A. C. Hargrove, Sr., and his son A. C. Hargrove, Jr., "met sudden death on 15 March 1942 when a fast passenger train and an extra freight on the NC&StL Railway crashed head-on near Denver in Humphreys County. The father was on duty as a fireman of the passenger train and his son was firing on the freight. The collision, one of the most serious on this division of the railroad since 1918 when locomotives of two passenger trains ran together near Nashville on Dutchman's Hill, killing 100 or more. A. C. Jr., began firing two years ago, making his first trip with his grandfather Robert Hargrove on the Centerville Branch." They were both buried in Dickson Union Cemetery.

Mrs. Mary Elizabeth Moore Powers died 5 February 1945 and was buried in Dickson Union Cemetery. She was born 10 October 1866, the daughter of a Confederate soldier Virgil Burke Moore, and she was the widow of John W. Powers. (Note: She was the writer's paternal grandmother.)

Robinson's Chapel Methodist Church is to be dedicated Sunday. (Nashville Tennessean 26 May 1944.)

Sensing Brothers 4641, VFW, organized December 1945 with about 50 members. The post was named in honor of Clifford Sensing, member of Company E, 117th Infantry, who was killed in the European Theater of War and Arnold "Tookie" Sensing, who died as a prisoner of war in the Philippines. They were the sons of Mr. and Mrs. Drury Sensing of the Dull community. The first officers were Lt. Wilbur F. Marsh, commander; Robert Lee, senior vice commander; William Henry, junior vice commander; and Wilson Fussell, quartermaster. (Dickson County Herald, 23 Dec. 1965.)

1946

Disastrous fire in January at White Bluff destroyed a church, two residences, two grocery stores, eight living apartments, a beauty shop, barber shop, a cafe, and a notion shop. The fire of January 8 was estimated at $300,000 and originated in a service station employee's acetylene torch he was repairing. The Methodist Church, erected 1927 at a cost of $16,500.00 was burned. It had only recently been remodeled.

MRS. LAURA HOPKINS RITES HELD SATURDAY.--"Funeral services for Mrs. Laura Knight Hopkins, 80, widow of the late F. S. Hopkins, were held at 3:00 o'clock Saturday afternoon at the Dickson Cumberland Presbyterian Church, of which the deceased was a member, conducted by the pastor, Rev. M. C. Powers, and burial was in Union Cemetery.

"Mrs. Hopkins died at her Center Avenue home here at 1:00 o'clock, Thursday afternoon, June 20, 1946, from a heart stroke she suffered a week previous.

"Born in Erin, Tenn., Mrs. Hopkins moved many years ago to Dickson, where her husband became engaged in the plumbing business. He died 19 years ago.

"Her survivors include two daughters, Miss Lula Belle Hopkins of Dickson and Mrs. Iris McClain of Florence, Ala., and two brothers. R. H.

and T. T. Knight, both of Erin; also one granddaughter."
(Note: The writer was the unnamed granddaughter.)

An earlier clipping, dated June 1929, is also on the same page in the family scrapbook as the above one:

"MEMORIAL FOR ODDFELLOWS.--A service of memoriam for Oddfellows was held at First Presbyterian Church in Dickson last Sunday under joint auspices of Harmony Lodge I.O.O.F. and its Auxiliary of Rebekahs. W. M. Hannah, Past Grand Secretary, was the principal speaker, being introduced by H. T. Cowan. Mrs. Hannah also gave a brief but interesting talk, praising the work of the Dickson Rebekah Lodge.

"Mrs. J. Max Cowan, in her charming manner, sang a beautiful solo, with Mrs. Robert Hearne the accompanist. At the conclusion of the service at the church the Oddfellows marched to Union Cemetery where flowers were placed on the graves of the following deceased Oddfellows: William Choate, William Askins, G. T. Collier, Charles Chappell, J. T. Easley, V. I. Hopkins, F. S. Hopkins, Pitt Henslee, E. E. Lovell, M. V. Little, H. S. Murphree, C. J. Martin, G. W. Mullins, Calvin Martin, J. F. McCaul, William Patterson, D. O. Page, John Ryan, C. E. Sager, W. S. Scott, Jacob Sesler, George Shaffer, I. N. Shannon, W. T. Turner, J. M. Thompson, T. M. Taylor, C. C. Turner, Charles Underhill, J. T. Warren, R. E. Wolfe and A. M. Woodard."

1948

On 16 January 1948 there was a 12-inch snow.

In January 1948 "Friends Join in Golden Wedding Anniversary of Mr. and Mrs. Adcox.--More that 150 friends saluted Mr. and Mrs. W. H. Adcox in the celebration of their 50th wedding anniversary, the festivities being held at their home on Center Avenue December 26 (1947). All of the children were in the receiving line to welcome guests. Punch was served from a sterling silver punch bowl, flanked by silver candelabra burning white tapers. The honorees have lived in Dickson most of their married life. Mr. Adcox has been superintendent of the city's Light and Water Department for many years and has established an enviable record at his position.

"The following members of the family assisted in the hospitality: Mr. and Mrs. Adcox, Mr. and Mrs. A. S. Wilson, Radburn, N. J., and son, Stuart Wilson of Los Angeles; Mr. and Mrs. E. M. Adcox, Hohenwald, and the former's daughter and son, Mrs. E. W. McCord and James Murry Adcox, Mr. and Mrs. H. E. Bolen, Tampa, Fla.; Mr. and Mrs. R. O. Fitzgerald, Syracuse, N. Y.; Mrs. Joe Parrish and daughter, Jo Ann, Winnetka, Ill.; Mr. and Mrs. John Allen Baker and daughters, Alice Ann and Corinne Allen of Gallatin, and Mr. and Mrs. Bob Nicks and son, Stephen."

1950

James A. Weems elected county judge at the age of 29 years. He served until 1958.

1951

Robert Lee Littleton, young attorney of Dickson, was elected to the Tennessee General Assembly. He served in the 77th, 78th and 79th sessions of the legislature.

St. Christopher's Catholic Church was completed and dedicated 17 June 1951.

This is the year given in some sources when the Boy Scouts were organized in Dickson.

1952

On 14 October 1952 Jesse R. Cooksey was reported missing in action in Korea. By 1969 there had been no further word received about him, according to an old newspaper clipping.

1953

Frank G. Clement began the first of his three terms as Governor of Tennessee, serving until 1959. He served again 1963-1967.

1955

W/O Herschel B. Daniels was killed when his fighter plane went out of control in the Mediterranean Sea. (Hickman County Times, 24 Nov. 1955.)

Radio station WDKN went on the air 1 January 1955 with William A. Potts as president and station manager. (Dickson County Herald, 1 Nov. 1979.)

Harry Davis, longtime active in local politics, died this year. Dickson Union had been started on his boyhood homeplace.

1956

On 20 January 1956 the Dickson County Historical Society was organized at the War Memorial Building. Judge James A. Weems acted as temporary chairman. J. B. White was elected president; Dr. Robert Corlew, vice-president; Mrs. Floyd Williams, secretary-treasurer.

The advisory committee was composed of Ray Stuart, Mrs. Joe B. Weems, Miss Willie G. McMillan, H. O. Anderson and Hartwell Gentry.

Charter members were: Mrs. Joe B. Weems, Miss Jamie Weems, Judge James Weems, Ray Stuart, Wiley Russell, Robert Corlew, H. O. Anderson, Randall Clayburn, Mr. and Mrs. Minor Stuart, Mr. and Mrs. J. B. White, Miss Bessie Greer, Clifton Goodlett, Miss Eleanora Miller, Miss Lola Miller, Hartwell Gentry, Wilbur F. Marsh, Mr. and Mrs. Robert Harrington, Kenneth Mitchell, Mrs. Floyd Williams, Mrs. Clifton Goodlett, Mrs. Ray Stuart, Mr. and Mrs. Edward Sugg, Billy Sugg, Mrs. Eddie Swank, Mrs. Mary S. Corlew, Henry Collier Leech, Slayden Weaver, Patty W. Speight, Olin Wright, Lucy Wright, Mrs. Ann Smith, Billy Raymond, Jimmy Clemmer, J. M. Clement, Mrs. Grace Still, Larry Jobe, Neil Jobe, Mrs. Karene Harris, Miss Mable Miller, Mrs. Sara Wishart, Mrs. Elizabeth Chapman, T. H. Richardson, Mrs. Vina Mitchell, Mrs. Lester McCaslin, Mrs. Albert Hines, Miss Anna Belle Clement, D. L. Castleman, Mrs. Wayne Radford, Wayne Radford, Mrs. Hartwell Gentry, Floyd Williams, Dr. Mary Baxter Cook, Miss Gertrude Borchert, Emmett Bibb, Edwin E. Foster, Stanley Martin, J. B. Worthy, Bob Hickerson, Mrs. Iris Hopkins McClain, Jill Knight Garrett, Miss Ruthelma Buckner, Miss Mary Ella Sensing, Mrs. Carlton Scott, Jimmy Scott, R. A. Freeman, Mrs. R. E. Corlew, and Thurman Sensing.

Dr. R. P. Beasley was the mayor of Dickson this year and plans were announced for a new lake to be across Highway 70 from the present lake. The land had been purchased from Hattie and Lilly Hurt and Ed Vanleer and contained approximately 70 acres. Superintendent Van Corlew estimated a 100 million gallon lake could be built here. He also said at present the water system had 1,375 customers.

Drs. L. C., W. M., and J. T. Jackson, operators of Jackson Clinic, were making plans for a 50-bed hospital, to cost more than a half-million dollars. For ten years they had operated a 22-bed clinic on North Main Street.

Clyde Buckner was elected president of the Dickson Chamber of Commerce with Jess Walker Beasley, first vice-president, J. R. Gilmore, second vice-president, and W. A. (Bill) Potts as secretary-treasurer.

1958

Goodlark Hospital was built this year.

In January 1958 the Old Timers program began in Clemore Pharmacy by Warren Medley. Since then Old Timers Day has developed into a large celebration with parades and other activities and attracts thousands each year.

Herman O. Powers, 73, died 28 July 1958. (Note: Uncle of the writer.)

1963
Dr. W. J. Sugg, 91, died 19 March 1963. During his years of practice he had delivered about 5,000 babies. He was among the oldest members of the Dickson First Methodist Church. He also served several terms as alderman of the third ward.

1965
The Dickson County Historical Society was reorganized 3 April 1965 and Clifton Goodlett was elected president. Mrs. Ernest Page was vice-pres., and Mrs. Floyd Williams, secretary-treasurer.

1966
Francis Craig, composer and orchestra leader, died in Nashville. He was native of Dickson County and his father was onetime Methodist minister here.

1967
On 28 Feb. 1967 Stephen Miles was killed in Vietnam. Other Dickson County Vietnam War casualties included William L. Marlin, Jimmy M. Logan, James C. Alderidge, George W. Coone, Bennie Underhill, Gene Davidson. (Note: A complete listing of Vietnam war deaths may be found in the military records section of this book.)

1968
Dickson County Herald was sold to Community Newspaper, Inc. (Dickson County Herald, 2 Jan. 1969.)

1969
Former governor Frank G. Clement was killed in car wreck 4 November 1969.

Mrs. Albert Hines retired as the librarian for the Dickson County Public Library. She had served 31 years.

1973
The Town of Dickson became the City of Dickson.

A new $278,000 public library opened January 1973 with Sue Grant as the librarian. A monument to Dickson County's war dead was placed in front of the library as a memorial.

In February of this year a big fire did much damage in downtown Dickson.

1974
The population of Dickson County was 25,751.

Claude Powers retired as the circuit court clerk of Dickson County. He had served 40 years, 10 terms, being elected 1934. (Nashville Tennessean 17 June 1974.)

1975
The population of Dickson County was 26,188.

1976
A new courthouse was built in Charlotte. On the 4 July 1976 the local DAR Chapter dedicated a marker to the soldiers of the American Revolution buried in Dickson County. The salute was given by Judge William Field and the principal address delivered by Dr. Robert Corlew. The Bicentennial Chairman for Dickson County was Judge William Leech, and John McCowan was the chairman for Dickson. (Dickson Free Press, 19 May 1976.)

In the elections held this year Doyle Wall was elected sheriff. Goodlark Hospital was dedicated August 15. (Dickson Free Press, 11 August 1976.)

The new armory was dedicated 15 August 1976. (Dickson Free Press, 18 August 1976.)

In the presidential election this year Dickson County voted for Jimmy Carter: 6,655; and for Gerald Ford, 2,285. (Dickson Free Press, 10 Nov. 1976.)

1977

Jean Daugherty was elected magistrate for the 11th Civil District of Dickson County. (Dickson Free Press, 1 June 1977.)

The police dog Max was killed in line of duty and buried at the pet cemetery in Maury County, Tennessee.

1980

Dickson County Humane Society organized.

Parade Magazine came to Dickson County and H. I. Siegel closed after 47 years.

Five men were indicted for rape in January 1980, three of them charged also with kidnapping.

1982

As of 18 May 1982 the following office holders are in the courthouse at Charlotte:

    County Judge - William Field
    Circuit Court Clerk - Bobby Allen
    Clerk and Master - Nancy Miller
    County Assessor - Clyde Davis
    County Court Clerk - William Brazzell
    General Session Judge - Durwood Moore
    General Session Clerk - Nancy Moore
    Register of Deeds - Clyde Buckner
    Sheriff - Doyle Wall
    Trustee - Jewel Bishop
    Superintendent of Education - William E. Sullivan
    County Road Engineer - William Fiser
    Register at Large - Emma Greer
    Planning and Safety - W. B. Lightfoot
    Chancellor - Alex Darnell
    Circuit Court Judges - Robert Burch and Leonard Mastin
    Child Guidance - Wayne Sanders
    Assistant Attorney General - Ken Adkins*

The mayors of the cities in Dickson County this year are:

    Mayor of Dickson - Dan Buckner
    Mayor of White Bluff - J. G. Brown
    Mayor of Burns - Joe Daugherty
    Mayor of Charlotte - Ronnie Greer
    Mayor of Vanleer - Paul Reynolds**

The Dickson Recorder is Peggy Mason.

State Senator Anna Belle Clement O'Brien announced her candidacy for the nomination of Governor of Tennessee on the Democratic ticket. She was formerly of Dickson and sister of the late governor, Frank G. Clement.

---

*This list prepared by Nancy Moore, General Session Clerk.
**This list prepared by Miss Ruth Eleazer, Dickson County historian.

XI

A STROLL THROUGH DICKSON COUNTY HISTORY

As a child and well into my teens, I spent every summer with my grandmother, Laura Knight Hopkins, and my aunt, Lula Belle Hopkins, in Dickson. For one brief period during a family illness I lived with them and attended Oakmont School. I have waded in Piney, I have been to Pond, I have been in a car hopelessly stuck in a ford on Yellow Creek, and I know where Abiff, Burns, Iron Hill, Eno, and other places are in the county. My knowledge was increased considerably when my mother, Iris Hopkins McClain, and I began copying all the cemeteries in the county.

I can remember those summers very well. Many times we rode "way out" in the country" to an abandoned, or at least seldom used, frame church. Located in a deep hollow, shaded by trees, this was a picturesque and cool spot. Untouched.

But it was also a historic piece of ground. My grandmother always called it the "Birthplace", and it was years before I understood why.

It literally was the birthplace of a church because here in Feb. 1810 the Cumberland Presbyterian Church was born. Three men, Finis Ewing, Samuel King, and Samuel McAdow met in the log home of McAdow and after a night spent in prayer they founded the church, rejecting the more formal doctrine of the Presbyterian Church.

For many years the Birthplace spot served as a camp ground for religious camp meetings, and in 1891 the frame church was built. An oil painting of the original log Birthplace still hangs in my aunt's home-- it was painted when the first church still stood. And a church bench from the frame church is also at my aunt's home.

Today the Birthplace is in the heart of Montgomery Bell Park and a log replica of Samuel McAdow's original cabin has been built on the site. It is furnished with period pieces.

Later I learned that my neighbor in Columbia, William R. Peebles, was the superintendent of the park when the log cabin was reconstructed in 1939. He went through the woods and checked many of the trees for the cabin.

The McAdow family spring can be reached by a bridge over the creek, a replica of the original bridge. By plundering through the woods in this area, you can find an old road which led to Burns a few miles away.

About 1815 the land about McAdow's old cabin was purchased by Richard C. Napier, and Laurel Furnace was operated here for many years. They say it is still possible to find some of the furnace ruins and residue of iron ore in the brush here.

In recent years a small chapel of Crab Orchard stone has been built near the cabin and services are held here at various times. The chapel has become popular for weddings.

There are five cemeteries on the park property: Ladd, Jackson, McCutcheon, Hall, and Richardson. Perhaps the most interesting is the Jackson-Eleazer Cemetery on the side of the main road in the park. A stone at the grave of a man who owned the furnace at one time has an engraving of old Laurel Furnace on it. Such engravings are rare and seem to be found on the stones of ironmasters. I have seen four of these in time: one on Montgomery Bell's stone in Cheatham County, one on the stone of John L. Sullivan in Humphreys County, one on the stone of Stephen Eleazer in the Stuart Cemetery in Dickson County, as well as the one on Epps Jackson's marker in Montgomery Bell Park.

People who lived here during the battle of Fort Donelson--which has to be at least 60 or so miles away in Stewart County--remembered they could hear the roar of the cannons and sometimes felt the jar from the firing. The furnace ground had also served as a musterground for the soldiers (Confederates) going off to war.

Following the fall of Fort Donelson in 1862, some of the retreating Confederate soldiers camped near the furnace overnight. A young boy living here at the time recalled in later years there were thousands of soldiers. They burned all the fence rails around hundreds of acres here. The men were cold and miserable and needed something for firewood.

But it is with the forming of the Cumberland Presbyterian Church the park is most associated.

Mrs. E. E. Littleton and Mr. Kenneth Johnson of Dickson furnished me with a copy of a deed to the Birthplace property:

For and in consideration of the high regard and esteem I entertain for the "Cumberland Presbyterian Church" as a separate denomination of churches and for other good and suffient considerations I have this day given, granted, bargained and sold and do by these presents give, grant, bargain, sell and convey to A. J. Parish, Wm. C. Collier, James M. Larkins and Wm. A. James Trustees, appointed by the "Charlotte Presbytery" of the "Cumberland Presbyterian Church" and their successors as such a certain tract or parcel of land in the State of Tennessee, Dickson County, and District 5 near "Laurel Furnace" containing by estimation five and one-half acres and boundaries follow to wit:

Beginning at a large white Oak Marked "C.P.C." running thence North five Poles to a Red Oak, thence North of East 53 degees, forty-six Poles to a wild Plum Tree, thence East of South 55 degrees, eighteen Poles, to a Chinky-Pin Oak, thence South of West 52 degrees, fifty-five Poles to a Turkey Oak, thence North twelve Poles to the beginning. Which boundaries include and embrace the old homestead of the Rev. Samuel McAdoo, decd., at whose house the first Presbytery of the "Cumberland Presbyterian Church" was organized, to have and to hold the same to the said A. J. Parish, Wm. C. Collier, James M. Larkins and Wm. A. James, Trustees, for the "Charlotte Presbytery" and their successors as such for the use and benefit of said Presbytery.

I covenant with the said Trustees that I am lawfully seized of said land and have a good right to convey it and that the same is unincumbered. I do defend the title to said land and every part thereof to the said Trustees and their successors as such for the use and benefit of the "Charlotte Presbytery" of the "Cumberland Presbyterian Church" against the lawful claims of all persons whatsoever. This 21st day of July 1856.

W. C. Napier (seal)

Test.
Tho. McNeely
W. J. Mathis

So far, within in two pages, the name of one of the church's founders has appeared as Samuel McAdow and Samuel McAdoo. According to <u>Sketches of Prominent Tennesseans</u>, by William S. Spear, published 1888, page 166: "The Rev. Samuel McAdoo (autography changed to McAdoo)...was a Presbyterian minister, and he, together with Rev. Finis Ewing and Ephraim McLain, of Kentucky, and Samuel King of Alabama, met at Mr. McAdow's residence and constituted a presbytery, thereby organizing and founding the Cumberland Presbyterian church in Dickson county, Tennessee, February 4, 1810."

The Tennessee Historical Commission erected a historical marker on Highway 70 at the Montgomery Bell Park entrance. The legend on this marker reads:

BIRTH OF A CHURCH

1.1 miles southwest is a restoration of the log cabin in which Finis Ewing, Samuel King and Samuel McAdoo organized the Cumberland Presbyterian Church on Feb. 4, 1810. The congregation was made up of secedent members of the Presbyterian Church and others in the area.

My grandmother was a devoted member of the Dickson Cumberland Presbyterian Church and I attended church here in the summers, even though I was an Episcopalian.

As Dickson is associated with many firsts in my life, some of the "firsts" took place at this church. Here I attended my first revival; here I attended the first wedding; here I attended the first funeral.

My grandfather Frank Stephen Hopkins married my grandmother Laura Elizabeth Knight in Houston County. They lived in Houston County for several years where their four children were born: Mittie May, Lula Belle, Frank Basil, and my mother Iris. Mittie died in her "second summer" and was buried in the McMillan Cemetery at Erin.

In November 1900 my grandparents with their family moved to Dickson. They lived first in a house on South Main Street, directly across from the W. H. Walker house, which was still standing a few years ago. They lived there one year and then moved to High Street, between Chestnut and Broad, living here for five years.

In July 1906 they moved to 425 Center Avenue, Dickson, where my aunt Lula Belle still lives. My grandfather bought the house from J. D. and Maggie Burney. The house was possibly built by W. A. and Maggie Dull, who sold it to William M. Garton and his wife Permelia T. The Gartons in 1894 sold it to G. W. and Maggie Loftis, who sold it in 1896 to Mrs. Maggie Byers. The Burneys came from around Cumberland Furnace the best my family remembers.

Mother remembers this house as having three rooms and being "on stilts"--we have a picture of this house in our album. My grandfather made additions and improvements to the place. Lula Belle remembers the yard was full of some sort of blue wild flowers when they moved here.

In 1926 my grandfather had the old house torn down and built a new one. While the new one was being built they rented a house on South Main. I think I was living with them at the time as I have a vague recollection of going to see the house while it was under construction.

The new house, where Lula Belle lives, was built of rock. One rock is a small marble slab, originally a tombstone for Fred Thomas, Mother's cat. His grave is under the driveway today.

In researching the old newspapers, I have found the following about my grandfather:

GETS THUMB AND FINGER CUT OFF - Dickson Herald, Friday 25 September 1908

Frank Hopkins happened to have the misfortune of getting his thumb and forefinger cut off while dressing some wagon rims at the Dickson Blacksmith and Machine Shops, Tuesday morning. His thumb was cut off at the last joint. Other fingers beside the forefinger were badly cut. His many friends regret the misfortune.

Lula Belle says he owned the machine shop part of this firm and that one finger never healed from the accident.

TOWN OF DICKSON - 1910

The recently released 1910 Census of Dickson County gives the residents of the town of Dickson during my mother's girlhood there. The following is the listing of the white population. Information given includes: household number; name of head of household or the relation of those in the house to the head of household; age; number of years married; and for the wife the number of children she has had and the number of them living, which will be indicated as 3/3; birthplace, birthplace of father, birthplace of mother, to be indicated as TN/TN/TN, standing for Tennessee, Tennessee (father), Tennessee (mother); occupation; and other information.

This enumerator also checked the marriage column as M1, or M2, indicating the number of marriages--but not for all households.

The census began 15 April 1910 and Alberta Scott was given as the enumerator. The name Tracy R. Heaberton was written immediately before the first household.

1
SENSING, Wilson T., head, 58, married 19 years, TN/TN/TN/ salesman, grocery store
____, Della, wife, 45, married 19 years, 3/3, TN/TN/TN/, teacher, kindergarten
____, Alva, daughter, age 18, TN/TN/TN
____, Azelle, daughter, age 17, TN/TN/TN
____, Edna, daughter, age 14, TN/TN/TN

2
HARRIS, Oury, head, age 36, married 7 years, KY/KY/KY, cashier, bank
____, Leona, wife, age 31, married 7 years, 3/3, KY/KY/KY
____, Clarence C., son, age 11, KY/KY/KY
____, Lorena, age 8, daughter, Ky/KY/KY
____, Ruth, daughter, age 3, KY/KY/KY

3
SENSING, Gardner H., head, age 37, married 10 years, TN/TN/TN, merchant hardware
____, Margret E., wife, 34, m1, married 10 years, 3/2, TN/PA/PA
____, Wendell, son, age 4, TN/TN/TN
____, Henry G., son, age 3, TN/TN/TN
McCREARY, Ben F., brother-in-law, 25, single, TN/PA/PA, rural carrier, U. S. Mail

4
CRAIN, John T., head, age 49, M1, married 17 years, TN,U.S./Ireland, inspector, lumber company
____, Lee K., wife, age 43, married 17 years, KY, KY, KY
____, Egbert, son, age 13, TN/TN/KY
____, Eloise, daughter, age 9, TN/TN/Ky
____, Thomas, son, age 7, TN/TN/KY
____, Dick, son, age 5, TN/TN/KY
____, Malcomb E., age 3, son, TN/TN/KY

5
TORRY, Henry M., head, age 38, M1, married 7 years, MISS/MISS/MISS., minister, Methodist Church
____, Lousie H., wife, age 35, married 7 years, 3/3, PA/PA/PA
 (Note: Her name spelled this way on census.)
____, Paul O., son, age 6, TN/MISS/PA
____, Lois A., daughter, age 4, TN/MISS/PA
____, Mary A., daughter, age 2, TN/MISS/PA

6
SWEET, Sherman, head, age 45, M1, married 17 years, IND/IND/ENGLISH miller, roller mill
____, Sarah E., wife, age 48, married 17 years, IND/IND/IND
____, Dickson, adopted son, age 2, TN/IND/IND

7
HELBURG, Lewis C., head, age 31, m2, OHIO/GERMAN/GERMAN, carpenter,
          house
____, Adel S., wife, age 27, m1, married 0 years, MICH/MICH/CAN.ENGLISH

     (Note: For those birthplaces that were non-American, the enumerator
     would write: Ger. German or Can. English. We have shortened
     this in most cases to one word.)

8
SMITH, Henry L., head, age 46, M1, married 22 years, GA/GA/GA, agent,
          depot
____, Dollie B., wife, age 45, married 22 years, 3/3, VA/VA/VA
____, Anna, daughter, age 21, TN/GA/VA, saleswoman, dry goods store
____, Clayton, daughter, age 20, TN/Ga/Va
____, Elizabeth, daughter, age 14, TN/GA/VA
GUN, Dollie, niece, age 4, TN/TN/Va

9
ALEXANDER, Celia, head of household, female, age 64, widowed, 12/8,
          TN/TN/TN
____, Tennie, daughter, age 38, single, TN/TN/TN, millner, millinery store
____, Ernest, son, age 22, single, TN/TN/TN, salesman, retail grocery

10
BERRY, Walter, head, age 29, M1, married 4 years, TN/TN/TN, salesman,
          hardware
____, Carrie, wife, age 21, married 4 years, TN/TN/TN
____, Dimple, daughter, 3/12, TN/TN/TN
     (Note: 3/12 meant the child was 3 months old.)

11
MILLER, Clay A., head, age 29, M2, married 1 years, TN/TN/TN, driver,
          livery barn
____, Mary, wife, age 29, M1, married 1 year, 1/0, TN/TN/TN
WALKER, Nannie, mother in law, age 57, widowed, 6/4, TN/TN/TN

12
BRINKLEY, Daniel, head, age 38, M2, married 3 years, TN/NC/TN, minister,
          Baptist Church
____, Ruth, wife, age 22, M1, married 3 years, 1/1, TN/TN/TN
____, Obed, son, age 7 years, TN/TN/TN
____, Robert D., son, age 1 year, TN/TN/TN

                         COLLEGE STREET
12/13
BAKER, Thomas J., head, age 40, M1, married 13 years, TN/TN/TN,
          minister, Methodist
____Mary M., wife, age 33, M1, married 13 years, 3/3, TN/TN/TN
____, Thomas B., son, age 12, TN/TN/TN
____, Mary M., daughter, age 9, TN/TN/TN
____, Robert B., son, age 4, TN/TN/TN

13/14
FENTRESS, Cecil D., head, age 32, M1, married 13 years, TN/TN/TN,
          agent, insurance
____, Ada L, wife, age 31, M1, married 13 years, 1/1, TN/TN/TN
____, Alline E., daughter, age 8, TN/TN/TN

14/15
HOOPER, Melvil W., head, age 66, M1, married 40 years, TN/TN/TN
____, Alice, wife, age 57, M1, married 40 years, 4/4, TN/VA/VA
SIZEMORE, Claude H., son-in-law, age 38, M1, married 12 years, TN/TN/TN
          overseer, depot, transft. dept.
____, Jessie O. (or Jossie?), daughter, age 33, married 12 years, 1/1,
          TN/TN/TN
____, Hooper A., grandson, age 9, TN/TN/TN
____, Sarah A., boarder, age 76, widow, 3/2, TN/TN/TN

350

15/16
HOPKINS, Fannie, head, female, age 38, widow, 4/4, TN/TN/TN, own income
____, Floy W., daughter, age 18, TN/TN/TN
____, Glen A., daughter, age 13, TN/TN/TN
____, Wren L., daughter, age 11, TN/TN/TN
____Ray M., son, age 7, TN/TN/TN

16/17
LENARD, Will H., head, age 49, M1, married 18 years, KY/NY/NY, sawery, stave factory
____, Callie, wife, age 39, M1, married 18 years, 4/4, TN/TN/TN
____, Lucille, daughter, age 10, TN/KY/TN
____, Luther, son, age 4, TN/KY/TN
____, Percy, son, age 5, TN/KY/TN
____, Wilber, son, age 4/12, TN/KY/TN

17/18
LOGGINS, Thomas B., head, age 47, m1, married 20 years, MISS/ALA/TN, professor, college
____, Ada C., wife, age 45, M1, married 20 years, 1/1, MISS/NC/IRELAND
____, Beth C., daughter, age 19, MISS/MISS/MISS
HALL, Josie, servant (black), age 32, M1, married 4 years, 0/0, TN/VA/GA, servant, private family
DONEGAN, Mary E., servant, age 47, single, TN/TN/TN, housekeeper, college hall
OUTLAW, Maude, servant, age 20, single, TN/TN/TN, waiter, college dining hall
CATHEY, Maude, servant, (black), age 20, single, TN/TN/TN, dishwasher, college dining hall
HANNAH, Maggie, servant (black), age 30, single, TN/TN/TN, cook, college dining hall

18/19
HUNT, Emmet S., head, age 43, M1, married 16 years, TN/TN/TN, cashier, bank
____, Ida F., wife, age 36, M1, 2/2, married 16 years, TN/KY/TN
____, Christine, daughter, age 14, TN/TN/TN
____, Neal, son, age 12, TN/TN/TN

19/20
McMURRY, Will H., head, age 43, M1, married 16 years, TN/TN/TN, president, bank
____, Gertrude, wife, age 34, M1, married 16 years, 3/3, TN/TN/TN
____, George, son, age 15, TN/TN/TN
____, Charlie, son, age 12, TN/TN/TN
____, Kate, daughter, age 8, TN/TN/TN
MEADOW, Will, boarder, age 23, single, TN/TN/TN, cashier, bank

20/21
TALLEY, James M., head, age 71, M1, married 42 years, TN/VA/UNKNOWN, recorder, city, marked "CA"
____, Kate, wife, age 63, M1, 42 years married, 10/6, TN/TN/TN
McCAULEY, Will, brother-in-law, age 72, single, TN/TN/TN, own income, marked "CA"

(Note: There was a column on this census to be checked if the men had served in either the Union Army or the Confederate Army during the Civil War. The two men in this household were marrked "CA" for the Confederate Army.)

21/22
MOORE, William A., head, age 30, M1, married 10 years, KY/KT/TN, inspector, lumber company
____, Lola G., wife, age 24, M1, married 10 years, 1/1, TN/TN/TN
____, William A., son, 11/12, TN/TN/TN

__/23
HAGGARD, Jim J., head, age 42, M1, married 20 years, TN/TN/TN, commercial trader, wholesale house
____, Wilton J., wife, age 39, M1, married 20 years, 0/0, TN/TN/TN

22/24
BOYTE, Robert T., head, age 34, M1, married 13 years, TN/TN/TN, cashier,
          bank
____, Dora, wife, age 33, married 13 years, 4/3, TN/NC/TN
____, Margret, daughter, age 6, TN/TN/TN
____, Virginia, daughter, age 5, TN/TN/TN
____, Kathleen, daughter, age 2, TN/TN/TN

23/25
LIGGETT, William R., head, age 51, M1, married 20 years, TN/TN/TN,
          salesman, hardware store
____, Nannie, wife, age 40, M1, married 20 years, /
____, Wade, son, age 16, TN/TN/TN
____, May, daughter, age 13, TN/TN/TN

24/26
TIDWELL, James E., head, age 42, M2, married 6 years, TN/TN/TN,
          merchant, retail grocery
____, Martha J., wife, age 33, M2, married 6 years, 3/3, TN/TN/TN
____, Delmar, son, age 20, single, TN/TN/TN, salesman, grocery store
____, Ella, daughter, age 18, single, TN/TN/TN
WALP, Clara, step-daughter, age 17, TN/TN/TN
____, Bessie, step-daughter, age 10, TN/TN/TN

25/27
SMITH, John M., head, age 38, M1, married 9 years, VA/VA/Ireland
          manager, lumber company
____, Lueela E., wife, age 28, M1, married 9 years, 0/0, TN/TN/TN

26/28
SUGGS, John B., head, age 35, M1, TN/TN/TN, inspector, lumber company
____, Josie, wife, age 32, M1, married 12 years, 4/4, TN/TN/TN
____, Irene, daughter, age 10, TN/TN/TN
____, Layton, son, age 9, TN/TN/TN
____, Thelma, daughter, age 7, TN/TN/TN

___/29
SWIFT, Mollie C., head, widow, age 50, 9/5, TN/TN/TN
____, John R., son, age 26, single, TN/TN/TN, carpenter, railroad bridge
____, Katie, daughter, age 23, single, TN/TN/TN

27/30
LOWERY, Henry W., head, age 74, M2, married 37 years, TN/TN/TN, own
          income
____, Eunice, wife, age 54, M1, married 37 years, 3/3, TN/TN/TN

28/31
RIDINGS, Dannie, (female), age 42, head, widow, TN/MISS/TN, own income
____, Lucile, daughter, age 16, TN/TN/TN

29/32
BROWN, John, head, 69 years, M1, married 42 years, TN/TN/TN, none
____, Isadora, wife, age 62, M1, married 42 years, 7/7, TN/TN/TN
____, Kelly, son, age 36, single, TN/TN/TN, farmer, general farm
____, Clayton, son, age 24, single, TN/TN/TN, lineman, telephone company

30/33
THOMPSON, Horatio, head, age 42, M1, married 14 years, TN/TN/TN,
          editor, newspaper
____, Lettie, wife, age 31, M1, married 14 years, 5/4, TN/TN/LA
____, Brice, son, age 10, TN/TN/TN
____, Bessie, daughter, age 8, TN/TN/TN
____, Mary, daughter, age 5, TN/TN/TN
____Mildred, daughter, 7/12, TN/TN/TN

31/34
LOGGINS, Lettie, head, female, age 40, widow, 5/5, TN/TN/TN, own income
____, Blanche, daughter, age 13, TN/TN/TN
____, Glen, daughter, age 10, TN/TN/TN
continued on next page

31/34, continued
___, Sarah, daughter, age 8, TN/TN/TN
___, Eddie, son, age 6, TN/TN/TN
NESBITT, Will, boarder, age 32, M1, married 6 years, TN/TN/TN, manager, telephone company
___, Effie, boarder, age 28, M1, married 6 years, 1/1, TN/TN/TN
___, Edward, boarder, age 1-2/12, KY/TN/TN
RAGAN, Fulton, cousin, age 17, TN/TN/TN, lineman, telephone company

32/35
FALKNER, Joseph, head, age 34, M1, married 11 years, TN/TN/TN, traveling auditor, NC&StL Railraod
___, Donnie, wife, age 27, M1, married 11 years, 1/1, TN/TN/TN
___, May Eunice, daughter, age 9, TN/TN/TN

__/36
TAYLOR, Thomas M., head, age 30, M1, married 2 years, TN/TN/TN, salesman retail furniture
___, Fannie E., wife, age 28, M1, married 2 years, 1/1, TN/TN/TN
___, Annie B., daughter, age 8/12, TN/TN/TN

33/37
WRIGHT, Lucius D., head, age 59, M2, married 33 years, TN/TN/TN, dentist, own office
___, Nannie, wife, age 22, M1, married 33 years, 2/2, TN/TN/TN
  (Note: wife's age ne3ds to be rechecked as it is believed to be in error, possibly should be 52.)

34/38
SHAWL, Ike, head, age 33, M1, married 5 years, PA/PA/PA, blacksmith, own shop
___, Nancy, wife, age 22, M1, married 5 years, 2/2, TN/TN/TN
___, Ralph, son, age 3, TN/PA/TN
___, Hazel, daughter, age 1-6/12, TN/PA/TN
ELDRIDGE, Charlie, brother-in-law, age 24, single, TN/TN/TN, barber, barber shop
_____, (no name given), sister-in-law, age 19, single, TN/TN/TN

35/39
MOORE, John, head, age 57, M1, married 22 years, TN/TN/TN, photographer, own shop
___, Mary, wife, M2, age 48, married 22 years, 7/5, TN/TN/TN, photographer, own shop
___, Ethel, daughter, age 18, single, TN/TN/TN
___, May, daughter, age 17, TN/TN/TN
___, Frank, son, age 14, TN/TN/TN
___Bessie, daughter, age 5, TN/TN/TN

36/40
HARPER, Thomas, head, age 42, M3, married 6 years, TN/VA/TN, physician, own office
___, Nellie A., wife, age 30, M1, married 6 years, 3/3, TN/Ohio/KY
___, Albert E., son, age 5, TN/TN/TN
___Thomas, son, age 3, TN/TN/TN
___, Elmer, son, age 10/12, TN/TN/TN
BROCK, Minnie, sister-in-law, age 33, single, TN/Ohio/KY
___, Clyde, brother-in-law, age 22, single, TN/Ohio/KY, none

37/41
CROCKET, George N., head, age 28, M1, married 1 year, TN/TN/TN, railway postal clerk, government
___, Annie E., wife, age 21, M1, married 1 years, TN/TN/TN
___, Rebekah, daughter, 8/12 years, TN/TN/TN

38/42
SCOTT, Albert, head, age 50, M1, married 31 years, ILL/PA/PA, postmaster, government
___, Agusta A., age 51, M1, married 31 years, 4/4, PA/PA/PA
___, Bessie E., daughter, age 24, single, TN/Ill/PA
continued on next page

38/42, continued
___, Charlie, son, age 21, M1, married 1 years TN/ILL/PA, stenographer,
          contractor
___, Flora, daughter-in-law, age 19, M1, married 1 year, 1/1, TN/TN/TN
___, Dorothy, granddaughter, 5/12 years, TN/TN/TN
WILSON, Charlie, son-in-law, age 28, M1, married 2 yea4s, VA/VA/VA, none
___, Jaunita, daughter, age 28, M1, married 2 years, TN/ILL/PA, assis-
          tant postmistress, government

39/42
SELF, Will A., head, age 49, M1, age 23, TN/TN/TN, retail merchant,
          grocery store
___, Nannie J., wife, age 44, M1, married 23 years, 7/5, TN/Va/TN
___, Osie, daughter, age 22, single, TN/TN/TN
___, Horace H., son, age 21, single, TN/TN/TN, bookkeeper, bank
___, Cecil, son, age 17, TN/TN/TN, lineman, telephone company
___, Mable, daughter, age 14, TN/TN/TN
___, Gertrude, daughter, age 12, TN/TN/TN
COLEMAN, Nannie, sister-in-law, age 53, single, TN/VA/TN

40/44
JOSLIN, Raymon, head, age 28, M1, married 3 years, TN/TN/TN, retail
          merchant, clothing store employee
___, Bertha, wife, age 27, M1, married 3 years, TN/PA/PA
___, Martha, daughter, age 1-8/12, TN/TN/TN

41/45
TIDWELL, Silvester, age 56, M2, married 4 years, TN/TN/TN, own income
___, Martha, wife, age 47, M1, married 4 years, 0/0, TN/TN/TN

COLLEGE STREET ENDS
CHURCH STREET BEGINS

42/46
GRIGSBY, Rosa Lee, age 55, widow, 8/6, TN/TN/TN
___, Virgil, son, age 30, single, TN/TN/TN
___, Clyde, son, age 24, single, TN/TN/TN, none
___, Ilena, daughter, age 22, single, TN/TN/TN, none
___, Buchanan, son, age 18, single, TN/TN/TN, salesman, retail grocery
___, Katherine, daughter, age 15, TN/TN/TN

43/47
LOVELL, Carrell M., age 60, M1, married 31 years, TN/TN/NC, physician,
          own office
___, Maggie, wife, age 55, M1, married 31 years, 2/1, Ohio/SCOT. ENGLISH
          SCOT. ENGLISH
WISHART, Sara, daughter, age 28, M1, married 6 years, 2/2, TN/TN/Ohio
___, Marguerite, granddaughter, age 4, TN/MO/TN
___, Morton E., grandson, age 2, KY/MO/TN
HAGEY, Jennie G., sister-in-law, age 58, widow, 0/0, OHIO/SCOT. ENGLISH/
          SCOT. ENGLISH.

44/48
WARREN, Thomas, age 61, M1, married 31 years, TN/TN/TN, agent,
          insurance company
___, Josie, wife, age 50, M1, married 31 years, TN/TN/TN
___, Cleveland, son, age 17, single, TN/TN/TN

45/49
GUERIN, Claude H., age 31, M1, married 5 years, TN/TN/TN, physician,
          own office
___, Mayme, wife, age 25, M1, married 5 years, 0/0, TN/TN/TN
RICHARDSON, Eva, servant (white), age 13, single, TN/TN/TN, servant,
          private family.

46/50
SHEELY, John, age 57, M2, married 23 years, PA/GERMANY/GERMANY
          policeman, city
___, Fannie, wife, age 45, M1, married 23 years, 6/6, TN/TN/TN
continued on next page

46/50 continued
___, Bessie, daughter, age 21, single, TN/PA/TN
___, John, son, age 13, TN/PA/TN
___, Curtis, son, age 11, TN/PA/TN
___, Huron, age 9, TN/PA/TN
___, Walton, son, age 6, TN/PA/TN

47/51
LEECH, Earl L., head, age 44, M1, married 19 years, TN/TN/TN, agent, depot
___, Elizabeth, wife, age 43, M1, married 19 years, 7/7, TN/TN/TN
___, Glen S., daughter, age 18, TN/TN/TN
___, Morris E., son, age 16, TN/TN/TN
___, Rye H., son, age 13, TN/TN/TN
___, Claggett H., son, age 10, TN/TN/TN
___, Lenard C., son, age 7, TN/TN/TN
___, Mayme G., daughter, age 4, TN/TN/TN
___, Virginia, daughter, age 4/12, TN/TN/TN

48/52
COPELAND, Frank, age 30, M1, married 9 years, TN/TN/TN, collector, whiskey house
___, Eva, wife, age 29, M1, 1/1, TN/Miss/TN
___, Burton, daughter, age 6, TN/TN/TN

49/53
WOODS, Nancy E., age 64, widow, 5/4, TN/VA/TN
___, Mollie, daughter, age 35, single, TN/TN/TN
___, Ida, daughter, age 25, single, TN/TN/TN
___, Campbell, son, age 21, single, TN/TN/TN, laborer, lumber company

50/54
COLLINS, George C., age 45, M2, married 20 years, TN/TN/TN, retail merchant, furniture
___, Emma, wife, age 41, M1, married 20 years, 1/1, TN/ILL/TN
___, George, Jr., son age 19, single, TN/TN/TN, retail merchant, furniture
NELSON, Rebecca, mother-in-law, age 66, widow, 5/3, TN/VA/VA
NESBITT, Pleasant, servant, age 22, widowed, TN/TN/TN, driver, delivery wagon

51/55
FAULKNER, Charles, age 50, M1, TN/TN/TN, commercial traveler, lumber company
___, Mary, wife, age 40, M1, married 21 years, 3/2, TN/VA/VA
___, Madlen, daughter, age 20, TN/TN/TN
___, William G., son, age 11, TN/TN/TN

52/56
NALLS, James, age 75, M1, married 48 years, TN/NC/NC, shoemaker, own shop
___, Rosina, age 64, M1, married 48 years, 9/7, TN/NC/NC

53/57
SWANSON, Donnie (black), age 55, widow, 5/2, TN/TN/TN, laundress at home

54/58
DAVIS, Harry, age 40, M1, married 17 years, PA/PA/PA, carpenter, house
___, Dovie, age 40, M1, married 17 years, TN/TN/TN
___, Thelma, daughter, age 6, TN/PA/PA ?

55/59
GREEN, John, age 38, M1, married 16 years, TN/TN/TN, foreman, stave mill
___, Mary, age 37, M1, married 16 years, 2/2, TN/PA/PA
___, Hubert, son, age 15, TN/TN/TN
___, Naomi, daughter, age 11, TN/TN/TN

56/60
MILES, Stephen M., age 67, M1, married 6 years, PA/CONN/CONN own income
___, Emma C., age 58, M1, married 6 years, 2/1, NY/NY/NY
      (Note: This entry may be in error.)

57/61
MARTIN, Robert, age 35, M1, married 8 years, TN/TN/TN, fireman on
           locomotive
___, Maggie, wife, age 36, M1, married 8 years, 0/0, TN/PA/PA

58/62
CHAPPELL, Wade, head, age 27, M1, married 6 years, TN/TN/TN, painter,
           railroad
___, Edna, wife, age 25, M1, married 6 years, 3/3, TN/PA/PA
___, Maggie, daughter, age 5, TN/TN/TN
___, Iro, daughter, age 3, TN/TN/TN
___, Roy, son, age 8/12, TN/TN/TN

                    SYLVIS STREET BEGINS

59/63
PAGE, John H., age 50, M1, married 31 years, TN/TN/TN, hostler, NC&StL
           Railroad
___, Linda, wife, age 50, M1, married 31 years, 7/7, TN/NC/TN
___, John J., son, age 14, TN/TN/TN
___, Haggard, son, age 10, TN/TN/TN
FOSTER, Eugene F., son-in-law, age 30, M1, married 8 years, Tn/Tn/Tn,
           electrician, telephone company
___, Lesbie, daughter, age 26, M1, married 8 years, 3/1, TN/TN/TN
___, Eugene, Jr., grandson, 8/12 years, TN/TN/TN

60/64
ALLISON, James, age 48, M1, married 21 years, TN/TN/TN, dragman, own
           team
___, Mary E., wife, age 38, M1, married 21 years, 6/6, TN/TN/TN
___, Nellie, daughter, age 20, single, TN/TN/TN
___Monroe, son, age 18, single, TN/TN/TN, carpenter, house
___, Elsie, daughter, age 15, single, TN/TN/TN
___, Jessie, daughter, age 9, TN/TN/TN
___, Granville, son, age 6, TN/TN/TN
___, Murry, son, age 3, TN/TN/TN

61/65
LUNN, James, age 62, M2, married 6 years, TN/TN/TN, none
___, Nancy, wife, age 57, M2, married 6 years, 1/1, TN/TN/TN
___, Dorsey, son, age 15, TN/TN/TN
___, Nannie, daughter, age 14, TN/TN/TN

62/66
HOOSIER, James, head, age 38, M1, married 17 years, TN/TN/TN, foreman of
           railroad crew
___, Lucy, wife, age 38, M1, married 17 years, 3/3, TN/TN/TN
___, Ollie, daughter, age 14, TN/TN/TN (Note: name also looked like
           Ottie.)
___, Ovel, son, age 11, TN/TN/TN
___, Oliver, son, age 5, TN/TN/TN

63/67
MORGAN, Sarah, single, age 45, IND/IND/IND, laundress at home
___, Willie, daughter, age 18, TN/US/IND
___, Lizzie, daughter, age 15, TN/US/IND
___, Thomas, son, age 9, TN/US/IND
___, Willie B., granddaughter, age 6/12, TN/US/TN

64/68
McMILLIAN, William, age 64, M1, married 33 years, TN/TN/TN, clerk and
           master, chancery court
___, Susie, wife, age 54, M1, married 33 years, 10/7, TN/TN/TN
continued on next page

356

64/68 continued
McMILLIAN, Charlie, son, age 17, single, TN/TN/TN
___, Willie G., daughter, age 9, TN/TN/TN

POPULAR STREET BEGINS

65/69
GIBSON, John H., head, age 50, M1, married 28 years, TN/TN/TN, machinist engine house
___, Meldel, wife, age 42, M1, married 28 years, 6/5, TN/TN/TN
___, Willie, daughter, age 20, single, TN/TN/TN
___, Erin, son, age 19, single, TN/TN/TN
___, John, son, age 12, TN/TN/TN
___, Annie M., daughter, age 9, TN/TN/TN
___, Jerald, son, age 6, TN/TN/TN
___, Sammie, daughter-in-law, age 21, widow, 0/0, TN/TN/TN

66/70
COWAN, Florence, head, age 56, widow, 6/6, NC/MD/NC
___, Turner H., son, age 31, single, NC/NC/NC, manager, lumber company
___, Daisey, daughter, age 28, single, NC/NC/NC
___, Horace J., son, age 22, single, NC/NC/NC
___, James, son, age 24, single, NC/NC/NC
___, Floyd, age 20, son, single, NC/NC/NC

67/71
PRINCE, William, head, age 33, M1, married 9 years, TN/TN/TN, teacher, college
___, Elizabeth, wife, age 28, M1, married 9 years, TN/TN/TN
___, Melba, daughter, age 2, TN/TN/TN

68/72
BARRNETT, Mannye, male, age 41, M1, married 11 years, NEB/NEB/NEB laborer, odd jobs
___, Bessie, wife, age 30, M1, married 11 years, 5/5, TN/TN/TN
___, Leroy, son, 10, TN/NEB/TN
___, Eudora, daughter, age 8, TN/NEB/TN
___, Mayme, daughter, age 6, TN/NEB/TN
___, Charlie, son, age 3, TN/NEB/TN
___, John, son, age 10/12, TN/NEB/TN

69/73
RYAN, Orpha (female), head, age 40, widow, 6/5, TN/OHIO/OHIO
___, Mike, son, age 20, single, TN/TN/TN, fireman, locomotive
___, Joe, son, age 19, single, TN/TN/TN, newsboy, locomotive
___, Edna, daughter, age 12, TN/TN/TN
___, Jim, son, age 9, TN/TN/TN
___, Opal, daughter, age 3, TN/TN/TN

70/74
GALLOWAY, John, head, age 30, M1, married 8 years, TN/PA/TN, tie inspector, railroad
___, Nettie, age 23, wife, M1, married 8 years, 3/3, TN/TN/TN
___, J. T., son, age 7, TN/TN/TN
___, Percy, son, age 5, TN/TN/TN
___, Eloise, daughter, age 3, TN/TN/TN

71/75
KISSLER, John, head, age 33, M1, married 13 years, OHIO/IND/OHIO, manager, monument company
___, Pearl, wife, age 32, M1, married 13 years, 4/4, OHIO/OHIO/OHIO
___, Charlie R., son, age 12, TN/IND/OHIO
___, Daniel, son, age 9, TN/IND/OHIO
___, Annie G., daughter, age 6, TN/IND/OHIO
___, William, son, age 3, TN/IND/OHIO
COOK, William, father-in-law, age 83, single, CANADA ENGLISH_____
(Note: Some of this information believed to be in error.)

OLIVE STREET BEGINS

72/76
SYLVIS, James, age 25, M1, married 6 years, TN/TN/TN, driver, livery
           barn
___, Orzona (Arzona?), wife, age 29, M1, married 6 years, 2/2, TN/TN/TN
___, Lillie, daughter, age 8, TN/TN/TN
___, Glayds, daughter, age 1-4/12, TN/TN/TN

73/77
NEIGHBORS, James T., head, age 42, M1, married 19 years, TN/TN/TN,
           lineman, telephone company
___, Rosa L., wife, age 39, M1, married 19 years, 6/6, TN/TN/TN
___, Pearl, daughter, age 18, TN/TN/TN
___, Myrtle, daughter, age 15, TN/TN/TN
___, Eugene, son, age 10, TN/TN/TN
___, Nina, daughter, age 5, TN/TN/TN
___, Leon, son, age 2, TN/TN/TN
___, Milton, son, age 9/12, TN/TN/TN

74/78
PATE, Lenard, head, age 53, M1, married 20 years, TN/TN/TN, farmer,
      general farm
___, Bettie, wife, age 47, M1, married 20 years, 5/5, TN/TN/TN
___, Isabelle, daughter, age 18, TN/TN/TN
___, Freda, daughter, age 16, TN/TN/TN
___, Lenard, son, age 14, TN/TN/TN
___, Ruby, daughter, age 12, TN/TN/TN
___, Mable, daughter, age 8, TN/TN/TN

75/79
MILLER, Cora L., female, head, divorced, 6/6, TN/TN/TN, laundress, at
        home
___, Oscar, son, age 17, TN/TN/TN, laborer, factory
___, Hubert, son, age 11, TN/TN/TN
___, Walter, son, age 8, TN/TN/TN
___, Cora, daughter, age 6, TN/TN/TN
STEWART, Lela, daughter, divorced, age 20, 1/1, TN/TN/TN
___, John, grandson, age 7/12, TN/TN/TN

76/80
REEVES, William E., head, age 36, M2, married 10 years, ILL/TN/TN,
        carpenter, house
___, Fannie, wife, age 34, M2, married 10 years, 4/4, TN/TN/TN
___, Lucile, daughter, age 8, TN/ILL/TN
___, Charlie, son, age 6, TN/ILL/TN
___, Howard, son, age 3/12, TN/ILL/TN
WOODSIDE, Auther L., stepson, age 11, TN/TN/TN

77/81
HALFACRE, Jefferson, head, age 35, M1, married 13 years, TN/US/US,
          patternmaker, factory
___, Annie M., wife, age 24, M1, married 13 years, 4/4, TN/TN/TN
___, Hank B., son, age 9, TN/TN/TN
___, Cordell, son, age 7, TN/TN/TN
___, Lee, son, age 4, TN/TN/TN
___, Alice, daughter, age 2, TN/TN/TN

78/82
MARSH, Dave (black), head, age 60, M1, married 35 years, TN/TN/TN,
       laborer, lumber yard
___, Cathrine, wife, black, age 50, married 35 years, 12/4, TN/TN/TN
       laundress at home
___, Hettie, 18, mu, age 18, granddaughter, TN/TN/TN
___, Clayton, age 15, black, grandson, TN/TN/TN
___, Zollie, age 9, black, grandson, TN/TN/TN
___, Blanch, age 8, black, granddaughter, TN/TN/TN
___, Harry, grandson, TN/TN/TN, black
___, Claude, grandson, Tn/TN/TN, black

79/82
RAMEY, Wash, black, age 50, widowed, porter, depot
    household, not copied

80/84
JOHNSTON, James W., head, age 67, M1, married 32 years, PA/PA/PA
___, Lizzie, wife, age 63, M1, married 32 years, 6/5, PA/PA/PA

                         CHARLOTTE STREET

81/85
FREEMAN, Joseph, head, age 57, M1, married 36 years, PA/PA/PA, foreman,
    carpenter, NC&StL railroad
___, Hattie, wife, age __, M1, married 36 years, 10/6, PA/PA/PA
___, Henry, age 31, son, widowed, TN/PA/PA, painter, house
___, Percy, son, age 21, TN/PA/PA
___, Louise, daughter, age 18, TN/PA/PA
___, Samuel, son, age 16, TN/PA/PA
___, Doris, granddaughter, age 7, TN/TN/TN

82/86
LOCKE, Joseph, head, age 47, M1, married 20 years, TN/TN/TN, jeweler,
    own shop
___, Lizzie, wife, age 38, M1, married 20 years, 8/8, TN/PA/PA
___, Joseph, Jr., son, age 18, TN/TN/TN
___, Maggie, daughter, age 16, TN/TN/TN
___, Bessie, daughter, age 14, TN/TN/TN
___, Homer, son, age 12, TN/TN/TN
___, Cecil, son, age 9, TN/TN/TN
___, Maude, daughter, age 7, TN/TN/TN
___, Glen, son, age 4, TN/Tn/TN
___, Howard, son, age 2, TN/TN/TN

83/87
ROBINSON, James, head, age 58, widowed, PA/PA/PA, proprietor, meat shop
___, Charlie, son, age 33, single, TN/PA/PA, butcher, meat shop
___, Elsie, daughter, age 28, single, TN/PA/PA, none
___, Walace, son, age 16, TN/PA/PA, driver, delivery wagon

84/88
WILLIAMS, Otho H., head, age 58, M1, married 28 years, TN/TN/TN,
    optometrist, own office
___, Emma, wife, age 53, M1, married 28 years, 0/0, KY/KY/KY
___, Trissie M., female, adopted, age 26, single, Ky/KY/KY

85/89
HELBURG, Thedore, head, M1, age 30, married 3 years, OHIO/GERMANY/
    GERMANY, trader, livestock
___, Erma, wife, age 30, M1, married 3 years, 2/1, TN/TN/TN
___, Annie Lee, daughter, age 1-4/12, TN/OHIO/TN

86/90
PADGETT, Millard F., head, age 54, M1, married 34 years, KY/KY/KY,
    overseer, stave mill
___, Malissa, wife, age 50, M1, married 34 years, 5/5/, KY/KY/KY
___, Anna, daughter, age 27, single, KY/KY/KY
___, Monte, son, age 25, single, KY/KY/KY, laborer, stave mill
___, Clyde, son, age 22, single, KY/KY/KY, bookkeeper, stave mill
___, Keith, son, age 18, Ky/KY/KY

87/91
WALKER, Billie, head, age 29, M1, married 7 years, TN/TN/TN, baggage
    master, baggage car
___, Ophelia, wife, age 26, M1, married 7 years, 1/1, TN/TN/TN
___, Earnestine, daughter, age 6, TN/TN/TN

88/92
MILLER, Matt, head, age 38, M1, married 15 years, TN/TN/TN, driver,
    livery barn
continued next page

88/92 continued
MILLER, Nora, wife, age 39, M1, married 15 years, 4/3, TN/TN/TN
____, Gertrude, daughter, age 12, TN/TN/TN
____, Eloise, daughter, age 8, TN/TN/TN
____, Murvel, daughter, age____, TN/TN/TN

89/93
MORAN, Maggie, black, age 50, widow, 7/5, TN/TN/TN, cook, boarding house
____, Rhoda, daughter, age 36, single, TN, TN, TN, servant, black

90/94
BAKER, John W., head, age 49, M1, married 27 years, TN/TN/TN, farmer
____, Inez B., wife, age 49, M1, married 27 years, 0/0, TEXAS/ALA/KY

91/95
EWELL, Ruth, head, age 60, widow, 5/1, PA/PA/PA, laundress, at home
____, Emma, daughter, age 20, single, TN/TN/PA

92/96
DAVIES, William J., head, age 45, widowed, KY/KY/KY, teacher, college
____, Alice, sister, age 54, KY/KY/KY
____, Clyde, son, age 6, KY/KY/KY

93/97
PETTY, William, head, age 60, M1, married 41 years, TN/NC/NC, farmer, general farm
____, Mary, age 60, wife, M1, married 41 years, 12/11, TN/TN/GA
____, Fannie, daughter, age 32, TN/TN/TN
____, Wilson, daughter, age 21, single, TN/TN/TN
____, Bessie, daughter, age 17, TN/TN/TN
____, Effie, daughter, age 14, TN/TN/TN

RICKERT AVENUE

94/98
MOODY, Silas C., head, age 57, M1, married 26 years, KY/KY/KY, engineer, factory
____, Nannie, wife, age 48, M1, married 26 years, 7/5, MO/PORTUGAL/NC
____, Elzie L., son, age 18, MO/KY/MO, laborer, factory
____John W., son, age 15, MO/KY/MO, delivery boy, grocery store
____, Eunice, daughter, age 12, MO/KY/MO

95/99
BEASLEY, William, head, age 24, M1, married 5 years, TN/TN/TN, plumber, city water works
____, Nattie P., wife, age 22, M1, married 5 years, 1/1, MO/KY/MO
____, Norine F., daughter, age 1-10/12, TN/TN/MO

96/100
PETTY, Frank, head, age 24, M1, married 5 years, TN/TN/TN, blacksmith, own shop
____, Jettie, wife, age 22, M1, married 5 years, 4/1, TN/TN/TN
____, Mason E., son, age 6/12, TN/TN/TN

97/101
RICKERT, Abner, head, age 51, M1, married 29 years, PA/PA/PA, farmer, general farm
____, Bena, wife, age 48, M1, married 29 years, 13/7, TN/NY/TN
____, Blanche, daughter, age 17, TN/PA/TN
____, Gertrude, daughter, age 15, TN/PA/TN
____Gordon, son, age 10, TN/PA/TN

98/102
BEARS, Nicholas, head, age 49, M1, married 26 years, PA/PA/Pa, driller, wells
____, Alice, wife, age 46, M1, married 26 years, 9/8, PA/PA/PA
____, Rosa E., daughter, age 20, TN/PA/PA
____, Ella M., daughter, age 18, TN/PA/PA   continued on next page

98/102 continued
BEARS, Amy G., daughter, age 16, TN/PA/PA
___, Guy W., son, age 13, TN/PA/PA
___, Harry L., son, age 8, TN/PA/PA
___, Robin E., son, age 5, PN/PA/PA

99/103
JONES, Will L., head, age 52, M1, married 28 years, TN/VA/TN, retail
    merchant, grocery store
___, Laura, wife, age 46, married 28 years, 7/7, MO/VA/KY
___, Dick, son, age 27, TN/TN/MO, fireman, locomotive
___, Frank, son, age 22, TN/TN/MO
___, Madie, daughter, age 18, TN/TN/MO
___, Edna, daughter, age 14, TN/TN/MO

100/104
MILLER, Jesse, head, age 23, single, TN/TN/TN, driver, livery barn
___, Sallie, sister, age 25, single, TN/TN/TN

101/105
WALKER, Harriett, head, age 78, widow, 8/7, TN/NC/NC
___, Wiley, son, age 43, single, TN/VA/TN, physician, own office
___, Ella, daughter, age 28, single, TN/VA/TN
EASLEY, Susie, daughter, age 39, widow, 0/0, TN/VA/TN

102/106
RAY, Charlie, head, age 45, M2, married 12 years, PA/PA/PA, retail
  merchant, grocery
___, Jennie C., wife, age 35, M1, married 12 years, 6/5, PA/PA/PA
___, Jennie S., daughter, age 20, single, TN/Pa/Pa
___, Hubert O., son, age 19, single, TN/PA/PA, salesman, grocery store
___, James, son, age 12, TN/PA/PA
___, Eugene, son, age 10, TN/PA/PA
___, William, son, age 8, TN/PA/PA
___, Ralph, son, age 6, TN/PA/PA
___, Edith S., daughter, age 5, TN/PA/PA

102/107
TOLAR, Henry L., head, age 40, M1, married 5 years, TN/TN/TN
      salesman, hardware
___, Anna E., wife, age 25, M1, married 5 years, TN/TN/TN
JOSLIN, Hester, companion, age 8, TN/TN/TN

103/108
TAYLOR, Joseph R., head, age 66, M1, married 46 years, TN/TN/TN, own
    income
___, Mary E., wife, age 70, M1, married 46 years, 7/7, TN/TN/TN
___, Mamie L., daughter, age 35, single, TN/TN/TN

104/109
HUDSON, Dan R., head, age 38, M1, married 15 years, TN/TN/TN, laborer,
  foundry
___, Ellen, wife, age 33, M1, married 15 years, 7/6, TN/TN/TN
___, Ella, daughter, age 14, TN/TN/TN
___Bertha M., daughter, age 12, TN/TN/TN
___Effie, daughter, age 7, TN/TN/TN
___Lucile, daughter, age 4, TN/TN/TN
___Ruth, daughter, age 3, TN/TN/TN
___Irene, age 3/12, TN/TN/TN, daughter

105/110
ROGERS, William T., head, age 52, widowed, married 27 years, KY/KY/KY
  miller, rolling mill
___, Lelia, daughter, age 24, single, KY/KY/KY
___, Phinous, son, age 22, single, KY/KY/KY
___, Lester, son, age 20, single, KY/KY/KY, bookkeeper, lumber company
___, Lida, daughter, age 17, KY/KY/KY
___, Walter, son, age 15, KY/KY/KY
___, Lucien, son, age 13, KY/KY/KY
VANDERVOIT, Anna, servant, age 48, single, PA/PA/PA, housekeeper

106/111
BALLARD, John B., head, age 49, M1, married 28 years, ARK/ARK/ARK
          painter, house
___, Sophia, wife, age 40, M1, married 23 years, 4/4, TN/TN/TN
___, Robert, son, age 20, TN/ARK/TN, painter, house
___, Horace, son, age 16, TN/ARK/TN, painter, house
___, Clayton, son, age 14, TN/ARK/TN
CAIN, John, grandson, age 3, TN/TN/TN

107/112
PULLEY, Jim, head, age 31, M2, married 3 years, TN/TN/TN, laborer,
          Standard Oil
___, Minnie, wife, age 22, M2, married 3 years, 2/2, TN/ARK/TN
___, Lenard, son, age 14, TN/TN/TN, delivery boy, grocery store
___, John, son, age 12, TN/TN/TN, laborer, bottle works
___, Ernest, son, age 10, TN/TN/TN
___, Lucile, daughter, age 7, TN/TN/TN
___, Harry, son, age 1-4/12, TN/TN/TN

108/113
HUDSON, Elvin, head, age 37, M2, married 14 years, TN/TN/TN, laborer,
          ice plant
___, Eliza, wife, age 45, M2, married 14 years, 6/6, TEX/TN/TN
___, Susise, daughter, age 13, TN/TN/TN
___, Myrtle, daughter, age 11, TN/TEXAS/TN
___, Dollie, L., daughter, age 2, TN/TEXAS/TN
DODSON, Jennie, stepdaughter, age 20, single, TN/VA/TN
___, Emma, stepdaughter, age 18, single, TN/TN/TN

109/114
COLLIER, William, head, age 43, widow, TN/TN/TN, laborer, factory
___, Herman, son, age 20, single, TN/TN/TN, laborer, lumber company
___, Bessie, daughter, age 19, TN/TN/TN, single
MILLER, Tulah, sister-in-law, age 44, divorced, married 18 years, 1/1,
    TN/TN/TN

110/115
MATHIS, Dan, head, age 29, M1, married 3 years, TN/TN/TN, agent,
    insurance
___, Daisy, wife, age 25, M1, married 3 years, TN/TN/TN
SPENCER, Doyle, nephew, age 13, TN/TN/TN, delivery boy, meat market

111/116
BATES, Richard, head, age 26, M1, married 2 years, TN/TN/TN, brakeman,
    locomotive
___, Myrtle, age 32, wife, M1, married 2 years, TN/TN/TN
ANDERSON, Millie, mother-in-law, age 69, widow, TN/TN/TN

112/117
DAVIS, Mellie (female), head, 52, widow, 3/2, WISC/NY/PA
___, Marvin, son, age 18, single, TN/TN/WISC, salesman, drug store

113/118
TROTTER, John M., head, age 66, M1, married 42 years, TN/TN/TN, own
    income
___, Martha, wife, age 64, M1, married 42 years, 1/1, TN/TN/TN
WILSON, Dee A., niece, age 19, single, TN/TN/TN

114/119
BEASLEY, Mike, head, age 45, M1, married 25 years, TN/TN/TN, air brake
    inspector, NCStL railroad
___Lois, wife, age 39, M1, married 25 years, 10/7, TN/OHIO/TN
___, Vera, 18, daughter, single, TN/TN/TN
___, Cheatham, 15, son, TN/TN/TN, driver, Standard Oil Company
___, Jessie, daughter, age 11, TN/TN/TN
___, Farris, son, age 9, TN/TN/TN
___Troy, son, age 6, TN/TN/TN
___, Pearl, daughter, age 5, TN/TN/TN

115/120
DUNN, John, tailor, black household, not copied

116/121
LONG, Whit, black household, not copied

117/122
LUCKY, Will, black household, not copied

118/123
CARR, Bob, black household, not copied

119/124
ROTH, Billie, head, age 46, M2, married 16 years, PA/PA/GERMANY,
    carpenter, house
___, Nettie, wife, age 36, M1, married 16 years, 6/5, TN/TN/TN
___, Lena, daughter, age 18, single, TN/PA/TN
___, Pearl, daughter, TN/TN/TN, age 12
___, Mable, daughter, age 10, TN/TN/TN
___, Lewis, son, age 7, TN/TN/TN
___, Robert, son, age 6/12, TN/TN/TN
DOAKE, Mary, aunt, age 74, single, TN/TN/TN

120/125
MARCH, John, black household, not copied

121/126
BELL, Jude, black household, not copied

122/127
RICHARD, Aden, black household, not copied

123/128
LEECH, Ransom, head, age 39, M1, married 18 years, TN/TN/TN, lawyer,
    general practice
___, Abel, wife, age 44, M1, married 18 years, 4/4, TN/TN/TN
___ Robert, son, age 17, TN/TN/TN
___, Sarah, daughter, age 13, TN/TN/TN
___, Dudley, son, age 10, TN/TN/TN
___, Murray, son, age 6, TN/TN/TN

124/129
JOHNSTON, John, head, age 35, M1, married 9 years, TN/PA/PA, merchant,
    hardware
___, Odie (?), wife, age 29, M2, married 9 years, 3/3, TN/TN/TN
___, Louise, daughter, age 8, TN/TN/TN
___, Paul, son, age 7, TN/TN/TN
___, Maud L., daughter, age 5, TN/TN/TN
ANDREWS, Bettie, aunt, age 64, M1, TN/TN/TN
___, Ephraim, uncle, age 84, M1, TN/TN/TN

125/130
GOSSETT, John, head, M1, age 36, married 11 years, TN/TN/TN,
    engineer, locomotive
___, Laura, wife, M1, age 25, married 11 years, 2/2, TN/TN/TN
___, Rollie, son, age 8, TN/TN/TN
___, Walker (Watker?), son, age 5, TN/TN/TN
___, Freddie, niece, age 17, TN/TN/TN

126/131
STITT, George, head, age 37, M1, married 20 years, TN/PA/PA, conductor
    railroad train
___, Hattie, wife, age 34, M1, married 20 years, 4/4, TN/TN/TN
___, Claude, son, age 18, TN/TN/TN
___, Nola, M., daughter, age 15, TN/TN/TN
___, Annie M., daughter, age 12, TN/TN/TN
___, Mary D., daughter, age 9, TN/TN/TN

127/132
EDWARDS, Anna R., head, age 64, widow, 8/2, TN/TN/TN
LYAL, Eva, granddaughter, age 14, TN/TN/TN
BEASLEY, Lester, grandson, age 14, TN/TN/TN

128/133
LOVELL, Joe, head, age 45, widowed, TN/TN/TN, engineer, locomotive
____, Hershal, daughter, age 17, single, TN/TN/TN
____, Harrison, son, age 15, TN/TN/TN

129/134
NALLS, Jeff, head, age 30, M1, married 10 years, TN/TN/TN, brakeman, railroad train
____, Stella, wife, age 27, M1, married 10 years, 1/1, TN/TN/ARK
____, Geraldine, daughter, age 6, TN/TN/TN

130/135
FULGHUM, Thomas, head, age 42, M1, married 15 years, TN/TN/TN, operator depot
____, Mable C., wife, age 36, M1, married 15 years, 4/4, TN/TN/TN
____, Harry J., son, age 13, TN/TN/TN
____, James E., son, age 11, TN/TN/TN
____, Glayds, daughter, age 8, TN/TN/TN
____Thomas, son, age 4, TN/TN/TN

MURRELL STREET

131/136
HOGIN, William M., head, age 66, M1, married 44 years, TN/TN/TN
____, Susan, wife, age 62, M1, married 44 years, 8/8, TN/TN/TN
____, Ray, son, age 22, single, TN/TN/TN, grader, lumber company

no household number but listed with above
DONEGAN, John S., age 51, M1, married 22 years, TN/TN/TN, laborer, odd jobs
____, Ida, wife, age 42, M1, married 22 years, 0/0, TN/TN/TN

132/137
BARKLEY, John, head, age 63, M1, married 22 years, MICH/GERMANY/MICH sawyer, factory
____, Mollie, wife, age 49, M1, married 22 years, 1/1, TN/TN/TN
____, Ernest, son, age 13, TN/MICH/TN

133/138
BALSBAUGH, Henry C., head, age 53, M2, married 7 years, PA/PA/PA colporteur, publishing house
____, Mary H., wife, age 40, M1, married 7 years, 0/0, TN/TN/KY

134/139
KILGORE, Robert, head, age 71, M1, married 42 years, OHIO/NY/PA, minister
____, Asenath, wife, age 70, M1, married 42 years, 3/2, MICH/PA/MICH
ALDRIDGE, Mary L., daughter, age 33, divorced, 3/3, IOWA/OHIO, MICH trained nurse, private family
____, Lenora, granddaughter, age 8, TN/IOWA/IOWA
____, Robert, grandson, age 6, TN/IOWA/IOWA
____, Charles, grandson, age 4, TN/IOWA/IOWA

135/140
ENGLISH, Alex D., head, age 53, M1, married 25 years, TN/TN/TN, laborer, lumber company
____, Kate W., wife, age 43, M1, married 25 years, 10/9, TN/TN/TN
____, Daniel E., son, age 20, single, TN/TN/TN
____, Walter, son, age 12, TN/TN/TN
____, Ewing, son, age 21, TN/TN/TN, lineman, telephone company
____, Robert, son, age 9, TN/TN/TN
____, Gardner, son, age 6, TN/TN/TN
____, Neil, age 4, TN/TN/TN, son
____, Clifford, son, age 1, TN/TN/TN

136/141
FREEMAN, Ralph, head, age 29, M1, married 7 years, TN/PA/NY, printer, printing office
___, Bessie, wife, age 29, M1, married 7 years, 1/1, TN/PA/TN
___, Lorena C., daughter, age 2/12, TN/TN/TN
___, Frank, brother, age 39, TN/PA/NY, printer, printing office

137/142
JACKSON, Epps, head, age 34, M1, married 3 years, TN/TN/TN, carpenter, house
___, Tennie, wife, age 30, M1, married 3 years, 0/0, TN/TN/TN

138/143
HOOPER, Frank, head, age 40, M1, married 22 years, TN/TN/TN, agent, insurance company
___, Emma, wife, age 44, married 22 years, M1, 9/7, TN/TN/TN
___, Rosa, daughter, age 18, TN/TN/TN
___, Versen, son, age 14, TN/TN/TN
___, Ruth, daughter, age 6, TN/TN/TN
___, Frank, Jr., son, age 3, TN/TN/TN
___, Richard, son, age 1, TN/TN/TN
___, Oscar, son, age 21, M1, married 1 year, TN/TN/TN, driver, livery barn
___, Katie, daughter-in-law, age 18, M1, married 1 year, 1/1, TN/TN/TN
___, Christine, granddaughter, age 8/12, TN/TN/TN

139/144
FUSSELL, William, head, 62, M1, married 39 years, TN/TN/TN, farmer, own farm
___, Missouri, wife, age 60, M1, married 39 years, 10/9, TN/TN/TN
___, Minnie, daughter, age 35, single, TN/TN/TN, milliner, millinery store
___, Leslie, son, age 14, TN/TN/TN
DICKSON, Omer, son-in-law, age 26, M1, married 0 years, TN/TN/TN, bookkeeper, telephone office
___, Ora, daughter, age 21, M1, married 0 years, 0/0, TN/TN/TN

140/145
SUGGS, William J., head, age 38, M1, married 13 years, TN/TN/TN, physician, own office
___, Lillie, wife, age 38, M1, married 13 years, 6/6, TN/TN/TN
___, William Jr., age 5, son, TN/TN/TN (age in question)
___, Norrise, son, age 10, TN/TN/TN
___, Dollie, daughter, age 8, TN/TN/TN
___, Thomas T., son, age 5, TN/TN/TN
___, Wilbur F., son, age 4, TN/TN/TN
___, Edward, son, age 11/12, TN/TN/TN
NORRISE, Minnie, sister-in-law, age 32, single, TN/TN/TN

141/146
LITTLE, Addie S., head, age 50, M2, 4/4, TN/TN/TN
LARKINS, Mayme, daughter, age 30, M1, married 12 years, 2/2, TN/TN/TN
___, Robert E., son-in-law, age 39, M1, married 12 years, TN/TN/TN
___, Edna, granddaughter, age 9, TN/TN/TN
___, Gertrude, granddaughter, age 5, TN/TN/TN

142/147
CULLUM, William, head, age 46, M1, married 26 years, TN/TN/TN, lawyer, general practice
___, Katie, wife, age 45, M1, married 26 years, 6/5, PA/PA/PA
___, Roy, son, age 21, single, TN/TN/PA
___, Merwyn, son, age 5, TN/TN/PA
___, Wilton, daughter, age 2, TN/TN/PA
___, Gordon, son, age 25, M2, TN/TN/PA, proprietor, job office
___, Allie, daughter-in-law, age 25, M1, TEXAS/US/PA
___, Thelma, granddaughter, age 1-7/12, TN/TN/TEXAS
SAGER, Romeo, son-in-law, age 23, M1, PA/PA/TN, baker, baker shop
___, Hazel, daughter, age 20, M1, TN/TN/PA

143/148
SCOTT, Harvey C., head, age 48, M1, married 34 years, PA/PA/PA,
    salesman, dry goods store
___, Minta Z., wife, age 54, M1, married 34 years, 6/4, PA/PA/PA
___, Alberta K., daughter, age 33, single, TN/PA/PA, saleswoman, dry
    goods store
___, Lynwood C., son, age 21, TN/PA/PA, carpenter, house

144/149
HAINES, Alonzo W., head, age 35, M1, married 0 years, IOWA/NJ/IOWA,
    treasurer, lumber company
___, Annie, wife, age 30, M1, married 0 years, VA/VA/MO

145/150
BROWN, Marsh, head, age 35, M1, married 11 years, TN/TN/TN, rural
    carrier, government
___, Willie, wife, age 30, M1, married 11 years, 2/2, TN/ILL/PA
___, Hubert, son, age 10, TN/TN/TN
___Cecil, son, age 8, TN/TN/TN

CULLOM STREET

146/151
SCOTT, George, age 31, M1, married 7 years, TN/PA/PA, carpenter, house
___, Lola, wife, age 27, M1, married 7 years, 4/4, TN/PA/OHIO
___, Carlton, son, age 6, TN/TN/TN
___, Weldon, son, age 5, TN/TN/TN
___, Mary L., daughter, age 2, TN/TN/TN
___, Clifford M., son, age 6/12, TN/TN/TN

147/152
DONALDSON, Hattie, head, widow, age 50, 7/6, OHIO/OHIO/OHIO
___, May, daughter, age 31, single, TN/PA/OHIO
___, Harry, son, age 23, single, PN/PA/OHIO, laborer, lumber company
___, Julia, daughter, age 18, single, TN/PA/OHIO
___, Rollie, son, age 16, TN/PA/OHIO

148/153
Saeger, Earl, head, age 39, M1, married 17 years, PA/PA/PA, manager,
    planing mill
___, Melvina, wife, age 35, M1, married 17 years, 4/4, TN/TN/TN
___, Bernard, son, age 13, TN/PA/TN
___, Bertha, daughter, age 10, TN/PA/TN
___, Charlie, son, age 5, TN/PA/TN
___, Alline, daughter, age 2, TN/PA/TN

149/154
COLEMAN, Thomas J., head, age 49, M1, married 18 years, TN/TN/TN,
    constable, city
___, Georgie L., wife, age 35, M1, married 18 years, 3/3, TN/TN/TN
___, Ruth, daughter, age 16, TN/TN/TN
___, Lucile, daughter, age 11, TN/TN/TN
___, Thomas F., son, age 2, TN/TN/TN
CHILDRESS, Thomas, father-in-law, age 76, M1, married 53 years, TN/NC/NC
___, Martha, mother-in-law, age 79, M1, married 53 years, 8/8, GA/GA/GA

150/155
ANKENY, Lewis J., head, age 54, M1, married 23 years, ILL/ILL/WISC,
    proprietor, restaurant
___, Mary M., wife, age 48, M1, married 23 years, 6/5, OHIO/CANADA/OHIO
___, Tolbert, son, age 21, single, TN/ILL/OHIO, cook, diner
___, John L., son, age 19, TN/ILL/OHIO
___, Julie C., daughter, age 17, TN/ILL/OHIO
___, Genevive M., daughter, age 15, TN/ILL/OHIO

151/156
GRIFFIN, Charlie T., head, age 24, M1, married 0 years, TN/TN/TN,
    salesman, hardware
___, Mable, wife, age 19, M1, married 0 years, TN/TN/TN

152/157
GRIFFIN, Edgar, head, age 25, M1, married 2 years, TN/TN/TN, bookkeeping, railroad office
___, Izora, wife, age 21, M1, married 2 years, TN/TN/TN
___, Carrie B., daughter, age 7/12, TN/TN/TN
___, Will, brother, age 21, single, TN/TN/TN, fireman, locomotive

153/158
GRAHAM, Jane H., head, 76, widow, 5/5, NY/IRELAND/SCOTLAND, none

___/159
GALLOWAY, Clementine, head, 71, widow, PA/MD/PA, own income

154/160
WALKER, James, head, age 49, M1, married 16 years, TN/TN/TN, laborer, odd jobs
___, Mattie, wife, age 39, M1, married 16 years, 9/8, TN/TN/TN, dressmaker, at home
___, Ramey, son, age 15, TN/TN/TN
___, Hettie, daughter, age 13, TN/TN/TN
___, Clarence, son, age 12, TN/TN/TN
___, James, son, age 10, TN/TN/TN
___, Cathrine, daughter, age 9, TN/TN/TN
___, Anna, daughter, age 6, TN/TN/TN
___, John F., son, age 5, TN/TN/TN
___, Jaunita, daughter, age 2, TN/TN/TN

155/161
KELLEY, Dallas, head, age 66, M1, married 40 years, TN/NC/NC, none
___, Tennie, wife, age 56, M1, married 40 years, 7/6, TN/NC/NC
___, Sallie, daughter, age 26, single, TN/TN/TN
___, Arch, son, age 22, single, TN/TN/TN

MAIN STREET

156/162
TOMLINSON, Horace, head, age 35, M1, married 14 years, TN/TN/TN, merchant, retail grocery store
___, Minnie, wife, age 33, M1, married 14 years, 5/5, TN/TN/TN
___, Dale, son, age 12, TN/TN/TN
___, Ruby, daughter, age 9, TN/TN/TN
___, Louise, daughter, age 6, TN/TN/TN
___, Aliene, daughter, age 4, TN/TN/TN
___ Eva May, daughter, age 6/12, TN/TN/TN

157/163
LITTLE, Luther, head, age 27, M1, married 4 years, TN/TN/ALA, baker, baker shop
___, Minnie, wife, age 21, M1, married 4 years, 1/1, TN/PA/TN
___, Larry E., son, age 1-10/12, TN/TN/TN

___/164
COLE, Parthenia A., head, age 69, widow, 6/2, TN/TN/NC, own income

158/165
GOSSETT, John M., head, age 37, M1, married 15 years, ARK/ARK/ARK, merchant, dry goods, retail
___, Mattie, wife, age 37, M1, married 15 years, TN/TN/TN

159/166
WALKER, Emma, head, age 44, M1, married 21 years, TN/TN/TN
___, Edwin, son, age 14, TN/TN/TN, laborer, farm
___, Pauline, daughter, age 13, TN/TN/TN

160/167
MURRELL, Tom J., head, age 85, widowed, TN/TN/TN, own income
MARTIN, Elenora, daughter, age 64, widow, TN/TN/TN
___, Connie, granddaughter, age 39, single, TN/TN/TN

161/168
BRIGHT, Frank L., head, age 55, M1, married 32 years, PA/PA/PA, rural
       mail carrier, government
___, Julia, wife, age 55, M1, married 32 years, 8/6, TN/MASS/TN
___, Frankie, son, age 27, single, TN/PA/TN, post office clerk, govt.
___, Lorena, daughter, age 25, single, TN/PA/TN, stenographer, lumber
       office
___, Vera, daughter, age 18, single, TN/PA/TN, none

162/169
MILLER, Fannie, head, age 49, widow, TN/TN/TN, own income

___/170
McKELVEY, Buren, head, age 23, M1, married 1 year, TN/TN/TN, brakeman,
       on train
___, Myrtle, wife, age 22, M1, married 1 year, 0/0, TN/TN/TN

163/171
CARTER, Mary R., head, age 50, widow, 2/2, OHIO/OHIO/OHIO, own income

164/172
NICHOLS, Marion, head, age 35, M1, married 9 years, TN/TN/TN, conductor,
       railway train
___, Pearl, wife, age 26, M1, married 9 years, 1/1, TN/TN/TN
___, Mary, daughter, age 8, TN/TN/TN

165/173
SANFORD, John, head, age 73, widowed, KY/KY/KY, none
___, Charlie, son, age 28, M1, married 2 years, TN/KY/TN, teamster, own
       team
___, May, daughter-in-law, age 23, M1, married 2 years, 1/1, TN/TN/TN
___, Junius, son, age 23, single, TN/KY/TN, bookkeeper, livery barn
___, Leon H., grandson, age 1-6/12, TN/TN/TN

166/174
SENSING, Lemuel, head, age 48, M1, married 16 years, TN/TN/TN, own
   income
___, Mary, wife, age 38, M1, married 16 years, 3/3, TN/TN/TN
___, Donald, son, age 15, TN/TN/TN
___, Thurman, son, age 10, TN/TN/TN
___, Wilbur, son, age 8, TN/TN/TN
STOKES, Kate, sister, age 36, widow, 2/2, TN/TN/TN
___, Clem, nephew, age 8, TN/TN/TN
STONE, Ernest, nephew, age 16, TN/TN/TN, farmer, general farm

167/175
RAY, Sarah, age 67, widow, 9/7, PA/PA/PA, none
___, Herman, son, age 41, single, PA/PA/PA, laborer, factory

168/176
HICKERSON, Tom H., head, age 42, M1, married 18 years, TN/TN/TN, none
___, Eunice, age 34, wife, M1, married 18 years, 5/5, TN/TN/TN, dress-
       maker, at home
___, Stella, age 16, TN/TN/TN, daughter
___, Adell, daughter, age 14, TN/TN/TN
___, Cleirton, son, age 17, TN/TN/TN, delivery boy, grocery store
___, Arthur, son, age 3, TN/TN/TN
___, Harry, son, age 8, TN/TN/TN

169/177
GRANDY, Belle, age 48, divorced, 1/1, PA/PA/PA, none
___, Ernest, son, age 22, single, TN/TN/PA, painter, railroad bridge

___/178
SHELTON, Mary R., age 47, widow, 0/0, TN/TN/TN, dressmaker at home

170/179
ESTERS, Dave, age 29, M1, married 8 years, TN/TN/TN, laborer, odd jobs.
___, Lida, wife, age 26, M1, married 8 years, 3/3, TN/TN/TN
___, Charlie H., son, age 6, TN/TN/TN
___, Horace, son, age 3, TN/TN/TN
___, Baxter, son, age 1, TN/TN/TN

171/180
CARROLL, Phines, age 38, M1, married 6 years, WASH/WASH/WASH/ proprietor livery barn
___, Edith, wife, age 28, M1, married 6 years, 2/2, ENG.ENGLISH/ENG.ENGLISH/ENG.ENGLISH
___, George, son, age 4, TEXAS/WASH/ENG
___, Hillary, son, age 1-10/12, TEXAS/WASH/ENG

172/181
ROAM, Charlie, porter, depot, wife Bettie; black household, not copied.

173/182
TAYLOR, Sarah, age 47, widow, 1/1, TN/TN/TN
BRAGG, Charlie, son, age 29, single, TN/TN/TN, painter, house.

174/182
SIMON, Fred, age 26, head, M1, married 5 years, NEB/NEB/NEB, proprietor, bottle works
___, Ethel, age 22, wife, M1, married 5 years, TN/TN/TN

___/184
SIMON, Melvin, head, age 24, M1, married 2 years, NEB/NEB/NEB, manager, bottle works
___, Donnie, wife, age 23, M1, married 2 years, 1/1, TN/TN/TN
___, Kenneth, son, age 1-3/12, TN/NEB/TN

175/185
LEMBKE, Rudolph, head, age 24, M1, married 2 years, GER.GERMAN/GER.GERMAN/GER.GERMAN, agent, lumber company
___, Hallie, wife, age 24, M1, married 2 years, 1/1, TN/TN/TN

176/186
HUGHS, Allison, head, age 40, M1, married 16 years, TN/TN/TN, commercial salesman, wholesale grocery
___, Lula, wife, age 37, M1, married 16 years, TN/TN/TN

177/187
ARNOLD, Holland, head, age 31, M1, married 6 years, TN/TN/TN, merchant, retrail dry goods
___, Annie, wife, age 21, M1, married 6 years, 1/1, TEXAS/MO/TEXAS
___, Truett, son, age 3, TEXAS/TN/TEXAS
___, Gertrude, sister, age 24, single, TN/TN/TN, saleswoman, dry goods store

178/188
MATHIS, James H., head, age 41, M1, married 15 years, TN/TN/TN, proprietor, drug store
___, Willie D., wife, age 35, M1, married 15 years, 6/5, TN/VA/TN
___, Walace, son, age 14, TN/TN/TN
___, Clay, son, age 12, TN/TN/TN
___, Elizabeth, daughter, age 9, TN/TN/TN
___, Jim D., son, age 7, TN/TN/TN
___, Will A., son, age 3, TN/TN/TN

179/189
TAYLOR, Aden A., head, age 26, M1, married 4 years, TN/TN/TN, no occup.
___, Bessie, age 23, wife, M1, married 4 years, 1/1, keeper, boarding house
___, Spicer, son, age 2, TN/TN/TN
RICHARDSON, Henry, boarder, age 48, single, TN/TN/NC, lawyer, general practice
TIDWELL, James, boarder, age 36, single, TN/TN/TN, laborer, odd jobs
continued on next page

DAVIS, Luther, boarder, age 34, M1, married 9 years, TN/TN/TN, engineer, ice plant
___, Tennessee, boarder, age 30, M1, married 9 years, 5/1, TN/TN/TN
___, John B., boarder, age 1, TN/TN/TN

180/190
HUDSON, Dennis, head, age 65, M2, married 46 years, TN/TN/TN, no occup.
___, Susan Be., wife, age 64, M1, married 46 years, 10/7, KY/KY/TN

181/191
HAYES, Jettie, female, head, age 32, single, TN/TN/TN, keeper, boarding house
HORD, Nettie, boarder, age 35, single, KY/KY/KY, teacher, music
HARRIS, Thomas, boarder, age 34, M1, married 11 years, KY/VA/TN, proprietor, retail dry goods
___, Ora, boarder, age 30, M1, married 11 years, 1/1, TN/TN/TN, saleswoman, dry goods store
___, Lillian, boarder, age 9, TN/KY/TN
BUFORD, Simeon, boarder, age 43, widowed, TEX/ALA/KY, agent, insurance company
___, Hattie, boarder, age 13, TEXAS/TEXAS/TN
GRAHAM, Ellen, servant, age 52, widow, 2/2, TN/TN/TN, servant, boarding house

182/192
SUTTON, Malinda, head, age 76, widow, TN/TN/TN, own income
MOIZE, Fennie, male, servant, age 30, single, TN/NC/NC, servant, private family
MOIZE, Julia, servant, age 25, single, TN/NC/NC, servant, private family

183/193
BUCKNER, William, head, age 23, M1, TEXAS/US/US, agent, medicine company
___, Clara, age 20, M1, 0/0, TN/TN/TN

184/194
TUCKER, James, head, age 42, M1, married 22 years, KY/TN/TN, proprietor restaurant
___, Mary, wife, age 37, M1, married 22 years, 8/3, TEX/TN/TEX
___, Pearl A., daughter, age 17, TN/KY/TEX
___, James C., son, age 13, TN/KY/TEX
___, Alton C., son, age 5, TN/KY/TEX

185/195
LARKINS, Asa, head, age 48, M1, married 17 years, TN/IRE.ENGLISH/TN
___, Carrie, wife, age 41, M2, married 17 years, 5/5, TN/TN/TN keeper, hotel
___, May, daughter, age 13, TN/TN/TN
___, Emmett, age 12, TN/TN/TN
___, Helen, daughter, age 11, TN/TN/TN
___, Baxter, son, age 8, TN/TN/TN
CONLEY, Iva, stepdaughter, age 19, single, TN/NY/TN
COOPER, Ashley, boarder, male, age 28, single, KY/KY/KY, mail clerk, train

186/196
EBERHART, Charles, head, age 40, M1, married 11 years; TN/GER.GERMAN/GER.GERMAN, proprietor, drug store
___, Parlena, wife, age 36, M1, married 11 years; TN/SWITZ.GERMAN/SWITZ. GERMAN; saleswoman, drug store
___, John J., son, age 10, TN/TN/TN
___, Gertrude, daughter, age 7, TN/TN/TN

___/197
CLEMENTS, Will, age 21, M1, TN/TN/TN, prescriptionist, drug store
___, Etta M., wife, age 18, M1, married 0 years, TN/TN/TN

187/198
MYATT, Albert, head, age 43, M1, married 23 years, TN/TN/TN, proprietor,
    drug store
___, Callie, wife, age 46, M1, married 23 years, 1/1, TN/TN/TN, sales-
    woman, drug store
___, Doy, daughter, age 20, single, TN/TN/TN

   (Note: The enumerator erred here as this was Mr. Myatt's second
    marriage.)

188/199
BLUE, Robert, brick mason; black household, not copied

189/200
WALKER, William, head, age 40, M1, married 17 years, TN/TN/TN, merchant,
    dry goods
___, Minnie, wife, age 39, M1, married 17 years, 1/1, TN/TN/TN
___Mary, daughter, age 11, TN/TN/TN

190/201
CUMMINS, John B., head, age 35, M1, married 12 years, TN/TN/TN, conduc-
    tor, train
___Amy, wife, age 30, M1, married 12 years, 4/3, TN/TN/TN
___, Louise, daughter, age 10, TN/TN/TN
___, Sam, son, age 8, TN/TN/TN
___, John, Jr., son, age 11/12, TN/TN/TN

191/202
NEWTON, Ben W., head, age 65, M1, married 28 years, NH/NH/NH, barber,
    own shop
___, Elizabeth, wife, age 60, M1, married 28 years, 0/0, ILL/PA/VERMONT

192/203
HENSLEY, Dora, head, age 52, widow, 3/2, TN/TN/TN, saleswoman, dry goods
___, Vallie, daughter, age 18, TN/TN/TN, stenographer, lumber company

193/204
WILKINSON, Claude, head, age 31, M1, married 7 years, TN/TN/TN, shipping
    clerk, wholesale house
___, Sammie, wife, age 25, M1, married 7 years, 1/1, TN/TN/TN
___, Viola, daughter, age 5, TN/TN/TN

194/205
PAGE, Dennis, head, age 28, M1, married 6 years, TN/TN/TN, police, city
___, Maggie, age 22, wife, M1, married 6 years, 3/3, TN/TN/TN
___, Eugene, son, age 4, TN/TN/TN
___, Lida, daughter, age 2, TN/TN/TN
___, Blanche, daughter, age 8/12, TN/TN/TN

195/206
GOSSETT, Sam B., head, age 55, M1, married 35 years, TN/TN/TN, carpenter,
    house
___, Fannie, wife, age 54, M1, married 35 years, TN/TN/TN
___, Alzo, son, age 27, widowed, TN/TN/TN, salesman, grocery store
___, Paul, grandson, age 6, TN/TN/TN

196/207
HOLLAND, Virgil, head, age 30, M1, married 6 years, TN/TN/TN, brakeman,
    train
___, Pearl, wife, age 28, M1, married 6 years, 0/0, TN/TN/TN

197/208
McELYEA, Tom, head, age 60, M1, married 32 years, TN/TN/TN, laborer,
    factory
___, Martha, wife, age 57, M1, married 32 years, TN/TN/TN
___, John, son, age 31, divorced, TN/TN/TN, barber, barber shop
___, Charlie, son, age 27, single, TN/TN/TN, carpenter, house
___, Lula, daughter, age 24, single, TN/TN/TN
WOOTEN, Hardie, boarder, age 35, single, TN/TN/TN, jewler, own shop
continued on next page

197/208, continued
OVERALL, Robert, boarder, age 30, widowed, TN/TN/TN, photographer, gallery
DUDLEY, Henry, boarder, age 22, single, TN/TN/TN, barber, barber shop

197/209
THOMAS, Jack, age 58, M2, mar. 23, TN/TN/TN, agent, insurance company
___, Kate, wife, age 53, M1, married 23 years, 0/0, TN/TN/TN

198/210
BROWN, Norman, age 27, M1, married 2 years, TN/TN/TN, bookkeeper, wholesale grocery
___, Georgenia, age 23, wife, M1, married 2 years, 2/1, ALA/IND/IND
___, Ala D., daughter, 3/12, TN/TN/ALA

199/211
SLAUGHTER, George W., head, age 56, M1, married 34 years, TN/TN/TN, carpenter, house
___, Missouri, wife, age 52, M1, married 34 years, 3/3, TN/TN/TN
___, Bert, son, age 22, single, TN/TN/TN, lineman, telephone company

200/212
HETHERINGTON, Joseph, head, age 49, M1, married 16 years, Eng.English/Eng.English/Eng.English, carpenter, railroad
___, Bonnie, wife, age 39, M1, married 16 years, 4/3, TN/TN/TN
___, Sarah W., daughter, age 15, TN/ENG/TN
___, Helen, daughter, age 11, TN/ENG/TN
___, George T., son, age 6, TN/ENG/TN

201/213
REED, John E., head, age 42, M1, married 21 years, TN/TN/TN, barber, own shop
___, Eula, wife, age 43, M1, married 21 years, 0/0, TN/TN/TN

202/214
HALLIBURTON, John, head, age 24, M1, married 2 years, TN/TN/TN, proprietor, livery barn
___, Bessie, wife, age 23, M1, married 2 years, 0/0, TN/TN/TN

203/215
DICKSON, Joe, head, age 24, M1, married 0 years, TN/TN/TN, manager, livery barn
___, Mable, wife, age 21, M1, married 0 years, 0/0, TN/TN/TN

204/216
PACK, Willard, head, age 31, M1, married 3 years, TN/TN/TN, blacksmith
___, Dollie, wife, age 25, M1, married 3 years, TN/TN/TN
___, Vivian, daughter, age 2, TN/TN/TN
DANIEL, Kate, sister-in-law, age 23, single, TN/TN/TN, teacher, school

205/217
WALTHOUR, Martha, age 74, widow, 1/1, PA/PA/PA
___, Hallie, granddaughter, age 25, single, TN/PA/TN, milliner, millinery store

206/218
McCALL, Lewis, head, age 26, M1, married 5 years, TN/TN/WISC, fireman, locomotive
___, Dell, wife, age 24, M1, married 5 years, 2/2, TN/TN/TN
___, Dorthy, daughter, age 3, TN/TN/TN
___, Marion, daughter, age 3/12, TN/TN/TN

207/219
GIBBS, James E., head, age 61, M2, married 24 years, IND/IND/IND, owner, stave mill
___, Cora, wife, age 41, M1, married 24 years, 8/7, IND/IND/IND
___, Hazel, age 21, daughter, single, IND/IND/IND
___, Carl, son, age 16, IND/IND/IND
___, Lee, son, age 14, TN/IND/IND
continued on next page

207/219, continued
___, Lena, daughter, age 14, TN/IND/IND
___, Val, son, age 11, TN/IND/IND
___, Lorena, daughter, age 8, TN/IND/IND

208/220
HOLLAND, Jesse, head, age 61, M1, married 3<u>1</u> years, TN/TN/TN, farmer, general farm
___, Nancy, age 59, wife, M1, married 3<u>9</u> years, TN/TN/TN

209/221
REDDEN, George, head, age 50, M1, married 27 years, TN/TN/TN, farmer, general farm
___, Amanda, wife, age 45, M1, married 27 years, 6/5, TN/NC/TN
___, Bertha, daughter, age 19, TN/TN/TN
___, Bessie, daughter, age 15, TN/TN/TN

210/222
ALLEN, Jack, head, age 81, M2, married 30 years, TN/VA/NC, own income
___, Pauline, wife, age 70, M2, married 30 years, 1/1, TN/VA/NC

211/223
PETWAY, Alex M., head, age 53, M1, married 30 years, TN/TN/NY, laborer, odd jobs
___, Nannie, wife, age 46, M1, married 30 years, 4/3, TN/TN/TN, dressmaker, at home
___, Ethel, daughter, age 24, single, TN/TN/TN, saleswoman, dry goods store
___, Lillie, daughter, age 21, single, TN/TN/TN
TALLEY, Albert, boarder, age 34, single, TN/TN/TN, operator, depot
ARMSTRONG, Morris, boarder, age 24, single, TN/TN/TN, operator, depot
KING, Bob, boarder, age 20, single, TN/TN/TN, farmer, own farm
FULMER, James E., boarder, age 22, single, TN/TN/TN
ROBERTS, James W., boarder, age 25, single, TN/TN/TN, commercial traveler, wholesale grocery

211/224
GILMORE, Tom L., head, age 28, M1, married 4 years, TN/TN/TN, brakeman, train
___, Emma, wife, age 23, M1, married 4 years, 2/2, TN/TN/TN
___, Ina, daughter, age 2, TN/TN/TN
___, Rollie, son, age 1, TN/TN/TN

212/225
GUPTON, Ed G., head, age 60, M1, married 30 years, TN/NC/TN, own farm, farmer
___, Nelie, wife, age 53, M1, married 30 years, 2/1, TN/TN/TN
WILLIAMS, Kane, black servant, age 17, single, TN/TN/TN

213/226
SAEGER, Henry, head, age 71, M1, married 48 years, PA/PA/PA, laborer, odd jobs
___, Margaret, wife, age 70, M1, married 48 years, 4/4, PA/PA/PA
___, Charlie, son, age 35, single, TN/PA/PA, carpenter, house
___, Susan, mother-in-law, age 94, widowed, PA/PA/PA

214/227
REEVES, Albert E., head, age 54, M2, married 6 years, TN/TN/TN, farmer, stock farm
___, Vandalia, wife age 47, M1, married 6 years, TN/TN/TN
___, Jessie P., son, age 18, single, TN/TN/TN, farmer, stock farm
___, Hugh, son, age 15, TN/TN/TN
HOBBS, Amanda, mother-in-law, age 73, widow, 2/1, TN/TN/NC
BIBB, Eliza, sister-in-law, age 70, single, TN/VA/NC

215/228
BROWN, Frank J., head, age 56, M2, married 28 years, TN/TN/TN, no occupation
___, Dockie, wife, age 52, M1, married 28 years, 5/4, TN/TN/TN
continued on next page

215/228, continued
____, Daimond, son, age 25, single, TN/TN/TN, laborer, telephone company
____, Homer, son, age 20, single, TN/TN/TN
____, Bunyan, son, age 15, TN/TN/TN

216/229
MARTIN, Robert J., head, age 43, M1, married 19 years, TN/TN/TN,
    laborer, lumber company
____, Maggie B., wife, age 37, M1, married 19 years, 8/6, TN/TN/TN
____, Hallo A., daughter, age 17, single, TN/TN/TN
____, Doy M., daughter, age 15, TN/TN/TN
____, Jessie May, daughter, age 12, TN/TN/TN
____, Maggie V., daughter, age 6, TN/TN/TN
____, Claude C., son, age 4, TN/TN/TN
____, Clyde D., son, age 7/12, TN/TN/TN

217/230
SCHMITTOU, Mattie, head, 83, widow, TN/TN/TN, own income

____/231
WADE, Charles W., head, age 43, M1, married 16 years, VA/VA/VA, farmer,
    own farm
____, Ora, wife, age 35, M1, married 16 years, 2/1, TN/TN/TN
____, Scott, son, age 13, TN/VA/TN

____/232
FIELDER, Cord W., head, age 34, single, TN/TN/TN, carpenter, house
____, Moody, brother, age 30, single, TN/TN/TN, watchman, mill
____, Hester, sister, age 28, divorced, TN/TN/TN
____, Leland, nephew, age 1-5/12, TN/TN/TN

218/233
DONEGAN, Scott W., head, age 62, single, TN/NC/VA, proprietor,
    restaurant
MARBLE, Edward, boarder, age 69, single, NY/NY/NY, waiter, restaurant
ADCOCK, Charles, boarder, age 17, single, TN/TN/TN, salesman, grocery
    store
BLUE, Cordelia, black servant, age 37, widow, 2/2, TN/TN/TN, cook,
    restaurant
____, Richard, black servant, age 14 single, TN/TN/TN, no occupation
____, Hershel, black servant, age 13, TN/TN/TN, no occupation
FRAHIER, Ed, boarder, age 41, single, TN/TN/TN, laborer, stave factory
CALL, Tobe, boarder, age 35, single, TN/OHIO/TN, plasterer, house
OWEN, Jessie, boarder, age 59, single, TN/TN/TN, laborer, stave factory
SPRINGER, Zollie, boarder, age 23, single, TN/TN/TN, merchant, grocery
    store

219/234
TURNER, Charlie M., head, age 55, M2, married 21 years, TN/SCOTLAND/
    SCOTLAND, assistant superintendent, NC&StL railroad
____, Minnie R., wife, age 45, M1, married 21 years, 2/1, TN/TN/TN
____, Carlton C., son, age 28, divorced, TN/TN/TN, engineer, locomotive
____, Charlie M., Jr., son, age 16, TN/TN/TN, no occupation
ROTH, Emma, servant, age 18, single, OHIO/SWITZ.GERMAN/SWITZ.GERMAN,
    servant, private family

220/235
WALL, Maggie, head, age 39, widow, 5/4, ARK/TN/TN, keeper, boarding house
____, Perry, son, age 19, single, TN/TN/ARK, bus driver, hotel
____, Ethel, age 13, daughter, TN/TN/ARK
____, Barnette, son, age 12, TN/TN/ARK
____, Henry, son, age 9, TN/TN/ARK
JONES, Pete, boarder, age 30, widowed, TN/TN/TN, operator, depot
____, Enlow, boarder, age 35, single, TN/TN/TN, operator, depot
WHITED, Rosco, boarder, age 22, single, TN/TN/TN, operator, depot
SWIFT, Tom, boarder, age 45, single, tN/TN/TN, agent, insurance company
BUTTREY, M., boarder, age 29, single, TN/TN/TN, policeman, railroad

221/236
CROWELL, Cephia (female), head, age 40, widow, 6/4, TN/TN/TN, keeps hotel
TURNABL, Orphant, daughter, 26 single, TN/TN/TN, labor, telephone co.
___, Willie, son, age 25, single, TN/TN/TN, butcher, meat shop
___, Highland, son, age 21, single, TN/TN/TN, no occupation
___, Bulah, daughter, age 15, TN/TN/TN

222/237
CHARLTON, Odell, head, age 43, M2, married 0 years, TN/TN/TN, carpenter, house
___, Lena, wife, age 19, M1, TN/TN/TN
___, James, son, age 12, TN/TN/TN
___, Hugh, son, age 9, TN/TN/TN
___, Elizabeth, daughter, age 3, TN/TN/TN

223/238
CLIFTON, Burl A., head, age 68, M1, married 43 years, TN/NC/NC, own income
___, Simtha, wife, age 69, M1, married 43 years, 4/4, KY/NC/NC

___/239
GOSSETT, Allen, head, age 40, M1, married 12 years, TN/TN/TN, laborer, railroad
___, Sallie, wife, age 32, M1, married 12 years, 3/2, TN/TN/TN
___, Lavonia, daughter, age 7, TN/TN/TN
___, Jewel, daughter, age 1-5/12, TN/TN/TN

224/240
CROSBY, Floyd W., head, age 59, M1, married 37 years, OHIO/OHIO/OHIO, manager, planing mill
___, Charlotte, wife, age 55, M1, married 37 years, 9/8, OHIO/OHIO/NY
___, Nellie, daughter, age 21 single, TN/OHIO/OHIO, teacher, private school
___, Fannie, daughter, age 19, single, TN/OHIO/OHIO, bookkeeper, planing mill
___, Bertha, daughter, age 17, TN/OHIO/OHIO
___, Howard, son, age 11, TN/OHIO/OHIO

225/241
BOX, Warren, head, age 61, M1, TN/TN/TN, black household
___, Julia, wife, 56, M1, 9/6, TN/TN/TN

226/242
CALHON, Mary, 64, widow, 5/2, MD/US/US, black household
___, Ella, daughter, 51, widow, 5/5, TN/TN/TN, laundress at home, black.

227/243
HILL, Harriett, black household, age 70, widow, 8/5, TN/TN/TN

228/244
GOSSETT, James P., head, age 39, M1, married 10 years, TN/TN/TN, carpenter, bridge
___, Eva, wife, age 30, M1, married 10 years, 2/2, TN/TN/TN
___Wendell, son, age 6, TN/TN/TN
___, Mary, daughter, age 2, TN/TN/TN

229/245
NEELY, Mina (female), head, age 43, widow, 4/4, TN/TN/UNKNOWN, own income
___, Bertha, daughter, age 21, divorced, 1/1, TN/TN/TN
___, Willtell (?), son, age 15, TN/TN/TN
___, Hugh, son, age 10, TN/TN/TN

RAILROAD STREET

230/246
RYAN, John, head, age 68, M1, married 35 years, IRE.ENGLISH/IRE. ENGLISH/ IRE.ENGLISH, cooper, cooperage
___, Jane, wife, age 58, M1, married 35 years, 1/0, OHIO/OHIO/OHIO
SHARP, Annie, friend, age 14, single, TN/TN/TN

___/___
TOMLINSON, Will A., age 50, M2, married 2 years, TN/TN/TN, retail
    merchant, dry goods
___, Ida, wife, age 38, M1, married 2 years, TN/VA/TN, saleswoman, dry
    goods store
___, Leon, son, age 13, TN/TN/TN
___, Lester, son, age 9, TN/TN/TN

231/247
HOGAN, Henry C., head, age 45, M1, married 20 years, TN/TN/TN,
    minister, Baptist
___, Minta D., wife, age 38, M1, married 20 years, 5/1, TN/TN/TN
___, Sophonia E., daughter, age 20, single, TN/TN/TN

232/248
COOK, James P., head, age 64, M2, married 13 years, TN/TN?TN, carpenter
    house
___, Callie, wife, age 45, M2, married 13 years, 8/6, TN/TN/TN
UNDERHILL, Reams, stepson, age 24, single, TN/TN/TN, brakeman, railroad
HINES, Grigsby, stepson, age 18, single, TN/TN/TN, driver, livery barn
___, Albert, stepson, age 13, TN/TN/TN
___, Gertrude, adopted, age 6, TN/TN/TN

233/249
McKINNON, Will H., head, age 40, M1, married 15 years, TN/NC/TN,
    house carpenter
___, Sallie, wife, age 39, M1, married 15 years, TN/TN/TN

234/250
BAKER, Susan, head, age 71, widow, 15/9, TN/TN/TN
___, Martha, daughter, age 40, single, TN/TN/TN
___, Mittie, daughter, age 30, single, TN/TN/TN
___, Cordelia, daughter, age 26, single, TN/TN/TN

235/251
HIETT, Jim, head, age 27, M1, married 3 years, TN/TN/TN, laborer,
    spoke factory
___, Anna B., wife, age 22, M1, married 3 years, 1/1, TN/TN/TN
___, Neta, daughter, age 1, TN/TN/TN

236/252
ADAMS, John H., head, age 74, M1, married 49 years, CN.ENGLISH/MAINE/
    CAN.ENGLISH, own income
___, Elizabeth A., wife, age 78, M1, married 49 years, TN/SC/GA

237/253
GORSE, Sarah, head, age 64, widow, NY/NY/NY, own income
BABCOCK, James, brother, age 67, widowed, NY/NY/NY

238/254
SELF, Dorsey T., head, age 50, M1, married 26 years, TN/TN/TN,
    proprietor, planing mill
___, Alice, wife, age 46, M1, married 26 years, 2/2, TN/VA/TN, none
___, Floyd, son, age 25, single, TN/TN/TN, none
___, Clyde, son, age 23, single, TN/TN/TN, bookkeeper, planing mill
___, Ophelia, mother, age 76, widow, TN/TN/TN

239/255
JACKSON, William L., head, age 45, M2, TN/TN/TN, minister, ME Church So.
___, Blanche, wife, age 39 single, married 1 year, 1/1, TN/TN/TN
___, Elizabeth S., daughter, age 4/12, TN/TN/TN
___, Thomas, adopted son, age 15, TN/TN/TN

240/256
BOONE, Almus, head, age 49, M1, married 25 years, TN/TN/TN, commercial
    traveler, wholesale grocery
___, Bettie, wife, age 47, M1, married 25 years, 5/5, ARK/TN/MISS
___, Alec, son, age 21, single, TN/TN/TN, salesman, dry goods store
___, Elsie, daughter, age 19, single, TN/TN/TN
continued on next page

240/256 continued
___, Baron, son, age 16, TN/TN/TN
___, Hortense, daughter, age 13, TN/TN/TN

241/257
ROBERTSON, William J., head, age 25, M1, married 1 year, TN/TN/TN,
    manager, telephone company
___, Pearl, wife, age 18, M1, married 1 year, 1/1, KY/KY/KY
___, Virgil L., son, age 9/12, TN/TN/KY

242/258
CLEMENT, James A., head, age 56, M2, married 10 years, TN/TN/TN, lawyer,
    general practice
___, Agnes A., wife, age 44, M2, married 10 years, TN/TN/TN
___, Newton, son, age 18, single, TN/TN/TN, operator, telephone company
___, Robert, son, age 9, TN/TN/TN
___, Archie, son, age 7, TN/TN/TN
___, Malcolm, son, age 6, TN/TN/TN
___, Ida A., daughter, age 3, TN/TN/TN
SHIPP, Dockie, step-daughter, age 16, TN/TN/TN

            WALNUT STREET BEGINS ABOUT HERE
(No separate mark made to show where street began.)

243/259
MORROW, Ed, head, age 36, M1, married 9 years, TN/TN/TN, salesman, dry
    goods store
___, Maggie, wife, age 30, married 9 years, 1/1, TN/TN/TN
___, Mareret, daughter, age 6, TN/TN/TN
DAVIS, Mary, mother-in-law, age 55, widow, 5/4, TN/TN/TN

244/260
TWOMEY, Robert M., head, age 34, M1, married 10 years, TN/TN/TN,
    blacksmith, blacksmith shop
___, Georgie, wife, age 33, M1, married 10 years, 2/2, TN/TN/TN
___, Mildred J., daughter, age 9, TN/TN/TN
___, Robert, Jr., son, age 5, TN/TN/TN

245/261
JONES, George, head, age 49, M1, married 18 years, TN/TN/TN, manager,
    wholesale groceries
___, Lucy Lee C., wife, age 48, M1, married 18 years, 5/3, TN/TN/IND
___, Georgia L., daughter, age 16, single, TN/TN/TN
___, Esther, daughter, age 12, TN/TN/TN
___, Erich C., son, age 13, TN/TN/TN

246/262
CLEMENS, Robert, 41, head, M1, married 5 years, VA/VA/VA, merchant,
    wholesale grocer
___, Maggie, wife, age 40, M1, married 5 years, 1/0, TN/PA/TN
BIVENS, Mary, mother-in-law, age 60, widow, 6/6, TN/TN/NY

247/263
PAYNE, Eugene, head, age 32, M1, married 7 years, TN/TN/TN, fireman,
    locomotive
___, Maud, wife, age 26, M1, married 7 years, 2/2, TN/TN/TN
___, Sarah, daughter, age 5, TN/TN/TN
___, Virginia, daughter, age 6/12, TN/TN/TN
HOOPER, Claud, brother-in-law, age 30, M1, TN/VA/TN, engineer, locomotive
___, Kate, sister-in-law, age 26, M1, TN/TN/TN

248/264
THOMAS, George, head, age 61, M1, married 26 years, IND/TN/TN, mail
    clerk, train
___, Pauline, wife, age 45, M1, married 26 years, 8/6, TN/TN/TN
___, Bert, son, age 19, single, TN/IND/TN
___, Emma, daughter, age 17, TN/IND/TN
___, Kate, daughter, age 13, TN/IND/TN
___, Pauline, daughter, age 10, TN/IND/TN
___, Carrie L., daughter, age 6, TN/IND/TN

249/265
CROW, Burnie H., head, age 33, M1, married 6 years, TN/TN/TN, manager,
    lumber company
____, Gertrude, wife, M1, age 32, married 6 years, 2/2, TN/TN/TN
____, Russell, son, age 5, TN/TN/TN
____, Louise, daughter, age 3, TN/TN/TN

250/266
JOSLIN, Dan, head, age 53, M2, married 17 years, TN/TN/TN, supervisor,
    railroad bridge crew
____, Texie, wife, age 35, M1, married 17 years, 5/3, TN/TN/TN
____, Otto, son, age 20, single, TN/TN/TN
____, Charlie, son, age 15, TN/TN/TN
____, Eula, daughter, age 10, TN/TN/TN
____, J. R., son, age 9, TN/TN/TN
____, Joe, nephew, age 2, TN/TN/TN

251/267
KELLOW, Dick, head, age 32, M1, married 3 years, TEX/TEX/TEX, commercial
    traveler, hardware
____, Jessie, wife, age 21, M1, married 3 years, 1/1, TN/KY/TN
____, Blanche, daughter, age 1-10/12, TN/TEX/TN

252/268
HOLLAND, Melvin, head, age 29, M1, married 3 years, nN/TN/TN, laborer,
    lumber company
____, Eva, wife, age 23, M1, married 3 years, 2/1, TN/TN/TN
____, Jessie A., daughter, age 6/12, TN/TN/TN

253/269
PETTY, Tom, head, age 32, M1, married 9 years, TN/TN/TN, power house
____, Lula, wife, age 28 M1, married 9 years, 3/3, TN/TN/TN
____, Myrtle, daughter, age 8, TN/TN/TN
____, Pauline, daughter, TN/TN/TN
____, Carlton, son, age 3, TN/TN/TN

253/270
WELCH, Martin, head, age 52, M2, married 31 years, KY/KY/KY, laborer,
    odd jobs
____, Susan, wife, age 60, M1, 4/2, TN/TN/TN
____, Marvin, son, age 23, single, TN/TN/TN, brakeman, train

254/271
APPLEGATE, Maggie, age 78, widow, TN/NC/VA, own income

____/272
DANIEL, Elijah, head, age 41, M2, married 8 years, TN/NC/TN, manager,
    wholesale grocery
____, Agnes, wife, age 33, M1, married 8 years, 3/2, TN/TN/TN
____, William, son, age 4, TN/TN/TN
____, Howard, son, age 2, TN/TN/TN
PHILIPS, Emma, servant, age 20, single, TN/TN/TN, servant, private
    family

255/273
SLAYDEN, George, head, age 42, M1, married 14 years, TN/TN/TN, dentist,
    own office
____, Yula, wife, age 36, M1, married 14 years, 1/1, MISS/MISS/ALA
____, Emma May, daughter, age 14, TN/TN/MISS

256/274
HOOPER, John W., head, age 42, M2, married 5 years, TN/TN/TN, foreman,
    railroad bridge
____, Sallie, wife, M1, married 5 years, 3/2, TN/TN/TN
____, Freddie L., daughter, age 15, TN/TN/TN
____, Paul, son, age 13, TN/TN/TN
____, Ruth, daughter, age 9, TN/TN/TN
____, Irma, daughter, age 4, TN/TN/TN
____, John, son, age 1-9/12, TN/TN/TN

257/275
MILLER, Jim P., black household, minister, AME

258/276
MOORE, Charity, black household

___/277
OAKLEY, Tom, black household

259/278
LEATHERMAN, William, black household

260/279
PERKINS, Maggie, black household

261/280
McALLISTER, Joe E., head, age 37, M1, married 17 years, TN/TN/TN, fireman, locomotive
___, Susie, wife, age 34, married 17 years, TN/TN/TN   7/7
___, Eula M., daughter, age 15, TN/TN/TN
___, John M., son, age 14, TN/TN/TN
___, James, son, age 12, TN/TN/TN
___, Joe, son, age 9, TN/TN/TN
___, Annie L., daughter, age 7, TN/TN/TN
___, Nettie C., daughter, age 3, TN/TN/TN
___, Eugene, son, age 7/12, TN/TN/TN

262/281
MYRES, Fidellar, head, age 40, M1, married 20 years, KY/KY/KY, manager, ice plant
___, Bettie, wife, age 36, M1, married 20 years, 1/1, KY/KY/KY
___, Frank, son, age 12, TN/TN/KY

263/282
BATES, Steve, head, age 40, M1, married 21 years, TN/TN/TN, fireman, locomotive
___, Sarah, wife, age 39, M1, married 21 years, 9/7, TN/TN/TN
___, Amy, daughter, 17, TN/TN/TN
___, Albert, son, age 16, TN/TN/TN
___, Wallace H., age 12, son, TN/TN/TN
___, Linnie, daughter, age 8, TN/TN/TN
___, Stephen G., son, age 6, TN/TN/TN
___, Carlton C., son, age 4, TN/TN/TN
___, Bessie L., daughter, age 2, TN/TN/TN

264/283
BADGE, Charlie, head, age 39, M1, married 16 years, PA/GER. GERMAN/ GER. GERMAN, engineer, locomotive
___, Margret E., wife, age 39, M1, married 16 years, 1/1, TN/TN/TN
___, Edith, daughter, age 15, TN/PA/TN

265/284
WILLIAMS, Aretas B., head, age 73, M1, married 53 years, TN/TN/TN own income
___, Mary M., wife, age 72, M1, married 53 years, 9/t, TN/TN/TN

266/285
SMITH, Thomas J., head, age 50, M1, married 25 years, TN/TN/TN, laborer, standard oil
___, Elnora, wife, age 50, M1, married 25 years, 3/3, TN/TN/TN
___, Grace, daughter, age 20, single, TN/TN/TN
___, Vera, daughter, age 17, single, TN/TN/TN

267/286
BRYANT, Jim, head, age 38, M1, married 16 years, TN/TN/TN, engineer, locomotive
___, Park, wife, age 32, M1, married 16 years, 3/3, TN/TN/TN
___, Glen B., son, age 14, TN/TN/TN
___, Mamie, daughter, age 12, TN/TN/TN
___, Jim, son, age 6, TN/TN/TN

268/287
HARGROVE, Bob, head, age 32, M1, married 13 years, TN/TN/TN, fireman,
    locomotive
____, Tishie, wife, age 30, M1, married 13 years, 4/3, TN/TN/TN
____, Clarence, son, age 12, TN/TN/TN
____, Curl, son, age 8, TN/TN/TN
____, Bertha, daughter, age 6, TN/TN/TN

269/288
BRADLEY, Isham B., head, age 42, M1, married 12 years, TN/TN/TN,
    minister, Christian church
____, Minnie Y., wife, age 36, M1, married 12 years, TN/ALA/ALA

270/289
DOZIER, Albert G., head, age 69, M1, married 38 years, TN/TN/TN,
    own income
____, Elizabeth R., wife, age 63, M1, married 38 years, 2/0, TN/TN/TN

271/290
SYLVIS, King, head, age 39, M2, married 12 years, TN/PA/PA, conductor,
    train
____, Naomi, wife, age 33, M1, married 12 years, 3/3, TN/TN/TN
____, Cecil, son, age 15, TN/TN/TN
____, Ella M., daughter, age 11, TN/TN/TN
____, Kathaline, daughter, age 8, TN/TN/TN
____, Beaulah, daughter, age 6, TN/TN/TN

272/291
FOREHAND, Mattie B., head, age 43, widow, 5/5, TN/GER.GERMAN/NC
____, Henry C., son, age 19, single, TN/TN/TN, brakeman, train
____, Mattie T., daughter, age 17, TN/TN/TN
____, John W., son, age 14, TN/TN/TN
____, Emma P., daughter, age 10, TN/TN/TN

273/292
BLACK, Jim, head, age 30, M1, married 6 years, TN/SCOT/SCOT, foreman,
    round house
____, Katie C., wife, age 29, M1, married 6 years, 2/1, TN/TN/TN
____, James R. (or K.), son, age 4, TN/TN/TN
RYAN, Tom, boarder, age 36, single, TN/IRE.IRISH/IRE.IRISH, engineer,
    locomotive

BRYANT HEIGHTS

274/293
GATEWOOD, Emma, head, age 61, widow, 5/3, VA/VA/VA
____, Annie, daughter, age 45, single, VA/VA/VA
PETTY, Dallas, son-in-law, age 58, M1, married 15 years, TN/TN/TN, none
____, Blanche, daughter, age 41, M2, married 15 years, 1/1, MO/VA/VA
    dressmaker at store
LARKINS, Maggie, sister, age 68, widow, VA/VA/VA, dressmaker, at store

275/294
LYAL, Edward, head, age 42, M2, married 11 years, TN/TN/TN, engineer,
    locomotive
____, Rosa, wife, age 33, M1, married 11 years, 0/0, TN/TN/TN
____, Addie, daughter, age 22, single, TN/TN/TN
____, Eva, daughter, age 19, single, TN/TN/TN
____, Annie, daughter, age 18, single, TN/TN/TN
____, Beatric, daughter, age 15, TN/TN/TN

276/295
DUNN, John W., head, age 34, M1, married 12 years, TN/TN/TN, overseer,
    oil house
____, Tennie, wife, age 35, M1, married 12 years, 1/1, TN/TN/TN
____, Sarah E., daughter, age 2/12, TN/TN/TN

277/296
BARNETT, Will A., head, age 37, M1, married 15 years, IND/IND/IND,
    retail merchant, clothing store
continued on next page

277/296 continued
BARNETT, Mattie, wife, age 36, M1, married 15 years, 4/4, TN/TN/OHIO
____, Anna B., daughter, age 13, TN/IND/TN
____, Mary, daughter, age 11, TN/IND/TN
____, Lorain, daughter, age 7, TN/IND/TN
____, Will, son, age 6, TN/IND/TN

SOUTH RAILROAD STREET

278/297
ROEDER, Mary, head, age 50, widow, 7/7, TN/TN/TN
____, Lela, daughter, age 19, single, TN/GER.GERMAN/TN
____, Nannie, daughter, age 18, single, TN/GER.GERMAN/TN
____, Cleve, son, age 16, TN/GER.GERMAN/TN
GALLOWAY, Dorsey J., son, age 29, single, TN/PA/TN, labor, factory
____, Will J., son, age 28, single, TN/PA/TN, labor, factory
____, Beaulah, daughter, age 26, single, TN/PA/TN, none
____, George, son, age 23, TN/PA/TN, laborer, factory

279/298
HOOVER, Wrott, head, age 28, M1, married 8 years, TN/TN/TN, flagman, train
____, Mary, wife, age 23, M1, married 8 years, 3/3, TN/TN/TN
____, Wina, daughter, age 6, TN/TN/TN
____, Annie, daughter, age 4, TN/TN/TN
____, Thomas E., son, age 10/12, TN/TN/TN

280/299
DUNN, Jake, head, age 34, married 9 years, M1, TN/TN/TN, conductor, locomotive
____, Sallie, wife, age 29, M1, married 9 years, 1/1, TN/TN/TN
____, Frank, son, age 5, TN/TN/TN

281/300
HATCHER, Alfred, head, age 33, M1, married 11 years, TN/TN/TN, laborer, factory
____, Emma, wife, age 32, M1, married 11 years, 5/5, TN/TN/TN
____, Thruston, son, age 11, TN/TN/TN
____, Earl, age 10, TN/TN/TN
____, Leslie, son, age 6, TN/TN/TN
____, Evonne, daughter, age 4, TN/TN/TN

282/301
REGISTER, John T., head, age 40, M1, married 19 years, TN/TN/TN, rural carrier, US mail
____, Mary E., wife, age 35, M1, married 19 years, 6/6, TN/TN/TN
____, Eunice, daughter, age 17, TN/TN/TN
____, Vester, daughter, age 16, TN/TN/TN
____, Vera, daughter, age 14, TN/TN/TN
____, Herbert, son, age 11, TN/TN/TN
____, Hubert, son, age 8, TN/TN/TN
____, John P., son, age 4, TN/TN/TN

283/302
HARRISON, Edward L., head, age 50, M1, married 25 years, TN/TN/TN, manager, lumber company
____, Mary E., wife, age 44, M1, married 25 years, 9/8, TN/TN/TN
____, Herman, son, age 23, single, TN/TN/TN, inspector, lumber company
____, Audrey, daughter, age 17, TN/TN/TN
____, Tommie, daughter, age 14, TN/TN/TN
____, Eva, daughter, age 10, TN/TN/TN
____, Mary, daughter, age 8, TN/TN/TN
____, Hinkle, son, age 7/12, TN/TN/TN

WADE AVENUE

284/303
EASLEY, Robert, head, age 48, M1, married 25 years, TN/TN/TN, supervisor, railroad

284/303, continued
EASLEY, Mellie, wife, age 47, M1, married 25 years, 8/8, PA/PA/VA
___, Tennie M., daughter, age 22, single, TN/TN/PA
___, Jack, son, age 20, single, TN/TN/PA
___, Ethel, daughter, age 18, single, TN/TN/PA, milliner, millinery store
___, Alma, daughter, age 16, TN/TN/PA
___, Suva, daughter, age 10, TN/TN/PA
___, Kathleen, daughter, age 9, TN/TN/PA
___, Maud L., daughter, age 8, TN/TN/PA
___, Turner, son, age 2, TN/TN/PA

285/304
RUSSELL, Frank, head, age 34, M1, married 11 years, TN/TN/TN, labor, factory
___, Eron, wife, age 34, M1, married 11 years, 0/0, TN/TN/TN

286/305
WOOD, Earnest, head, age 35, M1, married 16 years, TN/TN/TN, fireman, (or foreman?), planing mill
___, Maggie, age 25, M1, married 16 years, 1/0, TN/TN/TN
MAKEWALL, Mac, boarder, age 19, single, TN/TN/TN, laborer, planing mill
HUTTON, Dill, boarder, age 20, single, TN/TN/TN, laborer, planing mill
INAIL, Tom, boarder, age 42, widowed, TN/ENG.ENGLISH/TN, timber grader, spoke factory

287/306
CLARKE, Roy M., head, age 26, M1, married 6 years, TN/TN/TN, fireman, locomotive
___, Gertrude, wife, age 23, M1, married 6 years, 0/0, TN/TN/TN

288/307
DONEGAN, Lizzie, head, age 36, widow, 4/3, PA/GER.GERMAN/GER.GERMAN, own income
___, Lura, daughter, age 12, TN/TN/PA
___, Mary, daughter, age 10, TN/TN/PA
___, Robert L., son, age 6, TN/TN/PA
___, George, stepson, age 20, single, TN/TN/TN, stenographer, railroad office.

HIGH STREET

289/308
FREEMAN, Ellis, head, age 26, M1, married 4 years, TN/PA/PA, laborer, factory
___, Willie, wife, age 23, M1, married 4 years, 2/2, TN/TN/TN
___, Beulah, daughter, age 2, TN/TN/TN
___, Otto, son, age 4/12, TN/TN/TN

290/309
MYATT, Andrew, head, age 48, M2, married 4 years, TN/TN/TN, sawyer, factory
___, Kate A., wife, M1, married 4 years, 1/1, TN/TN/TN

291/310
CRAFT, Jim, head, age 40, M1, married 11 years, TN/TN/TN, laborer, stave factory
___, Annie, wife, age 39, M1, married 11 years, 0/0, TN/TN/TN
___, Frank, adopted child, age 5, TN/TN/TN

292/311
ASKINS, Mary T., head, age 57, widow, 3/1, TN/TN/TN, own income
SANDERS, Ruth, granddaughter, age 16, TN/TN/TN
___, Mary, granddaughter, age 9, TN/TN/TN

___/312
HAYSE, Haywood, head, age 40, M1, married 16 years, KY/VA/VA, laborer, stave factory
___, Annie, wife, age 33, M1, married 16 years, 0/0, KY/TN/NC

293/313
CAMEL, Mary A., head, age 48, widow, 8/2, OHIO/IRE/PA
___, Ralph, son, age 13, ARK/IND/OHIO
THOMPSON, Lee, son, age 23, single, KY/TN/OHIO, laborer, factory

294/314
SWANK, David L., head, age 46, M1, married 3 years, IND/OHIO/PA, teacher, music
___, Eddie, wife, age 37, M1, married 3 years, 0/0, TN/TN/TN

295/315
CREWS, Andrew J., age 46, M1, married 12 years, TN/TN/TN, carpenter, railroad bridge
___, Chacey, wife, age 26, M1, married 12 years, 5/3, TN/TN/TN
___, Mary A., daughter, age 9, TN/TN/TN
___, Dan, age 7, son, TN/TN/TN
___, Malcome, son, age 8/12, TN/TN/TN
JOSLIN, Martha, friend, age 82, widow, TN/TN/TN
PEELER, Rube, brother-in-law, age 23, single, TN/TN/TN, carpenter, railroad bridge

296/316
BATTS, William J., head, age 53, M2, married 13 years, TN/TN/TN, buyer, lumber company
___, Lizzie, wife, age 44, M2, married 13 years, 5/5, VA/VA/VA
___, Mary, daughter, age 12, TN/TN/VA
___, Lizzie, daughter, age 12, TN/TN/VA
___, Jack, son, age 6, TN/TN/VA
___, W. J., son, age 3, TN/TN/VA
HENSLEE, Edward, step-son, age 17, TN/KY/VA
BATTS, Robert, brother, age 64, single, TN/TN/TN, tobacco buyer, tobacco firm
BROWN, Martha J., mother-in-law, age 64, widow, VA/VA/VA

297/317
STEWART, Bettie U., 62, widow, 1/1, TN/TN/TN, own income

298/318
SHELTON, Major, head, age 35, M1, married 8 years, TN/TN/TN, laborer, stave factory
___, Emma, wife, age 34, M1, married 8 years, 4/4, TN/TN/PA
___, Winnie, daughter, age 7, TN/TN/TN
___, Nina M., daughter, age 5, TN/TN/TN
___, Jerome, son, age 3, TN/TN/TN
___, Oval, daughter, age 1, TN/TN/TN

299/319
REYNOLDS, Nannie, head, age 57, widow, 9/4, TN/VA/TN
___, Rosa, daughter, age 31, single, TN/IRE/TN, stenographer, railroad office
___, Ida, daughter, age 28, single, TN/IRE/TN, teacher, college
SMITH, Jeff D., brother, age 47, single, TN/TN/TN, laborer, bridge crew

300/320
JETT, Dan, head, age 47, M1, married 17 years, TN/TN/TN, engineer, mill
___, Alice, wife, age 39, M1, married 17 years, 5/4, TN/TN/TN
___, Mary E., daughter, age 16, TN/TN/TN
___, Paschel R., son, age 14, TN/TN/TN
___, Walter B., son, age 12, TN/TN/TN
___, Lesbie, daughter, age 4, TN/TN/TN

301/321
SHAWL, Levi, head, age 66, M2, married 23 years, OA/PA/PA, rural carrier US mail
___, Kate, 45, wife, M1, married 23 years, 7/7, PA/PA/PA
___, Andy, son, age 25, single, TN/PA/PA, blacksmith, blacksmith shop
___, Marie, daughter, age 22, single, TN/PA/PA
___, LeRoy, son, age 20, single, TN/PA/PA
___, Joe, son, age 18, single, TN/PA/PA, laborer, standard factory
continued on next page

301/321 continued
SHAWL, Dudey, son, age 15, TN/PA/PA
___, Lorena, daughter, age 11, TN/PA/PA
___, Wilma, daughter, age 8, TN/PA/PA
___, Elda, daughter, age 6, TN/PA/PA
___, Edgar, grandson, age 4, TN/TN/TN
STITT, Margret, mother-in-law, age 80, widow, PA/PA/PA

302/322
STROUD, Anson W., head, age 49, M1, married 23 years, TN/TN/TN,
    carpenter, house
___, Annie, wife, age 40, M1, married 23 years, 4/4, TN/TN/TN
___, Claude E., son, age 20, single, TN/TN/TN, teacher, school
___, Thomas B., son, age 18, single, TN/TN/TN, carpenter, house
___, Mable B., daughter, age 15, TN/TN/TN
___, Hobert N., son, age 10, TN/TN/TN

303/323
HOOPER, Paten, head, age 56, M2, married 3 years, TN/TN/TN, pump man,
    Standard Oil company
___, Etta, wife, age 32, M2, married 3 years, 3/3, TN/TN/TN
___, Maggie, daughter, age 19, single, TN/TN/TN
___, Floyd, son, age 10, TN/TN/TN
___, Aileene, daughter, age 1-11/12, TN/TN/TN
MYATT, Hattie, step-daughter, age 11, TN/TN/TN
___, Elbert, step-son, age 7, TN/TN/TN

304/324
WYNN, George, head, age 55, widowed, TN/TN/TN, merchant, retail grocery
___, Harry, son, age 24, single, TN/TN/TN
___, Lucy, daughter, age 18, single, TN/TN/TN
BOBBITT, Mattie, servant, age 52, single, TN/TN/TN, servant, private
    family

305/325
WILLIAM, Henry N., head, age 31, M1, married 4 years, TN/TN/TN, cashier
    stave factory
___, Cora, wife, age 30, M1, married 4 years, 0/0, TN/TN/TN

306/326
BAKER, John R., head, age 54, M1, married 22 years, TN/TN/TN, own
    income
___, Arminta, wife, age 43, M1, married 22 years, 3/2, TN/TN/TN
___, Ella L., daughter, age 19, TN/TN/TN
___, Hollie L., daughter, age 15, TN/TN/TN

307/327
PETTY, Oscar, head, age 26, M1, married 2 years, TN/TN/TN, laborer,
    spoke mill
___, Ethel, wife, age 19, M1, married 2 years, 1/1, TN/TN/TN
___, Eugene, son, age 1-3/12, TN/TN/TN

308/328
STEWART, Curtis L., head, age 53, M1, married 34 years, TN/TN/TN,
    trader, stock
___, Mollie, wife, age 51, M1, married 34 years, 4/4, TN/TN/TN
___, Lela, daughter, age 15, TN/TN/TN

309/329
WEAVER, Frank, head, age 41, M1, married 18 years, KY/VA/VA, night
    watchman, railroad
___, Kansas, wife, age 41, M1, married 18 years, 0/0, TN/TN/TN

310/330
BRUCE, Laura, head, age 46, widow, 4/2, TN/TN/TN, at home, laundress
___, Ercell, daughter, age 15, TN/TN/TN
___, Lettie, daughter, age 13, TN/TN/TN

SCOTT AVENUE

311/321
DULL, Maggie, head, age 47, widow, 4/4, PA/PA/PA, own income
____, Elsie, daughter, age 26, single, TN/PA/PA, millinery, millinery store
____, Willie, daughter, age 23, single, TN/PA/PA
____, Addie, daughter, age 18, single, TN/PA/PA
____, Gloyd, daughter, age 16, TN/PA/PA

312/332
ESTES, Earnest, head, age 36, M1, married 12 years, TN/TN/TN, commercial traveler, wholesale
____, Mary, wife, age 31, M1, married 12 years, 0/0, TN/TN/TN

313/333
MELTON, Robert E., head, age 51, M2, married 27 years, TN/ILL/TN, carpenter, house
____, Lucy E., age 28, M1, married 27 years, 5/4, TN/ILL/TN
____, Everett, son, age 22, single, TN/ILL/TN, laborer, factory
____, Nellie J., daughter, age 17, TN/ILL/TN
____, Mary J., daughter, age 13, TN/ILL/TN
____, Emmett, son, age 7, TN/ILL/TN
____, Lucy, daughter, age 5, TN/ILL/TN
____, Gracy D., daughter, age 2, TN/ILL/TN
____, Lorene, daughter, age 1, TN/ILL/TN

314/334
CRAIG, Claude, head, age 29, M1, married 11 years, TN/TN/TN, farmer, own farm
____, Eula, wife, age 30, M1, married 11 years, 4/3, TN/TN/TN
____, Nettie, daughter, age 11, TN/TN/TN
____, Claudie, son, age 6, TN/TN/TN
____, Elma, son, age 4, TN/TN/TN

315/335
SEXTON, Monroe, head, age 52, M1, married 20 years, TN/TN/TN, culler, stave mill
____, Lula, wife, age 37, M1, married 20 years, 2/2, TN/KY/KY
____, Homer, son, age 20, single, TN/TN/TN, laborer
____, Herman, son, age 17, TN/TN/TN

316/336
BOONE, Bratten, head, age 45, M2, married 10 years, TN/TN/TN, laborer, stave mill
____, Mary, wife, age 43, M1, married 10 years, 4/3, TN/TN/TN
____, Lundy, son, age 20, single, TN/TN/TN, laborer, stave mill
____, Doyle, son, age 18, TN/TN/TN, laborer, stave mill
____, Authur, son, age 13, TN/TN/TN
____, Willie, son, age 9, TN/TN/TN
____, Cecil, son, age 7, TN/TN/TN
____, Hattie M., daughter, age 2, TN/TN/TN

317/337
HOOPER, James, head; age 24, M1, married 5 years, TN/TN/TN, sawyer, stave mill
____, Julia, wife, age 24, M1, married 5 years, 2/2, TN/PA/TN
____, Ernest, son, age 4, TN/TN/TN
____, Donald, age 1, son, TN/TN/TN

318/338
SUMMERS, Jim B., head, age 35, M1, married 11 years, TN/TN/TN, farmer, general farm
____, Etta, wife, age 29, M1, married 11 years, 6/5, TN/TN/TN
____, Lillie, daughter, age 10, TN/TN/TN
____, Marshal, son, age 7, TN/TN/TN
____, Roy, son, age 5, TN/TN/TN
____, Jessie, daughter, age 3, TN/TN/TN
____, Hershal, son, age 10/12, TN/TN/TN

319/339
ALLEN, Mollie, head, age 38, widow, TN/TN/TN
____, Willie F., son, age 20, single, TN/TN/TN, painter, house

320/340
PENTECOST, Gabriel, head, age 43, M1, married 14 years, TN/VA/TN,
    merchant, dry goods
____, Emma, wife, age 35, M1, married 14 years, 1/1, OHIO/OHIO/OHIO
____, Mable, daughter, age 13, TN/TN/OHIO

BROAD STREET

321/341
JETT, James, head, age 49, M1, married 22 years, TN/TN/TN, foreman,
    stave mill
____, Mollie, wife, age 45, M1, married 22 years, 5/3, TN/TN/TN
____, Lawrence, son, age 18, single, TN/TN/TN
____, Lela, daughter, age 9, TN/TN/TN
____, Morris, son, age 6, TN/TN/TN

322/342
DAVIDSON, George, head, age 36, M1, married 9 years, TN/TN/TN, agent,
    insurance
____, Launa, wife, age 30, M2, married 9 years, 0/0, TN/TN/TN

323/343
SORENSON, Andrew, head, age 50, M1, married 21 years, DEN/DANISH/DEN.
    DANISH/DEN. DANISH, foreman, stave mill
____, Matilda, wife, agre 43, M1, married 21 years, 6/5, DEN.DANISH/
    DEN.DANISH/DEN.DANISH
____, Maren, daughter, age 19, TN/DEN/DEN
____, Sophia, daughter, age 18, TN/DEN/DEN
____, Anna, daughter, age 11, TN/DEN/DEN
____, Stella, daughter, age 8, TN/DEN/DEN
____, Arthur, son, age 3, TN/DEN/DEN

324/344
DAVIS, Will, head, age 52, M1, PA/PA/PA, undertaker, own shop
____, Etta, wife, age 50, M1, SC/TN/TN
____, Bessie, daughter, age 22, single, TN/PA/SC
(Note: No additional information on marriage years given in this entry.)

325/345
HUDSON, Newt, head, age 30, M2, married 4 years, TN/TN/TN, driver,
    livery barn
____, Jennie, wife, age 32, M1, married 4 years, 2/1, TN/TN/TN
____, Reba, daughter, age 5/12, nN/TN/TN

MULBERRY STREET

326/346
SHAWL, George, head, age 35, M1, married 7 years, PA/PA/PA, blacksmith,
    own shop
____, Hattie, wife, age 21, married 7 years, 2/2, TN/NEB/NEB
____, Leola, daughter, age 6, TN/PA/TN
____, Emma, daughter, age 3, TN/PA/TN

327/347
BROWN, Walter, head, age 21, M1, married 1 year, TN/TN/TN, merchant,
    retail shoe store
____, Nora, wife, age 19, M1, married 1 year, 0/0, TN/TN/TN

328/348
HENSON, Maggie, head, age 30, single, TN/TN/TN, no occupation

329/349
TIDWELL, Martha, head, age 54, widow, 10/3, TN/TN/TN, keeper, boarding
    house
____, Stella, granddaughter, age 15, TN/TN/TN
continued on next page

329/349 continued
DONALDSON, Meda, daughter, age 18, divorced, 1/1, TN/TN/TN
___, Annie L., granddaughter, age 2, TN/TN/TN

330/350
MORGAN, Thomas, physician, blackhousehold

331/351
LEATHERMAN, Pink, black household

332/352
WILLIAMS, Tom, black household

333/353
TURNER, Emett, black household

334/354
RAMEY, Van, black household

335/355
LENEERE, Lizzie, black household

336/356
VANZANT, Francis, black household

337/357
PORTER, Joe, black household

338/358
MANNING, Marion, black household

339/359
BELL, Liza, black household

340/361
HARDIN, Hugh, black household

342/362
MASON, Ben, black household

343/363
HOLT, Grigsby, black household

344/364
COX, Will, head, age 40, M1, married 13 years, TN/TN/TN, overseer,
    bridge crew
___, Mattie, wife, age 33, M1, married 13 years, 4/4, TN/TN/TN
___, Ottis, daughter, age 12, TN/TN/TN
___, Roy, son, age 10, TN/TN/TN
___, Dave, son, age 7, TN/TN/TN
___, Alfred, son, age 5, TN/TN/TN
TALLEY, Dave, father-in-law, age 67, M1, married 48 years, TN/TN/TN,
    carpenter, house
___, Ellen, mother-in-law, age 59, M1, married 48 years, 10/6, TN/TN/TN

345/365
MARTIN, Holt, black household

CENTER AVENUE

346/366
WIDENER, John A., head, age 50, M2, married 10 years, VA/VA/VA,
    foreman, planing mill
___, Carrie, wife, age 29, M1, married 10 years, 7/7, TN/TN/TN
___, Horace, son, age 9, TN/TN/TN
___, Raymond, son, age 7, TN/TN/TN
___, Ida M., daughter, age 5, TN/TN/TN
___, Lester, son, age 3, TN/TN/TN
___, Lelsie, son, age 3, TN/TN/TN
continued on next page

346/366 continued
WIDENER, Izora, daughter, age 3, TN/TN/TN
____, Thomas E., son, age 2/12, TN/TN/TN
____, Embler, son, age 18, TN/TN/TN

347/367
HOPKINS, Frank, head, age 44, M1, married 18 years, IND/IND/IND,
    foreman, spoke mill
____, Laura, wife, age 44, M1, married 18 years, 4/3, TN/TN/TN
____, Lula B., daughter, age 15, TN/TN/TN
____, Basil F., son, age 12, TN/TN/TN
____, Iris A., daughter, age 9, TN/TN/TN

(Note: this household was also marked as "owns own home, owned free of
mortgage. The Children's father's birthplace is marked as TN, on the
census, but this is in error.)

348/368
TEMPLE, William O., head, age 33, M1, married 10 years, TN/TN/TN,
    brakeman, railroad
____, Lelia, age 33, wife, M1, married 10 years, 3/3, TN/TN/TN
____, Aileen, daughter, age 9, TN/TN/TN
____, Mary, daughter, age 7, TN/TN/TN
____, Lois, daughter, age 3, TN/TN/TN

349/369
SUGGS, Rufus, head, age 69, M2, married 17 years, TN/TN/VA, farmer,
    own farm
____, Jennie, wife, age 66, M2, married 17 years, 0/0, TN/TN/TN
____, Emma, daughter, age 25, single, TN/TN/TN, stenographer, wholesale
    grocery
____, Mary, daughter, age 23, single, TN/TN/TN, stenographer for lawyer

350/370
WORK, Robert J., head, age 68, M1, married 46 years, TN/TN/TN, farmer,
    own farm
____, Melisia T., wife, age 67, M1, married 46 years, 8/8, TN/TN/TN
____, Sallie, daughter, age 39, single, TN/TN/TN, saleswoman, dry goods
    store

351/371
WILSON, Rachel, head, age 59, widow, 8/4, TN/NC/TN, dressmaker at home
____, Tommie, daughter, age 32, TN/TN/TN
____, Maggie, daughter, age 20, TN/TN/TN, teacher, music
____, Will, son, age 16, TN/TN/TN
STEELE, Susie, sister, age 54, single, TN/TN/TN

352/372
TAYLOR, Tom, head, age 60, M1, married 37 years, TN/TN/TN, farmer,
    general farm
____, Jennie, wife, age 60, M1, married 37 years, 10/10, TN/SC/TN
____, Eva, daughter, age 23, single, TN/TN/TN
____, Izora, daughter, age 21, single, TN/TN/TN
____, Talmage, son, age 19, single, TN/TN/TN
____, Kate, daughter, age 13, TN/TN/TN

353/373
HANLIN, Frank, head, age 34, M1, KY/IRE.RISH/VA, inspector, lumber co.
____, Lucy, wife, age 34, M1, TN/GER.GERMAN/GER.GERMAN
____, Stanley, son, age 7, TN/KY/TN
____, Eliose, daughter, age 3, TN/KY/TN

354/374
FLOWERS, Curl J., head, age 44, M2, married 1 year, TN/TN/TN, physician,
    own office
____, Maggie, wife, age 35, M1, married 1 year 1/1, TN/TN/TN
____, Harry, son, age 12, TN/TN/TN
____, Aubrey, son, age 11, TN/TN/TN
____, Herbert, son, age 9, TN/TN/TN
continued on next page

354/374 continued
FLOWERS, Louise, daughter, age 6, TN/TN/TN
___, Jarrett C., Jr., son, age 3/12, TN/TN/TN

355/375
ADCOCK, William H., head, age 31, M1, married 13 years, TN/TN/TN
    blacksmith, employee at blacksmith shop
___, Jennie A., wife, age 30, M1, married 13 years, 6/5, TN/TN/TN
___, Elbert M., son, age 10, TN/TN/TN
___, Nannie, daughter, age 8, TN/TN/TN
___, Zula, daughter, age 6, TN/TN/TN
___, Clara H., daughter, age 3, TN/TN/TN
___, Ludean, age 1-1/12, daughter, TN/TN/TN

356/376
FOSTER, Jake C., head, age 61, M1, married 33 years, TN/VA/VA, agent,
    real estate
___, Dollie C., wife, age 54, M1, married 33 years, 3/1, TN/TN/TN

357/377
WILSON, Robert, head, age 28, M1, married 9 years, TN/TN/TN, "lazy
    man", spoke factory
___, Dena, wife, age 26, M1, married 9 years, 2/1, KY/KY/KY
___, Cora A., daughter, age 4, TN/TN/KY

358/378
SAGER, Dan, head, age 62, M1, married 39 years, PA/PA/PA, foreman,
    carpenter crew
___, Arminta H., wife, age 60, M1, married 39 years, 9/6, TN/TN/TN
___, Guy M., grandson, age 6, TN/TN/TN
SISMON, Clarke, son-in-law, age 18, M1, married 0 years, NEB/NEB/NEB,
    lineman, telephone office
___, Nina, daughter, age 20, M1, married 0 years, TN/PA/TN

359/379
McCALL, James F., head, age 55, M1, married 27 years, TN/SCOT.IRISH/TN
    conductor, train
___, Etta, wife, age 48, M1, married 27 years, 8/6, WIS/ILL/WISC
___, Suzanne, daughter, age 22, TN/TN/WISC
___, Frank, son, age 14, TN/TN/WISC
___, Carrie, daughter, age 11, TN/TN/WISC
___, Ruth, daughter, TN/TN/WISC
___, Allie, niece, age 17, TN/TN/TN

360/384
COLLIER, George T., head, age 43, M2, married 10 years, TN/TN/TN,
    carpenter, house
___, Iris, wife, age 33, M1, married 10 years, 0/0, TN/TN/TN
___, Clyde, son, age 20, single, TN/TN/TN, painter, house
___, Lizzie, daughter, age 18, single, TN/TN/TN
___, Walter, son, age 16, TN/TN/TN
___, Holmes, son, age 11, TN/TN/TN

361/381
KANNARD, Will, head, age 36, M1, married 9 years, KY/IND/IND, lawyer,
    general practice
___, Minnie, wife, age 36, M1, married 9 years, 4/2, TN/TN/TN
___, Kenneth, son, age 7, TN/TN/TN
___, Keith, son, age 3, TN/TN/TN
___, Matilda, mother, age 58, widow, 2/2, IND/VA/VA

362/382
CRUTCHER, Will, head, age 42, M1, married 14 years, TN/TN/TN, none
___, Estelle, wife, age 31, M1, married 14 years, TN/TN/TN, milliner,
    own shop
___, Lorene, daughter, age 11, TN/TN/TN
___, Hester A., mother, age 66, widow, 3/3, TN/TN/TN

363/383
MARTIN, Calvin, head, age 42, M1, married 23 years, TN/TN/TN, black-
    smith, railroad
___, Susie, wife, age 40, M1, married 23 years, 5/5, TN/TN/TN
___, Etta, daughter, age 20, divorced, 0/0, TN/TN/TN
___, Jerome C., son, age 17, TN/TN/TN
___, Charlie, son, age 14, TN/TN/TN
___, Susie, daughter, age 11, TN/TN/TN

364/384
BURCH, Bob, head, age 39, M1, married 18 years, TN/TN/TN, inspector,
    lumber company
___, Lula, wife, age 36, M1, married 18 years, 4/3, TN/TN/TN
___, Clyde B., son, age 17, TN/TN/TN
___, Jack, son, age 11, TN/TN/TN
___, Lucille, daughter, age 3, TN/TN/TN
NIBLETT, Bertha, servant, black, age 18, TN/TN/TN, servant, private
    family

365/385
BEASLEY, Dan E., head, age 47, M2, married 9 years, TN/TN/TN, merchant,
    hardware
___, Mary G., wife, age 47, M2, married 9 years, 0/0, MO/TN/TN
___, Ida, daughter, age 21, TN/TN/TN, stenographer, bank
___, Annie, daughter, age 17, TN/TN/TN
___, Mable, daughter, age 15, TN/TN/TN

366/386
HALBROOK, Tom J., head, age 41, M1, married 19 years, TN/TN/TN, merchant
    dry goods
___, Tishie, wife, age 36, M1, married 19 years, 4/4, TN/TN/TN
___, Clint, son, age 17, TN/TN/TN
___, Joe, son, age 12, TN/TN/TN
___, Forest, son, age 9, TN/TN/TN
___, Hazel, daughter, age 4, TN/TN/TN

367/387
MARTIN, James, head, age 42, M2, married 19 years, TN/TN/TN, blacksmith,
    own shop
___, Rosa, wife, age 39, M1, married 19 years, 3/0, TN/TN/TN

368/388
REED, Loyde M., head, age 31, M1, married 8 years, TN/TN/TN, carpenter,
    house
___, Mattie E., wife, age 33, M1, married 8 years, 2/1, TN/TN/TN
___, Bernice, daughter, age 7, TN/TN/TN

369/389
CLOYS, William, head, age 36, M1, married 6 years, TN/TN/TN, treasurer,
    ice plant
___, Ethel, wife, age 32, married 6 years, M1, 1/1, TN/KY/TN
___, Ruby, daughter, age 5, KY/TN/TN

370/390
HOLLEY, Jessie T., head, age 40, M1, married 14 years, TN/TN/TN
___, Dell J., wife, age 36, M1, married 14 years, 2/2, OHIO/CAN.ENGLISH/
    OHIO
___, Anna, daughter, age 13, TN/TN/OHIO
___, Jesse, son, age 12, TN/TN/OHIO

371/391
DODSON, Washington, head, age 52, M1, married 28 years, TN/TN/TN, over-
    seer, concrete works
___, Mary, wife, age 54, M1, married 28 years, TN/TN/TN
___, Perry, son, age 24, single, TN/TN/TN, laborer, concrete work
MYETT, Percy, son-in-law, age 27, M1, married 5 years, TN/TN/TN, book-
    keeper, wholesale house
___, Samantha, daughter, age 27, M2, married 5 years, 1/1, TN/TN/TN
___, Beulah M., granddaughter, age 8, TN/TN/TN

372/392
LOVELL, James T., head, age 53, M1, married 30 years, TN/TN/TN,
    carpenter, house
___, Minnie, wife, age 47, M1, married 30 years, 12/2, WIS/WIS/WIS
___, Geraldine, granddaughter, age 6, TN/TN/TN

373/393
LEATHERS, Allison, head, age 43, M1, married 16 years, PA/PA/PA, owner,
    handle factory
___, Emma, wife, age 37, M1, married 16 years, 5/5, PA/PA/PA
___, John B., son, age 15, PA/PA/PA
___, Harry R., son, age 14, PA/PA/PA
___, Allison H., son, age 8, TN/PA/PA
___, Fannie, daughter, age 6, TN/PA/PA
___, Emma R., daughter, age 2, TN/PA/PA

374/394
MARTIN, John, head, age 37, M1, married 11 years, TN/TN/TN, blacksmith,
    own shop
___, Sallie, wife, age 30, M1, married 11 years, 0/0, TN/TN/TN
BARLETT, Odel, sister-in-law, age 17, TN/TN/TN

375/395
BOYTE, Charlie, head, age 31, M1, married 9 years, TN/TN/TN, manager,
    poultry, produce house
___, Callie, wife, age 31, M1, married 9 years, 3/3, TN/TN/TN
___, Charlie M., son, age 8, TN/TN/TN
___, Mary E., daughter, age 7, TN/TN/TN
___, Hazel, daughter, age 5, TN/TN/TN
GODWIN, Mary D., aunt, age 69, widow, TN/TN/TN

376/396
SEAY, Dick R., head, age 69, M1, married 35 years, VA/VA/VA, own income
___, Margret, wife, age 54, M1, married 35 years, PA/PA/PA

377/397
SEAY, Charles D., head, age 30, M1, married 8 years, KY/VA/PA, engineer,
    locomotive
___, Blanche, wife, age 28, M1, married 8 years, 2/2, TN/TN/TN
___, Henry T., son, age 7, TN/KY/TN
___, Robert A., son, age 4, TN/KY/TN

378/398
PRIN, (?), Narsissia, head, age 60, widow, 9/5, TN/TN/TN, keeping
    boarding house
___, Willie, son, age 25, single, TN/TN/TN, no occupation
TEMPLE, Fred, son-in-law, age 27, M1, married 3 years, TN/TN/TN, fireman
    locomotive
___, Polly, daughter, age 24, M1, married 3 years, 2/2, TN/TN/TN
___, Delle, daughter, age 3, TN/TN/TN
___, Fredie, son, age 11/12, TN/TN/TN
ALLEN, William, father, age 83, widowed, TN/NC/NC
BROWN, Decatur, boarder, age 25, widowed, TN/TN/TN, miller, roller mill
SHARP, Jake, boarder, age 29, TN/TN/TN, brakeman, train
POWERS, Charlie, boarder, age 31, single, TN/TN/TN, salesman, restaurant
GILMORE, Jim, boarder, age 27, single, TN/TN/TN, brakeman, train

379/399
TURNER, Will T., head, age 39, M1, married 18 years, TN/TN/TN
    engineer, locomotive
___, Bertha, wife, age 35, M1, married 18 years, 0/0, TN/TN/TN
___, Lucile, adopted, age 12, TN/TN/TN

380/400
SMITH, Clayton, head, age 50, M1, married 19 years, TN/TN/GA,
    dispatcher, train
___, Alice, wife, age 37, M1, married 19 years, 1/1, TN/TN/TN
___, Ouida, daughter, age 18, single, TN/TN/TN
WILSON, W., father, age 83, widowed, TN/US/US
(Note: Or this could be Wilson W. Smith--notes impossible to decipher)

381/401
SMITH, Tom M., head, age 43, M2, married 0 years, TN/TN/TN, paymaster,
    interstate, cooper
___, Mayme L., wife, age 41, M2, married 0 years, 2/2, TN/TN/TN
STANFIL, Willie M., daughter, age 12, TN/TN/TN

382/402
EASLEY, William T., head, age 50, M1, married 16 years, TN/TN/TN,
    salesman, hardware
___, Birdie, wife, age 32, M1, married 16 years, 1/1, TN/TN/TN
___, Edna, daughter, age 6, TN/TN/TN

383/403
HALBROOK, Mary E., age 65, widow, 4/4, TN/TN/TN
___, Mary, daughter, age 40, single, TN/TN/TN, saleswoman, dry goods
    store

384/404
SMITH, Lyda, age 47, widow, 2/2, TN/TN/TN, operator, telephone company

385/405
SALMON, William T., age 34, single, KY/VA/KY, minister, church

386/406
BELLEMY, George, age 61, widowed, ENG.ENGLISH/ENG.ENGLISH/ENG.ENGLISH,
    manager, livery barn

387/407
MARTIN, Fletcher, head, age 30, M1, married 10 years, TN/TN/TN,
    conductor, train
___, Mamie, wife, age 24, M1, married 10 years, 4/3, TN/TN/TN
___, Claude, son, age 8, TN/TN/TN
___, Tilford, son, age 5, TN/TN/TN
___, Raymon, son, age 1-6/12, TN/TN/TN
NICKS, Thomas, boarder, age 22, single, TN/TN/TN, engineer, pump house

388/408
CATHEY, Lou, black household, laundress

389/409
CALDWELL, Henry, black household, driver, dray

MCKINZIE STREET

390/410
TAYLOR, Marvin, head, age 33, M1, married 11 years, TN/TN/TN, farmer,
    general farmer
___, Minerva, wife, age 32, M1, married 11 years, 2/2, TN/TN/TN
___, Allen, daughter, age 10, TN/TN/TN
___, Roland, son, age 7, TN/TN/TN

391/411
CONANT, Larry, head, age 24, M1, married 1 years, TN/OHIO/OHIO,
    proprietor, bakery shop
___, Irene, age 20, wife, M1, married 1 year, 0/0, TN/IT.ITALIAN/IT.
    ITALIAN

392/412
STEELE, John, head, age 41, M1, married 13 years, TN/TN/TN, car repair-
    er, round house
___, Ida, wife, age 31, M1, married 13 years, 5/5, TN/TN/TN
___, Bryan, son, age 12, TN/TN/TN
___, Ruby, daughter, age 10, TN/TN/TN
___, Loyal, son, age 6, TN/TN/TN
___, Robert, son, age 4, TN/TN/TN
___, Mary, daughter, age 9/12, TN/TN/TN

393/413
RAMEY, Allen, black household

394/414
GRIMES, Alfred, black household

"Here ends the enumeration of the Town of Dickson."

The above listing contains the names of all the people living within the bounds of the Town of Dickson, with the exception of the black households. Several additional pages, not copied for this work, were marked the suburbs of Dickson. An example is given as follows:

WEST DICKSON SUBURB
South of the Railroad, District 5

143/145
HUDSON, K. W., female, age 46, widow, 10/8, TN/TN/TN
___, Luther, son, age 21, single, TN/TN/TN, lathman, factory
___, Claude, son, age 18, TN/TN/TN, lathman, factory
___, Della, daughter, age 17, TN/TN/TN
___, Beulah, daughter, age 15, TN/TN/TN
___, Pearl, daughter, age 10, TN/TN/TN
___, Blanche, daughter, age 11, TN/TN/TN
___, Ruby, daughter, age 8, TN/TN/TN
(The above household was that of Keziah McClurkan Rushing Hudson, even though her initials are given as K. W.)

***

INDEX

Compiled by
Texas City Ancestry Searchers
Texas City, Texas

ABERCROMBIE, J. H. 327
ABERNATHY, Gilbert T. 313
ABNER, ___ 187
  John 186
ABNEY, ___ 187
  Elias 187,306
  John 186
  Paul 144,235
  Rhoda 306
  William 303,307
ACOFF, Elizabeth 72
ACUFF, Carter 140,159,191
  Cate 191
  Charles 187
  Elizabeth 159,307
  Hamilton 187
  Hansellow 191
  Maria 19
  Nancy 238
ADAMS, Benjamin 131,146,
    147,151,161
  Betty G. 198
  Carl 234
  Charley C. 198
  Cinthy 53
  Cora Hattie 198
  Elizabeth A. 376
  Emma A. 198
  Enola Ann 198
  George 78,307
  Hodge 52,80
  Howel 151,153,154,174
  Howell 52,53,80,132,136,
    139,169,240,242
  J. A. 280
  J. I. J. 195
  James 224,319
  James B. 198
  Jane 102
  Jesse R. 198
  John 78,83,93,147,184,
    188,190,263,302,305,
    310
  John H. 376
  Joseph A. 198
  Kitchen 113
  Lallie 297
  Lewis Wade 198
  Lillah 53
  Lottie 327
  Mage 316
  Martha 105
  Martha Mathis 198
  Mattie L. 198
  McKinley 234
  Mildred 299
  Montgomery 195
  Nancy 6,19,52,80,305
  Nelson 198,297
  Odell 299
  Reaves 53
  Reeves 80
  Samuel 63,72,78,310
  Sarah 42,53,72
  Sil 78,198
  Silvester 78,96,156,
    166,170
  Stephen 326
  Susannah 9
  Susannah W. 8
  Syl 316
  Tho. 78
  Thomas 186
  Vella B. 298
  Vera 298
  W. M. 330
  W. T. 195,199

ADAMS (cont.)
  William 52,57,74,80,81,
    176,181,186,191,312
  William M. 198
  William W. 198
ADAMSON, W. L. 14
  William S. 310
ADCOCK, Arthur 282
  Betty 295
  C. G. 99
  Carby 287
  Charles 374
  Clara H. 389
  Clovis 290
  Curtis 234,340
  David W. 31
  Dolly M. 64
  Eddie 282
  Edward H. 11
  Elbert M. 389
  Elizabeth 43
  Elvin 327
  George 94
  George W. 13
  Henderson 11,64,309
  J. W. 195
  Jesse 40
  Jessie 309
  Jennie A. 389
  John 94
  Jonathan 309
  Ludean 389
  Manis 290
  Marion 282
  Martin V. 195
  Mittie 287
  Nancy 43
  Nannie 389
  Polly M. 40
  Randolph 281
  Rebecca Ann 26
  Sarah 199
  Sarah A. 43
  Sonny 283
  Stephen 309
  T. B. 195
  Thomas Benton 195,199
  W. M. 329
  Will 281
  William 41
  William H. 389
  Zula 389
ADCOX, E. M. Mr. & Mrs.
    342
  James Murry 342
  W. H. 336,342
ADENGE, Jonathan 131
ADKINS, Abner 17,312
  Abraham 11
  Drewry 182,313
  Drury 76,78,187,306
  E. 318
  Ezra 334
  Ken 345
  Mable 334
  Nancy 17
  William 11,37
  William J. P. 38,39
ADKINSON, John B. 306
  William 27
AGEE, James 189
AGLEMORE, David 9
AIMS, James 115
  Thomas 115
AKIN, W. V. 140
  William N. 132
ALBERT, Lulie 327

ALBRIGHT, James M. 28,312
  John A. 195
ALDERIDGE, James C. 235,
    344
ALDRIDGE, Charles 364
  Lenora 364
  Mary L. 364
  Robert 364
ALEXANDER, Celia 350
  Ernest 350
  J. N. 321
  James 158,160
  Jesse 57
  John F. 202
  Joseph 304
  Sarah 304
  Tennie 350
ALHEIGHT, E. W. 294
ALISON, ___ 193,199
  William 75
ALLEN, A. J. 199,224,319
  Archibald 162
  Barnebese 153
  Bobby 345
  Carr. 303
  Clyde 293
  Elizabeth 17
  Eveline 31
  Felix 172,174,177,190
  Gabriel 140,165,303
  Gladys 292
  Herman 292
  Irene 292
  Jack 373
  Jacob 188
  James 264
  James R. 7,313
  Jesse 223
  Jessie 333
  John 127,159,306
  Mary 284
  Mollie 386
  Pauline 373
  Ora 292
  Richard 137,140,163,164
  V. S. 9,13
  Valentine S. 298
  Volintine J. 311
  William 115,119,120,173,
    188,191,391
  Willie F. 386
  Zelma 292
ALLEY, Benjamin 160
ALLISON, Elsie 356
  Granville 356
  J. M. 330
  James 356
  Jessie 356
  Mary E. 356
  Monroe 356
  Murry 356
  Nellie 356
ALLMAN, ___ 298
  Clarence M. 17
  Fannie 289
  Iva 295
ALMON, James 77
ALSBROOK, Thomas 48
ALSPAUGH, Ann 281
  Emory, Jr. 282
  Joe 282
  Joseph 199
  Josiah Clifton 195
  Vina 295
ALSTON, John 133
  Samuel B. 311
ANDERSON, ___ 113

ANDERSON (cont.)
    Dr. 234
  Alex 305
  Alexander 235
  B. C. 225
  Daniel W. 44
  Ealum 75
  Elizabeth 16
  Elkanah 190
  Gladys 291
  Glenn 283,291
  H. O. 343
  Hazel 282
  Hiram 75
  Isaac 47
  John 32,190
  Lavena 39
  Levi 78,169,306
  Lucas 3
  Mary H. 99
  Millie 362
  Peggy 306
  Sarah 307
  Sherman 295
  Timothy 141,174
  W. G. 197,199
  Widow 325
  Will 325
  William 153,223,305
  William M. 223
  William P. 115,117,119, 120
  William Paterson 119
ANDREWS, Agness 87
  Agusta 84
  B. T. 195,225
  Benjamin 75,84,87,154, 158,177,304
  Bettie 363
  Dan 295
  E. 231
  E. G. 103
  Ephraim 363
  F. A. 202
  Gabrael 311
  Gabriel 21
  Louisa 15
  Martha E. 218
  P. 225
  P. H. 104
  Peterson 16
  Terrell 15
ANGLIN, Aaron 61
  Cornelius 61
  Elizabeth 61,98,309
  George 61
  J. C. 39,42,44,47
  J. W. 199
  John 61,98,309
  John C. 61,98
  Margaret 61
  Nancy 61
  Sally C. 61
  William 35,61
ANGLING, Sally 11
ANKENY,   248
  Genevive M. 366
  J. L. 248,325
  John L. 366
  Julie C. 366
  Lewis J. 366
  Mary M. 366
  Tolbert 366
ANNIS, Louise 293
ANTHONY E. M. 277
  Esther 218
APPLEGATE, Maggie 378
APPLETON, James 190
  Priscilla 44
ARCHER, James 131,133
  John H. 133,139,175,237
  Ruther 83
  Stevison 312

ARCHER (cont.)
  Thomas 131,133,156,166, 170
ARMOUR, Robert 305
  William 78,305
ARMS, John 273
ARMSTRONG, George W. 72
  James 21,72
  John 72
  Joseph M. 72
  Martin 118,126
  Morris 373
  Samuel 72
  Thomas 72,310
  William 56
ARNOLD, Annie 369
  Aron 81
  Elisha 190,191
  Emeline 29
  Ephraim 185,305
  Ephrm 81
  Ezra 81
  Gertrude 369
  Holland 369
  Israel 185,188
  James 147,177,191
  John 81,188,189
  Martin 21
  Thomas 81,185,188,189
  Truett 369
  Wyatt 81,188
ARRINGTON, Elizabeth 6
  James 19
ARTERBURN, Rev. F. T. 269
ARTRESS, Frank H. 297
ASHWORTH, Bill 275
  Eli 33
  Fred W. 234
  James 310
  John C. 33
  Mattie 282
  Nancy 17
  Richard 234
ASKINS, Mary T. 382
  William 342
ATKINS, Drury 192
  Howard 270
  Lauren 278
ATKINSON, Q. C. 17
  Quintus C. 17,69
  Thomas 197,199
ATLEE, E. G. 283
ATWOOD, James 10
AUSTIN, Abraham J. 70,71
  Betty 281
  C. W. 7,14
  Charles Van Buren 195
  David 79,306
  Dicey 323
  Eliza 43
  George Wyatt 195
  H. G. 195
  Howard 292
  Jody 281
  John 25
  John B. 45
  Joseph 78
  Lucinda 46
  Margaret 49,282
  Marie 282
  Marjorie 294
  Martha 70
  May 57
  Nancy 8
  Philip W. 7,11,14
  Samuel 312
  Samuel D. 306
  William 76,186,265,305, 310,327
  William G. 57,310
AVERETT, Walter 100
  Alice 107
AVERITT, Lawrence 286

ALVERITT (cont.)
  Martha Halliburton (Mrs.) 336
  N. C. 113
  S. K. 318
AVERITTE, Annie Mae 299
  Billy 298
  Lawrence 299
  Leon 298
AYRES,   231
BABCOCK, James 376
BACHMAN, Emma Jean 295
BACON, Barton 13
  Benedict 306
  Easter 324
  Jane 57
  Sally 57
  Sarah R. 13
BADGE,   277
  Charles 328
  Charlie 379
  Mrs. Charles Jr. 218
  Edith 379
  Margret E. 379
BADGER, Felix 38
BAGGET, Sarah 12
BAGGETT, Elias 17
  James 28
BAGETT, Josiah 47
BAGLEY, Cornelius 310
  William 188
BAGWELL, Ella E. 212
  J. M. 104
BAIL, Pat 197,199
BAILEY, William 12
BAILS, H. D. 41
BAILY, Elizabeth J. 47
  Lucinda 38
  Maryann 12
  Pat 199
BAIRD, Joseph 131
  William 307
BAKER,   Mr. 226
  Absalom 54,57,134,237, 309
  Absolum, Jr. 124
  Alice Ann 342
  Alton 294,299
  Ann 20
  Argain (?) 64
  Arminta 384
  Armstrong 64,309
  Aubrey 334
  B. 281
  Beckah 56
  Benjamin 53,96,122,124, 160,161,237,309
  Buck 282
  C. A. 64
  Casader 17
  Cave J. 64
  Charles 185,188,311
  Charles A. 8,14
  Claud 45
  Claud G. 107
  Cordelia 376
  Corinne Allen 342
  E. R. 89
  Elijah 91
  Elizabeth 97
  Ella 287
  Ella L. 384
  Emma 296
  Ethel 287
  Felix G. 64
  Fordie 287
  Francis 141
  George Washington 195
  Harriet 108
  Hollie L. 384
  Inez B. 360
  Isabell 296
  J. R. 330

BAKER (cont.)
  J. T. 322
  J. W. 107
  James 190
  James M. 29
  Jane 53,96,97,101,306
  John 56,96,137,138,160,
    161,173,185,191,306,
    309
  John A. 34,53,78,80,178,
    239
  John Allen 342
  John Carlos 341
  John R. 384
  John W. 56,174,360
  Johnnie 327
  Lula 327
  Martha 376
  Mary 306
  Mary A. 42
  Mary Ann 64
  Mary Emma 295
  Mary M. 350
  Mittie 376
  Monroe 287
  Nancy 34,53,96,309
  Nelly 53
  Nicholas 186,304
  Norman T. 64
  Patsey 53
  Peggy 78
  Polly 7
  R. Jane 48
  Rebecca 56
  Richmond 89,237
  Robert 189,193,197,199,
    327
  Robert B. 350
  Roy 282
  Roy, Jr. 282
  Sally 53
  Samuel 225
  Stephen 193,199
  Susan 112,376
  Susan C. 111
  Thomas 195
  Thomas B. 350
  Thomas J. 350
  Tom 100
  W. L. 193,199
  Wiley J. 195
  William 21,53,56,65,97,
    141,144,173,174,312
  William L. 42,174,313
  William N. 234
  William S. 6
BAKLEY, J. S. 223
BALDIN, Levi 313
  Margaret 45
BALDWIN, Aaron 186
  Edna 289
  Margaret 45
  Ozell 289
  Pheby 180
BALL, Franklin F. 309
BALLARD, Abram 72
  Clayton 362
  Horace 362
  J. B. 248,325
  John B. 362
  Lucy 72
  Robert 362
  Sophia 362
  Theophilus 72
BALSBAUGH, Henry C. 364
  Mary H. 364
BALTHORP, Mary 12,64
BALTHORPE, W. T. 193,199
BALTHROP, Alonzo 334
  Edward 312
  Elizabeth 214
  Frances 97
  Francis 78,306

BALTHROP (cont.)
  James C. 312
  Maybelle 334
  Thomas 312
  Thomas G. 14
  W. W. 97
  Willey 312
  William 95,97,298,305,
    311
  William, Jr. 17,305
  Willie 59,64,74,88,97,
    305
BALTHROPE, James C. 28
  William C. 46
BANDOLF, James R. 191
BANOCHET, C. 102
BARBEE, Asa 309
BARBER, John B. 190
BAREFIELD, Daniel 174
BARFIELD, James 190
BARKLEY, Ernest 364
  John 364
  Mollie 364
BARLETT, Odel 391
BARN, Richard 191
BARNARD, Elizabeth S. 16
BARNES, Charles 129,130,
    160,173
  Hezekiah 148
  Thomas H. 16
  William 311
BARNETT, Anna B. 381
  Elizabeth 32
  Lorain 381
  Mary 381
  Mattie 381
  W. A. 329
  W. C. 277
  Will 381
  Will A. 380
BARR, Hezekiah 116,135
BARRNETT, Bessie 357
  Charlie 357
  Eudora 357
  John 357
  Leroy 357
  Mannye 357
  Mayme 357
BARROW, Martha 49
  William 135
BARTEE, Elizabeth 16
  Jasper B. 71
  Jesse W. 64
  John H. 71
  Mary 22
  Sally 17
  Sarah 313
  Susan 19
  William B. 10
BARTER, Sarah 29
BARTHE, John 304
BARTON, Benjamin 155,187
  John 187
  Samuel 168,179
  William B. 190
BASS, Hartwell 76
BATEMAN, Essie 282
  Jeremiah 32
  Myrtle 282
  Ned 316
  Theny 50
  Tresa 49
  Walter 297
  William D. 35
BATES, Albert 379
  Amy 379
  Bessie L. 379
  Carlton C. 379
  Cheatham 334
  Linnie 379
  Myrtle 362
  Richard 362
  S. C. 106

BATES (cont.)
  Stephen G. 379
  Steve 379
  Sarah 379
  Wallace H. 379
BATSON, Calvin S. 33
  Ivie 289
  R. 15,19,20
  Richard 79,162,180,192,
    304,315
  Thomas 57,162,303
  Zachriah 41
BATTS, Jack 383
  Lizzie 383
  Mary 383
  Robert 383
  W. J. 383
  William J. 383
BATTSON, Richard 135
  Thomas 116,135
BAUGHAM, Christian 305
BAUGHMAN, Abraham 17,311
  C. 237
BAULDIN, Margaret 45
BAXTER, Donnie Mai 295
  E. D. 193
  James 85,197
  Martha A. 21
  Robert 58
BAYER, J. H. 295
BAYS, Jesse 185
BEAR, Percy 282
  Walter 282
BEARD, Andrew 56
  William 49
BEARS, Alice 360
  Amy G. 361
  Ella M. 360
  Guy W. 361
  Harry L. 361
  Nicholas 360
  Robin E. 361
  Rosa E. 360
BEASLEY, Annie 390
  Cheatham 362
  Dan 334,336
  Dan E. 390
  Dane 333,336
  Farris 362
  Florence 292
  Girlie 288
  H. C. 279
  Ida 390
  Jess Walker 343
  Jessie 362
  Joe Dotson 288
  Lester 364
  Lois 362
  Mable 390
  Mary G. 390
  Mike 362
  Nattie P. 360
  Norine F. 360
  Pearl 362
  Dr. R. P. 343
  Riley 199
  Troy 362
  Vera 362
  William 327,360
BEAUMOND, Milly 224
BEAUMONT, Milly 319
BEAVERS, Andy 163
BECHER, Rev. Charles 267
BECK, Andrew J. 66
  Bessie 290,291
  Crawford C. 225
  David C. 66
  Edgar 291
  Fredrick 129
  Hinchey 291
  Howell 295
  Jesse 66,67,68,87,192,
    311

BECK (cont.)
   John 117,131,133
   John E. 117,137
   John T. 66,195
   Judy 66
   Martha J. 41
   Mary 109
   Maude 295
   Myrtle 282
   Paul 291
   Pearl 282
   William J. 66
   Willie Mai 281
BEDFORD, Benjamin 78,190,
   237
   T. O. 274
   Teracy 237
   Terasy 239
BELL, ___ 283
   Blount M. 62
   Cuthbert 191
   Elisha 35,65
   Elizabeth W. 24
   Emma 331
   Eveline D. 323
   Fay 331
   George 116
   J. M. 266
   James 192,255
   James L. 185,191
   Jane 66,311
   Jane P. 62
   Jim 325
   John J. 62,65,154,312
   John P. 62
   Jude 363
   Liza 387
   Marceannia 62,68
   Mary 322
   Mary Ann 62,65
   Mary Ross 65
   Montgomery 116,346
   Montogery 62,65,66,68,
     75,151,154,156,170,
     242,244,245,254,255,
     262,265,277,283,302,
     303,307
   Nancy 9,62
   Nancy K. 62
   Nancy S. 62
   Robert 114,115,117,120,
     131,178
   S., Jr. 13,15
   Sarah B. 40
   Sarah E. 40
   Shaderick 170,172
   Shadrach 75,306
   Shadrick 65,311
   Thomas 11,65,75,294,311
   Thomas Drue 62,65,68,
   V. F. 65
   William 30,40
   William B. 70,313
   Wilson 322
BELLAMY, J. P. 14
BELLAR, George 392
BELLAR, Robert 234
   Robert M. 339
BENELL, James 119
BENHAM, John 145,191
BENNETT, Thomas 311
   Hosey 14
   Hozy 312
   Micajah 307
BENTLEY, Minnie 289
   Opal 289
   Sally 105
BENTSON, Reuben 176
BERNARD, John 307
BERRINGER, C. 2
BERRY, Aline 297
   Arthur 297
   Ben 297

BERRY (cont.)
   Carrie 350
   Dimple 350
   Lewis 77,82,191,238
   Lucian 234,339
   M. 26,27,29,33,38,95
   M. T. 72
   Martha A. P. 42
   Michael 21,43,97,264,
     310
   Michel 96
   Nancy 72
   Nallie 293
   Ray 293
   Richard H. 174
   Sarah 72
   Susanna 77
   Walter 350
   Warner 340
BERRYMAN, Lavern 298
   Myrtle 298
BERTHELL, John 46
BETHNY, Jacob 140
   Matthew 140
   Thomas 140
BETTS, Mr. 3
   Charles 68
   James A. 223
   William 122
BETTY, Edd 294
   Elergy 294
   Tennessee 294
BETZ, J. A. 223
   James A. 223
BEVAN, Charles D.
   Harry L. 328,329
BEVANS, Clara 331
   Myra 331
BIBB, Clara 327
   David 192,305
   Eliza 373
   Elizabeth 30,64,204
   Emmett 343
   Henry A. 35
   James 68,310
   John G. 68
   John M. 23,26
   Miner 86
   Minor 30,55,64,68,83,94,
     143,144,145,151,163,
     173,176,177,178,261,
     302,303,305,310
   N. 326
   Nancy 27,68
   Robert 311
   Robert F. 68
   Sadie 283
   Sam 260
   Samuel A. 71
   Sarah 305
   Vernon 30
BIGG, Samuel A. 48
BILBREY, Dale 269
BILL, Buffalo 328
BILLINGS, Daniel 55
BILLUPS, Daniel D. 22
   Margarett 22
BINKLEY, Araminta 69
   Elise 69
   Emalin 69
   Franklin M. 311
   H. H. Rev. 269
   H. J. 70
   Henry J. 25,26,312
   J. T. 197,199
   Juanita 295
   Morris 69
   Parile 69
   W. H. 195,197,199
BINKLY, H. J. 27,28,31,32,
     35,37,39
   Henry 93
   Nancy L. 43

BINUM, Tapley 95
BIRD, Nancy 309
   William C. 308
BINGHAM, Lissa T. 222
BIRMINGHAM, Lucy 219
BISHOP, ___ 282
   Arthur K. 340
   Billy 282
   Dorothy 282
   E. 30,44,67
   Eddie 287
   Eldridge 283
   Eliza 100
   Ellinor 36
   Empson 26,30,40,186,323
   Forrest 283
   Fronia 289
   Hattie 283
   James 283
   Jewel 345
   John 44,312
   Katherine 283
   Mildred 283
   Parion 31
   Press 199
   Rosa 287
   Ruby 283
   Sammy 282
   Stacy 31
   Susie 287
   Tena 289
BISSENGER, Bert 281
BISSINGER, Bessie 295
   Blanche 291
   Callie 291
   Euzella 293
   Freddy 295
   Hubert 295
   Myrtle 291,292
   Vergie 291
BITER, Ginnett 49
   John M. 29
BIVENS, Mary 377
BLACK, Andrew 241
   Elizabeth 59
   James 185,274
   James L. 234
   James R. 380
   Jim 380
   Katie C. 380
   Martin 127
   Rebecca 15
   Robert 105
   Sampson 87
   William 59
BLACKBURN, Benjamin 306
   Gideon Rev. 275
   John R. 195
   Sarah 309
BLACKFAN, Jesse 158,159,
     173
   John 158
   Thomas 159
   William 158,159
BLACKWELL, J. J. 328
   James 37
   Lilah Pearl 295
   Micajah 42
BLADES, W. A. 269,274
BLAIR, John 129
BLAKE, Mollie 290
   Wells 313,316
   William 306
BLAKELY, Wright 14
BLALOCK, Henry 190
BLANET, Wilson 189
BLANKENSHIP, I. C. 27
BLANKS, James 191
   Maggie 211
BLEADSOE, Cintha 40
BLEDSOE, Alice 291
   B. L. 80
   Barnabas L. 56

BLEDSOE (cont.)
  Barney B. 306
  Barney L. 56
  Giles J. 56
  Isaac 157
  Jane 18
  Lucinda 21
  Pinkney T. 56,306
  Rebecca 11
  Rebina 56
  Susannah 10
  Thomas 195
BLOCKLEY, G. 91
  Gustavus 17,94
  Lucretia 26,94
  Thadeus 94
BLOCKY, Lueslia 28
BLOUNT, John Gray 116,141,
    146,154,159
  Margaret 52,238,307
  Thomas 141,146
  William 127
  William R. 73
  Willie 137,154,159
BLUE, Cordelia 374
  Hershel 374
  Richard 374
  Robert 371
BLUNT, Parthenia 35
  William R. 312
BOARD, Joseph 120
BOAZ, Mattie 290,293
  Robert E. 234
BOBBITT, Mattie 384
BOGGS, Kate 277
BOHANNAN, Robert 313
BOLEN, H. E. 342
BOLES, Charles 305
  Sampson 305
  Thomas 116,120,122
BOMAR, Alice 290
BOND, Lewis 160
BONDS, Drury 189
  Robert 14
  Sarah 54
BONE, Elizabeth 41
  Gavon 307
  Isaac 12,312
  Rebecca 45
  Thomas 234,339
  William 313
BOOKER, Charles 294
  Gladis 294
  J. A. 197,199
  John 197,199
  Levicy 238
  Lillian 292
  Margaret Sue 292
  Melba 295
  P. R. 128
  Paul 294
  Robert 309
  Wilson 294
BOON, John 150
  Spier 188
BOONE, Alec 376
  Almus 376
  Authur 385
  Baron 377
  Bettie 376
  Mrs. Bettie 268
  Bratten 385
  Cecil 385
  Doyle 385
  Eddie Lee 331
  Elsie 331,376
  Elizabeth 294
  Forrest 294
  Hattie M. 385
  Hortense 377
  Katie 281
  Lundy 385
  Mary 385

BOONE (cont.)
  William P. 227
  Willie 385
BOOTHE, John 185
BORCHERT, Bessie 295
  Colista 291
  Cordan 295
  Gertrude 281,343
  Harvey 295
  Lola 295
  Nannie 295
  Percy 295
  Winfred 295
BORCHET, Christian 323
BORUM, William 317
BOSWELL, Miles 77
BOULDIN, Daisy 298
BOUTE, W. R. 271
BOWDEN, Willard 297
BOWE, Eliza 110
BOWEN, Agnes 299
  Allen 158,179,186,192,
    306,309
  Alvie 299
  Angeline 31
  Artie 288
  Artie Weems, Mrs. 299
  Benjamin 24,310
  Buford 299
  C. S. 9
  Carlton 290,299
  Caroline 224
  Charles 299
  Christine 294
  Christopher 69
  Clarence 292,299
  Claude 299
  Dewey 281,299
  Eldridge 186,306
  Emily I. 28
  Etta 290
  Fannie 299
  Ferbe 299
  George 53
  George A. 74
  Hickman 299
  Homer 299
  J. A. 86
  James 299
  Joe 294
  Mrs. Joe Puckett 290
  John 68,293
  Jordan 93
  Jordan A. 90
  Lawry 299
  Martha A. 42
  Mary 11,293
  Mary Ann 68
  Nancy 24
  Nyomy 18
  Reas 68
  Reece 168,172,202,253,
    305,310
  Richard 299
  Robert Thomas 299
  Rosannah J. 202
  Samuel D. 46,68
  Sarah 60,202,309
  Sarah Strong Browen 202
  Velma 299
  William 299
  Zallie 293
BOWER, Billie 211
  Nellie 211
BOWERS, Horace J. 199
  I. M. 200,326
  Isaac M. 199
  Julia 199
  Mary 200
  Maude 199
  Minnie 200
  Paul 200
  Paul R. 199

BOWERS (cont.)
  Sophiah B. 22
BOWKER, S. F. 328
  Samuel 3
BOWLES, Robert 191
  Sampson 191
BOWLS, Sampson 304
BOX, Boshie 305
  Julia 375
  Warren 375
BOYCE, ____ K. 42
BOYD, Bobby 277
  Catherine 41
  James 64
  John M. 35
  Joseph 190
  Matilda Ann 64
  Mary Jane 35,50
BOYKIN, Mary C. 21
BOYLE, Sarry 151
BOYT, Bob 324
BOYTE, Callie 391
  Charlie 291
  Charlie M. 391
  Dora 352
  Elijah 191
  Hazel 391
  Kathleen 352
  Margret 352
  Mary E. 391
  Robert T. 352
  Virginia 352
BRACKEN, ____ 232
BRACKETT, Benjamin 138,141
BRADFORD, Alice 299
  B. J. 139
  Crawford 191
  Elmer 234,290,340
  Elton 290
  Evelyn 295
  Hella 191
  James 239
  Lillian 290
  Roena 74,99
  William 290
BRADLEY, G. 166
  Gee 164
  Isham B. 380
  John 89,187
  Minnie Y. 380
BRADSHAW, Ephraim 127
  Solomon 148
BRAGG, Charlie 369
BRAHAN, John 149,172
  Mary 172
  Polly 172
BRAKE, Billy Joe 295
  Dr. J. G. 324
  Mollie 291,295
BRAME, Edward 306
BRANDON, Matthew 129
BRANNON, Frank 290
BRASHER, William 60,152,
    153,158
BRASHIER, William 79
BRASIER, Man 91
BRASURE, William 306
BRATTON, W. M. 284
BRAZEAL, George 20,54,239,
    306
BRAZELL, Emaline 105
BRAZIL, George 309
  Jackson 309
  Margaret 309
  Richard 312
BRAZZEL, Isom 315
BRAZELL, Allen 34
BRAZZELL, Bessie 287
  Carby 287
  Clarnece 292
  Coleman 287
  Della 282,292
  Elmer 282,292

BRAZZELL (cont.)
  Eva 295
  George 151
  Jackson 27
  John 194,200
  Lucinda 42
  Rachel 26
  Richmond 25
  Ritha 45
  Wesley 287
  William 345
BREADING, Esom 75
BRECKENRIDGE, James D.240
  Tennessee 240
BREEDEN, Lawrence 234
BRENIZER, Rick 265
BREWER, Allen 115
  Elizabeth 7
  Dr. James H. 83
  John 64,75,85,177,310
  Jno. 175
  Mary Ann 64
  Rep 118
  Ress 118
  S. 136,140,144,163,165,
    177
  Sally 175
  Sarah 39
  Sarah Elizabeth 64
  Starling 118,120
  Sterling 6,75,76,131,
    135,151,156,244,302,
    303,304
  Susan 64
BRIANT, James 87
BRIER, Patsy 60
BRIGGS, Nancy 41
BRIGHAM, Louisa 239
BRIGHT, Frank 327
  Frank L. 368
  Frankie 368
  Julia 368
  Lorena 328,368
  Vera 368
BRIM, A. J. 225
  Andrew Jackson 35,71
  Jackson 50
  William B. 225
BRIMM, Edward 176
BRIN, Andrew Jackson 35
BRINGHAM, Martha 14
BRINKES, D. R. 107
BRINKLEY, David 350
  Obed 350
  Robert D. 350
  Ruth 350
  T. C. 21
  T. M., Jr, 108
BRINN, Peggy 10
BROCK, Clyde 353
  John 8,14
  Minnie 353
  Robert 111
  Russell 186
BRODIE, Thomas 171
BROOKS, Jason 252,272
  Mathew 143
BROUGHTER, Samuel 37
BROW, A. Y. 200
BROWEN, Sarah Strong 202
BROWN,   248,325
  Capt. 322
  A. A. 69,96,318
  A. Y. 197
  Aaron 194,200
  Abner 150
  Adam 189
  Ala D. 372
  Alexander 307,312
  Alf 296
  Alford 311
  Andrew A. 313
  Anna 291

BROWN (cont.)
  Asa A. 55,305
  Asa Madison 55
  Azelia 18
  B. F. 195
  Beadie 291
  Ben 260
  Benjamin F. 223
  Benjamin Franklin 200,
    337
  Bulah 283
  Bunyan 374
  Cecil 291,366
  Charles 190
  Charles W. 60
  Clarence 292
  Claude 292
  Clayton 352
  Clyde 291
  Clude 291
  Corbitt 291
  D. R. 108
  Daimond 374
  Daniel 66
  David 133
  Decatur 391
  Dewey 292
  Dockie 373
  Doye 291
  Edith Mai 282
  Eliza 46
  Eliza Ann 34
  Elizabeth 32
  Elizabeth Ann 19
  Elsie Mai 282
  Elton 287,291
  Emmett 291
  Eva 292
  Fate 291
  Frances 133,146
  Francis 175,179,186
  Francis, Sr. 157
  Frank J. 373
  Fred 292
  Freeman 283
  G. W. 111
  Genie 291
  George 129
  George C. 46
  George Washington 223
  Georgenia 372
  Gilbert 298
  Grace 281
  Hannah E. 48
  Helen 292
  Homer 374
  Hubert 366
  Ida Mae 294
  Isaac 146,179,186,187
  Isadora 352
  J. E. 195
  J. G. 345
  J. H. 194,200
  J. J. 195
  James 28,42,58,68,115,
    119,129,170,188,189
  James M. 200
  Jane 65
  Jemisha 55
  Jesse 137
  Jim 66
  Joe 282
  Joe H. 234,339
  Julia 299
  John 35,37,38,39,42,47,
    48,49,64,68,72,77,81,
    87,118,141,146,155,
    161,162,177,181,202,
    261,271,294,302,311,
    352
  John, Sr. 311
  John B. 77,133,134,175,
    179,189,306
  John Humphreys 55

BROWN (cont.)
  John R. 48
  John S. 305
  John W. 11
  Jonathan 305
  Joseph 34,122,139,190
  Joshua 17
  Kelly 352
  Lela 298
  Lera 292
  Mrs. Lucinda 103
  Lular 110
  Lynn 292,295
  Mamie 292,295
  Margaret 12,42,209,250,
    270
  Mark 292,295
  Marsh 366
  Martha 68
  Martha J. 383
  Marvin 291
  Mary 291
  Minerva 292
  Minnie 292
  Dr. Morgan 137
  Nancy 22
  Noel 291
  Nora 386
  Norman 372
  Odie 291
  Orville 298
  Otho 298
  Polly 15
  Rachel 77,291,305
  Reuben 44
  Robert H. 14,15,21,77,
    97
  Rosser 77
  Ruth 291
  S. C. 195
  Sally 290
  Sam 1,267
  Samuel 9,276
  Sarah 21
  Sary 44
  Solomon 68
  Spencer 77,175,179,307
  Susan 14,106
  Susie 291
  T. 6,14
  Thomas 40,57,65,175,181,
    186
  Thurman 291
  Tillman 291
  Tommie 291
  Tommy 292
  Trula 291
  Turner 291
  Vegie 292
  Victor 338
  Wade 291
  Walter 386
  Wiley 194,200
  William 75,173,260
  William F. 77
  William P. 14
  Willie 366
  Wilma 290
BROWNING, Anna 327
  Archie 234
  B. W. 224
  C. 105
  Julia 299
  Millicent 112
  W. A. 224
  William Luther 234
BROYLES, V. L. 295
BRUCE,   226,227
  Benjamin 306
  Billie 290
  Charles 290
  D. 101
  Ella 288

BRUCE (cont.)
  Ercell 384
  George W. 32
  James W. 340
  John 157,288
  Laura 384
  Lemuel 309,322
  Lettie 384
  Loyd 299
  Margie 290
  Molly 288
  Nannie 299
  Nola 288
  S. D. 226,227
  Sarah 309
  Spartan 17,309
  Will 288
BRUMMET, William 312
BRUNET, Frank 234
BRUNETTE, Mary 290
BRUNS, David 70
  Emaline 70
BRYAN, Davis 63
  Harry 294
  J. R. 2,200,324
  James 284
  Jesse H. 39
  John 63
  Kedar 162,178
  Maggie E. 200
  Malinda Lenox 200
  Mattie M. 200
  Robert T. 200
  Sammy 294
  Thomas 312
  W. P. P. C. 200
BRYANT, Bell 290,299
  Belle 292,293,295
  Benjamin 312
  Mrs. Cecil 328
  Glen B. 379
  Hollie 288,293
  J. B. 328
  J. H. 274
  J. P. 108
  J. W. 194,200
  Jim 379
  Mamie 379
  Mary 83
  N. A. D. 42
  Park 379
BRYSON, Sarah L. 44
BUCHANAN, Allen 234
  E. A. 49
  James A. 115
  Ray 294
BUCKNER, Clara 370
  Clyde 343,345
  Clyde T. 234
  Dan 345
  Neil 295
  Ruthelma 343
  William 370
BUFORD, E. E. 264
  Hattie 331,370
  John C. 195,202
  Simeon 370
BUGG, Allen
  Chanie 53
  Delinda 12
  Dorcas 53
  Elizabeth 53
  Henry 53
  Jeremiah 53
  John 53
  Margaret 11
  Samuel 25,53,64,190,
    307,309
  Stiles 53,306
  William 53
  Willis 53,189
BUGGS, Style 187
BULL, Balaam 189,307

BULL (cont.)
  Eudora G. 111
  James 313
  Jeremiah 43
BULLARD, Mark 307
BULLIAN, John 191
  Thomas 191
BULLICK, William 306
BULLION, Henry 40,310
  Nancy 8
  Thomas 52,160,307
  William 160,169,182,310
BULLOCK, Addie 201
  James 8
  John A. 86
BUMPASS, Amanda 223
  Eliza T. 34
  John 189
  Thompkins 189
BUNCH, Andrew 322
  David 186,188
  Joseph 175
  Julia 322
  L. C. 322
BUQUO, Agness 331
  Clyde 329
  Edward 268
  G. W. 268
  H. C. 268
  Mary Agness 268
  Mary F. 268
  R. L. 268
BURCH, Bob 390
  Clyde B. 390
  Jack 390
  Lucille 390
  Lula 390
  Robert 345
BURFORD, Benjamin W. 14
BURGAN, Betsy 142,148
  John 123,132,146
BURGASS, Ann 112
BURGES, Helen 293
BURGESS, Araminta 36
  Auzey 306
  Charles 298
  Geneva 299
  Harvey 298
  John 29,80
  Joseph 42
  Larry L. 234
  Leon 298
  Margaret 10
  Margie 299
  Ozzy 310
  Patsy 9
  Polly 7,80
  Robert 297
BURGIE, Jane 21
  Jane A. 45
  Mrs. M. E. 102
  Nell 333
BURGIS, David 311
BURGISS, Elisha 312
BURKETT, Ephraim 164,190
  Sarah 52
  Susanna 164
  Thomas 52
BURKHART, Peter 197
BURNEY, J. D. 194,348
  Maggie 348
BURNS, _____ 243
  Caroline Jane 26
  Cyrus J. 312
  Elida 32
  Frances 38
  Hugh 47
  Larra 312
  Laura 305
  Thomas W. 223
BURPO, Lorenzo 27
BURPOE, Lorenzy 312
BURTON, Ambesse 61,305

BURTON (cont.)
  Ambrose H. 238
  Charles H. 9
  Crissie 19,20
  H. H. 79
  John H. 118
  Martin H. 78,188,306
  Polly 61
  R. H. 18
  Reuben P. H. 79
  Robert 313
  S. H. 18
  W. D. H. 79
  W. H. 194,202
  William H. 174
BUSBY, John 178
  Micajah 169,306
  Mills 169
  Robert 188
BUSH, Jesse 287
  Mary 287
  Nannie 287
  Tom 287
BUSSELLE, Absalom T. 200
BUTLER, Aaron 104
  Burrel R. 78
  Charles 187
  Elizabeth 239,304
  John 195
  Joshua 187
BUTTREY, Alfred 292
  Arthur 292
  Clara 291
  Clarence 295
  Dausey 292
  Docia 292
  Dorsey 234
  Mrs. Florence Ann 333
  Frances 295
  M. 374
  M. D. 327
  Ruth 292,333
  Sam 292
  Thelma 291
  Washington G. L. 33
  William G. W. 202
  William George D. 195
BYERS, John 310
  Maggie 348
BYNUM, Elizabeth 310
  H. J. 295
BYRN, Allie 287,297
  James 297
  S. M. 200
  William 297
BYRNE, Neil W. 33
  Tommy 270
BYRON, James 309
CAIN, John 362
  William 96
CALDWELL, Dr. _____ 172
  A. 63,167
  A. B. 224
  Abraham 242,302
  Abram 52,58,60,72,129,
    144,305,312
  Andrew 151,172
  Dorrie Sue 295
  David 159
  Edward 49
  Elizabeth 30,47
  Elizabeth W. 65
  Ella Mae 296
  Emaline 72
  Henry 392
  J. H. 270
  Jack 273
  James 189
  John 310
  John Campbell Crawford
    72
  John H. 48
  Joseph 123

CALDWELL (cont.)
  Maryann 23
  Melberry 110
  Nancy 72
  Oscar Dunreth 195
  P. O. 224,297
  Polly 72
  R. W. 327
  Reney 113
  Robert 14
  Roger 246
  Shaw. 269,274
  Thomas M. 24
  William 38,137,138,140,
    151,153,160,170,172,
    177
CALHON, Ella 375
  Mary 375
CALL, Addie 287
  C. F. 102
  Ellis 287
  Ethel 287
  Robert P. 105,223
  Tobe 374
CALLIER, Howell 53
CAMEL, Mary A. 383
  Ralph 383
CAMES, John 306
CAMP, James 6
CAMPBELL, A. 130
  Alexander 91,282,299
  Alexr 310
  Amy 179
  Benoni 244
  Charles 153,168,177,179
  Donald 298
  Edmond 187
  James 179
  John 179
  Matthew 191
  Mildred 298
  Susan D. 200
CAMPLER, Rafred. 305
CANE, William 30
CANNON, David 114
  G. G. 199
  Henry 114
  Newton 234,299
  Newton E. 340
CANON, Robert 165
CANTRELL,_____ 113
CAPPS, Charles T. 234
  Sterling 194,202
  William 127
CAR, Meckins 310
CARBON, B. B. 55
CARD, Joseph 155
CARICK, John 152
CARINGTON, Archibald 75
  John 75
  John, Sr. 75
CARMION, Anthony G. 311
CARNELL, Ira 102
CARNES, Jacob 19
CARNEY, Floyd 281
  Forrest 282
  Ham 282
  Velma 282
CARNS, Thomas 119,120
CAROLAND, Richard 42
CAROOTH, James 311
CAROTHERS, Andrew 169,170
  James 8,18
  John 179
CARPENTER, John 147
  John B. 67
  Mary 67
CARR, Beechie 281
  Bob 363
  George W. 201
  Gideon 235
  Iva 291
  J. T. 202

CARR (cont.)
  John B. 62,71,296,311
  John Bluford 201
  M. 22
  Martha 48
  Mickins 56,58
  Sarah 35
  Solomon 21
  Susan Hamner 201
  Susanna 71
  T. J. 108
  Tennessee Porter 201
  Thomas J. 195,201
  William H. 71,284
CARROTHERS, John 15
CARRINGTON, William 75
CARROLL, Decima 297
  Edith 369
  Elizabeth 62
  Ellington 36
  George 369
  H. M. 280
  Hillary 369
  J. J. 201
  James Jackson 195
  John C. 312
  Mary 291
  Mary J. 43
  Nancy 41
  Phines 369
  Robert 46
  Sally 306
  Sarah Jane 49,222
  Susan 49
  William 40,85,311
CARRUTHE, James 12
CARSON, John 49
CARTEO, Amanda M. 33
CARTER, Abetha P. 12
  Armour 295
  Dr. B. M. 3
  B. N. 57
  Belfield N. 311
  Catherine 44
  Essie 282
  Frank 282
  Granville 42
  Hettice 295
  James 46,58,311
  James L. 234
  Jeff T. 234
  Jim 282
  Jimmy 344
  Mary R. 368
  Nancy 12
  Sally 282
  Walter 282
  Will 282
  William C. 234
  William T. 62
CARTON, Cerba 292
CARUTH, Sally 12
CARUTHERS, John 180
  John, Jr. 155
  William 155,174
CARVER, Jane 107
  Neil 107
CARVIN, William 108
CARY, Francis 190
CASE, Francis 23
  Sarah 23
CASEY, Hixum 181
CASKEY, John R. 306
CASTELMAN, Ira
CASTLEMAN, A. G. 273
  D. L. 343
  David 312
  Edna 298
  John 37
  Nancy 37
  W. S. 274
CASWELL, William 127,130
CATES, William 144

CATHEY, Archibald 310
  Archie 194,201
  Archy 57
  Bessie 298
  Daniel 26,57,310
  David 57
  Dolly 27,57
  Elias Newton 195
  Flora 282
  George 57,307
  Horace 282
  Iva 291,296
  J. D., Jr. 276
  Jane 57
  John 57
  John R. 47,57
  Joshua 57,225,310
  Leo 291
  Lorene 282
  Lou 392
  Margaret 310
  Marguerite 44
  Martin 31,57
  Maude 351
  Maudie 282
  Newton 201
  Nolan 291
  Paul 298
  Peggy 57
  S. 225
  Samuel 40,57
  W. J. 194,201
CATLIN, Herbert 271
CATRON,_____ Judge 67,308
CAVENDER, George Bryant
  195
  Mack 234
CAVIDSON, Calvin 194
CAYCE, Mary C. 199
CEE, Hack 182
CEPHART, Perry A. 47
CHADEWICK, James E. 223
CHADOCK, Permelia 10
CHADWICK, J. A. 102
CHAMBERLAIN D. C. 65,68
CHAMBERS, Polly 306
  William 186
CHAMY, Sarah 108
CHANCE, Robert 190
CHANDLER,_____ 293
  Allie 282
  Alvin 282
  Howard 282
  Pearl 282
  R. D. 295
  Ruth 282
CHAPLIN, William H. 271
CHAPMAN, Elizabeth 343
  Louisa 42
CHAPPEL, Dorothy 336
  W. H. 225
CHAPPELL,_____ Moore 211
  Charles 211,294,342
  Drury 30
  Edna 356
  Ella 321
  George M. 340
  Iro 356
  Maggie 356
  Nancy 43
  Roy 356
  Wade 356
CHARLES, Hardin 306
CHARLESWORTH, Dr._____ 329
CHARLTON, Christiana 47
  Edwin 281
  Elizabeth 375
  Hugh 375
  James 375
  Lena 375
  Odell 375
  W. C. 280
CHAUDOIN, Leuallen 17

CHAUDOIN (cont.)
  R. 30
  Reuben 10,11,13,14,15,
    17,18,21,22,29,35
CHEATHAM, ___ 199
  Anderson 135
  Francis 327
  John B. 125
CHESTER, A. J. 201
  C. B. 193,201
  Claiborne 201
  J. A. 201
  John 322
  Joseph H. 39
CHESTNUT, Sam 212
CHEW, Lucille 282
CHICESTER, Cirus 197
CHICHESTER, Cyrus 48,201
CHILD, Smith 166
CHILDRESS, Betsy 117
  Elizabeth 117
  John 117,131,153
  Martha 366
  Mitchell 188
  Nathaniel 309
  Stephen 134,136,150,151
  T. M. 195,202
  Thomas 130,366
CHISENHALL, Alexander 86
CHIZENHALL, Alexander 307
CHOAT, James 86,94
  John 163
  Joseph 86
  Thomas 121
CHOATE, ___ 332
  Aaron 183
  Albert 292
  Ed. 282
  Eleanor 60,310
  Elizabeth 17
  Ethel 292
  Evie 292
  G. W. 48
  Hattie 282
  Henry 282
  Isaiah 51
  Jackson 310
  James 14,103,224,311,
    319
  James M. 274
  James Marion 201
  John 60,304
  John H. 60
  Joseph 88,310
  Leslie 282
  Lester 282
  Linda 282
  Lucresa 17,19
  Marvin 274,292
  Mary 292
  Mary Duke 201
  Ola 292
  Palia 107
  Peter 17,60,310
  S. E. 201
  S. J. 17
  Squire J. 60,68
  Thomas 173,183
  Virgil 292
  Vernie 282
  Walter 292
  William 342
  Zelmer Jones 291
CHRISMAN, George 43
  Joseph 25
CHRISTER, Serlane 24
CHRISTIAN, D. 136,140
  Donna M. 48
  Drewry 183
  Drury 140,154,155,158,
    162,165,166,170,171,
    177,178,263,304
  Elizabeth 22

CHRISTIAN (cont.)
  J. H. 21,332
  J. W. 23
  James 186
  James W. 270,304,311
  Jesse 145
  Jesse G. 52,181
  Letticia B. 38
  Paralee D. 25
CHRISTMAN, Rachel 22
CHRISTY, Harman 313
  Ita (?) 310
  Martha 43
CHRISWELL, Andrew 189
CHUN, Roy 283
CHRUCHILL, Mrs. John 329
CIMBARD, John 136
CLAGHORN, Robert 306
CLAIBORNE, Thomas 137,138,
  146
CLARDY, James 320
  Lucy J. 45
  P. 320
CLARK, A. D. 333
  Abija 189
  Benjamin 23,134,304,310
  C. H. 201
  George 23,110,116,131,
    135,136,156,166,235,
    244,253,302,305,307,
    311
  George W. 72,195
  J. C. 100
  J. W. 322
  Jane 59,72,268
  Martha 7
  Mary 8,105,153
  O. V. 333
  Paralee 49
  Richardson L. 59
  Serena 290
  Thomas 48
  Tobias 304
  William 11,163,191
  William L. 232
CLARKE, Gertrude 384
  Roy M. 382
  William 171
CLARKSTON, Joshua 26
CLAXGON, Joshua 311
CLAY, Nancy Anne 35
  Robert T. 38
  Sally 63
CLAYBURN, Randall 343
CLEGHORN, Robert 304
CLEMENS, Maggie 377
  Robert 377
CLEMENT, Agnes Shipp 293
  Anna Belle 295,343
  Archie 377
  Frank G. 333,343,344,
    345
  Ida 333
  J. A. 271
  J. M. 343
  James A. 377
  Reba 336
  Robert 333,377
  Robert S. 326
  W. A., Sr. 331
CLEMENTS, Agnes A. 377
  Etta M. 370
  Ida A. 377
  Malcolm 377
  Mary 202
  Newton 377
  Robert 268
  W. 128
  Will 370
  Wm. R. B. 159
CLEMMER, Jimmy 343
CLEMMONS, Mary J. 45
CLERK, William 167

CLIFF, Barny 79
CLIFT, John 118
  Sary 121
  Thomas 166
CLIFTON, Addie Bullock 201
  Ann 290
  Annie 293
  Arthur 293
  B. A. 201,202
  Bertie 293
  Burl A. 375
  Burrel A. 195
  Carl 293
  Clara Mae 290
  Elton 294
  Eva 290
  J. W. 194,201,204
  James K. 22,309
  James Kirby 195
  Jim 330
  Jimmy 290
  John J. 309
  Noah 293
  Ruby 293
  Samuel J. 234
  Smitha 375
  William 311
CLIMER, Charles Elbert 195
CLINARD, A. W. 269,335
  Z. N. 269,274
CLINE, Almira White 202
  Catherine Stewart 202
  George H. 195,202
CLINTON, Mrs. 3
CLOUD, Joseph F. 304
CLOYS, Ethel 390
  Ruby 390
  William 390
CLYMER, C. J. 194,201,204
COART, John 173
COBB, C. C. 68
COBBLER, Martin H. 30
COCHRAN, A. D. 24
  Jaretha Caroline 64
  William 114,123,150
COCK, Richard 162
COCKE, James 14
  John 146
  Richard 56,86,135,162
  Spilsby 310
  William 115
COCKS, Richard 307
COFFEE, Mrs. 4
COFFY, Joseph 310
COLDWELL, W. 69
COLE, Chesla O. 80
  Estha 338
  Henry 32
  J. E. 281
  Nonnie Powers 215
  Parthenia A. 367
  William 215
COLEMAN, Alex R. 316
  Allene 295
  Anne 41
  Daniel 166,182,306
  Elizabeth 61
  George L. 366
  Harriet A. 48
  Henry 38
  Jane E. 33
  Jesse 26
  John 247,306,316,321
  John W. 35,312
  Joseph 172
  Lucile 366
  Moses 85
  Nannie 354
  Ruth 366
  Thomas 73
  Thomas F. 366
  Thomas J. 366
  Tom 247,321

COLEMAN (cont.)
  W. S. 48,49,61,68
  William S. 60,85,94,310
  William W. 190
COLEY, John M. 311
COLLIER, B. A. 3,14,17
  B. H. 69
  Bessie 362
  Bethel 293
  Christopher C. 202
  Clyde 389
  Darius 311
  Elizabeth 29
  G. T. 342
  George T. 389
  Herman 362
  Holmes 389
  Iris 389
  J. M. 195
  John C. 64,69,72,298,
    307,311
  Lizzie 389
  M. E. 101
  Mary C. 22
  Mary Clements 202
  Mary J. 43
  Nathan 14
  Robert 91
  Sarah 35
  T. J. 22
  T. L. 11,13,111
  Theodore L. 298
  Thos. 75,307
  Tho. W. 18,91,311
  Tom 271
  Vera 293
  Walter 389
  William 4,362
  Wm. C. 347
  Willie 294
  Willis 9,90
COLLINS, Emma 355
  Frederic 305
  George, Jr. 355
  George, Sr. 271
  George C. 355
  Hazard 193,202
  James P. 12
  Lewis 157,187,188
  Lewis D. 27
  Tillis 305
  William 122
COLMAN, Joseph 117
COLTHARP, William H. 14
COLWELL, Andrew 172
  William 172
COMBS, William 168,179
COMER, Adaline 79
  E. A. 78
  Mark M. 78
  R. E. 78,80,83
COMES, Milly 41
  Reuben 56
CONANT, _____ 2
  Irene 392
  Larry 392
  W. J. 324
  Will 247,321
CONLEY, Iva 370
CONNELL, Charlotte 118
  Gilbert 291
  William 117,118
CONNELLEY, Christopher 173
CONNELLY, Peter 187
CONNER, John E. 313
  Moses 313
  Nathaniel 313
CONNERS, Pat 197,202
CONNLEY, Carl 273
COOK, Callie 376
  Collier 298
  Cynthia A. 73
  Gilford 310

COOK (cont.)
  James 86,310
  James P. 376
  James W. 39
  John 191
  John M. 340
  Mary A. 39
  Dr. Mary Baxter 271,343
  Parthenia 29
  William 142,357
  William Loch 339
  William Richard 195
COOKE, Peter 86
COOKSEY, A. J. 318
  Andrew 190
  Fannie 324
  George 311
  George T. 58,61,72,92
  Jesse R. 342
  Jesse Rook 234
  Lucinda 9
  Mary 297
  Pheba 61,304
  Phebe Anne 45
  Philip 94
COOLEY, George 191
  Richard 191
  Victoria A. Wyly 213
  Rev. W. M. 273
COON, Ada 293
  George 36
COONE, George W. 344
  George W., Jr. 235
COOPER, Allie 288
  Ashley 378
  John 21,185,187,188
  Lemmie 288
  Lilly 287
COPELAND, Burton 355
  Eva 355
  Frank 355
  John 106
  Jenet 53
COPPAGE, Alexander 313
  John J. 305
CORBAN, Burrell B. 69
  Stephen 119
  Wilkins 311
  William 119
CORBIN, Helen 298
  Percy 298
CORBITT, Clinton 283
  Dorothy 283
  Will, Jr. 283
CORDING, Jerome B. 202
  Rosannah J. Bowen 202
  Sarah Bowen 202
COREY, Nancy 79
CORLEW, Ada B. 205
  Benjamin 72,266
  Bernard T. 340
  Catherine 205
  Elizabeth 209
  James 204
  John 28
  John Randolph 195
  Leona 205
  Lucinda 204
  Mrs. Mary S. 343
  Melvina 214
  Parks 282
  Mrs. R. E. 343
  Richard D. 205
  Robert 317,343,344
  Robert E. 301
  Van 343
  William H. 110
CORMAN, Pat 205
CORNELL, Nancy 33
CORNET, Hiram 17
COROMNY, James 306
CORY, G. S. 105
COTHAIN, Tilford 265

COTHAM, J. H. 15
COTTINHAM, William 188
COULN, Richard 42
COULTER, Dane 279
  J. A. 99
COUNCIL, Aquilla 79
  Eliza 18
  James 79
  Lisa 79
  Lovy 20,60
  Lydia 11
  Martha 19
  Patsy 79
  Willis 79,195
COUNCILE, Rebecca 79
COWAN, _____ 270,338
  Daisey 357
  Daisy 294
  Florence 357
  Florence E. Turner 202
  Floyd 357
  H. T. 342
  Horace 270
  Horace J. 357
  James 357
  Mrs. J. Max 342
  John Max 195
  John Maxwell 202
  Margaret 78
  Turner H. 357
COX, _____ 231,284
  Alfred 387
  Benjamin 75
  Callie 212
  Cendarella 75
  Dave 387
  George 313
  J. C. 330
  James 309
  Mattie 387
  Ottis 387
  Roy 387
  S. A. 194,202
  Samuel W. 245
  Thomas 75
  W. J. 194,202
  Will 387
  William 138,190,224,253,
    306,310,319
  William James 109
  Winnefred 75
CRABTREE, John P. 143
CRAFT, Annie 382
  Frank 382
  Franklin 309
  G. R. 85
  George R. 57
  James 57
  James A. 13
  Jesse 57,84,128,137,303
  Jim 382
  Margaret 57
  Nannie 222
  Samuel 85
CRAGE, Eli 188
  John 188
CRAGEHEAD, Alexr. 121
CRAIG, Benjamin R. 27
  Claude 268
  Claudie 385
  Earl 275
  Elma 385
  Eula 385
  Francis 344
  J. E. 195
  James 135,141
  John 165,168,169,253
  Nettie 385
CRAIGE, Benjamin R. 312
CRAIN, Dick 349
  Egbert 349
  Eloise 349
  John T. 349

CRAIN (cont.)
  Lee K. 349
  Malcomb E. 349
  Rebecca 42
  Thomas 349
CRANE, John 191,306
CRATTY, Bertha 292
  Blanche 292
  Clarence 292
  Ilma 292
  Mary 292
  Warren 292
CRAWFORD, ____ 203
  Benoni 305
  Christine 334
  Daniel 87
  David 8,163
  Fannie 253
  Thomas 130
CREACH, Penelope 25
  William 25
CREECH, Gordon 299
  Lenorah 110
  Louisa 31
  Thomas 112,225
  William 225,309
  Willie 113
CRENSHAW, David 9
CREWDSON, William 311
CREWS, Andrew J. 383
  Barbary H. 58
  Benja 82,84
  Benjamin 75,145,189,
    190,304
  Chacey 383
  Dan 383
  Dolly 23
  Elizabeth T. 58
  John 82,190,304
  Lavina C. 39
  Lucinda 82
  Malcome 383
  Mary A. 383
  Peter M. 82
  Pleasant 186,304,311
  Sarah 31
  Sarah Ann B. 58
  Seaborn 311
  Seburn 75,82,304
  Vance S. 58
  William 190
CRICK, Ira 289
CRICKMAN, Edith 298
  John Thomas 298
CRISMAN, Susannah 74
CRITTENDEN, William 309
CROCKET, Annie E. 353
  George N. 353
  Rev. Henry 324
  Rebekah 353
  William 184
CROCKETT, ____ Judge 289
  Judge W. 29
CROOK, William 280
CROSBY, Bertha 375
  Charlotte 375
  Fannie 375
  Floyd W. 375
  Howard 375
  J. F. 338
  Nellie 375
CROSON, A. J. H. 224
CROSS, Henon 232
  John 187
  Noah 42
CROSSNOE, Thomas 146,176,
    178,186
CROSSWELL, Nimrod 137
CROTZER, W. T. 329
CROUCH, Dr. W. H. 289
CROW, Allen G. 43
  Burnie H. 378
  Douglas 282

CROW (cont.)
  Eli 58,76,116
  Mrs. Eliza 106
  Elizabeth 58
  Era Fussell 290
  George 281
  Gertrude 378
  Jessie 311
  John 35
  Louise 378
  M. B. 194,203
  M. M. 271
  Martha Anne 31
  Nancy 40
  Rollen 290
  Russell 378
CROWDER, Bertie 288
  Ivan 288
  Stella 288
CROWELL, Cephia 375
  Mrs. Dee 246
  William Penn 223
CRUICK (?), Davidson 59
CRUMP, F. J. 277
CRUMPLER, Ann 310
  Dicy 32
  Eliza 14,204
  Elizabeth 14
  John G. 30,310
  Mathew 136,146
  Matthew 57,75,304,311
  Matthew J. 14,311
  Newt. 17
  Raiford 168
  Raford M. 310
  Rafred 305
  Raifred 57
  Raiford 136
CRUNK, Davidson 312
  W. C. 111
  Wm. C. 197
  William C. 203
CRUTCHER, A. H. 2,245
  Elizabeth 14
  Estelle 389
  Hester A. 389
  J. P. 195
  Lorene 389
  Tho. 119
  Will 389
CUGH, Lucy 32
CULLOM, Robert 280
CUMMUM, Allie 365
  E. G. 195
  E. M. 74,103
  Gordon 365
  J. H. 225
  Katie 365
  Merwyn 365
  Roy 365
  Thelma 365
  W. E. 247,321,329
  William 365
  Wilton 365
CUMMINGS, James 9
CUMMINS, Amy 371
  Benj. 78
  John, Jr. 371
  John B. 371
  Louise 371
  Sam 371
  W. J. 247,321
CUNIFF, Hattie 281,290
  Mike 290
CUNNIFF, Hattie 292
CUNNINGHAM, A. J. 194,203
  Alice Jane 299
  Andrew 49
  E. L. 194,203
  Elijah W. 63
  Gideon 311
  James 11,62,96
  Jesse 306

CUNNINGHAM (cont.)
  Joe 299
  John 62,96,281,306,311
  Malissa 203
  Malissa P. 71
  Martha J. 34
  Mary 9
  Nathaniel 14,62,71,85,
    203,311
  Sarah 62
  Thomas 11,13,14,62,85,
    312
  William 62
  Willis 310
CURRY, David 187
  Mrs. Frank 333
  John 139
  William 160
CURTIS, Ada 295
  F. 223
  James Alford 195
  Joel 316
  John 188
CUTHERN, Gains F. 109
DAILY, D. A. 327
  Nannie 327
DAINS, Samuel A. 21
DALTON, Frances M. 37
DANE, Joseph 30
  Nancy 28
DANEE, Annie Laurie 295
DANIEL, Mr. ____ 324
  Mrs. 293
  Agnes 378
  Benjamin 235
  Claude 282
  Clayton 287
  Elijah 378
  Elizabeth 44,104,112
  Ennis 287
  Eunice 287
  Faustina 297
  Glynn 282
  Harris 297
  Harris Greer 297
  Howard 378
  J. 45
  J. J. 194,203
  Jas. 63,64,73
  James 10,21,24,25,26,31,
    32,33,34,35,36,38,40,
    44,47,48,49,73,118,
    306,310
  Jesse 45,112
  Jessie 318
  Joe 203
  John 85,238,306
  Joseph 129
  Joseph T. 311
  Kate 372
  Loyd 282
  Mary 288
  Matilda 238
  Phoebe 45
  Polly 297
  Robert E. 234
  Rosie 282
  Ruth 289
  Sally 14,238
  Sarah E. 36
  Tennessee Dickson 198
  W. H. 318,327
  W. R. 225
  William 297,378
  Willie 11
  Woodrow 57
  Woodson 312
  Mrs. Z. E. 327
  Zellie Ray 280
DANIELS, Herschel B. 343
  James 192
  Jesse 246
DANNAH, Solomon 311

DANSBY, M. E. 283
DARBY, George 174
DARNELL, Alex 345
DARR, Elizabeth 307
DARROW, B. M. G. 38
  Benjamin 28,32,38,40,
    235
  Benjamin, Jr. 14,18
  Benjamin, Sen. 17
DAUBENSPECK, D. F. 223
DAUGHERTY, Jean 345
  Joe 345
DAUGHTERTY, Martin 197
DAUGHTERY, James 31
DAVE, Joseph 30
  Nancy 28
DAVENPORT, Chancery 77
DAVID, C. 140
  Claudius 119
  Elizabeth 53,304
  Isaac 152
  James, J.P. 39
  L. C. 160
  L. Claudius 53,160,170
  Leon 297
  William 271
DAVIDLE, C. 137
DAVIDSON, _____ 53
  Abraham 85,305
  Alexander 180
  Aquilla 55
  Artemica 43
  Calvin 203
  David 62
  Elijah 31,62,95
  Elizabeth 8,55,59
  Gene 344
  Geo. 89
  George 14,59,86,89,94,
    235,243,304,312,386
  Green 202,203
  H. A. 225
  Henry 62
  Howell 312
  Howell H. 21,25
  J. M. 225
  J. W. 194,203
  James 33,62,85,188
  James M. 32
  Jane 8
  Jay 270
  Jesse 85
  John 53,55,62,84,95,
    131,135,152,156,186,
    188,242,244,302,311
  Joseph 55,56,62,84,164,
    237,305
  Josiah 306
  Launa 386
  M. 48
  M. V. 100
  Malilda 62
  Mary 61,62
  Mary Jane 29
  Peggy 62
  Pernelia 94
  S. B. 73
  Mrs. Sallie 103
  Sarah 21,25,62,79,85,
    265,312
  Susan 94
  Thomas 79,85,190,202,
    203,242
  V. Eugene 235
  Vilet 311
  Violet 62,296
  William 43,62,75
DAVIE, James H. 76
  William Richardson 130
DAVIES, Alice 360
  Clyde 360
  William J. 360
DAVIS, _____ 148

DAVIS (cont.)
  Andrew 189
  Ara 289
  Archibald 124
  Bessie 386
  Carl 269,289
  Catherine 204
  Clyde 345
  Dovie 355
  Edward 289
  Elizabeth 13
  Etta 386
  Frederick 235
  George 330
  Gideon 45,68
  Golden 289
  Harry 338,343,355
  Hattie 329
  Henry 135
  Huldy 312
  Isaac 85,87
  J. 248,330,331
  J. K. 202,203
  James 117
  John 51,122,123,132,
    143,145,158,163,175,
    178,180,307
  John A. 183
  John Ashe 154,181
  John B. 370
  Josiah Knox 195
  Kiziah 33
  Luther 370
  Mamie 218
  Marvin 362
  Mary 97,377
  Maryann 17
  Mellie 362
  Moses 186
  Nancy 28
  Nelson 203
  O'Neal 297
  Paralee 44
  Rebecca Harvey 203
  Robert V. 340
  Sophia W. 163
  Tennessee 370
  Thelma 295,355
  W. J. 284
  Wiley 40,64,68
  Will 386
  Will F. 339
  William 129,149,154,
    170,181
  Willie 186
  Willis 306,311
DAVY, Ashburn 188
DAWSON, Ben W. 203
  John 326
  Larkin 77,137,140,306
  W. L. 75,76
  Willis A. 82
DE___, Jesse 305
DEADRICK, Thomas 77
DEAL, Leegie 295
  Lola 295
  Lora 295
DEAN, _____ 232
  Hazel 299
  Jim 271
  Katherine 299
  Opal 293
  Robert 130
DEASON, _____ 125,298,299
  Albert 299
  C. P. 113
  Imogene 298
  John 5
  Maudie 293
  Mildred 299
  Montine 299
  Sara 295
  W. R. 195

DEASON (cont.)
  Warren 299
DE BUSK, Evelyn 298
DEBUSK, Marion 291
  Thelma 291
  W. A. 299
DECKER, Silas 279,280
DE HAVEN, George W. 324
DELOACH, Simon 49,86,190,
    191,310
DELONAS, William 195
DE LONES, Mary Connell 291
DEMERY, Robert 311
  William 311
DENNING, Elizabeth 323
DENNIS, L. R., M.G. 44
DENVER, Duke 252
DEPRIEST, Hugh 37
  Leland 283
DERRYBERRY, Rev. J. H. 275
DESHAZER, Susan 47
  William G. 94
DICKERSON, Caleb 156
  Edwin 195
  Edwin Hayes 203
  James 252
  Winnie Tate 203
DICKINS, J. W. 232
DICKINSON, Calep 145
  John 120
DICKISON, Caleb 144
DICKS, Artimeca 36
  Artimissa 36
  John P. 312
DICKSON, _____ 109
  A. 81
  Abigail 52
  Abner 51,148,154
  Adam 78
  Alexr. 80
  Alexander 54,55,75,77,
    78,83,145,167,167,305
  Alvin 297
  Anderson W. 115
  Ann 51
  Caleb 143,153
  Christopher 266
  Christopher W. 69
  David 5,51,130,135,136,
    138,147,154,156,181,
    303
  Edward 115,126,135,164
  Elisha 160
  Eliza 14
  Elizabeth A. 33
  Elizabeth Jane 13,51
  Fannie 299
  Henry 112
  Hugh 51,78,82,116,135,
    169,185,305,313
  Hugh, Jr. 306
  J. C. 296
  J. E. 113
  J. W. 71
  James 51,117,120,133,
    145,154,162,164,169,
    170,172,176,178,182,
    242,266,313
  James D. 310
  James W. 78
  Jane 51,134,151
  Joe 372
  John 78,82,88,114,126,
    134,135,139,157,158,
    164,169,178,182,183,
    305,313
  John B. 43
  Joseph 51,68,78,82,130,
    165,186,235
  Jos. A. 9,65
  Joseph Morrison 61
  L. A. 296
  Laura 299

DICKSON (cont.)
  Leven 167,187
  Levin 51,86,87,180,238,
    255
  Mable 372
  Malinda 35
  Martha 68,69,164,310
  Mary 298
  Mary Julia 297
  Michael 51,120,128,130,
    133,134,146,151
  Minerva J. 213
  Molten 253
  Molton 5,6,8,9,10,12,13,
    19,51,68,130,135,136,
    145,164,172,181,283,
    302,305
  Nancy 30
  Nollie 234
  Omer 365
  Ora 365
  Peggy 60,61
  Priscilla 68
  Rachel Ann Elizabeth 61
  Rebecca C. 24
  Robert 6,51,60,78,82,88,
    139,147,167,170,191,
    305
  Robert Patton 61
  Robertson 304
  Ruben 9
  Sadie 299
  T. R. 326
  Thomas 313
  Thos. K. 112
  Thurman 297
  W. H. 203,268
  William 1,51,115,149,
    169,301
  William, Jr. 132
  William Hendry 195
DICUS, James 190
DIEN, Caber 44
DIKEMAN, Mrs. 247,321
DILLAHAY, Nancy 312
  Nathan 168
DILLAHUNT, Sam 66
DILLARD, Ardie 295
  Hamer 292
  Hubert 300
  Rev. J. A. 274
  John 195,260,289,291
  Lula 295
  Richard 291
  Ruby 291,292
  Sam 291
DILLEHA, Nancy 213
DILLEHAY, Alford 33
  Alfred 94
  John G. 191
  Nancy 52,91,94
  Nancy, Jr. 94
  Nancy Anne 40
  Nathan 52,91,93,94,129,
    181,183,242,305
  Phelissan 94
  Philemon 94
  Starling 120,132,133
  Sterling 53
DILLIARD, B. D. 225
DILLIHAY, Robert 36,94
DILLGARD, John 225
DINING, John 143
DINNICK, Peter 148
DISINPORT, Chancey 55
DISMUKES, G. C. 200
DIXON, Levin 52,163,177
DOACK, William 116
DOAK, William 303
DOAKE, Mary 363
  William 134,138,139
DOBSON, Demps 225
DODD, Nora 295

DODGE, E. W. 259
DODSON, Abraham 158
  C. C. 64
  Catherine Davis 204
  Eliza C. Hopkins 204
  Emma 362
  George C. 224
  Gerome 95
  J. A. 204
  J. E. 195
  James M. 65,66
  Jennie 362
  Joseph C. 11
  Manervia 27
  Mary 390
  Mary A. E. Laird 204
  Newton 44
  Perry 390
  R. 101
  Susan 65
  Washington 390
  William 192,204,311,
    323
  William B. 305
DOLTON, Robert 39
DONALDSON, Annie L. 387
  Harry 366
  Hattie 366
  Julie 366
  May 366
  Meda 387
  Rawleigh 234
  Rollie 366
DONE, Joseph 30
DONEGAN, _____ 277
  A. J. 326
  Ada 327
  Albeth 295
  Alice 290
  Ann 290
  Arnold 287
  Cecil 290
  Clara 287
  Clint 299
  Dewey 287
  Diamond 287
  Elizabeth 8
  Emaline 205
  Ewel 287,290
  Genevieve 290
  George 382
  Graham 290
  Hattie 288
  Ida 364
  J. C. 324
  J. M. 290
  J. W. 105
  James 290
  Jim 287
  John 296
  John S. 364
  Josephine 204
  June 290
  Leona 287
  Lillie 287
  Linda 299
  Lizzie 382
  Lloyd 287
  Lou Dora 290
  Lura 382
  Marson 294
  Mary 382
  Mary E. 351
  Mattie 299
  McKinley 299
  Mildred 290
  Morrison 288
  Myrtle 287
  N. R. 102
  Novie 290
  Robert L. 382
  Rosa 287
  Roxie 287

DONEGAN (cont.)
  Roy 293
  Scott W. 374
  Verlie 295
  Walton 287
  William 205
DONELSON, Dora 211
  Colonel John 301
DONNEGAN, J. C. 245
DONNEHUE, Lt. _____ 225
DONNELLY, L. B. 294
DONNIGAN, William 307
DOOLY, Thomas 197,204
DORCH, Isaack 92
  William H. 92
DORTCH, Isaac 69
  Martha 69
DOTSON, _____ 334
  David G. 40
  Elijah 9
  Emma 292
  George 316
  George C. 225,319
  George G. 312
  J. C. 106
  James J. 9
  Jeanetta 218
  John 316
  John W. 195,225
  Leonard 334
  Monroe G. 39
  Nancy 9,10
  Sarah 39
  Thomas 204
  W. B. 9,11,16,19,20,29
  William C. 49
DOTY, Bertha 288
  Brown 334
  James 288
  Job P. 27
  Jobe 311
  John A. 195
  Lee 288
  Nellie 288
  Robert 190,239
  Tom 288
  William 239
DOUGHERTY, J. W. 178
  Martin 193
DOUGLAS, Alfred H. 42
  Catherine 25
  David 195
  James 180,188,237,239,
    244
  Martha 54
DOUGLASS, James 118,253,
    305
DOW, Lorenzo 265
DOWDEN, Bud 274
  Sarah 313
DOWNS, Henry 116
  Henry D. 116
DOXY, Jeremiah 150
DOZIER, A. L. 202
  Albert 380
  Elizabeth R. 380
  Joseph 13
DRAKE, George 57
  J. R. 86
  James 57,85
  Mary 57,85,306
  R. 145
  Robert 117,122,130,136,
    137,143,159,242
DRANE, S. 268
  Mrs. Stonewall 218
DREWRY, John 122
  Morgan 122,163
DRIVER, Abner 75
DROUILLARD, Ada Sorg Mrs.
    333
  Florence Kirkman 277
  J. P. 246,333

DROUILLARD (cont.)
  James P. 277
DRUMMOND, James M. 58
  Margaret G. 8
  Peggy 58,88
  Thomas 58,304
  William 58,88
  Z. 86
  Zaccheus 76
  Zacheus 58
DRUMMONDS, Anna 29
  Margaret 92,310
  Minerva 16
  Thomas 76
  Ths., Jr. 88
  Mrs. Zack 248
DRURY, John 115,116,146
  Morgan 147,161,164
DUDLEY, Dolly 7
  Gurtha 293
  Henry 372
  Hudson 8,306
  Hutson 256,302
  Louise 283
  Lucy 293
  Mary 68
  Nicholas 61,256
  Polly 7
  Pullen A. 41
  Tina 293
  William 310
  Willie 293
  Willis 61
DUFF, Nathaniel L. 43
DUGAN, Emaline 101
  J. A. 273
DUGGAN, George 287
  Sissy 287
  Vickey 287
  J. J. 295
DUGGER, Mary 105
  Sterling 112
DUKE, B. C. 65
  Bennet 312
  Bennett C. 25
  Betsy Ann 204
  Charlotte 45,55,64
  Dabney 311
  Davie Ewell 204
  Felix 287
  G. M. 246
  G. W. 22
  Gideon 204
  Green W. 64
  Henry 317
  M. J. 335
  Martha 49
  Mary 201
  Mary P. G. 65
  Maudie 204
  Mike 275
  Mordy Johnson 204
  Nancy 7
  Paulina Edward 204
  Pauline Hooper 204
  Robert 55,64,65,75,151,
    306,311
  Susan 22
DUKES, Julia 14
DULL, Addie 385
  Elsie 385
  Gloyd 385
  Ira 249
  Maggie 348,385
  Mollie 288
  W. A. 348
  Willie 385
DUNAGAN, Hyram 186
  John 94
  Madison 96
  Sharp 96
  Stanford 96
  William 70

DUNAWAY, Harvey 49
  Nancy 49
  Rebecca 47
  Robert L. 31,74
DUNCAN, Billy M. 339
  Jack 294
DUNIGAN, Charles 239
  James 17,53,239
DUNLAP, Captain Robert U.
    204
DUNN, _____ 226
  Dolly 30
  Elizabeth 295
  Frank 381
  Gus 271
  Jake 381
  James 271
  Jasper 271
  John 271,363
  John W. 380
  Lubie 299
  M. 24
  Richard D. 149
  Sallie 381
  Sarah E. 380
  Tennie 380
  William 151
DUNNAGAN, Benjamin B. 86
  Charles S. 80
  Elizabeth 108
  James 80,138,156,162,
    174
  John 156,174,256
  Louise 283
  M. 108
  Nelson 15
  Thomas 190
  William 84,85,156
DUNNAWAY, Caroline 310
DUNNEGAN, Adeline 215
  Alcy 25,53
  Andrew 53
  Benjamin B. 43
  Blount 32
  Charles 53,74
  Elizabeth 47,53
  Jane 34
  John 53
  Lydia 32
  Madison 27
  Manias 44
  Margaret 45
  Mary 25
  Matilda 53
  Menerva 44
  Parthena 32
  Sam R. 234
  Sharp 20,34
  Stanford 25,36
  Susannah 53
  William 53
DUNNEVANT, George 17
DUNNEVIN, George 29
DUNNIGAN, Andrew 309
  Charles 306,309
  Henderson 309
  John 306,309
  Liddy 309
  Madison 309
  Mary 309
  Nelson 21
  William 309
  William S. 309
DUNNING, John X. 55,58
  Margery 115
  Robert 115,116,120,131,
    132,133,135,156,158,
    160,244,302
DUNNINGTON, T. J. 194
DUNNIVAN, George 311
DURAN, Martha 39
DURAND, Martha 39
DURARD, Edney 36

DURARD (cont.)
  Elizabeth J. 49
DURELL, John 307
DURHAM, Pauline 298
  Stella Rachel 298
  W. A. 298
DURIN, Amanda 30
  Thomas 310
DURRARD, Martha 39
DURRETT, Rev. John 271
DUVAUGH, Paul 39
DUVAUL, Paul 39
DWYER, Rev. J. B. 269
DYE, John 59
DYER, James 190
EACUFF, John 132
EADES, Martha A. 48
EARLE, Mary 74
EASLEY, Alma 382
  Amy 80
  Andrew 202
  Benjamin 78
  Birdie 392
  Bob 202,204
  Catherine L. 220
  Edna 392
  Elbert 336
  Eliza O. (or C.) 56
  Elizabeth 80
  Emaline 56
  Ethel 382
  J. T. 342
  Jack 382
  James V. 56
  John 202
  John H. 56
  John Wesley 195
  Kathleen 382
  Mary Elizabeth 336
  Maud L. 382
  Mellie 382
  Millington 156,159
  Moses 56,80,83
  Robert 381
  Sarah 207
  Susie 361
  Suva 382
  Tennie M. 382
  Tully 294
  Turner 382
  William T. 392
EASLY, William 99
EASON, Bethery 77
  Bethina 77
  Calvin W. 53,77,174,180,
    191,306
  Carter B. 186
  Carter F. 77
  Carter T. 166,169,181
  James 77,306
  Joseph 86,166,168,169,
    174,186,238,256,306
  Joseph, Jr. 169,181
  Joseph, Sr. 181
  Joseph B. 306
  Joseph J. 53,77,180,238,
    304
  Mills 77,166,186,187
  Taffinous 53
EAST, G. H. 284
EASTES, Jesse 25
  Jessie 310
EATHERAGE, Joseph 18
  Willie 18
EASTON, Christian T. 118
EATON, Lucy 57
  Richard 145,169,173,174
EBERHART, Charles 370
  Gertrude 370
  John J. 370
  Parlena 370
ECCLES, Charles I. 329,332
EDDES, Martha A. 48

EDGE, John 114
EDGERTON, Graham 298
  Marjoribanks 298
EDGIN, James W. 234,341
EDISON, Thomas 331
EDMONDSON, Robert 114
EDMUNDSON, Kate 280
EDNEY, Jean 282
  June 282
EDWARD, Naoma 306
EDWARDS, ____ 293,317
  A. 87
  Adonijah 75,87,304
  Alfred 86
  Alford 87,90
  Alvin 293
  Anna R. 364
  Bettie 214
  Dan 293
  Dillie R. 102
  Ednonijah 84
  Enoch 188
  George 137
  George C. 10
  Jesse 22,24,30,34,37,
    40,46
  John 44,75,87,144,316
  John D. 10,51
  Joseph 188,306
  L. C. 140
  Lucinda 40
  Lucy 103
  Lucy Ann 66
  Mortimer 192
  Nancy 10
  Paulina 204
  Philip M. 234
  Sally 10,26,90
  Sandford 187,305
  Sarah 38,87
  Sellman 71
  Selman 143,161,170,182,
    183,306
  Silmond Capt. 242
  Silmons 310
  Thomas 75,191,192,304,
    311
  William 53,80,144,306
EGERTON, Graham 326,329
  Miss Mary 329
ELDER, Dilly 102,105
ELDRIDGE, ____ 353
  Charlie 353
ELEAZER, ____ 346
  Amanda 38
  Benjamin F. 204
  Elizabeth 204,333
  Elizabeth Bibb 204
  Frances 282
  George 204
  J. H. 274
  John D. 204
  John P. 104
  Jim 329
  Miner 225
  Ruth 273,274,345
  S. G. 195
  Sallie C. 204
  Sarah 94,311
  Sarah M. 31
  Stephen 94,95,346
  Stephen G. 204
  Stephen Gibson 204
  Steve 218,225
  Susan 40
  Susan O. Woodard 204
  Susie Ann 204
  V. J. 273,274
  Vanessa 298
  Venessa 274
  W. D. 197
  W. R. 274
  William D. 204

ELEAZER (cont.)
  William M. 204
  Zula 274
ELLINGTON, Gov. Buford 267
ELIOT, Samuel 120,121
ELIOTT, Tennessee 72
ELLIOT, Samuel 122,161
ELLIOTT, Alfred 38
  Andrew 151
  Charlie 297
  Nancy 7
  Samuel 137,138,140,147
  Wall 287,297
ELLIS, Altha 299
  Arthur J. 90
  Catherine 26
  E. B. 93
  Edward B. 90
  Elizabeth 50
  Ephraim 305
  Ephrim 90
  Erasmus J. 90
  Ernest 299
  Eveline 33
  Francis 190
  Francis S. 140,160,167,
    189,304
  Frank 244
  George Anne 41
  J. Erasmus 14,19
  James 48
  Jesse 307
  John 244
  John E. 29
  M. T. 13
  Mary Ann 24
  Mary M. 90
  Michael T. 90,312
  Nancy W. 59,312
  Ransom 59,88
  Ray 299
  Sarah B. 90
  Thomas 59,93,97,305,312
  W. D. 93
  W. E. 251
  William C. 96
  William D. O. 90
  William E. 24,312
  William M. 34
ELLISON, Hugh 74
  John 46
  Lydia 74
ELROD, Jacob J. 195
EMERSON, Judge 308
EMERY, N. R. 70
ENGLAND, Amanda 210
  Anderson 95,190,192,306,
    309
  Anny 41
  Betsy 53
  Clarence 287
  Elmer 287
  Glover 287
  Harry 295
  James E. 37
  Mary Helen 283
  Matilda 210
  Memory 32
  Miles 96
  Nelly 322
  Washington 96,309
  Wesley 287
  William M. 31
  Zuma 234
ENGLISH, A. D. 268
  Alex D. 364
  Clifford 364
  Daniel E. 364
  Ewing 364
  Exie 295
  Gardner 364
  Kate W. 364
  Mrs. Katie W. 268

ENGLISH (cont.)
  Neil 364
  Robert 364
  Walter 364
ENMERS, Ethel 327
ENOCH, Edwards 187
  James 58,191
ENLOW, James 191
EPHRAIM, Mary 55
EPLEY, Wayne 269,275,278
EPPERSONM Asa 306
  James 12,87
  Jesse 174,175,190,306
  John 52,188
EPPES, Richard Sgt. 235
EPPS, George 195
  George P. Y. 204
  Richard 158
  Wyatt 192
ERRANTON, J. C. 281,288,
    295
  Joel 32,288,290,295,309
  Walter 284,295
  Wash 288
  Willa 282
  Willie 290
ERWIN, John 129
  Joseph 118,122
ESTEP. James 189
ESTERS, Baxter 369
  Charlie H. 369
  Dave 369
  Horace 369
  Lida 369
  William 225
ESTES, Alex 328
  Allie 282
  Cam 287
  Clara 282
  Earnest 385
  Elijah 188
  Elsie 282
  Evie 282
  G. G. 195
  Herbert 292
  Lexie 282
  Lucy 287
  Ludie 287
  Mary 385
  Richard A. 38
  Solomon 194,204
  W. G. 49
ETHEAIDGE, Williber 7
ETHERAGE, A. 192
ETHEREDGE, William 46
ETHERIDGE, Acres 188
  Burwell 307
  Jackson 236
  James 236
  Nancy 236
  Nathan 236
  Phillip 236
  Sally 236
  William 194,204
  Willoughby 7,236,307
ETHERIGE, Mary 105
ETHERLEY, Rebecca 30
ETHREDGE, Martha 46
ETHRIDGE, Acheus 305
  Archius 312
  Hattie 328
  Jeremiah 188
  Jim 315
  John 35,195
  Joseph 313
  Kindrick 313
  Willoby 312,313
EUBANK, Mrs. 4
  Edward 30,32
  Eliza Crumpler 204
  J. 39
  John 14,21,22,24,25,27,
    28,29,31,33,34,35,36,
    37,39,42,204

EUBANK (cont.)
  Josephine Donegan 204
  Lucinda Corlew 204
  Mary Alyce 295
  R. D. 204
  R. G. 204
  Rafe 198,204
  Robert 198,204
EUBANKS, E. G. 193
  John 311
  N. H. 298
EVANS, Amy 25
  C. E. 284
  C. F. 320
  Caleb 62,95
  Elizabeth 117
  Elizabeth J. 40
  George 149,163,171,179,
    188,191,306,309
  George, Sr. 78
  George M. 42
  Jacob 57,60,64,310
  James W. 44
  Jane 53,323
  John 154,168,169,180,
    305
  John B. 38
  Lewis 26,53,78,179,190,
    239,310
  Margaret 53,306
  Mary 64
  Nancy C. 43
  Peggy 78
  Richard 56
  Susan 79
  W. H. 41
  William 79,185,304
EVERETT, Aquilla 312
  Elizabeth 46
  Joel D. 44
  Nancy A. 72
EVINS, Elizabeth 10
  Frankey 70
  George 239
  Jacob 152
  John 156
  Lewis 17,239
  Peggy 239
EWELL, Dovie 204
  Emma 360
  H. L. 109
  Ruth 360
  William 109
EWING, Evelyn 334
  Finis 267,346,347,348
  Harvey, Jr. 334,338
  Howard 295
  John L. 149
  Nathan 149
EXUM, John 75
EZZELL, Jane 68
FAFAN, James 126
FAGAN, Robert L. 270
FAIN, F. L. 197,205
FALKNER, Donnie 353
  Joseph 353
  May Eunice 353
FAMBROUGHT, Robert 75
FAN, Rolly 85
FANE, Eliza 34
FANN, Raleigh 84
  Rolly 85
FARMER, Samuel 66
FARRAR, Charles C. S. 236
  Christopher C. S. 236
  Cyprian 171,172,307
  Elizabeth 16
  F. 150,169
  Field 3,11,14,18,21,92,
    135,143,147,155,156,
    168,236,253,304
  Jane 69
  M. W. 95

FARRAR (cont.)
  Margaret 6
  Martha W. 28,236
  Matilda 11
FARRELL, Charles 337
FARRICE, Bryant 134
FARRIOR, Bryan 116
FARRIS, John 190
  Robert 190
FATE, Samuel 305
FAULKNER, Charles 355
  Madlen 355
  Mary 355
  William G. 355
FAWCETT, Felix 18
FELTS, Ellis 265,280
FENTRESS, Absalom 160
  Ada L. 350
  Alline E. 350
  Cecil 271
  Cecil D. 350
  David 187,192,306
  James 135,147,302
  W. S. 251
  William 57
  William S. 312
FEREBEE, Burnard 292
  Mary 292
FERGUSON, ____ 319
  Isham 182
  Jasper R. 41
  Moses 132,143
  Rogal 77,128,172
FERREL, Alvin 293
  David 293
FERRELL, Bass 193
  Clarence 297
  George 289
  James 306
  Jesse 289
  Maria 7
  Mildred 283
  Myrtle 298
  Sarah 28
  Walker 297
FERRIBY, ____ 148
FERRILL, Mary C. 103
FEW, Amanda 288
  Annie 287,331
  Bess 288
  Bessie 288
  Betty 288
  Elsie 288
  Floy 288
  Floyd 288
  George W. 309
  Grace 288
  Hardy 288
  Harris 295
  Herman 287
  James 250,309
  Jasper 288
  Lowell 288
  Myrtle 287
  Nellie 287
  Orland 288
  Oscar 288
  R. L. 287
  Tom 287
  Virgie 288
  Virgil 288
  Wash 287
  William 309
  Zackie 287
FIELD, Monroe 234
  Thomas C. 234
  William 345
  Judge William 344
FIELDER, Ada 299
  Alma 298
  Altha Claire 288
  Bessie Lu 290
  Billy 290

FIELDER (cont.)
  Burton 288,294
  Carson
  Claude 294
  Connie 334
  Cord W. 374
  Dalie 326
  Dan 293
  Donald 290
  Emma Jean 290
  Evie 293
  Gertrude 294
  Grace 294
  Hershel 290
  Hester 374
  Hulan 288,294
  J. W. 326,329
  Johnny 281,287
  Julian 290
  Kenneth 294
  Leland 374
  Lorene 290
  Lovey 298
  Loyd 299
  Mabel 288
  Martin 288,294
  Milas 299
  Moody 374
  Nannie 288
  Onita 290
  Opan 290
  Scott 334
  Silas 288
  Tinnie Pearl 294
  Virgil 299
  Willie 299
FIELDS, Curtis 287
  Dee 287
  Linnie 287
  Marshall 295
FILSON, Duel 283
  J. R. 283
FINCH, Austin 234
  Peter 112
FINLEY, James 311
  Silvester 68
  Thomas 68
  William 41
FINLY, Elizabeth West 62,
    68
  James 62,65
FINNEY, Tobert 136
FISER, William 345
FITTS, Billy 292
  Ruth 292
FITZGERALD, Edward 193,205
  R. O. 342
FLACK, William 183
FLAIRTY, Roger 198,205
FLANARY, Thomas 72,78
FLANNARY, Thomas 309
FLANNERY, Angeline 45
  Charlotty 38
  Eklkanah 309
  Thomas 47
FLEET, Elizabeth 43
  Estelle 299
  Rosie 299
  William 26,312
FLEMING, Isaac 60
FLETCHER, Dorothy 30
  W. H. 330
FLINN, Barna 150
FLOWERS, Andrew 306
  Aubrey 388
  Curl J. 388
  Harry 388
  Herbert 388
  Jarrett C. 389
  Louise 389
  Maggie 388
FLY, Sarah M. 31
FOLK, Christopher 129

FORAN, John 114
FORD, D. S. 25,26,27,96
  Daniel S. 311
  Gerald 344
  Gynath 280
  Jesse 198,206
  Jesse M. 206
  John 96,206,311
  Martha 96
  Paul 278
  Sarah 206
  Sarah R. 27
  Susannah 311
  W. D. 194,206
FOREHAND, Emma P. 380
  Henry C. 380
  John W. 380
  Mattie B. 380
  Mattie T. 380
  Susan Ann 72
FORREST, _____ 226,227,230
  General N. B. 203
FORSEE, Stephen P. 9
FORSEY, Stephen 12
  Nancy 12
FORSYTHE, Jacob 307
  Jerry M. 195
  Jno 57,187,190,307
  John 34
  Rachel 18
  William 131
FORTNER, John Estes 195
  W. S. 322
  William 76
FORUEN, John T. 108
FOSSEN, E. Van 327
FOSTER, A. 146
  Augustus 105
  B. 203
  David 133
  Dollie C. 389
  Edwin E. 343
  Eugene F. 356
  G. M. 326
  Gus 295
  J. C. 74,330
  Jake C. 389
  James 51
  Jonathan 205
  Margaret 24
  Nathan 55,77,83
  Wesley B. 234
  Willis 310
FOURD, Rebech 23
FOWLER, Caroline 30
  Flemming H. 310
  Francis 312
  Francis E. 14,18,26
  J. E. 330
  Jefferson 42
  Richard 34
  Ruby 288
  Thornton 288
FOWLKES, Bettie 102
  Jimmie 260
FOWLKS, E. A. 107
FRAHIER, Ed 374
FRANCE, Gideon 190
  William 179,180,307
FRANCES, Edward 51
  Gideon 51,109
  John 51
FRANCIS, Matthew 238
FRANKLIN, Howard 234
FRASER, David 322
FRASHER, David 61,97,309
  Marthena
  P. 195
  W. P. A. 195
FRASIER, M. H. 194,206
  N. C. 206
  Serena P. 216
FRASURE, John 304

FRAZIER, _____ 242
  Anval 293
  Bonnie 293
  Clara Fielder 281
  Darlean 293
  David 206
  Elizabeth 206
  Frank 295
  Mrs. Frank 295
  John 304
  Loyd 292
  Morgan 206
  Nicholas 206
FREELING, Henry 123
FREEMAN, _____ 2
  Addie 289
  Annie 111
  Bessie 365
  Beulah 382
  Buncels 61
  Cecil 289
  Doris 359
  Ellis 382
  Frank 365
  Gilbert 289
  Hannah 61,91
  Hardy 136,176
  Hattie 289,359
  Henry 359
  Howell 61,91,92,93,235,
    306
  J. R. 193,206
  Jeramiah 61
  John 111
  Joseph 359
  Lorena C. 365
  Louise 359
  Norman 289
  Otto 382
  Percy 359
  R. A. 258,332,343
  Ralph 365
  Ralph A. 331
  Sam 247,321
  Samuel 359
  William 61,189,190
  William B. 306
  Willie 382
FRENCH, William 85
FREY, Geneva 298
  Johnny 297
  Maud 297
  Shearon 298
FRIERSON, James L. 195
FRIEUDENTHAL, Dr. Gustie
  Augustus 223
FROST, _____ 231
  Nannie 298
FRY, Martin 113
FUGHN, Alfred 21
FULCHER, Elizabeth D. 8,87
  John J. 87
FULFER, Joseph 30
FULGHAM, Martha 99
FULGHUM, Glayds 364
  Harry J. 364
  J. T. 284
  James E. 364
  Mable C. 364
  Thomas 364
FULKS, Ned 272
FULTZ, Susan M. 99
FULLER, Jonathan 15
  Joseph 30
FULLERTON, Jane 5
FULMER, James E. 373
FUNDERBUNK, Mary 70
FUQUA, Andrew 287
  James 75
  James H. 13
  Luke 271
  Oneida 295
  Tommie 287

FUQUA (cont.)
  Tommy 287
FURANCE, Laurel 346
FUSSELL, A. A. 44
  Alma 290
  Bill 290
  Catherine 290
  Claude 292
  Clyde 287
  Delilah 306
  Edna 290
  Elbert Ray 290
  Emps 287
  Evelyn 294
  Forrest 287
  Harden 290
  Harrison 76
  Imogene 290
  J. E. 202
  John 238,290
  John W. 45
  Leslie 365
  Lloyd 292
  Lucy 58,287
  Lula 293
  Malcolm 290
  Mary 30,287
  Missouri 365
  Moses 58,305
  Myrtice 287
  Neil 295
  Norman 287
  Oscar 287
  Paul 287
  Ray 287
  Velma 290
  Verda 287
  W. W. 71
  William 58,307,365
  Willis 190
  Wilson 341
  Wyatt 53,58
  Wyett 190
FUZZEL, William 310
GABILL, Mary 176
GAFFORD, Elizabeth 33
  J. P. 225
  J. T. 198,205
  John P. 72
  Malilda 19
  Martha Caroline 35
  Michael 307
  W. G. 198,205
  William 311
GAILEY, Edwin 54
GAINES, Flavia 284
GALLIGAN, James T. 270
GALLIGHY, D. A. 317
GALLION, George 85,129,143,
    311
  George C. 250
GALLISON, George 82
GALLOWAY, Beaulah 381
  Clementine 367
  Dorsey J. 381
  Eloise 357
  George 381
  Henry 194,205
  J. T. 357
  J. W. 194,205
  James M. 15
  John 310,357
  Nettie 357
  Percy 357
  Will J. 381
GAMBILL, Mrs. 42
  Mildred Sullivan 4,23,
    50
GAMBLE, John 307
  Nancy B. 43
GAMBLES, John 311
GAMMELL, William 307
GAMMILL, Moses 6

GANNAWAY, Richard P. 266
GARDEN, R. O. 271
GARDNER, Charity E. 211
    Rev. H. M. 268
    Jesse 307
GARFIELD, J. A. 227
GARLAND, Jesse 75,198,205,
    225
GARNER, C. E. 276
    Henry 313
    John 182
    William 250
GARRET, Elizabeth 313
    Martha 66
    Phenius 66
    William 84,311
GARRETT, Diane
    Jill 4,51
    Jill Knight 343
    Lonnie 288
    Lucinda W. 10
    Malachi 189
    Maliachie 188
    Martha Ann 69
    Pearl 288
    Sarah 21,57,69
    Sary 57
    Valley 288
    William 32,33,35,36,40,
        42,48,69
    William, Senr. 57
GARTIER, D. P. 194,205
GARTON, Albert 290
    Allie 291
    Annie 284
    Audie 298
    Bee 300
    Bessie 291
    Burt 300
    Cacy 300
    Calley 300
    Cardon 291
    Carl 295
    Day 290
    Daye 290
    Elizabeth 70,300
    Erin 300
    Henry 18,68,312
    Herbert 293
    Ida 291
    Jessie 292
    John 261,305,311
    John, Jr. 312
    Kizziah 70
    Lloyd 334
    Lona 206
    Lorene 290
    Louisiana 200
    Lucille 290
    Marie 282
    Mark 31,296
    Martin 9,12,15,195,216,
        311
    Marton 44
    Mary 298
    Maude 293,299
    Moses 195,198,206
    Nettie 282
    Olie 300
    Paul 298
    Permelia T. 348
    Richard 15,296,311
    Ruby 298,300
    Sallie 101
    Thelma 290
    Thurman 300
    Vernon 300
    William M. 348
    Wilma 282
    Z. T. 71
    Zachariah 12,311
GARVER, Samuel M. 307
GARY, F. M. 195

GASTON, Matthew 132
GATES, John 186
    William 186
GATEWOOD, Annie 380
    Emma 333,380
    Frank 284
    John F. 195
GATTIS, William 168
GAY, William 109
GEE, Edmund 89
    Edmund W. 88
    Mary 89
GENIER, Jennet 51
GENOVESE, Vince 337
GENSING, Authur 110
GENTRY, Allie F. 234
    Anderson 7,65,311
    Anne 39
    Anney 65
    Arnold 281
    Basil 295
    Benajah 9,30,63,65,311
    Birdie 295
    Christine 282
    D. C. 194,205
    Dora 274
    Earl 282
    Eliza 35
    Erline 291
    Estella 292
    Eulon 295
    Hartwell 343
    Irene 295
    Jane 30,40
    Lovine 291
    Lucind 47
    Lucinda 65
    Lucy 311
    Martha 25
    Mary Ann 8
    Mathew 35,39
    Matthew L. 65
    Nancy 30
    Needham 292
    Odie 295
    Paul Turner 282
    Seth 282
    Susan
    Thelma 291
    Tho. 65,177,181,261,305,
        311
    Thomas 173
    W. 79
    Walter C. 30
    William 59,60,76,92,96,
        183,261,304,305
    William T. 312
GEORGE, Brinkley 93,309
    Daniel D. 62
    E. 330
    Emelina 23
    Joseph 309
    Sally 10
    Solomon 25
GERMAIN, William 140
GERMAN, Wm. 118
GERRON, Robert M. 234
GHEHAN, John 192
GIBBINS, William 167
GIBBONS, G. T. 326
GIBBS, Carl 372
    Cora 372
    Hazel 331,372
    James E. 372
    John 75
    Lee 372
    Lena 373
    Lorena 373
    Mary Jane 48
    Val 373
GIBSON, Annie M. 357
    Erin 357
    Jerald 357

GIBSON (cont.)
    John 357
    John H. 357
    Meldel 357
    Nancy 17
    R. M. 195
    Sammie 357
    William 188
    Willie 357
GIDEON, Enoch 76
GIFFIN, Andrew 129,191
    Isaac 38
    John 79
    William 118,129,141,153,
        191,305
GILASPIE, James 116,121
GILBERT, Miss _____ 294
    Rev. _____ 326
    Benjamin 147,161,173,
        174,186,305
    Buena 326
    Charles 145,147,174,177,
        235,306
    Dick 197,205
    Elizabeth 66
    H. G. 289
    Henry M. 311
    Henry Madison 56
    James 62
    James Monroe 56
    John 147,166
    John W. 266
    M. 225
    Mabel 19,56,62,304
    Nancy 85
    Nancy V. 58
    Nathan 56,62,95
    Nichols 62
    Nicy 56,85
    Peter 145,161,166,187,
        206
    Rosanna 62
    Sally 14
    Temperance 56
    Tempy 62
    Thos. 85
    Thomas 29,56,66,192
    Tommie 296
    William 56,61,62,85
    Wilson 304
GILBURN, James 75
GILL, J. D. 195
    John William 195
    Michael D. 73
    Neut 298
GILLEM, Gen. _____ 229
    Brigadier Gen. Alvan 261
GILLESPIE, Alma 292
GILLIAM, Ida 287
    James 330
    James E. 319
    Lee 287
GILLILAN, James E. 224
GILLISON, Roger 164
GILLOCK, James W. 195
GILMER, Hubert 294
GILMORE, Claborne 293
    Emma 373
    Ina 373
    J. A. 74
    Mrs. J. A. 105
    J. R. 343
    James 59,310
    Jim 391
    Katrine 293
    Louie 112
    Matthew 59,125,243,304
    Rollie 373
    Tom L. 373
    Vera 293
GILMOUR, William 146
GILPON, John 190
GINGER, George 82

GINNY, _____ 144
GIRT, Robert 126
GIVENS, Reuben 15
GIVIN, William 52,53
GIVINS, James 15,310
GLASGOW, Mr. _____ 3,4
  Earnest 291
  James 115
  John 128
  Pat 198
  Virgie Jones 291
GLASS, Albert F. 108
  Daniel 41
  Delbert 298
  James 311
  Martha 47
  Parthena 42
GLEAVES, Araminty 22
  Elizabeth 69,91,93,312
  Emily 91
  Ezekiel S. 69
  Isabella T. 13,69
  Lizzie 300
  Mathew 91,93
  William 93
  William D. 69
GLENN, William C. 25
GLOVER, J. D. 326
  Luther 291
GOAD, Mrs. Belle S. 333
GODWIN, George M. 195
  Mary D. 391
GOFF, Herman 270
GOINS, Henderson 270
GOLLADAY, Samuel 9
GOOD, Gustavus 226
  William 36,189
GOODGINE, Christine 283
  Edward 283
GOODIN, Reubin 310
  Sarah 310
GOODINE, Gibson 283
GOODLETT, Clifton 343
GOODRICH, Dolly 83
  Dorothy 81,88
  J. 81
  James 83,88,151,161,163,
    168,170
GOODMAN, Sam Virgil 234
GOODRICH, Alice 54
  Allen 75
  Caroline 29
  Charlotte 54,75
  Dorothy 54,75
  George Jackson 54
  Henry 25,26,306,309
  J. P. 195
  James 54,75,134,140,150,
    263,265,305
  Jane 64
  John 54,60,75
  John K. 309
  L. S. 320
  Martha 9
  Patsy 54,75
  William H. 54,75
GOODRIDGE, James 313
  William W. 313
GOODRITCH, James 178
GOODWIN, Beal 83,89,192
  Carl 283
  Elizabeth 304
  James 283
  John 194,205
  Loyd 283
  Lucy 33,60
  Mary 26
  Nancy 40
  Peter 60,119,192,307
  Reuben 9
  Sal 60
  Sally 60
  Sam 117
  William 33,60,76

GORDAN, Rebecca 68
GORDON, Captain _____ 211
  Harry 205
  John, Jr. 137
GORDEN, John A. 276
GORIN, Elizabeth 37
  T. R. 251
GORMAN, Marcus 198,205
  Pat 198
GORSE, E. 101
  Sarah 376
GOSS, Delila 15
GOSSETT, Allen 375
  Alzo 371
  Eleanor 323
  Eva 375
  Fannie 371
  Freddie 363
  Henry 309
  James P. 375
  Jewel 375
  John 271,363
  John M. 332,367
  Kris 294
  Laura 363
  Lavonia 375
  Mary 375
  Mattie 367
  Paul 371
  Rollie 363
  Ronald 292
  Sallie 375
  Sam B. 371
  Walker 363
  Wendell 375
GOSSTER, James 13
GOULD, James 3,28,66
  Martha 66
GOWER, Russell 3,119,140,
    301
GRACE, John 323
GRAHAM, Ellen 370
  Esb_____ 191
  Jane H. 367
  Jesse 309
  Lucyanah 41
  Roberta Russell 5,6
  Solomon 53
  Z. J. 74
GRANDY, Belle 368
  Ernest 368
  Mrs. Letty 268
GRANGER, Alford P. 311
GRANT, Charles 295
  J. W. 279
  James 295
  Pauline 294
  Sue 344
GRANTUM, M. 194,205
GRAVES, Annie 295
  James 9
  Selina 11
  Thomas 76,191,243,306
  W. S. 68
GRAVET, Henry 11
GRAVETT, Henry 171,172
  John 171,172
  William 172
GRAY, Alexander 130
  B. 13
  Benjamin 310
  Charlie 289
  D. 7,8,16,17,25,28,29,
    63
  David, M.G. 9,19,24,26,
    31,39,40,42,43,48,55,
    59,63,64,65,70,305,
    309
  Delilah 310
  Elizabeth 35
  Ethelbert T. 12
  G. W. 47,225
  George 309

GRAY (cont.)
  George W. 21
  Hesekiah 21
  Hezekiah 309
  Jeremiah 15,25,181
  John 127,161
  John L. 234
  Jonas 199
  Laura 199
  M. W. 24,25
  Mack, Jr. 289
  Nathaniel 15
  Rosanah 309
  Rosannah 48
  Sara 199
  Thomas 116,125,166,168
  W. M. 100
  William 45,309
  William G. 15
GRAYBILL, Dorris 295
GRAYHAM, Joseph 128
GREGG, J. C. 194,205
GREGGORY, Edmond 155
GREEN, Blanche 211
  Doctor 166
  Gardner 69
  Hubert 355
  J. W. 34
  Jackson 110
  James West 132
  John 313,355
  John W. 29
  Martha 8
  Mary 355
  Naomi 355
  Sarah 23
  Susan 311
  William 68
  Capt. William R. 205
GREENLEE, Elvira Parlee
    217
GREER, _____ 328
  Mrs. _____ 271
  Alexr. 124
  Ben 292
  Miss Bessie 343
  Burton 292
  Carroll 43
  Charlotte 290
  Dell 290
  Dorothy 290
  Earlie 292
  Emma 345
  Faustina 292
  James 198,205
  Jennie 292
  Joseph 122,124
  Karen 290
  Ronnie 345
  Tommy 282
  W. H. 330
  Wed 292
GRESHAM, Austin 190
GREY, Jeremiah 182,191
GRIFFIN, Andrew J. 34
  Carrie B. 367
  Charlie T. 366
  Dosea Ann 63
  Edger 367
  Elinor 237
  Eliza Jean 63
  Isaac 38,63
  Izora 367
  J. D. 245
  Mable 366
  P. S. 195
  Will 367
  William 237,311,305
GRIFFING, William 134
GRIFFITH, Joseph F. 12
GRIGGS, John 187
GRIGORY, Sally 56
  Stephen 79

GRIGSBY, Buchanan 354
　Clyde 354
　Dorcas Wyly 206
　F. C. Hassell 206
　H. L. 332,333
　Harris 206
　Ilena 354
　J. W. 329
　James P. 206
　John W. 206,329
　Katherine 354
　Kelly 206
　Mabel 206
　Rosa Lee 354
　Rosa McNeilly 206
　Samuel 206
　Samuel W. 206
　T. 211
　Theodosia 206
　Thomas K. 70,205,206
　Thomas Kinley 195
　Virgil 354
　W. L. 326
　Judge W. L. 248,325
　William L. 206
GRIMES, Alfred 393
　C., J.P. 49
　Cornelius, J.P. 28
　Elizabeth 30
　Henry 79,122,145
　Henry, Sr. 82,150
　Isaac G. 150
　J. 198
　J. P. 195
　Jacob 79
　Jay Cook 7
　John 79,82,117,142,150
　John P. 206
　Katharine 79,82
　P. 198
　Preston J. 206
　Reuben 15
GRIMMITT, Benjamin 76,80,
　　239
　Josiah 76
　William 186
GRISSOM, ___ 79
　Austin 263
GROGAN, Clement 9
GROUND, Al 270
GROVE, George 15
　Isaac 96
GROVER, Selina 11
GROVES, ___ 319
　Albert III
　George 311
　Isaac 311
　Joe 204
　John 69
　Joseph 67,69
　Mary Francis 69
　Paulina Edwards Duke 204
　Pearl 281
GRYMES, C. 31,48,71,96,97
　Cathrine 8
　Cornelius 310
　Elizabeth 110
　John 9,10,11,12,13,18,
　　19,22,96,145,180,182,
　　311
　John, Sr. 310
　Joseph 311
　Mary A. 41
　Missianianah 311
　Missoniah 6,236
　Nancy 12
　Rebecca 40
　William 6,236
GUERIN, Claude H. 354
　Henry H. 313
　Mayme 354
GULLEDGE, Weldon 265
GUN, Dollie 350

GUNN, A. C. 26
　A. J. 195
　A. M. 272
　Abijah 187
　Andrew C. 22
　Charles 190,312,306
　Elisha 77,98,187,190,
　　256,307,309
　G. W. 45
　James 238,306
　Jefferson 15
　John 125
　Lawson 190,192,256,309
　Madison 312
　Malinda 15,44
　Mary 17
　Reuben 53
　Robert S. B. 30
　Sarah 37
　Tabitha 25
　William 17,52,53,57,
　　191,307
　William M. 26
GUNTER, Martha 44
　Willie I. 28
GUNTHER, Mr. ___ 251
GUPTON, Nelie 373
　Ed G. 373
GURTE, Robert 126
GUSTIN, Nancy 323
GUSTON, Elizabeth 112
GUTHERIE, William 33
GUTHREY, Eliza 72
GUTHRIE, Bertie 299
　Mattie 299
GUTTON, Martha 110
GUYE, Rev. Dean 267
GWIN, Edward 139,160,167,
　　176
　Edwin 153
　John 160
HADDEN, Jane 12
HADDER, Joseph 127
HADDON, William B. 177,
　　181,236
HADEN, William E. 306
HADLEY, Joshua 117,126
HADRICK, Thomas 191
HAFT, Jacob 12,236
　Mary Ann 12,236
HAGAN, Murt 300
HAGAR, Bettie 287
　Hettie 287
　Mary 287
HAGEWOOD, Jesse 44
　Madge 299
　N. P. 43
　Polly 32
HAGEY, Jennie G. 354
　William 323
HAGGARD, Jim J. 351
　Wilton J. 351
HAGLER, James 188
HAGOOD, E. T. 195
　Madge 293
HAGUEWOOD, Tabbetha 22
HAGWOOD, Elizabeth 30
HAIL, Polly Ann 63
HAILEY, Avie 289
　Carl 289
　Emma 289
　Hattie 289
　Isaac 48
　Melvin 289
　Orman 294
HAINES, Alonzo W. 366
　Annie 366
HALBROOK, Clint 390
　Forest 390
　Hazel 390
　J. T. 328
　Joe 390
　Mary 392

HALBROOK (cont.)
　Mary E. 392
　Tishie 390
　Tom J. 390
HALE, Ethel 292
　Fannie 292
　John 175,179
　Nancy 240
　Thomas C. 240
　Tom 337
　Warren 34
　William 130
HALEY, Andrew 309
　Cynthia 32
　Isaac 309
　Isaach 48
　Isenias 185
　Thomas 192
HALFACRE, Alice 358
　Annie M. 358
　Cordell 358
　Hank B. 358
　Jefferson 358
　Lee 358
HALFORD, Andy 184
HALL, ___ 215,322,346
　Ann 282
　B. B. 225
　B. F. 225
　Ben Frank 195
　Benjamin B. 11,15,70,310
　Berrman 54
　Berryman 307
　Betsy 238
　Betty Sue 282
　Clayton T. 26
　David 54,307
　Delsie 334
　Dorothy Bell 282
　Earline 282
　Elizabeth M. 54
　Emeline 37
　Emma 45
　Ezra 281
　Frank 99,336
　Garret 310
　Hallie 334
　Henry 28,57,84,90,190,
　　306
　Isaac 45
　J. B., Sr. 225
　J. M., Jr. 103
　James 310
　James E. 234
　James H. 48
　Jesse 54,80,84,121,138,
　　146,147,150,151,192,
　　305,306,310
　John, Jr. 225
　John H. 225
　John M. 224
　Johnny 334
　Joseph 15,17,54,57,84,
　　86,88,89,90,225,306,
　　312
　Joseph W. 150
　Joshua 54
　Josie 351
　Leamon 334
　Lyndell 282
　Marshall 326,327
　Martha 29,54
　Mary 17
　Mary Ann 219
　Mary V. 33
　Mathew P. 46
　Minnie 281
　N. M. 34,70,225
　Nancy 57,306
　Nancy Ann 19,23
　Ora 282
　Ruby 334
　Susanna 54,80,307

HALL (cont.)
  Susannah 84
  W. C. 225
  Wesley 54
  William 41,225,307
HALLIBURTON, Allen 15,31
  Ambrose 305
  Arrabella 45
  Bessie 372
  Charles 43,312
  Chrisstie 20
  Edward 269
  Humphries 41,313
  John 118,372
  John D. 33
  Leon 293
  Lucy L. 29
  Lucy Lee 19
  M. 78
  Margaret S. 28
  Martha 336
  Martin 20,90,97,118,
    144,167,310
  Martin H. 306
  Martin Turner 50
  Nancy 56
  Nancy Ann 19
  R. J. 18
  R. P. 15,37,38,47,48
  Reuben P. 50
  Robert 36
  S. H. 18
  William 144
HALY, Mark 136
HAM, Clint 327
  J. W. 194,206
HAMBLETON, Andrew 189
  Isaiah 142
  Thomas 119,123
HAMBRICK, George 45
  Hiram 310
  James C. 30,44
  Jeramiah 97
  Jerry 18
  Mary I. 38
  Sarah 40
  William 310
  Yelverton 189
HAMILTON, ___ 128
  Amand 17
  Andrew 150,154,160,185,
    190,304
  Carrie 289
  Charlie 291
  Clyde 287
  Mrs. Clyde 288
  Dolma 289
  Earl 289
  Elvin 299
  Emmett 299
  Ida Mabel 299
  Joe 289
  Lilly 289
  Margaret V. 8
  Minor 289
  Nancy 62
  P. H. 317
  Thomas 119,137,138,139,
    140
  Vester 287
HAMLET, Burrell 75
HAMLIN, Allen 312
HAMM, Curtis 297
  Ethel 297
HAMMON, Samuel 195
  William 73
HAMMOND, Clara 23
  Israel 176
  John 186
  Mary 45
  Robert 186
HAMMONDS, Thomas 39
  William 311

HAMMONS, Sam 260
  Sammie 295
HAMNER, Susan 201
HAMON, Noel 176
HAMOND, Israel 136
HAMPTON, Elizabeth 48
  John 49
  Lester 295
  Nancy 41
  Waid 38
HANCOCK, Aaron 191
HAND, Delila 26
  Frances 49
  G. W. 104
  John 307
  Patsy 19
  W. 29,30,34,36,62
  William 18,25,27,29,30,
    31,32,36,38,42,46,
    170,304
HANDLIN, I. N. 206
  Joseph 78
  T. J. 206
  William 144
HANKINS, Nancy J. 313
HANKS, E., M.G. 38
  Milly 70
  Sallie 211
HANLEY, ___ 277
HANLIN, Eliose 388
  Frank 388
  Lucy 388
  Stanley 388
HANNA, James 52,187
  John 151,158,191
HANNAH, Frank 198,206
  Maggie 351
  W. M. 342
HANSON, James G. 38
HARBARD, Martin 73
HARBINSON, Evelyn 290
HARBISON, Chester 292
  Keith 290
HARDAWAY, Mary A. 108
HARDEMAN, James F. 15
  Nicholas P. 66
  Peter 167,178,189
  Susanna 167
  Thomas 51
HARDEWICK, Jonathan P.
HARDIN, Charlie 328
  Faustine B. 71
  Henry 177
  Hugh 387
  J. 49
  Joab 34,71
  Lorena W. 71
  Minerva J. 71
  Sarah Ann 71
HARDWICK, Benjamin 91,94
  Dillard 21
  Elizabeth 91,94
  J. P. 91
  Joyce P. 14,16,22
  Lydia H. B. 20
HARDWICKE, Eliza J. 26
HARDY, A. J. 289
  Jacob 305
  N. 172
  Nehemiah 239,305
  Thomas K. 57
  William Parrott 136,
    176
HARE, John 126
HARGETT, Frederick 155
HARGROVE, A. C., Jr. 341
  A. C., Sr. 341
  Bertha 380
  Bob 380
  Clarence 380
  Curl 380
  Eldridge 171,175
  Tishie 380

HARID, Keziah 311
  William 311
HARKLEROAD, Daniel 116
HARMACK, Walter R. 109
HARMAN, John 189
HARMON, Gilly 7
  Israel 154,156,159
  Lewis 7
HARMS, Sally 63
HARNBRICK, Jeremiah 310
  Uriah 310
  Yelvington 310
HARNES, Thos. 311
HARNISH, James 275
HARNS, E. 63
  Mark 63
  William 63
HARPER, Albert E. 353
  Althea 298
  Elmer 353
  Nellie A. 353
  Robert 154,169,253,307
  Ruth 298
  Thomas 353
HARRELL, Dona 218
  Elmer 299
  Jeanetta Dotson 218
  Joe 299
  John 218
  Juanita 295
  Nora 287
HARRINGTON, Robert 343
HARRIS, ___ 288
  Abner 119
  Ann 16
  Britton 37
  Buckner 67,90,312
  Burgess 15,76,89,90,
    120,124,165,173,175,
    310
  Carl 289
  Claiborn 134,135
  Clarence C. 349
  Daniel 83,86,305
  Darrel Y. 54
  Donel Y. 305
  Dorrell Y. 188
  Dorris 288,298
  Eliza Anne 36
  Elizabeth 10
  Emma L. 321
  Garner 288
  George T. 48
  Geraldine 288
  Gillium 130
  Isaac 75,76,137,165,182
  J. T. 194,206
  Jane 76
  Jessie 287
  John 12,42,89,149,304,
    311
  Joseph 21,90
  Karene 343
  Kathleen
  L. F. 74
  Lenny 13
  Leona 349
  Lillian 370
  Lorena 349
  Lorene 298
  M. G. 328
  Maggie 199
  Mark 25,65,73,311
  Mary 74
  Mary Ann 287
  Melvin 296,299,328
  Mumford 134
  Nissie 287
  Olif 27
  Ora 370
  Orey 332
  Oury 349
  Plummer W. 15

HARRIS (cont.)
  Polly 39
  Randolph 78,185
  Randolph R. 305
  Robert P. 54
  Ruth 349
  Samuel 145
  Sarah 19
  Silas 173,312
  Sinna 16
  Stephen 185,188,305
  T. J. 195
  Thomas 90,170,370
  Thomas W. 199
  W. M. 338
  Walter 74,287
  Wayne 287
  William 74,90,173,194,
    206
HARRISON, Audrey 381
  Edward L. 381
  Eva 381
  Herman 381
  Hinkle 381
  Mary 381
  Mary E. 381
  P. 6
  Tommie 381
  W. T. 321
HARROD, M. G. 194,206
HARSHMAN, John D. 323
HART, Pleasant 76
HARTLEY, James 306
HARTMAN, A. M. 328
HARTMANN, Charles 339
HORTON, Rev. W. H. 328
HARTZOG, Richard 36
HARVEY, Charles 271
  Elizabeth 69
  Lt. Gilbert B. 230
  Lem 118
  Lemual 118
  Lemuel 131
  Nancy 28
  Oney 110
  Rebecca 203
  Sarah 70
HARVILLE, Jennie 295
HARVY, Elizabeth 313
  Oney 313
HARWARD, Henry 309
HARWELL, W. L. 274
HASLEY, Abraham 21,112
  Mary C. 21
  Nancy 15
HASSEL, Eugene 293
  Madeline 293
HASSELL, Casy 89
  Cordie 293
  F. C. 206
  Floyd 293
  John 89
  W. B. 195
HATCHER, Alfred 249,381
  Earl 381
  Emma 381
  Evonne 381
  John 316
  Leslie 381
  Lou 209
  Thruston 381
  Zeke 316
HATFIELD, James 182
  William P. 182
HATLEY, N. G. 196
  Rye 104
  Stanford 310
HAWK, Zilla 102
HAWKINS, _____ 228
  Gov. _____ 320
  A. W. 318
  Marlin 340
  Marlin H. 340

HAWKINS (cont.)
  Nancy 32
HAY, Benjamin 30
  Susannah 35
HAYDEN, Richard B. 9
  T. 252
HAYES, Allen 288
  Benjamin 296
  C. L. 207
  Caroline 296
  Clara 288
  Cordis 296
  Elizabeth 154,156
  Ellis 288
  Eva 296
  James 154
  James B. 44
  Jeston 296
  Jettie 370
  John 38
  Lucy R. 39
  Mat 324
  Melvin 288
  Mildred 296
  Minor B. 64
  Nora 288
  Oliver B. 157
  Sally 296
  Thomas 154
  Virginia 295
  W. A. 196
HAYGOOD, Madge 290
HAYLE, Mathew J. 45
HAYNES, Daisy 287
  Elliott 287
  Henry 133
  Lurline 287
  Rachel J. 279
HAYS, Archie 83
  James 83
  James W. 22
  John 80,83,144,156,173,
    175,185,192,305
  Robert 139,156
  William J. 312
HAYSE, Annie 382
  Haywood 382
HAYWOOD, Judge _____ 308
  John 311
  Nicholas 9
HEABERTON, Tracy R. 349
HEADER, Thomas, Jr. 138
HEADLEE, E. A. 17
HEARD, Anne 295
  Bettie 268
  Sophia 28
  Tom 268
HEARN, Mrs. _____ 329
HEARNE, Robert, Mrs. 342
HEART, Pleasant 187
HEATH, _____ 223
  Abel 207,310
  Abijah 189
  Abraham 192
  Blurrel 198,207
  Bob B. 223
  Burrel 207
  Burril J. 207
  Delila 207
  George 226
  Isaac 192
  Rev. J. M. 272
  James 226
  John 192,197,207
  Joseph 226
  Julia Ann McCormick 223
  Samuel 37,223
  William W. 223
HEATHERINGTON, Joseph 248,
    325
HEATON, Robert 69
HEDGE, I. W. 38
  J. W. 38,42

HEDGE (cont.)
  John A. 74
  Lewis 47,74
  Malinda 32
  Mary 20,47
  Samuel 37
  William 306,309
HEDGES, Charlie 53
  Polly 53
HEFFINGTON, Richard 298
HELBERG, _____ 277
  Annie Lee 295
HELBURG, Adel S. 350
  Annie 359
  Erma 359
  Lewis C. 350
  Thedore 359
HELM, Mr. _____ 319
HEMMERLY, Helen 288
HENDERSON, G. 130
  H. H. 196,198,207
  Julia 110
HENDRICKS, Elizabeth 313
  James 313
  John 168,307
  Thomas 165,168,169
  Thornton 49
  William 304
  William H. 38
HENDRIX, John 153
  Thomas 153
HENNEY, Joseph 136
HENRY, F. B. 196
  Nanna 326
  Oney 304
  Rachel 39
  T. G. 268,270
  William 341
HENSLEE, _____ 207,248
  Dora M. Pickles 207
  Edward 277,383
  Floy 207
  Iva 331
  J. G. 330
  Dr. J. T. 207
  Joab 207
  Lipe 284
  M. F. Lipe 207
  Nancy Justice 207
  Pitt 207,330,331,332,
    333,342
  Vallie 331
HANSLES, _____ 325
HENSLEY, Dora 371
  Harmon 130
  Iva 207
  Vallie 371
HENSLY, John 187,188
HENSON, Harriet 29
  Jacob 150
  Maggie 386
HERBISON, Ellet 300
  Ellis 234
  Henry 287
  Marie 295
  Pearl 287
  R. B. 196
  Ruby 300
HERISON, James G. 312
HERLY, John 123
HERNDON, Benjamin 126
HERRIGES, Miss _____ 295
HERRIN, E. 139
  Gabriel 139
HERRON, George 260
HESBITT, James 197
HETHERINGTON, Bonnie 372
  George T. 372
  Helen 372
  Joseph 372
  Sarah W. 372
HEWITT, R. 130
HEWSTON, Sarah 91

HEZEND, Moses 128
HICKERSON, Adell 368
  Arthur 368
  Asa 297
  Billy 297
  Bob 343
  Cleirton 368
  Cyrena 33
  Daniel 306,311
  Elizabeth 44
  Emeline 31
  Eunice 368
  Ezekial 311
  Ezekiel 10,70,305
  Harry 368
  Henry 71,310
  Lucy 298
  Margaret 45
  Pauline 298
  Rhoda 34
  Sally Ann 27
  Sarah 110
  Seletia 10
  Stella 368
  Tom H. 368
  William 305,310
HICKMAN, Amanda 96
  Mrs. John P. 218
  Thomas 126,139,157,158
HICKS, A. V. 49
  A. W. 57
  Abner 127
  Americus 12
  Mrs. Cora C. 329
  Corine 298
  Daniel 127,182
  Elbert J. 41
  Elbert Jackson 41
  Etta 327
  J. B. 41
  James 59,60,82,263,295,
    305,310
  James Ed 327
  John 190
  John L. 59
  Lewis 127
  Margaret 153
  Mary 327
  Mollie 248
  R. H. 247,324,325,329
  R. M. 248
  Rena 35
  Rob 298
  S. 41
  W. R. 32,33,34
  William R. 312
  Winefred 53
  Zebeedee 155,156
HIETT, Anna B. 376
  Jim 376
  Neta 376
HIGGENBOTHAM, Caleb 186
  Luvica 31
  Midd ___ 186
  W. 181
HIGGENBOTTOM, Caleb 181
HIGGINBOTHAM, ___ 229
HIGHLAND, Henry 120,304
HIGHTOWER, Amanda 323
  Caty 77
  George 77,82,84
  George 8,240,304
  James 77,85,150,189,
    192,311
  Kitty 240
  Martha 239
  Mary 30
  Mary J. 26
  Polly 239
  Robert T. 75,77
  William 12,64,77,189,
    192,239,240,304,310
HIGINBOTTOM, Middleton 305

HILAND, Benjamin 60
  George W. 85,310
HILL, Barsheba Jane 13
  Cardin 45
  Cardine P. 45
  Caroline 45
  Elizabeth 19
  Harriett 375
  Isaac 23,39,67,185,192,
    305,311,312
  J. 32,33
  John G. 28,97,312
  John L. 266
  Mary 37
  Rebecca 54
  Robert 73
  Thomas 119,137,140
  William 49,129
HILLEY, Hamor 56
HILLIARD, Ann R. 208
HILLMAN, Daniel 313,318
HINDS, John 93
HINES, Albert 376
  Mrs. Albert 343,344
  Gertrude 376
  Grigsby 376
HINSLEY, John 188
HINSON, Elizabeth 11
  Henry W. 79
  J. G. 44,273
  James G. 9,35,38,41,46,
    47,90
  Jerome B. 21,90
  John 61,78,305
  Mag 333
  Mariah 14
  Martha 255,273
  T. H. 318
  Thomas 313
  Thomas H. 9,26,90,273
HINTON, Elizabeth Boyd 69
  John 278
  John J. 69
  Rachael Adeline 69
  Richard B. 69
HITE, John W. 14
HOBBS, Amanda 373
  Flora 295
  Joel 117
  Minerva J. 28
  Wilhelm Marion 196
HOBER, M. 327
  Sarah M. 327
HOBS, Joel M. 310
  John 141
HODDEN, William 188
HODGE, Charles 162
  William 161,173
HODGES, John 84,161,187,
    306
  William 52,143,177,178
HODGINS, Abraham 235
HOG, John Baptist 137
  Samuel 137
  Thomas 137
HOGAN, A. 174
  A. C. 68
  Abraham 256
  Daniel 52
  David 129,136,138,140,
    131,142,151,154,155,
    162,167,169,174,178,
    190
  Henry C. 376
  Martha 21
  Minta D. 376
  Oran D. 76
  Orrin D. 89
  Phil 321
  Rebecca 89
  Sophonia E. 376
  William 76
HOGG, John 302

HOGG, John B. 119
  John Baptist 123
  Samuel 123,119
  Thomas 123,124,125,119
HOGIN, Dimple 282
  Lilburn 282
  Morg 260
  Ray 291,364
  Ruth 281
  Susan 364
  Susie 291
  W. M. 202,218
  William M. 364
HODGINS, Nancy 53
HOGLE, ___ 231
HOGUES, Mary 14
HOGWOOD, Amy 62
  Edny 15
  John 18
HOLAND, Henry J. 312
HOLBROOK, Hazel 295
  Lura 295
HOLD, James 307
HOLDER, David 265
HOLLAND, ___ 242,332,334
  Agnes 299
  Annie 293
  Bessie 292
  Claude 293
  Clement 291
  Delila 60
  Edd 293
  Elvin 293
  Ernest 292
  Eva 378
  Ferebe 25
  Frances 35
  Green 77,188
  Hardie 334
  Hardy 60,293
  Jack 291
  James 18,60
  Jane 15
  Jesse 373
  Jesse G. 40
  Jessie A. 378
  Jewel 291
  John 1,27,60,116,134,
    136,148,244,302,309
  Lee 293
  Loyd 293
  Mark 60,187
  Martha 309
  Mary 60,293
  Melvin 378
  Myrtle 293
  Nancy 373
  Palestine 212
  Pearl 371
  Percy 293
  Perny 334
  Phebe 15,17
  Rosa 293
  Roscoe 282
  S. G. 328,330,332,333
  Sally 60
  Teresa 18
  Thomas 141
  Virgil 371
  Wesley 46,108
HOLLANDSWORTH, William 306
HOLLEY, Ann 56
  Anna 390
  Dell J. 390
  Edward 312
  J. 196
  J. B. 74
  J. T. 271
  Jesse 390
  Jessie T. 390
  M. 136
  Thomas 131
HOLLINGSWORTH, William 79

HOLLINS, John 324
HOLLIS, Joseph 105
HOLLOWAY, Mark 190
HOLLY, Delila 38
  Edward 44,55
  Edward D. 45
  Nancy G. 18
  Sophia 55
  Susan 42
HOLMES, J. R. 279
HOLT, Grigsby 387
  Isham P. 10
  James 156
  James M. 67
  John 186
  Laban 189,307
  Mary Ruth 292
  Simon 129,153
  Sterling 292
  Thomas L. 41
  W. C. 271
HOMER, Elizabeth 307
  James 307
HOOD, ___ 242
  Charles 290
  Conroy 288
  Johnny Paul 234
  Lee 290
  Morgan 63,86,166,173,
    235,256,306
  Thurman 288
  William R. 234
HOOK, George 125
  Alfred 7
HOOKS, Curtis 175
HOOPER, A. 196
  A. N. 112
  Aileene 384
  Alice 350
  B. D. 110
  Bailey 116
  Billie 316
  Bow 328
  Mrs. Bow 218
  Bowers 328
  Bruce 297
  Christine 365
  Claud 377
  Mrs. Claude 218,337
  Dickson 297
  Demps 316
  Donald 385
  Edgy 19
  Edith 297
  Ellinor 54
  Emma 365
  Ernest 385
  Etta 384
  Fannie L. 207
  Floyd 384
  Frank 365
  Frank, Jr. 365
  Freddie L. 378
  Gene 297
  Hershel 287
  Irma 378
  J. D. 112
  J. M. 207
  J. O. 74,103,207
  James 80,385
  Jep 204
  Jessie Owen 196
  Jimmie 316
  John 225,378
  John W. 378
  Julia 385
  Katie 365,377
  Langford R. 316
  Lester 297
  Lottie 287
  Lovel 225
  M. W. 280
  Maggie 384

HOOPER (cont.)
  Mary 296,298
  Mary G. 207
  Melvil W. 350
  Met 287
  Mollie Tidwell 293
  N. 78
  N. W. 112
  Nimrod 80
  Oscar 365
  Paten 384
  Paul 378
  Pauline 204
  Pearlis 234
  Ray 287
  Richard 365
  Rosa 365
  Ruth 365,378
  Sallie 378
  Scott 287
  Simpson Homes 196
  Susan Hogins 207
  T. J. 196
  Versen 365
  W. M. 101
  William 183,307,316
  William R. 207
  Woodrow 297
HOOSIER, James 356
  Lucy 356
  Oliver 356
  Ottie 356
  Ovel 356
HOOVER, Annie 381
  Mary 381
  Thomas E. 381
  Wina 381
  Wrott 381
HOPKINS, Arthur 324
  Basil 335
  Basil F. 388
  Eliza C. 204
  F. S. 332,341,342
  Fannie 351
  Floy W. 351
  Frank 334,348,388
  Mrs. Frank 113,335
  Frank Basil 348
  Frank S. 335
  Frank Stephen 209,348
  Gene 265
  Glen A. 351
  Iris 294,297,333,335,
    341,348
  Iris A. 388
  Laura 388
  Laura Knight 346
  Mrs. Laura 341
  Laura Elizabeth Knight
    209
  Mrs. Laura K. 335
  Mrs. Laura Knight 268
  Lula B. 388
  Lula Belle 2,4,113,218,
    251,268,269,271,331,
    335,341,346,348
  Mat 324
  Mattie May 348
  Ray M. 351
  V. I. 342
  W. A. 248,325
  Wren L. 351
HOPPER, D. 81
  Mary 81
  Mary Ann 79,81,84
  Z. 81
  Zachariah 188,189
HOPSON, Nelson 234
HORD, Miss ___ 268
  Nettie 331,370
HORN, Mary E. 43
  Theophilas 7
HORNER, Elizabeth 58,307

HORNER (cont.)
  George 118
  George H. 309
  George Wyatt 58
  H. B. 330
  Haywood 94
  Howard 290
  James 58,307
  John 114,115
  Juanita 283
  Lucretia 309
  Lucy 58
  Sally 58
  Sarah 39
  W. H. 39
HORSELY, Abraham 312
  Berryman R. 312
  Sam 163
  Stephen 149,168,310
HOSAY, Charles G. 271
HOSLEY, ___ 112
  Abraham 112
  S. 120
  Samuel 139,170
  Stephen 305
HOSTLEY, Samuel 156
  Stephen 172
HOUSE, Abigail 252
  John W. 194,207
HOUSTON, Anne 236
  Bixler 113
  Bruce 295
  Charles 22
  Edward 176,236,304
  Eloise 295
  Emily 236
  Herbert M. 271
  Isabella 236
  Madaline 282
  Martha 135,310
  Minerva 221
  Minervy 236
  Nelly 236
  Patsy 236
  Roberta 299
  Sally 236,299
  Sarah 310
  William 86,236,307
HOWARD, Abraham 239
  Allen 191,305
  Charles 188
  Edmond 173,303,307
  Edward 188
  Isaiah 188
  Jane 239
  John 239
  Nancy 239
  Polly 239
  Richard 166,189,239
  Robert 188,189
  W. B. 194,207
  William 12
HOWEL, Robert
HOWELL, Abner 306
  Alemelick 173
  Alexander 176
  David 51
  James 224,319
  R. C. 330
  Ros 106
HUBARD, Moses 128
HUBBARD, Eli 79,189,237
HOBS, Bain 190
  William 190
HUCHEL, Rev. Jack 267
HUDDLESTON, John 169
  Jonathan 186
HUDGENS, James H. 207
  Mary Jane 207
HUDGINS, Abner 92,95
  Elizabeth 48
  Herbert 288
  James 33,192,193

HUDGINS (cont.)
  Joseph 12
  Thomas 12,310
  Walter T. 234
  William 15,92,310
HUDSON, Capt. _____ 187
  Araminta 67
  Baker 53,76,165
  Bertha M. 361
  Beulah 393
  Blanche 393
  C. 81
  Carry M. 53
  Chamerlain 157
  Christopher 15,55,88
  Christopher C. 63,89,
    316
  Claude 393
  Comfert T. 72
  Cut B. 156
  Cuthbert 52,55,72,76,
    87,89,147,151,153,
    158,162,164,167,169,
    173,180,181,183,186,
    239,242,256,305
  Dan R. 361
  Della 393
  Dennis 370
  Doct. _____ 15
  Dollie L. 362
  Dowsey 157
  E. W. 234
  Edgar W. 340
  Effie 361
  Eliza 362
  Elizabeth 40
  Ella 361
  Ellen 361
  Elsie 292,294
  Elvin 362
  Frances C. 40
  George 281
  Grace 295
  Henry 303,305
  Ilma 292,298
  Irene 361
  J. R. 62,67
  J. T. 326
  Mrs. Jack 5
  James 46,305
  James D. 29,36
  Jennie 386
  John 93,94
  John R. 64,312
  John W. 26
  Judith J. 53
  K. W. 393
  Keziah McClurkan Rushing
    393
  Lucile 361
  Lucy 55,76,84,89
  Luther 393
  Mary 31,93
  Mary F. 5
  Minerva 31
  Myrtle 362
  Nancy 93
  Nancy E. 49
  Newt 386
  Paul 292
  Pearl 393
  Polly 60
  Reba 386
  Rebecca B. 53
  Robert Anderson 196
  Ruby 292,393
  Ruth 361
  Susan 55
  Susan Be. 370
  Susan D. 89
  Susie 362
  Taffincous 53
  Thomas 86,186,191,240,
    305

HUDSON (cont.)
  W. R. 326,329
  William 56,79,93,94,
    144,151,162,164,165,
    171,181,235,240,306
  William, Jr. 162,163,
    164,165,183
  William, Sr. 165
  William J. 15,53
HUDSPETH, J. A. 196
HUFF, Annie 299
  Clorene 299
  Jacob 263
  Lillie 299
HUFFT, Jacob 12
HUGES, Isaac 53
HUGGINS, J. M. 196
  William 113
HUGH, James 234
  Robert 78
HUGHES, A. C. 284,332
  David 130,303
  David D. 51
  Edwina Madison 62
  J. Bev. 16,62
  John Bev. 98
  Lemuel Horace 62
  Lewis T. 69
  Lula 284
  Martha 100,104
  Mary 51
  Nancy Newton 62
  Sallie 275
  T. P., Jr. 107.309
  William Granville 62
HUGHS, Allison 369
  Elizabeth 44
  Frederick 45
  John 47
  Lula 369
HUGINS, F. M. 196,198,207
HUGO, Jesse 86
HULISSA, Emily 72
HULL, Eve Ann 11
HULME, Tho. 68
HUM____, Robert 186
HUMBLE, G. 191
  George 188
  John 22
HUMPHREIS, John H. 306
HUMPHREY, _____ 3
  William Pearce 303
HUMPHREYS, Elijah 15,309
  Elizabeth Pearce 303
  G. W. 18
  Horatio 54,55,78,174
  John 52,53,54,55,56,
    120,129,134,140,141,
    166,167,173,175
  John H. 188
  John Howard 54
  Jno. 163
  Parry W. 263
  Stokely 55
HUMPHRIES, George W. 18
  H. G. 133
  Horatio 78
  Mary E. 41
  P. W. 131
  William 45
HUNDLY, T. V. 144
HUNSLEE, Bay 109
HUNT, _____ 316,332
  Albert P. 208
  Ann R. Hilliard 208
  Christine 351
  Edward 309
  Emmet S. 351
  Prof. F. E. 321
  Hartwell Slayden 208
  Ida F. 351
  James C. 208
  James Maurice 208

HUNT (cont.)
  James Morris 208
  John Franklin 208
  Mary 89,316
  Memican 313
  Morris 271
  Neal 351
  Noel Clarence 208
  R. N. Q. 39
  Robert B. 208
  S. E. 218,247,284,294,
    329,330
  Serenia Parthenia
    Slayden 208
  Solomon 208
  Solomon E. 208
  Spencer 74
  Spencer T. 76,81,87,88,
    89,312,313,315,316
  Theodosia E. 208
  William T. 208
HUNTER, Albert 23,31
  Alexander 75,144,187,
    304,311
  Allen 10,64,187,312
  Annie 327
  Burrel 312
  Burrell 15
  Charlotty G. 45
  Dury 10
  Elizabeth 14
  Elizabeth A. 47
  Francis 192
  Gaskey 306
  Gurtie 291
  Henry 186
  Isaac 15,28,140,144,304
  J. P. 193,208
  Jacob 75
  James 25,306,311
  James N. 32
  James W. 30
  John 161
  Joseph 237
  Joseph L. 75
  Kizziah C. 25
  Lance 291
  Luna 291
  Martin 7
  Nancy 32
  Patunel 311
  Pitts 197,208
  Sarah 27
  Susannah 237
  Thomas 53,188,191,306
  Tom 269
  W. A. 13,17,45,98
  Washington 13,45,69,71,
    75,82,95,98,190,304,
    312
  William 16
HURT, B. F. 100
  Billy 294
  David 295
  Hattie 343
  Lilly 343
  Marion 271
  William 295
HUSTON, Mariah C. 41
  William 91,284,320
HUTCHENSON, Donny 264
  George 280
HUTCHERSON, Alma 300
  Dixy 300
HUTCHESON, Genevieve 298
  George 224,319
  Joe 260
  John T. 306
  John W. 10
  Miles 10,73
HUTCHINS, Arrington 17
HUTCHINSON, John 295
  Marthy E. 111

HUTCHINSON (cont.)
  Stella S. 111
HUTCHISON, ___ 108
  F. C. 106
  Miles 312
  Mrs. Minta 106
HUTSON, Charles 309
  Isaac 119
  James 86
  Nancy 309
  Susan 88
  William 309
HUTTON, Comer 248
  Dill 382
  Miss Eunice 252
  Francis 186,303
  Rev. H. M. 252
  Henry 264
  Henry M. 29,272
  J. H. 325
  J. N. 248
  John Brady 234
  L. W. 225
  Mary E. 291
  Parson 225
  W. E. 337
  Z. D. 225
  Zack 298,208
HUTTSON, Mr. & Mrs. 322
HYDE, John H. 244,304
HYLAND, Henry 174,182
HYLTON, Daniel 119,121
  William 121
HYRE, Frederick 128
INAIL, Tom 382
INGRAM, Jesse C. 69
  Sary 176
INMAN, John 187
  William B. 309
IRBY, James 312
  John 310
  Pleasant 77,186,238
  Sarah A. 32
  Washington 26,312
  William 15,312
IRVIN, D. 82
  David 140
  John 140
IRWIN, Mrs. ___ 322
  David 87,176
  Ellenor 89
  William 322
ISAAC, Turner 318
ISAM, L. Roy (or Ray) 192
IVES, James 52
  Solomon 116
IVEY, Elijah 306
IVY, Isaac 73
JACKSON, ___ 25,186,227,
  228,252,254,346
  Alvin 291
  Andrew 114,185,245,315
  Arlie 295
  Billy 289
  Blanche 376
  Burrell 67,312
  Carley 295
  Coleman 54,59
  Edna 295
  Eliza R. 33
  Elizabeth 59,110
  Elizabeth S. 376
  Epps 31,68,189,193,198,
    208,242,253,302,307,
    312,346,365
  Epsey Ann 68
  Frances 54
  G. T. 198,208
  Green 8,310,311
  Howard 299
  J. T. 343
  J. V. 196,198,208
  James G. 40,68

JACKSON (cont.)
  Jane 112
  John 68,253,287,312
  John V. 274
  L. C. Dr. 343
  Layton 275
  Lillian 291
  Marion 225
  Martha Ann 104
  Mary 64,86,310
  Mary A. 46
  Mary Jane 39
  Milbria Larkins 291,299
  Ora 295
  Peter 312
  R. A. 160
  Ribhard P. 68
  Richard 304,311
  Richard P. 208
  Robert 68,306
  Sallie 107
  Sallie Hughes 275
  Samuel 142,173
  Sarah 68
  Sarah C. 46
  Sarah M. 64,74,219
  Stonewall 217
  T. A. 196
  Tennie 365
  Thomas 197,208,376
  Van J. 68
  Virgil 295
  W. H. 332
  W. M. 343
  Walter Bell 299
  Wesley 29
  William L. 376
  Wm. M. 68
  Willis 30,64,86,88,178,
    307
JAKES, Robert 75
JAMERSON, Robert 188
JAMES, Aaron 116,135,228,
    235,305
  Abah 56
  Aby 54
  Amos 54,56,76,305
  Benjamin 161,184
  Bessie 282
  Elijah 186,187
  Elijah, Jr. 54,76
  Enoch 54,56,76,82,86
  Enos 86,170,172,187,305
  Essie 282
  Finetta B. 27
  Hugh 282
  Ida P. 228
  Jamay 54
  James 49,73
  John 18,31,192,282,312
  Joshua 54,56,76,82,153,
    156,165,177,179
  Mary 30,73,311
  Nancy 313
  R. A. W. 197
  Rachel Walker 291
  Captain Robert A. W.
    208
  Sally 54
  Sarah 313
  Sarah E. 323
  T. H. W. 266
  T. N. 73
  Thomas 54,190
  Tucker 54
  Virgie 282
  W. A. 43
  William 54,192,238,262,
    291,299,311
  Wm. A. 347
JAMESON, Robert 115,141
JAMISON, I. C. 99
  Robert 115,183,191

JARMAN, Robert 283
  William 166
JARNAGAN, Thomas 312
  William 313
JARNAGIN, Susanna C. 24
  William 23
JARNEGAN, Jesse 161
JARNIGAN, Thomas 24,28,29
  Unity 56
JARRATT, Thomas 3
JARRETT, Malinda 10
  T. G. 196
JEMSON, Downs 313
JENKINS, ___ 339
  Alsey 101
  Robert 312
  Walter 312
JENNINGS, J. M. 196
  Mary 44
JERNIGAN, J. W. 265
  Jesse 176
  Thomas 22,79,306
  W. C. 18
JETT, Alice 383
  D. S. 268
  Dan 383
  James 386
  Lawrence 286
  Lela 386
  Lesbie 383
  Mary 269
  Mary E. 383
  Mollie 386
  Morris 386
  Paschel R. 383
  Walter B. 383
JOBE, Mrs. A. P. 296
  Bill 298
  Henreitti 289
  Kate Anna 299
  Larry 343
  Maud 289
  Neil 343
  Ruth May 298
JOHN, David J. 284
JOHNSON, ___ 233,282,332
  A. L. M. 281
  Amy 60
  Benjamin 53
  Billie June 282
  Caroline 26
  Charles 122
  Charlotte 20
  Charloty 60
  Cholaty 60
  Christine 282
  Dunkin 52
  Elizabeth 17,22
  Evelyn 282
  Frances 32
  Francis 309
  Granville M., Sr. 208
  Grover 282
  H. N. 273
  Henry 41,127
  Hudson 84,85,114,144,
    242
  Hutson 90,305
  Isaac 76,82,304
  J. B. 196
  J. L. 281
  J. S. 333
  J. T. 196
  J. W. 223,330
  Jacob H. 208
  James T. 196
  Joel S. 60,90
  John 15,19,60,85,90,306
  John J. 107,208
  John Parcy 282
  John Pinkerton 196
  Johnathan 51,155,309
  Kenneth 347

JOHNSON (cont.)
  L. P. 281
  Louise 294,333
  Lucinda 20
  Lucinda J. 42
  Martha Jane 66
  Maurine 298
  Milton 261
  Morel 298
  Patsey 60,90
  Pauline 282
  R. A. 274
  Richard 80,82,305
  Rubin 188
  Samuel 52
  Shirley 282
  Stephen B. 60.90
  Susan 311
  Talmadge 282
  Thomas 90,125
  Rev. Thomas Andrew 272
  Thomas M. 60
  W. H. 36
  Webster 295
  William 15,27,49,60,70,
    71,78,82,87,90,136,
    307,312
  William H. 11,52
  Willis 311,317
  Willis R. 196
JOHNSTON, Isaac 53
  Jacob 53
  James 35
  James W. 359
  Jennie 143
  John 128,363
  Lizzie 359
  Louise 363
  Maud L. 363
  Nathl 122
  Nathaniel 129,137
  Odie 363
  Paul 363
  Polly 52
  R. A. 273
  Samuel 52
  Thomas 190
  William 189
JOINER, Harmon 21
JOIST, Thomas 198,208
JONES, A. B. 158
  Dr. Aaron 228
  Alexander 192,312,323
  Anna 32
  Benjamin 22
  Beulah Glasgow 291
  Burrell 144
  Caroline 16
  Charles P. 75
  Charles S. 225
  Clyde 282,293
  D. C. 225
  Daniel M. 25
  David 44
  Dick 361
  Drury 18
  Drury C. 44
  Earnest A. 326
  Eckford 291
  Edna 361
  Elijah 182,304
  Eliza 17
  Elizabeth 52
  Elizabeth J. 47
  Elvis 291
  Enlow 374
  Erich C. 377
  Ernest 293
  Esta 294
  Ester 52
  Esther 377
  Ethel 293
  Francis 261

JONES (cont.)
  Frank 361
  George 271,377
  Georgia L. 377
  Giles 75,144,158,304
  Henry 18
  Henry D. 36
  Howard 293
  J. 95
  James 32,139,144,158,
    290,312,304
  James Madison 58
  James Yell 196
  Jane 58,312
  Jefferson 312
  John 11,24,44,52,58,115,
    121,144,164,186,192,
    305,311
  John, Jr. 58,165
  John, Senr. 165
  John H. 27
  Joseph 311
  Joshua 58,305
  Josiah 58,186,187
  Laura 282,361
  Lucy Lee C. 377
  Mable 290
  Madie 361
  Margaret 313
  Martha 25,28,42
  Mrs. Marvin 268
  Mildred 294
  Moses H. 40
  Myrtle 290,293
  Nancy 23,52
  Patsey 144
  Peggy 16
  Pete 374
  Polly 144
  Rebecca 323
  Reuben 186,187,242
  Rheuben 10,52
  Sam 329
  Sarah 25,35
  Sarah E. 40
  Sealum 52
  Thomas 33,42,180,190,
    243,304,312
  Thomas J. 12,52,98
  Thomas Jefferson 58
  W. E. 273
  W. M. 208
  Will L. 361
  William 58,81,237
  Willie 21
JONNAUL, _____ 228
JORDAN, _____ 285
  Aney 48
  Brittannia W. 54
  Ezekiel 46
  George W. 54,61,75
  Jesse 74
  John 260,263
  John Augustus 54
  John P. 74
  M. 198,208
  Martha 49
  Mary 54
  Minnie Hogins 207
  Nancy 48
  Norflet 312
  Peter 123
  Robert West 54
  Sarah 47
  Sarah Agnes 74
  Seth B. 54,75,82
  Syntha 28
  T. C. 207
  W. W. 328
  Warren 67
  Berry 194,208
JORNEGAN, Robert 304
JOSLIN, _____ 160,161,332

JOSLIN (cont.)
  Albert 310
  Albert N. 26
  Ben 244
  Benjamin 117,124,132,
    136,140,150,152,157,
    162
  Bertha 354
  Charlie 378
  Dan 330,332,378
  Elizabeth Jane 64
  Eula 378
  Gabe 79,253,302
  Gabriel 98,310
  H. W. 28
  Henderson 98,310
  Hester 361
  J. R. 378
  James 64
  Joe 378
  John 124,165,238,307
  Martha 38,333,354,383
  Mary Margaret 64
  Otto 378
  Patsy 98
  Raymon 354
  Rebecca 238
  Susan E. 42
  T. C. H. 327
  Texie 378
  W. B. 21,196
  William 134,192
  William B. 310
  Willie B. 37
JOURDAN, John 70
  Warren 68,73
JURRELL, Thomas, Sr. 307
JUSTER, Richard 185
JUSTICE, June 104
  Nancy 207
  Richard 185
  T. L. 102
  Thomas L. 196
KANNARD, Keith 389
  Kenneth 389
  Matilda 389
  Minnie 389
  Will 389
KARNES, Jacob A. 64
KARY, Francis 187
KAUFFMAN, _____ 315
  William 313
KEEL, Walter 282
KEELE, M. H. 327
  Marion 297
KELLAM, Eleanor 74
  Lucy 74
  Susan 74
  William H. 74
KELLER, Albert 270
KELLEY, Arch 367
  Dallas 367
  Ebenezer 162,306
  Noah 184
  Sallie 367
  Tennie 367
  W. P. 338
KELLOM, Edward 165
KELLOW, Blanche 378
  Dick 378
  Jessie 378
KELLY, A. B. 271
  Ebenezer 55,76,83,135
  George 86
  John 76,77
  Patrick 185
  Polly B. 15
  Rachel 55,83
  Susannah 76
  Thomas J. 14,16,21,26,
    98
  Woodrow W. 234

KELSEY, Eugene 202
   William T. 196
KELSY, William 101
KEMBLE, James R. 33
KEMP, Joseph 126
   Warren 298
KENABLE, James R. 33
KENEDY, Pat 198,208
KENNEDY, John 91
   Margaret 11,91
KEPHART, F. T. 198,208
   Florence 325
   Martha T. 34
   Mary Anne 36
   Perry A. 47
KERAGEN, Williams 58
KERLEY, James T. 311
   Ted 275
KERR, ____ 228
   Alex 280
   Alexander 224
   Alexander Kerr 319
KERRAGIN, W. 57
KEY, Thomas 305
KEYS, Eady 66
   Tom 66
KILGORE, Asenath 364
   Robert 364
KILLEBREW, J. B., Col. 327
   Mary 58
KILLEY, William 135
KILLINGSWORTH, Elizabeth 137
   William 123,137
KILLPATRICK, James 169
KILPATRICK, Ebenezer 191
KIMBLE, Joseph 59,159,305
KIMBREL, William 309
KIMBRELL, Henry 187
   John 131
KIMBRO, ____ Moore 211
   Docia 293
   Dollie Bell 290
   Ernest 292
   Fatha 41
   Jimmy 211
   Joe 208,293
   M. D. 276
   Maude 293
   Nathaniel 12,309
   Noel 293
   Rachel 323
   Serena King 208
   Sim 293
   Ward 290
KIMBROUGH, Fatha 41
   James 43
   Sarah 21
KIME, Michael 170
KINDLE, Richard 21
KING, Alexander 161
   Alford 309
   Alfred 22
   Amos 47
   Anderson 15,309
   Armour 306
   Bob 373
   Catren 161
   Elizabeth 307
   Fanny 15
   Fentress 208
   Garrison 310
   Henry 15,44
   Isaac 41
   Isabella 78,305
   Isaiah 41,47
   James 77,78,158,160,161,
     238
   Mrs. James 238
   James, Jr. 161
   James P. 12
   John 78,90,128,161,187
   Joseph 305

KING (cont.)
   Martha 305
   Martin 198,209
   Nancy 161
   Patrick 161
   Rachael 41
   Randy 279
   Rebecca 47
   Robert 161
   S. 160
   S. T. 20
   Samuel 78,158,161,267,
     307,309,346,347,348
   Serena 208
   William 13,26,57,161,
     237
KINNEY, John 171,175
KIPHART, Henry 311
KIRK, Goodwin 76
   J. L. 76
   J. W. 180
   James 76,306
   James M. 71,76,192
   Jesse L. 76,305
   Mary 209
   Polly 64
   W. M. 209
   William 64,76,310
   William M. 209
   Young 239,305
KIRKMAN, Florence 246,333
KIRWINE, ____ 226
KISSLER, Annie G. 357
   Charlie R. 357
   Daniel 357
   John 357
   Pearl 357
   William 357
KIZER, Benjamin 189
KLYCE, Rev. ____ 277
KNIGHT, Charles Nichols 209
   Cynthia Thomas 209
   Dora Nichols 209
   Elizabeth 209
   Elizabeth Knight 209
   Elizabeth Nichols 209
   George Wade 209
   J. Robert 209
   John 75
   Johnnie 209
   Joshua Y. 32
   Laura 268,341
   Laura Elizabeth 209,348
   Lou Hatcher 209
   Margaret Brown 209
   Mollie McMillan 209
   Mollie Taylor 209
   Naomy 6
   R. H. 341,342
   Robert Horace 209
   Mrs. T. D. 338
   T. T. 342
   Thomas 338
   Thomas Terry 209
   Wade Hampton 209
   William Benjamin 209
   William J. 91,313
KNIGHTON, James 179
KNOTT, Charles L. 234
KOEN, Henry B. 57
KOLB, Charles 154
   Martin 179
   P. 179
KOON, Polly 59
KRANE, Matthias 305
KRATCHMAN, Charles 294
KRETCHMAN, Christelle 334
   Delbert 334
   Derbert 298
KYES, George 129
KYLE, Absasder 8
   Alexander 8

KYLE (cont.)
   Flora 41
LACKEY, Rev. J. F. 268
LADD, ____ 346
   Edith Jane 295
   Eunice 288
   Geneva 288
   John 310,324
   Malcolm 282
   Roy 282
   Thomas 48
   Walter 281
LAIN, John 307
   John H. 72
   Rufus C. 72
LAIRD, Mary A. E. 204
LAKERAY, William 187
LAMASTER, William 11,312
LAMASTUS, Dudley B. 234,
     339
   John 302
LAMAY, Eugene 334
LAMB, George 125,131,152
   James 275
   James Shelton, Jr. 339
   Mike 234
   Polley 152
   Richard Napier
     Claiborne 152
LAMBERT, Aaron 124,126,129,
     166,169,172,173,238,
     239
LAMPLEY, A. J. 196,325
   Caroline 47
   Jacob 62,73,296,312
   John T. 37,73
   Joseph 73,155,305,312
   Mary 33
   Nancy 73
   Rebecca 62,73
   Till 260
   William 40
   William C. 73
   Zilphia 73
LAND, Lou Ella 334
LANDERSON, Emaline 22
   James 22
LANDRITH, Nancy 63
LANE, Alma 334
   Boogie 298
   Elias 242
   Frances 295
   Garrett 130
   Harden 334
   Hermie 297
   Jackie 298
   Leroy 292
   Liddy 237
   Lou Ella 298
   M. J. 95
   Mary 334
   Mary A. 44
   Millington J. 95,96,97
   Odie 334
   Polly 90
   Robert 298
   Rufus 107
   Talmage 334
   Thelma 298
   Thomas 96,103,196,197,
     209
   W. M. 270
   William 310
   Wineford 95
   Winnefred 29
LANERUM, Shepherd 306
LANGFORD, Jarrett 30
   John 311
   Moses 88
LANGHAM, John 118
LANIER, Isaac H. 6,306
   Pherson 297
   Robert 126

LANKERSON, Samuel 15
LANKFORD, Alice 291
  Billy E. 235
  D. 260
  Dillard H. 196
  Francis 20
  Harriett 37
  Howard 282
  J. W. H. 194,209
  James D. 234
  Jarrett N. 30
  Jeff 277
  Jemima 41
  John 85,90,113
  Lawrence 194,209
  Laurana 37
  Lurena 37
  Lurline 291
  Parish 85
  Parrish 90
  Robert 194,209
  Sarah 20
  T. P. 106
  Wayne 264
  William P. 48
LARKENS, James 135,136,140,
  148
LARKIN, John 116,118,235
  Sarah 23
LARKINS, Allie 104
  Asa 370
  B. F. 28
  Baxter 370
  Benjamin F. 48,310
  C. 225
  Carla Walker 299
  Carrie 370
  Catharine 93,98,310
  Charlie 292
  Clark 266
  Claude 282
  Clyde 292
  Delphia Jane 72
  Dorothy Mae 294
  E. E. 71,266
  Ebenezar 33
  Edna 365
  Elizabeth Corlew 209
  Ella 325
  Elzr. Newton 98
  Emmett 370
  Ersher 326
  Ewing 326
  Mrs. F. K. 102
  Francis 20
  G. W. 75
  George W. 18,310
  Gertrude 365
  H. C. 65
  H. J. 326
  Helen 370
  Howe C. 98
  Ione 294
  J. H. 196,198,209
  J. J. 196
  J. M. 69,193,209
  James 18,79,176,177,198,
    209,238,253,294,305,
    310,323
  James M. 98,347
  John 26,28,79,96,122,
    136,154,176,180,182,
    253,302,306,310
  John, Jr. 118,121,124,
    134,177
  John, Sr. 118,121,122,
    124,131,148,154,175,
    177,306
  John M. 65,234
  Joseph 29,75,79,93,97,
    98,175,180,185,306
  Joseph Henry 209
  Karen 295

LARKINS (cont.)
  Laura Ann 98
  Lena 292
  Louise 295
  Maggie 380
  Margaret 212,213
  Marshall 68,292
  Martha 70
  Mary 28,106
  Mary Louise 293
  May 370
  Mayme 365
  Melvin 295
  Odell Jackson 291
  Ora 292
  Paul 295
  R. A. 101
  Robert 79,175,180,191,
    225,292,307
  Robert E. 365
  S. P. 202
  S. T. 268,273
  Samuel Putnam 196
  Sarah E. 211
  Stella 292
  T. B. 106
  Virgie 281
  Wellington 326
  William M. 35
  Wilma 295
LASLEY, George 188
LATHAM, Bryan 313
  Elizabeth 44
  J. B. 193,209
  William S. 45
LATIMER, Joseph 329
  L. E. 100
LAUGHLIN, Isabell 10
  Jane 9
  Lyndon 10,11
  Susan 11
LAW, Benjamin 17
  Jacob S. 44
  John 311
LAWERNCE, Samuel 74
LAWRENCE, Dock 198,209
  Hal 198,209
  J. B. 196,209
  Joe 198,209
LAWS, Aaron 81,145,151,177,
    180,181,186,187,311
  Aron 22
  Feraby 81
  Pheraby 81
LAYNE, Dudley W. 61
  Robert 31
LEA, Matthew 75
LEACH, Edward 154
  L. L., Jr. 109
LEATHERMAN, Pink 387
  William 379
LEATHERS, A. H. 284,338
  Allison 391
  Allison H. 391
  Emma 391
  Emma R. 391
  Fannie 391
  Harry R. 391
  John B. 391
  Mahala 44
  Mary Ann 295
LE COMTE, Christine 290
  Frank 290
  Louise 290
  Lucille 290
LEDBETTER, George William
    292
LEE, Amanda 67
  Cecil 299
  Clyde 288
  Eliza 36
  Gosham 187
  Howard 278

LEE (cont.)
  James 24,313
  John 146,187
  Mary 288
  Mrs. Mat 104
  Nancy J. 110
  Robert 294,341
  Russell 299
  T. H. 109
  Samuel B. 67
  William 28
LEECH, ____ 268
  Abel 363
  Buck 297
  Charles 298
  Claggett H. 355
  D. R. 266
  Daniel 61,71,302,304,
    310
  Daniel R. 225
  Dudley 363
  Earl 297
  Earl L. 355
  Elizabeth 355
  Finis W. 22
  Glen S. 355
  Henry Collier 343
  Jacob 302,306
  L. E. 271
  Lenard C. 355
  Leonard Lane 266
  Manerva 34
  Mary 295
  Mayme G. 355
  Morris E. 355
  Murray 363
  O. R. 197
  R. L. 326,329
  Ransom 363
  Robert 363
  Rye H. 355
  Sarah 363
  Susan 28
  Virginia 355
  W. B. 252,330
  Hon. W. H. 329
  W. M. 336
  Judge William 344
LEEDON, G. W. 231
LEEK, Henry 63
  Josiah 63
  Minah 63
  Randolph 63
LEFTWICH, C. H. 268
LEFTWICK, Helen 299
  Margaret 299
  Robert 29
LEGGETT, John M. 16
LEGGIT, Nannie L. Hogins
    207
  W. R. 207
LEGITT, Henry 311
LEHMAN, John A. 313,316
LEIGH, George W. 22
  John W. 190,305
LE LOACH, Simon 192
LEMASTUS, John 263
  William Henry 196
LEMBKE, Hallie 369
  Rudolph 369
LENARD, Callie 351
  Lucille 351
  Luther 351
  Percy 351
  Wilber 351
  Will H. 351
LENEERE, Lizzie 387
LENZY, Branton C. 325
LESTER, Fon 176
  Fountain 5,66,91
  Sarah Ann 66
LESTHER, Tennessee 110
LEWIS, ____ 188

LEWIS (cont.)
  Aaron 185,188
  Amos 192,305
  Anthony G. 32
  Antoinette 45
  Arena 27
  Benjamin 189
  Delila 18
  Dilday 37
  Edna 38
  Enoch 187
  George 22,159,188,306,
    313
  George B. 31
  Hugh 52,186,187
  James 16,46,185
  James, Sr. 155
  James G. 196
  John 55,119,120,136,
    168,185,191,306
  Mrs. Leora 271
  Lydia 23
  M. L. 313
  Martha 35
  Mary E. 24
  Mary G. 27
  Mearian 142
  Pleas 326
  Rachel 36
  Richard 125
  Samuel 185
  Susie 326
  Wherriot 160
  William 56,225,304,311
  William P. 18
  William T. 136,139,148
  Willis E. 312
  Yen 37
  Zen 37
LIGGET, Henry R. 56
LIGGETT, May 352
  Nannie 352
  Wade 352
  William R. 352
LIGHT, George 86,88,306
  Michael 56,306
  Peter 86,310
  William 187,304
LIGHTFOOT, W. B. 345
LIGHTNER, Lewis 275
LILLY, Blake 296
LIN, Joseph 122
LINCOLN, President 225
LINDLEY, John 132
LINDSAY, J. M. 194,209
LINDSEY, Effie 292
  J. B. 193
  John 225
  W. R. H. 198,210
LINK, Benjamin 35
  Catherine 44
  Mariah 27
  Mary 41
  Nancy 311
  Robert 194,210
LINKS, John 192
LINN, Joseph 117
LINSEY, John 22
  Ramsey 33
  William Henry Harrison
    196
LINSY, Jackson 100
LINZY, Ezekiah 313
  John 311
  W. H. 210
LIPE, M. F. 207
LITLE, Robert 157
LITTLE, Addie S. 365
  Larry E. 367
  Luther 367
  M. V. 223,342
  Minnie 367
LITTLETON, Billie Boyd 113

LITTLETON (cont.)
  E. E. (Bill) 269
  Mrs. E. E. 347
  J. D. 298
  J. T. 113
  Olene 298
LIVINGSTON, Charlotte 57
LIVINGSTONE, R. 85
LIVINGSTON, Robert 3,55,
    188,240,307,310
LLEWELLYN, Clifford A. 234
LLOYD, Caroline 36
  Elisha 31
  Hopkins 44
  James 36
  James W. 34,38
LOCK, John 130,135
LOCKALIER, Lovet 304
LOCKE, Bessie 359
  Cecil 359
  Glen 359
  Homer 359
  Howard 359
  Joseph 359
  Juanita 294
  Joseph 359
  Maggie 359
  Maude 359
LOCKILEAR, Lucy 310
LOCKNEY, John, Jr. 305
LODAGE, Lewis 140
LOFTEN, Syloira 312
  William 225
LOFTIN, Milton 309
LOFTIS, Cinthia 56
  Cinthy 212
  Fereba 56
  G. W. 348
  Maggie 348
  Martin 56,57,83,88
  Milton 11,56,57
  Pheba V. 56
  Pheraby 83
  Rella E. 56
  Samuel M. 56
  Sinthy 29
  William 56,57
LOFTON, Thomas 76
  William 16
LOGAN, Daniel 192
  Jimmy M. 235,344
  Rev. W. C. 268
LOGGINS, Ada C. 351
  Beth C. 351
  Betty 243,282
  Blanche 352
  Clarence 282
  Daniel 282
  Douglas 282
  Dovie 282
  Eddie 282,353
  Glen 243,289,352
  Hick 297
  James 12,61,311
  Lem 287
  Lettie 352
  Lorena 282
  Mary 282,288
  Maude 287
  Priscilla 82
  Ruth 282,298
  Sara 282
  Sarah 353
  T. B. 284
  Thomas B. 351
  William 189
LOKALUS, John 304
LOMAX, William 6
LONG, Alfred 196,198,210
  Dick 252
  Irene 295
  Josephine 210
  May 282

LONG (cont.)
  Miles 15,28,92,95,210,
    310
  Nancy 29
  Ruby 283
  Tenor 282
  Whit 363
  William 22,310
  William Carlton 234
LOTT, Fanny 66
  Judia Adonia 66
  Leroy 66
  Margaret Anabella 66
  Mary Jane 66
  Melissa 66
LOVEACHE, Tennessee 53
LOVEL, ____ 113
LOVELADY, Jane 306,312
LOVELL, Dr. C. M. 247,321,
    324
  Carrell M. 354
  Crafford 36,309
  E. E. 342
  Ella Jones 291
  Ezra 334
  George W. C. 47
  Geraldine 391
  Harrison 364
  Hershal 364
  J. G. 74
  James T. 391
  Joe 364
  Maggie 354
  Maggie Connell 291
  Minnie 391
  Robert B. 210
LOVING, William 155,164
LOW, John 114,115,130
LOWDER, John 189
LOWE, James Y. 234
  John 120
  W. W. 226
LOWELL, M. G. 327
LOWERY, Eunice 352
  Henry W. 352
  W. H. 196,202
LOYD, Amelia 309
  William 312
LUCAS, Allen 75
  Anderson 119,140,301
  Andrew 119
  Ann 307
  Benjamin 124
  Edward 140,304
  James Harold 290
  John 75,238
  Mary 290,323
  Mose 329
  William 177
LUCKETT, James 165
LUCKY, Will 363
LUKE, John 53,192
  William 31
LUKEROY, John, Sr. 306
LUKROY, Isaac 237
LUMPLEY, S. G. 108
LUMSDEN, Jesse 150,164,169
LUNN, Callie Sparkman 210
  Dorsey 356
  James 202,210,356
  John A. 196,210
  Mollie White 210
  Myrtle 287
  Nancy 356
  Nannie 356
  Paul 287
  Terrell 210
LUTHER, ____ 242
  Mrs. Amanda 102
  Bessie 292,298
  Bill 298
  Blanche 291
  Cecil 298

LUTHER (cont.)
  Clayton 291
  Edgar 291
  Elizabeth 27
  Emma 295
  Eulalia 300
  Eulia 283
  Eva 291
  Freddie 298
  George 309
  Grover 288,293
  Helen 298
  Horace 334
  Hubert 293
  Jacob 16
  John 311,317
  John W. 234,340
  Junior 298
  Loretta 298
  Lucille 298
  Lucy 210
  Mary 43
  N. J. 210
  Patsey 43
  Robert 298
  Sarah Jane 32
  Mrs. T. 322
  Travis 210,309
  Vally 292
LUTON, Will 287
LUTTREL, Nancy Ann 211
LYAL, Addie 380
  Annie 380
  Beatric 380
  Edward 380
  Eva 364,380
  Rosa 380
LYLE, Justin 234
  Molly 299
  Toby 299
  Richard 299
  William 10,311
LYLES, Bea 292
  Edd 292
  Nellie 292
LYONS, Patrick 120,130
LYTLE, Robert 157,162
MABEN, John 307
MABIN, John 53,235
MAC GOWAN, Edward 175
MACK, James Clark 294
MACKBEE, Rezdon 192
MACLIN, Benjamin 54
MADDEN, Ephraim 236
  Ephraim A. 16
  Frances 303
  Minerva 236
  Patrick H. 23,313
  Robert 303,305
  Wm. B. 304
MADDIN, Absolum 185
  Jane 313
MADON, Robert 181
MAHAN, Rebecca 42
  William 140
MAHLEY, David 93
MAJOR, D. S. 206
  Theodosia Grigsby 206
MAKEWALL, Mac 382
MALEGIN, Minerva 60
MALLORY, Capt. ____ 197
  Jane 48
  Mary A. 36
  Mary Ann 36
  Pleasant T. 210
  W. J. 193
  William 252
  Captain William J. 210
MALONE, Jackson 19
MALOY, Thomas 120
MALTON, Michael 151,154,
  166,170
MALUGAN, John 186

MANEY, Frank 200
MANGLIN, E. B. 194,210
MANGRUM, Luther 290
MANLEY, Isaac 192
  Jeanette 290
  Molly 211
  Robert L. 272
  Walter 234
MANLY, Hugh 194,210
  S. A. 105
MANN, John 122,166
  Robert 125
MANNER, Joseph 52
MANNERS, John 190
MANNING, Joseph 180,234
  Marion 387
MANOR, Jobe 188
MARABLE, Annie E. 54
  Henry 54
  Henry H. 75,76,306
  John H. 57,59,72,87
MARAN, Robert 190
MARBLE, Edward 374
MARCH, Jennette 29
  John 363
  Mineyard 56
MARLIN, William L. 235,344
MARSH, Ann 56
  Aquilla 210
  Blanch 358
  Cathrine 358
  Claude 358
  Clayton 358
  D. M. 196
  Dave 358
  E. 223
  Elijah 39
  Elizabeth 53
  Emiline 103
  Gilbert 27,56,160,161,
    305,310
  Harry 358
  Hettie 358
  Jacob 304
  Joel 160,161,306,307
  John 33,310
  Margaret
  Solomon 296,311
  Thomas 210
  W. G. 194,210
  Wilbur F. 341,343
  William 18,40,198,210,
    310
  Zollie 358
MARSHALL, Eddie 277
  Rev. H. H. 289
  J. G. 48
  Reverend James 26
  John 186
MARTIN, ____ 166
  Alex 164
  Alexander 90,178
  Amanda England 210
  Ambrose 189
  Archibald 16,157
  Billy 292
  Bradley 90
  C. J. 342
  Calvin 342,390
  Cave Johnson 196
  Cecil 292
  Charlie 390
  Claude 392
  Claude C. 374
  Clyde D. 374
  Connie 367
  Cora D. 210
  Daniel W. 312
  Doy M. 374
  Edgar 292
  Edward F. 210
  Elenora 367
  Elizabeth 18

MARTIN (cont.)
  Emily 29
  Emily M. 210
  Etta 390
  Eunice A. 210
  Fletcher 392
  Fordie 287
  Francis 303
  George 57
  Hallio A. 374
  Henry 309
  Hester L. 210
  Holt 387
  I. F. 196
  J. C. 2
  J. D. 196
  J. T. 196
  James 51,93,97,117,122,
    132,133,142,143,153,
    167,168,182,253,306,
    390
  Jeremiah G. 310
  Jerome C. 390
  Jessie May 374
  John 391
  John E. 210
  John L. 28,87,88,93,310
  John S. 73,87
  John Shelby 196
  Jones D. 210
  Ludova J. 210
  Mrs. Lula 268
  Maggie 356
  Maggie B. 374
  Maggie V. 374
  Mamie 392
  Margaret Ann 214
  Marshall 292
  Mary 24
  Mary D. 87
  Mary Jean 295
  Matilda M. England 210
  Minerva 73
  Oscar 234
  Oscar Lee 340
  R. 102
  Rachel 93,97,310
  Raymon 392
  Robert 74,87,88,356
  Robert J. 374
  Rosa 390
  Roy 234,282
  Sallie 291
  Sam 288
  Samuel 191
  Samuel J. Tilden 210
  Stanley 343
  Susie 390
  Thomas 90,118,131,132,
    143,158,160,296,303,
    313
  Tilford 392
  Rev. W. M. 267
  William 154,189
  William E. 234
  William M. 210
  Zallie 292
MARTON, Bessie 327
MARVIN, Bishop E. E. 273
MASH, Joel 190
MASON, Ben 387
  Bennett 196
  Caleb 235
  Edmund 54
  Peggy 345
  Rebecca 54
  William 54
MASSEE, Indiana A. 21
MASSEY, Mr. ____ 3
  Absalon 309
  Elizabeth 61
  Enoch 307
  Jeremiah 188

MASSEY (cont.)
  Joel 56,188
  Milberry 35
MASSIE, Absolem 310
  Absalom 28
  Absolum 92
  John 61
  John C. 304
  Thomas 92
  William 78
MASTIN, Leonard 345
MATCHETT, John 117
MATHAS, Isiah 190
  James 190
MATHEW, D. N. 278
MATHEWS, Lucinda 28
  Thomas 92,127,145,146,
    305,311
  William 278
MATHIS, ____ 211
  Betty Lynn 282
  Clay 369
  Daisy 362
  Dan 362
  Drew 193,198,210
  Elizabeth 369
  James H. 369
  Jim D. 369
  John 100,198,211
  Kinchen 323
  Louisa Roberts 211
  Louise 290
  Mable 294,295
  Mary 211
  Mary Knox 282
  Nellie Bowen 211
  Ross 282
  Sarah 103
  Sarah E. Larkins 211
  Sarah F. 42
  Sue 282
  Thomas 198
  W. J. 42,196,211,247,
    321,347
  W. M. 278
  Walace 369
  Will A. 369
  William J. 12,211
  Willie D. 369
  Wilson J. 41,72,211,310
  Woodrow 290
MATLOCK, Allene 282
  Benjamin 188
  Caswell 134,141
  Charles B. 190
  Dureon 35
  James 22,305,311
  James B. 190
  John 36,311
  L. B. 174
  Leo 282
  Lewis 196,211
  Luke 60,86
  Lula 282
  Malinda 32
  Milberry 28
  Mimey 282
  Miriah 72
  Ruby 282
  Smyth 188
  Will 282
  William 19,72,310
MATTHEWS, Andrew Jackson
    61
  Emilla 61
  George T. 61
  Isam 127
  James 170
  Jane W. 215
  John T. 196
  Lollea 61
  Mary Sensing 211
  Milly 311

MATTHEWS (cont.)
  Ruth 289
  Thomas 10,61,166,170
  William 211
MAXEY, A. B. 196
MAXWELL, Jane 52
  Jess 52
  John 129,162,178
MAY, ____ 228
  James 227
  Jesse 55,78,135,180,
    184,305
  John 180,182,305,312
  Jonathan 188
  Michael 316
  Nancy 304
  Starling 180
  Sterling 78,132,133,
    135,183,306
  Susan 5
  Thomas 81,188,190
  Thomtas 110
  William 305
MAYBOURN, John 235
MAYFIELD, W. E. 196
MAYHEW, C. P. 269
MAYS, Agnes 290
  Mrs. Agnes Holland 299
  John 7
  John, Jr. 65
MC ADOO, Mrs. ____ 85
  Bettie 213
  D. 55
  David 52,188,192,304
  David O. 306
  E. A. 12
  Evans 306
  Ezra 305
  J. 171
  John 52,85,176,179,188,
    191,237,304,310
  John, Jr. 155
  Margaret 52
  Martha 85
  Mary 52
  Michael 187
  Samuel 1,52,146,217,267,
    332,347,348
  William 85
MC ADOW, David 121,155
  John, Senr. 177
  Samuel 182,273,274,346,
    347
MC ALISTER, Governor Hill
    336
  John 186
  Millie Rogers 212
  Robert M. 212
MC ALLISTER, Annie L. 379
  David 186
  Eugene 379
  Eula M. 379
  James 379
  Joe 379
  Joe E. 379
  John M. 379
  Nettie C. 379
  Susie 379
MC ARRY, Nathl. 134
MC BRIDE, Samuel 137
MC CADIN, Franklin 311
MC CALL, Allie 389
  Carrie 389
  Daniel 310
  Dell 372
  Dorothy 372
  Etta 389
  Frank 389
  James F. 389
  John B. 194,212
  Lewis 372
  Margaret P. 14
  Marion 372

MC CALL (cont.)
  Ruth 389
  Suzanne 389
MC CALLESTER, Adam W. 16
MC CALLISTER, James 169
  James, Jr. 145
  John 186
  William, Sr. 145
MC CALLUM, Robert 307
MC CAMMON, James W. 57
MC CAMON, Hugh 116
MC CANN, James 130
MC CARVER, Cecelia 43
MC CASHIN, John 296
MC CASLAND, ____ 271
MC CASLIN, Alfred Andrew
    243
  B. 225
  B. F. 202
  B. T. 196
  Benjamin 26
  Benjamin F. 26
  Elizabeth 323
  John 8,27,28,29,30,35,
    310
  L. F. 338
  Mrs. Lester 343
  Nancy 28
  Susan 38
MC CAUL, Dorothy 295
  J. F. 342
  L. A. 331
  M. L. 225,248
  Marian 295
MC CAULEY, Doney 322
  James 130,307
  John 130,164
  Katie 219
  W. H. 196,202
  Will 351
  William H. 212
MC CAULLEY, Henry 322
MC CAULY, James 306
  Solomon 48
MC CLAIN, Mrs. Iris 341
  Iris Hopkins 4,334,343,
    346
  Jill 336
  John 188
MC CLANAHAN, David 190
  James 304
MC CLANE, Mary 307
MC CLEARY, Dr. T. F. 321
MC CLELEND, James 153
MC CLELLAND, Agness 52
  Frances 52
  Francis 135,143,171,174,
    191
  Herbert H. 234
  J. R. 193,212,330
  James 52,143,147,160,
    168
  Jane 52,306
  Nancy 147
  Nelly 236
  Nelson 11,86,236,237,
    307,310
  Rebecca 35,312
  Robert H. 212,310
  Sally 236
  Thomas 52,86
  William 52,160,187,191
MC CLENDON, Simon 24
  William 164
MC CLENNEN, Francis 177
MC CLERKIN, Hugh 37,40
MC CLINTOCK, Robert 188
MC CLISH, Jane 145
  John 122,129,142,145,150
  William 142,143
MC CLOUD, Anguish 305
MC CLURE, Mrs. Delila 103
  J. E. 103

MC CLURE (cont.)
　Robert W. 16,69
MC CLURKAN, H. 251
　Hugh 72
　Jack 299
　James 154,169,182
　Matthew 132,143,154,169,
　　182
　Paul G. 340
　Samuel Brison 196
MC CLURKIN, James 131
MC COIN, William 32
MC COLLISTER, George 306
　James 305
MC COLLOM, Elizabeth 24
MC COLLUM, George 16
　George K. 234
　James 68
　James M. 47
　Levi 9,89,92
　Love 316
　Patten S. 92
　Patton S. 89
　R. H. 83,89
　Robert H. 89
　Sarah P. 89
　Susan 68
MC COLY, John 86
MC COMBS, R. W. 275
MC COMMAK, John 80
MC CONNEL, Joshua 134
MC CORD, Calvin McDonald
　　196
　Catherine 334
　E. W. 342
　Mary 334
　Westell 334
　William 83
MC CORKLE, Jo. 119
MC CORMAC, John 307
MC CORMACK, Ed 225
　Edward 27
　Julia Anne 37
MC CORMICK, Edward 310
　Julia Ann 223
　T. M. 102
MC CORPIN, Mr. _____ 290
　Bessie 290
　Ed 290
　Estell 290
　Evelyn 290
　Claud 290
　Martie 281
　Vardie 289
MC COWAN, John 344
MC COY, Bessie 282
　Rev. Dr. Don 270
　Harland 292
　Hazel 282
　Pearl 282
MC CRARY, Joseph 56
MC CREAREY, Nathaniel 118
MC CREARY, _____ 277
　Ben F. 349
　Dr. T. F. 247,275
MC CREENEY, William 7
MC CRORY, Hugh 186
　James 212
　Polly 179
MC CUTCHAN, James 179
MC CUTCHEON, _____ 346
MC DANIEL, Alexander 240
　Arthur 292
　Artie 292
　Barbara 292
　Clement 139
　Howard 292
　J. W. 268,270
　Lorene 292
　Lula Mae 292
　Margaret 292
　William 139
MC DERMAN, Sally 81

MC DOLE, John 38
MC DOWELL, Nelson 150
MC DURMITT, James 27
MC ELHINEY, Allie 287
　B. S. 272
　Cecil 339
　Cecil R. 234
　D. D. 298
　Gracie 298
　Gretchel 287
　John 223,272
　Lizzie 100
　Vera 298
MC ELHINNEY, William C.
　　223
MC ELROY, John 131
MC ELYEA, Charlie 371
　John 371
　Lula 371
　Martha 371
　Tom 371
　Thomas Benton 196
MC ENNERIE, James 32
MC ENROE, Pat 316
MC FARLAND, John T. 321
　W. B. 25,74
　Walker 157
　William 275
MC CALUGHEY, Alexander 187
MC GAVOCK, R. M. 119
MC FAW, Joe 263
MC GEE, James 160
　Micajah 304
　O'Kelly 309
MC GOWEN, Ed 120
　Edward 178
　John 100,120
MC GRAW, Cornelius 140,
　　144,160
　David 130,139,142,144,
　　148
　Isaac 148
　Judy 148
　Rachel 148
MC GUIRE, Johnie 316
MC HENRY, Archd 182
　John 185
　Peggy 304
MC INTIRE, Billy 282
　Florence 282
　Paul 282
MC KAY, Samuel 188
MC KEAN, Joseph 139
MC KECHNIE, John 225
MC KEE, James 54,186,188,
　　191,239
　Polly 124
MC KEEN, Joseph 121
MC KEETHEN, Neel 157
MC KELVEY, Buren 368
　Myrtle 368
MC KEY, James 307
MC KINLEY, Esther 83
MC KINNEY, Wilson 144
MC KINNON, Sallie 376
　Will H. 376
MC LAIN, Ephraim 347
　Margaret 35
MC LAUGHLIN, Israel 310
　James 232
　Mary Jane 49
　Nancy 63
　W. C. 330
　Winnie 333
MC LEAN, Angus 77
MC LELLAND, James 79
MC LENDON, William 181
MC MAHAN, A. M. 198,212
　G. W. 212
　Isabella 37
　Jimmy 292
　Minerva 212
MC MENN, Oliver 33

MC MILLAN, Archibald 128,
　　157
　Daniel 157
　John 166
　M. 80
　Mollie 209
　Polly 20
　William G. 295,343
　William Gilbert 298
MC MILLEN, John 138,139,
　　146,149
MC MILLIAN, Mary 110
　Charlie 357
　Susie 356
　William 356
　Willie G. 357
MC MILLIN, A. 136
MC MULLIN, William 242
MC MURRAY, Agness 183
　Robert 183
　Thomas 88,93,166,178,
　　183
　W. H. 284,324
　Washington 88,183
MC MURRY, Charlie 351
　Cynthia 50
　George 351
　Gertrude 351
　Gilly 57
　James 237
　Kate 284,351
　Rebecca 35
　Sally 237
　Sinthey 237
　Thomas 50,61,141,312
　W. H. 330
　Mrs. W. H. 218
　Washington 237
　Will H. 351
　William 7,8,11,27,79,
　　88,188,237,307,311
MC MURTREY, James 188,189
　John 188
MC NABS, John 34
MC NAIRY, Alexander Duval
　　232,233
　Hugh 182
　John 153
　Miss Eliza 5
　Robert 122
　William H. 233
MC NARY, _____ 231
　Robert 139,147
MC NEAL, J. R. 106
MC NEALLY, Sophia B. 67
MC NEELLY, Hugh 154
　James 34
　John E. 87
　Robert 22,69,70
　Tho. 347
MC NEIL, J. R. 202
　John R. 196
MC NEILEY, William 22
MC NEILLEY, Hugh 307
MC NEILLY, Charles M. 212
　Ella E. Bagwell 212
　Felix W. 212
　G. W. 212
　Hugh 143
　Hugh J. 193,212
　James 198,212
　Rev. James H. 212
　James Hugh 66,213
　John 69
　John Hugh 122
　Lucien 212
　Margaret Larkins 212,
　　213
　Mary 73
　Mary Russell Weatherford
　　213
　R. M. 67
　Robert 65,66,67,72,73,
　　212,213,310,313

MC NEILLY (cont.)
  Rosa 206
  Mrs. Sam Chestnut 212
  Thos. 63,67,72,73,199,
    225,310
  Thomas Lucien 212
MC NICHOLS, Mrs. Ann 104
MC NICKOLS, Thomas 196
MC NIELEY, Thomas 23,69,71
MC NOBS, John 34
MC QUERTER, Mrs. Annie 268
  Reuben 316
MC QUISTON, Thomas 173
MC QUISTON, Benjamin 129
  Thomas 118
  Thomas, Sr. 129
MC RAE, John L. 166,305
MC RONE, Thomas 79
MC WILLIAMS, ____ 18,247,
  321
  Rev. E. L. 268
  Frances 167
  Kitty 292
MEACHAM, L. 327
MEAD, Sarah 71
MEADOR, John A. 196
MEADOW, Edward L. 335
  Mary Alice 294
  Will 351
MEANS, James 115
MEDINS, E. A. 10
MEDLOCK, John 10
  Luke 306
MEEK, Adam 51
  Agness 51
  Alice 292
  Christopher 312
  Clara 281,291
  Cletus 291
  Cora 291
  Edd 282
  Elizabeth 51
  Eunice 291
  Ira Addison 147
  Jim 327
  John 16,311
  Joshua 51
  Josiah 133,137,307
  Leeta 281
  Leta 291
  Lucille 292
  M. H. 43
  Margaret 51,132,133,
    137,169
  Moses 51,133,137,143,
    158,167,168,169,191,
    211
  Pauline 291
  Mrs. Susie 106
MEEKE, Margaret 166
MEEKER, Benjamin 7
MEEKS, Bobby 294
MELONE, Jackson 19
MELTON, Emmett 385
  Everett 385
  Gracy D. 385
  James 80
  John 80
  Lorene 385
  Lucy 385
  Lucy E. 385
  Mary J. 385
  Massy 80
  Nellie J. 385
  Robert 80
  Robert E. 385
  Ted 295
MELUGEN, James 306
  Joseph 306
MELUGIN, James 188
  Joseph 164
  Jonathan 306
MENDERS, Molly 325

MENTLO, ____ 322
MEREDITH, Joseph 139
MERFRE, Robert 139
MERICK, Moreland 75
MERRILL, Holloway N. 77
MERS, Jacob 123
MESSER, Benjamin 124
MEYER, Rebecca 47
MICHAEL, Roger 276
MICKEL, John 36
  Sally 14
MICKLE, Robert 313
MIDDLESON, James 145
MIDDLETON, James 116,126,
    133,162,167
  Martha 61
  Samuel 125,126
MIERS, Simon 92,146,181
MILAM, Blanche Green 211
  Captain J. K. 211
  Soloman 76
MILAS, Edmund 187
MILES, Emma C. 356
  Marilla 42
  Stephen 344
  Stephen M. 356
  William H. 311
MILLAR, William, Junr. 118
MILLER, Annie Louise 299
  Arthur 284
  Catherine 49
  Clay A. 350
  Clyde 297
  Cora 103,358
  Cora L. 358
  E. E. 248,325
  Eleanora Miss 343
  Eloise 360
  Eugene 299
  Fannie 368
  Fred 107
  George 116
  Gertrude 360
  Gideon 192
  H. T. V. 334
  Hart 274
  Henrietta 295
  Hubert 358
  J. N. 25
  Jacob W. 116,128,140,
    141
  Jacob West 116
  James M. 192
  Jesse 361
  Jim P. 379
  John 35
  Lincoln 299
  Lola 298,343
  Louise E. 102
  Mable 295,343
  Madison 310
  Mary 350
  Matt 359
  Murvel 360
  N. E. 326
  Nancy 345
  Nora 360
  Oscar 358
  Pete 202
  Peter A. 196
  R. 133
  Sallie 361
  Silas 138,167,168
  Silas H. 143,153
  Thomas J. 12
  Tulah 362
  V. A. 103
  Vera 295
  Verge 271
  W. 131
  W. C. 196
  W. M. 272
  Walter 358

MILLER (cont.)
  William 22,25,118,132,
    133,153,157,160,171,
    174,190,305,311
  William, Jr. 132,133,
    144,160,167
  William, Sr. 138,147,
    160,166,167
  William T. 234
  Willie 29
  Willis 310
MILLS, Rev. ____ 263
  Benjamin 157,183
  Cave 323
  Daniel 278
  Edward 186,187
  Gelford 312
  Gibson 189
  Gipson 79
  Griffin 162
  John 186
  Mary Ann Jane 27
  Mary E. 44
  Randell 36
  Randolph 278
  William 161,188,265
MINOR, C. 22
  Charles 69
  Henry 128
  John 69
MISCON, Anne 38
MISEN, E. A. 9
MITCHEL, Samuel 57
MITCHELL, Adalina 21,71
  Alexr. 131
  Asenatha 71
  Ballard 71,196
  Benjamin Franklin 71
  Bobby 295
  Dona 291
  Elizabeth 38
  George 71,164,166,186,
    188,305,311
  George, Jr. 305
  Henrietta 104
  J. D. 106
  Jack 295
  John 111,187,235
  John D. 70,71
  Josephus 71
  Kenneth 343
  Martha 37,71
  Mary 37
  Mary B. 23
  Minor 71
  Robert B. 22,227
  Samuel 175,306
  Sherman 291
  Thomas 119,175,307
  Van J. 234,340
  Mrs. Vina 343
  W. D. 49
  William 311
  William M. 29,312
  Winey 313
MIXON, Anne 38
  Charles 12,307,312
  Dora 102
  John 16
MOAK, Andrew 75
MOBLEY, David 93
MOCKBEE, John 178,182
MODING, Robert 305
MOIZE, Fennie 370
  Huelett 287
  Julia 370
MOLLOY, Thomas 149
MOLTON, Abraham 51
  James 186
  Jane 186
  M. C. 185
  Michael 51,79,136,140,
    150,185,186,283,303

MOLTON (cont.)
  Sarah 51,186
  Sarah Ann Jane 51
MONK, Andrew 32
  Mary 309
MONROE, _____ 271
  Dollie E. 110
  John B. 211
  Johnson 211
  L. G. 243
  Nancy Ann Luttrel 211
  Owen 31
  Sallie Hanks 211
MONTAGUE, John 7
MONTFLORENCE, John Cole 153
MONTGOMERY, Jane 236
  John 58,69,92,94,236
  Thomas 72
MOODY, Andrew 188
  Charity E. Gardner 211
  Elizie L. 360
  Eunice 360
  James Martin 211
  James W. 171
  John 151
  John W. 360
  Maggie Blanks 211
  Nannie 360
  Silas C. 360
  W. A. 72,322
  W. G. 327
  William 211
MOORE, _____ 211,245
  Barbara Frances Rowland 211
  Bessie 353
  Carl 294
  Charity 379
  Christine 294
  Clatie 294
  Daniel 57,58,305,311
  Durwood 345
  Ed 272
  Eddie 294
  Elias 14
  Elijah 234,293
  Elizabeth 23
  Ethel 331,353
  Fanny 119
  Frank 353
  Frank B. 196
  George W. 319
  George Washington 224
  Gully 119
  H. B. 22
  Hazel 290
  Homer 294
  Hubert 294
  Ira 211
  Isaiah 52
  J. 35,44
  J. B. 211
  J. T. 248,325
  James 211
  Jean 290
  Jessie R. 223
  Jewel 290
  John 187,211,306,353
  Jordan 28,34
  Junior 290
  Lizzie 293
  Lola G. 351
  Lou 292
  Louisa 36
  Lucy Redden 211
  M. L. 230
  Mary 211,353
  Mary Elizabeth 211,215, 341
  Maude 248,325
  Millie 287,290
  Molly Manley 211

MOORE (cont.)
  Nancy 345
  Norman 294
  Robert 12,57
  Robert E. 211
  Roy 294
  T. F. 67
  Tarleton F. 67
  Thomas 311
  Virgil 294
  Virgil Burke 211,341
  Virgil Burke, Jr. 211
  W. Frank 211
  Wade 294
  William 115,121,133, 136,141,150,159,172, 190,211,351
  William A. 351
  Zollie 294
MOOREHOUSE, Philemon 19
MORAN, John 306
  Maggie 360
  Rhoda 360
MORAND, John 161
MORGAN, _____ 226
  A. H. 22
  Buford 292
  Caleb 10,18
  Dr. Charles 74
  Dodson 109
  Elsie 292
  Dr. H. A. 336
  Hiram 26
  J. W. 292
  James M. 22
  Jane 44
  Joseph 189
  Lizzie 356
  Mathew 36
  Matthew 151
  Novalene 292
  Sarah 356
  Thomas 292,356,387
  Tommy 292
  William 87
  Willie 356
  Willie B. 356
MORISETT, William 124
MOROW, W. 124
MORRESET, William 305
MORRIS, _____ 329
  And. T. 97
  Carter 311
  Elizabeth 12,15,77
  Gilford 93
  Guilford 22
  H. 7
  Hilery 94
  Hillory 92
  Holloway 306
  James K. 311
  Reverend James T. 27
  Jesse 180,181,183,185, 188
  John 89,94,193,311
  John T. 97
  Joseph 28,65,75,97,312
  Katie Bell 331
  Lucy G. 97
  Matthew 311
  Nancy 32
  Sam 242
  Samuel 185
  Susan 92,312
  Susannah 47,89
  Tho. C. 73
  William 58,89,93,143, 188,305
MORRISET, Elly 17
  Isaac 312
  William 313
MORRISETT, Charity 162
  John 124,150,152,165, 178,183

MORRISETTE, John 150
  William J. 155
MORRISON, Betsy 60
  Charity 6
  Elizabeth 60,61,91
  Mary 5
  Noble 79
  Peggy 6
  Rachel 5,6,60
  Thomas 150
  W. P. 294,295
  Will 294
  William 5,6,54,60,72, 78,83,91,93,134,150, 159,174,182,183,235, 306
  William, Jr. 6,61
MORRISS, William 303
MORROW, Ed 329,377
  John 177,181
  Maggie 377
  Mareret 377
  Thomas 178
  William 19
MORTON, Dora Donelson 211
  George H. 211
  Marguerite 211
  N. B. 2
  Thomas D. 211
MOSELY, Henry 189
  Susan 42
MOSER, David 75
MOSIER, Benjamin J. 49
MOSLEY, Daniel 35
  Martha 39
  Mary T. 48
MOTT, Daniel 126
MOULDEN, Michael 277
MOULDER, Abraham 303
  Polly 303
MULHEMIS, Frank 27
MULLINS, G. W. 104,342
  George 271
  J. B. 252
MURCHISON, Ed 271
MURDOCK, Allen 123
MURFRE, Edward 83
MURFREE, Elizabeth 83
  Polly 83
MURPHEY, William 334
MURPHREE, Col. _____ 164
  H. S. 342
  Hardy 136,182
  Rebecca Katherine 215
MURPHEY, Stephen
MURPHREY, Stephen 118
MURPHY, _____ 231,299
  Hubert 299
  John 324
  Mary 38,312
  Mildred 299
  Mintie Weems 290
  Richard 24,36
  Stephen 263
  Thomas 29
MURRAY, Henry Allen 196
MURREL, Thomas, Jr. 305
MURRELL, _____ 334
  Belle 328,329
  Benjamin 9
  Burket 9,10
  Burkett 309
  Eliza 9
  Elizabeth 27
  Georgie 287
  Harry 234
  Henry 288
  J. D. 327
  J. T. 202
  John 19,310
  Kisiah 32,97
  Lela 288
  Lucy 22

MURRELL (cont.)
  Lula 288
  Mary 7,97
  Mary A. M. 6
  Maude 329
  Mick 288
  Richard 9,10,57,96,97,
    155,165,307,309
  Rosaetta 287
  Susannah 97
  T. J. 103
  Thomas 43,60,72,74,150,
    165,178,310
  Thomas, Sr. 150
  Tom J. 367
  Wesley 288
  William S. 6,75,77,305
MURREY, Gertrude Talley
    219
  W. H. 219
MURRILL, Rev. Thomas 5,72
MURRY, Cyrus 39,40,42,312
  John 190
  Mary Wheeler 333
MUSGROVE, Ann 212
  D. 193
  David 198,212
  Obadiah 212
MYATT, ___ 109,212,248,
    325
  A. 247,321
  Ab 330
  Albert 371
  Alsey 310
  Alston 45
  Andrew 382
  Andrew J. 19,24,309
  Ben 262
  Bradley 212
  Burwell 8,62
  C. A. 332
  Callie 371
  Callie Cox 212
  Cinthy Loftis 12
  Cynthia 42
  Doy 371
  Edith 282
  Edy 24
  Elbert 384
  Eldridge 62,309
  Elizabeth 61,63,65
  Glen 294
  H. 8
  Harriet 19
  Hattie 384
  J. A. 330,332,333
  J. F. 212
  James C. 19
  Jones Albert 212
  K. 8,10,21,24,25,27,31,
    32,33
  Kate A. 382
  Kinderick 29,62,212,
    307,309
  Louisa 29
  Margaret 295
  Mary 27,45,309
  Matthew 64
  Morgan 99
  Murrell 310
  Nancy 6,216
  Palestine Holland 212
  Polly 11,62
  Ramie 293
  Reddick 309
  Ruby 293
  Sarah 39,43
  Sarah Russell 212
  Stella Vey 282
  Th. 11
  Virgil 282
  W. J. 196
  William Jack 196

MYATT (cont.)
  Willie 293,306,309
MYER, Simon 305
MYERS, Jacob 48
  John 129
  Mrs. Nancy 324
  Sally 8
  Simon 58
  William 108
MYETT, Beulah M. 390
  Dolly 11
  Percy 390
  Samantha 390
MYRES, Bettie 379
  Fidellar 379
  Frank 379
NAIL, Ben 255
  Joseph 255
  Nathan 304,306
  Rufus 198,213
NALE, Joseph 181
NALL, Elisha J. D. 196
  James 202
  John 184
  Joseph 7
  N. 198,213
  Nathan 306
  Thomas 156
  William 156,184
  Williamson 225
NALLS, Alexander 190
  Geraldine 364
  James 355
  Jane 31
  Jeff 364
  Nathan 261
  Reuben 191
  Richard 306
  Rosina 355
  Stella 364
  William 10
NAPIER, Dr. ___ 3,254
  Alonzo 213
  Araminta 15
  Bettie McAdoo 213
  Blunt R. 66
  Cassander 58
  Charlotte 59,66
  Charlotte Mary 59
  Clarence 213
  E. C. 122
  E. W. 66,67,82,125
  Elias 125,131
  Elias W. 77,159,238,
    262,304,305,313
  George F. 175,176,304,
    307
  H. A. 92
  Hannah 59
  Henry 213
  Henry A. C. 57,67,85,
    89,304,312
  Henry A. L. 304
  J. W. 10,12,13,14,16,
    17,64,95,176
  James 192
  James R. 8,59,66,307
  Jennetta 58
  John 213,304
  John W. 64,66,67,85
  Leroy W. 59,66
  Madison C. 59,66
  Mary 213
  Mary J. 213
  Mary Jane 36
  Nancy J. 213
  R. C. 115,117,120,122,
    123,128,151,167,190,
    307
  R. H. 198
  Dr. R. S. 213
  Richard 82,125,126,
    152,175,176,235,242,
    302,303,304

NAPIER (cont.)
  Richard, Sr. 80,307
  Richard C. 125,152,178,
    187,283
  Richard Claiborne 59,
    66,182
  Richard S. 213
  Robert Henry 213
  Miss Sally Fox 5
  T. A. 226,318
  Thomas 67,117,125,131
  Thomas Alonzo 213
  Victoria A. Wyly 213
  W. C. 347
  W. Z. Russell 213
  William C. 67
  William H. 66,67,213,
    312
NAPPIER, R. C. 159
NASH, J. W. R. 194,213
NAWL, William 182
NAWLS, Nathan 261
NEBLEBO, ___ 113
NEBLETT, Ann 330
  Benjamin 189
  Cyrns 289
  Dick 297
  Capt. Edward 189
  Joseph 214
  R. P. 196
  W. H. 266,270
NEELEY, John 306
  Mrs. Minnie 268
  James D. 340
NEELY, Bertha 375
  Hugh 375
  Mina 375
  Willtell 375
NEIGHBORS, Eugene 358
  James T. 358
  Leon 358
  Milton 358
  Myrtle 358
  Nina 358
  Pearl 358
  Rosa L. 358
NELSON, Alexander 139
  Addie 289
  Alfred 289
  Celia 289
  Dwight 266
  Guy 289,293
  I. M. 326
  Jacob 309
  John 162
  Leslie 251
  Mattie 289
  Rebecca 355
  Robert 117,162
  Sarah 293
  Mrs. Tenn. 326
  William 130
NESBET, Jeremiah 115
NESBIT, Mrs. ___ 113
  Nathan 128,133,141,188,
    236
NESBITT, A. 39
  A. F. 40
  Adeline 12
  Allen 12,35,37,38,39,
    48,59,60,63,65,70,71,
    72,192,310
  Andrew 187
  Andrew F. 73,213
  Athie 234
  B. F. 338
  Betsy 73
  Betsy Ann 73
  Catherine M. 73
  Cornelia Moore White
    213,214
  Edward 353
  Effie 353

NESBITT (cont.)
  Harvey 33
  Henry 283
  Hugh 287
  James 3,304
  James A. 29,310
  Jane 33
  Jeremiah 73,120,138,
    177,180,190,263,305,
    312
  Jerry 263,302
  Jerry M. 213
  Joe 198,213
  John 51,63,73,79,121,
    129,138,140,142,150,
    168,174,177,191,235,
    242,306
  John, Jr. 302,305
  John, Sr. 306
  John B. 112
  John C. 73
  Joseph 26,73,191,307,
    312
  Katherine Powers 215
  Lavenia 287
  Louis W. 215
  M. G. 330
  Mamie 287
  Margaret 73,79
  Martha 73
  Martha Susan 213
  Minerva J. Dickson 213
  N. 140
  Nancy 310
  Nancy A. S. 43
  Nancy Dilleha 213
  Nancy W. 73
  Nathan 69,115,120,161,
    168,177,181,182,191,
    263,304,313
  Nellie 287
  O. 69
  Pleasant 355
  R. 138
  R. C. 145
  R. S. 318
  Ruvell E. 213
  Richard C. 138
  Robert 51,63,65,145,
    191,235,242,301,304,
    307
  Robert, Sr. 305,310
  Robert A. S. 310
  Robert P. 187
  Roberts S. 27,73
  Roger 299
  Sallie 217
  Sally 73
  Sally Sligh 213
  Samuel 65,183,237,304
  Thomas 63,79,190,192,
    310
  Will 353
  William A. 73
  William J. A. 213
  William T. 213
  William Thomas 214
  Zudie Ellis 213
NEVILLE, Granderson D. 310
  H. C. 284,320
  George 132
NEWBERRY, James 214
  Joe M. 214
  Lou Martha 214
NEWHOUSE, Lonnda 106
NEWMAN, Francis 94
  Frankey 312
  Henry 39,94,97
  Jesse 36
  John 94,97
  Mary 33
  Susan 39
NEWSOM, Francis 75

NEWSON, Robert 311
NEWTON, B. A. 223
  Ben W. 371
  Elizabeth 371
NIBLACK, Edward 192
NIBLETT, Bertha 390
NICHOL, Andrew 17
NICHOLS, Cassander 31
  Dora 209
  Elizabeth 209
  Hugh 163,253
  James K. 214
  John 118,119,129,306
  Katherine 291
  Marion 368
  Mary 368
  Nicholas H. 312
  Pearl 368
  Sarah 163
  T. W. 318
  William H. 312
NICHOLSON, James 123
  Robert 271
NICKELL, Curley 333
NICKS, A. P. 225,318
  A. V. 70
  Albert 282
  Alice 219
  B. W. S. 271
  Mrs. & Mrs. Bob 342
  Carney 281,282,295
  Clarence 287
  Dallas 287
  Dee 282
  Elder 323
  Emma 113
  F. 326
  Frank 214
  Henry 282
  Ida 295
  Margaret Ann Martin
    214
  Marshall 287
  Mary 282
  Melvina Corlew 214
  N. P. 225
  Ora 295
  Parter 282
  Peggy 288
  Reba 295
  Stephen 342
  Thomas 392
  Tolbert Fanning 214
  William A. 214
NIGHT, William 189
NIMMO, Allen C. 304
NIMO, Allen C. 239
NISBETT, Nancy 13
NISBITT, John 114
NITE, John W. 14
NIXON, Charles 312
NOLAND, George 12
  Philip B. 304
  Robert 75
  Thomas 304
NOLEN, Betty Melinda 60
  Cary 61
  Charity 60
  James 87
  Malinda 19
  Philip 94
  Susannah 19
NOLIN, Elizabeth M. 19
  Robert 6
  Robert 42
NOLL, Nicholas 213
  Rufus 193,213
NOLLY, Anderson 173
NOONER, Preston 120
NORMAN, J. 233
  Martha Anne 33
  Mary A. 37
  Simpson A. 34

NORMAN (cont.)
  William 312
NORRIS, Alford B. 312
  Benjamin 155
  Betsy 52
  Daisy 214
  Daniel B. 12
  Dollie Ann Thompson 214
  Donie Alice 214
  Elizabeth Balthrop 214
  Ellinor 52
  Ezekiah 52
  Ezekiel 79,129,150,151,
    168,180,181,183,303
  George 125
  Hugh 307
  James 155,186,187
  Jane 51,77,96,161,169,
    306
  Jennie 214
  Jesse 52,78,180,181,
    183,185,312
  John 51,52
  Lillie Ann 214
  Mary 214
  Mary E. 46
  Milton 214
  Minnie 214
  Nancy 96
  Robert 51,52,79,82,125,
    129,181,185
  Sarah N. 48
  Susan 312
  Susannah 79,82,305
  W. W. 96
  William 79,115,128,129,
    161,168,169,170,181,
    303
  William J. 214
  William W. 13,51,52,214,
    310
NORRISE, Minnie 365
NORSWORTHY, John 13,19,20,
    21,91,95,312
  Parthenia 16
  Susannah 58
  William 95,312
  Willie 97
  Willis 19,55,95,96,188,
    305
NORTHAN, John 136
NORTHERN, John 304,312
  Margaret 25
NOWLES, Elizabeth 70
NOYSWETHER, Molly 315
NUSON, William 189
OAKLEY, Bartlet A. 38
  Bertha 289
  Bonnie 292
  Curtis A., Sr. 214
  Curtis Alexander 196
  Elizabeth 100
  Emaline 24
  Frank 234
  George 312
  George W. 36
  Sgt. J. W. 214
  James 234
  James C. 196
  James Coleman 214
  James H. 29
  James W. 111
  James Wash 196
  Nancy Westmoreland 214
  Oscar 292
  Peter 323
  Robert 310
  Rosanna 294
  Tom 379
  William 36,100
O'BRIEN, Anna Belle Clement
    345
O'CONNELL, John 198,214

O'CONNER, _____ 193,214
ODELL, Clatie Donegan 281,
  299
ODIL, John 136
OFFTEN, Samuel 192
OGDEN, John W. 42
OGLESBY, Rubin 189
O'KELLY, Bartlet A. 38
  Emaline 24
  William 36
OLINGER, Susie 112
OLIPHANT, Edna Ruth 282
  Edward Lynn 282
  Katherine 282
  Leonard 281
  Lucille 282
  Maurice 282
  Theo 282
OLIVER, Drury 147,192
  Elizabeth 15
  Elizabeth H. 12
  George W. 313
  Giles J. 43
  James 12,310
  Mary Anne 35
  Susan 27,28
  Thomas M. 165
ORGAIN, Richard 295
  William H. 196
ORMSBY, Robert 160,178
ORR, _____ 231
ORTEN, Samuel 181
OSBORN, John 214
  W. J. 214
OSBORNE, _____ 284
  Tom 257
OSBURN, Brackin 289
  James 234
  John 198
  W. J. 198
OSTRANDER, Andy L. 234
OTTENVILLE, Idella 284
OUTLAW, Dr. Drew A. 7
  George 189
  Grover 234
  Harriet 57
  John 87
  Marguerite 57
  Mrs. Mary Ann Eliza 89
  Maude 351
  W. P. 196
  William 137,159
OVERALL, Robert 372
OVERBY, John T. 330
OVERTON, Elizabeth 52
  Gabriel 52,81,156,180,
    186,187
  Hugh 287
  Katie 110
  Robert 52
  Stanton 287
  Thomas 22,59,67,68,266,
    311
OWEN, Mr. _____ 295
  J. M. 198,214
  Jesse 198,214
  Jessie 374
  Joseph 310
OWENS, J. P. 338
  John 193
  John, Sr. 223
  John H. 43
  Leonard 266
  Martha 49
  Maurice 283
  Tennessee 48
  Thomas 42
OWINGS, Henry 115
OZMENT, Jonathan 148
  Sally 81
PA____, Garner 299
PACK, Betty 294,336
  Dollie 372

PACK (cont.)
  Elizabeth 323
  Garland 337
  Luella 300
  Philip 234
  Virginia 336
  Vivian 372
  Willard 372
PADGETT, Anna 359
  Clyde 359
  H. B. 196
  Keith 359
  Malissa 359
  Mildred F. 359
  Monte 359
  Rev. T. H. 274
PAFFORD, William 139
PAGE, Absolum 135
  Beulinda 279
  Blanche 371
  D. O. 342
  Dennis 371
  Mrs. Ernest 344
  Eugene 371
  Eugene, Jr. 356
  Haggard 356
  J. J. 196
  John H. 356
  John J. 356
  Lesbie 356
  Lida 371
  Linda 356
  Maggie 371
  Michaci 306
PAINTER, Rollie 323
PALISTRANT, Shirley Ann
  336
PALMER, _____ 298
  C. B. 298
  Henry S. 7
  Hester 49,331
  Judson 331
  Thomas 3,38,39,310
PANE, Pryor 307
PANNEL, Thomas 153,165,
  168,174
PANNELL, Eliza B. 6
  Thomas 142,144,178,304
PARCHMAN, Bert 294
PARCHMENT, Helen 290
  Linward 290
  Lynwood 290
  Thomas 290
PARDUE, A. E. 214
  Bettie Edwards 214
  Billy 234
  Erilla Reeves 214
  Fannie 111
  Hardin 287
  Loyd 287
  Mary 287
  May 111
  Oliver 214
  Rosco 287
PARISH, A. J. 347
  Eleaner 183,190,237
  Howel 86,192
  Huel 86
PARK, Joseph 130
PARKER, _____ 176,279
  Ceborn 40
  Charles 120
  Cynthia Ann 256
  Daniel 52,70,86,87,138,
    143,145,177,178,181,
    237,238
  Daniel, Jr. 143,163
  David 52
  Ebon 305
  George, Sr. 139,144
  Hannah 70
  Hiram 10
  Homer 215

PARKER (cont.)
  Hulda May 70
  J. A. 117
  J. T. 198,215
  James M. 177
  Jesse 80
  John 12,16,19,70,123,
    134,140,145,146,173,
    177,181,236,256
  John, Sr. 255
  Joseph 41
  Joseph A. 41
  Keziah 15
  Martha 27,236
  Moses 70,81,153,255,
    256,260,261,296,305,
    311,323
  Quanah 256
  Samuel 116,134,136
  T. J. 196,215
  Thomas 215
  W. P. 326
  William 133,172,182,
    243,296,303,311
  William J. 12,70
PARKIN, Ebon 305
PARKS, H. 37
  Hamilton 30
PARNELL, George 29
  J. C. 198,215
  John 240
  Thomas 244
PARRISH, Rev. _____ 17
  A. J. 318
  Aaron 192
  Aaron J. 24
  Eleanor 77,78,170,305
  Elinor 8
  Eliza 39
  Ellenor 84
  Ezekiel 38
  Francis 313
  H. 9,14,15,16,17,18,21
  Hewel 11,92
  Hewell 97,185,306
  Howell 172,183
  Huel 77,78,81,84,312
  Irwin 312
  Isaac 313
  JoAnn 342
  Mrs. Joe 342
  John C. 44
  John G. 44
  Joseph 192
  N. C. 69
  Overton L. 19
  Sarah C. 25
  Wiatt 170,183
  Widow 77
  Wyatt 77,78,84,92,188,
    305
PARROTT, Alice 100
  John 77,82,239,240,304
  Julia Anne 33
  Lettuce 77
  Letty 21
  Manoah 31
  Susan 46
PARROTTE, J. N. 326
PASCHAL, Alxr 311
  Gilford G. 311
  Helena Anne 40
  Henry 44
PASCHALL, Elizabeth G. 48
  G. G. 28
  J. 48
  J. P. 49
  J. S. 48
  L. S. 49
  Sarah 31,36
PASCHELL, E. A. 93
  Elisha 93,95
  Elizabeth 93

PASCHELL (cont.)
  Gilford 95
  Nancy 93
  Ramey 93
PASHELL, Middy 93
PASSMORE, David 59,67,76,
  82,92,235,239,305
  John 160
PATE, Bettie 358
  Freda 358
  Isabelle 358
  Lenard 358
  Mable 358
  Ruby 358
PATEY, Randall 340
  Randel 234
PATTEN, J. J. 333
  J. T. 333
PATTENY, William 187
PATTERSON, Miss_____ 295
  Ann 62
  Babel 307
  Elizabeth 9
  James 170
  John T. 44,54,55,313
  Polly 60
  Polly W. 7,54
  Rachel 60,61
  Robert 6,22,60,306
  Robert, Jr. 313
  Robert, Sr. 313
  Sophia 30
  Thomas 38
  W. H. 202
  William 187,313,342
  William M. 20,22,44
  William T. 41,180,189
PATTON, Isaac 118
  Robert T. 187
  Thomas 151,165,171,175,
    179
PAULK, Mrs. G. P. 295
PAXTON, Alice 303
  John 121,303
PAYNE,_____ 362
  Albert B. 256
  E. S. 332
  Eugene 377
  Mrs. Eugene 218
  Joseph 313
  Maud 377
  Nancy 22
  Pryor 240
  Sarah 377
  Thomas, J. P. 40
  Virginia 377
PEACOCK, William 79,133,
  140,142,154,158,167,
  175,178,244
PEAKE, John 186
  S. H. 13
PEARCE, Jeremiah 310
PEARSALE, Jane 51
  Lucy 51
PEARSALL, Benjamin 80,239,
  305
  Edward 6,51,97,136,140,
    150,170,172,181,182
  J. 6
  Jeremiah 51,130,138,
    145,154,163,263
  Patience 51
  Sally 6
  William 303
PEARSELL, Edward 153,154,
  161,162,163
PEARSON, William 304
PEASON, Ann 16
PEEBLES, James C. 30
  William R. 346
PEELER, Jake 296
  Rube 383
  William E. 234

PEELER (cont.)
  William Edward 334
PENDAGRASS, William 99
PENDERGRASS,_____ 324
  Elijah F. 25
  J. 9,10,11,12,22,31,32
  John 76,261,312
  John Harvey 70
  Lucretia 32
  M. E. 327
  Manley 46
  Martha 101
  Martha A. 43
  Rilly 70
  Sarah Elizabeth 70
  Van Buren 70
  William 312
  William E. 65,70,296,
    312
PENDOR, W. 15
PENEL, Thomas 119
PENNINGTON, J. B. 266
PENTECOST, Dolly 287
  Emma 386
  G. L. 333
  Gabriel 386
  George 44
  Mable 386
  Mariah Annah 44
  Mary 287
  Maryah Annah 44
  Sue 287
PENTICOST, Scarborough 317
  William 311
PERDUE, Willie 327
PERIGIN, John 312
PERKER, Joseph 41
PERKINS, Ebben 155
  Edward 305
  Ephraim 190
  Horace 272,274
  Jacob 155
  Joshua 19
  Maggie 379
  Wright 186
PERRY, Hollie 295
  Isaiah 13
  James 141
  John H. 296,311
  Nathaniel 114
  Nehemiah 123
  Patsy 9
  Paul 294
  Ruffin 62,296,311
  Sally 57
  Samuel 141,166,170
  Thornton 44
  Tilman 305
PERSEL, Benjamin 185
PERSONS, Thomas 131,156
  William 156
PERY, Tilman 86
PETTY, Adeline Dunnegan
  Alexander 187
  Ambrose 86
  Berry 327
  Bessie 360
  Blanche 380
  Carlton 378
  Dallas 380
  Daniel C. 234
  Dolly Steele 5
  Ebenezer 307
  Effie 360
  Elizabeth 11,36,47
  Epsia 288
  Eugene 384
  Fannie 360
  Frank 360
  G. H. 196
  Gabrael 43
  Gabral 90

PETTY (cont.)
  Gabriel 10,86,94,309
  George C. 13,94,95
  Gilbert 294
  Gilbert Holland 215
  Henry A. 47
  Jacob 27,309
  James D. 23,94
  James D., Jr. 309
  James D., Sr. 309
  James M. 86
  Jettie 360
  John A. 10,35,36,94,309
  Jonathan 86,87,94,309
  Joshua 41
  Kisiah 13
  Lee 282
  Leonard 288
  Lester 288
  Lewis L. 44
  Louis L. 44
  Lula 378
  Magdaline Knox 220
  Marvell M. 37
  Mary 360
  Mason E. 360
  Millington M. 42
  Myrtle 378
  Oscar 384
  Pauline 378
  Peggy 86
  Samuel 86,87
  Sinthey 8
  Sollomon 94
  Solomon 309
  Thomas 26,235,256,302,
    309
  Tom 378
  William 47,360
  William K. 23
  Wilson 360
PETWAY, Alex M. 373
  Ethel 373,384
  Lillie 373
  Nannie 373
PHELPS, Doug 269
  Myrtle 296
PHILIPS, Eldridge N. 310
  Emma 378
  Rev. G. W. 274
PHILLIPS,_____ 246,271
  Abraham 311
  Albert 246
  C. J. 215
  Clifford 289
  Eleanor 63
  Jane W. Matthews 215
  John W. 215
  M. 35
  Peter 131,185
  Slayden 335
  Tony 335
  William 19,29,134
PHIPPS, Nancy 68
PICKERING, Horace 291
PICKET, John 90,94,188
  Rebecca 90,312
PICKETT, Edward 191,263,
  307
  H. E. 318
  Henry 247
  J. J. 318
  William 247,318,321
PICKLES, Dora M. 207
PIERCE, Jesse 189
  Leburn 294
PILES, Leonard P. 179
PINEGAR, Abner 12
  Daniel Z. 13
  Elizabeth 36
  Joseph 59
  Leonard 59,90
  Martin 36

PINEGAR (cont.)
　Susan 309
　Susannah 59
　William 10,59,309
PINER, Thomas 7
　William 19
PINES, Thomas 312
　William 313
PINIGAR, Mary 13
PINION, Oscar 335
PINKERTON, D. T. 202
　David Thomas 215
　Mrs. Dolka Weatherspoon 215
　Rebecca Katherine Murphree 215
　W. L. 331
　William 311
PINSON, Aaron 38
　Harey 310
　Moses 310
PIPKIN, Steward 81,145,146,180,255,305
　Stuart 181,239
PIPKINS, Jacob 305
　Stuart 186
PIPPIN, Mr. _____ 281
PITCHFORCE, John 187,188,191
PLANT, John 135,161,188
　William 135,161,184,188,189
　Williamson 235,263
POLK, Thomas 119
PONDER, Archibald 61,83,84
POPE, J. A. 276
　Phoebia 112
PORCH, Delila 71
　Henry S. 71
　William Silons 196
PORTER, Mrs. _____ 322
　Charlie 336
　Elizabeth 9
　F. M. 273
　J. 36,37,40
　J. K. 101
　Joe 387
　John 48,62,63,65,256,296,311
　John W. 311
　Mary E. 69
　Matilda 69
　Reese 142
　Samuel M. 69
　Samuel S. 64
　T. M. 274
　Tennessee 201
　William 19,69,192,310
PORTWOOD, _____ 248,325
POTENGALE, John 10
POTTER, Annie 296
　John 189
　P. P. 318
　William 188
　Zadock 313
POTTS, E. M. 47
　Harriett 49
　Henry 309
　W. A. (Bill) 343
　W. D. 107
　William A. 343
POUNDS, Mintie 295
POWELL, _____ 111
　Dilly Ann 105
　George 54,143,144,146,147,153,156,176,177,178,179,305
　Richard 188
POWERS, _____ 299
　Annie Sanders 215
　Arthur 79
　Charlie 391
　Claude 344

POWERS (cont.)
　David 215
　Eudora 215
　Fagin 215
　Fredonia 215
　Harrison W. 215
　Herman O. 343
　Mrs. Iris (Hopkins) 335
　Rev. J. E. 274
　J. Thomas 215
　James 215,326
　James Cobin 215
　James S. 91
　John W. 341
　John William 211,215
　Juanita 295
　Katherine 215
　Lewis 135,157,164
　Lois 294
　M. C. 269
　Margaret Rogers 215
　Martha 215
　Martha Powers 215
　Mary Elizabeth Moore 211,215,341
　Mary Virginia Winters 215
　Nancy 33
　Nannie 215
　Nannie Roland 215
　Ollie 215
　Rebecca 15
　Rebecca C. 11
　Thomas J. 215
　Warner 289
　William 185,306,310
POYNER, Amanda Bumpass 223
　Thomas 63
　William Dillard 223
PRATER, Beede 20
PRATT, Henry 313
PRELLER, Archibald 87
PRICE, Andrew 30
　Asia 78
　Barham 37
　Charlotte 310
　Cullin 30
　Dan 323
　Drew 169
　Drewry 161
　Drury 78,81,306
　Harriet 29
　James 78
　Joseph 28
　Joseph E. 112
　Joshua 81,184,188
　Mary Ann 110
　Phoebe 31
　Sally 81
　Sarah 78
　Thomas 81
　Willis A. 81
　Wyatt 310
PRICHARD, Cary 68
　John 68
　Richard 68
PRIMM, Horatio Clagett 196
　Shadrick 185
PRIN, Narsissia 391
　Willie 391
PRINCE, Elizabeth 357
　Melba 357
　Ray 270
　William 357
PROCKTOR, Henderson 31
PROCTOR, _____ 319
　Abba 48
　Mrs. Amanda 104
　Gwen 288
　Helen 288
　Joshua 49
　Marvin 289
　William 288

PROVINE, Alexander 145
　John 145
PRUIT, Portan 39
PRUITT, A. D. 276
　Keith 267
　Ned 316
PRYOR, Lydia 30
　William 178
PUCKET, Jacob 76,80
PUCKETT, Arena 33
　Ceborn 40
　Jacob 305,311
　Mary Ann 26
PULLEN, A. 12,15,20
　Archibald 54,58,67,93
　J. C. 40,42,44
　James 16,70
　James C. 30,35,67
　John A. 67
　N. B. 12
　Nelson B. 67
　Polly 67
　William 19,67,261
PULLEY, Ernest 362
　Harry 362
　Jim 362
　John 362
　Lenard 362
　Lucile 362
　Minnie 362
PULLIN, Archibald 76,306,311
　James 310
PULLY, Jesse 78
PURKINS, Jacob 155
　Jacob H. 7
PURNELL, George 311
PURSLEY, W. G. Capt. 340
PUTNAM, D. U. 196
QUIN, Micahel 172
RABOURN, John 145
RABURN, Green 100
RACHER, Thomas 131
RADFORD, Wayne 343
RAE, Agnes 56
　Elizabeth 56
RAGAN, Alner H. 310
　Ann M. 8
　B. G. 86
　Birdie 293
　Elizabeth 89
　Elthia 293
　Fulton 353
　George 46,50
　Georgia 293
　Graves 76
　Hosey M. B. 7
　James W. 313
　Jesse 92,159,305
　John W. 24
　Joseph W. 10
　Lloyd 282
　Lucile 282
　Martha E. 27,45
　Mary E. 34
　Nallison 81
　Nancy 43
　Nathan 89,129,181,305
　Patience 58
　Polly 25
　Thomas J. 12,312
　Valeria 293
　William 81,187,307,313
RAGLAND, H. 142,144,148
　Henry 148
　Martha B. 62
RAIBURN, John 169
RAIL, James 143,153
RAINES, John George 153,156
　Mary S. 111
RAINEY, Ammon 292
　Bill 292

RAINEY (cont.)
  Freda Mae 292
  Joe Billy 295
  Susan 31
RAINIER, John George 178
RAINS, J. D. 294
  Oda 294
  Rosa 294
RAINWATER, Willis 17
RALPH, Peter 75
RALSTON, Isaac 127
RAMEY, Allen 392
  Isaac 19
  Van 387
  Wash 359
RAMSEY, John 134,137,159,
    176
  Miles 159
  Mill 124
  Mills 134,137,176
RANDLE, Richard 23
RANDOLF, James B. 192
  Thomas 192
RANDOLPH, Benjamin Fits 157
  Benjamin Fitz 123,162
RANEY, William R. 24
RANIE, John 322
RANIER, John George 147,
    179
RANSOM, Etta Mai 293
RAPE, Barbra 70
  Daniel 70
  Gustavus 70,94,235,312
  Henry 51,70
  Jacob 70
  John 70
  Peter 70
RASBERY, Jacob 78
RASCOE, Alexander 13
RAWLS, Rev. Benjamin 30
  William B. 31
RAWLSTON, Kathleen 296
RAWORTH, B. 68
  Edward 75
  Egbert 68
  George 32,312
  George F. 11,13,32,33
  Mary T. 31
RAY, Charlie 361
  Edith S. 361
  Eugene 361
  Herman 368
  Hubert 287
  Hubert O. 361
  James 361
  Jennie C. 361
  Jennie S. 361
  Ralph 361
  Sarah 368
  Susan 15
  Virginia 289
  William 361
RAYBURN, _____ 331
  Mrs. W. W. 331
RAYMOND, Billy 343
  Eliakim 160
  Elickim 236
  Lindsey 297
  Nellie Dee 297
  Orville 297
  Orville, Jr. 297
  Willie Van 297
RAYMOR, Mills 136
RAYNER, Miles 176
RAYNOR, Miles 176
READ, James 77,148,154,156,
    166,237
  John 154,156,160,173,
    181,307
  Rebecca 77,237
  William 77,133,148,156,
    164,237
READER, J. L. 194,215

READER (cont.)
  Mary 59
  Mary J. 15
READS, John 159
REAM, Lewis 191
REASONS, William 178
REAVACE, William 82
RECORD, David 27,66,98,312
RECTOR, James Madison 196
REDDEN, Amanda 373
  Bertha 373
  Bessie 373
  Blanche 295
  Cannon 338
  Elizabeth 33
  Ernest 293
  Frank 292
  G. C. 332
  George 373
  Hubert 281
  Isaac 261
  James 8
  Jim 327
  John 261
  John Wiley 196
  Lucy 211
  Sam 261
  William 14
REDDIN, George W. 309
  Lucy 309
REECE, Permelia Ann 30
REED, Bernice 390
  Ealic Ramey 334
  Eula 372
  Euvals Hunter 291
  James 166
  John 132,191,244
  John E. 372
  Loyde M. 390
  Mattie E. 390
REEDER, _____ Hall 315
  Alma 215
  Almira Ann Walp 215
  Edward 215
  Eliza 106
  Elmer 215
  Elzina 215
  J. H. L. 196,215
  Jacob H. 311
  John 215
  John Ernest 215
  Joseph E. 215
  Kate 215
  Liza 291
  O. A. 337
  Roma 215
REEP, Alberta 287
  Florell 287
  Henry 275
  Roland 287
REES, Porter 133
REESE, David O. 310
REEVES, _____ 288
  Albert E. 373
  Augustine 37
  Austin 37
  Benjamin 154
  Bill 288
  Charles 191
  Charlie 358
  Erilla 214
  Fannie 358
  Howard 358
  Hugh 336,373
  Jessie P. 373
  John 152
  John Andrew 196
  Lucile 358
  Reena 37
  Vandalia 373
  William E. 358
REGISTER, Edward 298
  Eunice 381

REGISTER (cont.)
  Herbert 381
  Hubert 381
  Jimmie 298
  John 298
  John P. 381
  John T. 381
  Loretta 298
  Leamon 298
  Mary E. 381
  T. S. 105
  Thad 292
  Vera 381
  Vesta 293
  Vester 381
RENFRO, Peter 137,142,145
RENFROE, Peter 122
RENSHAW, Benjamin 190
  Elijah 158,171,190
RANSLOW, William E. 10
RENTFRO, Jane 142,145
REVER, Charles 304
REYNOLDS, Amos 54,55,150,
    303
  Carolina 24,55
  Charles L. 323
  Clarida 54
  Clinton 55
  Clifton 299
  Elgie 299
  Garfield 299
  George 75
  Ida 383
  J. B. 133,141,146
  James 39,279
  Jane 60,61
  John 57,79,83,86,158,
    161,166,171,174,235,
    254,307
  John, Jr. 175
  John, Sr. 57,175
  John G. 49
  John S. 23,312
  John Severe 55
  L. 13
  M. 78
  Mark 54,57,77,188,305
  Martha 43
  Martha Ann Allbright
    216
  Martha C. 73
  Nancy 57
  Nancy H. 8
  Nannie 383
  Paul 345
  Rosa 383
  S. H. 196
  Solomon 60
  Solomon J. 13,312
  Sophia 54,55,303
  Susannah 57,83,86,90
  Thomas M. 26
  Rev. W. A. 215
  William 56,83,150,235,
    263
  William D. 26
  William T. 59,79,188,
    313
  William W. 147
RHEA, John W. 43
  Standford D. 19
RHINEHART, Martha A. 22
RHOADS, James 238
RHODES, Moses 43
RICE, Dan 196,323
  Daniel 216
  Harnett 172
  John 120,144,188
  Jim D. 294
  Lela 294
  Susan 37
RICHARD, Aden 363
  Elvira Parlee Greenlee
    217

RICHARDS, Betty 295
RICHARDSON, _____ 59,346
  A. J. 198
  Andrew J. 216
  Arthur 292
  Augustin 91,157
  Augustine 151,152,159
  Austin 91,93,94,305
  B. W. 194,216
  Bartholomew 16,310
  Belius 59,72
  Clara 281
  Cive 225
  Edward 149
  Eliza 54
  Elizabeth 22,52,58,59,76
  Elizabeth J. 62
  Elizabeth Jane 32
  Emma 292
  Esquire 225
  Eva 354
  Ezra 282
  Frances 52
  Frankey 59
  Fuller 282
  Gilla 281
  H. C. 329
  H. J. 225
  H. R. 68
  Hazel 282
  Henry 75,369
  Henry C. 329
  Hudson J. 35
  Hutson 19
  Ida 292
  James Joy 59
  James W. 33
  Jewell 282
  Jim 281
  John 59,89,179,180
  Jordan 76
  Jordan M. 58
  Jordan W. A. 58
  Jorden 54
  Kate 219
  Labeus 240,306
  Labius 59,72,144
  Lebbius Wilkins 59,60
  Lebuis 89
  Lee 292
  Lewis 109
  Louisiana 48
  M. T. 193,216
  Mary 12,54
  Mary A. 58
  Morton 281
  Nancy 35
  Nancy I. 39
  Nancy J. 39
  Polly 54,58
  Mrs. R. 89
  R. J. 99
  Rebecca Ann 58
  Rodney 281
  Sally 53,54
  Samuel 185,192,304
  Sandy D. 19
  Sarah 282
  Squire 96,310
  Stephen D. 12
  Stephen Dailey 59
  Stith 54,58,59,61,76
  Susan 27,312
  T. H. 343
  Tho. 79
  Thomas 52,55,59,144
  Thomas E. 58,59
  Thomas M. 39
  Turner 198,216
  W. T. 268
  W. Turner 214
  William 21,54,75,311

RICHARDSON (cont.)
  William Turner 196
  Winnefred 52,53,72,73,93,94,95,96,304,310
  Woodrow 270
RICHDSON, _____ 109
RICHMOND, Elvira Parlee Greenlee 217
RICKELL, John 306
RICKER, William 327
RICKERS, Frank 328
RICKERT, A. G. 327,339
  Abb 339
  Abner 360
  Bena 360
  Blanche 360
  Gertrude 360
  Gordon 360
RICKETT, John 324
RICKLE, Jonas 166
RIDGEWAY, Clemmie 292
  Pearl 291
RIDINGS, Dannie 352
  E. W. 330
  Lucile 284,352
  Solomon 39
RIETHMEIR, John 196
RIEVES, Jesse 41
RIGBY, William, Jr. 136
RIGGON, Margrit 111
RIGGS, John 278
RIGHT, Thomas 118
RINER, John George 141
RIORDAN, Edward 340
RITCHERSON, John 19
  Willie Mai 295
RITCHISON, Donald 335
  Rachel 298
ROACH, Elvin 298
ROAM, Charlie 369
ROBARDS, Huling 242
ROBB, Charles 165,179
ROBBINS, John 46
ROBBS, Martin 165
  Nancy 40
  Peter 165
ROBERSON, Huse 134
ROBERTS, Dr. A. 83
  Alice 100
  Augustian 311
  Delila 221
  Dempsey 239
  Dempsy 80
  Emmie 287
  Elisha 121
  Isaac 116
  James W. 373
  Lorene 287
  Louisa 211
  Louise 12
  Obediah 157
  Robert 190
  Rook 298
  S. 260
  Sarah E. 42
  Shook 298
  Veny 80
  W. M. 216
  William 196,216
  Wm. H. 191
ROBERTSON, Abraham 118,124,152,162,165,167,305
  Almond 293
  Ann 66
  B. C. 69,70
  Benjamin C. 57,66,67,312
  Benjamin J. 66
  C. 159,178
  Charles 8,18,23,311
  Charles P. 192
  Charlotte 244
  Christian 75,244,303,304

ROBERTSON (cont.)
  Christopher W. 66
  D. L. 193,216
  Daniel 23
  David Gay 196
  Edward A. 66
  Elijah 122,125,131
  Elizabeth 117
  Feliso 27
  Felix 311
  Franklin 37
  George 311
  Graham 271
  James 8,51,115,116,118,121,122,129,130,132,138,139,145,146,151,152,153,158,165,167,177,180,183,187,245,254,301,302,313
  James, Jr. 144
  Jewell 299
  John 191,291,306
  John H. 66
  Jonathan F. 122
  Kenneth 299
  M. C. C. 75
  Maggie 293
  Mark 10,312
  Martha 14,18
  Martha D. 66
  Mary Lee 298
  Michael 179
  Olin 293
  Ollen 293
  Pauline 293
  Payton 115
  Pearl 377
  Richard 161,179
  S. G. 332,333
  Sarah J. 46
  Virgil L. 377
  Wilkerson 9
  William 306
  William B. 115
  William J. 377
ROBESON, Sally Jane 50
ROBINS, Ella 293
ROBINSON, Abraham 117,186
  Charlie 359
  David 128,158,161,291,305,312
  Rev. E. U. 257
  Elsie 359
  J. B. 322,327
  James 177,359
  Jane 26
  Joseph 117
  Margaret Hite 295
  Michael 177
  Peyton 59
  Robt. 327
  Walace 359
  William 161,186
  Willie McGee 293
ROBISON, B. C. 3
  Guy 293
  Sammy 293
  Samuel 161
ROCHE, Mary G. 22
ROCHELLE, Jasper 216
  W. L. 283,334,335
ROCKEY, Johnetta 287
  Nellie 287
ROCKY, Sue 295
RODGERS, B. F. 104,262
  John 230
  P. 171
ROEBUCK, John 238
ROEDER, Cleve 381
  Lela 381
  Mary 381
  Nannie 381
ROGAN, John W. 312

ROGERS, A. A. C. 34
  Callum 19,91,312
  E. 77
  Edward 312
  Edward M. 29
  Edward Moore 19
  Elias 305
  Elizabeth 77,81,240
  Fannie 323
  Henry R. 19,20
  J. M. 216
  James 50,238,305
  Jesse 77
  Joel 312
  John 83
  Jonathan 188
  Jones 305
  Joseph 305
  Lelia 361
  Lester 361
  Lida 284,361
  Linda 331
  Lucien 361
  Margaret 215
  Mary 134
  Millie 212
  Phinous 361
  Robert 77,81,189,240
  T. 323
  Thomas 253,323
  Tom 258
  Vernon 338
  Rev. W. R. 274
  W. T. 284
  Walter 361
  Widow 77
  William 134,137
  William T. 361
ROLAND, Nannie 215
  Young W. 305
ROOK, William 72
ROOKER, Anne 30
  C. 40,41,42,46,47,48
  Caleb 34,36,65,311
  Elizabeth 32
  James B. 47
  John W. 216
  Mary E. 25
ROPER, _____ 168
  Thomas 155,179
  William 155,164
ROSE, Mrs. _____ 84
  A. 78
  Alexr. 84
  Alexander 306
  Elizabeth 28
  Emily 78
  Polly 78
  R. H. 225
  Thomas 122,310
ROSECRANS, General _____
    226,227
ROSS, _____ 227
  Alexr 84
  Daniel 116,118,120,131
  David 118,151
  George 57,58,90,91,95,
    123,131,143,306
  James M. 22,24,57,86,
    90,91,95,122,123,305
  Jesse S. 121,123,124,
    139,167,168,169,173,
    181,186
  John 123,151
  John H. 317
  Martha 8
  Mary 143
  Susanna 169
  W. B. 44,47,48
  W. J. H. 317
  William B. 31,88,89,
    121,150,151,161,162,
    165,180,253

ROTH, _____ 332
  Billie 363
  Emma 374
  Lena 363
  Lewis 363
  Mable 334,363
  Nettie 363
  Pearl 295,363
  Robert 363
ROWELL, Andrew 128
  D. A. 74
ROWLAND, _____ 228
  Barbara Frances 211
ROY, Abel 8
  Ephraim 306
  Meredith 13
ROYAL, James 143
RUCKER, Caleb 264
RUDOLPH, A. D. 269
  Mrs. A. D. 113
RUMAN, Eliakiam 240
RUMSEY, James B. 339
RUSHING, David 185
  David, Jr. 13
  Jacob 80,305
  Mary 54
  Richard 185
  Susan M. Springer 216
  William 75
  William W. 216
RUSHTON, Letha Fay 295
RUSKIN, John 259
RUSS, Angeline S. 13
RUSSEL, Lewis 124,158,160,
    162,165
RUSSELL, _____ 242
  Alfred 83
  Augustine 218
  Christopher H. 311
  Elizabeth 43,46,89
  Eron 382
  Frank 382
  George 28,41,124,160,
    162
  James 3,75,119,140,301
  Jesse 5,162,165,178,
    183,189,239,305
  John 328
  L. 11,12,13,15,16,17,
    21,24,25,26,27,29,31,
    32,36,38,39,41,44,47
  Lemuel 6,76,88,89,165
  Lemuel J. 309
  Lemuel S. 216
  Lewis 138
  Lynn 280
  Martha 21
  Mary 28
  Nancy 323
  Nancy Myatt 216
  Paul 293
  Polly F. 53
  Rebecca 24
  Sallie 293
  Samuel 150,157,306
  Sarah 212
  Sarah M. Sugg 216
  Serena P. Frasier 216
  Thomas 165
  W. Z. 213
  Wiley 343
  Wiley M. 216
  William 25,117,118,124,
    147,152,162,165,167,
    183,303
  Willis 165
RUSSHIN, Curlie 287
  Earlie 287
RUTHERFORD, _____ 113
RUTHLEDGE, David 16,312
RUTLEDGE, John 306,309
RYAL, William 117
RYAN, D. 100

RYAN (cont.)
  Edna 357
  Jane 375
  Jim 357
  Joe 357
  John 342,375
  Mike 357
  Opal 357
  Orpha 357
  Tom 380
  W. P. 47
RYE, Benjamin 31,189
  Cassander 34
  James R. 45
  John 29
  Joseph 305,312
  Nancy 29
  Peggy 58
  Sarah B. 53
  Solomon 53,163,164,189,
    306,313
  Solomon, Jr. 184
  Tristam 8
  William 53,84,86,307
SADLER, Rev. S. A. 269
SAEGAR, Dave 281
  Bobby 295
  Earl 271
SAEGER, Alline 366
  Bernard 366
  Bertha 366
  Charlie 366,373
  Earl 366
  Henry 373
  Margaret 373
  Melvina 366
  Susan 373
SAGER, Albert 290
  Arminta H. 389
  C. E. 342
  Dan 279,389
  Ed 273
  Guy M. 389
  Hazel 365
  Margaret 290
  Romeo 365
  Susan 106
ST. CLAIR, J. K. 262
SALE, Eliza 7
SALMAN, Rev. W. T. 268
SALMON, James 116
  William T. 392
SAMUEL, James 62
  Phamata 62
  Polly 62
SANDERS, Annie 215
  Benjamin 59
  Carter 292
  Elias 47
  Elizabeth 20,35
  H. W. 195,216
  John 68,103,155,310
  John J. 196,216
  L. D. 327
  Lyda 30
  Lytha 30
  Margaret 297
  Martha 104,106
  Mary 382
  Ruth 382
  Samuel W. 68
  Sarah A. 47
  Sytha 30
  Thomas B. 274
  Van 292
  Wayne 345
  William 155
SANDERSON, Elizabeth 27
  Emelia 98
  Emily 98
  Jacob 98,312
  James 98
  Miley 98

SANDERSON (cont.)
  Milly 98
  Nancy 8
  Robert 98
SANDFORD, Hardy 177
SANFORD, Charlie 368
  Hester 100
  Jessie 329
  John 368
  Junius 368
  Leon H. 368
  May 368
SANKER, Edna Sue 283
  Hazel 283
  Sophie 327
SANSOM, Barbara 57,85
  David N. 57
  Dorrel N. 57
  Richard D. 57,75,85
  William C. 57,85
SARRETT, Wilson M.
SAUNDERS, M. F. 216
SAUNDERSON, Jacob 239
SAYGER, Fred 107
SCHMITTOU, Clyde 296
  F. V. 78
  F. F. V. 39
  Francis V. 39,56,57,
    204,307
  Gertrude 299
  Lavina 240
  M. C. 101
  Martha C. V. 74
  Mattie 374
  Nettie 296
  Normank 340
  O. S. V. 41,47,48,49,
    71,312
  Othie 296
  R. L. V. 225
  Vera 296
  William R. V. 44
SCHWARTZ, Rev. Michael
  270
SCOTT, _____ 248,271,328
  A. L. 329,332
  Albert 353
  Alberta 349
  Alberta K. 366
  Agusta A. 353
  Alice 327
  Ann 328
  Arthur 156
  Bessie E. 353
  Carlton 366
  Mrs. Carlton 343
  Caroline 28
  Charlie 354
  Clifford M. 366
  Courtney 331
  Dorothy 354
  Flora 354
  G. L. 335
  G. W. 70
  George 32,366
  George W. 39
  Harvey C. 366
  James 188,288
  Jas. D. 97
  James L. 160,178,183
  Jimmy 343
  John 138,162,307
  John N. 16,53,95,310
  John W. 58,97
  Lola 366
  Lynwood C. 366
  Mary L. 366
  Mary S. 97
  Minta Z. 366
  Nehemiah 7,57,146,149,
    188,191,305
  Parthenia 97
  Robert 191,198,216

SCOTT (cont.)
  Robert A. 168
  Rosamond P. 78
  Sally C. 95
  Sarah C. 97
  Sue 329
  W. S. 342
  Weldon 366
  William 58
  William D. 97
SCRUGS, M. 100
SCULL, John Gambier 125,
  128
SCULLY, Col. _____ 226
SEAL, Abson 196
  James 175
  Rachael 46
SEALS, Adelade 14
  Anna Elizabeth 299
  Drury 28
  Elizabeth Jane 70
  James 153,170,183
  John 79,183,306
  Nicholas 114
  Palatira 79
  Peter 79,245,308
  William 183
SEARCY, Bennett 120,153
  R. 119,149
  Robert 119,121,137,146
SEARS, E. 296
  Elizabeth 113
  Hannah 25
  Hiram 42,217
  Indiana 46
  Kissiah 42
  Moses 32
  Richard 196,216
SEAT, Rosamund 190
SEATON, Austen 306
SEAY, Armistead 217
  Blanche 391
  Charles D. 391
  Charlie 217
  Dick R. 391
  Henry T. 391
  Margret 391
  Martha 217
  Richard H. 196,217
  Robert A. 391
  William 313
SECTION, Jeremiah 132
SEEL, Horace N., Jr. 234
SEGRAVES, John 179
  Joseph 179
SEIGEL, Henry I. 338
SELEVANT, Jeremiah 181
SELF, _____ 147
  A. 78
  Abraham 61,77,92,307,
    312
  Alice 376
  Ashburn 188
  Cecil 354
  Clyde 376
  Dorsey T. 376
  Elizabeth 38
  Floyd 376
  Gertrude 354
  H. H. 332,333
  Horace 271
  Horace H. 340,354
  James M. 10
  Mable 354
  Martha 61
  Nannie J. 354
  Ophelia 376
  Osie 354
  Peter 8
  Samuel 10,77,144,239,
    307
  Sarah Anne 36
  Susan 40,64

SELF (cont.)
  W. A. 247,320
  Will A. 354
  William S. 312
SELFE, Happy 9
SELLARS, Edward 311
  Isaac 174,182
  Ruth 28
  Samuel 261,312
SELLERS, David 42
  John 93
  Samuel 191,307
  William 8
SENSING, Alva 349
  Ann 269
  Archibald 23,311,306
  Archie Benton 196,217
  Arnold 234,339,341
  Authur 110
  Azelle 349
  Benjamin 234
  Clifford 340,341
  Della 349
  Dolly 288
  Donald 284,368
  Drewsillar B. 70
  Drury 341
  Edna 288,349
  Erl. 269
  Gardner 271
  Gardner H. 349
  George W. 196,217
  Henry G. 349
  J. H. 193,217
  Mrs. John D. 297
  John Henry 70
  L. M. 328,330,333
  Lem 271
  Lemuel 368
  Lon M. 251
  Margaret Ann 70
  Margret E. 349
  Mary 211,368
  Miss Mary Ella 343
  McIndry G. 313
  McKindree Gardner 70
  Mekindra G. 23
  Polly Wilding 70
  Raymond 288
  Ruby 288
  Ruth 300
  Sally Bell 288
  Sara Sue 289
  Thurman 343,368
  W. M. (Bill) 275
  Wendell 349
  Wilbur 368
  Wiley Powel 70
  William 23,104
  William D. 311
  William H. 69,74
  Wilson T. 349
  Zorie 271
SERIN, A. 175
SESLER, Henry 329
  Jacob 342
  Tommy 267
SESSOMS, Jno. 136
SETGREAVE, Joseph 179
SETTLE, David 13
SEWELL, William 20
SEXTON, Herman 385
  Homer 385
  Jeremiah 132
  Lula 385
  Monroe 385
SEYMOUR, O. J. 295
SHACKELFORD, J. W. 8
  Roger 152
SHACKLETT, H. E. 198,217
SHADDOCK, Elizabeth 8
  Gabriel 307
SHADERICK, Prudy 13

SHADICK, Gabrael 311
SHADOWEN, Lenallen 17
  Reuben 313
  Ruben 35
  Tennessee A. 42
SHADOWIN, Lewallen 312
SHADRICK, Tennessee A. 42
SHAFFER, George 342
SHANNON, I. N. 197,202,342
  Isaac N. 217
SHARP, Annie 375
  Benjamin 59
  Jake 391
  James D. 51
  Maryann 14
  Wilson 284
SHAW, Colin 117
  Daniel 119,128
  J. W. 279,322
  Solomon H. 13
SHAWL, ___ 277
  Andy 383
  Dudey 384
  Dudley 234
  Edgar 384
  Elda 384
  Emma 386
  George 386
  Hattie 386
  Hazel 353
  Ike 353
  J. W. 294
  Joe 383
  Kate 383
  L. 223
  Leola 386
  LeRoy 383
  Levi 223,383
  Lorena 384
  Marie 383
  Nancy 353
  Ralph 353
  Wilma 384
SHEARING, Daniel M. 310
SHEARMAN, Daniel 211
SHEARON, Ann 90
  George W. 7
  Jesse 90
  Thomas W. 97,98
  William 97
SHEEHAN, Jerry 316
SHEELY, Bessie 355
  Curtis 294,355
  Fannie 354
  Huron 355
  John 354,355
  Walton 355
SHEFFIELD, Mrs. Ella Lee 50
SHEHAN, John 188
  Lewis 191
SHELBY, ___ 90,191
  Isaac L. 13,87
  Sally 87
  William 87,90,165,190
SHELEY, ___ 328
  John 271,332
  John C. 234
SHELLEY, ___ 191
SHELTON, Abel 91
  Abner B. 10,71
  Albert G. 36
  Betsy 238
  Coleman 313
  Eleanor 74
  Elizabeth 307
  Emma 383
  George 81,187,188,189,313
  James 81,306
  Jerome 383
  Jessee 312
  Joel 186,188

SHELTON (cont.)
  John 158
  John B. 44
  John H. 30
  John M. 35
  Joseph 37
  Julia Ann 27
  Lenora 218
  Louisa 33
  Major 383
  Mary R. 368
  Nancy M. 39
  Nina M. 383
  Oval 383
  Polly 10
  Robert 304,306
  Thomas 34
  William 60,61,313
  William, Jr. 161
  William H. 74
  Winnie 383
SHEPARD, Paul
SHEPHERD, Henry 146
  Will 329
  William 146
SHERON, Bettie 267,268
SHERRIN, Perthenia 6
SHERWOOD, David 102
SHEWMAKER, Faney 56
SHIP, Josiah 134
SHIPP, Dockie 284,377
SHIRLEY, Carrie 287
  Mabel 287
SHP, Joseph 153
SHORES, Reuben 255
  Reubin 164
  William 255
  William, Sr. 164
SHRIEBER, Ella 336
  Pauline 336
SHROM, J. C. 327
SHROPSHIRE, David 190,304
  Elizabeth 19,58
  H. J. 86
  Hudson 192
  Hutson 305
  Joel 78,139,144,167,180
  John 86
  Polley 304
  Polly 78,79,84
SHUTE, Asa 174
  John 115
  Philip 174
SHYSTER, John 191
SIEGEL, H. I. 336
  Henry I. 336
SIGMORE, J. W. 195,217
SIKES, John 63
  Levina 63
  Nancy 63
SILVERS, John 161,177
SIMMONS, ___ 183
  Elisha 185
  James 185,243
  Lester 288
  O. B. 231
  Richard D. 306
  Robert 152,153,161,190,242
  Thomas 147,306
  William B. 35,60
SIMMS, William 82
SIMON, Donnie 369
  Ethel 369
  Fred 369
  Kenneth 369
  Melvin 369
SIMONS, William 298
SIMPKINS, Lizzie May 104
  P. W. 69
SIMPSON, A. B. 316
  Amy 282
  Edward M. 20

SIMPSON (cont.)
  Elizabeth 51
  Evie 292
  John 127,157,292
  John R. 13,18,51
  Kathleen 292
  Nathaniel 80
  Otis 326
  Polly 13
  Robert 75
  Thomas 51,150,170,307
  William 34,188
SIMS, Benjamin 25,312
  Hicksey R. 15
  James 190
  Polly 82,306
  William 85
SINKS, Elizabeth 78
  Drury 310
  Hartwell 46
  Henry 78
  Jessee 313
  Olive 47
  Powell 78
  Zachariah 78
SINSABAUGH, George 322
SISMON, Clarke 389
  Nina 389
SITTON, Paul 277
SIZEMORE, Claude 331
  Claude H. 350
  Hooper 350
  James 264
  Jessie O. 350
  Jones W. 217
  Jossie 350
  Richmond Baker 217
  Rufus 196
  Rufus Hix 217
  S. A. 106
  Sallie 113,217,268
  Sarah A. 350
  William E. 234
SKEGGS, George 234
SKELTON, A. B. 318
  Abel 88,89
  Abner 311
  Abner B. 96
  Alfred 96
  Archibald 71,88,89,311
  J. M. 318
  James Morris 218
  John 307
  John M. 71
  Lenora Shelton 218
  Mariah Allen 71
  Mary 96
  Sarah 71
  Sarah Elizabeth Alfred 71
SKINNER, John 136
  William 159
SKIPPER, Samuel 23
SLATTON, Archibald 307
SLAUGHTER, Bert 362
  Edgar 268
  George W. 372
  Missouri 372
SLAYDEN, Mr. ___ 280
  Adella 218
  Augustine Russell 218
  Daniel E. 17
  David E. 17
  Dilly A. E. 46
  Durina 26
  Emma 378
  F. A. 8
  G. A. 329,330
  George 378
  H. M. 64
  Hartwell 218
  Hartwell M. 65,312
  Jane May 218

SLAYDEN (cont.)
  Dr. John D. 218
  John J. 111
  Joseph 113
  Joseph S. 27
  Letsey C. 11
  Mayor 328
  Serenia Parthenia 208
  Tolbert 33
  Travis E. 11,20,310
  W. M. 218
  William 242
  William E. 60,79,312
  Yula 378
SLIGH, Sally 213
SLOAN, David 128,133,145
  Gibson 136
  James 224,319
SMILEY, Bud 327
SMITH, ____ 3,271,332
  Abner 94,97,311
  Alice 391
  Alice M. Talley 219
  Aline 282,295
  Amanda M. 49
  Andrew 165,182,185,191,
    242
  Andrew J. 213
  Anita 295
  Mrs. Ann 343
  Anna 350
  Austin Willis 218
  Bartholomew 51,72,120,
    153,165,235,253,305,
    310
  Benjamin 187,312
  Bessie 284
  Clarice 291
  Clayton 218,219,328,
    350,391
  Cordelia 292
  Cordell 269
  Mrs. Dollie 328
  Dollie B. 350
  Dorcus 51
  Dorothy 72
  E. L. 107
  Earl 289
  Edward 37,77,153,176,
    182,186,187,238,304,
    310
  Edward J. 81
  Edwin 289
  Eleazer 253
  Elisha 56,77,239,240
  Elizabeth 46,236,350
  Elnora 379
  Erin 174
  Eudora 215
  Ezekiel 94,97
  Ezkil 240
  Frances 240
  Frank 327
  G. W. 16,72,95,224
  George 76,98,158
  George L. 28
  Grace 379
  Gray W. 236
  Henry L. 350
  Hickory 271
  Ida P. (James) 228
  Isaac 75,215
  Izetta 289,295
  J. M. 225,332
  Jackson 16,72,92,95
  James 77,105,157,175,
    189,305,312,318
  James Montgomery 196
  Jasper 240
  Jean 295
  Jeff D. 383
  Jeremiah 41
  Jewell 292

SMITH (cont.)
  Joel 187
  John 20,155,228
  Rev. John L. 275
  John M. 352
  John T. 164
  Jonathan K. T. 4
  Josiah 189
  Kattie 296
  Lizzie 327
  Lockie 7
  Loyd 282
  Lueela E. 352
  Lyda 392
  M. M. 46
  Madison H. 72
  Malinda 43
  Margaret 26
  Martin 223,327
  Martin V. B. 196
  Mary Ann 30
  Mathew J. 42
  Mayme L. 392
  Moses 51,120,239
  Mumford 92,95,253
  Mumsford 51,59
  Nancy 18,20,240
  Nancy A. 44
  Newton 240
  "Old Hickory" 218
  Oliver 135
  Orena 296
  Ouida 391
  Polly 77
  Prier H. 313
  Pryor H. 25
  Rebecca Wylie 218
  Richard 311
  Ronnie 275
  Ruby 296
  Samuel 115
  Sarah 77,312
  Sarah C. 36
  Sealy 81
  Stephen 270,311
  Susanna 51
  Tennessee 38,240
  Thomas 32,77,306
  Thomas C. 57,312
  Thomas J. 379
  Tom M. 392
  Rev. Uriah 35
  Vera 379
  Victor 292
  W. B. 65
  W. E. 273
  W. W. 197,202,218
  William 20,72,127,133,
    138,146,157,229
  Willis 134
  Wilson W. 391
  Winn B. 218,312
SMITTO, Abegal 18
SNEEDSVILLE, ____ 2
SNIDER, Joe 269
  John 121
SNYTH, ____ 147
SOMMERVILLE, Fredonia
  Powers 215
  Hunt 215
SOMMEVILLE, Jno. 114
SORENSON, Andrew 386
  Anna 386
  Arthur 386
  Maren 386
  Matilda 386
  Sophia 386
  Stella 386
SORRY, Allen 189
SOUTHERLAND, Alexander 33
  Dona Harrell 218
  Edward T. 40
  George 307,310

SOUTHERLAND (cont.)
  Henry 13,24,310
  J. 225
  John 13,218,310
  Mary Ann Williams 218
  Nancy 34
  R. E. 78
  Rob A. 218
  Robert A. 196
SOWELL, John 306
  Samuel 17
SPAHR, Raymond 234
SPAN, P. A. 197
SPANN, Allen 282
  Dottie 282
  Will Allen 337
SPARKMAN, Callie 210
SPARKS, Hardy 80
  Samuel 160,168,178,183,
    305
SPATS, John T. 13
SPEAR, Isaac 172
  William S. 347
SPEARS, James 309
  William 31
  Willis W. 42
SPEIGHT, Albert 10,75,310
  Alice Nicks 219
  Allis U. 71
  Alsey 86
  Alsey S. 88
  Clyde 297
  Elizabeth 39
  Emeline 34
  Emily C. 71
  Jesse 75
  Jesse M. 86,88,312
  John 312
  John T. 13,16
  Mabel 289
  Martha E. Andrews 218
  Paradise 71
  Patty W. 343
  Sarah J. 46
  Surrena 29
  Wesley 196,218
  William 16,70,71,154,
    165,303
SPEIGHTS, ____ 271
SPENCE, Jerome 232
SPENCER, Celia 108
  Clark 185,188,237
  Clint 300
  Daniel 62,92,93,101,311
  Doyle 362
  Edgar 291
  Ellenor 312
  Emma 291
  H. A. 105
  High 260
  Hiram A. 196
  James 62
  John 131,140,154,191,
    244,302,303
  John S. 1,307
  M. B. 327
  Mary 62
  Mollie 281
  Pet 281
  Ruby 300
  Sam 260
  Sammie 282
  Samuel 10
  Thomas 54
  William 62
  Z. C. 108
SPICER, A. D. 300
  Alex 300
  Archie 300,340
  Aurena 37
  Buford K. 340
  Burl 257,300
  Burwell B. 316

SPICER (cont.)
  Charlotte 31
  Clabourn 307
  Clark 295
  Cletis 295
  Curdon 295
  Eugene 300
  Gracy 10
  Grover 288
  Joseph 20,310
  M. A. 327
  Oliver 68,311
  Rebecca 47
  Rons 288
  Ruby 288
  Russell 322
  Sally 18
  Tinsley 295
  Ulysses 234
  Will 300
  William M. 340
  Willie 295
SPIERY, Claiborne 188
SPIVY, Clark 191
SPRADLIN, A. O. 194,219
  John 178
  Obediah 192,313
  William J. 26
SPRADLING, Caroline 323
  Hazel 299
  John 174
SPRAGUE, Delpho 329
SPRINGER, Bill 271
  Emmogene 283
  George 281
  Gladys 287
  Joe 290
  Leola 298
  London 322
  Louise 295
  Millie Moore 281
  Olin 299
  Susan M. 216
  W. D. 102
  Zollie 374
STACEY, Mr. _____ 279
  A. H. 196
  Maggie Jones 291
STACKER, Martha J. 69
STADEN, Travice 20
STAFFORD, Cealy 238
  John 54,58,165,166,168,
    174,176,177,178,179,
    242,305
  Permelia Annis 11
  William 187
STALEY, Elizabeth 103
  Hattie 298
  James 48,196
STALLCUP, _____ 313
STANDEFER, Mrs. Jewel B.
  309
STANFIELD, Elizabeth 54
  John 23
STANFIL, Willie M. 392
STANLEY, James 310
STARK, _____ 271
  Florence 100
  Thomas 40
STARNES, Henry 312
STARNS, Evia 334
  John 87
STEEL, James 253,266
  Robert 266
STEELE, Bob 219
  Bryan 392
  Ida 392
  J. D. 19
  James 146,151,196,302
  James M. 274
  John 392
  Lizzie 292
  Loyal 392

STEELE (cont.)
  Margaret J. 310
  Mary 392
  Mary Anne 31
  Robert 392
  Robert D. 196
  Ruby 392
  Susie 388
  Thomas 32
  William A. 25
STELLEY, Jesse 48
STEP, John 13
  William 10
STEPHENS, Clara White 293
  D. S. 290
  John 96,290,311
  Mable 290
  Scott 330
STEPPEE, Rev. Terry 270
STEVENS, Dimple 298
  John 139
  Ruth 298
  Scott 298
  W. H. 231
STEWARD, Buck 288
STEWART, Abraham 10
  Alena 237
  Alex 288
  Andrew 97
  B. B. 156
  Bettie U. 383
  Billy 294
  Carter 287
  Catherine 202
  Charles 124,125,127,
    141,162,178,244,302
  Curtis L. 384
  D. 51
  Duncan 115,120,125
  E. W. 338
  Florence 292
  Herman 292
  James 51,178
  Jane 51
  Janie 288
  John 51,159,188,358
  Lela 358,384
  Lizzie 292
  Marcus B. 311
  Mollie 384
  Nolen 178
  Oliver 288
  Pearl 288
  Peter B. 237
  Sampson 20
  Susan 64
  Tengnal 178
  Thomas 288
  W. H. 194,219
STILL, Mrs. Grace 343
STINNETT, Sigma Fay 295
STINSON, Ammon 292
  Arlis 292
  Corrinne 292
  J. W. 292
  Marie 292
  Roy 340
  Roy L. 234
  Walker 292
STITT, Annie 363
  Claude 363
  George 363
  Hattie 363
  Margaret 384
  Mary D. 363
  Nola 363
STOCKELY, W. A. 193
STOKES, Albert 299
  Carrie 299
  Clem 368
  Geneva 299
  Granville 234,298
  Helen 297

STOKES (cont.)
  Imogene 299
  James B. 40,49
  John 111,311
  John Hugh 234
  Kate 368
STOKEY, John 11
  John J. C. 312
  M. A. 219
STONE, Alene 295
  Benjamin 36,67
  Dolly 51,167
  E. H. 199,330
  Elizabeth 51,167,168,
    183
  Ernest 368
  H. 91
  Hardeman 9,11,51,90,158
  Henry 310
  Jack A. 269
  John 11
  John H. 5,51,64,124,
    144,167,171,178,304
  Kate Richardson 219
  Marable 148
  Marbel 190
  Marble 51,58,167,171,
    174,177,183,244,306
  Mary 32,67
  Mill 154
  Nancy 307
  Mrs. R. B. 267
  Robert B. 219
  Sarah M. Jackson 219
  Solomon 51,158
  Susannah 25,51
  William 51,120,131,137,
    148,151,152,154,157,
    158,159,162,165,166,
    167,168,169,171,180,
    183,253,283,305
  William, Senr. 168
STOREY, John 313
STORY, Anna 110
  F. L. 332
  Henry 183,297
  John 7,21
  Leona 297
  Littleton 7
  Louie E. 234,340
  Samuel 187
  Turner 190
  W. M. 328
STRAHAN, John 172
STRAYHORN, Alfred M. 12
STREET, Abraham 192
  Abram 64
  Ailsey 64
  David 64
  David B. 313
  David G. 196,219
  Elzilma 287
  F. M. 193,219
  H. W. 196,219
  J. C. 193,219
  Jackonias 64
  Jeremiah 312
  Mary 222
  Moses 64,192,306,313
  Moses B. 311
  Rowena 287
  Techoniac (?) 64
STREETMAN, Thomas Jefferson
  196
  William 334
STRINGFELLOW, James 49
  John M. 49
  Robert 51
STRONG, Christopher 68,69,
  140,142,143,158,163,
  164,168,181,182,235,
  238,253,260,307,310
  Major _____ 169,303

STRONG (cont.)
  Martha 5
  Rosannah 68
  Samuel 134
STROUD, A. B. 49
  A. V. 49
  A. W. 49,103
  Annie 384
  Anson W. 384
  Ara 20
  Claude 287
  Claude E. 384
  Hobert N. 384
  Jane 87,90,311
  Jesse 86,87,90,146,147,
    176,186
  Jourdan 161
  Mable B. 384
  Thomas 305
  Thomas B. 384
  Willis 311
STUART, Dr. _____ 260
  Mrs. _____ 94
  Alex 271
  Aline Smith 281
  Charles 115,121
  Harris 282
  J. M. 198,219
  J. R. 101
  John Minor 196
  M. B. 25,27,30,31,33,71
  Marcus B. 30,33
  Minor 299,343
  Olin D. 234
  Oneida 282
  Ray 343
  Richard 282
  Robert 94
  Sally 26
  Thomas 115
  U. T. 69
  William 138
STUMP, C. 174
STURDIVANT, B. 84
  Benjamin 170,305
  Nancy 54
SUCHARS, James 151
SUGG, Ann 295
  Annie Lee 295
  Aquilla 238
  Billy 343
  Caey J. 111
  Carl 293
  Dolly 333
  Edward 343
  Ella Hogins 207
  H. S. 74
  Howell 238
  J. B. 292
  Dr. J. T. 207
  Joel D. 295
  John 108
  Josiah 153,238
  Mary 45,238
  Mollie 297
  N. R. 107,329
  Nancy 44,80
  Nathaniel W. 219
  Noah 75,238
  Polly 105
  Quintus 219
  Quintess C. 219
  S. W. 194,219
  Sally 238
  Sarah M. 216
  Tom 295
  Tom T. 295
  Dr. W. J. 271,344
  William 80,177,238
SUGGS, Dollie 365
  Edward 365
  Emma 388
  George W. 43

SUGGS (cont.)
  Harriett A. 47
  Irene 352
  Jennie 388
  John B. 352
  Josie 352
  Layton 352
  Lillie 365
  Mary 388
  Norrise 365
  Rufus 388
  Thelma 352
  Thomas T. 365
  Wilbur F. 365
  William 190
  William, Jr. 365
  William J. 365
SUITES, Mary 62
SULLIVAN, Annie 287
  Arreva Thompson 23
  Claude 287
  E. A. 274
  Earl 295
  Elisha 239
  Elizabeth Jane 43
  Elley 90
  G. 296
  George 79,90,92,93,304,
    310
  Hallie 294
  Harvel 294
  Irsle 295
  John 90
  John L. 346
  Nancy 40,70,90,92,93,
    239,305
  Odell 295
  Owen 63,90,312
  Percy 295
  Perry 294
  Valerie 295
  William E. 345
  Zachariah 90
SULLIVANT, Jesse 133
  John 20,23
  William 133,148
  William, Sr. 136
SUMMERS, Benjn 313
  Etta 385
  Hershal 385
  Jessie 385
  Jim B. 385
  Lillie 385
  M. C. 196
  Marshal 385
  Roy 385
SURGERNER, Grant 287
SUTER, William 188
SUTHERLAND, W. H. 106
SUTTON, Buckley 114
  J. R. 99,330
  Laura 18
  Laurel 18
  Malinda 370
  Moses A. 37
  Ransard 100
  Sarah J. 11
SWAIN, Geneva 5
  W. M. 328
SWAN, Edward 190
  Mary 113
SWANK, David L. 383
  Eddie 383
  Mrs. Eddie 343
SWANSON, Dona 248,253,332
  Donnie 355
  Edward 52
  Jeff 248,253,318
SWEANY, James 17
SWEANEY, Lucy 25
SWEENEY, Herman 276
SWEENY, Albert G. 32
  Caroline 31

SWEET, Dickson 349
  Sarah E. 349
  Sherman 349
SWIFT, Absolem 313
  Absalom 189
  Benjamin 47,192
  Erin T. 24
  Ervin 24
  Irene 289
  James M. 35
  John R. 352
  Katie 352
  Lloyd 289
  Mary A. 323
  Mollie C. 352
  Susannah 311
  Thomas 82,189
  Tom 374
SWINNEY, John 75
  Lucinda 238
SWISHER, Green H. 310
SYKES, A. D. 269
  Rev. A. H. 274
SYLVIS, _____ 277
  Beaulah 380
  Cecil 390
  Ella M. 380
  Glayds 358
  James 358
  Kate 277
  Kathaline 380
  King 380
  Levi 101
  Lillie 358
  Naomi 390
  Orzona 358
SYMS, Jeffry 189
SYVUS, Sarah 109
TABOR, James 163,164,171,
    176
  Russell 163,164,171
TAGGERT, James 83
TAILOR, Benjamin 92
  Berryman 92
  Lockey 92
  N. C. 95
TAIT, Larkin 191
  William 119,131
TALBOT, John L. 124
  Thomas 124
  Thos. 119
TALBOTT, Thomas 155
TALLENT, Herbert S. 340
TALLEY, Albert 373
  Alice M. 219
  Bertha 219
  C. M. 219
  Dave 387
  Ellen 387
  Ella 324
  George F. 324
  Gertrude 219
  J. M. 197,202,279
  James M. 219,351
  James M., Jr. 219
  Kate 351
  Lucy Birmingham 219
  William 219,265,277
  William M. 219
TALLY, Katie McCauley 219
TANN, Raleigh 84
TANNER, J. H. 225
  Mary A. 108
TAPLEY, James 86
TATAM, M. E. 107
TATE, Anderson 43
  Eleanor 89
  Larkin 188,306
  Nancy 46
  Samuel 20,37,40,41,42,
    43,47,49,89
  William 193
  Winnie 203

TATOM, Ann 53
  Anne 30
  Benjamin M. 39
  Benjamin N. 39
  Caroline 38
  Ed L. 219
  Elizabeth 18,52
  G. W. 18,32,33,34,64
  George W. 9,310
  Green 309
  James 30,176,309
  John 158
  John, Sr. 175
  Polly 13
  Rebecca 26
  Richardson 53
  Sarah 27
  Stephen 144,171,179
  Susan 39
  William 175,192,304,312
  Willis 14
TATTOM, William 175
TATUM, Mrs. Bruce 75,241
  Eddie 287
  Eliza 59
  G. W. 92,96
  George 76
  George W. 60,95
  Howel 137,149
  Howell 173
  James 162,165,192,306
  Jessie 287
  John 76,78,191,235,307
  John, Sr. 306
  Murry 287
  Peter 306
  Richard 76
  Stephen 157,306
  Wesley 287
  Wilkins 76,91
  William 78,144,164,188,
    191,235
  William, Jr. 305
  William, Sr. 305
TAUNT, Thomas 127
TAYLOR, Aden A. 369
  Allen 191,392
  Annabelle 295
  Annie B. 353
  Aretus 234
  B. 97
  Rev. B. M. 273
  Barley 225
  Berry 101
  Bessie 369
  Charles B. 311
  Claiborne 63
  Clyde M. 234
  D. 78
  Daniel 8,63,87,145,312
  Dick 197,219
  Drury 80
  Edm. 171
  Edmond 146,180,184,188
  Edmund 183
  Edward 80,191,237,238,
    239
  Eva 388
  Fannie E. 353
  Gibson 310
  Henry 327
  I. B. 43
  Izara 287
  Izora 388
  Jack 271
  James 71,80,237,305
  Jane 294
  Jennie 388
  Jimmy 295
  John 80
  Jonathan 219
  Joseph R. 361
  Kate 287,388

TAYLOR (cont.)
  Lockey 80,97,305,312
  Mamie L. 361
  Marvin 332,392
  Mary Alice 295
  Mary Ann 63
  Mary Ann Hall 219
  Mary E. 361
  Matilda 236
  Minerva 392
  Mollie 209
  Nicholas 11
  Nicholas C. 236,311
  Ralph 276
  Roland 392
  Samuel 145,146,151,181
  Sarah 369
  Spicer 369
  T. M. 342
  Talmage 332,388
  Talmadge 287
  Thomas M. 353
  Thomas G. 71
  Thomas S. 11
  Tom 271,332,388
  Vudus 282
  W. 225
  W. R. 38
  Welton 193,219
  William 75,243,304
  William Henry 197,220
TEAGUE, William 307
TEAL, Charles 253
  Edward 163
  George, Sr. 115,121,163
  James 139
TEALE, Edward 305
  George, Sr. 253
TEAS, _____ 263
  Charles 116,120,123,125,
    134
  Charles W. 151
  James 59,115,120,121,
    123
  Joseph 125
  William 115,120,121,123,
    125,132,180,303
TEASES, _____ 120
TEDFORD, Capt. _____ 197
  James 42,309
  Knott 187
  Quilla 187
  William 187
  Zaphina 9
TEMPLE, Aileen 388
  Delle 391
  Fred 391
  Fredie 391
  Lelia 388
  Lois 388
  Mary 388
  Polly 391
  William 128
  William O. 388
TENNEL, George 139
TENNY, Marcus D. 231
TERRELL, _____ 233
TERRILL, Joseph R. 220
TERRY, Edmond 13
  Edward 309
  Prescilla L. 26
THACKER, John 189
THATCH, Fostina 291
THEDFORD, J. R. "Dick" 220
  J. W. B. 195,220
  James 39,47,60,66,306,
    307
  Nancy 47
  Sarah 41
  William 16
  William R. 220
THERMAN, Carter 66
  Dock 66

THERMAN (cont.)
  Elizabeth 66
  James 66
  John 66
  July Ann 66
  Richard 66
  William 66
  William J. 66
THOMAS, Aline 282
  Asa 131
  Benjamin 123,125
  Bert 377
  Buford 282
  Carrie L. 377
  Catherine L. Easley 220
  Cynthia 209
  Eliza 9
  Emma 377
  George 377
  H. C. 220
  Henry 334
  J. A. 197,202,220,247,
    320
  Jack 372
  James 192
  James Gee 90
  James M. 307
  Jane 175
  John 312
  John C. 55,189
  John W. 85
  Kate 372,377
  M. B. 194,220
  Maggie S. 220
  Mary 55
  Minor B. 220
  Pauline 377
  Sarah 90
  Stephen 55,83,84,86
  William 53,55,75,187,
    190,306
  William M. 304
THOMASON, Eliza 19
  James 324
  Jonathan 20
THOMPKINS, Silas 305
THOMPSON, A. N. 219,220,
    273,274
  A. N., Jr. 273,274
  Alice 269
  Allen 137,150
  Amos 20
  Arrena 23
  Augustin 83,84
  Bessie 352
  Brice 352
  Carl 281
  Charles 62,98,161,163,
    164,235,261,263,305
  Dollie Ann 214
  Ed 274
  Ed, Jr. 274
  F. F. 268
  Floye 281
  H. C. 332
  Horatio 352
  Hubert 291
  Inez 291
  J. B. 197
  J. L. 195,220
  J. M. 195,220,342
  James 62,98,188,305
  James B. 220
  James J. 220
  Jason 117,133
  Jeremiah 64,312
  Jiles 181
  John 62,154,192
  Kendrick 281
  Lee 383
  Lettie 352
  Lewis 310
  Lewis P. 220

THOMPSON (cont.)
  Lucy Ann 66
  Mary 62,312,352
  Maybelle 282
  Mildred 352
  Nancy Sally 62
  Nannie 281
  Nathan P. 176
  Nettie 282
  Richard 66
  S. A. 225
  S. F. 279
  Samuel 168
  Sherod 305
  Silas 39
  Thelma 281
  Thomas 118,154,177
  Vara 291
  William 35,67,188,294
  William L. 311
THORN, Daniel 23,313
THORNTON, Esther 56
  J. 63,83,88
  Joseph 83
  Josiah 56,61
  Reubin 309
  W. E. 107
THRELKELD, Elbert 147
  Elijah 142,155,163,169, 183
TIBBS, Buster 298
TIDWELL, _____ 295
  Alice 291
  Aquilla 55,56,84,311
  Arthur 291
  B. 296
  Benjamin 16,72,194,220, 311
  Bertie 218
  C. J. 327
  C. M. 194,220
  Cane 281
  Celina 79
  Connie 291
  Cora S. 109
  Delmar 352
  Docie 281
  Doye 292
  Edgar 300
  Edmond 235,237,261
  Edmond, Jr. 311
  Edmond, Sr. 311
  Edmund 55,164
  Edmund, Sr. 305
  Edward 55,79,302
  Eli 137
  Ella 295,352
  Ellis 292
  Ely 296,312
  Evelyn 292,296
  F. F. 74,109,197,202
  Frances 92
  Francis 62,93
  Franklin Fulton 220
  George 9
  George L. 234
  Gladden 20
  Gladys 282
  Harley 279
  Harmon 291
  Hassie 281,292
  Hazel 292
  Homer 291
  Houston 265
  Huldy 30,93,312
  Isaah 163,311
  Isaiah 158,306
  Isedore 109
  Isiah 65,255
  J. B. 275
  James 62,79,82,83,96, 158,161,177,255,369
  James E. 352

TIDWELL (cont.)
  Jensey 31
  Jim 260
  John 62
  John K. 62
  Johnnie Mai 291
  Josiah 220
  Knot W. 23
  Knott 161
  Landon C. 234
  Levena 26
  Levi 79,83,304,305
  Levy 82
  Lucinda 72,225
  M. E. 99
  Magdaline Knox Petty 220
  Malachi 310
  Malichi 8
  Mansel 38
  Mark 281,290,299
  Martha 354,386
  Martha J. 352
  Mary 35,46,62,296,312
  Matilda 9,16
  Maude 281
  Michael 20,311
  Monncy 18
  Mose 17,18,28,72,207, 243,260,311
  Nancy 79,82
  Nara 299
  Ollie 300
  Ora 281
  Oscar 281
  Paul 281,282
  Rebecca C. 33
  Rebecker 65
  Richard 237
  Robert 187,188
  S. C. 327
  S. M. 197
  Silas 72,84,194,220, 296,311
  Silvester 354
  Spencer 291
  Stella 386
  Susan 207
  Thelma 292
  Vara 291
  Vera 291,292
  Zilpak 48
TIGER, Louis 86
TILLEY, George 310
  John 192
  Lucy A. 44
  Robert 289
TILLY, George 86
  Lucinda 38
  Lucretia 36
  Martha 44
  Mary 26
TILMAN, Mrs. J. F. 218
TIMON, Charles 309
TINSLEY, Eliza 21
TIPPET, George 159
  William 304
TIPTON, Carrol 295
  Dorothy 334
  Gladys 334
  S. J. 101
  Willie Mai 334
TISER, Elis 177
TOLAND, Isaac 167,188
  Jacob 167
  Jacob, Jr. 167
TOLAR, Anna E. 361
  Daniel 305
  George 288
  Henry L. 361
  Lem 288
  Lucille 288
  S. M. 198,220

TOLER, Daniel 313
  Edney 16
  Eleanor Jane 50
  Furney 310
  John 306
  Mary Ann 28
  William W. 12
TOLLER, Nancy 12
TOLLINGER, Wilma 283
TOMLIN, Nathaniel 260
TOMLINSON, Aliene 367
  Arleen 295
  Dale 367
  Eddie Ray 282
  Eva May 367
  Horace 367
  Ida 376
  Leon 376
  Lester 376
  Louise 367
  Minnie 367
  Nathaniel 260
  Ruby 367
  Will A. 376
TOMPKINS, Isaac 155
  Silas 155,237,238
TORBET, Harmas 161
TORRY, Henry M. 349
  Lois A. 349
  Louise H. 349
  Mary A. 349
  Paul O. 349
TOTTY, Adell 291
  Bennie 292
  Lera 291
  Lois 291
  Thomas L. 220
  Thomas S. 197
  William 138
TRATTER, Sylvanus 197,221
TRAYWICK, Goodman 162,171
  Nancy 171
TRIBBLE, A. 80
  Absalom 80,305
  Jesse 305
  Shaderick 169
  Spilsby 148,171,174
TROLLINGER, Elizabeth 283
  Mary 283
TROTTER, Claud 293
  Cleo 299
  Henrietta E. 37
  James 146,311
  John M. 362
  Laverne 299
  Martha 362
  Tunley 293
  Zelma 293
TRUBY, Anna M. 200
TUBB, Daniel 61
  George 61,92,94,162,182, 235,253,304
  Isaac 61,94,304
  James 61
  James, Jr. 165
  John 155,235
  Nathan 61,94,304
  Richard 61,153
TUBBS, Samuel 163,171
TUCKER, _____ 242
  Alfred 273
  Alton C. 370
  Daisy 290
  Diamond 292
  Francis 14
  Ida Pearl 290
  Jacob 61
  James 370
  James C. 370
  James M. 11,60,311
  Jane 60
  John 60,93,188,305
  John, Jnr. 166

TUCKER (cont.)
  John M. 93
  Lewis 60
  Louisa C. 26
  Mary 370
  Mary Ann 60
  Pearl A. 370
  Samuel 156
  Wiley 290
  William C. 60
TUGGLE, Joe W. 234
TUMMINS, Elsie 334
  Floyd 298
  Raymond 298
  Ruby 298
TURLEY, Will B. 80
TURMAN, William 155
TURNABL, Bulah 375
  Highland 375
  Orphant 375
  Willie 375
TURNER, ____ 15,272,299
  A. B. J. Turner 39
  Amanda 111
  Arabella 41
  Bertha 391
  Bertha Talley 219
  Bob 327
  C. C. 342
  C. M. 247,321,330,331,
    332
  Charlie M., Jr. 374
  E. 78
  Elisha 5,78,147,306
  Elizabeth 7,55
  Emett 387
  Florence E. 202
  George 38,77,263,276,
    316
  H. W. 10,18,25,26,27,
    28,29,40,78,79,93
  Howard 55
  Howard W. 7,14,18,21,
    55,61,78,83,90,93,
    185,188,307
  Ike 316
  J. A. 330
  J. T. 318
  J. W. 332
  Jane 13
  Jesse 12,13,90
  Jesse, Jr. 306
  John 25,55,76,77,78,
    120,121,138,147,177,
    188,235,276
  John, Sr. 306
  John T. 312
  Lucile 391
  Maggie 107
  Mahaley 21
  Marry 18
  Polly 18
  Rachel T. 10
  Richard 78,316
  S. 8,10
  Samuel 55,77,78,79,147,
    156,168,169,307
  Susan May 5
  Thomas 190,219
  Mrs. Tom 218
  W. B. 318
  W. T. 103,332,342
  Will T. 391
  William 55,57,75,138,
    188,304
  William D. 78,156,166,
    170,306,312
  Wylie 316
TWOMEY, Georgie 377
  Mildred 289,290,335
  Mildred J. 377
  Robert, Jr. 377
  Robert M. 377

TYCER, Ellis 152,235,305,
    312
  Louisa 33
  Letticia 24
  Sims 72
TYLER, Don 275
UNDERHILL, B. B. 335
  Bennie 344
  C. H. 328
  Charles 342
  Daniel 305
  G. W. 102
  James 296
  John 296,311
  Lorra 108
  Minerva 12
  Nancy 7
  Reams 376
  William 12
UNDERWOOD, Howell 312
  Jeremiah 313
  Leamon 234
  Mary 46
  William 49
  Willie 304
  Willis 312
UNOWN, Blake 290
URUCE, John 306
USELTON, Lavert 292
VALENTINE, Benjamin 122,
    135,305
  Berry 78
  Hardy 122,135,164
  Mary Anne 31
  William 188,313
VAN, Martha V. 296
VANCE, Samuel 154
VANDERVOIT, Anna 361
VANDERWATER, John 311
VANHOOK, Aaron 76,77,78,
    169,188,305
  Amander 76
  Ashburn 77,236,305,310
  Eliza 42
  Elizabeth 34
  Elmena 7
  John R. 48,224,319
  Lucy 76,78
  Robert 76,77,306,312
  Samuel 221
  Victoria 34
VANLANDINGHAM, ____ 285,
    286
  Francis 70
  Martha Y. 296
  Mary Amanda 37
  Susannah C. 36
VAN LEER, ____ 227,246
VANLEER, A. W. 307,313
  Anthony 302
  Anthony W. 245
  B. W. 6
  Betsy 6
  Earsley 289
  Ed 343
  Wayne 44
VAN LEW, ____ 227
VAN RUTLEDGE, Nancy 42
VANSKIKE, ____ 232
VAN ZANT, Francis 387
VARNAL, William 188
VARRELL, Mary 62
VAUGHN, David 189
  Jacob 185
VENABLE, J. R. 197,221
VENTRESS, Abner 84
VETTER, Adrain 298
  Albert 298
  Layman 298
  Ramey 298
  Wilbert 298
VETTERS, Adrain F. 234
  Albert 334

VETTERS, Mildred 334
  Westell 334
VICK, Elizabeth 71,72
  Susan 10
VINCENT, James 171,305
VINEYARD, Augie 294,299
  B. J. 113
  Buddy 288
  Callie Weems 290
  Cordie 322
  Debbie 288
  Doye 287
  Florence 288
  Floyd 288
  Gina 299
  Hester 288
  Hubert 293
  Ivan 293
  John 167
  Lillian 269,290,292,298
  Lucille 288
  Lucy 288
  Mary 47
  Matilda 27
  Mood 288
  Patience 309
  Rufus 287
  True 293
  Willie 294,299
  Zack 287
VINSON, Hannah 80
VOORHIES, ____ 3
  J. 9,11,12,15,17,20,64,
    95
  Jacob 3,6,98,236,282,
    311
  Margaret 236
VOS, Joseph 255
VOWELL, Myrtle
WADDLE, James 146
  John 138,139,146,149,
    166
WADE, Charles W. 374
  David 8
  Lucia 284
  Ora 374
  Scott 374
  W. T. 284
WADKINS, Minerva 18
  Thomas 11
WAGONER, J. T. 50
  W. A. 50
WALDIN, Anna 29
WALKER, Achilles 190
  Allen 119,128
  Anna 34,367
  Ben 287
  Benjamin 9,190,296,312
  Benjamin, Sr. 147
  Berryman 11,310
  Betsy Jane 53
  Billie 359
  Cathrine 367
  Charles 114,115,120
  Clara 287,290
  Clarence 367
  Cynthia A. 39
  Dimple 287
  E. V. 221
  Earnestine 359
  Eden 191
  Edwin 367
  Eliza 34
  Elizabeth 76,82,85,121,
    153,167
  Elijah 20
  Elizabeth 25,58,73,305,
    307,310
  Elizabeth Jane 26,72
  Ella 361
  Elmore 305
  Emma 367
  Fanny 63

WALKER (cont.)
  Dr. Frank 271
  Fredonia 45
  George 82,119,121,125
  George H. 76,87
  Harriett 361
  Henry 310
  Herman 291
  Hettie 367
  I. 163
  Irene 287
  Isaac 53,120,235,306,
    312
  J. 136
  J. L. 195,221
  J. N. 195,221
  Jacob 76,188,304
  James 53,116,122,136,
    141,188,191,307,310,
    367
  Jaunita 367
  Jeremiah 120,138
  John 41,134,136,142,
    186,189,190,304
  John B. 58,59,85,186,
    192,305,313
  John F. 367
  John K. 85
  John V. 73
  Joseph 15,17,136,140,
    153,190,238
  Lakin 114,115
  Lee 292
  Lucinda A. 48
  Margaret 282
  Marnerva 53
  Martha 73
  Martha T. 73
  Mary 287,294,371
  Maryann 21
  Mattie 367
  May S. 58
  Mildred 299
  Minerva Houston 221
  Minnie 371
  Nancy 323
  Nancy Ann 21,53
  Nannie 350
  Ophelia 359
  Palitha 49
  Pauline 367
  Prillee Viena 53
  R. 195,221
  Ramey 367
  Rebecca 306
  Sally 53,72,238,266
  Samuel 116,121
  Samuel Thomas 221
  Sarah 5
  Sarah R. 58,312
  Scott 287
  Sim 136
  Simeon 121
  Simmons S. 190
  Simon 167
  Simon Holt 141
  Simpson S. 190
  Stella 292
  Susannah 15
  Van 121
  Vienna 72
  Viola 292
  W. H. 294,328,335,348
  W. W. 45,328
  William 128,163,371
  William L. 296
  Willis 78,186,307,312
  Wineford 24
  Winney 53
  Zachariah 167
WALL, Alma 289
  Alva 289
  Ammon 289

WALL (cont.)
  Anna 29
  Arthur 289
  Barnette 374
  Buena 289
  Burges 156
  Burgess 28,306,313
  Mrs. C. L. 335
  Clara 289
  Doyle 344,345
  Ellen 289
  Ernest 289
  Ethel 374
  Grady 289
  Grigsby 289
  Henry 374
  Hershell 289
  Irene 289
  Jesse 26
  Joel 11
  Lavana 289
  Leonard 289,299
  Louis 289
  Louise 289
  Maggie 374
  Mary 53
  Novella 289
  Patsy 7
  Pearl 289
  Perry 374
  Polly 29
  Rebecca 289
  William 251,304
  Wilson 289
WALLACE, Adell 334
  Barney 42
  David 143,161,171,239
  Elizabeth 56
  Isaac 191
  Lucy 37
  Maggie Lee 334
  Nancy 36
  Rebecca 313
  Ruby 334
  Ruth 334
  Thurman C. 334
  Virgil M. 340
  William A. 340
WALLER, David 310
WALLS, Burgess 189
  David 43
  John 193,221
  Nancy 306
WALP. Alene 282
  Almira Ann 215
  Bessie 352
  Clara 352
  Corinne 282
  Ed 282
  Frances 282
  Grady 282
  Lloyd 282
WALTHOUR, Hallie 372
  J. R. 100
  Martha 372
WALTON, Jesse 30
  John B. 48
  Mack 234
WARD, Eliza 307
  Freda 105
  John 114,120,306
  Jonathan 311
  Lynon 266
  Robert 188
  Stephen 146,152,170
  Thomas 188
  William 85,122,149,253,
    303,307,311
WARNER, Joseph 246
WARREN, Albert 290
  Buford 290
  Charles 46
  Cleveland 354

WARREN (cont.)
  J. T. 342
  Josie 354
  Ollie Powers 215
  Thomas 354
  Will 215
WARTERS, Phebe M. 10
  Racheal M. 10
WASH, A. D. 221
WASHINGTON, E. W. 252
  Foster 252
  Guy 221
WATERS, Benjamin C. 235,
    309
  John 151
WATKINS, Ichabod 164
  Isaiah 188
  James 15,17
  John 190,309
  Phebee 29
  Richard 192
  Thomas 309
  Will 289
WATSON, A. W. 106
  Aft 325
  David 13
  Didamy 37
  Harrison 13
  James 114,150,156,218,
    307
  Jefferson 13
  Lott 126
  Thomas T. 85
  William 37,188,189
WATTS, Edward 79,161,173
  F. O. 330
  Luna Pickering 291
  Remellia 295
WAUGH, Richard 1,10,12,19,
    58,150,152,154,304
WAY, Nancy 304
  Robert 189
  Wicoy 304
WAYLAND, Henry 188
  J. A. 259,328
WAYNICK, Amanda 293
  Andrew J. 37
  Benjamin 43
  Bethel 299
  David 35
  Dewey 337
  Evie 299
  Forrest 293
  Franklin 256
  Lenard 47
  Mrs. Maude 337
  Rizbah 38
  Senard 47
  Sidney 293
WEAKLEY, Alma Jean 295
  Benjamin 160,162
  David 13,23,93,311
  David C. 312
  Elizabeth 34
  John 57,311
  John A. 29
  Joshua 5
  Mary 60
  Pauline 299
  Polly 199
  R. 118,160,172
  Robert 75,95,119,130,
    137,138,156
  Robert H. 34
  Samuel 138
  W. T. 221
  Walter 296
  William 123,144
  William T. 46
WEALSH, John 317
WEATHERBED, Francis 138
WEATHERFORD, Mary Russell
    213

WEATHERSPOON, Polka 215
WEAVER, Alver 299
　Charles 337
　Dane 107
　Dorcas 53
　Francis 10
　Frank 384
　Hartwell 86,188,307
　John C. 47
　John L. 221
　Kansas 384
　Martha 53
　Mrs. Mary Lee 337
　Maurice 299
　Nannie 299
　Slayden 343
　W. L. 327
WEBB, M. 85
　Robert 306
　William 305
WEBSTER, Olive C. 44
　William 192
WEEMS, ___ 27
　Benjamin W. 47
　Bryant 290
　C. T. 197,221
　Clara 293
　Mrs. Dockie Shipp 333
　G. W. 221
　Gladys 288
　James A. 342,343
　Miss Jamie 343
　Joe B. 271,343
　T. W. 327
　Tom 292
　Violetta 336
　Washington 192
WEINS, ___ 27
WELCH, Ada 300
　Arnold 298
　Bates 334
　Earnest Olin 300
　Hattie 298
　John 27,197,221
　John S. 221
　M. C. 327
　Mark 234,291
　Martin 378
　Marvin 378
　Mike 334
　Odell 334
　Ola 334
　Susan 378
　Susanna 221
　Thomas 9
　Wesley 197,221
WELKER, Anna 34
　John 44
　Matilda 24
WELLS, Benjamin 310
　David 43
　Elizabeth 43
　Hayden 146,147,151,161
　Haydon 150
　John J. 188
　John T. 305
　M. 85
　Martin 147
　Thomas 290
　William H. 40
WERT, Henry 171
WEST, Albert 334
　Anderson 142,155,163,
　　168,177,183
　Arabella C. 17
　Arter 302
　Elizabeth 41,75,240,
　　306,313
　George 69,78,80,83,84,
　　128
　Georgia Anne 34
　Henry 171
　Isaac 131,135,153,183,
　　306

WEST (cont.)
　Isaac, Jr. 135,168
　Isaac, Sr. 142,155,160,
　　183,303
　Isaac D. 69
　Isham 309
　J. B. 334
　James 11,14,75,80,83,
　　87,89,144,192
　John 52,76,168,190,
　　306,315
　John C. 28,76
　Louisa B. 16
　Mary 22
　Mary Ann Eliza 7
　Nancy 69
　Napoleon 87
　Napoleon B. 89
　Napolian B. 87
　Polly 307
　Randell 334
　Sarah 37
　Robert 61,69,75,79,82,
　　156,159,261,263,305,
　　313
　Robert C. 17
　Sally 52,57,69,76
　Samuel 76
　Sary 76
　William 192,306
　William B. 75,77,144,
　　167,239
　William H. 75,89
　William U. 240
WESTMORELAND, Nancy 214
WETHERFORD, Stephen 84
WHARTON, Irma Lee 5
　J. 114
WHATLEY, Reason B. 310
　Sarah J. 44
WHATLY, Eliza 44
WHEELER, ___ 226,227
　Thomas M. 33
WHISENHUNT, David 32
WHISTENHUNT, Elizabeth 13
WHITAKER, Sebron 41
WHITE, Alexr. 124
　Alexander 9
　Almira 202
　Andrew Jackson 320
　Bedy 49
　Beedy 98
　Benjamin 63
　Billy 297
　Mrs. Billy 289
　Blanche 281
　Mrs. Callie 248
　Chapman 63
　Charles 63,231
　Clara 281,290,292,293
　Cornelia Moore 213,214
　Crage 63
　Daniel 63,197,221
　Dardy 300
　David 63
　E. W. 197,202,221
　Elizabeth 9,40,63
　Essie
　Etta 300
　Frances 289
　Glenn 300
　Haney 313
　Henry 27
　Irene 282
　J. B. 300,343
　J. P. 197
　Jack 320
　James 63,122
　James B. 313
　James P. 222
　James S. 63
　James T. 35,311
　Jesse 63,282

WHITE (cont.)
　John 10,33,63,237
　Joseph F. 31,68
　Joshua 58,63,187,296,
　　305,311
　Luvina 31
　Mrs. M. G. 327
　Mahala 63
　Martha 63,282
　Martha S. 26
　Mary 39
　Mary B. 70,71,108
　Medy 187
　Mollie 210
　Moses T. 57
　Nancy 38,63
　Narvie 281
　Otho 282
　Polly 63
　R. F. 105
　Ralph 289
　Reubin 23,70,312
　Roney 63
　Sarah G. 15,25
　T. W. 296
　Tula 300
　Uda 300
　W. A. 289
　W. H. 194,222
　W. M. 197,198,222
　W. S. 70,71
　William 9,12,15,20,23,
　　25,26,28,30,70,98,137,
　　181,187,261,305,311
WHITED, Rosco 374
WHITEHEAD, Abraham 160
　Drucilla 56
　Ebenezer 305,312
　Elinezer 312
　Mary 11
WHITEMER, Mrs. Mary M. 337
WHITFIELD, Thomas 280
　Wilkins 75
WHITLEDGE, Robert 55
WHITLACK, A. P. 295
WHITMILL, Blount 172
　Davy S. 53
　Drew S. 170
　Elizabeth West 169,170
　Jno. S. 160
　Thomas 304
　Thomas Blount 169
　Thomas W. 170
WHITNEY, John 104
WHITSETT, Robert 84
　S. C. 278
WHITSITT, John S. 38
　Samuel 37
WHITSON, Josephine 290
　Marie 290
WHITTIER, George D. 323
WHITTOCK, Ro. C. 96
WHITWELL, Ann 62
　Robert 57,86,89,90,306
　Thomas 190
WHITWILL, Thomas 181
WHITWORTH, Philmore 189
WHIZENHUNT, Henry 32
WHIZZENHUNT, Henry 312
WICKOFF, William 162
　William, Jr. 162
WICKS, Amos 106
　Luther 288
WIDENER, Carrie 387
　Embler 388
　Horace 387
　Ida M. 387
　Izora 388
　John A. 387
　Lelsie 387
　Lester 387
　Raymond 387

WIDENER (cont.)
  Thomas E. 388
WIGGIN, Cany 82
  John Permote 149
WIGGINS, Casy 304
WILCHER, Earl 272
WILCOX, Charles B. 192
  Wayne N. 192
WILES, Marilla 42
WILEY, Adderson Jasper 61
  Allen 17
  Ann 63,65
  David 61,97,98
  Ebenezer 61,63
  Eli 63
  Gaston 61
  Hazel 290
  J. K. P. 195,222
  Jesse 61
  Jim 257
  John H. 72
  John M. 40
  Jonathan 61
  Josiah 63
  Levi 17
  Louson 61
  Percy 293
  Tom 292
  William 63,98,235
WILKEN, John 311
WILKERSON, John 305
WILKIAS, Julia Anne 33
WILKINS, Alexander 71
  Alexandria 309
  Charles A. 311
  Gracie 281
  Marvin 269
  N. F. 71
  Nora 292
  Orville 222
  Napoleon F. 31
  Robert A. 71
  Sarah M. 71
  Thomas 292
WILKINSON, Calude 371
  Sammie 371
  Viola 371
WILKISON, William J. 311
WILLEY, ____ 242
  Bernard 297
  Delila Roberts 221
  Dennis 297
  Edna 297
  Elizabeth 60
  F. C. 245
  Felix Emps 221
  John 52,70,106,306
  Joseph 55
  Mary 312
  Polly 55,60
  Thomas 77,312
  Washington 60
  William 60,310
  William, Sr. 305,310
  William D. 225,310
  Willis 77,192,305,310
WILLIAM, Cora 384
  Henry 61,303
  Henry N. 384
  Capt. Joseph 188,189
WILLIAMS, ____ 109,125,
   147
  A. B. 202,222,257
  Aley 62
  Allen 133
  Allison 192
  Allonie A. 222
  Mrs. Annie Lee 267
  Aretas B. 379
  Benjamin 58,85
  Caleb 192
  Catherine 40
  Charlotte 90

WILLIAMS (cont.)
  Christian Scott 58
  Coleman 262
  D. H. 84
  Dan H. 149
  Daniel 58,87,88,91,115,
   116,121,137,139,146,
   149,174,175,192,235,
   245,263,305
  Daniel H. 52,58,62,305,
   312
  Daniel Hicks 149
  Drury 43
  Eddie 218
  Elisha 244,304
  Emma 359
  Ester E. 62
  Ewell 329
  F. G. 197,198,222
  Floyd 343,344
  G. L. 315
  Garland 240
  George Coleman 222
  George Washington 20
  H. B. H. 312
  H. K. 197
  H. Newt 271
  Henry A. B. 16,58
  Henry B. H. 33
  Henry E. 183
  Henry Kephart 222
  Ida 322
  J. J. 77
  J. W. 194,222
  James 58,165
  James F. 271
  Jas. Jno. 171
  Jane A. 47
  Jesse 87
  Rev. Jim 260
  Joanna 64
  John S. 9
  John T. 57
  Jones 89
  Joseph 58,81,139,149,
   305
  Joseph J. 224,319
  Kane 373
  Louis 104
  Lydia Ann 69
  Maggie 295
  Margaret R. 58
  Martha 165
  Mary Ann 13,218,295,336
  Mary Anne 38
  Mary H. 39
  Mary M. 379
  Mary Street 222
  Nancy 41,65
  Nathan 135,155
  Otho H. 359
  Permelia 57
  Plummer 312
  R. 165
  Rebecca 336
  Richard N. 89,92,188
  Richard Nixon 58
  Robert 188,310
  Robert F. 75
  Robert T. 34
  Sally 7
  Sarah Jane Carroll 222
  Simon 8
  Steven 193,198,222
  Thomas 58,76,149,161,
   163,174,183,191,192,
   197,306
  Thomas N. 37
  Thomas W. 222
  Tom 113,335,387
  Trissie 359
  W. B. 329
  W. H. 313

WILLIAMS (cont.)
  Wesley 30
  Wesley A. 65
  William 305
WILLIAMSON, ____ 154
  Hugh 115
  Dr. Hugh 126,127,162,
   163
WILLIAMSTON, Mary 22
WILLIAS, Augustan 180
  Houston 180
WILLIE, Allen 309
  John 242
  Josiah 309
  Nancy 41
  William 242
WILLIS, James 188
WILLS, B. D. 182
  Berry 293
  Benjamin F. 45
  C. D. 74
  Deal 294
  Earl 294
  Floyd 294
  Fred 294
  Houston 299
  Irene 290
  Mrs. Lunora Moore 299
  Martha 21
  Williams 327
WILLSON, Adam 122,124,139
  Ben 124
  Benjamin 124
  David 170,172
  J. 172
  James 122,124,144,171
  John 124
  Joseph 124,151
  William 124
WILLY, Eliza 38
  Martha 48,70
  Mary 45,70
  Michael B. 70
  Nancy 37
  Pilly 70
  Rhoda 44
  William 86
  Willis 70,188
  Willis Carroll 70
WILSON, A. D. 342
  Adam 55,119,122,306
  Albert 284
  Albert G. 36
  Alex 188
  Benjamin 122
  Caroline 9
  Charlie 354
  Christopher 304
  Cora A. 389
  David 116
  Dee A. 362
  Dena 389
  E. B. 284
  Eliza 9
  James 55,85,116
  James, Jr. 144
  John 55,306
  John B. 111
  John M. 11
  Joseph 55,150
  Lizzie 102
  Lucrenia 55
  Lucretia 55
  Maggie 331,388
  Margaret 55
  Mary 62
  Mary Eliza 66
  Nancy 55
  Nancy Ann 19
  Nicholas 304
  Polly 57
  Rachel 388
  Robert 188,389

WILSON (cont.)
  Sarah 109
  Stuart 342
  Thomas 307
  Tommie 388
  W. 391
  Will 388
  William 134
  William Wesley 222
  Zacheus 116
WIMBERLY, Claude 287
  G. W. 197,222
WIMMS, Washington T. 309
WIMS, John 187,307
WINFRED, W. S. 225
WINFREY, W. E. 222
  William 222,223
WINGATE, J. 163
  Joseph 132,171,172,303
  William 185,237
  William H. 236
WINNS, ____ 27
  Washington 27
WINSTEAD, Charles 78
  Dave 316
  David 11,316
WINTERS, Mary Virginia 215
WIRT, Henry 149
WISEMAN, Stacy 44
  Thomas 31
WISENHUNT, David 32
WISHART, Marguerite 354
  Morton E. 354
  Sara 354
  Mrs. Sara 218,343
WOLF, Elosie 102
  R. E. 101
WOLFE, Etta Kate 299
  R. E. 342
WOMACK, D. 26
WOOD, C. 242
  Earnest 382
  Edwin 175
  John 134
  Joseph 122
  Josiah 225
  Maggie 382
  Rainy 331
  Titus 125
  West 77.185,239,240
WOODARD, Jesse 73,74
  Selkirk 234
  Susan O. 204
WOODDY, William 108
WOODE, Elijah 80
WOODS, Campbell 355
  Ida 355
  James 161
  John 168,242
  Mollie 355
  Nancy E. 355
  Patrick 161,176
WOODSIDE, Auther L. 358
WOODSON, Rev. W. N. 274
WOODWARD, ____ 227
  A. 73
  A. M. 342
  Benjamin 73,74
  Elizabeth 73
  George B. 73
  Harriet 73
  J. D. 36
  Jessee 311
  John D. 48,74
  Sarah 74
  William 73
  William Waynen Harriet 73
WOODY, John 247,321
  William A. 251
WOOTEN, Hardie 371
WOOTSON, David 129
WORK, ____ 328

WORK (cont.)
  Agnes 292,293
  Andrew 68
  Beatrice 290
  Brunnetta 73
  Catherine 68
  Clara Donegan 299
  Irene 293
  J. R. 223
  James Robert 290
  John H. 74
  Lissa T. Bingham 222
  Marie 295
  Melisia T. 388
  R. J. 197
  R. T. 202
  Robert J. 222,388
  Robert John F. 68
  Sallie 388
  Sally 288,299
  Samuel 68
WORLEY, Henry 187
  James 262
WORLY, Henry 180
WORTHY, J. B. 262,343
WRENNE, J. T. 113
  Snow 113
WRIGHT, Charles 294,298,334
  Elizabeth 9
  Frank 316
  George 158,187,237
  George, Jr. 81
  George, Sr. 78
  Isaac 175
  J. 157
  John 78,81,158,237,239,305
  John F. 319
  John Franklin 222,224
  John H. 24,54,309
  L. D. 197,202,222,248,331,332
  Lucius D. 353
  Lucy 343
  Milton 271
  Mrs. Monsie 269
  Nancy 78,81
  Nannie 353
  Nannie Craft 222
  Olin 343
  Robert 121
  Thomas 131,132,137,138,156,158,160,166,169,171
  W. M. 197,222
  William 175,185,222,307
WYAT, James 122
WYATT, Eugene 282
  J. F. 222
  Mildred 282
  William 223
WYBURN, Mrs. Bert Tidwell 281
WYET, James 124
WYLIE, Rebecca 218
WYLY, Dorcas 206
  Victoria A. 213
WYMAN, J. L. 284
WYMS, Matilda 27
  W. T. 27
WYNN, ____ 27,248,325
  George 384
  Harry 384
  James 109,325
  Lucy 384
WYNNS, Iva Henslee 207
  Lucy 331
  Minnie 331
VOSS, Joseph 139,141
XRON, John 39
YANCY, Mary 295
YARBROUGH, Thomas Luis 223

YARRELL, Mary 95
YATEMAN, Eliza 66
  John 66
YATES, C. H. 280
  Doyl 294
  Doyle 288
  E. S. 263
  Earl 288,294
  Fanning 15,27,65,309
  Granville 289
  James 309
  Jason 198,223
  Jethro 309
  Leamon 288,294
  Martha 99
  Miley 15
  Mollie Rogers 293
  Myrtle 288
  Nancy 46
  Ola 293
YEATES, James 20
  William 13
YOUNG, Bates 295
  Benjamin 63
  Daniel M. 21
  Edward S. 32
  James 182,192,312
  John 174
  Lance 295
  M. Q. 225
  Sam 99
  T. B. 172
  Thomas A. 82,84
  W. B. 13,20,85,251
  William 11,192
  William B. 87,312
YOUREE, Hazel 295
  ____, Adam 190
  Allen 304
  Amanuel 66
  Andrew Jackson 66
  Angeline 66
  Anne 182
  Barry 77
  Bob 66
  Burrell 67
  Charity 66
  Chloe 181
  Creecy 66
  Derry 178
  Elbert 111
  Eliza 66
  Emmaline 66
  Esther 183
  Francis 67
  Isaiah B. 181
  Jack 66
  James E. 191
  James Monroe 66
  Jane 63,65,66
  Jenira 55
  Jerusha 238
  Jo 75
  John H. 190
  Judy 66,67
  Kiah 67
  Lizza 66
  London 66
  Louanna 60
  Malilda 63
  Martha A. 26
  Mary 63,315
  Only 66
  Peggy 55,66
  Perry 66
  Phebe 61
  Prince 63
  Richard C. 42
  Sally 180
  Simon 66,67
  Solomon 66
  Tho. Benton 66
  Wiley 308

_____, William Carroll 66
_____ William H. 48

SLAVES

Adam 145
Armstead 138
Becky 129
Daniel 148
Elizabeth 91
Humble 136
Jack 142
Mary 90
Milly 91
Stephen 86
Viney 148

www.ingramcontent.com/pod-product-compliance
Lightning Source LLC
Chambersburg PA
CBHW020634300426
44112CB00007B/111